Great American Drives *of the West*

Fodor's Travel Publications
New York Toronto London Sydney Auckland
www.fodors.com

Fodor's Great American Drives of the West

Editor: Carissa Bluestone

Editorial Contributors: Shelley Arenas (ID), Gina Bacon (WA), Michele Bardsley (NV), Lisa Dunford (AR, LA, TX), Tom Griffith (ND, SD), Marilyn Haddrill (NM, TX), Pat Hansen (MT), Cindy Hirschfeld (CO), Kathryn Knudson (MN), Janet Lowe (UT), Diana Lambdin Meyer (IA, MO, NE), Carrie Miner (AZ), Cindy Mines (KS, OK), Janna Mock-Lopez (OR), Candy Moulton (WY), Laura Randall (CA), John Vlahides (CA)

Maps: Rebecca Baer, Robert Blake, David Lindroth, Todd Pasini

Design: Siobhan O'Hare

Cover Photograph: Craig Aurness/Corbis

Production/Manufacturing: Angela L. McLean

Copyright

Second Edition

ISBN 1–4000–1372–0

ISSN 1538–7615

Special Sales

This book is available for special discounts for bulk purchases for sales promotions or premiums. Special editions, including personalized covers, excerpts of existing books, and corporate imprints, can be created in large quantities for special needs. For more information, write to Special Markets/Premium Sales, 1745 Broadway, MD 6-2, New York, NY 10019 or e-mail specialmarkets@randomhouse.com.

PRINTED IN THE UNITED STATES OF AMERICA

10 9 8 7 6 5 4 3 2

CONTENTS

Great American Drives

For some, driving is a means to get from one destination to the next as fast as Mother Nature, the roads, and the law will permit. If this is how you drive, you've picked up the wrong book.

If, for you, driving *is* the destination, and you pull over for reasons that don't necessarily involve food, fuel, or driving faster than the law permits, congratulate yourself on finding this guide. Inside are all the tools you'll need to plan perfect road trips in the 22 glorious states west of the Mississippi River.

Every chapter includes easy-to-follow, point-by-point driving tours, corresponding maps, and specific rules of the road. And since this wouldn't be a Fodor's guide without reviews, we give you more than 1,400 listings for attractions, restaurants, and hotels along the way.

These drives set you on specific paths, but by all means allow yourself a few detours. Because as wonderful as it is to know the correct exit, it can be serendipitous to turn off elsewhere to discover that hole-in-the-wall diner with transcendent tomato soup, or a gallery crammed with dusty local curiosities. After all, it's this sense of adventure that helped shape the Great American Drives you have in your hands.

How to Use This Book

Alphabetical organization should make it a snap to navigate through these pages. Still, in putting them together, we've made certain decisions and used certain terms you need to know about.

ORGANIZATION

Following each tour are alphabetical, town-by-town listings with additional information about many of the sights mentioned in the tours, as well as listings for other attractions in those towns. We've also included information on nearby restaurants and hotels.

Attractions, restaurants, and hotels are listed under the nearest town covered in the tour.

Parks and forests are sometimes listed under the main access point.

Exact street addresses are provided whenever possible; when they are not available or applicable, directions and/or cross-streets are indicated.

FODOR'S CHOICE

Stars denote sights, restaurants, and hotels that are the best in a given region or price category.

RESTAURANTS

We have provided restaurant listings for almost every town mentioned in these drives. Restaurants are arranged alphabetically; price categories are indicated at the end of each review.

CATEGORY	COST*
$$$$	OVER $25
$$$	$20–$25
$$	$12–$20
$	$7–$12
¢	UNDER $7

Prices are for one main course at dinner.

Dress: Assume that no jackets or ties are required for men unless specified.
Meals and hours: Assume that restaurants are open for lunch and dinner unless otherwise noted. We always indicate days closed.
Reservations: They are always a good idea. We don't mention them unless they're essential or are not accepted.

HOTELS

Hotels are listed only for towns we suggest as overnight stops. Properties are arranged alphabetically; price categories are indicated at the end of each review.

CATEGORY	COST*
$$$$	OVER $200
$$$	$150–$200
$$	$100–$150
$	$50–$100
¢	UNDER $50

cost of a double room for two during peak season, excluding tax and service charges.

Bear in mind that the prices gathered for this book are for standard double hotel or motel rooms, and you may pay more for suites or cabins. If a property we recommend is comprised only of suites, cabins, and other atypical lodgings, assume that the given price category applies.
AP: American Plan. The rate includes all meals. AP may be an option or it may be the only meal plan available.
Baths: You'll find private bathrooms with bathtubs unless otherwise noted.
BP: Breakfast Plan. The rate includes a full breakfast.
CP: Continental Plan. The rate includes a Continental breakfast.
Exercising: We mention any exercise equipment even when there's no designated exercise area; if you want a dedicated facility, look for "gym."
Facilities: We list what's available but don't note charges for use. When pricing accommodations, always ask what's included.
FAP: Full American Plan. The rate includes all meals.

Hot tub: This term denotes hot tubs, Jacuzzis, and whirlpools.

MAP: Modified American Plan. Rates at these properties include two meals.

Opening and closing: Assume that properties are open year-round unless otherwise noted.

Pets: Assume that pets are not welcomed, unless we note otherwise.

Telephones: Assume that you'll find them unless otherwise indicated.

NATIONAL PARKS

National parks protect and preserve the treasures of America's heritage, and they're always worth visiting. Many warrant a long detour. If your drive brings you to many national parks, consider purchasing the National Parks Pass ($50), which gets you and your companions (only one pass is required per vehicle) free admission to all parks for one year. (Camping and parking are extra.) A large percentage of the proceeds from sales of the pass helps fund park projects. Both the Golden Age Passport ($10), for those 62 and older, and the Golden Access Passport (free), for travelers with disabilities, entitle holders to free entry to all national parks, plus 50% off fees for the use of the many park facilities and services. You must show proof of age and of U.S. citizenship or permanent residency (such as a U.S. passport, driver's license, or birth certificate) and, if requesting Golden Access, proof of your disability. You must get your Golden Access or Golden Age passport in person; the former is available at all federal recreation areas, the latter at federal recreation areas that charge fees.

You may purchase the National Parks Pass by mail, by phone, or through the Internet. For information, contact the National Park Service (Department of the Interior, 1849 C St. NW, Washington, DC 20240-0001, 202/208–4747, www.nps.gov). To buy the National Parks Pass, write to The National Park Foundation, Attention: Park Pass, Box 34108, Washington, DC 20043-4108, call 888/GO–PARKS, or visit www.national-parks.org.

IMPORTANT TIP

Although all prices, opening times, and other details in this book are based on information supplied to us at press time, changes occur all the time in the travel world, and Fodor's cannot accept responsibility for facts that become outdated or for inadvertent errors or omissions. So always confirm information when it matters, especially if you're making a special detour to visit a specific place.

LET US HEAR FROM YOU

Keeping a travel guide fresh and up-to-date is a big job, and we welcome any and all comments. We'd love to have your thoughts on places we've listed, and we're interested in hearing about your own special finds, even the ones in your own backyard. Our guides are thoroughly updated for each new edition, and we're always adding new information, so your feedback is vital. Contact us via e-mail in care of editors@fodors.com (specifying the name of the book on the subject line) or via snail mail care of Great American Drives of the West editor, Fodor's Travel Publications, 1745 Broadway, New York, NY 10019. We look forward to hearing from you.

Regina

SASKATCHEWAN

MANITOBA

Winnipeg

ONTARIO

Lake Superior

NORTH DAKOTA

North Dakota Frontier

Fargo

MINNESOTA

Duluth

NTANA

Billings

Bozeman Trail

er River to the Parks

SOUTH DAKOTA

Bismarck

Missouri R.

MING

Historic Trails Trek

Cheyenne

Denver

Colorado's Heartland

COLORADO

Pierre

Black Hills and Badlands

The Fur Trade and the Oregon Trail

NEBRASKA

Lincoln

Omaha

WISCONSIN

Minneapolis

St. Paul

Green Bay

Great River Road Along US 61

Iowa Great River Road

IOWA

Des Moines

Missouri Caves

Topeka

The Santa Fe Trail Along US 56

Kansas City

Jefferson City

Lake Michigan

Madison

Milwaukee

Lake Michigan

Chicago

Springfield

St. Louis

Ohio R.

ILLINOIS

MISSOURI

Mississippi R.

KANSAS

Circling Northern New Mexico

Santa Fe

NEW MEXICO

OKLAHOMA

Oklahoma City

Amarillo

Tulsa

Ouachita National Forest Along US 59

ARKANSAS

Little Rock

Memphis

Mississippi R.

n the Trail of lly the Kid

El Paso

Big Bend Country Tour

UA

Rio Grande

TEXAS

Bandera to New Braunfels

Austin

San Antonio

Dallas

Scenic 7 Byway

MISSISSIPPI

Jackson

Baton Rouge

Mississippi River Plantations

New Orleans

LOUISIANA

Houston

Kingsville to Aransas National Wildlife Refuge

COAHUILA

Gulf of Mexico

ARIZONA

PAINTED DESERT AND NAVAJO COUNTRY
FROM CAMERON TO THE THIRD MESA

Distance: 430 mi Time: 3 days
Overnight Breaks: Kayenta, Chinle

The stark beauty of the Navajolands and the Hopi Mesas dominate the remote reaches of the northeastern corner of the state. This region is dominated by the 27,000-square-mi Navajo Nation, which stretches into Utah and New Mexico. Although it's the largest reservation in the United States—an area larger than Vermont, New Hampshire, Massachusetts, Connecticut and Rhode Island combined—the Navajo Nation is sparsely populated with only 260,000 residents living in a few select population centers and in hogans (log and mud dwellings) scattered across the vast Colorado Plateau. With its stark topographic features—yawning canyons, piercing mountains, and haunting valleys—the area inspires awe with its fierce beauty. Surrounded on all sides by the Navajo Nation, the Hopi Reservation is home to 10,000 tribal members. The Hopi primarily live in their ancestral homes on and around First, Second, and Third Mesas. The Hopi people keep to themselves, but still attract attention with their elaborate ceremonies, some of which are open to the public.

Etiquette is a key concern when visiting any reservation. Keep in mind that each reservation operates under its own government and that in some areas, off-road driving, hiking, and rock climbing are forbidden. Photography and videotaping also are unwelcome in many situations. Hopi villages and ceremonies may not be photographed nor sketched, nor their sounds recorded. If you attend a Hopi dance, remember that many of them are sacred religious ceremonies and act as you would if you were attending a church service—no talking and no applause. Many Navajos also prefer their privacy and will, in many cases, post signs asking visitors to refrain from photographing their property. In no instance should you take photographs of Navajo people or their homes without their permission; if they allow you to photograph them, expect to pay a small fee.

Summer is hot on the Colorado Plateau, making the cooler spring or fall months the best time to take this scenic drive. If you do visit in the summer, be sure to bring a raincoat as afternoon storms are commonplace. Also keep in mind that the Navajo

Nation observes daylight saving time from early April to late October, whereas the rest of Arizona does not.

❶ The **Cameron Trading Post** is a good place to get your bearings and pick up maps before you begin your journey. There's a large arts-and-crafts store, where you'll find Navajo and Hopi pottery, jewelry, baskets, and rugs. There are also a restaurant, lodgings, and a gas station at the historic trading post. When you're fueled up, take U.S. 89 north from Cameron. You'll drive through the west end of the Painted Desert, a vision of subtle, almost harsh beauty, with windswept plains and mesas, isolated buttes, and barren valleys in pastel patterns. Continue for approximately 16 mi though this surreal multicolored landscape until you reach U.S. 160, which will take you to Tuba City. A short detour off U.S. 89 at Milepost 316 will lead you to Dinosaur Tracks, the preserved footprints of what is thought to have been a dilophosaurus.

❷ Back on U.S. 160, you'll come to **Tuba City.** The landscape around the town includes sediments deposited 200 million years ago in an ancient ocean. There's a small trading post on Main Street, and it's a good place to stop for gas before heading on. Tuba City is also the home of the administrative center for the **Navajo Indian Reservation.**

❸ **Keet Seel,** which means "broken pottery" in Navajo, is a 160-room ruin open to 20 visitors a day (between Memorial Day and Labor Day, when a ranger is on duty). A ladder leads up into the cliff dwelling where you can walk the ancient streets and peek into smoke-darkened rooms. The hike to the actual ruins is a vigorous 17 mi round-trip, but it's possible to obtain a free permit to camp overnight if you call ahead.

❹ A shorter hike to **Betatakin** (Navajo for "ledge house") is possible, but it, too, is strenuous—a steep 5-mi guided hike offered to 25 people per tour from late May through September. Most visitors simply walk the $1/2$-mi Sandal Trail from the visitor center for a good view of these ruins. However, those who hike down to the site will get an impressive view of the crumbling 135-room ruin nestled in a sandstone arch measuring 450 feet high and 370 feet wide.

❺ **Kayenta,** about 30 mi to the northeast of Navajo National Monument (north of U.S. 160 on U.S. 163) is a good base for touring the monument and is also a good place to spend the night. If you decide to add a day to your itinerary, you can take a side trip to Monument Valley, which is 29 mi north of Kayenta on U.S. 163.

❻ The next leg of the trip turns south into the heart of Navajolands. Head back to U.S. 160 and proceed for approximately 10 mi to Route 59. Take Route 59 southeast for approximately 40 mi to the tiny town of Many Farms. From Many Farms, head south on U.S. 191 to **Chinle.** From here, you can begin your exploration of Canyon de Chelly (pronounced *d'shay*), which is 3 mi east of Chinle on Route 7.

Like most of the land within the sacred boundaries of the Navajolands, **Canyon de Chelly**—a deep-cut gorge, which was, according to Navajo legend, created by huge wallowing beasts (with walls rippled by a giant hummingbird's wings) and home to the wise Spiderwoman—echoes with the heartbeat of the Navajo people. In some places, the dramatic sandstone walls reach up 1,000 feet to turquoise skies. Ancient Anasazi pictographs adorn many of the cliffs in the national park and are, in themselves, worth a guided trip into the gorge. Canyon de Chelly and the adjoining Canyon del Muerto are home to more than 7,000 archaeological sites, some dating back 4,500 years. If you take a guided tour into the canyon, you'll discover lush pasture, streams, peach orchards, and occupied hogans.

Take the **South Rim Drive** (Route 7) from the visitor center, a 36-mi round-trip that travels to Spider Rock, Tsegi, and Junction overlooks. You'll also be able to make a stop at White House Overlook, where you'll find the trailhead of the only hike to the bottom of the canyon that visitors are permitted to take without a guide. You can hike down this steep, but short (1¼ mi) path in less than an hour (leave a little more time for the uphill return).

Chinle is an ideal place to spend the night after a day of exploring the canyon and its environs.

7 Take U.S. 191 south out of Chinle. Drive for about 30 mi to Route 264 and then head east for a few miles toward **Ganado** and the **Hubbell Trading Post National Historic Site.** The Hubbell Trading Post continues to cling to its rich past, still operating much as it did when John Lorenzo Hubbell opened the doors of the post's first two-room structure in 1883. At the height of Hubbell's career, he operated more than 30 posts on the Navajo reservation, two wholesale houses, and several curio shops on the California coast. Today, the Hubbell Trading Post in Ganado stands as a testament to the Hubbell empire as the oldest continuously operating trading post on the Navajo Reservation. You can take a guided tour of the Hubbell house and outbuildings or stop by the visitor center—where you can watch a Navajo weaver at work on a traditional loom.

8 Continue west on Route 264 for approximately 60 mi to the **Hopi Indian Reservation.** The Hopi, a Puebloan people, trace their roots back to the Anasazi (or ancestral Puebloan) presence at Wupatki near Flagstaff, Navajo National Monument, and

Canyon de Chelly, among other sites. The Hopi people primarily live in villages grouped on and around three narrow plateaus—dubbed by early European explorers as First Mesa, Second Mesa, and Third Mesa—all of which are connected by a 37-mi strip of Route 264. The village at Old Oraibi on Third Mesa dates back to 1150 and is known as the oldest continuously inhabited community in the United States.

❾ The **First Mesa** contains the villages of Walpi, Sichomovi, and Hano, but you should stop at the **visitor center** to get your bearings before tour the area. To get here, follow the signs to First Mesa villages; you'll see the visitor center at the top of the mesa. Request a guide to help you tour Walpi, a tiny community with fewer than 10 families.

❿ Continue west on Route 264 for approximately 6 mi to the **Second Mesa,** the center of which is the **Hopi Cultural Center.** Here you'll find a compelling museum that traces the Hopi people's turbulent history. There's also a restaurant on the premises that serves such traditional Hopi dishes as *nok qui vi* (a lamb hominy and green chili stew), blue-corn pancakes, and fry bread.

⓫ At the **Third Mesa,** the **Office of Public Relations** has a wealth of information on local ceremonies and dances held year-round throughout the Hopi Reservation.

To return to Cameron, continue west on Route 264; at the junction with U.S. 160, make a left. Continue for about 5 mi until you reach U.S. 89 south, which will take you back to Cameron in less than an hour.

Chinle

Canyon de Chelly National Monument. In the northeast corner of the state, this 83,840-acre national park protects two main canyons. The 26-mi-long Canyon de Chelly and 35-mi-long Canyon del Muerto are a network of deeply sculpted sandstone passages all accessed by a narrow 30 foot entrance. You can view the canyons from the North and South Rim drives (each of which takes about two hours round-trip), hike a well-marked trail to the White House Ruin, or take guided tours of the canyon

ARIZONA RULES OF THE ROAD

License Requirements: To drive in Arizona you must be at least 16 years old and have a valid driver's license.

Right Turn on Red: You may make a right turn on red *after* a full stop, unless there is a sign prohibiting it.

Seat Belt and Helmet Laws: If you are sitting in the front seat of any vehicle, the law requires you to wear your seat belt. Kids age 4 and under must be strapped into an approved safety seat. Anyone under the age of 18 is required to wear a helmet while riding on a motorcycle.

Speed Limits: Speed limits in Arizona go as high as 75 mph on many interstates, but tend to remain at 55 mph on most of the reservation's highways. Be sure to check speed limit signs carefully and often.

For More Information: Department of Public Safety | 602/223-2000 | www.dps.state.az.us/.

floors. The canyons have been occupied by various tribes over the past 2,000 years, and the Navajo have claimed this drainage system as their home since they first settled here in AD 1700. The visitor center is 3 mi east of Chinle. | Navajo Rte. 7 | 928/674–5500 | www.nps.gov/cach | Free | Visitor center: May–Sept., daily 8–6; Oct.–Apr., daily 8–5.

The 36-mi round-trip around the rim of Canyon de Chelly on **South Rim Drive** includes seven overlooks, from which you can see different cliff dwellings and geological formations, including the White House, one of the largest ruins in the canyon, and Spider Rock, which the Navajo people believe is the home of the benevolent deity Spider Woman (who among other things taught the Navajo the art of weaving). | Canyon de Chelly | 928/674–5500 visitor center | www.nps.gov/cach | Daily.

On the **North Rim Drive,** you'll drive 34-mi round-trip along the rim of Canyon del Muerto. Among the stops are Antelope House, where you can spy Black Rock Canyon, and Massacre Cave Overlook, where more than 100 Navajo people were killed by Spanish soldiers in 1805. This drive turns into Route 64 or you can turn around at the Massacre Cave Overlook and retrace the route back to the visitor center. | Canyon de Chelly | 928/674–5500 visitor center | www.nps.gov/cach | Daily.

With 60 rooms in the lower section and another 20 tucked away in the cliff, the **White House,** an ancestral Puebloan structure, housed as many as 100 people at a time during the years between 1060 and 1275. Its name comes from the white-plaster covering the upper portion of the ruins. If you look closely you'll see hand and toeholds chipped into canyon walls, which were used to access the dwelling. Note that the 2½-mi round-trip trail leading down to the ruin is the only part of the canyon that can be visited without a Navajo guide. | Canyon de Chelly | 928/674–5500 visitor center | www.nps.gov/cach | Free | Daily.

Dining

Garcia's Restaurant. American. This is one of the few full-service restaurants in the area and the best place in town for a bite to eat. The menu includes burgers, chicken, steaks, ribs, pasta, and traditional Navajo food. The dining room gets packed fast, however; if you end up waiting in line, you'll have time for a quick browse in the adjacent gift shop or a chance to check out the local artwork decorating the restaurant. Breakfast served. | Holiday Inn Canyon de Chelly, Navajo Rte. 7 | 928/674–5000 | AE, D, DC, MC, V | $–$$

Junction Restaurant. Native American. Both Navajo and American cuisines are served in three dining areas at this restaurant in the Best Western Inn. One dining area features photographs of the Navajo code talkers from WW II, and, elsewhere, you'll see photos of Navajos in traditional dress hanging alongside a beautiful array of rugs available for purchase. The local favorite here is the mutton stew. | Navajo Rte. 7 | 928/674–8443 | AE, D, DC, MC, V | $–$$

Pizza Edge. Pizza. This is the best place in Chinle to grab a slice. The menu also includes sandwiches and hot wings. | Basha's Shopping Center, U.S. 191 | 928/674–3366 | AE, D, DC, MC, V | Closed Sun. | ¢–$$

Lodging

Best Western Inn. The farthest Chinle property from the canyon's entrance, this basic motel is a last resort if you are unable to book a room elsewhere. The Junction Restaurant serves up a little bit of everything—Navajo, Mexican, American, and Continental. Restaurant, room service, cable TV, pool, business services. | 100 Main St., 86503 | 928/674–5874 or 800/327–0354 | fax 928/674–3715 | www.bestwestern.com | 99 rooms | AE, D, DC, MC, V | $

Holiday Inn Canyon de Chelly. Part of the historic Garcia Trading Post is incorporated into the restaurant and gift shop of this standard motel, ½ mi from the entrance to Canyon de Chelly. The rooms are basic but comfortable and they all have balconies or patios for a quiet respite. Garcia's Restaurant is on-site. Restaurant, room service, cable TV, pool, business services. | Navajo Rte. 7, 86503 | 928/674–5000 or 800/465–4329 | fax 928/674–8264 | www.holiday-inn.com | 108 rooms | AE, D, DC, MC, V | $–$$

Thunderbird Lodge. The red-adobe building—under a grove of cottonwood trees at the mouth of Canyon de Chelly—is a popular place to stay in Chinle, partly because of its proximity to the canyon and partly because of the historical presence of the 1896 stone-and-wood trading post that now serves as the lodge's cafeteria-style restaurant. A gift shop and a rug room feature the work of Navajo artists and weavers. The lodge also offers half- and full-day jeep tours into the canyons. Restaurant, cable TV, business services, airport shuttle. | Navajo Rte. 7, 86503 | 928/674–5841 or 800/679–2473 | fax 928/674–5844 | www.tbirdlodge.com | 72 rooms | AE, D, DC, MC, V | $–$$

Ganado

Hubbell Trading Post National Historic Site. A walk though the preserved 1880s buildings at the Hubbell Trading Post is a walk through time itself. Fine imported European furnishings still grace the five-bedroom home, which is carpeted with Navajo rugs and decorated with Native American artwork. A few retired national parks horses occupy the massive barn and the trading post itself still runs much as it did in the 1870s, catering to Navajo, Zuni, Hopi, and other tribal members. Nearby, a visitor center offers books on the region and interaction with one of the Hubbell weavers. | Rte. 264 | 928/755–3475 | www.nps.gov/hutr | Free | Daily 8–5.

Dining

Ramon's Restaurant. Native American. The menu focuses on Native American food, but this small, comfortable restaurant also serves Mexican and American specialties. Local favorites here include the Navajo burger and Navajo tacos. | Hwy. 264 | 928/755–3404 | No credit cards | Closed Sun. No dinner Sat. | ¢–$

Hopi Reservation

Guided Walking Tour of First Mesa. Take a one-hour guided walk through the First Mesa village of Sichomovi with a Hopi guide and learn about daily life of the Hopi people. On the tour you'll discover the history of the Hopi, see artists at work, walk past the spring and farms, and even learn the secrets of the bread ovens where the famously delicious piki bread is cooked. | Punsi Hall Visitor's Center, First Mesa | 928/737–2262 | $8 | Daily 9–4.

Guided Walking Tour of Oraibi. Bertram Tsavadawa, an Oraibi native, will take you on a four-hour tour through the oldest continually inhabited settlement in North America, sharing with you the village's history, facts about Hopi culture, and the secrets behind the area's largest collection of petroglyphs. | 928/734–9544 or 928/306–7849 | $85 | By appointment.

Hopi Museum. This comprehensive museum illuminates the history of this ancient culture, along with the wide variety of arts and crafts produced by the Hopi peoples, including the famous pottery of the First Mesa, coiled plaques from Second Mesa, and wicker plaques from Third Mesa. Artists from all three mesas create colorful katsina carvings, silver overlay jewelry, and sifter baskets. | Second Mesa | 928/734–6650 | $3 | Mon.–Sat. 8–5, Sun. 8–4.

Dining

Hopi Cultural Center. Native American. This is the best place to stop if you want to try some Hopi dishes. The casual restaurant is also a favorite of Hopi residents; blue-corn pancakes for breakfast and hominy stew with piki bread for lunch are favorites. They also serve a basic American menu, with sandwiches, salads and burgers. | Second Mesa | 928/734–2401 | AE, D, DC, MC, V | ¢–$

Kayenta

Monument Valley Navajo Tribal Park. A 17-mi bumpy dirt road is the only section of this arid landscape open to the public without a native guide. There are 11 scenic viewpoints along the way, but outside of these areas, the Navajo strictly forbid visitors from getting out of their cars at any point and signs warn against leaving the selected parking areas. The Navajo first came to this region in the late 15th century. Since that time, they were only parted from its stark beauty after their forced removal to New Mexico between 1864 and 1868. Ninety years later, the Navajo Tribal Council designated the 29,816-acre Monument Valley Navajo Tribal Park to preserve the lifestyle of the Navajos residing within its boundaries. | Visitor center: off U.S. 163 | 435/727–5870 | $5 | Daily sunrise–sunset.

Navajo Code Talkers Exhibit. In Kayenta's Burger King restaurant, an exhibit of World War II memorabilia honors the Navajo code talkers of the Pacific campaign. These Navajo Marines sent and received military orders and dispatches in the Navajo language, a code the Japanese could not break. Outside there are several Native American structures that you can walk through, including a traditional Navajo hogan. | U.S. 160, ¹/₂ mi west of U.S. 163 | 928/697–3170 | Free | Daily 7 AM–10 PM.

Navajo National Monument. The sandstone walls of the extensive Tsegi Canyon system cradle the remains of an ancient civilization that inhabited lands now part of the vast Navajo Nation. Deep within these sandstone canyons lie three 13th-century cliff dwellings now protected by the monument—Inscription House, Betatakin, and Keet Seel. You can take a 5-mi round-trip hike led daily by Navajo guides to the base of a looming cave measuring 450 feet high and 370 feet wide. Nestled inside are the crumbling ruins of Betatakin. An 18¹/₂-mi round-trip hike into a tributary canyon of the system leads to Keet Seel, one of the largest and best-preserved cliff dwellings in the state. The location of Inscription House is kept secret in hopes of preserving the small dwelling. The monument's visitor center houses a small museum, exhibits of prehistoric pottery, and a crafts shop (9 mi north of U.S. 160, about 20 mi southeast of Kayenta). Reservations are required for hiking permits to Keet Seel. Tickets for the hike to Betatakin are issued on a first-come, first-serve basis for both the 8:15 AM and 11 AM guided hikes. You can pick up tickets at the visitor center—at the Black Mesa junction, turn north off U.S. 160 onto Route 564, which will lead you right to the center. | Rte. 564 | www.nps.gov/nava | Free | 928/672–2700 | Daily 8–5.

Dining

Anasazi Inn Restaurant. Native American. Ten miles west of Kayenta, this is a good place to go for a quiet, peaceful meal. Basic in comfort and decor, this restaurant is more of a diner than a traditional sit-down restaurant. The Navajo fry bread roast beef sandwiches and tacos are especially tasty and will sate even the largest of appetites. Breakfast served. | U.S. 160 | 928/697–3793 | AE, D, DC, MC, V | $

Golden Sands Restaurant. American. In this unassuming place next door to the Best Western Wetherill, you can get hot and cold sandwiches, Navajo tacos, Navajo beef, and traditional mutton stew. | U.S. 163 | 928/697–3684 | No credit cards | ¢–$

Lodging

Best Western Wetherill Inn. This two-story motel, named for John Wetherill, a frontiersman who discovered prehistoric Native American ruins in Arizona, is on the north side of Kayenta. Rooms are basic with Southwestern decor. Cable TV, pool, business services. | U.S. 163, 86033 | 928/697–3231 or 800/780–7234 | fax 928/697–3233 | www.bestwestern.com | 54 rooms | AE, D, DC, MC, V | $–$$

Goulding's Monument Valley Trading Post & Lodge. The John Wayne films *Stagecoach* and *Fort Apache* were set here. The original trading post includes a museum with movie memorabilia. The two-story motel offers basic, comfortable rooms with spectacular views of Monument Valley. Goulding's also runs a campground, a grocery store, and a convenience store. 2 restaurants, minibars, in-room VCRs, pool, laundry facilities, some pets allowed. | Indian Rte. 42, UT 84536 | 435/727–3231 or 800/874–0902 | fax 435/727–3344 | www.gouldings.com | 19 rooms in lodge, 41 motel rooms, 2 cabins | AE, D, DC, MC, V | $–$$$

Hampton Inn Navajo Nation. This three-story chain property has a friendly staff and immaculate rooms, plus it's close to all the local attractions. The gift shop sells some Navajo crafts. Restaurant, room service, in-room data ports, cable TV, pool. | U.S. 160, 86033 | 928/697–3170 or 800/426–7866 | fax 928/697–3189 | www.hamptoninn.com | 73 rooms | AE, D, DC, MC, V | $–$$

Tuba City
Cameron Trading Post. Twenty-nine miles southwest of Tuba City you'll find Native American arts and crafts at this historic enterprise, which sells authentic Navajo and Hopi art and jewelry. Come armed with knowledge of Native American artisanship if you're looking at high-ticket items, some of which are sold at a separate gallery. Also at the post are a restaurant, cafeteria, grocery store, butcher shop, and post office. | U.S. 89 at Rte. 64 | 928/679–2231 | Daily 7 AM–9 PM.

Dinosaur Tracks. Some well-preserved dilophosaurus tracks can be viewed at this site about $5\frac{1}{2}$ mi west of Tuba City, between Mileposts 316 and 317 of U.S. 160. | U.S. 160 | No phone | Free | Daily.

Tuba City Trading Post. Founded in the 1880s, this octagonal trading post sells authentic Navajo, Hopi, and Zuni rugs, pottery, baskets, and jewelry, as well as groceries. | Main St. and Moenabe Rd. | 928/283–5441 | Mon.–Sat. 8–5, Sun. 9–5.

Dining
Hogan Restaurant. Southwestern. Next to the Quality Inn Tuba City, this spot serves mostly Southwestern and Mexican dishes, including chicken enchiladas and beef tamales. Breakfast served. | Main St. (Hwy. 264) | 928/283–5260 | AE, D, DC, MC, V | ¢–$

Kate's Café. American/Casual. This is a local favorite and is known for catering to a wide range of tastes with everything from sizable salads to steak and shrimp. Try Kate's Club or the Baja Burger ($\frac{1}{3}$-lb hamburger topped with bacon, jack cheese, avocado, lettuce and tomato). You may have to wait a bit for seating. Breakfast served. | Edgewater and Main Sts. | 928/283–6773 | No credit cards | ¢–$

Tuba City Truck Stop Cafe. American. Fast service and hearty home cooking distinguish this stop. Try the Navajo vegetarian taco, a mix of beans, lettuce, sliced tomatoes, shredded cheese, and green chilies served open-face on succulent fry bread. Or you might consider mutton stew served with fry bread and hominy. Breakfast served. | Hwy. 264 at U.S. 160 | 928/283–4975 | MC, V | $

THE CANYONLANDS
FLAGSTAFF TO SEDONA ON I-40 AND U.S. 89

Distance: 289 mi   Time: 3 days
Overnight Breaks: Grand Canyon Village, Prescott, Sedona

This is canyon country, with Grand Canyon National Park as the centerpiece. At the base of Mount Humphreys, the state's highest mountain, Flagstaff is a mecca for outdoor enthusiasts and a great base for exploring the many wonders abounding in this marvelous region. Farther south in Prescott, you'll discover Arizona's first capital city and the mountain town's role in the development of the state. A jaunt to the thriving arts communities of Jerome and Sedona round out a long weekend of fresh air and local color. The high season in Sedona is spring and fall; Flagstaff is most crowded in summer.

1 Start in **Flagstaff.** This sleepy college town of almost 60,000, home to Northern Arizona University, is a growing destination for skiers and hikers alike. Flagstaff has more than 200 restaurants and dozens of hotels and motels, as well as a fascinating arboretum, an observatory, and a good symphony. But much of Flagstaff's popularity stems from a nearby neighbor—only about 90 mi from the South Rim of the Grand Canyon, Flagstaff has always been a good base for exploring the canyon and surrounding area. Get your bearings, then head out along U.S. 89. On the way to Grand Canyon, **Sunset Crater** and **Wupatki National Monument** are interesting side trips. The former, a volcano that erupted more than 900 years ago, is 15 mi north of Flagstaff. The latter is situated in the shadow of the San Francisco Peaks, once home to traders and farmers of the Anasazi (more accurately known as the ancestral Puebloan) and Sinagua people, or Hisatsinom, as their contemporary Hopi descendants call them.

2 Fifty-two miles north of Flagstaff, U.S. 89 meets up with Route 64, which will take you to the East Entrance Station near Desert View at **Grand Canyon National Park.** You can get a quick taste of this magnificent park by driving the scenic 26-mi drive along the South Rim to the South Entrance Station or you can spend several days here exploring the splendor of Nature at her finest.

3 When you're ready to leave the park, continue 53 mi south on Route 64 down to **Williams.** Named for the mountain man Bill Williams, a trapper in the 1820s and 1830s, Williams was founded when the railroad passed through in 1882. It's a small town less than an hour from the Grand Canyon and is a reasonable place to stay if everything closer to the canyon is full. Williams's Main Street is historic Route 66; in fact, the town wasn't bypassed by I–40 until 1984. This is a popular area for hiking, hunting, and fishing.

4 From Williams, take I–40 16 mi to U.S. 89 and then head south 52 mi to **Prescott.** Named the first capital of Arizona Territory in 1864, Prescott was settled by Northeasterners with interests in local gold. They brought with them a New England architectural style still visible today. Despite a devastating downtown fire in 1900, Prescott remains the Southwest's richest store of New England–style architecture; in fact, it's been called the "West's most Eastern town" by some. At an elevation of 5,300 feet, it's one refuge where Phoenix residents can escape the summertime heat, and it's also a popular retirement community, given the temperate climate and low cost of living. The **Yavapai Indian Reservation** is outside the town limits.

5 After spending the night in Prescott, head north on Alternate Route 89 and follow it 26 mi to **Jerome.** Eugene Jerome, a frontier financier, agreed to fund a speculative mining venture here, with the condition that the town be named after him. Jerome was once known as the Billion Dollar Copper Camp, and in 1903 a New York reporter called Jerome "the wickedest town in America" because of its disproportionate number of saloons. After the last mines closed in 1953, the population shrank to 50, making it a true ghost town. Now there are about 500 inhabitants, but you'll find about 50 retail establishments. It is somewhat ramshackle, but still charming because it has held off such invasions as convenience stores. Nearby

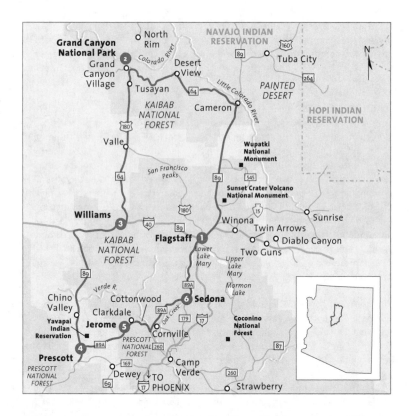

Cottonwood, named for the trees that line the washes here, is a good base for exploring **Dead Horse Ranch State Park,** a 325-acre preserve that offers both high desert and wetlands habitats.

6 Another 28 mi on Alternate Route 89 will bring you to **Sedona,** one of the most unabashedly beautiful places in the state. To the east and south, red rock formations with such evocative names as Cathedral Rock and Bell Rock jut up into the clear blue sky, their dazzling colors intensified by dark-green pine forests. In the 1960s Sedona became an art colony, and art remains the town's primary industry. Of a population of around 9,200 full-time residents, there are at least 300 professional artists and around 50 galleries. Stay overnight in Sedona and drive the 27 mi back to Flagstaff the next day, staying on Alternate Route 89 for one of the prettiest drives in the state.

Flagstaff

Arizona Snowbowl and Summer Resort. This popular downhill ski resort is 14 mi northwest of Flagstaff. One of Flagstaff's most popular winter attractions, the Snowbowl has 30 runs, four chairlifts, and a vertical drop of 2,300 feet. Though almost a fifth of the runs are classified for advanced skiers, the skiing here is more suited to beginners and intermediates. In summer you can hike and picnic and take the Sky Ride at Agassiz Lodge, which climbs to 11,500 feet in 25 minutes for spectacular views of Coconino National Forest. Additionally, you can take trail rides through the forest with MacDonalds Ranch Trail Rides, which also offers hayrides and cookouts. | Snowbowl Rd. | 928/779–1951, 928/774–4481 for trail rides | www.arizonasnowbowl.com | Sky Ride $10, Trail rides $27 | Skiing: mid-Dec.–mid-Apr., daily 9–4; Sky Ride: Memorial

Day–Labor Day, daily 10–4; Labor Day–mid-Oct., Fri.–Sun. 10–4; Trail rides: Memorial Day–Labor Day, daily 9–5 (last ride leaves at 5).

Coconino National Forest. Encompassing 1.8 million acres, Coconino National Forest rises on all sides at the outskirts of Sedona and Flagstaff. Its rugged alpine terrain is cool in summer and very cold in winter. There are extensive hiking trails as well as picnic facilities. | Supervisor's Office, 2323 E. Greenlaw La. | www.fs.fed.us/r3/coconino | 928/527–3600 | Free | Office weekdays 7:30–4:30; forest daily.

Peaks Ranger Station. This district office north of Flagstaff has useful hiking and recreational guides to the Coconino National Forest. | 5075 N. U.S. 89 | 928/526–0866 | www.fs.fed.us/r3/coconino | Free | Office weekdays 7:30–4:30; forest daily.

Historic Downtown District. Some excellent examples of Victorian, Tudor Revival, and early art deco architecture give a feel for life in this former logging and railroad town. | Between Beaver and San Francisco Sts. | 928/774–4505 | Free | Daily.

The Tudor Revival–style **Santa Fe Depot** was constructed in the early 1900s. Today, it houses the historic district's visitor center, where a walking-tour map of the area is available. It's still a working Amtrak station. | 1 E. Rte. 66 | 928/774–4505 | Free | Daily.

Lowell Observatory. Clyde Tombaugh discovered Pluto at this historic 1894 observatory 1 mi west of Flagstaff; other work here led to the theory of an expanding universe. At the Steele Visitor Center, you can view astronomy exhibits, hear lectures, and look at the sun through a solar telescope. Throughout the year, the observatory is open for night viewing and special presentations, but the days and hours vary monthly. Take Interstate 17 to Milton Street. | 1400 W. Mars Hill Rd. | www.lowell.edu | 928/774–2096 | $4, separate admission for night viewing | Apr.–Oct., daily 9–5; Nov.–Mar., daily noon–5; night viewing varies monthly.

Museum of Northern Arizona. This museum 3 mi north of Flagstaff is highly regarded for its research in the natural and cultural history of the Colorado Plateau. Artifacts tell the story of life here from 15,000 BC to the present. There is an actual Hopi kiva ceremonial room (not a replica) as well as katsinas and other Native American arts and crafts. | 3101 N. Fort Valley Rd. (U.S. 180) | 928/774–5211 | www.musnaz.org | $5 | Daily 9–5.

Riordan Mansion State Historic Park. This park is a testament to Flagstaff's logging days. Its central attraction is a 13,000-square-foot, 40-room Arts and Crafts mansion built in 1904 for timber moguls Michael and Timothy Riordan. It was designed by Charles Whittlesley, who also built the El Tovar Hotel at the Grand Canyon. Everything on display—family photos, furniture, and the like—is original to the house; much of the furniture is by Gustav Stickley. Guided tours are available on the hour. Take I–40 (exit 190) or I–17 (exit Milton Road). | 409 Riordan Rd. | www.pr.state.az.us | 928/779–4395 | $6 | May–Oct., daily 8:30–5; Nov.–Apr., daily 10:30–5.

Sunset Crater Volcano National Monument. This 1,000-foot cinder cone 17 mi north of Flagstaff was an active volcano 900 years ago. Its final eruption contained iron and sulfur, which lends the rim a glow reminiscent of a sunset, hence the crater's name. You can hike around, but not into, the crater. Take U.S. 89 north for 12 mi; turn right onto the road marked "Sunset Crater," and go another 2 mi to the visitor center. | Sunset Crater-Wupatki Loop Rd. | www.nps.gov/sucr | 928/526–0502 | $5 (includes admission to Wupatki National Monument) | Mid-May–Sept., daily 8–6; Oct.–mid-May, daily 9–5.

Walnut Canyon National Monument. The more than 300 cliff dwellings built by the Sinagua were abandoned around 1300, but they weren't discovered by Europeans until 1883. If you take the 1-mi Island Trail from the visitor center, you can descend 185 feet and actually walk inside some of the dwellings, getting a good sense of what life might have been like back then. Guides conduct tours on Wednesday, Saturday, and Sunday from Memorial Day through Labor Day. Go 7 mi east of Flagstaff on I–40 to exit 204, then 3 mi south. | Walnut Canyon Rd. | www.nps.gov/waca | 928/526–3367 or 928/556–7152 | $5 | June–Aug., daily 8–6; Mar.–May and Sept.–Nov., daily 8–5; Dec.–Feb., daily 9–5.

Wupatki National Monument. This site 30 mi north of Flagstaff via U.S. 89 was once home to a group of Sinagua, established when nearby Sunset Crater erupted some 900 years ago. The immediate area was settled around 1100 but was abandoned by 1250. Wupatki means "tall house" in the Hopi language—the largest dwelling here was three stories high. Three other ruins can be visited, but others are closed to the public. Go north on U.S. 89 for 12 mi; turn right onto the road marked "Sunset Crater," and go 20 mi beyond the Sunset Crater Visitor Center. | Sunset Crater–Wupatki Loop Rd. | www.nps.gov/wupa | 928/774–9541 or 800/842–7293 | $5 (includes admission to Sunset Crater) | Mid-May–Sept., daily 8–6; Sept.–mid-May, daily 9–5.

Dining

Beaver Street Brewery. American/Casual. Popular among the wood-fired pizzas here is the Enchanted Forest, with Brie, artichoke pesto, Portobello mushrooms, roasted red peppers, and spinach. Whichever pie you order, expect serious amounts of garlic. Sandwiches, such as the Southwestern chicken with three types of cheese, come with a hefty portion of tasty fries. Among the excellent microbrews, the raspberry ale is a local favorite. An outdoor beer garden opens up in summer. | 11 S. Beaver St., Downtown | 928/779–0079 | AE, D, DC, MC, V | $–$$

Café Espress. American/Casual. The menu is largely vegetarian at this natural-foods restaurant. Stir-fried vegetables, pasta dishes, Mediterranean salads, tempeh burgers, pita pizzas, fish or chicken specials, and wonderful baked goods made on the premises all come at prices that will make you feel good, too. | 16 N. San Francisco St., Downtown | 928/774–0541 | MC, V | $

Pasto. Italian. This downtown Italian restaurant—two intimate dining rooms in adjacent historic buildings—is popular with a young crowd for good food at reasonable prices. Such southern Italian standards as lasagna and spaghetti with meatballs appear on the menu along with more innovative fare, such as artichoke orzo and salmon Caesar salad. | 19 E. Aspen St., Downtown | 928/779–1937 | MC, V | No lunch Sept.–May | $–$$

Salsa Brava. Mexican. This cheerful Mexican restaurant, with light-wood booths and colorful designs, eschews heavy Sonoran-style fare in favor of the grilled dishes found in Guadalajara. The fish tacos are particularly good, and this place has the only salsa bar in town. On weekends, come for a huevos rancheros breakfast. | 1800 S. Milton Rd., Downtown | 928/774–1083 | AE, MC, V | $

Grand Canyon National Park

★ **Desert View Drive.** The breathtaking Desert View Drive proceeds east for about 25 mi along the South Rim from Desert View to Grand Canyon Village. There are four marked picnic areas along the route and rest rooms at Tusayan Museum and Desert View. This is the road you come into the park on if you enter at the East Entrance. A fee of $20 per vehicle (regardless of the number of passengers) is collected at the East Entrance near Cameron and also at the South Entrance near Tusayan. This fee is for one week's access. The entrance gates are open 24 hours but are generally staffed from about 7 AM to 7 PM. If you arrive when there's no one at the gate, you may enter legally without paying.

Desert View and the Watchtower make for a climactic final stop if you are driving Desert View Drive from Grand Canyon Village—or a dramatic beginning if you enter the park through the East Entrance. From the top of the 70-foot stone-and-mortar Watchtower, even the muted hues of the distant Painted Desert to the east and the 3,000-foot-high Vermilion Cliffs rising from a high plateau near the Utah border are visible. In the chasm below, angling to the north toward Marble Canyon, you can see an imposing stretch of the Colorado River. The Watchtower houses a glass-enclosed observatory with powerful telescopes. Desert View originally served as a trading post; now the building is a small museum and information center. | Desert View Dr., Grand Canyon | 928/638–2736, 928/638–2360 trading post | Entrance fee $20, Watchtower 25¢ | Watchtower and museum daily 9–5.

Grandview Point. At an altitude of 7,496 feet, Grandview Point, with large stands of ponderosa pine, piñon pine, oak, and juniper, is one of the best overlooks in the canyon. To the northeast is a group of dominant buttes, including Krishna Shrine, Vishnu Temple, Rama Shrine, and Shiva Temple. A short stretch of the Colorado River is also visible. Directly below the point and accessible by the rugged Grandview Trail is Horseshoe Mesa, where you can see ruins of the Last Chance Copper Mine. Grandview Point was also the site of the Grandview Hotel, constructed in the late 1890s but closed in 1908; logs salvaged from the hotel were used for the Kiva Room of the Desert View and the Watchtower. | Off Desert View Dr.

Lipan Point. A mile northeast of Tusayan Ruin, Lipan Point is the canyon's widest. From here you can get an astonishing visual profile of the gorge's geologic history, with a view of every eroded layer of the canyon. You can also see Unkar Delta, where a wide creek joins the Colorado to form powerful rapids and a broad beach. Ancestral Puebloan farmers worked the Unkar Delta for hundreds of years, growing corn, beans, squash, and melons. | Off Desert View Dr.

Moran Point. This overlook was named for American landscape artist Thomas Moran, who painted Grand Canyon scenes from many points on the rim but was especially fond of the light and shadows at this location. He first visited the canyon with John Wesley Powell in 1873, and his vivid canvases helped persuade Congress to create a national park at the Grand Canyon. It's fitting that Moran Point is a favorite spot for photographers and painters. | Off Desert View Dr.

Navajo Point. The 7,461-foot-high point is the probable site of the first Spanish descent into the canyon in 1540. Just west of Navajo Point—the highest natural elevation on the South Rim, at 7,498 feet—is the head of the unmaintained Tanner Trail, a rugged route once favored by prospectors, rustlers (it's also called Horsethief Trail), and bootleggers.

Tusayan Ruin and Museum. Three miles east of Moran Point on the south side of the highway is this archaeological site, which contains evidence of early habitation in the Grand Canyon. *Tusayan* comes from a Hopi phrase meaning "country of isolated buttes," which certainly describes the scenery. The partially intact rock dwellings here were occupied for roughly 20 years around AD 1200 by 30 or so Native American hunters, farmers, and gatherers. They eventually moved on like so many others, perhaps pressured by drought and depletion of natural resources. The museum displays artifacts, models of the dwellings, and exhibits on modern tribes of the region. Free 30-minute guided tours—as many as five during the summer—are given daily. | Desert View Dr., 3 mi east of Moran Point, Grand Canyon | 928/638–2305 | Free | Daily 9–5.

Yaki Point. Here you can get an exceptional view of Wotan's Throne, a majestic flattop butte named by François Matthes, a U.S. Geological Survey scientist who developed the first topographical map of the Grand Canyon. Due north is Buddha Temple, capped by limestone. Newton Butte, with its flat top of red sandstone, lies to the east. At Yaki Point the popular South Kaibab Trail starts the descent to the Inner Gorge, crosses the Colorado over a steel suspension bridge, and wends its way to rustic Phantom Ranch, the only lodging facility at the bottom of the Grand Canyon. If you plan to go more than a mile, carry water with you. If you encounter a mule train, the animals have the right-of-way. Move to the inside of the trail and wait as they pass. Yaki Point is accessible only by the park shuttle bus most of the year. Sometimes, during winter months when visitation is low, the road is open to private vehicles. | Rte. 64, east of Grand Canyon Village.

Dining

Arizona Room. Steak. This casual Southwestern-style steak house serves chicken, steak, and seafood. The food is standard fare, but the canyon views from the dining room add to the flavor of the evening. The restaurant opens at 4:30 PM. | Bright Angel Lodge, West Rim Dr., Grand Canyon Village | 928/638–2631 | Reservations not accepted | AE, D, DC, MC, V | Closed Jan.–mid-Feb. | $–$$

Amfac Cafeteria. American. Locals and park employees favor the home-style food at Yavapai Lodge in Grand Canyon Village, which offers dining on a budget. Fast-food favorites here include the fried chicken, chicken potpie, and fried catfish. The cafeteria also serves up other basics including pastries, burgers, pizza, and pasta. Breakfast served. | Grand Canyon Village | 928/638–2631 | Reservations not accepted | AE, D, DC, MC, V | ¢

El Tovar Dining Room. American. Modeled after a European hunting lodge, this rustic 19th-century dining room built of hand-hewn logs is worth a visit in itself. El Tovar dishes up some fantastic fare including hickory-smoked rainbow trout served with a wild rice salad and topped with an apple–pine nut salsa. Another favorite is the restaurant's New York strip steak framed with buttermilk, cornmeal, onion rings, and pepper Jack au gratin potatoes. | El Tovar Hotel, West Rim Dr., Grand Canyon Village | 928/638–2631 Ext. 6432 | Reservations essential | AE, D, DC, MC, V | $$–$$$

Lodging

Bright Angel Lodge. Famed architect Mary Jane Colter designed this 1935 log-and-stone structure, which sits within a few yards of the canyon rim and blends superbly with the natural environment. Bright Angel offers as much atmosphere as El Tovar for about half the price. Accommodations are in motel-style rooms or cabins. Most rooms in the main lodge share baths; cabins, some with fireplaces and/or canyon views (No. 6158 has both), are scattered among the pines. Expect historic charm and bargain prices but not luxury. The Bright Angel restaurant serves family-style meals all day; the Arizona Room serves dinner only. Restaurant, coffee shop, bar; no a/c, no room phones, no room TVs. | West Rim Dr., Grand Canyon Village | Box 699, Grand Canyon 86023 | 303/297–2757 reservations only, 928/638–2631 Ext. 6284 direct to hotel (no reservations) | fax 303/297–3175 reservations only, 928/638–2876 direct to hotel (no reservations) | www.grandcanyonlodges.com | 30 rooms, 13 with ½ bath, 6 with shared bath; 42 cabins | AE, D, DC, MC, V | $–$$

El Tovar Hotel. A registered National Historic Landmark, El Tovar was built in 1905 of Oregon pine logs and native stone. The hotel's proximity to all of the local facilities, its European hunting lodge atmosphere and its renowned dining room make this the best place to stay on the South Rim. It's usually booked well in advance, though it's easier to get a room here during winter months. Only three suites have canyon views—and these are usually booked two years in advance—but you can enjoy the view anytime from the cocktail lounge's back porch. Restaurant, room service, some refrigerators, some in-room hot tubs, bar; no smoking. | West Rim Dr., Grand Canyon Village | Box 699, Grand Canyon 86023 | 303/297–2757 reservations only, 928/638–2631 Ext. 6384 direct to hotel (no reservations) | fax 303/297–3175 reservations only, 928/638–2855 direct to hotel (no reservations) | www.grandcanyonlodges.com | 70 rooms, 8 suites | AE, D, DC, MC, V | $$–$$$$

Kachina Lodge. This contemporary motel-style lodge is next to the El Tovar Hotel in Grand Canyon Village. Half of the rooms have a partial canyon view for a $10 premium. This property is a good choice for families and for people with physical disabilities. Check in at El Tovar to the east. Kids under 16 stay free. No-smoking rooms; no a/c, no room TVs. | West Rim Dr., Grand Canyon Village | Box 699, Grand Canyon 86023 | 303/297–2757 reservations only, 928/638–2631 Ext. 6384 direct to hotel (no reservations) | fax 303/297–3175 reservations only | www.grandcanyonlodges.com | 50 rooms | AE, D, DC, MC, V | $$

Thunderbird Lodge. This motel is next to Bright Angel Lodge in Grand Canyon Village. For a little extra money, you can get a room with a partial view of the canyon. All rooms have two queen beds. Check in at Bright Angel Lodge, the next hotel to the west. Kids under 16 stay free. No-smoking rooms; no a/c, no room phones, no room TVs. | West Rim Dr., Grand Canyon Village | Box 699, Grand Canyon 86023 | 303/297–2757 (reservations only), 928/638–2631 direct to hotel (no reservations) | fax 303/297–3175 reservations only | www.grandcanyonlodges.com | 55 rooms | AE, D, DC, MC, V | $$

Jerome

Gold King Mine and Ghost Town. Remnants of the mining operation 1 mi north of Jerome include an old shaft, a miner's hut, a worker's baseball field, and a boarding-house, though it's sometimes hard to sort out the history from the junk. | Perkinsville Rd. | 928/634–0053 | www.jeromechamber.com/gold_king_mine.htm | $4 | Daily 9–5.

Jerome State Historic Park. This park has a museum with displays on mining and minerals and the history of Jerome, all housed in the home of James S. Douglas, the owner of the Little Daisy Copper Mine. Of the three mining museums in town, this is the most comprehensive. There are also picnic facilities. | Douglas Rd. | 928/634–5381 | www.pr.state.az.us/parkhtml/jerome.html | $4 | Daily 8–5.

Mine Museum. This small museum houses a collection of mining stock certificates and is staffed by the Jerome Historical Society. | 200 Main St. | 928/634–5477 | $2 | Daily 9–4:30.

Dining

Flatiron Cafe. American/Casual. Drop by this small, eclectic eatery with 1950s-style diner tables, old advertising memorabilia, and Mexican folk art for an afternoon snack, a strong cup of coffee, or healthful sandwiches like black-bean hummus with feta cheese. An outdoor patio across the street offers views of the valley and canyons below. Breakfast served. | 416 Main St. | 928/634–2733 | No credit cards | No dinner | ¢–$

Jerome Brewery. American/Casual. This casual, attractive restaurant is in an old fire station and serves good beer, sandwiches, burgers, pastas, and espresso. | 111 Main St. | 928/639–8477 | MC, V | ¢–$

Jerome Palace. American/Casual. After climbing up the stairs from Main Street to this former boarding house, you'll be ready for hearty burgers, cheesesteaks, and ribs. Outdoor dining is available on a deck that overlooks the Verde Valley. | 410 Clark St. | 928/634–0554 | MC, V | $–$$

Prescott

Courthouse Plaza. In the heart of the city, this plaza is bounded by Gurley and Goodwin streets to the north and south and by Cortez and Montezuma streets to the west and east. The 1916 Yavapai County Courthouse is still standing tall, and it is protected by an equestrian bronze of turn-of-the-20th-century journalist and lawmaker Bucky O'Neill. | 928/445–2000 or 800/266–7534 | Free | Daily.

Phippen Museum of Western Art. This museum 5 mi north of downtown features the work of many prominent artists of the West in its permanent collection. But the focus is the paintings and bronze sculptures of George Phippen. | 4701 U.S. 89 N | 928/778–1385 | www.phippenmuseum.com | $5 | Wed.–Mon. 10–4.

★**Prescott National Forest.** You can hike and camp on the million or more acres of forest land here that surround the town of Prescott, which is in the Bradshaw Ranger District. The winding road from Jerome to Prescott through the forest is one of

Arizona's most breathtaking mountain drives. | Ranger District office: 344 S. Cortez St. | 928/445–1762 | Free | Forest daily; district office weekdays 8–4:30.

Sharlot Hall Museum. Named for historian and poet Sharlot Hall, this museum constitutes three fully restored period homes and an original ponderosa pine cabin that once housed the territorial governor. | 415 W. Gurley St. | 928/445–3122 | $5 | Mon.–Sat. 10–5, Sun. 1–5.

Smoki Museum. This 1935 stone and log building houses a fine collection of Native American artifacts. Though the items on exhibit are genuine, the museum is named for a fictitious tribe, invented in 1921 by Anglos who wanted to draw visitors to Prescott. | 147 N. Arizona St. | 928/445–1230 | $2 | Mon.–Sat. 11–4, Sun. 1–4.

Whiskey Row. This stretch of Montezuma Street flanks Courthouse Plaza's west side. In its heyday it held 20 saloons and prostitution houses; nowadays the historic bars just provide a respite from the street's many boutiques. | Montezuma St. at Courthouse Plaza | Free | Daily.

Dining

El Charro Restaurant. Mexican. This is where you'll find the best Mexican food in town, mostly heavy Sonoran food. The restaurant has been open since 1959, and the enchiladas, fajitas, and basic soft tacos are perennial customer favorites. The salsa has been tamed over the years, but ask for hot sauce and your wish will be granted. | 120 N. Montezuma St. | 928/445–7130 | AE, MC, V | ¢–$

The Palace. American. Legend has it that the patrons who saved the Palace's ornately carved 1880s Brunswick bar from a Whiskey Row fire in 1900 continued drinking at it while the rest of the row burned across the street. Whatever the case, the bar remains the centerpiece of the beautifully restored turn-of-the-20th-century structure, with a high, tin-embossed ceiling. Steaks and chops are the stars here, but the grilled fish and hearty corn chowder are fine, too. | 120 S. Montezuma St. | 928/541–1996 | AE, MC, V | $–$$

Prescott Brewing Company. American. Good beer, good food, good service, and good prices—for a casual meal, it's hard to beat this cheerful, multilevel restaurant. In addition to the chili, fish-and-chips, and British-style bangers (sausage) and mash, you'll also find vegetarian enchiladas made with tofu. | 130 W. Gurley St. | 928/771–2795 | AE, D, DC, MC, V | $–$$

Zuma's Woodfire Café. Italian. One of the more sophisticated restaurants in town, Zuma's offers pizzas made in a wood-burning oven, with such toppings as goat cheese, grilled onions, and fresh basil. The large menu also includes salads, pastas, and grilled meats and fish. | 124 N. Montezuma St. | 928/541–1400 | AE, D, MC, V | $–$$

Lodging

Hassayampa Inn. Built in 1927 for early automobile travelers, the Hassayampa Inn oozes character (be sure to look up at the hand-painted ceiling in the lobby). Some rooms still have the original furnishings. Restaurant, bar. | 122 E. Gurley St., 86301 | 928/778–9434, 800/322–1927 in AZ | fax 928/445–8590 | www.hassayampainn.com | 58 rooms, 10 suites | AE, D, DC, MC, V | BP | $$–$$$

Hotel St. Michael. Don't expect serenity on the busiest corner of Courthouse Plaza, but for low rates and historic charm it's hard to beat this hotel. In operation since 1900, the inn has rooms with 1920s wallpaper and furnishings; some face the plaza and others look out on Thumb Butte. The first-floor Caffé St. Michael serves great coffee and croissants. Coffee shop, shop. | 205 W. Gurley St., 86303 | 928/776–1999 or 800/678–3757 | fax 928/776–7318 | 71 rooms | AE, D, MC, V | $

Hotel Vendome. This World War I–era hostelry has seen miners, health seekers, and such celebrities as cowboy star Tom Mix walk through its doors. Old-fashioned touches, including the original claw-foot tubs, remain. Like many other historic hotels, the Vendome has its obligatory resident ghost (her room costs slightly more). Only a block from Courthouse Plaza, this is a good choice for those who want to combine sightseeing, modern comforts, and good value. Dining room, cable TV. | 230 Cortez St., 86303 | 928/776–0900 or 888/468–3583 | fax 928/771–0395 | www.vendomehotel.com | 16 rooms, 4 suites | AE, D, DC, MC, V | CP | $–$$

Sedona

Chapel of the Holy Cross. Commissioned by Marguerite Brunwige Staude in 1956, this modern landmark south of town is one of the most stunning churches in the Southwest. Set on a red-rock peak, the church and surroundings provide spectacular views of Sedona. | 780 Chapel Rd. | 928/282–4069 | Free | Daily.

★ **Oak Creek Canyon.** This wooded, primarily evergreen canyon, with Oak Creek gurgling through it, begins 1 mi north of Sedona and continues to Flagstaff. Here you'll find camping, fishing, and hiking. | N. Hwy. 89A | 928/282–7722 or 800/288–7336 | Free | Daily.

Pink Jeep Tours. One of the more popular companies in town, Pink Jeep has permits that give them access to trails that other companies can't use. You can choose from a number of tours that highlight everything from the Mogollon Rim to Honanki, an ancient Native American cliff dwelling. | 204 N. Hwy. 89A | 928/282–5000 or 800/873–3662 | www.pinkJeep.com | $40–$95 | Daily 7–5.

Rainbow Trout Farm. You'll get a cane pole, hook, and bait for a buck. Any trout under 8 inches is yours to keep for free. Bigger ones cost $3 to $6. The staff will clean and pack your fish for 50¢. | 3500 N. Hwy. 89A | 928/282–3379 | $1 | Labor Day–Memorial Day, daily 9–5; Memorial Day–Labor Day, daily 8–6.

Red Rock State Park. This 286-acre nature preserve is 2 mi west of Sedona on Highway 89A. Feel free to go on nature walks or a bird-watching excursion, but swimming is not permitted. | 4050 Red Rock Loop Rd. | 928/282–6907 | www.pr.state.az.us | $6 per vehicle with up to four people; $1 each additional person | May–Aug., daily 8–8; Sept. and Apr., daily 8–6; Oct.–Mar., daily 8–5.

Slide Rock State Park. A natural-rock slide that deposits you into a swimming hole is the lure at this state park 6 mi north of town, along with an apple orchard and picnic tables for lunching. In summer, traffic is extreme, and there will probably be a wait to get in. Bring jeans if you plan to slide. | 6871 N. Rte. 89A | 928/282–3034 | $8 per vehicle | Daily 8–7.

Tlaquepaque. Named for the Mexican village it was built to resemble, Tlaquepaque's shops and restaurants are decidedly upscale, and the complex has been planned so you won't be bombarded with endless rows of the same merchandise. | 336 Hwy. 179 | 928/282–4838 | www.tlaquepaque.net | Free | Daily 10–5.

Dining

Dahl & DiLuca. Italian. A husband-and-wife team—Andrea DiLuca and Lisa Dahl—has created one of the most popular Italian restaurants in town with this colorful, eclectic space. Andrea runs the kitchen, and Lisa meets and greets diners as they enter. Lisa also slips into the kitchen every day to make delicious homemade soups like white bean with ham and hearty minestrone. | 2321 W. Rte. 89A | 928/282–5219 | AE, D, MC, V | No lunch | $$–$$$

Heartline Café. Southwestern. Fresh flowers and innovative, modern cuisine are this attractive café's hallmarks. The oak-grilled salmon marinated in tequila and lime and the chicken breast with prickly-pear sauce are two options. Appealing vegetarian plates are also on the menu. | 1610 W. Rte. 89A | 928/282–0785 | AE, D, MC, V | No lunch Sun. | $$–$$$

Shugrue's Hillside. American. Almost everything is good here, which has made this one of the most popular restaurants in Sedona. Rack of lamb and filet mignon are prepared and presented simply. There's a small, thoughtful, and well-priced wine list as well. Don't be confused: Shugrue's Hillside is not owned by the same folks who own Shugrue's West, a less appealing restaurant. | 671 Rte. 179 | 928/282–5300 | AE, DC, MC, V | $$–$$$$

Thai Spices. Thai. This small, unadorned restaurant has a loyal following of vegetarians and health-food enthusiasts. The curries, especially red curry with tempeh, are delicious and can be prepared at the spice level of your choice. There's plenty here for carnivores, too: traditional pad thai with chicken is satisfying, and the spicy beef salad will make your hair stand on end. | 2986 W. Rte. 89A | 928/282–0599 | MC, V | ¢–$

Lodging

Alma de Sedona. One of Sedona's most enchanting B&Bs, this family operation has large rooms with spectacular views and ultracomfortable beds. All rooms have private entrances and patios, and you'll find bath salts and candles in the bathrooms. Some in-room hot tubs, cable TV, pool, meeting room; no smoking. | 50 Hozoni Dr., 86336 | 928/282–2737 or 800/923–2282 | fax 928/203–4141 | www.almadesedona.com | 12 rooms | AE, MC, V | BP | $$$–$$$$

The Canyon Wren. The best value in the Oak Creek Canyon area, this small B&B has freestanding cabins with views of the canyon walls. Cabins have private decks, fireplaces, and whirlpool tubs. Breakfast is a selection of delicious baked goods. In-room hot tubs, kitchens; no room TVs, no room phones. | 6425 N. Rte. 89A, 86336 | 928/282–6900 or 800/437–9736 | fax 928/282–6978 | www.canyonwrencabins.com | 4 cabins | AE, D, MC, V | CP | $$

L'Auberge de Sedona. This trilevel resort consists of a central lodge building; a motel-style structure called the Orchards, reached by means of an incline railway; and—the major attraction—cabins in the woods along Oak Creek. Rooms in the Orchards are less expensive—and more standard-motel issue—while rooms in the lodge are decorated in Provençal style. The large cabins along the creek have wood-burning fireplaces. 2 restaurants, pool, hot tub. | L'Auberge La. | Box B, 86336 | 928/282–1661 or 800/272–6777 | fax 928/282–2885 | www.lauberge.com | 69 rooms, 30 cabins | AE, D, DC, MC, V | $$$–$$$$

Quail Ridge Resort. One of the more affordable accommodations in the Sedona area, this small, family-oriented resort in the Village of Oak Creek is about 6½ mi south of town. It offers smaller rooms or separate, private A-frame chalets with kitchens. Picnic area, some kitchenettes, some microwaves, cable TV, 2 tennis courts, pool, hot tub, bicycles, hiking, laundry facilities, business services; no smoking. | 120 Canyon Circle Dr., 86351 | 928/284–9327 | fax 928/284–0832 | www.quailridgeresort.com | 4 rooms, 9 chalets | AE, D, MC, V | $–$$

Williams

Grand Canyon Railway. In 1989 the railway re-inaugurated service that had first been established in 1901; railcars date from the 1920s. This scenic train route runs 65 mi from the Williams Depot to the South Rim of the Grand Canyon (2½ hours each way). There are several classes of service; some tickets include food and beverages. The depot is worth a visit since there is a small railroad museum and a vintage train car to explore. | N. Grand Canyon Blvd. at Fray Marcos Blvd. | 800/843–8724 | $58–$147. Depot free | Departs daily at 10 AM, returning to Williams at 3:30.

Kaibab National Forest. This huge national forest around the Grand Canyon encompasses more than 1.6 million acres. Wildlife unique to the land include the mule deer and Kaibab squirrel. Forested with pines and sycamores, the area offers hiking, fishing (trout), and camping. | Headquarters: 800 S. 6th St. | www.fs.fed.us/r3/kai | 928/635–2681 | Free | Daily.

Williams Ski Area. Four slopes, open from mid-December through much of March, include one for beginners only. There are also cross-country trails. Go 1½ mi south on 4th Street, then 1½ mi west on Ski Area Road. | Ski Area Rd. | 928/635–9330 | www.williamsskiarea.com | Mid-Dec.–Mar., Thurs.–Sun. 9–5.

Dining

Cruisers Café 66. American. Icons from old Route 66 fill this renovated gas station. Favorite dishes include burgers, steaks, ribs, pizzas, salads, and of course, malts. | 233 W. Rte. 66 | 928/635–2445 | AE, D, MC, V | No lunch | $–$$

Grand Canyon Coffee Café. Café. You'll find good espresso drinks here, along with wonderful sandwiches on homemade focaccia. This is the home of the mountain man sandwich (piled-high roast beef with cheddar cheese and onions on Italian bread). Try an egg-cream soda with Ghirardelli chocolate if you're feeling nostalgic. Harley-Davidson artifacts fill the space, and some of them are for sale. | 125 W. Rte. 66 | 928/635–1255 | AE, MC, V | No dinner Jan.–Feb. | ¢

Pancho McGillicuddy's. Mexican. Dating from the late 1800s when it was originally the Cabinet Saloon, this restaurant is on the National Register of Historic places. Wood tables, faux Mexican windows with iron bars, and a fountain add to the experience. Combination shrimp, chicken, and beef fajitas and chimichangas are on the menu, but the specialty locals rave about are the "armadillo eggs"—deep-fried jalapeños stuffed with cheese. | 141 Railroad Ave. | 928/635–4150 | AE, D, MC, V | $–$$

Rod's Steak House. Steak. You can't miss the huge plastic Angus cow out front of this casual steak house known for charred steaks and prime rib (they have a tendency to overcook). The local favorite here is Rod's special charred steak, a hefty sirloin dipped in sugar and grilled over mesquite. | 301 E. Bill Williams Ave. | 928/635–2671 | MC, V | $–$$$

ARKANSAS

SCENIC 7 BYWAY
THROUGH THE OUACHITAS AND OZARKS

Distance: 295 mi   Time: 5 hours to several days
Overnight Breaks: Jasper, Harrison, Hot Springs, Russellville

A gentle roller-coaster ride, Scenic 7 Byway (Route 7) winds across undisturbed forests, through busy towns, and past small outposts, providing some breathtaking vistas in the process.

The route begins at Exit 78 of I-30, about 55 mi southwest of Little Rock, and goes 190 mi north to Harrison, crossing the Arkansas River about halfway along. The southern portion of Route 7 undulates across the Ouachita Mountains, whose folds and faults run in a rare east–west pattern rather than the north–south alignment common to most of the world's ranges. North of the Arkansas river town of Russellville, the highway's twists, turns, ups, and downs continue. Occasionally, the road rides the tops of mountain ridges for panoramic views before descending to wide valleys.

Be aware that hills and curves and occasional fog and snow can make the drive challenging, particularly in the northern portion of the journey. A fair amount of traffic can accumulate, especially near Hot Springs and Russellville; this is one of the main north–south routes through the hills. Take your time and explore some of the side roads if you're interested in even steeper grades and tighter turns.

❶ Heading north from Exit 78 of I-30 (north of Arkadelphia), **DeGray Lake** soon appears to the west. Surrounded by the Ouachita Mountains, its shoreline is dotted with campgrounds, rental cabins, and marinas. At **DeGray Lake Resort State Park,** on the lake's northeast shore, is a lodge with a restaurant and pool, a championship golf course, a full-service marina, and RV and tent campsites.

❷ From DeGray, Route 7 winds north through the countryside for approximately 25 mi toward Hot Springs. Just south of Hot Springs is the man-made **Lake Hamilton,** which has long been a favorite spot for vacationers, retirees, and residents desiring a water view. The highway passes the docks of the *Belle of Hot Springs,* an excursion boat that sails Lake Hamilton. There are shopping malls near the intersection with U.S. 270. Farther toward downtown Hot Springs you pass the **Oaklawn Racetrack and Jockey Club,** Arkansas's only thoroughbred track.

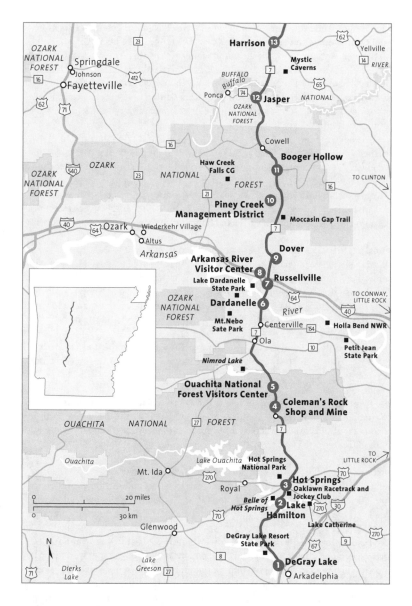

③ The thermal waters at **Hot Springs** have drawn visitors since prehistoric days. Bathhouse Row—eight turn-of-the-20th-century spa buildings in the heart of town—is the center of **Hot Springs National Park,** which also has a campground, 30 mi of hiking trails, and picnic areas in mountains and gorges. The visitor center and museum are in the restored Fordyce Bathhouse. Hot Springs has numerous accommodations worthy of an overnight stay.

④ Leaving Hot Springs, follow Route 7 up a sharp left turn on the byway (along U.S. 70), pass Gulfa Gorge, DeSoto Park, the Belvedere Country Club, and the tin-roof stands of Snow Springs Flea Market, which are full on weekends. Crystal boulders on a weathered, weedy stand mark the edge of Mountain Valley. Fifteen miles north of

Hot Springs is the tiny town of Blue Springs, which contains **Coleman's Rock Shop and Crystal Mines** and not much else. Coleman's is one of the biggest crystal shops in the area. Note that only the clear and white crystals are from Arkansas.

⑤ Jessieville has a handsome native-stone schoolhouse that was established in 1937. Staff at the **Ouachita National Forest Visitors Center,** a mile north, can provide information on the forest's trails, scenic drives, sport-utility-vehicle drives, and outdoor activities.

The next 40 mi through the Ouachita National Forest bring the fine views that earned Route 7 its scenic-byway status. Roadside signs point out picnic tables and trailheads. The route makes ear-popping descents and steep climbs as the Ouachitas loom taller and the valleys narrow. There are pretty crossings of Fourche LaFave River branches, and you can gaze south over Nimrod Lake and north across the Arkansas River valley. Past the village of Ola and the Petit Jean River, the environs of Centerville provide scenes of cattle and horses grazing in white-fenced pastures.

⑥ Crossing the flat Arkansas River floodplain, Route 7 enters the old river town of **Dardanelle,** where tall, bare Dardanelle Rock at its northern edge served as a landmark for explorers and pioneers. Among cottages and Victorian homes west of Route 7 on Front Street rises the ancient **Council Oak.** Beneath this imposing tree, now surrounded by a low iron fence, Chief Black Fox and other Cherokees reluctantly agreed to hand over part of their treaty-given lands along the river to white settlers in 1820.

⑦ Heading north again on Route 7 you come to **Russellville,** on the north side of the Arkansas River. Chain restaurants and motels abound and there are grocery stores to stock your cooler.

⑧ Just west of Route 7 and Russellville is the **Arkansas River Visitor Center,** in **Lake Dardanelle State Park.** The visitor center is operated by the U.S. Army Corps of Engineers at Old Post Road Park and sits above Dardanelle Lock and Dam, whose 54-foot lift makes it the largest on the river as it forms the 50-mi-long lake.

⑨ Across I–40 heading north out of Russellville, the Scenic 7 Byway passes the lakeside Shiloh Park. Roadside churches, used-car lots, retread tire outlets, homes, and a jerry-built flea market give way to forests and farms. Gradually the hills open into a wide valley where beef cattle graze, and 7 mi from the interstate, a green sign marks the town limits of **Dover,** the Pope County seat before it was moved to Russellville.

Beyond Dover to the north, the landscape returns to pastures and hay barns in a flat valley along **Illinois Bayou,** which carved cliffs into the limestone layers along its north side. The road runs uphill into mountain terrain, with more cliffs and slopes visible through the trees. The small town of Pleasant Valley is along the highway. A sign warns that the road is "Crooked and Steep Next 63 Miles" as it snakes uphill through a forest of pine and hardwoods. Road signs mark sharp curves and intersections.

⑩ Soon after Scenic 7 enters the Ozark National Forest's **Piney Creek Management District,** there's a turnoff to Long Pool Campground at a scenic spot with a natural pool in Big Piney Creek. The site has hiking trails, fishing, swimming, picnic areas, and a spot to launch canoes. Signs point out rental cabins and a private campground in the area.

⑪ Inside the forest, the road crosses Church Bell Ridge and passes the old Lane Cemetery. The Moccasin Gap horse trail leads west into the trees. The road, still winding uphill, slices through the limestone. The forest floor is strewn with rocks coated with green and gray lichen and moss. You may want to stop and pick up a ham or a wonderfully tacky souvenir in **Booger Hollow**—Pop. 7, Countin' One Coon Dog reads the town sign. Scenic 7 curves out of Booger Hollow along the top of a ridge, gaining a bit more altitude. There are more vistas—one of the finest is at a turnoff point called Rotary Ann, before you pass through Pelsor.

Scenic 7 soon passes into Newton County. A parking lot sits at an access point to the **Ozark Highlands Trail,** which runs 178 mi between Lake Fort Smith State Park and Tyler Bend Campground on the Buffalo River. The rustic Fairview campground is nearby. Continuing north you pass through Lurton, then farms carved into the top of a ridge.

⓬ In and around **Jasper** are several B&Bs and campgrounds that you might want to explore for an overnight break. A brake-check area and two runaway-truck ramps are at the ready as Scenic 7 curves and plummets downhill into the Newton County seat. The small town radiates from its weathered stone courthouse. Close by are churches, crafts shops, cafés, and **Arkansas House Bed and Breakfast.**

The journey from Jasper to Harrison is about 25 mi along Scenic 7. You cross the Little Buffalo River, then curve past the Ozark National River Visitor Center, RV parks, cabins, and shops as the road heads through the forests and bluffs lining the **Buffalo National River.** At the river crossing are an information station, a parking lot, and trailheads. Gravel roads lead to historic homesteads and churches, and it's possible to spot elk, which have been reintroduced to the region. On an uphill curve, a marker commemorates the site where stone was quarried in 1836 for Arkansas's contribution to the Washington Monument. Soon Scenic 7 passes Mystic Caverns, still beautiful despite heavy damage resulting from centuries of human use.

⓭ The terrain flattens as Scenic 7 heads into **Harrison.** RV camps, a smoked-meats store, and fast-food spots begin to appear between the farms. Harrison's population of 12,000 makes it seem a booming metropolis after the small Ozark communities. Restaurants, motels, and shops line its highways and circle its courthouse square.

From Harrison, Route 7 leads northeast to the shores of Bull Shoals Lake (42 mi). U.S. 62 takes you to Eureka Springs (43 mi) to the west and Mountain Home (50 mi) to the east; U.S. 65 goes north to Branson, Missouri (39 mi). With the Ozark Mountains surrounding you, there's not a bad route to take.

DeGray Lake

DeGray Lake Resort State Park. DeGray is a man-made 13,800-acre lake surrounded by the Ouachita Mountains, with cabins, camping, and marinas along its shores (the park itself encompasses 986 acres along the lakefront). You can rent ski boats, pontoon boats, and Jet Skis at the marina, and horses at the stables. There are five trails in the park; one of the most popular, the Green Heron, leaves from the visitor center near the beginning of the park road. An 18-hole golf course is north of the lake and 113 campsites are available. There are 10 Corps of Engineers campsites and day-use areas here. | 2027 State Park Entrance Rd., Bismarck | 501/865–2801 | www.degray.com | Free | Daily.

Dining

O'Keefes Fish Net. Seafood. Weekend evenings the parking lot is full of vehicles with boats in tow. The crowds inside are usually sunburned, finishing up a day on the lake with family-friendly service and large plates of fried seafood—grain-fed catfish, jumbo and baby shrimp, oysters, and crawfish. The steaks and burgers are just as good. | Rte. 7 at DeGray Lake | 870/246–7885 | D, MC, V | Closed Mon. No lunch Tues.–Sat. | $–$$

Lodging

DeGray Lake Resort. Wander along the lakeside path at this island lodge and enjoy the peace that descends on the water come nightfall. The low-lying building blends in with the woods around it—just enough of it has been cleared for a view of the lake. A maroon and blue color scheme dominates the modern rooms. You can take a dip in the large pool, or venture back down the road a couple of miles to the marina and golf course for activities. Restaurant, room service, cable TV, 18-hole golf course, 2 tennis courts, pool, gym, hot tub, fishing, hiking, business services, meeting rooms, no-smoking rooms. | 2027 State Park Entrance Rd., Bismarck 71929 | 501/865–2801 or 800/737–8355 | www.degray.com | 96 rooms | AE, D, MC, V | $

Harrison

Boone County Heritage Museum. Harrison's past comes alive with this museum's genealogy library, railroad room, Civil War artifacts, and Native American relics. | 110 S. Cherry St. | 870/741–3312 | $2 | Mar.–Nov., weekdays 10–4; Dec.–Feb., Thurs. 10–4.

Mystic Caverns. The upper level has enormous, well-lit formations, but has seen some wear from years of use. The lower level, Crystal Dome, is pristine—discovered 100 years after the former. Be warned that some may find the climb strenuous. There's a mineral museum and a gift shop on-site. | Rte. 7, 8 mi south of Harrison | 870/743–1739 | www.mysticcaverns.com | $11 | Mar.–May and Sept.–Oct., Mon.–Sat. 9–5; June–Aug., Mon.–Sat. 9–6; Nov.–Jan., Mon.–Sat. 9–4; Feb., Wed.–Sat. 10–4.

Dining

Ol' Rockhouse. Barbecue. This converted turn-of-the-20th-century home is filled with local memorabilia, including old school photographs and athletic trophies. You can also eat outside on the deck. Of the hickory-smoked meats on offer, brisket is most popular, but the steaks run a close second. | 416 S. Pine St. | 870/741–8047 | MC, V | No dinner Sun. | $

Catfish Wharf. American. Deep-fried and grilled catfish and hush puppies are the specialties at this casual, no-nonsense establishment with speedy service. For something

ARKANSAS RULES OF THE ROAD

License Requirements: Arkansas residents receive an intermediate license at 16, and a regular license at 18. Valid out-of-state and foreign driver's licenses are good in Arkansas.

Right Turn on Red: A right turn on red at a traffic signal is permitted *after* you come to a full stop and yield to pedestrians and other traffic, unless otherwise posted.

Seat Belt and Helmet Laws: State law requires all passengers to wear seat belts. All children under age five must wear safety restraints while the vehicle is in motion. Children under age four or weighing less than 40 pounds must be secured in an approved safety seat. Motorcycle drivers and passengers under the age of 20 are required to wear helmets.

Speed Limits: Speed limits on major freeways are from 60 to 70 mph.

Other Regulations: Vehicle headlights must be turned on when windshield wipers are on.

For More Information: Office of Motor Vehicles | 501/682–7059 | www.state.ar.us/dfa/motorvehicle/.

heavier, try the ribs or the burgers. | 1318 U.S. 62/65N | 870/741–9200 | D, MC, V | Closed Sun. | ¢–$

Lodging

Holiday Inn Express and Suites. This property has what is fair to expect from any Holiday Inn—clean, up-to-date rooms and public spaces. Two-bedroom suites are also available for a good price. The breakfast bar is an extended Continental with occasional hot items. Some kitchenettes, cable TV, indoor pool, hot tub, laundry facilities, business services, no-smoking rooms. | 117 Rte. 43 E, 72601 | 870/741–3636 | fax 870/741–8222 | www.hiexpress.com | 90 rooms, 23 suites | AE, D, DC, MC, V | CP | $

Lost Spur Guest Ranch. Daily trail rides and chuckwagon breakfasts cooked over a campfire are highlights of a stay at Lost Spur. The 116-acre ranch is on the banks of Crooked Creek, with opportunities for canoeing, swimming, and wade fishing (bring your own gear). Country cabins have two bedrooms and a combination of queen and bunk beds. All meals and activities are included in the rate. The ranch is 17 mi north of Harrison off Route 7. Dining room, refrigerators, pond, beach, fishing, basketball, horseback riding, horseshoes, volleyball, recreation room, children's programs (ages 6–16), playground; no room phones, no room TVs, no smoking. | 8148 Lost Spur Rd., 72601 | 870/743–7787 or 800/774–2414 | fax 870/743–6686 | www.lostspur.com | 2 rooms, 4 cabins | D, MC, V | Closed Nov.–Mar. | FAP | $$–$$$

Hot Springs

Belle of Hot Springs. The 400-passenger excursion boat sails Lake Hamilton for sightseeing, lunch, and ice-cream-social cruises. Evenings you can take a sunset dinner-dance cruise. | 5 mi south of Hot Springs | 5200 Central Ave. (Rte. 7) | 501/525–4438 | www.belleriverboat.com | $11–$30 | Feb.–Nov., daily.

Bukstaff Bathhouse. Operating since 1912, this is the only bathhouse on the row to still offer spa services. A typical bathing package includes a mineral bath in a whirlpool tub, a loofah scrub, and a 20-minute massage for $42. The bathhouse doesn't accept reservations. | 509 Central Ave. (Rte. 7) | 501/623–2308 | www.buckstaffbaths.com | Mar.–Nov., Mon.–Sat. 7–11:45 and 1:30–3; Dec.–Feb., weekdays 7–11:45 and 1:30–3, Sat. 7–11:45.

Coleman's Rock Shop & Crystal Mine. Register at the store to dig for crystals nearby (and keep what you find), or browse among table after table of those already cleaned and polished. The largest, imported pieces are outside. | 15 mi north of Hot Springs | 5837 Rte. 7, Blue Springs | 501/984–5328 | Daily 8–8.

★**Fordyce Bathhouse.** The restored bathhouse museum, in the most opulent building on Hot Springs National Park's Bathhouse Row, is also the park's visitor center. Stained-glass windows and an ornate fountain grace the original men's bathing area. After your tour (self- or ranger-guided), check out the film and the bookstore. | 369 Central Ave. (Rte. 7) | 501/624–3383 | www.nps.gov/hosp | Free | Daily 9–5.

Lake Catherine State Park. The Civilian Conservation Corps built the 17 modern, fully equipped cabins in this park. There are also hookups for RV and tent camping, rent-a-camp equipment, swimming, fishing, and from June to August, boat and horse rental. | Off Rte. 171, 5 mi south of Hot Springs, 1200 Catherine Park Rd. | 501/844–4176 | www.arkansasstateparks.com | Free | Daily dawn–dusk.

Lake Ouachita State Park. Swim, ski, scuba dive, rent a boat, fish, hike trails, and take part in interpretive programs on this 40,000-acre lake. The park is on the eastern tip. Fully equipped housekeeping cabins, RV and tent campsites, picnic areas, and a marina with boat rentals and supplies are on-site. | Off Rte. 227, 10 mi northeast of Hot Springs, 5451 Mountain Pine Rd., Mountain Pine | 501/767–9366 | www. arkansasstateparks.com | Free | Daily dawn–dusk.

Ouachita National Forest. The oldest and largest state forest in the United States has 1.6 million acres of woodland dotted with campsites, fishing areas, and picnic sites. Hiking trails include the 223-mi-long Ouachita National Recreation Trail, which runs from Talimina, OK, to Pinnacle Mountain State Park near Little Rock. | Ouachita National Recreational Trail access, 17 mi north of Hot Springs on Rte. 7 | 501/321–5202 | www.fs.fed.us | Free | Daily.

Dining

Bohemia. Eastern European. Bratwurst, herring, roast pork, and sauerbraten are some of the Germanic options at Bohemia. The Eastern European heritage of the owner-chef is evident not only in the menu, but in the collector's plates and original Czech art that adorn the walls. | 517 Park Ave. | 501/623–9661 | AE, D, MC, V | Closed Sun. No lunch Fri.–Mon. and Wed. | $–$$

Colonial Pancake House. Café. A line often forms outside this pancake house on weekends. Not to worry—someone will come and serve you coffee while you wait. The made-to-order pancakes and waffles come from the Colonial's own recipe. | 111 Central Ave. (Rte. 7) | 501/624–9273 | MC, V | Closed Mon. No dinner | ¢

Mollie's. American/Casual. You can get fried catfish, brisket, and a decent steak at this local favorite. The made-from-scratch soups are particularly good. Eat in the homey dining room or out on the patio. | 538 W. Grand Ave. | 501/623–6582 | AE, D, DC, MC, V | Closed Sun. | $–$$

Lodging

Arlington Resort Hotel and Spa. You'll find hot spring waters everywhere at the Arlington: in the large mountainside hot tub, in the lobby water fountain, at the third-floor spa (open to the public), and, for a little extra, piped into your bathtub. The spacious old rooms have Louis XIV–inspired furnishings; huge magnolias decorate the bedspreads and curtains. 2 restaurants, room service, some refrigerators, cable TV, golf privileges, pool, gym, hair salon, outdoor hot tub, spa, bar, video game room, shops, laundry service, business services, no-smoking floors. | 239 Central Ave. (Rte. 7), 71901 | 501/623–7771, 800/643–1502 outside AR | fax 501/623–2243 | www.arlingtonhotel.com | 439 rooms, 42 suites | AE, D, MC, V | $–$$$

Downtowner Hotel & Spa. The balconies of this affordable hotel one block north of bathhouse row face downtown Hot Springs' main strip. Traditional wood furnishings and small-scale florals decorate the rooms. As a guest you have first choice of appointments for the on-site bathhouse treatments. Restaurant, cable TV, pool, hair salon, outdoor hot tub, spa, shops, laundry services, no-smoking rooms. | 135 Central Ave. (Rte. 7), 71901 | 501/624–5521 or 800/251–1962 | fax 501/624–4635 | www.angelfire.com/ar/downtownerhs | 139 rooms | AE, D, DC, MC, V | ¢–$

1890s Williams House Bed and Breakfast. Walk through an etched-glass panel door into the Victorian era. The spacious foyer—with deep-red carpeting and an ornate carved-wood staircase—sets the tone for the whole mansion. The dining room, parlor, and the guest rooms are similarly outfitted with intricate woodwork, rich colors, and period antiques. The carriage house out back holds two suites. Cable TV, some in-room hot tubs, library; no smoking. | 420 Quapaw Ave., 71901 | 501/624–4275 or 800/756–4635 | fax 501/321–9466 | www.1890swilliamshouse.com | 6 rooms | AE, D, MC, V | BP | $$–$$$

Jasper

Lost Valley Canoes. Guides take small groups on 1- to 10-day Buffalo National River float trips. You stop to explore caves, bluffs, and trails along the way. Lodging is in campgrounds or cabins. | Off Rte. 74, 6 mi east of Jasper | Rte. 43 A, Ponca | 870/861–5522 | www.lostvalleycanoes.com.

Dining

Cliff House Inn Restaurant. Southern. For homemade biscuits, fried catfish, pinto beans with sugar-cured ham, and plain good Southern food, you've come to the right place. Rustic tools and knickknacks line the walls, including a circa-1932 boat motor, but the main distraction is undoubtedly the stunning view into the state's deepest natural valley. Breakfast is also served. | 4 mi south of Jasper on Rte. 7 | 870/446–2292 | DC, MC, V | Closed Nov.–mid-March. No dinner. | ¢–$

Dairy Diner. American. This family-owned diner is associated with the Arkansas House. Daily specials, including apricot chicken, round out a menu of casual comfort foods. | Rte. 7 at Rte. 74 | 870/446–5343 | AE, D, MC, V | ¢–$

Jasper Mercantile. Café. Breakfast is a draw here, but so are the banana splits, milk shakes, and ice-cream sodas from the fountain. For dinner, pasta, fried shrimp, and steaks are on the menu. The restaurant was once a general store and is still decorated as such. | 205 E. Court (Rte. 7) | 870/446–5775 | D, MC, V | ¢–$

Lodging

Arkansas House Bed and Breakfast. The Little Buffalo River flows behind this 1940s, two-story building made with native-cut limestone. Family heirlooms are placed carefully among the Victorian furnishings. Stone-sculpture animals play among the pools in the yard's rock garden. If he's out, you may visit with Coco, a friendly 500-pound bear who lives in an enclosure behind the house. Restaurant, some in-room hot tubs, some microwaves, some refrigerators, cable TV, in-room VCRs, laundry facilities. | 217 Rte. 7, 72641 | 870/446–5179 or 888/274–6873 | http://thearkansashouse.com | 2 rooms, 3 suites | AE, D, DC, MC, V | BP | $

Cliff House Inn. You feel like you're floating at the Cliff House, which is suspended on stilts over a huge, verdant valley. Country floral swags and wallpaper borders spruce up the standard motel rooms. The restaurant and gift shop are upstairs; the rooms are downstairs. Restaurant, shop; no room phones, no smoking. | 4 mi south of Jasper on Rte. 7 | HCR 31, Box 85, 72641 | 870/446–2292 | www.mcrush.com/cliffhouse | 5 rooms | D, MC, V | Closed Nov.–mid-Mar. | ¢–$

Ozarks Crawford's Cabins. Swing on your back porch and look into the woods adjoining the Ozark National Forest at Crawford's. The two dark-wood log cabins have full kitchens, woodwork throughout, stone floors, some bent-willow furniture, and handmade quilts. The Arkansan has two bedrooms, Bear Hollow has one. A reproduction of an old general store has a deli counter. Kitchens; no smoking. | 3 mi north of Jasper on Rte. 7 | HCR 31, Box 221, 72641 | 870/446–2478 | fax 870/446–5824 | www.buffalorivercountry.com | 2 cabins | AE, D, MC, V | $

Russellville

Arkansas River Visitor Center. "Renaissance of the River" exhibits explain the river's development and the Dardanelle Lock and Dam. RV camping, a boat ramp, tennis courts, a basketball court, a playground, a ball field, and a soccer–football field are on-site. | 1590 Lock and Dam Rd. | 479/968–5008 | www.usace.army.mil | Free | Weekdays 9–4.

Holla Bend National Wildlife Refuge. The 7,055-acre refuge is a wildlife-rich area that becomes a bird-watcher's paradise from November through February. Boat ramps provide access to Lodge Lake and the Arkansas River. | 11 mi southeast of Russellville | Rte. 155, Dardanelle | 479/229–4300 | www.southeast.fws.gov | Free | Daily.

Lake Dardanelle State Park. Created by damming the Arkansas River, this 34,000-acre body of water is a popular recreational lake as well as a barge channel. The park has two areas—Russellville (east of town on Lock and Dam Road) and Dardanelle (6 mi southeast of Russellville on Route 22). Both have marinas, campsites, picnic areas, and beaches. Interpretive programs are at the Russellville location only. | Office: 100 State Park Dr., Russellville | 479/967–5516 | www.arkansasstateparks.com | Free | Daily.

Mount Nebo State Park. Up a steep, zigzag road, the 3,000-acre Mount Nebo State Park offers spectacular views of the Arkansas River valley. The park has cabins, campsites, 14 mi of hiking trails, a swimming pool, tennis courts, picnic areas, playgrounds, pavilions, a small store with bicycle rentals, and a visitor center with exhibits. | Off Rte.155, 12 mi southwest of Russellville | 1 State Park Dr., Dardanelle | 479/229–3655 | www.arkansasstateparks.com | Free | Daily.

Nimrod Lake. Known for its excellent catfish, crappie, and white bass fishing, this 3,700-acre Army Corps of Engineers lake also has waterskiing, camping, picnicking, swimming, and hiking. It's off Route 7, 34 mi south of Russellville. | Rte. 60 | 479/272–4324 | www.swl.usace.army.mil | Free | Daily.

Dining
Guido's Deli. Delicatessens. A small dining area gives you the option of eating in or taking your purchases elsewhere for a picnic. Sandwiches and daily lunch specials are available. The desserts alone are worth stopping for—baklava, turtle cheese cake, bourbon pecan pie, and peanut butter–cup pie. | 113 N. El Paso Ave. | 479/967–8781 | No credit cards | Closed weekends. No dinner | ¢

Madame Wu's Hunan Restaurant. Chinese. A long menu includes Hunan and Szechuan dishes. For about $10, a family dinner comes with an egg roll, a crabmeat wonton, and your choice of main dish and a soup. | 914 S. Arkansas Ave. | 479/968–4569 | MC, V | No lunch Sat. | $–$$

Lodging
Holiday Inn. This two-story modern hotel is the closest one to Lake Dardanelle. A free shuttle will take you to the nearby marina or to the regional airport. Red pepper prime rib is the specialty of the on-site restaurant. Restaurant, room service, in-room data ports, cable TV, pool, business services, meeting rooms, airport shuttle, no-smoking rooms, some pets allowed. | 2407 N. Arkansas St. (Rte. 7), 72801 | phone/fax 479/968–4300 | www.holiday-inn.com | 149 rooms | AE, D, DC, MC, V | $

Mather Lodge. Overlooking Cedar Creek canyon, Mather Lodge is the focal point of Petit Jean State Park. The compact rooms have oak paneling and basic furnishings. One-, two-, and three-bedroom cabins are also available; September through March, make sure to ask for one with a fireplace. Restaurant, picnic area, some kitchens, 2 tennis courts, pool, lake, boating, marina, playground; no room phones, no room TVs. | Off Rte. 154, 25 mi southeast of Russellville | 1285 Mountain Rd., Morrilton 72110 | 501/727–5431 or 800/264-2462 | www.petitjeanstatepark.com | 24 rooms, 35 cabins | AE, D, MC, V | ¢–$

Mount Nebo State Park Cabins. Many of the park's stone-and-log cabins were constructed in the 1930s by the Civilian Conservation Corps, although the kitchens and bathrooms have been updated. Two more recent, A-frame cabins have three bedrooms and are more expensive to rent. Picnic area, kitchens, 2 tennis courts, pool, bicycles, hiking, shop, playground; no room phones, no room TVs. | Off Rte. 155, 12 mi southwest of Russellville | 1 State Park Dr., Dardanelle 72834 | 479/229–3655 | www.arkansasstateparks.com | 15 cabins | MC, V | $

CALIFORNIA

CALIFORNIA NORTH COAST
FROM SAN FRANCISCO TO REDWOOD NATIONAL PARK

Distance: 250–275 mi   Time: 7 days
Overnight Breaks: Eureka, Inverness, Gualala, Mendocino/Fort Bragg

Driving the California coast's Route 1 is a beautiful experience, especially if taken at a leisurely pace. Bear in mind that while distances seem short, there are many portions of the highway along which you won't want to drive faster than 20–40 mph. Also, your drive might be slowed down by seasonal influences—namely rain and early darkness in winter, and slow-moving travelers in summer. There's a lot more to the coast than what you see from the road, so leave time to explore.

Weather on the North Coast is unpredictable—December can yield a sunny beach day, while August can be unexpectedly cool. Still, the temperatures are always mild, making this a year-round trip. When you visit, though, determines what you'll see. The migration of the Pacific gray whales is a winter phenomenon, roughly from mid-December to early April. Autumn is the quietest time of year—a wonder, since the season's wild mushrooms, fresh crab, and Indian-summer produce bring out the best of local cuisine. Fog can be maddening in July and August, when it obscures views and dampens the warm weather.

❶ Depart from San Francisco and head north over the Golden Gate Bridge for approximately 10 mi, then proceed west (take the Mill Valley/Stinson Beach exit off U.S. 101 and follow signs) to **Muir Woods National Monument.** This is the world's most popular grove of old-growth *Sequoia sempervirens* (redwoods). If you can find a parking place at this popular spot, spend an hour or so hiking the manicured trails before leaving for Stinson Beach.

❷ **Stinson Beach,** approximately 8 mi north of Muir Woods National Monument on Route 1, is the most popular beach in Marin County. Compared with the pristine spots up north it might not seem dazzling, but it is a great place to sunbathe and walk a long, sandy shoreline.

❸ Driving north you'll pass from the Golden Gate National Recreation Area into **Point Reyes National Seashore.** Eager hikers can park and set off on any of the trails

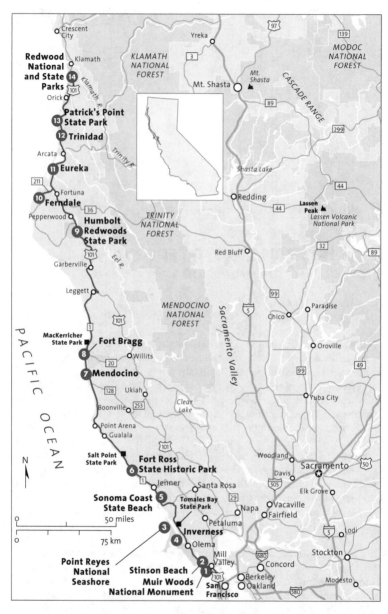

radiating out from Route 1. To reach the heart of the park, though, pass through Olema and head west on Bear Valley Road to the **Bear Valley Visitor Center.** The rangers here can advise you on everything from whale-watching to hiking and camping. Also, a short walk away there is a reconstructed Miwok village, which gives a view into the daily lives of the region's first human inhabitants.

4 Five miles north from the visitor center is **Inverness,** a sleepy town with the last delis and inns before Fort Ross State Historic Park. After town there is only the wild penin-sula, a land of rolling hills and long, empty beaches. Twenty miles from Inverness (about a 45-minute drive), the road ends at the **Point Reyes Lighthouse Visitors Center.** There are 300 steps from the cliff top to the lighthouse below, and the walk is often windy, but the tireless are rewarded with an outstanding view. Stay overnight in Inverness or, for more of a town, Point Reyes Station, which is north of Olema on Route 1.

❺ Thirty-two miles north of Point Reyes the road hits the ocean again at Bodega Bay. For 17 mi north of here stretches the entirely wild coast of the **Sonoma Coast State Beach,** actually a collection of beaches separated by bluffs and headlands. There are more than a dozen beaches, ranging from windy kite-flying spots to coves for private sunbathing. Better yet, most are visible from the highway, so you can pick the perfect one as you drive.

❻ Next you'll come to **Fort Ross State Historic Park,** 25 mi north of Bodega Bay via Route 1. Completed in 1821, Fort Ross was Russia's major fur-trading outpost in California. By 1841 Russian settlers had depleted the area's population of seals and otters and sold the post to John Sutter, later of Gold Rush fame. The state park service has reconstructed Fort Ross, including its Russian Orthodox chapel, a redwood stockade, the officer's barracks, and a blockhouse. Though the town of **Gualala,** 25 mi north, is nothing special, the area around it is. It's worth spending a night there, and even an extra day exploring the region.

❼ Continue 50 mi north on Route 1 to **Mendocino.** Logging created the first boom in this town, which flourished for most of the second half of the 19th century. As the timber industry declined in the early 20th century many residents left, but in the 1950s the gorgeous setting on a sea-swept promontory attracted the artists and crafts-people who have defined Mendocino since. Today, the tiny town is *the* North Coast vacation spot, with its chic shops, romantic inns, and exquisite restaurants.

Downtown is surrounded by the **Mendocino Headlands State Park,** which means you can walk right off Main Street onto a path to a tiny cove or grassy bluff. The 1850's Ford House serves as the park's visitor center and has a scale model of late-19th-century Mendocino.

❽ **Fort Bragg,** about 10 mi north of Mendocino on Route 1, has changed more than any other coastal town in the past few years. The decline in the timber industry is being offset in part by a boom in charter-boat excursions and other tourist pursuits. The city is also attracting many artists, some lured from Mendocino, where the cost of living is higher. Fort Bragg has a nightlife, which, while fairly tame, is really the only such scene between Point Reyes and Eureka.

MacKerricher State Park includes 10 mi of sandy beach and several square miles of dunes. You can often spot whales from the nearby headland between December and mid-April.

❾ **Humboldt Redwoods State Park,** 85 mi north of Fort Bragg on Route 1, is home to some of the area's giant redwoods. An easy driving tour is the Avenue of the Giants, which begins about 7 mi north of Garberville and winds north, more or less parallel to U.S. 101. Some of the tallest trees on the planet tower over this stretch of two-lane blacktop.

At the Humboldt Redwoods State Park Visitor Center brochures are available for a self-guided auto tour of the park; stops include short and long hikes into redwood groves.

❿ Fans of Victoriana might take an afternoon's detour to **Ferndale** (20 mi north on U.S. 101 and 8 mi west on Route 211) to see some of the best-preserved period homes in California. Walking tours and a local museum illuminate the area's 19th-century history.

⑪ North on Route 1 lies **Eureka,** the North Coast's largest city (population 28,500). This port has gone through cycles of boom and bust, first with mining and later with timber and fishing. Today tourism is breathing (some) new life into the area. If you exit U.S. 101 as it runs through town you'll find a growing hub of shops and restaurants, many housed in the well-preserved Victorian buildings that give Eureka an old-timey feel. Stay overnight in Eureka.

⑫ The town of **Trinidad,** 23 mi north via U.S. 101, got its name from the Spanish mariners who entered the bay on Trinity Sunday, June 9, 1775. The town became a principal trading post for the mining camps along the Klamath and Trinity rivers. As mining, and then whaling, faded, so did the luster of this former boomtown, but it still has good dining spots and several inns; spend the night at one of them.

⑬ **Patrick's Point State Park,** 5 mi north of Trinidad via U.S. 101, is the ultimate California coastal park. Its forested plateau almost 200 feet above the surf has stunning views of the Pacific and hiking trails through old-growth forest; its beaches range from sand to barnacle-covered rocks. Best of all, it's remote enough that there's rarely a crowd; on weekdays, you can nearly have the place to yourself.

⑭ **Redwood National and State Parks** are less than 20 mi north of Patrick's Point State Park. After 115 years of intensive logging, this 106,000-acre parcel of tall trees came under government protection in 1968, marking the California environmentalists' greatest victory over the timber industry.

At the **Redwood Information Center** you can get brochures, advice, and a free permit to drive up the steep, 17-mi road (the last 6 mi are gravel) to reach the Tall Trees Grove, where a 3-mi round-trip hiking trail leads to the world's first-, third-, and fifth-tallest redwoods.

To reach the entrance to **Prairie Creek Redwoods State Park** take the Prairie Parkway exit off the U.S. 101 bypass. Extra space has been paved alongside the

CALIFORNIA RULES OF THE ROAD

License Requirements: You must be at least 16 years old to get a driver's license in California. Persons with valid driver's licenses from other U.S. states and foreign countries are permitted to drive in the state.

Right Turn on Red: Unless otherwise posted, right turns on red are permitted *after* a full stop.

Seat Belt and Helmet Laws: All passengers are required to wear safety belts in the state of California. Children under age four or weighing less than 40 pounds must travel in an approved child safety seat. Motorcyclists must wear helmets.

Speed Limits: The maximum speed limit on California highways is 70 mph.

For More Information: California Highway Patrol | 916/657–7261 | www.chp.ca.gov.

parklands, providing fine vantage points from which to observe an imposing herd of Roosevelt elk grazing in the adjoining meadow.

To return to San Francisco drive south on U.S. 101/Route 1 for 250 mi.

Eureka

Sequoia Park and Zoo. You get a taste of nature, both native and exotic, in this 50-acre, redwood-filled zoo, which also has an aviary and municipal garden. | Glatt and W Sts. | 707/442–6552 | www.eurekawebs.com/zoo | Oct.–Apr., Tues.–Sun. 10–5; May–Sept., Tues.–Sun. 10–7.

To see Eureka's most stunning Victorians, head to M and L streets. Within a one-block radius, you'll find the dark and regal **Carter Mansion** (built in 1885), the frilly **Pink Lady** (built in 1889), and the **Carter House Bed and Breakfast,** a convincing replica of a San Francisco building that burned in the 1906 earthquake.

Dining

Café Waterfront. Seafood. This local favorite has a solid basic menu of burgers and steaks, but the real standouts are the daily seafood specials—lingcod, shrimp, and other treats fresh from the harbor across the street. The building, listed on the National Register of Historic Places, was a saloon and brothel until the 1950s. | 102 F St. | 707/443–9190 | MC, V | $–$$

★**Samoa Cookhouse.** American. A longtime loggers' hangout and local landmark, Samoa serves hearty, family-style meals at long, wooden tables. The menu is meat-heavy and pre-set, and consists of soup or salad, an entrée like roast pork or fried chicken, a side dish, and homemade desserts including apple pie and strawberry shortcake. From U.S. 101 cross Samoa Bridge, turn left onto Samoa Road, then left one block later onto Cookhouse Lane. | 79 Cookhouse La. | 707/442–1659 | AE, D, MC, V | $

Ramone's. American/Casual. Ramone's is a casual bakery and café in one. Light sandwiches are served from dawn to 6 PM. | 209 E St. | 707/442–6082 | MC, V | No dinner | ¢

Restaurant 301. Contemporary. Eureka's best dining spot is known for its outstanding wine list, which has so many vintages (including the owner's private label) that several rooms in the hotel upstairs have had to be converted into "cellars." Ingredients are also top-notch, with most hand-selected from the farmers' market and local cheese makers, fishermen, and ranchers or picked from the on-site garden. | 301 L St. | 707/444–8062 | AE, D, DC, MC, V | No lunch | $$–$$$$

Lodging

★**An Elegant Victorian Mansion.** Not only do Victorian furnishings fill each room, the innkeepers here may even greet you in vintage clothing. Entertainment includes croquet, silent movies, old records on a wind-up Victrola, and free tours of downtown in a 1930 model A coupé driven by the innkeeper. Sauna, bicycles, laundry service. | 1406 C St., 95501 | 707/444–3144 | fax 707/442–3295 | www.eureka-california.com | 3 rooms (2 with shared bath), 1 suite | MC, V | BP | $–$$$

Eureka Inn. The high-ceiling lobby, with its polished redwood beams, crystal chandeliers, and massive brick fireplace, still plays host to swing dances and, in season, a 22-foot Christmas tree. Less-expensive rooms are available in the motor annex across the street, which is far less charming but does have a pool, hot tub, and saunas. 2 restaurants, cable TV, pool, hot tub, saunas, 2 bars, business services, airport shuttle, some pets allowed. | 518 7th St., 95501 | 707/442–6441 or 800/862–4906 | fax 707/442–0637 | www.eurekainn.com | 95 rooms, 9 suites | AE, D, DC, MC, V | $

Weaver's Inn. A stately Colonial Revival house built in 1883 harbors this B&B, which is in a quiet residential area a few blocks from downtown Eureka and 1 mi east of the

Old Town area. Special touches include overstuffed, canopy beds in the rooms and a Japanese Contemplation Garden. Croquet, some pets allowed; no room phones. | 1440 B St., 95501 | 707/443–8119 or 800/992–8119 | fax 707/443–7923 | www.aweaversinn.com/weaversinn | 3 rooms, 1 suite | AE, D, DC, MC, V | BP | $–$$

Fort Bragg
★ **Mendocino Coast Botanical Gardens.** You can see pine forests, endless varieties of flowers, 100 species of birds, and 80 species of mushrooms at this 47-acre garden. The scenery along the 2 mi of trails changes constantly, ranging from vegetable beds to a dahlia extravaganza to native plants along a craggy ocean shore. Thanks to the mild climate, the gardens bloom year-round. | 18220 N. Rte. 1 | 707/964–4352 | www.gardenbythesea.org | $7.50 | Mar.–Oct., daily 9–5, Nov.–Feb., daily 9–4.

Dining
Headlands Coffee House. Café. Along with pastries, cheesecake, and biscotti to go with your coffee, you can order lasagna, chicken enchiladas, soups, stews, and sandwiches for lunch or dinner. Belgian waffles are breakfast favorites. Musicians perform most nights. | 120 E. Laurel St. | 707/964–1987 | D, MC, V | ¢–$

Mendo Bistro. Contemporary. On the second floor of the Company Store complex downtown, the town's sole hip restaurant serves oodles of noodles, made fresh on the premises. You might find on the menu rotini with sun-dried tomatoes; shells stuffed with spinach, Swiss chard, and ricotta; and sweet-potato gnocchi with Gorgonzola sauce. | 301 N. Main St. | 707/964–4974 | AE, D, DC, MC, V | No lunch | $–$$

The Restaurant. Contemporary. The name may be generic, but the space isn't— American cuisine is served in a dining room that doubles as an art gallery. The Restaurant is one of the few places in town serving Sunday brunch. | 418 N. Main St. | 707/ 964–9800 | MC, V | Closed Wed. No lunch | $$

Lodging
Beachcomber Motel. The inside of this nondescript motel is nothing thrilling, but most rooms have views of the ocean, and the ground-floor patios open onto grassy bluffs and trails leading 50 yards down to the beach. Propane grills are provided on the large observation deck. This is a nice, low-key alternative to pricey Mendocino. Cable TV, some in-room hot tubs, some kitchenettes, some pets allowed. | 1111 N. Main St., 95437 | 707/ 964–2402 or 800/400–7873 | fax 707/964–8925 | www.thebeachcombermotel.com | 72 rooms, 7 suites | AE, D, DC, MC, V | $–$$$

Gualala
★ **Manchester State Park.** This 5-mi sandy beach is the biggest and best in the area. Offshore are several surfing breaks, and the two creeks flowing into the ocean here offer fishermen runs of steelhead and salmon. Above the beach, trails lead through meadows where wildflowers bloom nearly year-round and tundra swans visit in winter. | Rte. 1 | 707/882–2463.

Point Arena Lighthouse. Just north of Point Arena, this is a good place for a dramatic view of the surf and, in winter, migrating whales. First constructed in 1870, the lighthouse was destroyed by the 1906 earthquake and rebuilt in 1907. It towers 115 feet above its base, which is already 50 feet above the sea. The small museum here has exhibits on local nautical history as well as art from the surrounding towns. | Rte. 1 | 707/882–2777 | $5 | Apr.–Sept., daily 10–4:30, Oct.–Mar., daily 10–3:30.

Salt Point State Park. Each of the three entrances at this 6,000-acre park has a different face. At Fisk Mill Cove, Bishop pines protect the picnic area and a short walk reveals a dramatic view of Sentinel Rock; the cliffs here have *tafonis*, caverns in the sandstone. Stump Beach offers a sandy beach and a grassy cliff for looking down on the surf. And at Gerstle Cove, seals sun themselves on the water, while the surrounding meadows of wild brush host more birds than humans. The highway isn't visible from within the park, making this a good place to stretch your legs and forget about driving. | Rte. 1 | 707/847–3221 | $4 per vehicle | Daily sunrise–sunset.

Dining

The Food Company. American/Casual. The backbone of this café's business is the picnic-ready prepared foods. Excellent wine, cheese, and fresh bread are always available to round out every meal. Nightly dinner specials are inventive—lamb pie with shallots, moussaka with Moroccan bread—and the gingersnaps are locally famous. Breakfast is served. | Rte. 1, ½ mi north of Gualala | 707/884–1400 | MC, V | Closed Tues.–Wed. | ¢–$

Laura's Bakery. Café. This *panaderia*, or Mexican bakery, behind the Gualala Hotel is so small you can easily miss it; look for the sign on the parking lot's south side. Inside are authentic Mexican baked goods, including guava empanadas and sugar-dusted wedding cookies. | Rte. 1 | 707/884–3175 | Closed Sun. | ¢

★**Pangaea.** Contemporary. The impeccable ingredients used at Pangaea are primarily local (and organic), but the food is a product of the owner-chef's world travels. The menu, which changes weekly, has been known to include "Hoisin Explosion" grilled quail with bitter greens and rice noodles and celery-root soup with Dungeness crab. | 39165 Rte. 1 | 707/884–9669 | MC, V | Closed Mon.–Tues. No lunch | $$–$$$

Lodging

Gualala Hotel. Gualala's oldest hotel has small, no-nonsense rooms furnished with well-worn antiques. Most rooms share baths. Rooms in the front have ocean views (and some street noise). The rustic first-floor saloon was one of Jack London's haunts. Restaurant, bar. | 39301 Rte. 1, 95445 | 707/884–3441 | fax 707/884–3908 | www.thegualalahotel.com | 19 rooms, 5 with bath | AE, D, MC, V | ¢–$

Old Milano Inn. This not-so-old hotel—the 1905 mansion burned a few years back—is one of the most beautiful sunset spots on the coast. Options include five cottages and one caboose, which has been converted into a funky, two-person retreat with a wood-burning stove. Four cottages have gas fireplaces, some have whirlpool tubs; all guests can soak in the ocean-view hot tub and listen for sea lions in the waters below. Room service, hot tub. | 38300 Rte. 1, 95445 | 707/884–3256 | fax 707/884–4249 | www.oldmilanohotel.com | 5 cottages, 1 caboose | MC, V | BP | $$–$$$$

★**St. Orres.** Two Russian-style cupolas distinguish the main house, which is further accented by balconies, stained-glass windows, and wood-inlaid towers. In the tranquil woods behind the house are clusters of cottages that somehow manage to feel both rustic and opulent; some have in-room saunas and wood-burning stoves. Part of the experience is dinner in the restaurant, a fixed-price meal that is fittingly decadent. Restaurant, some in-room hot tubs, some kitchenettes, hot tub, sauna, beach. | Rte. 1, 2 mi north of Gualala, 95445 | 707/884–3303 | fax 707/884–1840 | www.saintorres.com | 8 rooms with shared bath, 13 cottages | MC, V | BP | $–$$$$

Inverness

Johnson's Oyster Company. At this working oyster farm you can buy several sizes of the local shellfish, shucked or not. The set-up is less scenic than it is authentic: the small seating area is amidst the busy work area, but as employees bustle by they're happy to deftly demonstrate how to wield a shucking knife. | 17171 Sir Francis Drake Blvd. | 415/669–1149 | Tues.–Sat. 8–4.

★ **Point Reyes National Seashore.** Wild shorelines don't get much better than this: windswept headlands, dunes, tide pools, and secluded beaches on 65,300 acres of protected parkland. Inland, rolling hills and freshwater lakes link up with more than 140 mi of hiking and horse trails, many of which are open to bicycles. There are four hike-in campgrounds, and visitor centers at Bear Valley and the lighthouse. | Sir Francis Drake Blvd. | 415/464–5100 | www.nps.gov/pore | Daily dawn–dusk; lighthouse, Thurs.–Mon. 10–4:30.

Dining

Manka's Inverness Lodge Restaurant. American. This restaurant is commonly regarded as among the best in Northern California for its exceedingly handcrafted food—you'll feel like you're having dinner at a friend's house. Nearly all the kitchen's ingredients come from within 15 mi of the lodge, so the dinner menu, which is prix fixe only, changes daily according to what local farmers, fishermen, and foragers offer chef-owner Margaret Grade. | 30 Callendar Way | 415/669–1034 | Reservations essential | MC, V | Closed Tues.–Wed. No lunch | $$$$

Lodging

Blackthorne Inn. Built in 1982 from salvaged railway-station doors and timber from the San Francisco wharves, this inn is a combination of whimsy and sophistication. The giant tree house–like structure is bedecked with spiral staircases, a 3,500-square-foot deck, and a fireman's pole. The best room in the house is aptly named the Eagle's Nest, perched as it is in the octagonal tower that crowns the inn. Cable TV, hot tub, business services. | 266 Vallejo Ave., 94937 | 415/663–8621 | www.blackthorneinn.com | 5 rooms (2 with shared bath) | MC, V | BP | $$$$

Ten Inverness Way. Antiques, handmade quilts, and fresh flowers abound in this turn-of-the-20th-century shingle house one block from Tomales Bay. Rooms are painted in warm tones and accented with wicker furniture and quilts. Daily sunroom breakfasts might include warm buttermilk-spice coffee cake or banana pancakes. Dining room, hot tub, library; no room phones. | 10 Inverness Way, 94937 | 415/669–1648 | fax 415/669–7403 | www.teninvernessway.com | 5 rooms | MC, V | BP | $$$

Mendocino

Mendocino Art Center. This local cultural center has two galleries showing area artists' work, top-quality community theater productions, and arts-and-crafts fairs in summer and at Thanksgiving. Inspired visitors can participate by taking classes in ceramics and other crafts. | 45200 Little Lake St. | 707/937–5818 or 800/653–3328 | www.mendocinoartcenter.org | Daily, call for class and exhibit schedules.

Russian Gulch State Park. The craggy wilderness at this state park is a cross-section of the North Coast, offering a bit of everything. Take your pick from the forests of Russian Gulch Creek Canyon, the headlands that include a massive blowhole and the Devil's Punch Bowl (a large, collapsed sea cave with churning water), or a beach where you can swim, skin dive, and check out tidal pools. Inland, there is even a 36-foot-high waterfall. | Rte. 1 | 707/937–5804 | Apr.–Nov., daily dawn–dusk.

Dining

Café Beaujolais. French. Gardens surround this Victorian farmhouse, which has an intimate, woody dining room and an enclosed atrium where you can eat in the summer. Fresh French-inspired food with organic local ingredients is the specialty here.

Try the braised asparagus or roasted free-range chicken, duck, or lamb loin in herb crust with white beans, accompanied by homemade bread. Beer and wine are served. | 961 Ukiah St. | 707/937–5614 | MC, V | $$$

Lu's. American/Casual. The restaurant itself is no more than one person in a little shed, but the food is gargantuan—the burritos here require a fork. All ingredients are organic. Whether you eat at the tables in the sheltered, sunny garden or take the food to go, do it early—Lu's closes at 5:30. Note that on very rainy days, Lu's may be closed. | 45013 Ukiah St. | 707/937–4939 | No dinner | ¢–$

★ **MacCallum House.** Contemporary. Chef-owner Alan Kantor handcrafts all the menu's offerings, down to the ice cream. He procures ingredients from all over Northern California (he and the bartender even forage for mushrooms on days off), and the result is exceptional: chipotle chocolate truffles, huckleberry daiquiris, and duck—Kantor's favorite—with chanterelle risotto. | 45020 Albion St. | 707/937–0289 or 800/609–0492 | Reservations essential | AE, MC, V | Closed mid-Jan.–mid-Feb. | $$$–$$$$

Lodging

Agate Cove Inn. This 1860 inn outside town is on a half-acre garden on a bluff—perfect for whale-watching. Accommodations are in individually decorated cottages and two rooms in the farmhouse, where country breakfasts are prepared on an antique woodstove. Cable TV, in-room VCRs, massage, concierge, shop; no room phones. | 11201 N. Lansing St., 95460 | 707/937–0551 or 800/527–3111 | fax 707/937–0550 | www.agatecove.com | 10 rooms | AE, MC, V | BP | $$–$$$$

McElroy's Cottage Inn. Gardens surround the house, water tower, and cottage that make up this early 1900s Craftsman-style inn, which faces the ocean at the east end of the village of Mendocino. The rooms have radios and are stocked with books and games, and kids are very welcome here. The place is less dreamy than the B&B's downtown, but it's also less expensive. Minibars, some pets allowed; no smoking. | 998 Main St., 95460 | 707/937–1734 | www.mcelroysinn.com | 4 rooms | MC, V | CP | $

Mendocino Hotel. From the street this hotel looks like something out of the Wild West, with a period facade and a raised sidewalk. Inside, stained-glass lamps, polished wood, and Persian rugs lend the hotel a swank 19th-century appeal. Guest rooms are filled with antiques, and some have wood-burning fireplaces and private balconies. 2 restaurants, room service, bar, business services; no TV in some rooms. | 45080 Main St., 95460 | 707/937–0511 or 800/548–0513 | fax 707/937–0513 | www.mendocinohotel.com | 51 rooms (14 with shared bath), 6 suites | AE, MC, V | $$–$$$$

★ **Whitegate Inn.** With a white picket fence, a latticework gazebo, and a romantic garden, the Whitegate is picture-book Victorian. The wooden house with large bay windows, built in 1883, has 19th-century French and Victorian antiques, including the owner's collection of Civil War memorabilia. High ceilings, floral fabrics, and pastel walls define the luxurious rooms, all of which have fireplaces. Kids under 10 and pets are only allowed in the adjacent cottage. Cable TV, some refrigerators, Internet. | 499 Howard St., 95460 | 707/937–4892 or 800/531–7282 | fax 707/937–1131 | www.whitegateinn.com | 6 rooms, 1 cottage | AE, D, DC, MC, V | BP | $$–$$$$

Point Reyes Station

Point Reyes Farmers' Market. Point Reyes's gathering of growers and craftspeople in the heart of town is the outdoor social event of the week. | 15479 Rte. 1 | 415/663–1223 | June–Nov., Sat. 9–1.

Tomales Bay State Park. Sheltered coves, beaches, tidal marshes, and Bishop pine forests occupy much of this 2,000-acre park, which lies on both sides of the bay (north of Point

Reyes Station on Route 1 and north of Inverness on Pierce Point Road). The water here is calmer and warmer than the ocean, making this a popular area for swimming. Explore the area on foot or in a sea kayak, which you can rent in Inverness or Marshall. | 415/669–1140 | Daily dawn–dusk.

Dining

Bovine Bakery. Café. You can get lunch items like pizza and sandwiches at this popular bakery, but the real draws are the delectable pastries and sweets, which come hot from the oven throughout the day. | 11315 Rte. 1 | 415/663–9420 | No dinner | ¢

★ **Olema Inn.** Contemporary. A bright dining room and adjoining patio—which reaches out into an apple orchard—of an 1876 inn make up this charming restaurant. The food is centered around local produce, fresh seafood, and quality meats—some cured right in the kitchen. The menu changes often and is complemented by a solid wine list. | 10000 Sir Francis Drake Blvd., at Rte. 1, Olema | 415/663–9559 | www.theolemainn.com | AE, MC, V | $$–$$$

Tomales Bay Foods. American/Casual. There are three separate businesses here, providing one-stop shopping for gourmands: a stand with organic fruits and vegetables; a shop that sells artisanal cheeses (including some made in the building); and a kitchen that draws on both of its neighbors' products to create excellent sandwiches, salads, and soups. Dinner is available, but only until 6 PM. | 80 4th St. | 415/663–9335 | MC, V | Closed Mon.–Tues. | ¢–$

Trinidad

North Coast Adventures. Guided tours allow you to explore Trinidad Bay by kayak, from which you might catch sight of seals, sea birds, or whales. Note that previous kayak experience is required. | 707/677–3124 | fax 707/677–0603 | www.northcoastadventures.com | Apr.–Oct., daily 7–7.

Patrick's Point State Park. The 640-acre park, cloaked in fir, hemlock, red alder, and spruce, has trails to cliffs overlooking the Pacific and to the beaches below. It's a great spot for whale-watching, rock hunting, or exploring tide pools. Services include a reconstructed Indian village, bookstore, campgrounds, rental cabins, and several picnic areas. | 4150 Patrick's Point Dr. | 707/677–3570, 800/444–7275 (camping information) | www.cal-parks.ca.gov | Daily.

Dining

★ **Larrupin' Cafe.** American. Considered by many locals to be one of the best places to eat on the North Coast, this restaurant has earned widespread fame for its mesquite-grilled ribs and fresh-fish dishes. The bright yellow two-story building is on a quiet country road, 2 mi north of Trinidad. | 1658 Patrick's Point Dr. | 707/677–0230 | Reservations essential | No credit cards | May–Sept. closed Tues.–Wed., Oct.–Apr. closed Wed. No lunch | $$–$$$

SIERRA NATIONAL PARKS

*FROM THE YOSEMITE VALLEY TO KINGS CANYON
AND SEQUOIA NATIONAL PARKS*

Distance: 390 mi   Time: 5 days
Overnight Breaks: Kings Canyon, Yosemite Valley area

Yosemite, Kings Canyon, and Sequoia national parks are famous worldwide for their granite peaks, towering waterfalls, and giant sequoias. Summer is the most crowded season for all the parks, though things never get as hectic at Kings Canyon and Sequoia as they do at Yosemite. To avoid traffic and crowds at both parks, visit from mid-April through Memorial Day or from Labor Day to mid-October, when the parks are less busy and the weather is fine.

The waterfalls at Yosemite are at their most spectacular in May and June. By the end of summer, some will have dried up. They begin flowing again in late fall with the first storms, and during winter they may be hung with ice, a dramatic sight. Snow on the floor of Yosemite Valley is rarely ever deep, so you can camp there even in winter (January highs are in the mid-40s, lows in the mid-20s). Tioga Road is usually closed from late October through May; unless you ski or snowshoe in, you can't see Tuolumne Meadows at that time. The road to Glacier Point beyond the turnoff for Badger Pass is not cleared in winter, but it is groomed for cross-country skiing. In parts of Kings Canyon and Sequoia snow may remain on the ground into June; the flowers in the Giant Forest meadows hit their peak in June or July.

Plan on spending at least one night in Kings Canyon or Sequoia for a quick tour of the parks, but two or three nights is preferable for a leisurely exploration.

❶ Begin your tour at the **Foothills Visitor Center,** at Ash Mountain at the southern entrance to **Sequoia National Park.** You can get your bearings, pick up maps, and purchase tickets to **Crystal Cave,** your second (or possibly third) stop. Formed from limestone that metamorphosed into marble, stalactites and stalagmites of various shapes, sizes, and colors grow dramatically from the ceiling and floor. It's the best known of Sequoia's many caverns. Note that tickets are not sold at the cave; you must buy them at the Foothills or Lodgepole visitor centers.

Return to the Generals Highway and head to **Giant Forest,** where you can tour the **Giant Forest Museum** and see outstanding exhibits on the ecology of the giant sequoia. Afterward hit the short trails through groves of the huge trees. You can get the best views of them from the park's meadows, where flowers are in full bloom by June or July. The most famous sequoia in the area is the General Sherman Tree: weighing in at 2.7 million pounds, it has the greatest volume of any living thing in the world.

Moro Rock, an immense, granite monolith, lies along Moro Rock–Crescent Meadow Road. It rises 6,725 feet from the edge of the Giant Forest. Four hundred steps lead from an elevation of 6,425 feet to the top; the trail often climbs along narrow ledges over steep drops. The view from the top is striking. To the southwest you look down the Kaweah River to Three Rivers, Lake Kaweah, and—on clear days—the Central Valley and the Coast Range. To the northeast are views of the High Sierra. Thousands of feet below lies the middle fork of the Kaweah River.

❷ Within Sequoia National Park, **Lodgepole,** 5 mi north of the Giant Forest via Route 198, lies in a canyon on the Marble Fork of the Kaweah River. Lodgepole pines, rather than sequoias, grow here because the U-shape canyon directs air down from the high country that is too cold for the big trees but is just right for lodgepoles. The area has a campground and a post office open year-round. A snack bar, market and deli, public laundry, gift shop, and showers are open in the summer only.

The **Lodgepole Visitor Center** has extensive exhibits, a small theater where you can watch an orientation slide show, and a first-aid center. You can buy tickets for Crystal Cave, get advice from park rangers, purchase maps and books, and pick up wilderness permits (except during summer, when they're available from 7 to 4 at the permit office next door).

❸ From the Lodgepole Visitor Center, continue north on Route 198 for 20 mi to **Kings Canyon National Park** and **Grant Grove,** where you can pick up several trails and visit the **Gamlin Cabin,** an 1867 pioneer cabin that's listed on the National Register of Historic

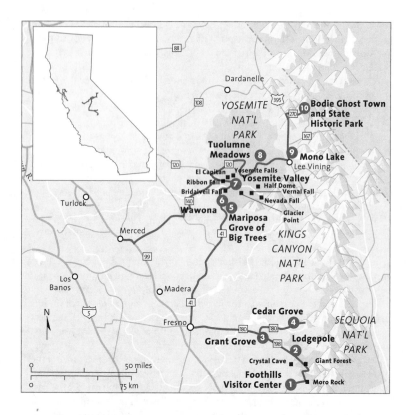

Places. Also within Grant Grove is the **Centennial Stump,** the remains of a huge sequoia cut for display at the 1876 Philadelphia Centennial Exhibition.

Grant Grove Village has a visitor center, a grocery store, campgrounds, a coffee shop, overnight lodging, and a horse rentals.

❹ Drive 30 mi east on Route 180 along the spectacular **Generals Highway.** On the hour-long drive from Grant Grove the road clings to cliffs along the way: watch out for falling rocks. Built by convict labor in the 1930s, the highway (usually closed from mid-October through April) passes the scars where large groves of sequoias were felled at the beginning of the 20th century. It runs along the south fork and through dry hills covered with yuccas that bloom in the summer. There are amazing views into the deepest gorge in the United States (deeper even than the Grand Canyon) at the confluence of the two forks.

Near the end of the road, you'll come to **Cedar Grove,** named for the incense cedars that grow in the area. The grove occupies the upper end of a glacial U-shape valley. While this valley lacks the towering waterfalls of Yosemite National Park, it's full of granite cliffs and monoliths similar to those at the more northern park. At Cedar Grove Village, there are campgrounds, lodgings, a small visitor center, a snack bar, a cafeteria, a convenience market, a gift shop, and horse rental. The area is open only between April and November. At the end of the highway, you can hike, camp, or turn right around for the drive back up the canyon.

❺ After spending the night in Kings Canyon, proceed north from Cedar Grove to **Yosemite National Park** (58 mi west to Fresno on Route 180, then 65 mi north on Route

41). After entering the park's South Entrance, if you've not had your fill of big trees, head to the **Mariposa Grove of Big Trees,** Yosemite's largest grove of giant sequoias. Visit on foot—trails all lead uphill—or, in summer, on one-hour tram rides. The Grizzly Giant, the oldest tree here, is estimated to be 2,700 years old. If the road to the grove is closed (which happens when the parking lot fills up), passengers are picked up by a shuttle near the gas station. The access road to the grove may also be closed by snow for extended periods from November to mid-May. You can still usually walk, snowshoe, or ski in.

❻ From the Mariposa Grove proceed northwest to **Wawona,** approximately 5 mi on Route 41. The historic buildings in **Pioneer Yosemite History Center** were moved to Wawona from their original sites in the park. From Wednesday through Sunday in summer, costumed docents re-create life in 19th-century Yosemite. Near the center are a post office, general store, and a gas station.

❼ Continue 22 mi north via Route 41 to the **Yosemite Valley area,** the park's main attraction, where you'll see the most famous sights. Get your bearings at the Valley Visitor Center, where you can view exhibits, pick up maps, and obtain information about the free shuttle buses that operate in the valley.

Yosemite is justly famous for its towering waterfalls and giant granite peaks. Be sure to see **Yosemite Falls**—actually three falls that combine to a height of 2,425 feet— the highest waterfall in North America and the fifth-highest in the world. **Bridalveil Fall,** a filmy fall of 620 feet that is often diverted as much as 20 feet one way or the other by the breeze, is the first view of Yosemite Valley for those who arrive via the Wawona Road. At 1,612 feet, **Ribbon Fall** is the highest single fall in North America, but also the first valley waterfall to dry up in summer; the rainwater and melted snow that create the slender fall evaporate quickly at this height. Fern-covered black rocks frame 317-foot **Vernal Fall,** and rainbows play in the spray at its base. The 594-foot **Nevada Fall** is the first major fall as the Merced River plunges out of the high country toward the eastern end of Yosemite Valley.

El Capitan, rising 3,593 feet above the valley, is the largest exposed granite monolith in the world, almost twice the height of the Rock of Gibraltar. Astounding **Half Dome** rises 4,733 feet from the valley floor to 8,842 feet. The west side of the dome is fractured vertically and cut away to form a 2,000-foot cliff. **Glacier Point** yields what may be the most spectacular vistas of the valley and the High Sierra—especially at sunset—that you can get without hiking. The Glacier Point Road leaves Wawona Road (Route 41) about 23 mi southwest of the valley; then it's a 16-mi drive into higher country.

You can't see everything in one day. Plan to spend one to three nights in one of the campgrounds or lodges in the park.

❽ After a good night's rest, start your 55-mi, 90-minute drive to **Tuolumne Meadows**; you'll travel west on Big Oak Flat Road to Route 120 (Tioga Road east). Tioga Road, the only route to Tuolumne Meadows, stays open until the first big snow of the year, usually about mid-October. Tuolumne Meadows is the largest subalpine meadow in the Sierra and the trailhead for many backpack trips into the High Sierra. There are campgrounds, a gas station, a store (with limited and expensive provisions), stables, a lodge, and a visitor center.

❾ Twenty miles east of Tuolumne Meadows, where Route 120 meets U.S. 395, you'll come to **Mono Lake.** Eerie tufa towers—calcium carbonate formations that often resemble castle turrets—rise from the impressive lake. Stop at the **Scenic Area Visitor Center** (north of Route 120 via U.S. 395) for information on trails and activities in the area.

10 From Mono Lake and Lee Vining, continue north on U.S. 395, then east on Route 270 for 23 mi to **Bodie Ghost Town and State Historic Park**—the last 3 mi are on unpaved roads; snow may close Route 270 in winter and early spring. Old shacks and shops, abandoned mine shafts, a Methodist church, the mining village of Rattlesnake Gulch, and the remains of a small Chinatown are among the sights. There's an excellent museum, and you can tour an old stamp mill (where ore was stamped into fine powder to extract gold and silver) and a ridge that contains many mine sites.

Return west on Route 120 back into Yosemite. Alternatively, continue north on U.S. 395 toward Reno and Lake Tahoe, or south on U.S. 395 toward Mt. Whitney and the backside of Kings Canyon and Sequoia National Parks.

Sequoia and Kings Canyon National Parks

Boyden Cavern. The Kern River runs through this canyon, which is deeper than the Grand Canyon. The seepage of its waters has created many caves in this area, well below the surface of the ground. If you can't make it to Crystal Cave in Sequoia, Boyden is a reasonable substitute, but the operations here aren't on par with those at the former. Tours depart on the hour. The caves are on the south side of Route 180, 10 mi west of Cedar Grove Village. | Rte. 180 | 209/736–2708 | www.caverntours.com/boydenrt.htm | $10 | Apr.–May and Oct.–Nov., daily 10–4; June–Sept., daily 10–5.

★**Cedar Grove.** The best view of this region is from the spectacular 30-mi descent along Kings Canyon Highway from Grant Grove to Roads End, where the highway ends, 6 mi east of Cedar Grove Village. Cedar Grove is a good place to sit on a rock next to the Kings River and enjoy a picnic. If you arrive in late afternoon, watch the sinking sun cover the granite in a golden wash. | www.nps.gov/seki | Mid-Apr.–early Nov.

★**Crystal Cave.** Buy a ticket at Foothills or Lodgepole visitor centers, in Sequoia National Park, then hike the scenic half mile along Cascade Creek to the cave. It's 9 mi off Generals Highway via a winding road not suitable for RVs. The 45-minute tour takes you from room to room on paved and lighted pathways, while water drips and echoes in the eerie subterranean spaces. | Crystal Cave Rd., off Generals Hwy., 12 mi north of Rte. 198 entrance | 559/565–3759 | www.sequoiahistory.org | $9 | Mid-May–Oct., daily 10–4.

Foothills, Lodgepole, and Grant Grove Visitor Centers. The year-round visitor centers have displays on park history, birds and beasts, and geology, as well as books, maps, and information about wilderness permits. Be sure to inquire about ranger-led walks and talks. Visitor centers extend their hours in summer, and shorten them in winter; call to confirm times. | 559/565–4212 Foothills, 559/565–3782 Lodgepole, 559/565–4307 Grant Grove, 559/565–3766 wilderness permits | www.nps.gov/seki | Daily 9–5.

General Grant Grove. Named for Ulysses S. Grant, this grove of trees on the north end of Generals Highway between the Giant Forest and Cedar Grove was the original grove designated as General Grant National Park in 1890. A walk along 1-mi Big Stump Trail, which starts near the park entrance, graphically demonstrates the toll heavy logging takes on wilderness. The General Grant Tree Trail, a paved 1/3-mi path through Grant Grove, winds past the General Grant, an enormous, 2,000-year-old sequoia, the world's third largest, designated "the nation's Christmas tree." | Kings Canyon Hwy. (Rte. 180), 4 mi from the Big Stump Entrance | 559/565–4307 | www.nps.gov/seki | Daily.

Giant Forest. The grove of giant sequoia, in Sequoia National Park, encircles five meadows, which are speckled with wildflowers mid-May through June. Take the Big Trees Trail, a paved, 2/3-mi-long wheelchair-accessible trail around Round Meadow. | Generals Hwy., 4 mi south of Lodgepole visitor center | Daily.

★ **Giant Forest Museum.** You'll find excellent exhibits on the ecology of the giant sequoia at the park's premier museum. Though housed in a historic building, it is entirely wheelchair accessible. | Generals Hwy., 4 mi south of Lodgepole visitor center | 559/565–4480 | Free | Memorial Day–mid-June daily 8–5; mid-June–Labor Day, daily 8–6; Labor Day–Memorial Day, daily 9–4:30.

Redwood Mountain Grove. This is the largest grove of giant sequoias in the world. As you head south through Kings Canyon toward Sequoia on Generals Highway, several paved turnouts allow you to look out over the treetops. The grove itself is accessible only on foot or by horseback. Drive 5 mi south of Grant Grove on Generals Highway, then turn right at Quail Flat; follow it 1½ mi to the Redwood Canyon trailhead.

Dining

Cedar Grove Restaurant. American/Casual. This cafeteria-style restaurant serves eggs at breakfast and sandwiches and hamburgers at lunch and dinner; also in the evening it offers several specials, such as chicken-fried steak and trout. | Cedar Grove Village | 559/565–0100 | AE, D, MC, V | Closed Oct.–May | ¢–$

Grant Grove Restaurant. American/Casual. The largest restaurant in Kings Canyon serves full breakfasts as well as hot entrées and sandwiches for lunch and dinner. Counter service is available. | Grant Grove Village | 559/335–5500 | AE, D, MC, V | ¢–$$

Stony Creek Restaurant. American/Casual. This family-style restaurant in Sequoia National Forest serves sandwiches and burgers for lunch, and pasta, fish, and steak for dinner. | Generals Hwy., 12 mi south of Grant Grove | 559/565–3909 | AE, D, MC, V | Closed mid-Oct.–May | ¢–$$

Wuksachi Lodge Dining Room. Contemporary. Huge windows that look out on the trees run the length of the high-ceiling dining room at Sequoia's only upscale restaurant, whose contemporary California menu borrows elements from European cooking. This is the best place to eat in either park. A breakfast buffet is served. | Generals Hwy., 2 mi north of Lodgepole Visitor Center | 559/565–4070 | Reservations essential | AE, D, DC, MC, V | $$–$$$

Lodging

Cedar Grove Lodge. Although the motel-style accommodations are close to the road, Cedar Grove manages to retain some quiet. The lodge is small, so book far in advance. Each room has two queen-size beds. Snack bar, some kitchenettes; no room TVs, no smoking. | Rte. 180, 93628 | 559/335–5500 or 866/522–6966 | fax 559/335–5507 | www.sequoia-kingscanyon.com | 21 rooms | AE, D, MC, V | Closed Nov.–Apr. | $–$$

Grant Grove Cabins. Some of the wood-paneled cabins here have private baths, but most have shared baths and woodstoves outdoors on the porch for cooking. If you like to rough it, you can opt for the rustic cabins (summer only), but note that there's no insulation, carpeting, or running water in these. You can also book a tent cabin (summer only), which has a canvas roof. Restaurant, picnic area; no smoking. | Rte. 180, Grant Grove Village, 4 mi east of the Big Stump entrance to Kings Canyon National Park | 559/335–5500 or 866/522–6966 | fax 559/335–5507 | www.sequoia-kingscanyon.com | 18 tent cabins, 27 rustic cabins, 9 cabins with bath | AE, D, MC, V | ¢–$

John Muir Lodge. This modern timber-sided lodge is in a wooded area near Grant Grove Village. Rooms all have queen beds and private baths. There's a comfortable lobby with a stone fireplace, but no restaurant—though you'll find eateries in nearby in the village. No a/c, no room TVs, no smoking. | Rte. 180, Grant Grove Village, 93628 | 559/335–5500 or 866/522–6966 | fax 559/335–5507 | www.sequoia-kingscanyon.com/johnmuir-lodge.html | 24 rooms, 6 suites | AE, D, MC, V | Closed Nov.–Apr. | $$

Stony Creek Lodge. Sitting among peaceful pines, Stony Creek is on national forest land between Grant Grove and Giant Forest. Rooms are plain but are carpeted and have private showers. There are a restaurant and a market in the lodge. Restaurant, cable TV with movies, shops; no a/c, no smoking. | Generals Hwy., 14 mi southwest of Grant Grove | 559/335–5500 or 866/522–6966 | fax 559/335–5507 | www.sequoia-kingscanyon.com/stonycreeklodge.html | 11 rooms | AE, D, MC, V | Closed Nov.–Apr. | CP | $

★ **Wuksachi Lodge.** Three cedar-and-stone lodge buildings have comfortable rooms with modern amenities. At 7,200 feet above sea level, many of them also have spectacular views of the surrounding mountains. Of all the lodgings in the two parks, this is the nicest. The lodge is 2 mi north of Lodgepole visitor center, 21 mi south of Grant Grove, and 22 mi north of the Ash Mountain Entrance. Restaurant, in-room data ports, hiking, cross-country skiing, bar; no a/c, no room TVs. | Generals Hwy., 93262 | 559/253–2199 or 888/252–5757 (reservations), 559/565–4070 (front desk) | fax 559/456–0542 | www.visitsequoia.com | 84 rooms, 18 suites | AE, D, DC, MC, V | $$$–$$$$

Yosemite National Park

Ahwahneechee Village. Tucked behind the Valley Visitor Center, a short loop trail of about 100 yards circles through a re-creation of an Ahwahneechee Native American village as it might have appeared in 1872, 21 years after the Native Americans' first contact with Europeans. Markers explain the lifestyle of Yosemite's first residents. Allow 30 minutes to see it all. | Yosemite Village | Free | Daily sunrise–sunset.

Ansel Adams Gallery. See the works of the master Yosemite photographer here; some of Adams's original prints are for sale and an elegant photography shop sells more prints and camera supplies. You can also sign up for photography workshops; see the gallery's Web site or call for details. There are private showings on Saturday. Take the Yosemite Village shuttle to stop 5 or 6. | Yosemite Village | 209/372–4413 or 800/568–7398 | www.anseladams.com | Free | Apr.–Oct., daily 9–6; Nov.–Mar., daily 9–5.

Mariposa Grove. Self-guided trails lead uphill through the massive cinnamon-red trunks, with interpretive signs explaining the ecology and threats to the sequoia ecosystem. There's also a guided, one-hour Big Trees Tram Tour; you can ride it through the grove or disembark at any point to hike back to the parking lot. | 209/372–0200 | $20 per car for a weekly park pass | Grove May–Oct., weather permitting; tram tour late spring–Aug., daily 9–4.

Pioneer Yosemite History Center. Several 19th-century buildings have been gathered together in Wawona to create this center. Learn about the people and events that shaped Yosemite's history. Ask about ranger-led walks and horse-drawn stage rides, which happen sporadically. | Rte. 41 near the South Entrance, Wawona | 209/375–9531 or 209/379–2646 | Free | Mid-June–Labor Day, Wed. 2–5, Thurs.–Sun. 10–1 and 2–5.

Valley Visitor Center. For maps, guides, and information from park rangers, be sure to stop at this helpful visitor center, which also has exhibits on the history of Yosemite Valley. A 1-mi paved loop trail, "A Changing Yosemite," charts the park's natural evolution. | Off Northside Dr. | 209/372–0299 | www.yosemitepark.com | Memorial Day–Labor Day, daily 8–6; Labor Day–Memorial Day, daily 9–5.

Dining

★ **Ahwahnee Dining Room.** American. This is the most dramatic dining room in Yosemite, if not California. The massive room has a 34-foot ceiling supported by immense sugar-pine beams and floor-to-ceiling windows. In the evening, everything glows with candle-light. At dinner, men are required to wear jackets, and jeans and sneakers are not permitted; breakfast and lunch are more casual. | Yosemite Valley, about 3/4 mi east of the visitor center | 209/372–1489 | Reservations essential | AE, D, DC, MC, V | $$$–$$$$

Food Court at Yosemite Lodge. American/Casual. Fast and convenient, the food court, open year-round, serves simple fare, ranging from hamburgers and pizzas to pastas, carved roasted meats, and salads at lunch and dinner. There's also a selection of beer and wine. At breakfast, enjoy pancakes and eggs made any way you like. | Yosemite Valley, about $3/4$ mi west of the visitor center | 209/372–1265 | AE, D, DC, MC, V | ¢–$

Mountain Room Restaurant. American. The food becomes secondary when you see Yosemite Falls through the wall of windows in this dining room in the Yosemite Lodge. Grilled trout, steak, and pasta dishes are but a few of the menu choices. A kids' menu is available. The lodge is about $3/4$ mi west of the visitor center. | Northside Dr., Yosemite Valley | 209/372–1281 | Reservations essential | AE, D, DC, MC, V | Closed weekdays from Thanksgiving to Easter except for holiday periods. No lunch | $$–$$$

Tuolumne Meadows Grill. Fast Food. This fast-food grill cooks up breakfast, lunch, and dinner; stop in for a quick meal before exploring the Meadows. | Tioga Rd. (Rte. 120) | 209/372–8426 | AE, D, DC, MC, V | Closed Oct.–Memorial Day | ¢

Wawona Dining Room. American. Watch deer graze on the meadow while dining in the romantic, candlelit dining room of the whitewashed Wawona Hotel, which dates from the late 1800s. The American-style cuisine favors California ingredients and flavors. Trout is a menu staple. There's also a Sunday brunch. Note that jackets are required at dinner. | Rte. 41, Wawona | 209/375–1425 | Reservations essential | AE, D, DC, MC, V | Closed weekdays Nov.–Easter, excluding holidays | $$–$$$$

Lodging

Camping in Yosemite. There are lots of camping sites in Yosemite (nearly 2,000 in summer, 400 year-round), and they fill up quickly, especially in the Valley. Reservations are required at most of Yosemite's campgrounds, especially in summer. You can reserve a site up to five months in advance; bookings made more than 21 days in advance require prepayment. Unless otherwise noted, book your site through the central NPS reservations office. Note that none of the campsites have RV hookups. | National Park Reservation Service, Box 1600, Cumberland, MD 21502 | 800/436–7275 | http://reservations.nps.gov | D, MC, V | ¢

Curry Village. In the shadow of Glacier point, this large community of cabins, tent cabins, and basic hotel rooms lies in a wooded area on the eastern end of Yosemite Valley. The one-room cabins, spartan but adequately furnished, are less expensive than Yosemite's hotels, but not all have private bathrooms. Tent cabins have wood frames and canvas walls and roof and share central bath and shower facilities. Linen service is provided; cooking is not allowed. Cafeteria, pizzeria, pool, bicycles, ice-skating; no a/c, no room phones, no room TVs. | South side of Southside Dr., Yosemite Valley | 559/252–4848 reservations, 209/372–8333 (front desk) | 19 rooms; 182 cabins, 102 with bath; 427 tent cabins | AE, D, DC, MC, V | $–$$

Housekeeping Camp. These rustic three-wall canvas "cabins," on a beach along the Merced River, are difficult to come by; reserving a year in advance is advised. They are not the prettiest sites in the valley, but they're good for travelers with RVs or those without a tent who want to camp. You can cook on gas stoves rented from the front desk. Toilets and showers are in a central building, and there's a camp store for provisions. Laundry facilities. | Southside Dr., $1/2$ mi west of Curry Village | 559/252–4848 | www.yosemitepark.com | 226 units | AE, D, MC, V | Closed Nov.–Apr. | $

Yosemite Lodge. This 1915 lodge is so close to Yosemite Falls that you can hear the water roar. Though it once housed the U.S. Army Cavalry, today it looks like a discrete 1950s motel-resort complex, with several satellite buildings painted brown and white to blend in with the landscape. Rooms are simple with two double beds, though larger "lodge rooms" also have dressing areas and balconies. Restaurant, cafeteria, fans, in-room data ports, pool, bicycles, bar, no-smoking rooms; no room TVs, no a/c. | North-side Dr., Yosemite Valley, about ³⁄₄ mi west of the visitor center | 559/252–4848 | fax 559/456–0542 | www.yosemitepark.com | 239 rooms | AE, D, DC, MC, V | $$

LOS ANGELES TO SAN DIEGO
QUINTESSENTIAL SOUTHERN CALIFORNIA ALONG THE PACIFIC COAST HIGHWAY

Distance: 140 mi   Time: 2–3 days
Overnight Breaks: Carlsbad, La Jolla

This drive exemplifies classic California: you'll pass quaint beachfront settlements, roadside cafés, and surf shops, and may find yourself in the middle of a minor local traffic jam or two, especially on weekends. In between the towns, there are breath-taking views of the Pacific Ocean and protected coastal land. It's a good drive any time of year, but winter brings the bluest skies to the Southern California coast and often means lower hotel prices and quieter beaches. Summer usually draws the largest crowds, with families dominating the sand and sidewalks.

❶ Depart from Los Angeles on I–710 south (from downtown) or I–405 south (from the beaches or airport). Twenty-one miles south of downtown, **Long Beach** is a bustling city in its own right and has plenty to explore, from landmark art deco buildings to artists' neighborhoods.

❷ From Long Beach, take Route 1, known locally as Pacific Coast Highway or PCH, 22 mi to **Corona del Mar,** a small jewel on the Pacific Coast. Like its neighbors to the north and south, this beachside village boasts tony stores and pricey restaurants.

❸ Continue on Route 1 for 7 mi to the laid-back resort town of **Laguna Beach.** Part bohemian artist colony, part gay enclave, Laguna Beach has a mix of artists, hippies, and counterculture dropouts as well as a quite wealthy, conservative component. The community has managed to maintain a balance between luxury tourism and communal values. For day trips, there are scores of art galleries, plenty of arts-and-crafts and antiques shops, and a very active swimming and surfing beach.

❹ From Laguna, follow Route 1 about 25 mi until it ends at San Clemente. Hop on I–5 south and continue another 25 mi to **Carlsbad.** (You can re-connect with the coastal highway in Oceanside, north of Carlsbad.) The strong suit of this small beach spot in southern Orange County is location, location, location. Gently sloping hillsides—covered each spring with buttercups—give way to vibrant wetlands at Batiquitos Lagoon, then to a stunning shoreline. This is a major flower-producing area and an antique-hunters paradise. Spend the night in Carlsbad.

❺ Continue on Route 1 for about 17 mi to **Del Mar.** Deemed the "Toast of the Coast," Del Mar is best known for its racetrack, chic shopping strip, celebrity visitors, and wide beaches. It has also become the headquarters for romantic hot-air-balloon excursions.

❻ Head south on the coastal highway another 10 mi, and it will bring you to the cove-hugging village of **La Jolla.** This oceanfront community is within the San Diego city limits but feels more like its own hamlet. It has long been known for its rugged coast, choice beaches, and sandstone cliffs etched and sculpted by endless wave action. Stay here if you want easy access to scuba diving, snorkeling, and surfing.

7 Take I–5 south about 15 mi, and you'll be in the heart of downtown **San Diego.** As the seventh-largest U.S. city, sunny San Diego is a giant, sprawling metropolis, yet it maintains a laid-back, small-town feel. Its bay-front location, sandy beaches, temperate climate, and unusually clean streets add credence to its self-proclaimed label as "America's finest city."

8 From downtown, you might want to continue on I–5 south towards the San Diego–Coronado Bay bridge, which links San Diego to the narrow isthmus of **Coronado.** This is one of Southern California's prettiest beach resorts, popular with tourists as well as full-time residents. It's also home to a U.S. Naval Air Station and many hotels, including the famous Hotel Del Coronado, recognizable to many from *Some Like it Hot* with Tony Curtis, Jack Lemmon, and Marilyn Monroe.

Carlsbad

Carlsbad State Beach. Joggers and skaters flock to the smooth, six-block promenade behind the seawall. There's also a sidewalk on the bluff above. This beach is narrow, but it's noted for surfing and swimming. Parking is free along the street, or you can use an ample pay lot at the beach's south end. A wheelchair-accessible rest room is available, but there are no showers or concessions. Turn right onto Carlsbad Village Drive from Highway 1 and follow Carlsbad Boulevard south. Parking is free along the street and in the lot at the south end. | Carlsbad Blvd. between Carlsbad Village Dr. and Tamarack Ave. | 760/438–3143 | $4 per vehicle.

★ **Legoland.** A 9-foot-tall red Lego brick dinosaur greets you at the entrance to this roller-coaster- and retail-filled Lego toys theme park, the first of its kind in the country. The park is best for children ages 3–12. | 1 Lego Dr. | 760/918–5346 | www.legolandca.com | $42 | June–Aug., daily 10–5; Sept.–May, Thurs.–Mon. 10–5.

Dining
Bellefleur Winery and Restaurant. Contemporary. Tuscan-inspired archways and photographs of vineyards complement white tablecloths at this stylish spot that has occasional live jazz. Peppercorn-crusted New York strip steak and roasted free-range chicken are favorites. | 5610 Paseo Del Norte | 760/603–1919 | fax 760/603–8465 | www.bellefleur.com | AE, D, DC, MC, V | $$–$$$

Fidel's Norte. Mexican. This family-run restaurant serves reliable Mexican dishes in a former movie studio. The chiles rellenos and hand-shaken margaritas make it a favorite. | 3033 Carlsbad Blvd. | 760/729–0903 | MC, V | ¢–$

Spirito's. Italian. This cozy restaurant serves fresh pasta and pizzas with interesting toppings like eggplant, pesto, and chicken parmigiana. Outdoor seating is available. | 300 Carlsbad Village Dr. | 760/720–1132 | D, MC, V | ¢–$

Vigilucci's Trattoria. Italian. Reminiscent of a Milanese trattoria, Vigilucci's is unpretentious and a comfortable choice for families. Try the *saltimbocca* (veal) or *cioppino* (mixed seafood on a bed of linguine). You can eat outdoors on a covered patio. | 505 1st St., Encinitas | 760/942–7332 | AE, D, DC, MC, V | $–$$$

Lodging
Carlsbad Inn Beach Resort. Set on a wide landscaped lawn in the center of town, this picturesque European-style inn is convenient to the beach. Some rooms have fireplaces. Picnic area, some kitchenettes, cable TV, in-room VCRs, pool, hot tubs, exercise equipment, children's programs, laundry facilities, business services. | 3075 Carlsbad Blvd., 92008 | 760/434–7020 or 800/235–3939 | fax 760/729–4853 | www.carlsbadinn.com | 62 rooms | AE, D, DC, MC, V | $$$–$$$$

Ocean Palms Beach Resort. This 1940s hotel offers beachfront studios and suites. It's in the west part of town close to dozens of restaurants and antiques stores. Picnic area, kitchenettes, cable TV, pool, hot tub, laundry facilities. | 2950 Ocean St., 92008 | 760/729–2493 or 888/802–3224 | fax 760/729–0579 | 56 rooms | AE, D, DC, MC, V | $–$$

Pelican Cove Inn. Rooms at this two-story inn are individually decorated and have gas fireplaces and feather beds; some have whirlpool tubs. It's two blocks from the beach and palm trees surround the grounds. Cable TV; no phones in some rooms, no smoking. | 320 Walnut Ave., 92008 | 760/434–5995 or 888/735–2683 | www.pelican-cove.com | 8 rooms | AE, MC, V | $–$$$

Surf Motel. This tidy two-story roadside motel is across the street from the beach and the promenade. Rooms are bright and spacious, if not terribly inspiring. Restaurant, some in-room hot tubs, some kitchenettes, minibars, cable TV, pool. | 3136 Carlsbad Blvd., 92008 | 760/729–7961 or 800/523–9170 | fax 760/434–6642 | www.surfmotelcarlsbad.com | 28 rooms | AE, D, DC, MC, V | $–$$

Corona Del Mar
Big Corona Beach. This is a great place to romp in the surf, join a game of volleyball, or just stroll along the seashore with your shoes off. The bluff overlooking the beach is called Lookout Point, and is a favorite among locals for watching the sun set over Catalina Island. | Marguerite Ave. at Ocean Blvd. | 949/644–3047 | Parking fee $6.

Dining

The Bungalow. Seafood. You can eat outside on the patio at this Craftsman-style restaurant known for its Australian lobster and high-quality steaks. Top dishes also include hazelnut-crusted Chilean sea bass and New York strip pepper steak. | 2441 E. Coast Hwy. | 949/673–6585 | AE, D, DC, MC, V | No lunch | $$$–$$$$

Quiet Woman. Continental. This British pub is known for its traditional English dishes, and also for pasta, seafood, lamb, burgers, and mesquite-grilled Black Angus steak. There's live entertainment Wednesday through Saturday. | 3224 E. Coast Hwy. | 949/640–7440 | AE, MC, V | No lunch weekends | $$–$$$

Coronado

Coronado City Beach. The sand is white, and the beach is dotted with small dunes where the kids can play. There are fire rings, rest rooms, and lifeguards on duty May–September. Free parking is available on Ocean Boulevard and its side streets. | 900 Ocean Blvd. | 619/522–7380 | Free | Daily.

★**Hotel Del Coronado.** "The Del" is an 1888 building with a rich history of celebrity guests including Marilyn Monroe and Frank Sinatra, and, it's rumored, a resident ghost. A newer building was added in 1977. You don't have to stay here to soak up its bustling, elegant atmosphere. Stroll through the rich, wood-panel lobby and outdoor public gardens, or order a drink and relax on the oceanfront veranda. | 1500 Orange Ave. | 619/435–6611 | fax 619/522–8262 | www.hoteldel.com.

Silver Strand State Beach. You can see 10 mi across to the Point Loma bluffs from here. You can go swimming, surf fishing, and clamming in the mild water. Pedestrian tunnels lead from the parking lot to the beach, which has rest rooms, fire pits, picnic tables, showers, and seasonal concession stands. | 5000 Rte. 75 | 619/435–5184 | $4 per vehicle | Daily 8 AM–9 PM.

Dining

Brigantine. Seafood. Swordfish, prime rib, and twin lobster tails are popular here at this local chain restaurant, which is more neighborhood pub than TGIF. The oyster bar is busy with an after-work crowd. A kids' menu is available. | 1333 Orange Ave. | 619/435–4166 | AE, DC, MC, V | No lunch weekends | $$–$$$

Peohe's. Contemporary. You'll have an outstanding view of the San Diego Harbor and skyline while sampling such creations as halibut with bananas and macadamia nuts and spicy-citrus scallops. A kids' menu is available. | 1201 1st St. | 619/437–4474 | AE, D, DC, MC, V | No dinner Sun. | $$–$$$$

Prince of Wales. American. The grill at Hotel Del Coronado has towering windows overlooking the ocean. It's a perfect setting for seafood—try the roasted sterling salmon, butter-poached Maine lobster, and halibut in lemongrass broth. Heavier fare, such as venison trio loin chop, rounds out the menu. A jazz pianist plays nightly. | 1500 Orange Ave. | 619/522–8818 | AE, D, DC, MC, V | No lunch | $$$–$$$$

Rhinoceros Café and Grill. Seafood. This restaurant's modest interior belies its top quality dishes—local favorites include filet mignon and the lobster bisque, which is said to be Coronado Island's best. | 1166 Orange Ave. | 619/435–2121 | AE, D, DC, MC, V | $–$$

Del Mar

Del Mar City Beach. The beach is long and picturesque, with grassy bluffs rising at either end. You'll find good swimming, surfing, and fishing here. The south end of the beach is near an Amtrak station. | 17th St. and Coast Blvd. | 858/793–5291 | Free | Daily.

Moonlight Beach. This small beach takes its name from Encinitas's early days when residents held nighttime picnics on the sand. The beach still offers lots of soft, clean sand, along with excellent recreational facilities. You can swim, surf, and play volleyball. | 400 B St., Encinitas | 760/633–2740 | Free | Daily.

San Elijo State Beach. A high bluff separates a 171-site campground from the beach below. The view from the heights is spectacular, and stairs are positioned along the long, narrow campground for beach access. The campground includes a bait shop, grocery store, rest rooms, and hot showers. | 2050 S. Coast Hwy. Cardiff | 760/753–5091 | $4 per vehicle | Daily dawn–dusk.

Swami's Beach. The wide, terraced reef extending out from the shore several hundred yards makes this narrow, sandy beach a great place for surfers and fisherman. The reef also attracts scuba divers and snorkelers. Swimming is great at the southern end, away from the reef. To reach the beach, you must take a long, steep stairway down from the bluffs above. | 1298 S. Coast Hwy., Cardiff | 760/633–2740 | Free | Daily.

Dining

Cuvee del Mar. Contemporary. The big, bright room with lots of windows and pictures of the lagoon makes a cheerful place for a meal. The restaurant overlooks the Torrey Pines State Park. Locals come for such dishes as the tempura shrimp, New York strip steak, and seared ahi tuna. Outside, tables with umbrellas overlook the lagoon. | 2334 Carmel Valley Rd. | 858/259–5878 | AE, D, DC, MC, V | $$–$$$

Epazote. Southwestern. The menu changes seasonally at this Southwestern-style restaurant. Specialties include ahi tuna with Thai shrimp salsa, lobster chimichangas, and fajitas. A large rock wall and an open kitchen make for an interesting interior. There's live jazz on Wednesday and reggae on Thursday. | 1555 Camino del Mar | 858/259–9966 | AE, DC, MC, V | $$–$$$

Poseidon Restaurant. American. The patio dining area at this beachfront restaurant is as large as the indoor dining room. The Pojo burger, a half-pound patty topped with cheese, cooked onions, and mushrooms, is a house specialty as are the fresh seafood entrées. | 1670 Coast Blvd. | 858/755–9345 | AE, D, DC, MC, V | $$–$$$$

Laguna Beach

Crystal Cove State Park. Biking and hiking trails are plentiful here, but the main attraction is the 1,000-acre underwater park for scuba divers and snorkelers. | 8471 N. Pacific Coast Hwy. | 949/494–3539 | fax 949/494–6911 | $5 | 6 AM–sunset.

Dining

A La Carte. Café. Though most people opt for takeout here, this restaurant also has a small dining area. You can get salads, sandwiches, a selection of vegetarian entrées, and great desserts any time; weekends an hors d'oeuvres bar is added to the lineup. Try the boneless breast of chicken with pasta in tequila-lime and cream sauce, or the Cajun fried chicken sandwich. | 1915 S. Coast Hwy. | 949/497–4927 | MC, V | ¢–$

Beach House. Seafood. This cozy little beach house of a restaurant is right on the water, so you might get a face full of spray at hightide. Naturally, seafood's the focus here, with such entrées as fresh Hawaiian ahi and lobster tails. If you don't want fish, there are still plenty of options, like prime rib and pasta. | 619 Sleepy Hollow La. | 949/494–9707 | AE, MC, V | $$–$$$$

Cafe Zinc. Contemporary. Laguna Beach locals gather on the plant-filled patio of this vegetarian breakfast-and-lunch café. Oatmeal is sprinkled with berries, poached eggs are dusted with herbs, and the juice is fresh squeezed. For lunch, try the mixed vegetable sandwich or one of the gourmet pizzas. | 350 Ocean Ave. | 949/494–2791 | No credit cards | No dinner | $

Las Brisas. Seafood. The candlelit cliff-side dining room overlooks Laguna's scenic, craggy, coastline. This romantic restaurant serves Mexican-influenced seafood and fish dishes, such as red snapper Veracruzano (a lightly breaded fillet, filled with shrimp, in spicy tomato sauce) and sautéed calamari medallions with green peppers and capers. | 361 Cliff Dr. | 949/497–5434 | AE, D, DC, MC, V | $$–$$$

La Jolla

★**La Jolla Cove.** The wooded spread that looks out over a shimmering blue inlet is what first attracted everyone to La Jolla, from Native Americans to the glitterati; it is the village's enduring cachet. You'll find the cove beyond where Girard Avenue dead-ends into Coast Boulevard, marked by towering palms that line a promenade. An underwater preserve at the north end of La Jolla Cove makes the adjoining beach the most popular one in the area. On summer days, the beach and water seem to disappear under the mass of bodies swimming, snorkeling, or sunbathing.

★**Museum of Contemporary Art.** A patterned terrazzo floor leads to galleries where the museum's permanent collection of post-1950s art and rotating exhibits are on display. Works by Andy Warhol, Robert Rauschenberg, Frank Stella, Joseph Cornell, and Jenny Holzer, to name a few, get major competition from the setting: you can look out from the top of a grand stairway onto a garden landscaped with rare 100-year-old California plant specimens. | 700 Prospect St. | 858/454–3541 | $6 | Fri.–Tues. 11–5, Thurs. 11–7.

Scripps Beach and Tidepools. This sandy beach is separated from La Jolla Shores only by the Scripps Pier. Here you will find numerous tide pools that offer a close-up view of marine life. You can look, but touching marine life is prohibited. To reach the tide pools, park in the Kellogg Park lot and walk north toward the pier. | Caminito del Oro | 619/235–1169 | Free | Daily.

Stephen Birch Aquarium-Museum. The aquarium contains marine life from both the warm tropical seas of the Pacific Ocean and the cold northern waters. During January through March, there are whale-watching boat rides and exhibits about migrating gray whales. | 2300 Expedition Way | 858/534–3474 | www.aquarium.ucsd.edu | $10 | Daily 9–5.

Torrey Pines State Beach. The coastline leading to Torrey Pines is as impressive as any in Southern California. The beach itself runs for nearly a mile between the Del Mar bluffs and the sandstone cliffs of the Torrey Pines State Preserve. Hiking trails lead to the cliffs, 300 feet above the ocean; trail maps are available at the park station. When the tide is out, it's possible to walk south all the way past the lifeguard towers to Black's Beach over rocky promontories. | 120600 N. Torrey Pines Rd. | 858/755–2063 | $4 per vehicle | 8 AM–dusk.

Windansea Beach. This narrow, rocky beach is considered one of Southern California's best for surfing. The smooth, rocky ledge that lines most of the beach makes for interesting exploration. There are no amenities, though lifeguards are stationed on the beach during the summer. Park along Neptune Place or in a small, unpaved lot at the end of Nautilus Road. | 619/235–1169 | Free | Daily.

Dining
Brockton Villa. Contemporary. This informal restaurant resides in a restored 1894 beach cottage with a wraparound veranda that overlooks La Jolla Cove and the ocean. The extensive menu includes pan-seared filet mignon and lobster tail stuffed with crabmeat. Sandwiches, salads, and some seafood dishes are available for lunch. | 1235 Coast Blvd. | 858/454–7393 | AE, D, MC, V | $$–$$$

Crab Catcher. Seafood. The Crab Catcher is set high on a cliff with a spectacular ocean view. Have the catch of the day stuffed with crab or try the coconut shrimp tempura. Next door is a sister café with a full bar. | 1298 Prospect St. | 858/454–9587 | AE, D, DC, MC, V | $$–$$$$

French Pastry Shop. Continental. As the name implies, the specialties here are the homemade breads and pastries, but the quiches, salads, pâtés, and assorted desserts are equally popular. There's a patio for open-air dining. | 5550 La Jolla Blvd. | 858/454–9094 | MC, V | No dinner Mon. | $

Piatti Ristorante. Italian. The interior is light and airy, with pastel murals of overflowing plates of pasta gracing the walls. A wood-burning oven turns out flavorful pizzas; creative pastas include wide saffron noodles with shrimp, fresh tomatoes, and arugula, and garlicky spaghetti served with clams in the shell. | 2182 Avenida de la Playa | 858/454–1589 | AE, D, MC, V | $–$$

Lodging
Bed and Breakfast Inn at La Jolla. Noted architect Irving Gill designed this beige stucco Cubist house, which was built in 1913. Attractive guest rooms have Laura Ashley fabrics and antiques, fireplaces, and ocean or garden views. The Museum of Contemporary Art is across the street and the beach is only a block away. Dining room, in-room data ports, some minibars; no TV in some rooms, no kids under 12, no smoking. | 7753 Draper Ave., 92307 | 858/456–2066 or 800/582–2466 | fax 858/456–1510 | www.innlajolla.com | 15 rooms | MC, V | BP | $$$–$$$$

Best Western Inn by the Sea. All rooms of this five-story tourist and business hotel amidst boutiques and restaurants have village or ocean views, many with private balconies. You can have your morning juice, coffee, and pastries in the breakfast room by the pool. Restaurant, some minibars, some microwaves, cable TV, outdoor pool. | 7830 Fay Ave., 92307 | 858/459–4461 or 800/526–4545 | fax 858/456–2578 | www.bestwestern.com/innbythesea | 132 rooms | AE, D, DC, MC, V | CP | $$–$$$

★ **La Jolla Torrey Pines Hilton.** The low-rise, high-class hotel blends discreetly into the Torrey Pines cliff top, looking almost insignificant until you step inside the luxurious lobby and gaze at the Pacific Ocean. The oversize accommodations are simple but elegant; ground-floor rooms have patios, all other rooms have balconies. Restaurant, room service, in-room data ports, in-room safes, minibars, cable TV, tennis courts, pool, exercise equipment, hot tub, bicycles, bar, children's programs (ages 5–12), business services. | 10950 N. Torrey Pines Rd., 92307 | 858/558–1500 | fax 858/450–4584 | 394 rooms | AE, D, DC, MC, V | $$–$$$$

Scripps Inn. You'd be wise to make reservations well in advance for this small, quiet inn, which has one of the village's best ocean views across La Jolla Cove. Cottagelike rooms and suites are decorated in different shades of white and have quirky configurations—yours might have a balcony with a view, a kitchen and dining area, or a fireplace. Some kitchenettes, minibars, cable TV, free parking. | 555 S. Coast Blvd. | 858/454–3391 | www.scrippsinn.com | 14 rooms | AE, D, DC, MC, V | CP | $$$–$$$$

Long Beach
★ **Aquarium of the Pacific.** The Long Beach Aquarium of the Pacific has over 550 species in 17 major living habitats and 30 smaller exhibits where you learn about the Pacific Ocean's three regions: Southern California/Baja; the Tropical Pacific; and the Northern Pacific. | 100 Aquarium Way | 562/590–3100 | www.aquariumofpacific.org/ | $14.95 | Daily 9–6.

Catalina Island. Beaches, rocky areas, restaurants, and shops greet you at this resort community on an island off the coast of Los Angeles. On Catalina you can enjoy hiking and water sports such as waterskiing, snorkeling, swimming, and diving. You'll have to take the Catalina Express from Long Beach to reach the island: from I–710, follow signs to downtown Long Beach and exit at Golden Shore, turn right at the stop sign and follow the road around to the terminal on the right. | Catalina Express: 320 Golden Shore Blvd. | 310/519–1212 or 800/995–4386 | www.catalina.com or www.catalinaexpress.com | Free | Daily.

Municipal Beach. More than 5 ¹/₂ mi of public beach winds along the waterfront on the west side of town, off Ocean Blvd. | 562/570–3215 | Free | Daily.

Museum of Latin American Art. This cultural center, in what was a silent-film studio in the '30s, is the only place in the western United States to exclusively show contemporary art from Mexico, Central America, South America, and the Spanish-speaking Caribbean. | 628 Alamitos Ave. | 562/437–1689 | fax 562/437–7043 | www.molaa.com | $5 | Tues.–Sat. 11:30–7, Sun. noon–6.

★ *Queen Mary* **Seaport.** Both a hotel and living museum of a past way of life and travel, the Queen Mary is a historic luxury liner now permanently docked at Long Beach. The Queen Mary has a wedding chapel, restaurants, and salons for private parties. Planning for the ship began in 1926 and the ship went into service in 1936. She served as a troop ship during World War II, then returned to private service until 1967, when she was permanently docked. | 1126 Queens Hwy. | 562/435–3511 | fax 562/437–4531 | www.queenmary.com | $25 | Daily 10–6.

Queenway Bay. This downtown, 300-acre oceanfront development includes the Long Beach Aquarium of the Pacific and Rainbow Harbor, home of the ships *Pilgrim of Newport*, *Californian*, and *American Pride*, as well as up to 50 commercial vessels with scheduled dinner cruises and various tours. A multilevel, 2,000-foot-long public esplanade surrounds the harbor, which is also within a landscaped park. There's also an IMAX theater. | Off Ocean Blvd. | 562/570–6684.

Dining

Mariposa. Mexican. Traditional Mexican entrées, from tacos and burritos to the fabled Oaxacan mole and fresh seafood, are the order of the day here. Street-side patio dining and live salsa music Friday and Saturday help make it a popular spot. | 110 Pine Ave. | 562/437–2119 | MC, V | $–$$$

Mum's. Contemporary. A pioneer in the redevelopment of downtown Long Beach, this swank, romantic restaurant has an outdoor patio with umbrella tables and a reputation for its eclectic California cuisine and sushi bar. On the menu are delectable options like sizzling scallops and seared-shrimp scampi with sticky-rice timbale. After dinner, go upstairs and check out Cohiba, Mum's dance hall and billiards club. | 144 Pine Ave. | 562/437–7700 | AE, D, DC, MC, V | $$–$$$$

Parker's Lighthouse. Seafood. This Long Beach landmark, built to look like a giant New England lighthouse, overlooks the Queen Mary and the marina. There are three different floors to dine on, including a circular bar at the top. Among the many selections, you'll find mesquite-grilled fresh fish, a seafood platter, and prime Black Angus beef. | 435 Shoreline Dr., No. 1 | 562/432–6500 | AE, D, DC, MC, V | $$–$$$$

San Diego

★ **Balboa Park.** Overlooking downtown and the Pacific Ocean, 1,200-acre Balboa Park is the cultural heart of San Diego, where you'll find most of the city's museums, the San Diego Zoo, restaurants, performance venues, and picnic areas. Parking near Balboa

Park's museums is no small accomplishment. If you end up parking a bit far from your destination, consider the stroll back through the greenery part of the day's recreational activities. Alternatively, you can park at Inspiration Point on the east side of the park, off Presidents Way. Free trams run from there to the museums every 8 to 10 minutes, 9:30–5:30 daily.

San Diego Zoo. Balboa Park's—and perhaps the city's—most famous attraction is the 100-acre San Diego Zoo and it deserves all the press it gets. Nearly 4,000 animals of some 800 diverse species roam in hospitable, expertly crafted habitats. | 2920 Zoo Dr. | 619/234–3153 | www.sandiegozoo.org | $19.50–$32 | Mid-May–Sept., daily 9–9; Sept.–mid-May, daily 9–4.

Cabrillo National Monument. This 144-acre preserve marks the site of the first European visit to the San Diego area, made by 16th-century explorer Juan Rodríguez Cabrillo. In 1913, public land was set aside to commemorate his discovery, and today the site, with its rugged cliffs and shores and outstanding overlooks, is one of the most frequently visited of all the national monuments. The moderately steep 2-mi Bayside Trail winds through coastal sage scrub, curving under the cliff-top lookouts and bringing you ever closer to the bay-front scenery. The western and southern cliffs are prime whale-watching territory in January and February. | 1800 Cabrillo Memorial Dr., Point Loma | 619/557–5450 | www.nps.gov/cabr | $5 per car, $3 per person entering on foot or by bicycle | Daily 9–5:15; hrs vary in summer.

Gaslamp Quarter. The 16-block National Historic District between 4th and 5th avenues from Broadway to Market Street contains most of San Diego's Victorian-style commercial buildings. Businesses thrived in this area in the latter part of the 19th century, but when the commercial district moved west, many of San Diego's first buildings fell into disrepair. During the early 1900s the quarter became known as the Stingaree district. Prostitutes picked up sailors in lively area taverns, and dance halls and crime flourished. Today former flophouses have become office buildings, shops, and restaurants.

William Heath Davis House. One of the first residences in town now serves as the information center for the historic district. Two-hour walking tours ($8) of the historic district leave from the house on Saturday at 11. The museum also sells detailed self-guided-tour maps ($2). | 410 Island Ave., at 4th Ave., Downtown | 619/233–4692 | Tues.–Sun. 11–3.

Maritime Museum. A must for anyone with an interest in nautical history, this collection of six restored ships affords a fascinating glimpse of San Diego during its heyday as a commercial seaport. The museum's headquarters is in the *Berkeley*, an 1898 ferryboat moored at the foot of Ash Street. The most historically significant of the six ships is the *Star of India*, an iron windjammer built in 1863, when iron ships were still a novelty. | 1492 N. Harbor Dr., Embarcadero | 619/234–9153 | www.sdmaritime.com | $7 (includes entry to all ships) | Daily 9–8 (until 9 in summer).

★**San Diego Museum of Art.** Known primarily for its Spanish baroque and Renaissance paintings, including works by El Greco, Goya, Rubens, and Jacob van Ruisdael, San Diego's most comprehensive art museum also has strong holdings of South Asian art, Indian miniatures, and contemporary California paintings. The Baldwin M. Baldwin collection includes more than 100 pieces by Toulouse-Lautrec. | Casa de Balboa, 1450 El Prado | 619/232–7931 | www.sdmart.org | $8 ($10–$12 for special exhibits) | Tues.–Sun. 10–6 (till 9 on Thurs.).

Dining

Café Eleven. French. The super-saver menu, which always includes roast duckling, has long drawn budget-minded San Diegans to this popular café. Specials, served Tuesday through Thursday and Sunday nights, may include trout, rack of lamb, or sesame chicken. Service is casual but excellent, and there's outdoor dining. | 1440 University Ave. | 619/260–8023 | AE, D, DC, MC, V | Closed Mon. No lunch | $$

★**El Agave.** Mexican. A charmer on the edge of historic Old Town, El Agave promises caring service, a bar stocked with hundreds of tequilas (a collection that El Agave claims is unrivaled in the United States), and a delicious, truly Mexican menu. Make a meal of such appetizers as crisp chicken tacos covered with thick, tart cream and rolled taquitos stuffed with shredded pork. Or save room for entrées like chicken in spicy Don Julio mole sauce, and terrific, crisp-skinned roast leg of pork. | 2304 San Diego Ave. | 619/220–0692 | AE, MC, V | $$–$$$$

★**Fish Market.** Seafood. Fresh mesquite-grilled fish is the specialty at this informal restaurant. There's also an excellent little sushi bar and good steamed clams and mussels. The view is stunning: enormous plate-glass windows look directly out onto the harbor. A more formal restaurant upstairs, the Top of the Market ($$$$), is expensive but worth the splurge. | 750 N. Harbor Dr. | 619/232–3474, 619/234–4867 for Top of the Market | AE, D, DC, MC, V | $–$$$

COLORADO

COLORADO'S HEARTLAND
GOLD AND SILVER COUNTRY TOUR

Distance: approximately 275 mi   Time: 1 or 2 days
Overnight Break: Breckenridge

In summer you can make this trip in a single day if you leave early and plan on getting back to Colorado Springs late. However, it's too much of a stretch in winter, when an overnight in Breckenridge is in order, giving ample time for more relaxed driving on potentially hazardous roads. Given the number of attractions to see on this tour, if you have the time, make it a two-day trip regardless.

❶ From **Colorado Springs** proceed northwest on U.S. 24 for 3 mi, then turn right on 30th Street and view the absolutely stunning **Garden of the Gods.** Take the time to drive through this geological wonderland, which has 1,350 acres of fantastic, 300-million-year-old red sandstone formations.

❷ Leaving the Garden of the Gods, follow U.S. 24 to **Manitou Springs,** outside the city limits of Colorado Springs. There tour the Manitou Cliff Dwellings, where the ancestral Puebloan Indians lived circa 1100. If you're up to a brisk walk, visit the **Cave of the Winds.** Underground tours (45 minutes and up) take you past millions of years of local geology. Bring a light jacket; the temperature of the cave is a constant 54°F.

❸ From Cave of the Winds, proceed west on U.S. 24 for another 21 mi until you enter the village of Florissant and see the sign pointing southward to **Florissant Fossil Beds National Monument,** where a 35-million-year-old redwood forest as well as lake-bottom plants and insects were perfectly preserved. Enjoy a ranger-led or self-guided walk on one of the well-marked trails. This little-known wonder is a boon for fossil buffs.

❹ Leaving the Fossil Beds, continue westward on U.S. 24 for 30 mi to Hartsel. (On your way you will cross Wilkerson Pass at an elevation of 9,507 feet) At Hartsel take Route 9 north for 17 mi to **Fairplay.** Here you may wish to visit the **South Park City Museum,** which contains more than 30 mining-era buildings, exhibits, and 60,000 artifacts.

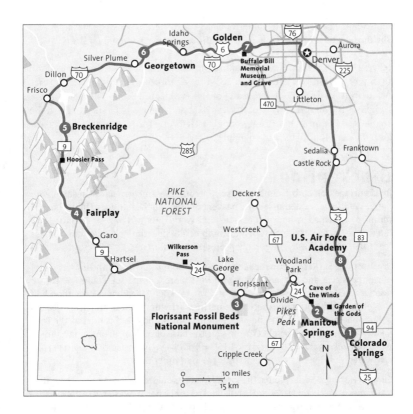

❺ From Fairplay, proceed north on Route 9, with a stop at the Bristlecone Pine Scenic Area to view these ancient trees at the base of 14,172-foot Mount Bross. Continue for 22 mi and drive over the 11,541-foot-high **Hoosier Pass** to reach **Breckenridge.** You'll marvel at the snowcapped peaks on all sides. There's plenty to do and see in Breckenridge, which had its beginnings in 1859 as a gold-rush boomtown and today attracts skiers and other vacationers. You can take a walking tour of the historic district and some of the outlying gold mines. Spend the night in Breckenridge.

❻ Leaving Breckenridge, take Route 9 north for 10 mi to its junction with I–70, and proceed east on I–70 for about 38 mi to historic **Georgetown.** Georgetown dates from 1859, when gold was discovered in the area. Since then the area has produced more than $200 million worth of precious metals. If you have the time, take a ride on the **Georgetown Loop Railroad,** a narrow-gauge steam train that ascends a steep grade to the neighboring town of Silver Plume. Also visit the **Hamill House Museum,** the restored home of Colorado state senator and silver mogul William A. Hamill, and the **Hotel de Paris Museum,** where period furnishings re-create a period of wealth and influence.

❼ When you leave Georgetown, it's a straight shot—and 29 mi—east along I–70 into Denver, which is certainly worth a stay. But since you only have a short amount of time on this tour, **Golden** should be your next stop. Take Exit 244, pick up U.S. 6, and proceed the 10 mi or so into the town that Coors beer and the **Colorado School of Mines,** both renowned throughout the world, put on the map. You can tour the **Coors Brewing Company** and watch as the ever-popular beer is being brewed. Mineral and mining history exhibits are on display at the **School of Mines' Geology Museum.** Learn more about scout and entertainer William F. Cody, better known as Buffalo Bill, at **The Buffalo Bill Memorial Museum and Grave,** 5 mi west of town off U.S. 6.

8 Leaving Golden, pick up U.S. 6 eastbound and follow it through Denver (about 12 mi) to its junction with I–25. Turn south on I–25 and proceed 50 mi to the **U.S. Air Force Academy** (take Exit 156B [North Gate] or Exit 150B [South Gate]). This magnificent campus is the Air Force's answer to West Point and Annapolis. Be sure and visit the chapel, which is an architectural wonder in itself. After leaving the Academy, take I–25 and proceed south back to Colorado Springs.

Breckenridge

Breckenridge Golf Club. Dramatically set, the course resembles a nature reserve, with native wildflowers and grasses and beaver ponds lining the fairways. This is the only municipally owned 27-hole golf course in the world designed by Jack Nicklaus. | 200 Clubhouse Dr. | 970/453–9104 | www.townofbreckenridge.com/golf/index.cfm | Greens fees $70–$110 | Mid-May–Aug., daily 7–6; Sept.-Oct., daily 9–5.

Breckenridge Ski Resort. America's second-most popular ski resort and a sister resort of Vail, Keystone, and Beaver Creek, is 1 mi west of Breckenridge off Route 9. The 2,228 skiable acres encompass Peaks 7, 8, 9, and 10 of the Ten Mile Range. More than half the terrain is advanced or expert. Summertime activities include miniature golf, an alpine slide, zip lines, a climbing wall, bungee jumps, and chairlift rides at the Peak 8 Fun Park, as well as horseback riding (at the base of Peak 9), hiking, and 35 mi of mountain biking trails at the ski area. | Ski Hill Rd. | 970/453–5000 or 800/404–3535 | www.breckenridge.com | Winter, daily 8:30–4; summer, daily 9–5.

Summit Historical Society Tours. The society conducts guided walking tours of the historical homes of Breckenridge. With 254 buildings on the National Register of Historic Places, the downtown comprises one of Colorado's largest National Historic Districts. | 309 N. Main St. | 970/453–9022 | www.summithistorical.org | $6 | Daily 9–5.

COLORADO RULES OF THE ROAD

License Requirements: The legal driving age in Colorado is 17. As a visitor driving an automobile in Colorado, you must have a valid driver's license from your home state.

Right Turn on Red: A driver can legally turn right on a red light *after* coming to a full stop.

Seat Belt and Helmet Laws: State law requires automobile drivers and passengers in the front seat of the vehicle to use seat belts. Children under four years old and under 40 pounds, regardless of where in the vehicle they are riding, must use an approved safety seat.

Speed Limits: Individual speed limits are posted along all major thoroughfares and in all municipalities. The interstate system, except where posted for lower rates, maintains a 75-mph speed limit.

For More Information: Colorado State Patrol | 303/239–4500.

Dining

Blue River Bistro. Italian. A large variety of pasta dishes, as well as traditionally prepared meat and seafood, graces the menu at this sophisticated Breckenridge standby. There's live music nightly. | 305 N. Main St. | 970/453–6974 | AE, D, DC, MC, V | $$–$$$

★ **Café Alpine.** Eclectic. Dishes, from black sesame–seared tuna sashimi to West Indies beef shoulder with plantain sweet potato mashers, change daily. The café, which also has a tapas bar, is in a late-1880s, three-story Victorian house. | 106 E. Adams St. | 970/ 453–8218 | AE, D, DC, MC, V | $$–$$$

Downstairs at Eric's. American. Local snowboarders mingle with visiting families at this sports bar–cum–eatery with 22 beers on tap. The menu includes pizzas, burgers, rotisserie chicken, and hearty sandwiches at down-to-earth prices. | 111 S. Main St. | 970/453–1401 | D, MC, V | $

Hearthstone. Continental. Lace curtains frame fabulous mountain views at this eatery in an 1889 house; walls are adorned with antique barn wood. Try the tilapia *pepita* (pumpkin seed–crusted tilapia fillet). Enjoy daily happy hour specials, from 4 to 6, on one of the four large decks overlooking the Breckenridge ski area. | 130 S. Ridge St. | 970/453–1148 | AE, DC, MC, V | No lunch | $$–$$$

Pierre's Riverwalk Café. French. Watch the chefs at work through the open kitchen at this elegant café. Try the Rocky Mountain trout, or the Colorado rack of lamb. Dine alfresco on a deck overlooking the Blue River and the Rocky Mountains. | 137 S. Main St. | 970/453–0989 | DC, MC, V | Closed May and early Nov. | $$$

Lodging

Allaire Timbers Inn. There are fabulous views of the Tenmile Range from the main deck of this stone-and-log B&B nestled in the woods. All rooms have private decks and king-size beds; the suites include gas fireplaces. In-room data ports, some in-room hot tubs, cable TV, hot tub, business services; no a/c, no kids under 13, no smoking. | 9511 S. Main St. (Rte. 9), 80424 | 970/453–7530 or 800/624–4904 | fax 970/453–8699 | www.allairetimbers.com | 8 rooms, 2 suites | AE, D, MC, V | BP | $$–$$$

★ **Bed and Breakfasts on North Main Street.** Three buildings—including two restored, historic cottages impeccably furnished with Victorian accents—comprise this property. An 1885 miner's house has five individual guest rooms. The romantic Willoughby Cottage sleeps two and has a gas fireplace, whirlpool tub, and kitchenette. And the newer timber-frame "barn" (really a house) on the Blue River has five lodge-style rooms, each with gas fireplace. Picnic area, some in-room data ports, some kitchenettes, some refrigerators, cable TV, some in-room VCRs, hot tub; no a/c, no phone in some rooms, no kids under 12, no smoking. | 303 N. Main St., 80424 | 970/453–2975 or 800/795–2975 | fax 970/453– 5258 | www.breckenridge-inn.com | 10 rooms, 1 cottage | AE, D, MC, V | BP | $$–$$$$

Great Divide. The Great Divide is 50 yards from the base of Peak 9 and two blocks from Main Street; it's also one of the few full-service hotels in Breckenridge. Expect large guest rooms, some with private balconies. Restaurant, in-room data ports, refrigera- tors, cable TV with movies and video games, indoor pool, hot tub, 3 outdoor hot tubs, health club, massage, ski shop, bar, meeting rooms, business services, no-smoking rooms; no a/c. | 550 Village Rd., 80424 | 970/453–4500 or 800/321–8444 | fax 970/453–0212 | www.greatdividelodge.com | 208 rooms | AE, D, DC, MC, V | $$

The Lodge and Spa at Breckenridge. The hillside setting of this lodge, 2 mi from town, delivers gorgeous vistas of the surrounding peaks. The interiors are upscale rustic, with hand-peeled log furniture and hand-painted armoires. The larger superior rooms have kitchenettes and gas fireplaces. A treatment at the on-site spa is the perfect antidote to car-ride kinks. Restaurant, in-room data ports, some kitchenettes, some in-room VCRs, cable TV, indoor pool, 2 indoor hot tubs, 2 outdoor hot tubs, health club, spa, meeting rooms, business services, some pets allowed; no smoking. | 112 Overlook Dr., 80424 | 970/453–9300 or 800/736–1607 | fax 970/453–0625 | www.thelodgeatbreck.com | 45 rooms, 1 suite | AE, D, DC, MC, V | CP | $$$–$$$$

Village at Breckenridge. The Village, a sprawling self-contained resort, practically stretches from Main Street to the ski area. The centerpiece is Maggie Pond, which serves as the area's only outdoor ice rink. Reserve a lodge room (the only ones in Breckenridge with air-conditioning, though you'll hardly need it), a studio with a full kitchen, or a one- to three-bedroom condominium with a full kitchen and fireplace. 2 restaurants, some in-room data ports, some kitchens, cable TV, some in-room VCRs, indoor-outdoor pool, 2 outdoor hot tubs, health club, downhill skiing, pub, business services, meeting rooms, no-smoking rooms; no a/c in some rooms. | 535 S. Park, 80424 | 970/453–2000 or 800/800–7829 | fax 970/453–3116 | www.villageatbreckenridge.com | 60 rooms, 101 studios, 92 condos | AE, D, DC, MC, V | $–$$$

Colorado Springs

★**The Broadmoor.** Even if you're not staying here, it's worth passing by the pink-stucco, Italianate Broadmoor complex, built in 1918 and still one of the world's great luxury resorts. You can also survey original owner Spencer Penrose's collection of antique carriages. | 1 Lake Ave. (I–25, Exit 138) | 719/634–7711 or 800/634–7711 | fax 719/577–5700 | www.broadmoor.com | Museum free | Museum Mon.–Sat. 10–5; Sun. 1–5.

Cheyenne Mountain Zoo. America's highest zoo (6,800 feet) has almost 600 animals, including some 40 endangered species; many of the animals live in natural settings. Admission includes the Will Rogers Shrine, a five-story granite tower with Western murals and photos of America's favorite cowboy. | 4250 Cheyenne Mountain Zoo Rd. | 719/633–9925 | fax 719/633–2254 | www.cmzoo.org | $12 | June–Sept., daily 9–6; Oct.–May, daily 9–5.

★**Colorado Springs Fine Arts Center.** Native American and Hispanic art, a collection of 19th- and 20th-century Western works, an art school, and a theater comprise this pueblo-style space. | 30 W. Dale St. | 719/634–5581 | fax 719/634–0570 | www.csfineartscenter.org | $5; free on Sat. | Tues.–Sat. 9–5, Sun. 1–5.

Pro Rodeo Hall of Fame and Museum of the American Cowboy. Learn about bronco-busting, bull-riding, and the men and women who compete in these events and more at the country's only museum dedicated to the wild world of professional rodeo. The heart of the museum, the Hall of Champions, contains photographs, personal memorabilia, trophies, and the original saddles, ropes, clothing, and hats worn by rodeo contestants. | 101 Pro Rodeo Dr. (I–25, Exit 147) | 719/528–4764 | fax 719/548–4874 | www.prorodeo.com | $6 | Daily 9–5.

★**Seven Falls.** As the name implies, seven waterfalls cascade down 181 feet of sheer granite cliff. Either walk up the 224 steps to view this natural wonder and access two nature trails or ride an elevator to a viewing platform. At night a light show illuminates South Cheyenne Canyon. | S. Cheyenne Canyon Rd. | 719/632–0765 | fax 719/632–0781 | www.sevenfalls.com | $8.25; $9.75 after 5 | Mid-Apr.–mid-June and mid-Aug.–Sept. 1, daily 8:30 AM–9:30 PM; mid-June–mid-Aug., daily 8:30 AM–10:30 PM; Sept. 2–late Oct., daily 9–5:15; late Oct.–mid-Apr., daily 9–4:15.

U.S. Air Force Academy. Since its establishment in 1954, the academy has graduated thousands of career Air Force men and women. Though much of the campus is off-limits to civilians, a visitor center has exhibits on cadet life; the architecturally striking, 17-spired chapel is also open to the public. There is a self-guided driving tour. | I–25, Exit 150B (South Gate) or 156B (North Gate) | 719/333–2025 or 800/955–4438 | fax 719/472–1420 | www.usafa.af.mil | Memorial Day–Labor Day, daily 9–6; Labor Day–Memorial Day, daily 9–5.

World Figure Skating Hall of Fame and Museum. Exhibits tell the story of figure skating through the years. You'll also find a library, artwork, skating memorabilia, and videos of memorable performances. The museum is adjacent to the U.S. Figure Skating Association headquarters. | 20 1st St. | 719/635–5200 | www.worldskatingmuseum.org | $3 | May–Oct., weekdays 10–4, Sat. 10–5; Nov.–Apr., Mon.–Sat. 10–4.

Dining

★**El Tesoro.** Southwestern. Southwestern paintings and photographs (for sale) adorn the exposed-brick walls. Enjoy northern New Mexican dishes such as *posole* (hominy), Santa Fe enchiladas, mango quesadillas, or a margarita made with fresh-squeezed lime juice and one of a large selection of tequilas. | 10 N. Sierra Madre | 719/471–0106 | AE, D, MC, V | Closed Sun. | $–$$

La Petite Maison. Contemporary. This romantic restaurant in a restored Victorian cottage offers two menus that change seasonally: one with more casual fare, such as pasta and sandwiches, the other with dishes that reflect classic French influences. Organic meats and produce are used whenever possible. | 1015 W. Colorado Ave. | 719/632–4887 | AE, D, DC, MC, V | Closed Sun. | $$–$$$

Penrose Room. French. The Broadmoor Hotel's famed Penrose Room is a luxurious place with grand chandeliers, rich velvet draperies, and majestic views of the city and mountains. Try the chateaubriand *Bouquetiére,* Colorado bone-in venison chop, and the restaurant's signature dessert soufflés. | Broadmoor Hotel, 1 Lake Ave. | 719/634–7711 | Reservations essential | Jacket required | AE, D, DC, MC, V | No lunch | $$$–$$$$

Fairplay

Monument to Prunes, a Burro. Prunes was a faithful burro who hauled supplies to area mines for more than 60 years, until his death in 1930. This graveside memorial includes his collar and a dinner bell that townsfolk would ring when they had food scraps for him. | Front St. next to the Hand Hotel | 719/836–2622 | Daily.

Pike National Forest and Bristlecone Pine Scenic Area. Fairplay is surrounded on three sides by this national forest, which has more than 1 million acres for hiking, fishing, and other activities. Stop by the South Park Ranger station for directions to the Bristlecone Pine Scenic Area off Route 9, where ancient, wind-stunted pine trees stand at the base of 14,172-foot Mount Bross. | 320 U.S. 285 (at Rte. 9) | 719/836–2031 | fax 719/836–3875 | www.fs.fed.us/r2/psicc | Free | Daily.

South Park City Museum. This restoration of an old mining town has 34 buildings and more than 60,000 artifacts dating from 1860 to 1900. | 100 4th St. | 719/836–2387 | www.southparkcity.org | $6.50 | Memorial Day–Labor Day, daily 9–7, Labor Day–mid-Oct., daily 9–5.

Dining

Front Street Café. Contemporary. This casual bistro is in a 1910 building. The frequently changing menu includes seafood, fresh pastas, and steaks. The Sunday brunch is very popular. | 435 Front St. | 719/836–7031 | D, MC, V | $$

Georgetown

Georgetown Loop Railroad and Historic Lebanon Silver Mine Tour. On this narrow-gauge steam train ride, you'll cross the reconstructed 95-foot-high Devil's Gate Bridge, an engineering marvel when it was built in 1884, and negotiate 14 twisting turns on the steep grade to Silver Plume. The optional silver mine tour gives a fascinating perspective on an integral part of the area's history. Reconstructed mining and railroad buildings from the late 1800s are highlights of this tour. The railroad travels 6 mi to Silver Plume. | 100 Loop Dr. | 303/569–2403 or 800/691–4386 | fax 303/569–2894 | www.georgetownloop.com | $15.50, $6 additional for mine tour | Late May–early Oct., daily 9–4; call for schedule. No mine tours after Labor Day.

Guanella Pass Scenic and Historic Byway. From Rose Street in Georgetown, drive south for almost 12 mi up a partly paved, partly gravel road to the 11,669-foot summit of Guanella Pass. From there, take in a classic Rocky Mountain vista, including 14,060-foot Mount Bierstadt to the east. In early fall, the aspen trees lining the road have golden leaves. Stop in at the Georgetown visitor center for more information. | 6th and Argentine Sts. | 303/569–2888 or 800/472–8230 | www.town.georgetown.co.us.

Hamill House Museum. See the elegantly restored home of Colorado state senator and silver magnate William A. Hamill, who made his fortune in silver. Period (late-19th-century) furnishings are displayed. | 305 Argentine St. | 303/569–2840 | www.historicgeorgetown.org | $5 | Memorial Day–Sept., daily 10–4; Oct.–Dec., Tues.–Sun. 10–4.

Hotel de Paris Museum. French immigrant and former miner Louis Dupuy opened this hotel in 1875 and watched it become one of the West's finest hostelries. Re-created rooms today convey its former splendor. | 409 6th St. | 303/569–2311 | www.hoteldeparismuseum.org | $4 | Memorial Day–Labor Day, daily 10–4:30; early-May–Memorial Day and Sept.–Dec., weekends noon–4.

Loveland Ski Area. This ski area 12 mi west of Georgetown has three quad, two triple, and four double chairlifts; two surface lifts; three terrain parks; 60 runs (the longest is 2 mi); a vertical drop of 2,410 feet; and a refreshingly low-key vibe. | I–70, Exit 216 | 303/571–5580 or 800/736–3754 | fax 303/571–5580 | www.skiloveland.com | Mid-Oct.–May, weekdays 9–4, weekends 8:30–4.

Watchable Wildlife Viewing Station. Your chances of spotting a bighorn sheep, Colorado's state animal, are good at this location, which is equipped with viewing scopes. | Rte. 6 at Georgetown Lake | Year-round.

Dining

Café Prague. Eastern European. This casual, family-run café offers hearty Eastern European classics such as schnitzel, roast pork with sauerkraut and dumplings, and Bohemian sauerbraten. Try the *palacinky*, sweet crepes with cream cheese and raisins, for dessert. | 511 Rose St. | 303/569–2861 | AE, D, MC, V | Closed Mon.–Tues. | $–$$

Happy Cooker. American/Casual. This homey, inexpensive spot is famous for its waffles (available with chicken or beef or the usual variety of sweet toppings) and decadent cinnamon buns. Breakfast is served all day; salads and sandwiches are also available. | 412 6th St. | 303/569–3166 | AE, D, DC, MC, V | No dinner | ¢–$

The Red Ram. American. Serving patrons for some five decades, this classic Western bar is known for its great half-pound hamburgers, ribs, and Mexican dishes. There's live music on weekends. | 606 6th St. | 303/569–2300 | AE, D, MC, V | $–$$

Golden

Astor House Museum. This was the first stone hotel west of the Mississippi (built in 1867); it was later used a boarding house up until the 1950s. Late Victorian-era furnishings are on display, as are changing exhibits on Western life. | 822 12th St. | 303/278–3557 | www.astorhousemuseum.org | $3 | Tues.–Sat. 10–4:30.

Buffalo Bill Memorial Museum and Grave. William "Buffalo Bill" Cody's final resting place is adjoined by a small museum and gift shop. It's worth the trip just for the beautiful drive up Lookout Mountain, accessible from 19th Street in Golden. | 987½

Lookout Mountain Rd. | 303/526–0747 | www.buffalobill.org | $3 | May–Oct., daily 9–5; Nov.–Apr., Tues.–Sun. 9–4.

Clear Creek History Park. The park interprets Colorado pioneer life in the late 1800s via restored buildings and replicas. Guided tours lasting about 45 minutes include demonstrations of wool spinning, blacksmithing, and gold panning. | 11th and Arapahoe Sts. | 303/278–3557 | fax 303/278–8916 | www.clearcreekhistorypark.org | $3 | June–Aug., Tues.–Sat. 10–4:30; May and Sept., Sat. 10–4:30.

Colorado Railroad Museum. This museum, outside the Golden city limits, is a must for railroad buffs. A replica of a depot from the 1880s has memorabilia, artifacts, and a working model railroad. | 17155 W. 44th Ave. | 303/279–4591 or 800/365–6263 | fax 303/279–4229 | www.crrm.org | $7 | June–Aug., daily 9–6; Sept.–May, daily 9–5.

Colorado School of Mines. Founded in 1874, this is one of the world's foremost mining engineering schools. More than 3,100 students attend annually. The lovely campus has an outstanding geology museum, as well as the National Earthquake Information Center. | 1500 Illinois St. | 303/273–3000 | www.mines.edu | Free.

Geology Museum. Minerals, ore, and gemstones from around the world, as well as mining history exhibits are on display here. | 136th and Maple Sts. | 303/273–3815 | fax 303/273–3859 | www.mines.edu/academic/geology/museum | Free | Late Aug.–early May, Mon.–Sat. 9–4, Sun 1–4; early May–late Aug., Mon.–Sat. 9—4.

Coors Brewing Company. Each year thousands of beer lovers make the pilgrimage to this venerable brewery, founded in 1873 by German immigrant Adolph Coors. It's now one of the largest breweries in the world—output exceeds 1½ million gallons a day. The 40-min walking tour includes an informal tasting for those 21 and over. | 13th and Ford Sts. | 303/277–2337 | www.coors.com | Free | Mon.–Sat. 10–4.

National Renewable Energy Laboratory. This U.S. Department of Energy lab investigates solar energy, wind power, alternative fuels, and energy-efficient building technologies. At the visitor center you can try out interactive exhibits and take a self-guided lab tour. | 15013 Denver West Pkwy. | 303/384–6565 | fax 303/384–6568 | www.nrel.gov/visitors_center | Free | Weekdays 9–noon and 1–4.

Dining

Hilltop Café. Eclectic. In a 1900 Victorian Four Square house, this popular, airy bistro offers a frequently updated menu of dishes such as orange soy–grilled buffalo flank steak or chili coriander–seared wild Alaskan salmon. Deli-style sandwiches and grilled cracker-crust pizza are available for lunch. | 1518 Washington Ave. | 303/279–8151 | fax 303/278–1583 | AE, D, DC, MC, V | Closed Sun. No lunch Sat. | $–$$$

Old Capitol Grill. American. The historic setting of Colorado's original territorial capitol building (circa 1861) is what makes this busy grill stand out. The food—steak, burgers, sandwiches, fajitas—is less impressive than the surroundings, but good nonetheless. | 1122 Washington Ave. | 303/279–6390 | AE, MC, V | $–$$

Table Mountain Inn Restaurant. Southwestern. The adobe Table Mountain Inn has a patio overlooking Main Street for summer dining, and a fireplace-warmed dining room for winter eating. Specialties include pine nut–crusted chicken with dried cherries, chicken-and-basil chiles rellenos, and smoked pork loin. | 1310 Washington Ave. | 303/216–8040 or 800/762–9898 | AE, D, DC, MC, V | $–$$

Manitou Springs

Cave of the Winds. This cave system, which has been open continuously since 1881, stretches for 2 mi. Three types of tours let you view the chambers and fantastic limestone formations according to your level of adventure. A nighttime laser show in summer illuminates adjacent Williams Canyon. | U.S. 24 | 719/685–5444 | www.caveofthewinds.com | $15 | Memorial Day–Labor Day, daily 9–9; Labor Day–Memorial Day, daily 10–5.

Florissant Fossil Beds National Monument. The monument highlights the remains of a 35-million-year-old lake that was filled in with volcanic ash, which in turn fossilized all of the resident insects and plants. Nearby are the remains of a petrified redwood forest that was covered by ash and similarly preserved. The grounds include picnic areas, 14 mi of nature trails, and a restored 19th-century Hornbek homestead. The beds are 22 mi west of Manitou Springs on U.S. 24. | County Rd. 1, Florissant | 719/748–3253 | www.nps.gov/flfo | $3 | June–Labor Day, daily 8–7; Labor Day–May, daily 8–4:30.

Garden of the Gods. This city park contains a collection of 300-million-year-old, vivid red sandstone formations, with descriptive names such as the Kissing Camels and the Three Graces. A visitor center has geologic and historic exhibits; from there either drive through the park or hike one of several short trails. | 1805 N. 30th St. | 719/634–6666 or 719/385–5940 | www.gardenofgods.com | Free | Visitor center, Labor Day–Memorial Day, daily 9–5; Memorial Day–Labor Day, daily 8–8.

Garden of the Gods Trading Post. At the south end of the park near Balanced Rock, this trading post—Colorado's largest—that dates back to the 1900's, sells Native American jewelry, Navajo rugs, Pueblo pottery, and katsina dolls. | 324 Beckers La. | 719/685–9045 or 800/874–4515 | fax 719/685–9377 | www.co-trading-post.com | Memorial Day–Labor Day, daily 8–8, Labor Day–Memorial Day, daily 9–5:30.

Manitou Cliff Dwellings Museums. Explore 40 rooms of ancestral Puebloan cliff dwellings dating to AD 1100, as well as a Pueblo-style museum of artifacts. In summer (June–August) traditional Native American dance performances are held several times a day. | On U.S. 24 | 719/685–5242 or 800/354–9971 | www.cliffdwellingsmuseum.com | $8 | June–Aug., daily 9–8; May and Sept., daily 9–6; Oct.–Apr., daily 9–5.

Pikes Peak. The best-known landmark in the entire state is this 14,110-foot mountain named after Zebulon Pike; though the peak is named after him, Pike never climbed it. Views from the top are expansive and inspired Katharine Lee Bates to write "America the Beautiful." | U.S. 24, Exit 141, Cascade | 719/385–7325 or 800/318–9505 | www.pikespeakcolorado.com | $10 | Memorial Day–Labor Day, daily 7–7; Labor Day–late-Sept., daily 7–5; Oct.–late-May, daily 9–3 (weather permitting).

Pikes Peak Cog Railway. Dating from 1891, this is the world's highest cog railroad. The round-trip up to the summit takes a little more than three hours, including some time at the top. The railroad makes up to eight round-trips daily during peak season (June–mid-August). | 515 Ruxton Ave. | 719/685–5401 | www.cograilway.com | $26.50 | Mid Apr.–early Jan., daily; call for exact train schedules.

Dining

Adam's Mountain Café. Eclectic. This intimate café focuses on flavorful vegetarian cuisine, though seafood and poultry dishes are on the menu, and uses only the freshest ingredients. There's live music several nights a week. Breakfast also served. | 1100 Cañon Ave. | 719/685–1430 | AE, D, MC, V | Closed Mon. Oct.–Apr. No dinner Sun.–Mon. | $–$$

Historic Stagecoach Inn. Steak. Built in 1881, the Stagecoach was in various incarnations a summer cottage, a stage stop, an electric-power plant, and the office for the local newspaper. Today you can dine indoors or outside by the banks of Fountain Creek. Specialties include slow-roasted buffalo and Rocky Mountain trout. | 702 Manitou Ave. | 719/685–9400 | AE, D, MC, V | No lunch | $$–$$$

IDAHO

LEWIS AND CLARK COUNTRY AND THE NORTH WOODS
FROM LOLO PASS TO SANDPOINT

Distance: 414 mi   Time: 4 days
Overnight Breaks: Coeur d'Alene or Sandpoint, Lewiston

Deep, cool woods sprinkled with lakes the color of a deep blue winter sky drape across the folded mountains of north-central Idaho and the slender Panhandle region.

You'll follow the path taken by early explorers as you drive through mountain ranges and the native lands of the Nez Perce tribe. After a stop at Hells Canyon—the state's lowest point and the site of an inland seaport—the route heads north through the north woods of Idaho, where the Coeur d'Alene tribe hunted and fished. Avoid this drive in the winter, when snow and wintry conditions can make the roads impassable.

❶ Begin your tour at Lolo Pass (on the Montana–Idaho border on U.S. 12). The new log cabin–style **Lolo Pass Visitors Center,** which opened in 2003 to commemorate the 200th anniversary of Lewis and Clark's expedition, has information and interpretive displays about the expedition and the Lolo Trail, which roughly parallels U.S. 12 and is the trail that the two explorers followed on their epic journey. Originally it was a trail used by the Lolo tribe to travel between the buffalo hunting grounds in Wyoming and the Weippe Prairie of Idaho. Remnants of the trail are still visible today. Roughly halfway to Grangeville, the **Lochsa Historical Ranger Station** recalls how rangers lived and operated one of the state's earliest U.S. Forest Service stations, which you could reach only on foot until the mid-1900s.

❷ Your drive from Lolo Pass to **Grangeville** will run 100 mi on U.S. 12 to Kooksia, then another 26 mi on Route 13. **White Bird Road,** as U.S. 95 is known between Grangeville and White Bird, was an engineering marvel when it was built in the late 1930s, climbing 4,429 feet in elevation. The **White Bird Hill Battlefield Auto Tour** recalls the fascinating story of the first battle of the Nez Perce War in the hills near White Bird. At the **White Bird Interpretive Shelter,** exhibits explain the battle.

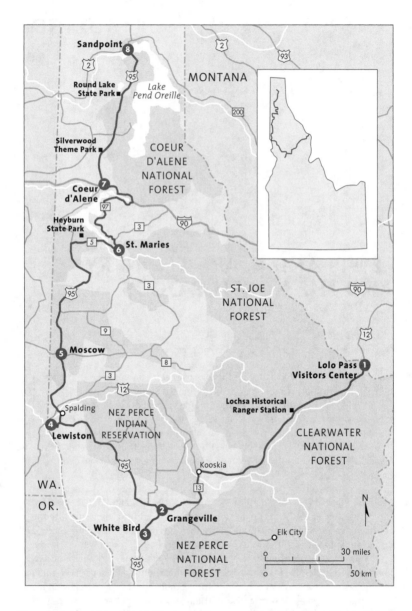

❸ At **White Bird** (12 mi south of Grangeville on U.S. 95), a gravel road, Route 493, will take you 12 mi to the northern rim of the continent's deepest gorge, Hells Canyon. At 1 mi deep, it surpasses even the Grand Canyon. **Pittsburg Landing** is the only year-round access point to the 71¹/₂-mi steep-walled basalt canyon. Picnic at the shady area near the river's edge. Explore the canyon by jet boat and raft on trips from one to six days.

❹ When you're finished at White Bird and Pittsburg Landing, backtrack 24 mi north to Grangeville, then 61 mi north on U.S. 95 to Spalding and the **Lewiston** area. Exhibits and artifacts tell the poignant story of the Nee-Me-Poo people or Nez Perce Indians and their legacy at the **Nez Perce National Historical Park and Museum.** Nez Perce

Chief Joseph is known for his words, "My heart is sick and sad. From where the sun now stands, I will fight no more forever." The park encompasses 38 sites in Idaho, Montana, Oregon, and Washington. The **Luna House Historical Museum** has exhibits on the history of Nez Perce County and the surrounding area. Among the displays is a pioneer kitchen in a building that was originally a hotel catering to miners en route to the northern goldfields. Spend a night or two in Lewiston.

❺ From Lewiston, proceed 28 mi north on U.S. 95 to **Moscow** and the **Appaloosa Museum and Heritage Center.** The museum highlights the history of Appaloosa horses, which the Nez Perce bred centuries ago. The **McConnell Mansion** was built in 1886 and reflects Eastlake, Queen Anne, and Victorian Gothic styles. Changing exhibits also tell the county history. The town is cradled by mountains to the east and the Palouse Hills to the west. Moscow is known as the dry pea and lentil capital of the world—the crops carpet the hills. From Moscow Mountain, a few miles northeast of town via Mountain View Road, you get a panoramic view of the area.

❻ Leaving Moscow, head 51 mi north on U.S. 95, then 19 mi east on Route 5 to **St. Maries** and **Heyburn State Park,** at the foot of sprawling Lake Coeur d'Alene on a small lake known as Chatcolet. Herons and ospreys are often seen nesting here. Six hiking trails cover 20 mi here, at the oldest state park in the Pacific Northwest.

❼ From Heyburn State Park, go 7 mi west on Route 5 to Plummer, then 28 mi north on I-95 to **Coeur d'Alene.** A busy vacation resort area surrounds much of the northern tip of the lake, which includes the world's only floating golf green. The lake is 2½ mi wide and 25 mi long, and is nestled in a glacially sculpted setting of soft mountains and pine forests. **Lake Coeur d'Alene Cruises, Inc.** takes visitors on two-hour sight-seeing tours and sunset dinner cruises, departing from the city dock. In town near the waterfront, the **Museum of North Idaho** has major exhibits on the region's rich history of Native American culture, steamboating, the logging industry, and nearby communities. Twenty miles north of town on U.S. 95 is **Silverwood Theme Park and Boulder Beach Water Park.** Silverwood is a charming Victorian-style park patterned after an 1880s mining town and the state's only amusement theme park. Supplementing the rides, games, and water park is an antique airplane museum. Spend the night in Coeur d'Alene or continue on to Sandpoint.

❽ From Coeur d'Alene, proceed 46 mi north on U.S. 95 into **Sandpoint.** The state's largest lake, **Pend Oreille,** is nearby, and dips to an amazing depth of 1,200 feet, making it an angler's paradise for big fish and "fish stories" about the lake's own "Nessie"— the "Pend Oreille Panhandler." When asked, locals can spin a tale or two about the fabled lake monster. The 65-mi-long lake has more than 300 mi of shoreline and at the northern end, the resort town of Sandpoint. The city beach features a sweeping stretch of sparkling white sand and a view to the east of Montana's Cabinet Mountains. Also along the lake is a shopper's paradise, the **Cedar St. Bridge,** with dozens of shops lining an enclosed rustic timbered bridge across Sand Creek. On the west side of the lake are tiny **Round Lake** and **Round Lake State Park,** one of the state's smallest. A little more than 140 acres of land surrounds the 58-acre lake. Since the lake is only 37 feet deep, it warms enough for comfortable swimming. Another state park, **Farragut State Park,** borders the southwest shore of the lake, about 25 mi south of Sandpoint. Once a naval training center, the park has historical displays about its role in World War II.

To return to Lolo Pass from Sandpoint, go south on U.S. 95 back to Coeur d'Alene. From there either backtrack, or head east on I-90 for about 165 mi to Missoula, Montana, and then proceed south on U.S. 93 into Lolo and west on U.S. 12 to the pass.

Coeur d'Alene

Canfield Mountain Trail System. More than 30 mi of trails are available to hikers, motor-cyclists, mountain bikers, and equestrians. Pick up a map at the ranger station. | Fernan Ranger District, 2502 E. Sherman Ave., east off I–90 | 208/664–2318 | Free.

Idaho Panhandle National Forests. The Panhandle Forest administers approximately half the total forested acres in the Panhandle region of Idaho. Notable are the old stands of cedars at Hanna Flats and Roosevelt Grove near Priest Lake, and the Settlers Grove of ancient cedars near Prichard and Hobo Cedar Grove near Clarkia. At the East Fork of Emerald Creek, 8 mi southeast of Route 3 near Clarkia, you can collect quality garnets for a fee. The Idaho Panhandle National Forests include the Coeur d'Alene and portions of the Kaniksu and St. Joe national forests. | 3815 Schreiber Way | 208/765–7223 Forest Supervisor's Office | fax 208/765–7307 | www.fs.fed.us/ipnf | $10 garnet digging permit; $5–$10 for campsite rentals | Daily dawn–dusk.

Lake Coeur d'Alene. Glaciers carved out the basin for this lake, elevation 2,152 feet, that extends south of town for about 25 mi. The lake is 2½ mi wide, tucked in among softly sculpted and forested mountains. Most of its water comes from the Coeur d'Alene, St. Joe, and St. Maries rivers, which rise along the Pend Oreille Divide and the Bitter-root Range. The highly developed shoreline offers lakeside restaurants, marinas, and hotels. | Daily dawn–dusk.

Museum of North Idaho. The museum's major exhibits highlight Native American culture, steamboats, the logging industry, railroads, recreation, and history of nearby communities. | 115 Northwest Blvd. | 208/664–3448 | www.museumni.org | $2 | Apr.–Oct., Tues.–Sat. 11–5.

　　Fort Sherman Museum. On the North Idaho College campus, this museum contains artifacts and information on Fort Sherman, which was founded in 1878. It also contains an original Forest Service smoke-chaser's cabin. | 208/664–3448 | Free with admission to the Museum of North Idaho | May–Sept., Tues.–Sat. 1–4:45.

Silverwood Theme Park and Boulder Beach Water Park. The theme of this amuse-ment park is an 1880s mining town. Within it are a narrow-gauge steam train, a wooden roller coaster, a log flume, and 24 other rides, including the newest roller-coaster ride Tremors, which spends much of the time in underground caves. Boulder Beach Water Park, which opened in 2003, has 12 acres of aquatic fun, including tube slides, a wave pool, river rides, and a water fortress for kids. | 26225 U.S. 95 N, Athol | 208/683–3400 | fax 208/683–2268 | www.silverwoodthemepark.com | $28 | Call for hrs.

Tubbs Hill. Come to this 120-acre wooded preserve to find century-old pine and fir trees, as well as hidden coves and beaches. Open to foot traffic only. You can pick up the trail at the south end of 3rd Street. | 208/769–2252 | Free | Daily dawn–dusk.

Dining

Beverly's. Contemporary. The inspired Northwest cuisine is made even more enjoyable by the lake views. The 7th-floor restaurant, part of the Coeur d'Alene Resort, has a contemporary design with copper and dark-wood accents. Try the grilled salmon drizzled with huckleberry salsa or the tenderloin of beef. | 115 S. 2nd St. | 208/765–4000 Ext. 23 | AE, D, MC, V | $$$–$$$$

Brix. Contemporary. Brix has a hip, sophisticated feel, with leather upholstery and cherry-wood tables. Many of the menu items are prepared in the brick oven, and you can watch the cooks in the open kitchen from your table. The menu highlights fresh, seasonal ingredients, with several kinds of fish, steaks, duck, and lamb. There's a nightclub downstairs open nightly. | 317 Sherman Ave. | 208/665–7407 | AE, D, MC, V | No lunch Sun. | $$–$$$$

Iron Horse. Contemporary. Old photographs and local memorabilia offer a slice of Idaho history in this fun family dining spot. The menu includes steaks, prime rib, seafood, and burgers. Weather permitting, you can eat on the patio. Enjoy live music Thursday–Saturday night. | 407 Sherman Ave. | 208/667–7314 | MC, V | $–$$

★**Stonegrill at Jimmy D's.** Contemporary. The work of local artists is showcased on the redbrick walls of this popular spot, where dinner is served by candlelight. The menu includes an extensive selection of low-fat cuts of steak, fish, seafood, and chicken. Your entrée is served to you on a personal Australian granite stone, heated to 752°F. | 320 Sherman Ave. | 208/664–9774 | AE, D, MC, V | $$–$$$

Lodging

★**Clark House on Hayden Lake.** When it was built in 1910 as the summer home of F. Lewis Clark and his wife Winifred, the 15,000-square-foot home was on 1,400 acres and was the most expensive home in Idaho. The guest rooms are furnished with antiques and heavy traditional furniture in ivory, black, and gold. Four rooms have fireplaces, and three overlook the garden or a small cedar forest. A formal, two-course breakfast is served and six-course candlelight dinners are available by reservation. Restaurant, hot tub, no-smoking rooms. | 5250 E. Hayden Lake Rd., 83835 | 208/772–3470 or 800/765–4593 | fax 208/772–6899 | www.clarkhouse.com | 10 rooms | AE, D, DC, MC, V | BP | $$–$$$$

Coeur d'Alene Resort. The plush rooms at this lakeside high-rise resort have either fireplaces or balconies with terrific views of the water. The lower-priced rooms are standard motel fare. The resort's golf course is well-known for its unique floating green. Take I–90 to Exit 11. 4 restaurants, minibars, cable TV with movies and video games, 18-hole golf course, pro shop, pool, gym, spa, Internet, business services, meeting rooms, no-smoking rooms. | 2nd and Front Sts., 83814 | 208/765–4000 or 800/688–5253 | fax 208/667–2707 | www.cdaresort.com | 336 rooms | AE, D, DC, MC, V | $$$–$$$$

Red Lion Templin's Hotel on the River. Old but well maintained, this hotel is a good choice if you plan to do a lot of hiking: it's a five-minute walk from the Centennial Trail, which runs from Coeur d'Alene to Spokane. Many rooms overlook the marina and private beach, and you can take a riverboat cruise on the paddle wheeler *West Coast River Queen* from here up the Spokane River. Take I–90 to Exit 5, about 9 mi east of Coeur d'Alene. Restaurant, picnic area, room service, in-room data ports, some microwaves, some refrigerators, cable TV, tennis courts, indoor pool, exercise equipment, hot tub, beach, dock, boating, marina, volleyball, lounge, laundry facilities, business services, meeting rooms, airport shuttle, some pets allowed (fee), no-smoking rooms. | 414 E. 1st Ave., Post Falls, 83854 | 208/773–1611 | fax 208/773–4192 | 167 rooms | AE, D, DC, MC, V | $–$$

Shilo Inn Suites. Part of a Northwest chain, this big hotel has spacious minisuites that include microwaves, refrigerators, and a wet bar. Other handy features, especially for families, include in-room video game and movie rentals and discount tickets to nearby Silverwood Theme Park. There are several sit-down and fast-food restaurants within walking distance. Take Exit 11 or 12 off I–90. In-room data ports, minibars, microwaves, refrigerators, cable TV with movies and video games, indoor pool, gym, hot tub, sauna, steam room, laundry facilities, airport shuttle, some pets allowed, no-smoking rooms. | 702 W. Appleway, 83814 | 208/664–2300 or 800/222–2244 | fax 208/667–2863 | www.shiloinns.com | 139 mini-suites | AE, D, DC, MC, V | CP | $

Grangeville

★**Nez Perce National Historical Park.** For thousands of years, the prairies and plateaus of north-central Idaho, northeastern Oregon, and southeastern Washington have been home to the Nez Perce. This park, which actually includes 38 sites in Idaho, Montana, Oregon, and Washington, interprets Nez Perce culture and history. At the visitor center near Spalding, you can enjoy audio-visual programs and, during the summer, attend daily talks. | Headquarters and Visitor Center, Spalding, 1 mi east on U.S. 12 | 208/843–2261 | www.nps.gov/nepe | Free | Spalding Visitor Center, June–Aug., daily 8–5:30; Sept.–May, daily 8–4:30.

White Bird Summit and Road. The Old White Bird Road can be seen en route to the summit on U.S. 95, south of Grangeville. This road was considered an engineering feat in its day, as its zigzags gained 4,429 feet in elevation within 14 mi. Paved in 1938, it is listed on the National Register of Historic Places. | 5 mi south on U.S. 95 | 208/843–2261 | Daily.

White Bird Hill Battlefield Auto Tour. The first battle of the Nez Perce War was fought here on June 17, 1877. Thirty-four soldiers were killed while the Nez Perce lost none. The visitor center in Spalding has maps you can use for a tour of the battlefield. The White Bird Interpretive Shelter has exhibits that explain the sequence of the battle. | 12 mi south on U.S. 95 | 208/843–2261 | Free | Daily dawn–dusk.

Dining

Oscar's Restaurant. American. The memorabilia and photos scattered throughout trace the town's history and make this almost as much a museum as a restaurant. Burgers, steaks, omelets, and other basic fare are available. | 101 E. Main St. | 208/983–2106 | MC, V | $–$$

Lewiston

Beamers Hells Canyon Tours and Excursions. If you're an outdoor-adventure lover, give Beamers a try. Jet-boat trips include a one-day tour ($52), which takes you 100 mi upriver to Rush Creek, past the end of navigation on the Snake River. The historic mail-run tour ($253 per person, including accommodations and meals) is offered year-round; boaters help deliver the U.S. mail to rugged canyon reaches as it's been done since 1919. The overnight is at Beamers' Copper Creek Lodge, and includes private modern cabin accommodations. It departs at 9 AM every Wednesday year-round for a two-day, one-night tour. | 700 Port St., Clarkston, WA | 800/522–6966 | www.hellscanyontours.com.

Hells Canyon National Recreation Area. The deepest canyon in North America, Hells Canyon plunges 7,913 feet. The terrain and wildlife habitats range from desert at the canyon floor to alpine in the mountains. Idaho's Seven Devils Mountains tower above one rim and Oregon's Wallowas above the other. You can see the gorge on a sight-seeing cruise, originating in Lewiston, or by raft or dory. Canyon rapids range from Class III to Class IV. Wildflowers bloom in spring; summer and fall are ideal for steelhead and sturgeon fishing. | Park office: 2535 Riverside Dr., Clarkston, WA | 509/758–0616, 509/758–1957 river info | www.fs.fed.us/hellscanyon | Free | Daily.

Cache Creek Ranch. At the very northern end of the area, the ranch was historically part of the Dobbins and Huffman sheep ranch that flourished in the 1930s, and is now a rest stop for river trips. It's reached by water only. The buildings are surrounded by lawns, a fruit orchard and a small visitor center. | 208/628–3916 | Free | Visitor Center: June–Sept., daily dawn–dusk.

Hells Canyon Creek. The primary launch point for float trips on the Snake River, this is also the only place in Hells Canyon where the Snake is accessible by a two-lane paved road. Pick up information at the staffed visitor center. | Forest Rd. 517, west of Riggins and HCNRA office | 208/628–3916 | Daily.

Kirkwood Historic Ranch. The historic ranch on Kirkwood Bar offers a glimpse of canyon life from the 1930s. Displays in the old bunkhouse contain historic and prehistoric artifacts. You can reach it by boat or trail only. Call ahead for road conditions. From the end of the road you hike 6 mi on the Snake River National Recreation Trail. | North of Riggins on U.S. 95, west on Forest Rd. 493 at White Bird, south on Forest Rd. 420, west on Forest Rd. 242, or drive to Pittsburg and hike | 208/628–3916 | Free | Daily dawn–dusk.

Pittsburg Landing. You reach this area via the only year-round public road leading to the Snake River. There is a concrete boat ramp and float apron for launching or takeout. | North of Riggins on U.S. 95, west on Forest Rd. 493 at White Bird | 208/628–3916 | Daily dawn–dusk.

Hells Gate State Park. Grassy open picnic areas are a big attraction at this park, which also has a large swimming beach, boating facilities, a volleyball area, trails, and campsites ($7–$22 per night) within 100 yards of the Snake River. The park connects with the Lewiston beltway bike path. The marina has more than 100 slips available on a daily to annual basis. If you're an angler, try the famous steelhead runs of the Snake during the fall and winter. Bird-watchers should keep an eye out for pheasants, quail, chukar, hawks, geese, ducks, and owls, as well as eagles, pelicans, herons, and swans. | 3620-A Snake River Ave. | 208/799–5015 office, 208/799–5016 marina | www.idahoparks.org | $3 per car.

Nez Perce County Museum. Formerly known as the Luna House, this house-museum is devoted to the history of Nez Perce County and its surrounding area. It contains reproductions of a pioneer kitchen and a typical room setting. | 306 3rd St. | 208/743–2535 | Donation suggested | Mar.–mid-Dec., Tues.–Sat. 10–4.

Winchester Lake State Park. More than one-fourth of the park's total area is water, in the form of a 103-acre lake. You can camp, hike, and picnic here during the summer, and in winter, if the weather's on your side, you can cross-country ski, ice-skate, or ice-fish. You might see white-tailed deer, beavers, raccoons, muskrats, and the painted turtle. Trails ring the lake, and there is an interpretive nature trail next to the park headquarters. The park has three yurts for rent ($35–$55 per night) available year-round. | Off I-95 near Winchester, or follow signs from town | 208/924–7563 | www.idahoparks.org | $3 per car | Daily.

Dining

Bojack's Broiler Pit. American. Casual dining and good food are the order of the day at this small but highly regarded restaurant. The house favorites are the prime rib and the shrimp salad. | 311 Main St. | 208/746–9532 | AE, D, MC, V | Closed Sun. | $–$$

Jonathan's. Contemporary. A solid mahogany bar anchors this spot; the menu is strong on Northwest-inspired dishes that draw heavily on fresh seafood and local beef and produce. | 1516 Main St. | 208/746–3438 | AE, MC, V | Closed Sun. No lunch Sat. | $$–$$$

Zany's Hollywood Grill. Contemporary. This offbeat restaurant has '50s decor, with jukeboxes and an old-fashioned soda counter, and a carousel horse, a bathtub, and other miscellany hanging from the ceiling. They serve some Mexican dishes, as well as steaks, chicken, burgers, salads, and pasta. | 2006 19th Ave. | 208/746–8131 | AE, D, MC, V | $

Lodging

Red Lion Hotel. Set on a hillside above the Clearwater River 1 mi from I–15, this hotel has a full-service athletic club, a sports bar, and its own microbrewery. All rooms have oversize bathrooms, and many have views of the Lewis/Clark Valley, Clearwater River, and Snake River. Restaurant, room service, in-room data ports, some microwaves, some refrigerators, cable TV with movies, pool, indoor pool, gym, hot tub, salon, bar, lounge, laundry facilities, business services, airport shuttle, some pets allowed, no-smoking rooms. | 621 21st St., 83501 | 208/799–1000 or 800/232–6730 | fax 208/748–1050 | www.redlionlewiston.com | 183 rooms | AE, D, DC, MC, V | $

Riverview Inn. This large, multistory hotel, 2 mi from U.S. 95, is older but comfortable. There are several restaurants within walking distance, and the river is nearby. Some rooms have balconies and river views. In-room data ports, some microwaves, refrigerators, cable TV, pool, lounge, meeting rooms, some pets allowed, no-smoking rooms. | 1325 Main St., 83501 | 208/746–3311 or 800/806–7666 | fax 208/746–7955 | 75 rooms | AE, D, DC, MC, V | CP | ¢

Sacajawea Select Inn. About 2 mi from U.S. 95 and near downtown, this older motel with well-maintained rooms is in a quiet area. The motel's restaurant, the Helm, serves simple, well-prepared food. Restaurant, some microwaves, refrigerators, in-room data ports, cable TV with movies, pool, exercise equipment, hot tub, bar, laundry facilities, business services, airport shuttle, some pets allowed (fee), no-smoking rooms. | 1824 Main St., 83501 | 208/746–1393 or 800/333–1393 | fax 208/746–3625 | www.selectinn.com/lewiston.html | 90 rooms | AE, D, DC, MC, V | CP | ¢–$

Moscow

Appaloosa Museum and Heritage Center. The Nez Perce tribes who lived in the area practiced selective horse breeding and produced large herds of high-quality horses, including Appaloosas. Regalia, saddles, and artifacts associated with the Appaloosa are on display. | 2720 W. Pullman Rd. | 208/882–5578 Ext. 279 | www.appaloosamuseum.org | Free | Tues.–Fri. 10–5, Sat. 10–4.

Latah County Historical Society McConnell Mansion. Built in 1886 by Idaho's third governor, the house is a combination of Eastlake, Queen Anne, and Victorian Gothic styles. On display are artifacts and Victorian-style furniture from the early 1900s to 1930s. The Latah County Historical Society, which presents changing exhibits on county history, is based here. | 110 S. Adams St. | 208/882–1004 | http://users.moscow.com/lchs/mansion.html | Free | Oct.–Apr., Tues.–Sat. 1–4; May–Sept., Tues.–Sat. 1–5.

Dining

Basilio's. Italian. This restaurant in the Moscow Hotel offers updated Italian cuisine in a bright dining room fitted with artwork from ceiling to floor. | 313 S. Main St. | 208/892–3848 | MC, V | $–$$

La Casa Lopez. Mexican. Massive margaritas and genuine south-of-the-border entrées are offered here at reasonable prices. Outdoor seating available. | 415 S. Main St. | 208/883–0536 | AE, MC, V | ¢–$

Sandpoint

Cedar Street Bridge. Inspired by Italy's Ponte Vecchio, this solar-heated structure constructed of massive tamarack logs, is one-of-a-kind in the U.S.—a marketplace built over a bridge. The promenade of shops spans Sand Creek and is anchored by the well-known catalog company Coldwater Creek, which has five separate stores here. There are an espresso bar, deli, gallery and other shops, as well as a wine bar with live music and free hors d'oeuvres on Friday evening. | 1st and Cedar Sts. | 208/263–2265 | Mon.–Sat. 9–7, Sun. 11–6.

Farragut State Park. One of Idaho's largest state parks at 4,000 acres, it edges Lake Pend Oreille and has several beaches. You might spot whitetail deer, badgers, black bears, coyotes, bobcats, and an occasional elk. You can hike, fish, boat, swim, and ride horses. It's 25 mi south of Sandpoint on Route 54 east off U.S. 95 | 13400 E. Ranger Rd., Athol | 208/683–2425 | www.idahoparks.org | $3 per car | Daily dawn–dusk.

Lake Pend Oreille. Idaho's largest and deepest (1,200 feet) lake is a recreational paradise, with boating, swimming, fishing, windsurfing, and other water sports. Head to Sandpoint's City Beach at the end of Bridge Street for sandy beaches and a lifeguarded swimming area. You can also play volleyball, tennis, horseshoes, and basketball, and grill your dinner on the barbecues. | Bridge St. | 208/263–3371 | Daily.

Round Lake State Park. This park is the product of glacial activity dating back 1 million years to the Pleistocene epoch. Take the 2-mi nature trail to get a close look at the many varieties of trees, plants, and wildlife. The park has educational events and guided walks. Winter activities include cross-country skiing, ice fishing, ice-skating, sledding, and snowshoeing. Small boats are allowed on the lake, but none with gas motors. The lake is 10 mi south of Sandpoint and 2 mi west of U.S. 95 on Dufort Road. | 208/263–3489 | www.idahoparks.org | $3 per car | Daily.

Dining

Ivano's Ristorante. Italian. Sandpoint's oldest family-owned restaurant serves up northern Italian fare and is a favorite among nearby Schweitzer Mountain's skiing crowd. Choose from more than a dozen pasta choices, as well as chicken, veal, and steak. There's a good selection of regional wines. Save room for homemade gelato. | Vintage Court, 1st and Pine Sts. | 208/263–0211 | AE, D, DC, MC, V | No lunch | $–$$

Panhandler Pies. American/Casual. This family-style restaurant serves up hearty portions of down-home favorites like meat loaf. The deep-fried scones are an unusual menu item. Be sure and save room for pie—there are 21 varieties. | 120 S. 1st Ave. | 208/263–2912 | MC, V | Closed Sun. | ¢–$

Power House Bar & Grill. Eclectic. This restaurant has a distinctive location, in the Old Power House building, north of the Long Bridge. Dine inside or alfresco on the lakeside deck. The menu includes burgers, steaks, seafood, slow-roasted chicken, salads, sandwiches, and breakfast specials on the weekends. There are several vegetarian options and a variety of "power" wraps—try the Southwestern chicken wrap with jalapeño cream sauce. | 120 E. Lake St. | 208/265–2449 | AE, D, DC, MC, V | $–$$

Lodging

Best Western Edgewater Resort. At this lakeside hotel, all rooms have views of the lake and mountains. Those on the upper levels have balconies, while the main level rooms have lakefront patios. There's a beach and dock right outside and marina and boat rentals nearby. You'll find downtown shopping a block away. The Beachhouse Bar & Grill is open every day for casual dining, with a daily happy hour, too. Restaurant, in-room data ports, cable TV with movies, some VCRs, indoor pool, gym, hot tub, beach, dock, lounge, meeting rooms, business services, some pets allowed (fee), no-smoking rooms. | 56 Bridge St., 83864 | 208/263–3194 or 800/635–2534 | fax 208/263–3194 | www.sandpointhotels.com/edgewater/ | 54 rooms | AE, D, DC, MC, V | CP | $

Inn at Sand Creek. This small, plush inn is connected to the Sand Creek Grill, an upscale restaurant with an innovative menu of fusion cuisine, and live jazz and blues music. There's an on-site spa, or you can arrange for a massage in the privacy of your suite. All of the suites have fireplaces; the largest has a kitchen and creek view. Children are welcome. Restaurant, some in-room data ports, some kitchens, cable TV, in-room VCRs, hot tub, some pets allowed (fee), no-smoking rooms. | 105 S. 1st Ave., 83864 | 208/255–2821 | www.innatsandcreek.com | 3 suites | MC, V | $$–$$$

Sandpoint Quality Inn. This economical inn is right off U.S. 95, within walking distance to downtown shopping and beaches. The rooms are pleasant and comfortable; for more space, splurge on a Jacuzzi suite. Family-style dining is available at the hotel's Fifth Avenue Restaurant. Ask about discount tickets for Silverwood Theme Park, Schweitzer Ski Resort, and nearby golfing. Restaurant, some in-room hot tubs, some microwaves, some refrigerators, cable TV with movies, some in-room VCRs, indoor pool, hot tub, lounge, business services, some pets allowed (fee), no-smoking rooms. | 807 N. 5th Ave., 83864 | 208/263–2111 or 800/635–2534 | fax 208/263–3289 | www.sandpointhotels.com/quality/ | 62 rooms | AE, D, DC, MC, V | ¢–$

St. Maries

Heyburn State Park. One of the more popular state parks, Heyburn spans 5,505 acres near Chatcolet Lake. At the west end of the lake are six hiking trails that at various points pass through stands of 400-year-old ponderosa pines. The Hawleys Landing Amphitheater presents lectures, slide shows, and other naturalist programs. Visit the Chatq'ele' Interpretive Center to see displays on local history and wildlife. The park has 132 campsites and two cabins available for rental ($85). Two-hour boat cruises ($12.50–$27.50) on the *Idaho* are offered several times a week, and include brunch and sunset dinner cruises. Shorter themed cruises are free for campers. | Between Plummer and St. Maries on Rte. 5 | 208/686–1308 | www.idahoparks.org | $3 per car | Daily.

St. Joe, Moyie, and Clearwater Rivers. The Moyie, St. Joe, and Clearwater rivers are popular for river excursions that take only a single day but still give you a white-water experience. The picturesque St. Joe has blue-green water and its banks are covered with moss and dotted with cedars. Beginning rafters learn to paddle here. The Clearwater is a quiet and scenic river with no rapids and is popular with families. | East of town on Rte. 5 | 208/476–4541 | Daily.

IOWA GREAT RIVER ROAD

FROM NEW ALBIN TO KEOKUK

Distance: 237 mi   Time: 2–3 days
Overnight Breaks: Burlington, Dubuque

The Great River Road is a 3,000-mi network of federal, state, and county roads that parallels the Mississippi River on both sides, from Canada to the Gulf of Mexico. The upper Mississippi River, dominated by Iowa countryside, offers spectacular scenery, charming communities, and interpretive centers that explain the impact of the Great River. The green paddle-wheel symbol found on maps and road signs is known throughout the region as the symbol of the Great River Road.

❶ Begin on Route 26 in **New Albin,** a quiet little town of dense forests and fertile farmland. From this area, the upper Iowa River flows into the Mississippi River.

❷ Continue 11 mi south on Route 26 to **Lansing,** where you should stop for your first look at the region known locally as Little Switzerland: During the Ice Age, when great glaciers carved out the Mississippi River valley, the hills in northeastern Iowa were not flattened like those in much of the area. From Mt. Hosmer Park, you can see for miles into Wisconsin and Minnesota.

❸ Leaving Lansing, the Great River Road departs Route 26 for a county road, X52, which is clearly marked. Within a few miles, you come to the village of Harpers Ferry, where you can access the 9,000-acre **Yellow River State Forest.** With additional access to approximately 3,000 acres of Mississippi River backwater, the forest is a good bet for hikers and anglers.

❹ Farther south X52 rejoins Route 26, and you'll come to the twin communities of **Marquette** and **McGregor.** Iowa's only National Monument, **Effigy Mounds,** is in this area. Here you'll see some 200 burial and ceremonial mounds created by prehistoric Native Americans between 500 BC and AD 1300. Effigy Mounds also has several hiking trails that provide views of the many tiny islands that comprise the upper Mississippi River valley.

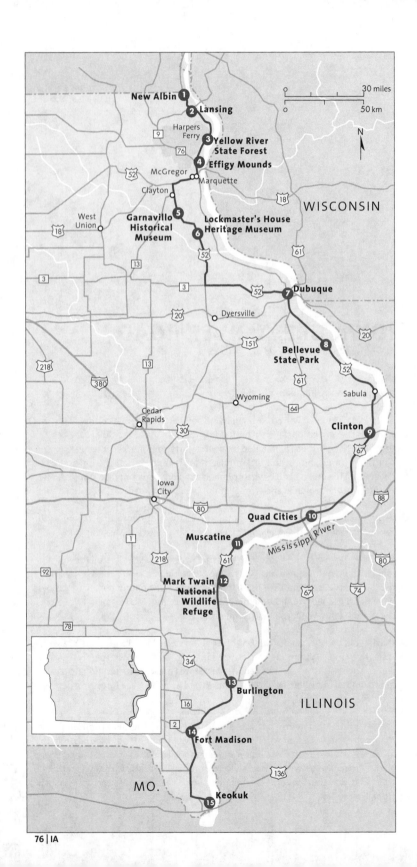

New Albin **1**

2 Lansing

Harpers
Ferry

9

76

3 Yellow River
State Forest

McGregor

4 Effigy Mounds

52

Marquette

Clayton

West
Union

18

5

Garnavillo
Historical
Museum

Lockmaster's House
Heritage Museum

6

52

18

WISCONSIN

61

13

3

3

52

7 Dubuque

20

Dyersville

151

20

8

Bellevue
State Park

52

13

61

Wyoming

64

Sabula

218

380

Cedar
Rapids

30

Clinton **9**

67

88

Iowa
City

80

Quad Cities **10**

74

80

1

Muscatine **11**

61

Mississippi River

67

218

92

12

Mark Twain
National
Wildlife
Refuge

78

34

13 Burlington

ILLINOIS

16

2

14 Fort Madison

136

MO.

Keokuk

15

Marquette is named for the French-Canadian explorer who, along with Louis Joliet, journeyed down the Mississippi River in the 1670s. Marquette is home to **Pikes Peak State Park,** which contains the highest bluff along the 1,100-mi path of the Great River. From the top of this 500-foot bluff, the confluence of the Wisconsin River and the mighty Mississippi may be seen to the south. To the north, there is a view of the twin suspension bridges that connect Iowa and Wisconsin.

Adjacent to Marquette is McGregor, a community of historic homes with a business district filled with antiques shops. Here you may wish to divert from the Great River Road for a jaunt around the **River Bluffs Scenic Byway,** which will take you along hilly U.S. 18 through Gunder, Clermont, and West Union. If you think Iowa is all flat farmland, this 40-mi roller-coaster journey will certainly prove you wrong.

5 You may continue on Route 26 where your next stop is the historic fishing village of Clayton, followed by Garnavillo, where you'll find numerous Native American artifacts in the **Garnavillo Historical Museum.**

6 At Guttenberg, Route 26 joins with U.S. 52 for a few miles. Park the car at Guttenberg, take a quick mile-long walk through River Park, and investigate the activities at Lock and Dam 10. The **Lockmaster's House Heritage Museum** is one of the few left along the river, providing a look inside the lives of those who built the lock and dam system. Guttenberg also has an art gallery and microbrewery, as well as several shops and restaurants in its historic downtown square.

7 About 20 mi southeast of Guttenberg along U.S. 52 is **Dubuque.** Depending on the number of stops you've made along the way, Dubuque may be your first overnight stay. You'll find numerous B&Bs and a surprisingly wide variety of restaurants here. There's also plenty to do in Dubuque. The America's River Project includes a water park, museums, aquarium, outdoor amphitheater, and hotel. You may also wish to explore the Dubuque Art Center or take a trolley or carriage ride around the city. You might also want to drive 25 mi west on U.S. 20 to **Dyersville** and play baseball at the *Field of Dreams* baseball field.

8 Leaving Dubuque south along U.S. 52, you'll come to the Luxembourger community of St. Donatus. Also on U.S. 52, in nearby Bellevue you can visit the butterfly garden at **Bellevue State Park.** The **Grant Wood Scenic Byway** is another diversion from the river. This 30-mi drive along Route 64 passes through the towns of Andrew, Maquoketa, and Preston. You may, however, decide to just continue driving south from Bellevue along U.S. 52 to Sabula, the only Iowa town on an island.

9 At Sabula, the Great River Road becomes U.S. 67, on which you should continue south to **Clinton.** Eagle Point Park is worth a stop, as it provides a view of the widest part of the Mississippi River, an impressive 3-mi-wide span of water. A casino and a showboat are docked in Clinton, but be sure to save time for the arboretum and museum as well.

10 From Clinton, continue south on U.S. 67 into the **Quad Cities** (Davenport and Bettendorf, Iowa, and Rock Island and Moline, Illinois). More riverboats and walking trails dominate the riverfront, along with Lock and Dam 15. Take time to drive onto **Arsenal Island** for a visit to the Rock Island Arsenal Museum and the Mississippi River Visitor's Center. Activities are numerous in the Quad Cities; you could chose to spend several days here or continue south on U.S. 61 to Muscatine, driving through great camping and boating communities such as Buffalo, Montpelier, and Fairport.

⑪ **Muscatine** is at a bend in the river where freshwater mussel shells accumulate; in the 1850s, German immigrants used the shells to build an enduring business of pearl button manufacturing, which put Muscatine on the map. Muscatine's **Mark Twain Overlook** provides one of the best views of the river during the course of this drive. Have your camera handy for shots of the bald eagles, tugboats, or the immense power of the Mississippi River.

⑫ Just south of Muscatine on U.S. 61 you'll enter Louisa County, with its **Mark Twain National Wildlife Refuge.** The refuge is marshy and filled with wetlands, a place enjoyed in the past by the Native Americans for hunting and fishing. In Toolesboro, you'll find a series of Native American burial mounds and a museum of Oneota culture.

⑬ From Toolesboro, the Great River Road moves inland a few miles until you reach **Burlington,** 25 mi to the south via U.S. 34. The Point of Burlington Welcome Center is on the riverfront in a 1928 building that once served the city and the commercial barge traffic stopping here.

⑭ The Great River Road returns to U.S. 61 at Burlington. Twenty miles south of Burlington on U.S. 61 is **Fort Madison,** the site of a full-scale replica of the old fort and a museum dedicated to the Great Flood of 1993.

⑮ Great River Road continues 25 mi south along U.S. 61 to **Keokuk,** the last town in Iowa before the road enters northeast Missouri. Another lock and dam is in Keokuk, as is the George M. Verity Riverboat Museum, a national cemetery, and Rand Park, which overlooks the river and is the burial site of Chief Keokuk.

To return to New Albin, take U.S. 218 north out of Keokuk. U.S. 218 north becomes I–380 around Iowa City. Take I–380 into Cedar Rapids, then pick up U.S. 151 out of Cedar Rapids to Route 13 north. Take Route 13 north to U.S. 52 and then take U.S. 52 to U.S. 18 east into Marquette. From Marquette you can follow the Great River Road again. Take Route 76 north to Route 364, then Route X52 to Route 26, which you'll pick up around Lansing. Route 26 will bring you back to New Albin.

IOWA RULES OF THE ROAD

License Requirements: To drive in Iowa, you must be at least 17 years old, although an instruction permit is possible at age 14, and an intermediate license may be granted at age 16.

Right Turn on Red: Right turns on red are allowed in Iowa *after* coming to a full and complete stop, unless otherwise posted.

Seat Belt and Helmet Laws: The driver and front seat occupants must wear a seat belt. Children under the age of three are required to be in a car safety seat. Children between the ages of three and six must be in either a car safety seat or a seat belt. Helmets are not required.

Speed Limits: The speed limit on rural Iowa interstates is 65 mph. In urban areas and on secondary roads, the speed limit is 55 mph, unless otherwise posted. Mopeds that operate over 25 mph are illegal in Iowa.

For More Information: Contact the **Iowa Motor Vehicle Information Center** | 800/532–1121 | www.dot.state.ia.us/mvd.

Burlington

Geode State Park. Geodes, with their hollow centers and sparkling quartz crystals, are Iowa's state rock and can be found in abundance in this park 12 mi west of Burlington. If you are not a rock hound you may enjoy the supervised swimming beach that rims Lake Geode, known for excellent largemouth bass, bluegill, and crappie fishing or the park's hiking and camping. | Rtes. 79/J20 | 319/392–4601 | www.state.ia.us/parks/goede.htm | Daily.

Heritage Hill National Historic District. Nearly 160 buildings in various architectural styles provide a sense of local history. Walking-tour brochures are available at the Port of Burlington Welcome Center. | North of downtown between Washington and High Sts. | 800/827–4837 | www.visit.burlington.ia.us | Free | Daily.

Phelps House. The original part of the historic home was built in 1851. Some original furnishings remain in the six-story Italianate-style structure, along with other artifacts of local history. | 521 Columbia St. | 319/753–2449 | $2 | May–Oct., weekends 1:30–4:30.

Snake Alley. A shortcut from Heritage Hill to downtown, Snake Alley is one of the crookedest streets in the world, on par with Lombard Street in San Francisco. | North of downtown between Washington and High Sts. | 800/827–4837 | www.snakealley.com | Daily.

Dining

Big Muddy's. American. Barbecued ribs are a hot item at this converted freight depot, which has a view of the river. Many locals arrive via motor boat and dock right in front of the restaurant. | 710 N. Front St. | 319/753–1699 | AE, D, DC, MC, V | $–$$

Martini's. Eclectic. Your choices range from Thai food to brick-oven pizza in this bustling spot in the Best Western Pizazz Motor Inn. There's also a Sunday brunch. | 3003 Weingard Dr. | 319/753–2291 | AE, D, DC, MC, V | No dinner Sun. | $–$$

Lodging

Best Western Pizazz Motor Inn. Burlington's only full-service hotel is in the northwest corner of town, north of U.S. 34 and U.S. 61. Most guest rooms are either poolside or have balconies overlooking the three-story indoor pool atrium. Restaurant, room service, in-room data ports, cable TV, in-room VCRs, indoor-outdoor pool, gym, hot tub, bar, recreation room, laundry facilities, business services, airport shuttle. | 3001 Winegard Dr. | 319/753–2223 or 800/528–1234 | fax 319/753–2224 | www.bestwestern.com | 151 rooms | AE, D, DC, MC, V | BP | $

Comfort Inn. This quiet, unassuming motel, 2 mi east of Snake Alley and the Mississippi River, is within walking distance of plenty of shops and restaurants. In-room data ports, cable TV, pool, business services. | 3051 Kirkwood Ave. | 319/753–0000 or 800/28–5150 | fax 319/753–0000 Ext. 301 | www.comfortinn.com | 52 rooms | AE, D, DC, MC, V | CP | $

Clinton

Bickelhaupt Arboretum. Browse 14 acres of labeled trees, perennials, and a medicinal plant display. | 340 S. 14th St. | 563/242–4771 | Free | Daily, dawn–dusk.

Eagle Point Park. A scenic road winds through this 205-acre park overlooking the Mississippi River at the northern edge of town, taking you past ball fields and a picnic area to a three-story stone observation tower built in the 1930s. | U.S. 67 | 563/243–1260 | www.ci.clinton.ia.us | Daily dawn–dusk.

Felix Adler Discovery Center. Celebrating the career of Clinton native and longtime Ringling Brothers clown Felix Adler, this museum's numerous attractions for children include a minigolf course, a rabbit house, a giant bubble machine, a dress-up corner, face-painting, and balloon animal–making demonstrations. | 501 11th Ave. S | 563/243–3600 | www.felixadler.com | $2 | Thurs.–Sat. 10–4.

Riverview Park. A band shell and picnic facilities are among the attractions of this 65-acre riverfront park. | 6th Ave. N | 563/243–1260 | www.ci.clinton.ia.us | Daily.

Mississippi Belle II. Also docked at Riverview Park is this 40-foot cruising riverboat with gambling and entertainment aboard. Children are allowed on the boat but must stay at a day-care center on the premises for no more than three hours. | 311 Riverview Dr. | 563/243–9000 or 800/457–9975 | http://mississippibelle.casinocity.com | Sun.–Thurs., 9 AM–2 AM; Fri–Sat., 9 AM–4 AM.

Dining

The Unicorn. Contemporary. Eclectic items fill the menu, like the Duke of Earl sandwich with turkey, melted Swiss, asparagus, and curry sauce. The local favorite is chicken salad with almonds served on homemade oatmeal bread. | 1004 N. 2nd St. | 563/242–7355 | AE, D, MC, V | Closed Sun. No dinner | ¢–$

Upper Mississippi Brewing Company. American. This historic brewing house, built in the early 1900s, serves steaks and sandwiches. | 132 6th Ave. S | 563/241–1275 | AE, D, MC, V | Closed Sun. | $–$$

Dubuque

Bellevue State Park. Tall cliffs in this 700-acre park 26 mi south of the town of Bellevue have fine views of the Mississippi River. You'll also find wooded walking trails, a butterfly sanctuary, and a nature center. | 24668 U.S. 52 | 563/872–3243 or 563/872–4019 | www.state.ia.us/parks | Daily dawn–dusk | Free.

Crystal Lake Cave. Discovered in 1868, this cave is about 5 mi south of town, off U.S. 52. It contains a "chapel room" and unusual geological formations like cave flowers and soda straws. | 7699 Crystal Lake Cave Dr. | 563/556–6451 or 563/872–4111 | www.crystallakecave.com | $9 | Memorial Day–Labor Day, daily 9–6; Labor Day–mid-Oct., weekdays 11–5, weekends 9–5.

Dubuque Art Center. The glass-curtain walls of this art museum look out onto downtown Dubuque's Washington Park. On display are traveling exhibits and regional artwork, including pieces by Iowa native Grant Wood, who captured the state on canvas during the 1930s and '40s. | 701 Locust St. | 563/557–1851 | $3 (Thurs. free) | Tues.–Fri. 10–5, weekends 1–4.

Fenelon Place Elevator. Traveling just 296 feet while elevating passengers 189 feet, this is the world's shortest, steepest railway. Built in 1882 and now providing both transportation and a view, this lift is also known as the Fourth Street Elevator. | 512 Fenelon Pl. | 563/582–6496 | www.dbq.com/fenplco | $1.50 | Apr.–Nov., daily 8 AM–10 PM.

★ **National Mississippi River Museum and Aquarium.** This multifaceted complex includes a river museum and aquarium, where you may float on a simulated log raft, pilot a riverboat, and explore a boat-building shop as you learn about 300 years of river history. You may get a little wet and lost in the fog during *River of Dreams*, an atmospheric film (involving split screens and fog machines) that tells the history of life on the river. | 350 E. 3rd St. | 563/557–9545 or 800/226–3369 | www.rivermuseum.com | $9 | Daily 10–6.

Trolleys of Dubuque, Inc. Old-fashioned trolleys depart at 12:30 from the welcome center at 3rd and Main streets and go to major Dubuque sights in a one-hour fully narrated tour. | 563/552–2896 | Apr.–Oct., daily.

Dining

Betty Jane Homemade Candies and Ice Cream Shoppe. Café. Family-owned and -operated since 1938, this candy shop is famous for homemade chocolates, particularly the "gremlin," a caramel, pecan, and chocolate confection. You can also choose from 66 flavors of ice cream. | 3049 Asbury Rd. | 563/582–4668 | MC, V | ¢–$

Dempsey's Steakhouse. Steak. Steak, pasta, and much of the artwork are for sale in this casual, downtown Irish pub–restaurant. A kid's menu is available. | 395 W. 9th St., at Bluff St. | 563/582–7057 | AE, D, MC, V | Closed Sun. No lunch Sat. | $$–$$$

Mario's. Italian. Opera and movie posters hang throughout this cozy, downtown eatery. House specialties include rich fettuccine Alfredo, veal scaloppine, and chicken marsala. | 1298 Main St. | 563/556–9424 | AE, D, DC, MC, V | Closed Sun. | $–$$$

Lodging
Grand Harbor Resort and Waterpark. This is the first indoor water park in Iowa, adjacent to the National Mississippi River Museum. Rooms are spacious with views of either the city or the Mississippi River. Rates include passes to the water park. Dining room, room service, minibars, microwaves, in-room data ports, some in-room hot tubs, cable TV, health club, recreation room, shop, children's programs, Internet, meeting rooms. | 350 Bell St., 52001 | 563/690–4000 or 866/690–4006 | www.grandharborresort.com | 193 rooms, 31 suites | AE, D, MC, V. | $–$$

Hancock House. Perched halfway up a bluff in the 11th Street Historic District is this meticulously restored lavender Victorian home. The large front porch has swings and comfy deck furniture. Some rooms have fireplaces. The inn's second-floor turret has a great view of the river. Some in-room hot tubs. | 1105 Grove Terr. | 563/557–8989 | fax 563/583–0813 | www.thehancockhouse.com | 9 rooms | AE, D, MC, V | BP | $–$$$

Holiday Inn. A freestanding fireplace dominates the spacious lobby of this downtown hotel. Some rooms have excellent views of the city and the area's surrounding bluffs. Restaurant, room service, some refrigerators, cable TV, pool, exercise equipment, hot tub, bar, business services, airport shuttle. | 450 Main St. | 563/556–2000 | fax 563/556–2303 | www.kinseth.com | 193 rooms | AE, D, DC, MC, V | $$

Dyersville
Field of Dreams **Movie Site.** The 1989 Academy Award–nominated movie was shot here, 3 mi northeast of town. Run the bases, play catch, or cheer from the bleachers, just as Kevin Costner did. | 29001 Lansing Rd. | 563/875–6012 | www.leftandcenterfod.com | Free | Apr.–Nov., daily 9–6.

St. Francis Xavier Basilica. One of only 33 basilicas in the country, this is one of the finest examples of Gothic architecture in the Midwest. The twin steeples rise 212 feet, but the 64 stained-glass windows get most of the attention. | 104 3rd St. SW | 563/875–7325 | $1 for guided tours | Daily 8–5. Guided tours by appointment.

Dining
The Palace. American/Casual. Popular for such comfort food as roasted chicken, stews, and soups, this old-fashioned saloon and bar is in the heart of downtown. If the weather is fair on Friday evenings you can grill your own steaks out on the deck. | 149 1st Ave. E | 563/875–2284 | No credit cards | ¢–$

Fort Madison
River View Park. River access, a marina, and an ice-skating rink are the attractions in this park on the eastern edge of town. | U.S. 61 and 6th St. | 319/372–7700 | Daily.

Old Fort Madison. Inside the park you'll also find a replica of the first military fort west of the Mississippi. There are daily military reenactments in summer and you can participate in such hands-on learning activities as candle making and basketry. | 319/

372–6318 | www.oldfortmadison.com | $5 | Memorial Day–Labor Day, Wed.–Sun., 9–5; Sept.–Oct., weekends 9:30–5.

Santa Fe Depot Historic Museum and Complex. Donated by the Santa Fe and Burlington Railroad, this museum contains 100 years of railroad history and the world's largest Sheaffer pen collection. | 9th and Ave. H | 319/372–7661 | www.visitfortmadison.com | Apr.–Sept., daily or by appointment.

The Great Flood of 1993. Inside the railroad museum is a smaller museum dedicated to the flood. Through TV footage, newspaper clippings, and photos, this museum recounts the flood and the devastation wreaked on communities in nine states as the Mississippi and Missouri Rivers, and their tributaries reached record levels.

Santa Fe Railway Bridge. On the east edge of town, this bridge from the 1920s is the largest double-decker swing-span bridge in the country. It's still functioning as a railway and an automobile bridge from Iowa into Illinois. | East edge of town | 800/210–8687 | Daily.

Dining

Ivy Bake Shop. Café. Breakfast treats at this bakery and café include blackberry scones, rhubarb brunch cake, cinnamon and pecan rolls, and a variety of muffins. Lunches include quiches, pasta dishes, and sandwiches. You can sip specialty coffee drinks, homemade lemonade, and brewed teas all day on the screened-in porch along Avenue G. | 622 7th St. | 319/372–9939 | MC, V | Closed Sun. No dinner | ¢

Keokuk

George M. Verity Riverboat Museum. You can visit the crew quarters or the pilot house of this dry-docked paddle-wheel 1920s steamboat in Victory Park, which also has exhibits on old-time life on the river. | 1st and Water Sts. | 319/524–4765 | $3 | Memorial Day–Labor Day, daily 9–5.

Grand Avenue. The Keokuk Convention and Tourism Bureau offers a "Walking Tour of Grand Avenue" map that will guide you past the beautiful homes on Grand and Orleans avenues—prestigious addresses for Keokuk's elite during the late 1800s and early 1900s. | Grand and Orleans Aves. | 319/524–5599 | www.keokuktourism.com | Daily.

Keokuk Dam/Observation Deck. A former bridge across the river here is now a covered observation deck, where you can look down and watch barges and other boats navigate the lock system of this, the longest lock and dam on the Mississippi River. It's also a great place to look for eagles in the winter. | End of N. Water St. | 319/524–4091 or 319/524–9660 | www.keokuktourism.com | Daily 7 AM–10:30 PM.

National Cemetery. Built in the 1860s, this is one of America's 12 original national cemeteries, and the only one in Iowa. There's a large Civil War section. | 1701 J St. | 319/524–5193 | Daily.

Rand Park. Community flower gardens, a fountain, and the burial site of Chief Keokuk, the city's Sauk–Fox namesake, fill this city park overlooking the Mississippi River. This is a popular spot for weddings in this region. | Between N. 14th and N. 17th Sts. | 319/524–5599 or 319/524–2050 | www.keokuktourism.com | Daily.

Dining

Hawkeye Restaurant. American. Barbecued ribs, barbecued prime rib, and chops are among the favorites at this eatery 2 mi north of town, but you can also get catfish, shrimp, and lobster. While you wait for your dinner, enjoy microbrews on tap or study the period photos of Keokuk. The lounge is open until 1 AM. | 105 N. Park Dr. | 319/524–7549 | AE, D, MC, V | $$–$$$

Marquette

Effigy Mounds National Monument. The 1,481-acre monument 3 mi north of Marquette contains 191 known prehistoric mounds of various shapes built by the Woodland Indians. Numerous scenic hiking trails are in the area. | 151 Rte. 76 | 563/873–3491 | www.nps.gov/efmo | Daily 8–4:30.

Lockmaster's House Heritage Museum. The only remaining lockmaster's house on the Mississippi is now a museum in Guttenberg about 21 mi southeast of Marquette. It displays period furnishings and photos and provides insight into the lives of those who built the lock and dam system. | Lock and Dam La., Guttenberg | 563/252–1531 | Free | Memorial Day–mid-Oct., Tues.–Sun. noon–4.

Pikes Peak State Park. You'll have a clear view of Wisconsin and Illinois from the park, on the highest bluff of the Mississippi, 5 mi southeast of town. Hikers will enjoy a waterfall along the trail, and lots of woodland areas. | 15316 Great River Rd. | 563/873–2341 | www.state.ia.us/parks | Daily.

Yellow River State Forest. This 8,503-acre forest 11 mi north of Marquette offers hiking, cross-country skiing, and more. The six trout streams are stocked each spring. | 729 State Forest Rd. | 563/586–2254 | www.iowadnr.com/forestry/yellowriver.html | Daily.

Dining

Alexander Café. American. Oversize chairs and large windows make for some fine river-gazing. This comfortable spot 1 mi south of Marquette, is known for its Saturday prime rib specials. | 213 Main St., McGregor | 563/873–3838 | AE, D, MC, V | $$–$$$

Muscatine

Mark Twain National Wildlife Refuge. Two of the four separate divisions of this refuge are south of Muscatine on County Route X61. Both the Big Timber Division (10 mi south of town) and the Louisa Division (14 mi south of town) are part of one of the most important flyways in the country, and offer wildlife observation, hiking trails, and educational programs. The Louisa Division closes for four and a half months out of the year to protect migrating birds. | Rte. X61 | 563/523–6982 | Big Timber: daily dawn–dusk; Louisa: Feb.–Sept. 15, daily dawn–dusk.

Pearl Button Museum. Pearl button manufacturing put this town on the map in the late 1800s; at the turn of the last century Muscatine produced a third of the world's buttons. | 206 W. 2nd St. | 563/263–1052 | www.pearlbuttoncapital.com | Free | Tues.–Sat. noon–4 or by appointment.

Saulsbury Bridge Recreation Area. You'll find a nature center, hunting and fishing areas, and a canoe transport service in this 675-acre county park. | 2007 Saulsbury Rd. | 563/649–3379 or 563/264–5922 | www.co.muscatine.ia.us/html/conservation-saulsbury.html | Apr.–Oct., daily; Nov.–Mar., Sun.–Fri.

Shady Creek Recreation Area. This 16-acre area 7 mi east of town on the Mississippi River is among the more popular of those managed by the Army Corps of Engineers. You'll find 53 modern campsites, a boat ramp, and activities throughout the year. | 1611 2nd Ave. | 563/263–7913 | www.mvr.usace.army.mil/missriver | Daily.

Wildcat Den State Park. One of the focal points of this park 12 mi east of Muscatine is the Pine Creek Grist Mill. Built in 1848, the mill is on the National Register of Historic Places. Hikers are attracted to trails that wind along bluffs above the river. | 1884 Wildcat Den Rd. | 563/263–4337 | www.state.ia.us/parks/wildcat.htm | Daily.

KANSAS

SANTA FE TRAIL ALONG U.S. 56
A DRIVE FROM EDGERTON TO ELKHART

Distance: 427 mi   Time: 3 days
Overnight Breaks: Council Grove, Dodge City

The Santa Fe Trail was opened in 1821 as a trade route between the United States east of the Missouri and the Mexican provinces. Hundreds of thousands of pioneers took this route, leaving wagon ruts that are still visible today. More than half of the Santa Fe Trail lies within the boundaries of Kansas, roughly following U.S. 56, starting near Edgerton, south of metropolitan Kansas City.

Because there isn't a lot of foliage along the route, spring, summer, and fall are all good seasons for this drive. Note that in winter, snowstorms can blow into western Kansas from Colorado without much notice.

❶ U.S. 56 and 183rd Street intersect in **Edgerton,** at about the point where the Santa Fe Trail separated from the Oregon Trail. The trail follows U.S. 56 west through Baldwin City, home of the **Ivan Boyd Prairie Preserve,** a great place to study the native grasses and flowers the pioneers encountered and one of several places where wagon ruts are still visible. About 65 mi farther west along U.S. 56, you'll come to the tiny community of Allen, founded in 1854. Here a cemetery holds 150 unmarked graves of pioneers. A toll bridge across 142 Creek and a mail station also operated here.

❷ West of Allen on U.S. 56 is **Council Grove,** home to 20 historic sites along the trail, including the Last Chance Store, a jail, a tree under which peace treaties were signed, and a mission school for Native Americans. Council Grove is another spot where wagon ruts are visible. To see the ruts, take U.S. 56 (Main Street) west to the city limits sign. Drive another 5 mi west, turn left (south) on a gravel road (1400 Road) and go a half mile. A sign indicates the ruts. (Note that the ruts are on private property, so don't go traipsing around the grounds.) Council Grove is a good place to spend the night.

❸ Continue following U.S. 56 through the towns of Herrington and McPherson to **Lyons.** The community about 30 mi west of McPherson is where the trail crosses Crow Creek. The **Coronado Quivira Museum** showcases life on the Santa Fe Trail and as far back as Coronado's explorations of the area in 1541. **Ralph's Ruts,** considered some of the finest examples of wagon ruts on the trail, are seven parallel paths on a farm north of U.S. 56 and east of Chase. Watch for signs.

❹ The trail continues along U.S. 56 and next passes through Ellinwood, where artifacts from the **Allison Fort Trading Post and Postal Relay Station** are preserved.

❺ The trail continues along the banks of the Arkansas River to the city of **Great Bend,** where you can see an excellent exhibit of Santa Fe Trail artifacts at the **Barton County Historical Society Museum and Village.** Great Bend is where the trail and U.S. 56 take a dramatic turn to the south, and you'll see the Citadel of the Prairie, a huge limestone rock nearly 70 feet high. A monument on the site tells the significance of the wagon trains reaching this point.

❻ Next on the route is the town of **Larned,** a must for those interested in the history of the Santa Fe Trail. Just 2 mi west of Larned on Route 156 is the **Santa Fe Trail Center,** the only research museum specifically designed to study the trail. Stop at the **Fort Larned National Historic Site,** established in 1859 to protect the mail coaches and travelers on the Santa Fe Trail, to see one of the best surviving examples of an Indian War–period fort. Ruts are clearly visible for miles near the old fort.

❼ Next along the trail is **Dodge City,** another must for anyone interested in the "real" Old West. In addition to details of life in "the wickedest city of the west," Dodge City is where you will find the largest continuous stretch of clearly defined tracks along the entire route of the trail. The tracks are 9 mi west of Dodge City on U.S. 50 (watch for the "Historic Marker" signs) and are impressive, even to teenagers and others not easily impressed on family vacations. Before getting out of Dodge, spend the night.

❽ The trail splits west of Dodge City at Cimarron: the southern route, known as the Cimarron Cut-off, was shorter but more dangerous and water was scarce. To see Wagon Bed Springs, the only dependable water source along this part of the trail, drive west on U.S. 56 about 25 mi until you reach Hugoton and turn north on to Route 25. The Santa Fe Trail and U.S. 56 leave Kansas, crossing into Oklahoma and New Mexico, at the **Cimarron National Grassland,** near Elkhart (approximately a two-hour drive along U.S. 56 from Dodge City). To take a self-guided tour of the grasslands, which cover key Santa Fe Trail sites in Morton County, pick up a map at the office at 242 East U.S. 56 in Elkhart; the office is open weekdays 8–5, but you can drive through the grasslands at any time.

Retracing your route on U.S. 56 is the fastest way to return to Kansas City.

Council Grove

Kaw Mission State Historic Site. Methodist Episcopal missionaries built this school for Kaw children in 1851, but today it showcases the heritage of the Kaw Indians, the Santa Fe Trail, and early Council Grove. | 500 N. Mission St. | 620/767–5410 | www.kshs.org/places/sites.htm | $3 | Tues.–Sat. 10–5, Sun. 1–5.

Old Calaboose. Calaboose is an old-fashioned word for jail, and this one is a replica of the original home for cowboys and homesteaders who got a little out of control during their visits to town. | 502 E. Main St. | 620/767–5882 | Daily.

Post Office Oak and Museum. Santa Fe Trail travelers left messages in a hole of this tree, which served as the area's official post office. The museum, in an 1864 brewery building, has agricultural and household artifacts from settlers. | E. Main St. | 620/767–5882 | Sun. 1–4 and by appointment.

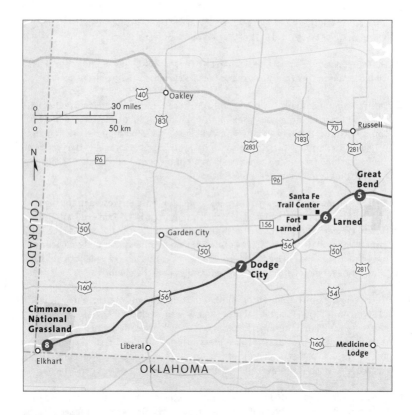

Dining

★**Hays House 1857 Restaurant & Tavern.** American. The oldest continuously operating restaurant west of the Mississippi was built in 1857 by Seth Hays (Daniel Boone's grandson) and is now a National Historic Landmark. Pictures of the building and area line the walls, and there are a few antique church pews that serve as booths. It's known for skillet-fried chicken, bone-in ham, prime rib (weekends only), and homemade breads and pies. There is a buffet on Sunday. | 112 W. Main St. | 620/767–5911 | D, MC, V | Closed Mon. | $–$$

Station Restaurant. American/Casual. Soup and made-to-order sandwiches are the staples here. Try the Railroad Hoagie (a hero with assorted meats and vegetables), ham and bean soup, strawberry pie, or pound cake. | 219 W. Main St. | 620/767–5619 | No credit cards | Closed weekends | $

Lodging

Cottage House. Built in 1867 as a cottage and blacksmith shop, this Prairie Victorian structure grew into a popular boarding house. The property, one block from Main Street, has two honeymoon cottages, rooms in the main house, and motel units. In-room data ports, some in-room hot tubs, some refrigerators, cable TV, meeting rooms, some pets allowed (fee). | 25 N. Neosho, 66846 | 620/767–6828 or 800/727–7903 | fax 620/767–6414 | www.cottagehousehotel.com | 40 rooms | AE, D, DC, MC, V | $

Flint Hills Bed and Breakfast. Relax on the porch swing or chat with fellow guests in the sitting room of this 1913 American four square house. The B&B has retained its original woodwork and floors. No TV in some rooms, no kids under 4, no smoking. | 613 W. Main St., 66846 | 620/767–6655 | www.flinthillsbedandbreakfast.com | 4 rooms | D, MC, V | BP | $

Dodge City

Boot Hill Museum. Climb up to Boot Hill to see the famous cemetery, so-named because cowboys were buried here immediately after gunfights—with their boots still on. The replica of Front Street as it was in 1876 houses exhibits such as "The Guns That Won the West." Summer entertainment includes stagecoach rides, Long Branch saloon shows, and gunfights at high noon. | Front St. | 620/227–8188 | www.boothill.org | $7 | Memorial Day–Labor Day, daily 8–8; Labor Day–Memorial Day, Mon.–Sat. 9–5, Sun. 1–5.

Dodge City Trolley. Narrated tours spotlight such sites as the Long Branch Saloon, Fort Dodge, and the Santa Fe Trail. | 400 W. Wyatt Earp Blvd. | 620/225–8186 | $5 | Memorial Day–Labor Day, daily at 9:30, 11, 1:30, and 3.

Fort Dodge. Several original buildings remain of the fort that supported this area from 1865–1882. It's 5 mi east of Dodge City. | 101 Pershing Ave. | 620/227–2121 | Memorial Day–Labor Day, daily 10–4; Labor Day–Memorial Day, daily 1–4.

★**Santa Fe Trail Tracks.** The wide-open prairie reveals the vastness of the pioneers' undertaking as miles of wagon ruts, found 9 mi west of Dodge City, stretch to the horizon. | On U.S. 50 | 620/227–8188 | Daily.

Dining

Casey's Cowtown Restaurant. American. A brick fireplace, antiques, and local art contribute to this steak house's casual atmosphere. Casey's is known for it's hand-cut Black Angus steaks. | 503 E. Trail | 620/227–5225 | AE, D, MC, V | $$

El Charro. Mexican. Mexican dishes such as enchiladas make this ranchlike restaurant with wooden tables and flowers a favorite. | 1209 W. Wyatt Earp Blvd. | 620/225–0371 | AE, D, MC, V | Closed Sun. | ¢–$

Freight House. American. The Freight House, which is in the restored Santa Fe Freight Depot, specializes in steaks, chicken, and seafood grilled over mesquite wood, as well as dry-aged steaks from the Dodge City Steak Co. You can eat in an original Pullman dining car. | 207 E. Wyatt Earp Blvd. | 620/227–6443 | AE, MC, V | Closed Sun. | $–$$

Lodging
Boot Hill Bed and Breakfast. You'll find rooms with such names as the Wild West, Miss Kitty, and Annie Oakley in this 1927 Dutch Colonial home. Most rooms are spacious, and some have cherrywood four-poster beds, fireplaces, and skylights. In-room data ports, cable TV, in-room VCRs; no smoking. | 603 W. Spruce St., 67801 | 620/225–7600 or 888/225–7655 | fax 620/225–6585 | www.boothilldodgecity.com | 6 rooms | AE, MC, V | BP | $–$$

Comfort Inn. This hotel is 1 mi from Boot Hill. The lobby, with its massive chandelier and curving oak stairway, makes you feel you're staying in something a little more personable than a chain hotel. Free wireless Internet is another perk. In-room data ports, some microwaves, some refrigerators, cable TV, indoor pool, hot tub, Internet, meeting rooms. | 2000 W. Wyatt Earp Blvd., 67801 | 620/338–8700 | fax 620/338–8412 | 54 rooms | AE, D, DC, MC, V | CP | $

Great Bend
Allison Fort Trading Post and Postal Relay Station. A historical marker is all that remains of this significant spot along the Santa Fe Trail. | U.S. 56, 2 mi east of Great Bend in Ellinwood | 620/792–2750 | Daily.

Barton County Historical Society Museum and Village. Ten buildings, including the first permanent house in Barton County, are vivid reminders of life here a century ago. | 85 U.S. 281 | 620/793–5125 | $2 | Apr.–Oct., Tues.–Sun. 1–5 and by appointment.

KANSAS RULES OF THE ROAD

License Requirements: Residents of Kansas with a farm permit may drive as early as 14 years of age. However, other drivers must be at least 16 years old, have completed driver's training, and have a valid license from their state of residence.

Right Turn on Red: A right turn on red is allowed in Kansas *after* coming to a full and complete stop unless otherwise posted.

Seat Belt and Helmet Laws: Seat belts are required for all front-seat passengers and all children ages 4–15; safety seats are required for children up to 4 years. Helmets are required for motorcyclists under 18 years of age and encouraged for adults.

Speed Limits: Speed limits on interstate and divided multilane highways are a maximum of 70 mph, on two-lane state and U.S. highways 65 mph, and on county roads 55 mph.

For More Information: Contact the **Kansas Department of Transportation** | 785/296–3566.

Cheyenne Bottoms. Designated a wetlands of international importance, this area north-east of Great Bend is an annual stopover point for nearly half a million migrating birds. More than 320 species have been identified in the 41,000-acre lowland. Take U.S. 281 north from Great Bend for about 5 mi, then east 2 mi on county blacktop; follow signs to the headquarters. | 56 N.E. 40 Rd. | 620/793–7730 | www.cheyennebottoms.net | Daily.

Coronado Quivira Museum. Upstairs exhibits chronicle settlement of the area from Coronado's explorations through the blazing of the Santa Fe Trail. See a rare piece of Spanish chain mail (circa 1500) uncovered in the county in 1940. A Quivira Indian exhibit shows a life-size replica of a grass lodge as it would have been in 1500. The museum is in Lyons, 30 mi east of Great Bend on U.S. 56. | 105 N. Lyon | 620/257–3941 | $2 | Mon.–Sat. 9–5, Sun. 1–5.

Quivira National Wildlife Refuge. More than 22,000 acres of prairie grasses, salt marshes, sand dunes, and canals are home to hundreds of thousands of waterfowl and mammals. Take U.S. 281 south from Great Bend for about 21 mi, then go 14 mi east on Northeast 70th Street and 1 mi north to the visitor center. | Rte. 3, Stafford | 620/486–2393 | www.cheyennebottoms.net | Daily; some seasonal closings.

★**Ralph's Ruts.** These seven parallel paths on the farm of Ralph Hathaway (considered a leading authority on the Santa Fe Trail) are thought to be some of the finest examples on the trail. The ruts are north of U.S. 56 and 4 mi west of Chase. | 4222 Ave. L, Chase | 620/938–2504 | By appointment.

Dining
Tenth Street Restaurant. Mexican. The cheerful Southwest-style interior here is complemented by tasty tacos, burritos, and chalupas. Order the hot made-to-order chips and the pork enchiladas, both popular with regulars. | 2210 10th St. | 620/793–3786 | No credit cards | Closed weekends | $

Larned
Fort Larned National Historic Site. The fort is known as the guardian of the Santa Fe Trail. Many of its buildings are original military structures. It's 6 mi west of Larned on Route 156. | Rte. 3 | 620/285–6911 | www.nps.gov/fols | $3 | Daily 8:30–5.

★**Santa Fe Trail Center.** See a portion of the original wagon ruts made by travelers on this route, as well as other artifacts from the 60 years of this commerce trail. The center is 2 mi west of Larned. | Rte. 156 | 620/285–2054 | www.larned.net/trailctr | $4 | Memorial Day–Labor Day, daily 9–5; Labor Day–Memorial Day, Tues.–Sun. 9–5.

Dining
Burgerteria. American. As the name implies, you'll find plenty of burgers on the menu, along with homemade fries and ice cream. Kids' menu available. | 417 W. 14th St. | 620/285–3135 | No credit cards | ¢–$

Walkers Steakhouse on the Santa Fe Trail. American. The specialty here is steak: cuts range from a fillet all the way up to a porterhouse. For the brave, there's mountain oysters (fried bull testicles) or an 80-ounce sirloin. If you've got room, try a piece of the homemade pie for dessert. For those looking for something lighter, Walkers also serves sandwiches, seafood, and has a salad bar. There's a buffet weekdays (for lunch) and weekend evenings. | 718 Fort Larned Ave. | 620/285–6226 | MC, V | $–$$

LOUISIANA

MISSISSIPPI RIVER PLANTATIONS
NEW ORLEANS TO ST. FRANCISVILLE

Distance: 183 mi Time: 3 days
Overnight Breaks: Destrehan to Plaquemine, New Roads, St. Francisville.

Antebellum mansions share the landscape with industrial complexes and shacks, making this drive a fascinating view of life along the Mississippi both from the 1800s and today. The historic manors are beautiful year-round, but especially when decorated for Christmas and in spring, when azaleas and magnolia trees are in bloom and gardens are splashed with fresh color. Spend your first night in New Orleans, then on the second night pick one of the plantation–museums that is also a bed-and-breakfast to stay in (tours included) before pushing on to St. Francisville or New Roads for the third night. Keep in mind that guided tours of the manor homes take at least an hour and may involve some waiting before your group is taken in. It's challenging to see more than three in one day.

Because of the many twists and turns as the River Road follows the Mississippi, directions such as "east" or "west" are pointless. Locals go with the flow, indicating either "downriver" (towards New Orleans) or "upriver" (towards Baton Rouge and beyond).

1 The great **River Road** is actually two roads tracing both sides of the Mississippi River, a vital trade route for almost two centuries, from **New Orleans** to Baton Rouge. The roads change route and highway designations as they go along.

2 For the first stop at **Destrehan Plantation,** take Exit 6 off I–310 and proceed ¼ mi downriver (towards New Orleans) on River Road. This Creole manor, with hand-hewn cypress timbers and a two-pitch roof, is one of the oldest plantation houses remaining in the Mississippi Valley. It was built in 1787 by planter and legislator Jean Noel Destrehan; a Greek Revival remodeling was completed in 1840. Pirate Jean Lafitte was a frequent visitor, which led to persistent rumors that treasure is buried behind the walls.

3 About 25 mi upriver from Destrehan on River Road, you come to Garyville and the **San Francisco Plantation House.** An ornate and colorful extravaganza, the San Francisco is famous for its hand-painted decorative ceilings and faux marbling. The name of the 1856 mansion was originally "Sans Frusquin," French slang for "without

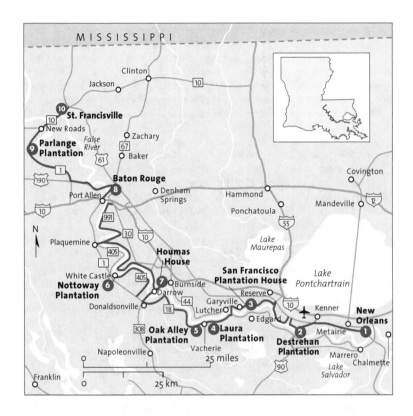

a penny in my pocket." That rueful claim came from planter Edmond Bozonier Marmillion, who had spared no expense in the construction of his home.

4 The Gramercy-Lutcher Bridge is 7 mi farther on: cross to the other bank, then continue 2 mi on Route 18 toward Vacherie. **Laura Plantation,** just off on Route 20, presents one of the liveliest and best-documented tours in the region, an unusual look at plantation life from the perspective of women, children, and slaves. The circa-1805 complex incorporates 11 buildings (one main manor house, plus assorted Creole cottages and slave quarters). The folktales of Br'er Rabbit, which originated in West Africa, were first recorded in America on this site in the 1870s.

5 **Oak Alley Plantation** is only 4 mi upriver from the Laura, back on Route 18. A ¼-mi avenue framed by twenty-eight live oaks leads from Route 18 to the Greek Revival manor. The trees, planted by an early settler, were already mature when the house was built in 1839 by planter Jacques Telesphore Roman. The antiques are not as impressive as in other river mansions, but you can spend the night in plantation cottages here.

6 From Oak Alley, follow Route 18 upriver past Donaldsonville, then pick up Route 1 to connect to Route 405. **Nottoway Plantation,** in White Castle, is the largest surviving antebellum manor in the South. The 53,000-square-foot main house, including a 65-foot grand white ballroom, attracts a lot of tourists. Built in 1859 by planter John Hampden Randolph, the Greek Revival–Italianate house is famous for its intricate plaster friezes, marble fireplaces, and hand-painted Dresden doorknobs. You can spend the night at Nottoway or grab a bite to eat at the inn.

❼ Back across the river, **Houmas House** once stood on the largest sugarcane plantation in the U.S., some 20,000 acres producing up to 20 million pounds of sugar per year. From White Castle take a shortcut back to Donaldsonville on Route 1 and cross the Sunshine Bridge, then head upriver on Route 44 to Route 942 in Burnside to get there. The 1840 Greek Revival mansion, built by planter John Preston Smith, is a showplace of the South, with its three-story spiral staircase and formal gardens. The nearby Cajun Village restaurant housed in former slave quarters is a great place to eat.

❽ Follow the curves of the river north to **Baton Rouge** (Route 30 is a shortcut). **Magnolia Mound Plantation,** south of I–10 on Route 30, stands on a ridge facing the Missis-sippi River. The 1791 French Creole house is furnished with Federal-style antiques from the 19th century. Farther east off I–10, **LSU Rural Life Museum** incorporates 20 build-ings from 19th-century Louisiana, transplanted from plantations and farms statewide, including an overseer's house, slave cabins, a blacksmith shop, a grist mill, and a country church with rustic homemade art.

❾ From Baton Rouge, take U.S. 190 west to Route 1 north to New Roads. **Parlange Planta-tion** in New Roads is one of the oldest French Colonial manors in Louisiana, and it continues to command a working plantation (sugar, cattle, pecans). The property is still owned and occupied by seventh- and eighth-generation descendants of the Marquis de Trenant, who built the house in 1750. It is open by appointment only.

❿ Drive east on Route 10 for approximately 5$^1/_2$ mi and take the ferry across the Missis-sippi to **St. Francisville.** On Route 10 east of town is one of the area's most distin-guished house-museums, **Rosedown Plantation,** on 1,000 acres, with 28 acres of historic gardens and 14 restored outbuildings, including the original hothouse, detached kitchen, barn, and doctor's office. The 1835 Greek Revival manor has been pains-takingly restored with all of its original furnishings. **Audubon State Historic Site,** off U.S. 61 south of town, once attracted naturalist John James Audubon, who painted 32 of his Birds of America while living here at Oakley Plantation House in the 1820s. The 1806 manor is now furnished in the style of the late Federal period, as it would have been when the artist was in residence. Hikers can follow his tracks through 100 acres of nature trails and woodlands. **Butler Greenwood Plantation,** on U.S. 61 north of St. Francisville, is still owned by members of its founding family, who often act as tour guides. The antebellum mansion, circa 1790, has a formal Victorian parlor.
From St. Francisville, take U.S. 61 south for approximately 20 mi to I–110 south toward Baton Rouge. Exit onto I–10 east and proceed for 75 mi back to New Orleans.

Baton Rouge
LSU Rural Life Museum. A compound of 19th-century buildings depicts pre-industrial Louisiana life, including a working plantation with a commissary, schoolhouse, sick house, gristmill, overseer's house, blacksmith's shop, open-kettle sugar mill, and church. Folk architecture is represented by a dog-trot cabin (with its two wings connected by a covered porch), Acadian cottage, and slave quarters, among others. Vintage vehicles and Native American artifacts are housed in a large barn. Classical statuary graces the 25-acre Windrush Gardens. | Essen La. at I–10 south | 225/765–2437 | fax 225/765–2639 | http://rurallife.lsu.edu | $7 | Daily 8:30–5.

Magnolia Mound Plantation. On 16 acres of the original 900, this 1791 French Creole manor has been restored as a house museum with quite a collection of Louisiana and Federal furnishings. Open-hearth cooking demonstrations in the reconstructed out-kitchen are held on Tuesday and Thursday from October through May. After the house tour, walk through the slave cabins and around the crop and herb gardens. If you'd like to find out more about the slaves' perspective, make a reservation (two weeks in advance) to join one of the "Beyond the Big House" tours. | 2161 Nicholson Dr. (Rte. 30) | 225/343–4955 | fax 225/343–6739 | www.magnoliamound.org | $8 | Mon.–Sat. 10–4, Sun. 1–4.

U.S.S. *Kidd*. Volunteer war veterans staff this World War II destroyer, which has been restored to its VJ Day configuration. Tours of the 369-foot ship include admission to the adjoining nautical museum with a submarine exhibit, ship models, and Veterans' Memorial Wall. | Off I–110, Government St. Exit | 305 S. River Rd. | 225/342–1942 | fax 225/342–2039 | www.usskidd.com | $6 | Daily 9–5.

Dining

Boutin's. Cajun/Creole. Walk into Boutin's and you're surrounded by a rustic bayou atmosphere. Cajun standards are on the menu—fried catfish, shrimp étouffée—but so are modern interpretations like crawfish enchiladas and a super spicy rib-eye steak. Live bands play Cajun tunes for dancing Monday through Saturday nights. | 8322 Bluebonnet Blvd. | 225/819–9862 | AE, D, DC, MC, V | $$

Mike Anderson's. Seafood. Generous seafood dishes are the selling point for this comfortable and casual family restaurant. A fried seafood platter has shrimp, oysters, catfish, crawfish tails, stuffed crab, and crab sticks; a broiled platter substitutes dishes like shrimp scampi and crab-stuffed mushrooms. | 1031 W. Lee Dr. | 225/766–7823 | AE, D, DC, MC, V | $$

Destrehan to Plaquemine

Destrehan Plantation. The pale yellow Destrehan was built in 1787 in Creole planta-tion style by Robin de Logny. During the Civil War, the Union took it over and used it as a Freedman's Bureau where former slaves were trained. The hipped roof with two pitches and wide galleries supported by columns is typical of plantations built by French planters. Look for it in the movie *Interview with the Vampire*, based on the novel by New Orleans author Anne Rice. | 13034 River Rd., Destrehan | 504/764–9315 | www.destrehanplantation.org | $10 | Daily 9–4.

LOUISIANA RULES OF THE ROAD

License Requirements: To drive in Louisiana, you must be at least 15 years old with a learner's permit or 16 years old with a valid driver's license. Residents of Canada and most other countries may drive as long as they have a valid driver's license from their home countries.

Right Turn on Red: Everywhere in the state you may make a right turn at a red light *after* a full stop unless otherwise posted.

Seat Belt and Helmet Laws: All drivers and front-seat passengers must wear seat belts. Children under age 13 must wear a seat belt at all times, whether seated in front or back; children under age 4 must ride in a federally approved child safety seat. Motor-cyclists may choose to ride without a helmet only if they are at least 21 years of age and carry a medical insurance policy with at least $10,000 in coverage. They are also required to keep their headlights and taillights on at all times.

Speed Limits: Louisiana's speed limits are 70 mph on interstate highways, 65 mph on controlled-access highways, 55 mph on state highways, and lower where posted.

For More Information: Contact the **Office of Motor Vehicles** | 877/368–5463 | http://omv.dps.state.la.us.

Houmas House. One of the most beautiful antebellum manors on the Mississippi is set in well-tended formal gardens on the River Road. The Greek Revival showplace is flanked by two octagonal wings, shaded by wide verandas and massive old oaks. It was built by Colonel John Preston, once master of a 20,000-acre plantation. Tours are led by docents in period gowns. | 40136 Rte. 942, Darrow | 504/891–9494 | www. houmashouse.com | $10 | Daily 10–5.

Laura Plantation. This is the most well-documented plantation in the state—there are more than 5,000 pages of records, diaries, and journals relating to the everyday operation of the place. The final owner, Laura Locoul Gore, never ran the plantation, but it was her grandmother and great-grandmother who developed the family's powerful position. Laura's memoirs have been turned into a book, which now informs the tour of the main house. Walks around the slave quarters and out buildings are self-guided unless you call ahead to join one of the tours that focuses on the slave experience. | 2247 River Rd. (Rte. 18), Vacherie | 225/265–7690 or 888/799–7690 | www. lauraplantation.com | $10 | Daily 9:30–5 (last tour at 4).

Nottoway Plantation. The tiny riverfront community of White Castle may have been named for this 53,000-square-foot, white Georgian Revival mansion, the largest remaining antebellum home in the South. It was built in 1859 by sugar planter John Hampden Randolph, and was later spared during the Civil War by a Union gunboat officer who had once been a houseguest. | 30970 Rte. 405, White Castle | 866/527–6884 | www.nottoway.com | $10 | Daily 9–5.

Oak Alley Plantation. The view between hundreds-of-years old oaks toward the manor house has been made famous by TV and movies: It's had cameos in *Days of Our Lives*, *Interview with the Vampire*, and *Primary Colors*. The oaks were planted in the 1700s by an unknown settler trying establish claim to the land; the home was built by later owners, the Romans. The interior is not as lavish or intricate as other homes on the river. Most of the antiques inside are not original to the home. | 3645 River Rd. (Rte. 18), Vacherie | 225/265–2151 | www.oakalleyplantation.com | $10 | Mar.–Oct., daily 9–5:30; Nov.–Feb., daily 9–5.

San Francisco Plantation House. Built in 1856 by planter Edmond Bozonier Marmillion, this mansion is an architectural confection lavished with gingerbread trim and bright pastels. The interior is just as ornate, with lofty rooms and famous ceiling frescoes heavily influenced by European styles. The plantation inspired a novel called *Steamboat Gothic*. | 2646 River Rd. (Rte. 44), Reserve | 504/535–2341 | www.sanfranciscoplantation.org | $10 | Daily 9:30–5.

Dining

The Cabin. Cajun/Creole. The restaurant and surrounding shops are in what were once slave quarters. Domestic artifacts, advertising paraphernalia, and farm implements adorn the rooms and grounds. With broiled snapper, oyster po'-boys, country fried steak, and red beans and rice, the kitchen serves something from all the influences in southern Louisiana. | Rtes. 44 and 22, Burnside | 225/473–3007 | www.thecajunvillage.com | AE, D, MC, V | No dinner Sun.–Mon. | ¢–$$

B&C Cajun Deli. Cajun. Great seafood gumbo and fried catfish are served at this casual place next to Laura Plantation. The owners are fishermen as well as good cooks and there's a seafood market on-site. | River Rd., Vacherie | 225/265–8356 | AE, D, MC, V | No dinner | ¢–$

Lodging

Madewood Plantation. Elegance surrounds but doesn't suffocate you at this off-the-beaten-track Greek Revival mansion. A four-course meal is included in your stay. Enjoy complimentary wine and cheese in the parlor before dinner—and after-dinner sherry in the music room. Rooms have antiques, but they are far from stuffy or overcrowded. The Nursery is particularly colorful with mandarin-orange walls and multicolor quilts. Though tours are given, there's no touristy gift shop, no hoards of visitors, and no cordoned off areas—just you, inhabiting a piece of another era. No room phones, no room TVs, no smoking. | 4250 Rte. 308 (7 mi south of Donaldsonville), Napoleonville 70390 | 985/369–7151 or 800/375–7151 | fax 985/369–9848 | www. madewood.com | 6 rooms, 2 suites | MC, V | FAP | $$$$

Nottoway Plantation. Overnight guests may stay in main-house bedrooms, the boys' wing, or the overseer's cottage. The federal blue Master Bedroom Suite on the third floor is furnished with original pieces that belonged to John Hampton Randolph, the first owner. Restaurant, cable TV, pool, library, shop, business services; no smoking. | 225/545–2730 | fax 225/545–8632 | www.nottoway.com | 13 rooms, 3 suites | AE, D, MC, V | CP | $$–$$$

Oak Alley Plantation. Cheery florals decorate cottages from the 1800s on the plantation grounds. You can stay in a one-room cottage with a fireplace (No. 5) or a roomy two-bedroom cottage, with living room, dining room, and full kitchen (No. 3). A tour of the manor house is included in your stay, and breakfast is served in the on-site restaurant. Restaurant, café, some kitchens, microwaves, refrigerators, shop; no room phones, no room TVs, no smoking. | 3645 River Rd. (Hwy. 18), Vacherie 70090 | 225/265–2151 | fax 225/265–7035 | www.oakalleyplantation.com | 5 cottages | AE, D, MC, V | BP | $$

New Orleans

Audubon Park. On the site of artist John James Audubon's former estate, the park was designed by Frederick Law Olmsted (who also laid out New York City's Central Park). It's a large, lush stretch of green that contains the world-class Audubon Zoo, picnic and play areas, a golf course, riding stables, a tennis court, a river view, and a 1.7-mi track for running, walking, or biking. | 6500 Magazine St. | 504/586–8777 | www.auduboninstitute.org | Park free, zoo $10 | Park daily dawn–dusk, zoo mid-Mar.–mid-Oct., weekdays 9:30–5, weekends 9:30–6; mid-Oct–mid-Mar., daily 9–5.

Beauregard-Keyes House. This stately 19th-century mansion with period furnishings was the temporary home of Confederate general P. G. T. Beauregard. The house and grounds had severely deteriorated in the 1940s when the well-known novelist Frances Parkinson Keyes moved in and helped restore it. Her studio at the back of the large courtyard remains intact. | 1113 Chartres St., French Quarter | 504/523–7257 | $5 | Mon.–Sat. 10–3, tours on the hr.

French Market. The oldest open-air market in the United States rambles along the riverfront from Jackson Square to Esplanade Avenue. Built on the site of an ancient Native American trading post, the series of colonnaded structures dates to 1813. Today the daily flea market provides an entertaining rummage for handmade masks, ethnic jewelry, and leather goods. | 1008 N. Peters St., French Quarter | 504/522–2621 | fax 504/596–3410 | Free | Daily.

★**Hermann–Grima Historic House.** Built in 1831, this is one of the earliest examples of American architecture in the French Quarter. The house was built for wealthy merchant Samuel Hermann and was occupied after 1844 by the family of Judge Felix Grima. You can tour the courtyard and stables, and open-hearth cooking demonstrations are held in the original kitchen every Thursday, October through May. | 820 St. Louis St., French Quarter | 504/525–5661 | www.gnofn.org~hggh | $6 | Tours weekdays 10–3:30.

Jackson Square. Surrounded by historic buildings and filled with plenty of the city's atmospheric street life, the heart of the French Quarter is today a beautifully landscaped park. Originally called the Place d'Armes, the square was founded in 1718 as a military marching ground. | Bounded by Decatur, St. Peter, St. Ann, and Chartres Sts., French Quarter | Daily dawn–dusk.

★ **Old Ursuline Convent.** The only example of true French Colonial architecture in the French Quarter (which is primarily Spanish in style) is also believed by many historians to be the oldest remaining structure in the lower Mississippi Valley. In addition to holding classes for wealthy Creole plantation children from upriver, it was also the first school on American soil to teach children of Native American and African heritage. | 1100 Chartres St. | 504/529–3040 | www.accesscom.net/ursuline | $5 | Weekdays 10–3, weekends 11:15–2.

Pitot House. One of the few surviving houses that lined Bayou St. John in the late 1700s, and the only plantation house in the city open to the public, Pitot House is named for James Pitot, who bought the property in 1810. Pitot built one of the first cotton presses in New Orleans and served as the city's mayor from 1804 to 1805. The house is noteworthy for its stucco-covered brick-between-post construction, an example of which is exposed on the second floor. | 1440 Moss St., Bayou St. John | 504/482–0312 | $5 | Wed.–Sat. 10–3; last tour at 2.

The Presbytère. One of twin Spanish Colonial–style buildings flanking St. Louis Cathedral, this one, on the right, now holds an outstanding exhibit about Mardi Gras. The building was originally designed to house the priests of the cathedral; instead, it served as a courthouse under the Spanish and later under the Americans. | Jackson Sq., French Quarter | 504/568–6968 | $5 | Tues.–Sun. 9–5.

St. Charles Avenue Streetcar. The electric cars, installed in 1923, are part of the oldest street railway system in the world, first powered by steam locomotives in 1835. The 13-mi Garden District round-trip along the tree-lined avenue full of stately mansions takes about 90 minutes to Tulane University and back. | Along St. Charles and Carrollton Aves., from Canal St. to Palmer Park | 504/248–3900 | $2 | Daily.

Dining

Acme Oyster and Seafood Restaurant. Seafood. A rough-edge classic in every way, this no-nonsense eatery near the edge of the French Quarter is a prime source of cool and salty raw oysters on the half-shell; shrimp, oyster, and hot roast beef po'boys; and red beans and rice. Expect a line during peak lunch and dinner hours. | 724 Iberville St. | 504/522–5973 | www.acmeoyster.com | Reservations not accepted | AE, D, DC, MC, V | ¢–$$

Central Grocery. Delicatessens. This old-fashioned Italian grocery store produces authentic muffulettas, one of the gastronomic gifts of the city's Italian immigrants. Good enough to challenge the po'boy as the local sandwich champs, they're made by filling round loaves of seeded bread with ham, salami, mozzarella, and a salad of marinated green olives. The grocery closes at 5:30 PM. | 923 Decatur St. | 504/523–1620 | No credit cards | No dinner | ¢–$

Herbsaint. Contemporary. Upscale food and downscale prices are among Herbsaint's assets. "Small plates" and side dishes such as charcuterie, crudités, a knock-'em-dead shrimp bisque, gumbos, and salads are mainstays. More substantial appetites are courted with pork tenderloin, beef short ribs, rib-eye steak, and salmon in a mustard-seed crust. | 701 St. Charles Ave. | 504/524–4114 | Reservations essential | AE, D, DC, MC, V | Closed Sun. No lunch Sat. | $$–$$$

★ **Praline Connection.** Southern. Down-home cooking in the Southern-Creole style is the forte of this rather quirky restaurant a couple of blocks from the French Quarter. The fried or stewed chicken, smothered pork chops, barbecue ribs, and collard greens are definitively done. To all this add moderate prices, a congenial staff, and a neat-as-a-pin dining room. | 542 Frenchmen St. | 504/943–3934 | AE, D, DC, MC, V | Closed Sat. | $–$$

New Roads

Parlange Plantation. This National Historic Landmark is a good example of the area's French Colonial architecture; the house is raised on a brick basement and the first story is surrounded by a wide verandas. Built in 1750 of native materials, it was framed by brick and cypress beams then plastered with *bousillage,* a traditional mixture of mud, moss, and deer hair. The working plantation is run by seventh- and eighth-generation members of the Parlange family and is rumored to be haunted. | 8211 False River Rd. (Rte. 1), 5 mi south of town | 225/638–8410 | $10 | By appointment only (make reservations a week in advance).

Pointe Coupee Parish Museum. There's no shortage of grand manors in the heart of plantation country, but here's a rare look at a typical middle-class home. The 1760 cottage is furnished with period antiques appropriate to a family of modest means. | 8348 False River Rd. (Rte. 1), 6 mi south of town | 225/638–7788 | Free | Daily 10–3.

Dining

Satterfield's Riverwalk. Seafood. Dine on the deck or head inside to the dining room, which has a fireplace and a glass wall overlooking False River. The building, a former Ford Motor Company dealership built in 1917, is on the National Register of Historic Places. Memorabilia in the street-front antiques store includes a 1927 Ford Model A and vintage photos of the dealership and town. Try the beef tenderloin topped with crabmeat or the trout with dill. | 108 E. Main St. | 225/638–5027 | AE, D, DC, MC, V | $$–$$$

Lodging

Mon Rêve. The three-story Creole plantation home was originally built by owner Joe Hinckley's great-grandfather in 1820. Joe and his wife, Cathi, rent out bedrooms with private baths, unless a suite is requested, in which case two bedrooms share a connecting bath. Period pieces furnish the house. Cable TV, dock, fishing; no room phones, no smoking. | 9825 False River Rd. (Rte. 1), 70760 | 225/638–7848 or 800/324–2738 | www.monreve-mydream.com | 3 rooms | D, MC, V | BP | $$

St. Francisville

Audubon State Historic Site–Oakley House. John James Audubon painted 32 of his Birds of America at Oakley House. The house was built in 1799 but is furnished in the style of the 1820s, when the artist lived here. You can also explore the detached plantation and weaving room, formal and kitchen gardens, two slave cabins, a barn, and 100 acres of forested grounds with a nature trail and picnic area. | 11788 Rte. 965, off U.S. 61 | 225/635–3739 or 888/677–2838 | www.crt.state.la.us | $2 | Daily 9–5.

Butler Greenwood Plantation. Members of the founding family guide tours at this National Register of Historic Places property, a 1790s plantation set in oak-shaded gardens. Rooms in the antebellum manor are furnished with original antiques, and there's a formal Victorian parlor. | 8345 U.S. 61 | 225/635–6312 | www.butlergreenwood.com | $5 | Daily 9–5.

Port Hudson State Historic Site. From May 23 to July 9, 1863, 6,800 Confederate soldiers defended this site against a Union force of 30,000. It was the longest siege in U.S. history and one of the first battles in which freed slaves fought alongside Union troops. Today interpretive displays tell the story as you walk through a portion of the battlefield, viewing towers, trenches, artillery, and a cemetery for more than 3,000 Union soldiers, most unknown. The site is off U.S. 61, 10 mi south of St. Francisville. | 756 W. Plains–Port Hudson Rd., Zachary | 225/654–3775 or 888/677–3400 | www.crt.state.la.us | $2 | Daily 9–5.

Rosedown Plantation. An oak alley leads to an 1835 manor on a 1,000-acre plantation. More than a dozen restored outbuildings include the original hothouse, barn, detached kitchen, doctor's office, and milk shed. Formal parterres, classical landscapes, and fine statuary make up the gardens. Tours of the house leave on the hour, the last one is at 4. | 12501 Rte. 10 (at U.S. 61) | 225/635–3332 | www.crt.state.la.us | $10 | Daily 9–5.

Dining
Steamboat Charley's Sports Bar and Grill. American/Casual. Belly up to the pine bar or shoot pool in one of the side rooms. The menu includes real root beer, burgers, rib-eye steaks, chicken-fried steak, fried or grilled shrimp, crawfish and oyster plates, and other casual eats. There's live country music Friday and Saturday. You can't miss the large neon sign out front after sunset, but in the daylight this gem seems to hide behind a car wash. | 7193 U.S. 61 | 225/635–0203 | AE, MC, V | ¢–$$

Lodging
Best Western St. Francis Hotel. This two-story hotel is set on a lake—where you can go fishing—but is within walking distance of historic downtown St. Francisville's shops and cafés. Rooms have pretty standard hotel decor, but they are up to date and clean. Dining room, cable TV with movies, in-room data ports, lake, fishing, lounge, video game room, laundry services, business services, meeting rooms, no-smoking rooms. | U.S. 61, 70775 | 225/635–3821 or 800/826–9931 | fax 225/635–4749 | www.bestwestern.com | 101 rooms | AE, D, DC, MC, V | CP | $.

Butler Greenwood Plantation. On the 50 acres of Butler Greenwood Plantation sits an assortment of cottages, all with kitchens or kitchenettes stocked with croissants, jam, juice, and coffee. The Old Kitchen, a two-bedroom cottage, was built in 1796; the Cook's Cottage, a studio, was built in the 1800s. Other quirky buildings include the Gazebo, a one-bedroom, six-sided structure with stained-glass windows, and the Dovecote, a three-story former windmill with two bedrooms. Kitchens, cable TV; no smoking. | 8345 U.S. 61, 70775 | 225/635–6312 | fax 225/635–6370 | www.butlergreenwood.com | 8 cottages | AE, D, DC, MC, V | CP | $$–$$$

GREAT RIVER ROAD ALONG U.S. 61
FROM RED WING TO LA CRESCENT

Distance: 107 mi   Time: 1–2 days
Overnight Break: Wabasha

On this portion of the Great River Road you'll follow the bluffs that hug the Mississippi River between Red Wing and La Crescent; some of Minnesota's oldest communities are here, river towns that came into their own during the steamboat era. This is a year-round tour, but the sights are especially beautiful in fall. In late winter you might see bald eagles.

❶ Begin in downtown **Red Wing,** near the intersection of U.S. 61 and U.S. 63. The town's most distinctive feature is **Barn Bluff,** a huge sandstone and dolomite formation that towers above town. You can park at the end of East 5th Street and climb trails to the top. Well-preserved Victorian architecture is one of Red Wing's biggest attractions. The **St. James Hotel** was built in 1875. The **Pottery District** (north of downtown off U.S. 61) surrounds the old Red Wing Stoneware Company factory and is now home to outlet stores, specialty shops, and galleries of local artisans.

❷ Your next stop is **Frontenac,** about 10 mi southeast of Red Wing on U.S. 61. Actually, Frontenac consists of two unincorporated communities: Old Frontenac and Frontenac Station. Old Frontenac was founded in 1839 and is a historic district. It includes the **Lakeside Hotel,** which is now part of a larger resort complex. In **Frontenac State Park** more than 200 animal species pass through during the spring and fall. In winter there's cross-country skiing on 6 mi of trails and snowmobiling on 8 mi of trails.

❸ Leaving Frontenac State Park, head 5 mi southeast on U.S. 61 into **Lake City.** The Great River Road follows the Mississippi shoreline closely here and provides panoramic views of Lake Pepin, which is actually a bulge in the river created by sediment downstream. The town's 2¹/₂-mi Riverwalk is a great place to enjoy the lake's scenery. This is the birthplace of waterskiing.

4 After you've explored Lake City, head southeast on U.S. 61 for approximately 11 mi to **Reads Landing.** It's hard to believe this was once a bustling staging area for rafts of sawmill-bound northern pine. One of the few reminders of Reads Landing's glory days is the 1870 brick schoolhouse that now houses the **Wabasha County Historical Society,** with displays of Mississippi River artifacts and Laura Ingalls Wilder memorabilia. Reads Landing also marks the northern boundary of the **Upper Mississippi River National Wildlife and Fish Refuge,** a huge, protected floodplain stretching south to Rock Island, Illinois.

5 **Wabasha** is 3 mi southeast of Reads Landing on U.S. 61. Here people boast that their home is both the oldest town in Minnesota and the setting for the movie *Grumpy Old Men* and its sequel. The **Anderson House,** built in 1856, is the oldest operating hotel in the state. Life in Wabasha is so tranquil that bald eagles build their nests along the river, sometimes within the city limits. The people at the **Eagle Watch Observatory** can help you spot the great birds. Spend the night in Wabasha.

6 Continue southeast out of Wabasha on U.S. 61 for 5 mi and you'll come to **Kellogg.** Try as you might, you'll find few signs that this was a turn-of-the-20th-century transportation hub. Among the remaining attractions is the **L.A.R.K. Toy Factory,** where woodcarvers create toys and carousel animals. **The Kellogg-Weaver Dunes Scientific and Natural Area** is home to one of the largest populations of the rare Blanding's turtle.

7 The mighty Mississippi goes in and out of view as you leave Kellogg and wind 31 mi southeast on U.S. 61 to **Winona.** Once there, your gaze will immediately rise to **Sugar**

Loaf Bluff, a huge chunk of limestone overlooking town that is reflected in **Lake Winona,** 500 feet below. More than two dozen downtown structures are listed on the National Register of Historic Places. Among them are the **Church of Saint Stanislaus Kostka** and the Egyptian Revival–style **Winona National and Savings Bank.**

❽ Leaving Winona, travel another 22 mi southeast on U.S. 61 to **La Crescent,** the self-proclaimed apple capital of Minnesota. Harvest time is a great time to follow **Apple Blossom Drive** (Route 29). From there you can enjoy a panoramic view of the Mississippi and choose from among the two dozen or so varieties of apples available at the orchards along the way.

Retrace your route along U.S. 61 to return to Red Wing.

Lake City

Hok-Si-La Municipal Park. Part of a major migratory flyway, these 160 acres (by far the city's largest park grounds) are among southeastern Minnesota's best bird-watching spots, particularly in early spring and late fall. You might see bald eagles, tundra swans, Canada geese, and Iceland gulls. Besides nature trails and a playground, the park has campsites, picnic areas, and a swimming beach. Most of the city's 500 mi of snowmobile trails, and all 40 mi of its ski trails, are part of this park. It's ½ mi northeast of downtown. | U.S. 61 | 877/525–3249 | www.lakecity.org.

McCahill Park. Playground equipment and a fishing pier are the highlights of this park. | U.S. 61 3 blocks south of U.S. 63 | 877/525–3249 | www.lakecity.org.

Ohuta Park. Playground facilities, picnic areas, and a swimming beach are all directly on the lakefront. | Lyon Ave. 3 blocks east of U.S. 61 | 877/525–3249 | www.lakecity.org.

Patton Park. One square block in size, the park has a central fountain, a quaint gazebo, and paved walking paths. | U.S. 61, 1 block south of U.S. 63 | 877/525–3249 | www.lakecity.org.

Roshen Park. Besides picnic areas for large and small groups, this park at the south end of town has tennis courts, playground equipment, and fine lake views. | U.S. 61 south end of town | 877/525–3249 | www.lakecity.org.

MINNESOTA RULES OF THE ROAD

License Requirements: To drive in Minnesota, you must be at least 16 years old and have a valid driver's license. Visitors to the state may drive in Minnesota as long as they have a valid license from their home state or country.

Right Turn on Red: Unless otherwise posted, you are permitted to make right turns on red *after* your vehicle has come to a complete stop. You must also be in the correct turn lane and your path must be clear.

Seat Belt and Helmet Laws: All drivers, front-seat passengers, and any other passengers ages 4 to 10 must wear seat belts. Children younger than four must ride in a federally approved safety seat. Motorcyclists must wear helmets.

Speed Limits: 65 mph is the speed limit on all interstate highways inside urban areas and on noninterstate freeways and expressways. The limit rises to 70 mph on interstates outside urban areas. In most other locations, the limit remains 55 mph.

For More Information: Contact the **Minnesota Department of Public Safety** | 651/282–6565.

Dining

Chickadee Cottage Tea Room & Restaurant. Continental. The traditional English cream tea is this cozy restaurant's signature. If you're looking for a full meal, the rotating European platters, creative salads, and hearty soups can be enjoyed with a variety of wines. Pick up homemade scones, muffins, or breads for the road. | 317 N. Lakeshore Dr. | 651/345–5155 or 888/321–5177 | D, V | Closed Nov.–Mar. No dinner | ¢–$

The Galley. American. Burgers and sandwiches are the mainstays at this family-style restaurant. You'll find the dining area full of locals, and the friendly, easygoing service will remind you why talking with a town's residents can make traveling so enjoyable. The breakfast is satisfying, if not memorable. | 110 E. Lyon Ave. | 651/345–9991 | AE, D, MC, V | ¢–$

Skyline on Pepin. American. With dining room windows facing Lake Pepin and the surrounding bluffs, eating at this supper club would be worth it for the view alone. However, the food *is* as good as the view. Known for its steaks and fresh seafood, the kitchen serves a surprisingly pleasing Italian menu. Locals favor the king crab legs on Friday night and the prime rib on Saturday. Definitely leave room for dessert. | 1702 N. Lakeshore Dr. | 651/345–5353 | AE, D, DC, MC, V | $–$$$

Red Wing

Cannon Valley Trail. Bikers, Rollerbladers, and hikers fill this 20-mi trail along the old Chicago Great Western railroad line, which connects Cannon Falls, Welch, and Red Wing. The main trailhead is about ½ mi east of Red Wing, off Route 52S on Route 19. Note that from April–October a "wheel pass" ($3 for a day pass or $12 for a season pass) is required for bikes and Rollerblades. | City Hall, 306 W. Mill Street, Cannon Falls | 507/263–0508 | www.cannonvalleytrail.com.

Goodhue County Historical Museum. Among the permanent exhibits are displays on local and regional history, Red Wing ceramics, and Prairie Island Native American artifacts. An extensive library, with more than 15,000 photos and 5,000 books, is used for historical and genealogical research. | 1166 Oak St. | 651/388–6024 | $5 | Tues.–Fri. 10–5, weekends 1–5.

Red Wing Pottery. The showroom of the original Red Wing Pottery factory, which opened in the late 1800s and closed in 1967, continues to sell what's left of the famous salt-glazed brown dinnerware, crocks, and jugs, as well as modern stoneware and gifts. The shop hosts local potters who work while visitors look on. | 1920 W. Main St. | 651/388–3562 or 800/228–0174 | Free | Mon.–Thurs. 8–6, Fri–Sat. 8–7, Sun. 9–5.

Soldiers Memorial Park–East End Recreation Area. The park has hiking trails, picnic areas, easy-to-explore caves, and a spectacular view. | E. 7th St., 1 mi south of downtown | 800/498–3444 | Daily.

Dining

Eagles Nest Coffee House. Café. Fresh baked muffins, cookies, and cinnamon rolls make it hard to remember this coffee shop also serves hearty breakfasts and sandwiches at lunchtime. The café closes at 5 PM on weekdays and 6 PM on weekends. | 314 Main St. | 651/388–1280 | No credit cards | No dinner | ¢–$

Liberty's. Continental. Over the years, this 1872 corner building has served as a saloon, shoe store, clothing store, pool hall, and (legend has it) a speakeasy and house of ill repute. Today, the kitchen serves three meals a day; a dinner special is slow-cooked prime rib au jus with horseradish sauce. There's also a Sunday brunch. | 303 W. 3rd St. | 651/388–8877 | AE, D, DC, MC, V | $–$$

Port of Red Wing. Contemporary. Forest green tablecloths, exposed brick, and dark-stained furniture accent this dining room in the downtown St. James Hotel. The menu changes seasonally, but summer dishes might include roasted rack of lamb with garlic-whipped potatoes and bourbon-rhubarb glaze, or Creole-style chicken with onions, peppers, and mushrooms in a spiced, red-wine tomato sauce. | 406 Main St. | 651/388–2846 or 800/252–1875 | AE, D, DC, MC, V | No lunch | $$–$$$

Staghead. Contemporary. Exposed brick walls, oak tables, and a pressed-tin ceiling are complemented by historic maps and paintings of Red Wing. Specialties include fresh fish, beef tenderloin, free-range chicken, and a grilled pork tenderloin with applewood-smoked bacon and sun-dried cherries in a sage demi-glaze. Thursday is all-Italian night. | 219 Bush St. | 651/388–6581 | D, MC, V | Closed Sun. No dinner Mon. | $–$$$

Wabasha

Eagle Watch. Wabasha's eagle population soars during fall and spring migrations, and this Audubon group is dedicated to fostering environmental stewardship and celebrating eagles. You can visit the eagle observation deck on the Mississippi River in downtown Wabasha, where volunteers explain eagle activity. | 152 Main St. | www.eaglewatch.org.

Historic Commercial District. Downtown Wabasha is listed on the National Register of Historic Places. Visit the city library for information on walking tours or to see a slide show. | 168 Alleghany Ave. | 651/565–3927.

Dining

Grandma Anderson's Dutch Kitchen. American. Fresh homemade breads, chicken noodle soup, baked raisin beans, stuffed beef rolls, and apple brandy pie are served family-style in a relaxed atmosphere. The Sunday breakfast buffet has a good variety of eggs, meats, fruits, and breads. | 333 W. Main St. | 651/565–4524 or 800/535–5467 | AE, D, MC, V | $–$$

Papa Tronnio's. American. This eatery, in the local bowling alley, serves up generous portions of roasted chicken, spaghetti, and shrimp. Pizzas and burgers are also available—if you're feeling adventurous, try the Reuben pizza. Plus, the extensive appetizer menu shouldn't be overlooked. | 218 2nd St. W | 651/565–3911 | MC, V | ¢–$$

★ **Slippery's.** American. Originally just a shack for beer, bait, and burgers, Slippery's was made famous by the movies *Grumpy Old Men* and *Grumpier Old Men*. The existing building dates back to 1979 when the shack burned down, and Slippery and his wife, Gladys, rebuilt it as a resort, with boat rentals and a gas dock. The menu is extensive and, in honor of the "Grumpy" movies, includes such items as "morons chicken" and the "putz burger." | 10 Church Ave. | 651/565–4748 | AE, D, MC, V | $–$$

Lodging

Bridgewaters B & B. This 1903 inn, one block off the Mississippi River, has a wraparound porch with wicker seating. The rooms, named for local bridges, have such nice touches as spoon-carved headboards; some have hot tubs or fireplaces. No smoking. | 136 Bridge Ave., 55981 | 651/565–4208 | www.bridgewatersbandb.com | 5 rooms (3 with private bath) | MC, V | CP | $–$$

Coffee Mill Inn & Suites. The Coffee Mill Inn is on 2 secluded acres at the base of Coffee Mill Bluff. Standard rooms have two double beds; four theme rooms, including "Grumpy Old Men" and "Bluff Country," have fireplaces, VCRs, and hot tubs. One spacious suite, sleeping eight, offers two baths, a deck, and a full kitchen. Cable TV, some pets allowed. | 50 Coulee Way (Rte. 60 just west of U.S. 61), 55981 | 651/565–4561 or 877/775–1366 | www.coffeemillinn.com | 16 rooms, 4 suites | AE, D, MC, V | CP | $–$$

Eagles on the River B&B. This B&B overlooks the Mississippi River, $^3/_4$ mi southeast of town. All rooms have CD players and CDs; some also have fireplaces and whirlpool tubs. Some in-room hot tubs. | 1000 E. Marina Dr., 55981 | 651/565–3417 or 800/684–6813 | www.eaglesontheriver.com | 4 rooms | AE, D, MC, V | CP | $$–$$$

Winona

Julius C. Wilkie Steamboat Center. A museum and a collection of miniature steamboats are aboard this full-size steamboat replica. It's at Levee Park, between Walnut and Johnson Streets on the Mississippi River. | 507/454–1254 | $2.50 | June–Labor Day, Wed.–Sun. 10–4.

Prairie Island Park and Nature Trail. Half of this municipal park is maintained in near-pristine condition, and has a 1-mi interpretive nature trail that stops by an enclosed deer park, a floodplain forest, and an observation deck overlooking a Mississippi River backwater slough. Also in the park are a visitor center, boat launches, picnic and camping areas, and playgrounds. | 1120 Curry Island Rd. | 507/452–8550 | Daily.

Upper Mississippi River National Wildlife and Fish Refuge. Extending 261 mi along the Mississippi River, from the Chippewa River in Wisconsin almost to Rock Island, Illinois, this is the longest wildlife refuge in the continental United States, providing a habitat for plants, fish, migratory birds, and other animals. | 51 E. 4th St. | 507/452–4232 | http:// midwest.fws.gov/uppermississippiriver/ | Free | Daily.

Winona County Historical Society Museum. In a former armory, the museum has extensive historical archives, plus exhibits on Native Americans, logging and lumbering, steamboats, transportation, and pioneer life. | 160 Johnson St. | 507/454–2723 | www. winona.msus.edu/historicalsociety | $3 | Weekdays 9–5, weekends noon–4.

    Bunnell House. Maintained by the Historical Society, Bunnell House is an example of rural Gothic architecture. It's built of northern white pine and contains furniture and objects from the mid to late 1800s. Guides walk you through three floors of pioneer life, describing the era when Native American canoes gave way to steamboats and game-trails became roads and highways for Euro-Americans. Bunnell House is 5 mi downriver from Winona, off U.S. 61, in Homer. | 507/452–7575 | www.winona. msus.edu/historicalsociety/sites/bunnell.asp | $3 | Memorial Day–Labor Day, Wed.–Fri. noon–5, Sat. 10–5, Sun. 1–5.

Dining

Beier's Family Food and Cocktails. American. On the west end of town, this casual spot serves breakfast until 3 PM and has a daily soup and salad bar, plus a popular prime rib sandwich. On Friday night, stop in for a reasonably priced all-you-can-eat buffet. | 405 Cottonwood Rd. (U.S. 61 and U.S. 14) | 507/452–3390 | MC, V | $–$$

Winona Steak House. Steak. Whether you order chicken, seafood, or beef—try the New York strip or rib eye—you will leave this steak house satisfied, both with the food and the reasonable tab. If you aren't in the mood for meat, fill up on the plentiful salad bar. Breakfast is served. | 3480 Service Dr. | 507/452–3968 | MC, V | $–$$

MISSOURI

MISSOURI CAVES
FROM HANNIBAL TO BRANSON

Distance: 275 mi   Time: 2–4 days
Overnight Breaks: Camdenton, Branson

Jesse James used Missouri's caves for hiding stolen treasure. More recently, some young couples have chosen to marry under their dripping stalactites. But even if you don't have such dramatic plans you shouldn't overlook Missouri's 5,000 caves.

Missouri's caves are accessible by foot, boat, or car. Some caves offer true wilderness experiences, while others have been developed for tourism, or as storage facilities, office space, and even restaurants and schools. When visiting any cave, remember to bring a light jacket, a pair of pants to change into if necessary, and your most comfortable shoes. The average temperature of the caves is a constant 55°F.

❶ The first cave to open for public tours was the **Mark Twain Cave** in 1886. Tom Sawyer and Becky Thatcher were lost in this cave, which is now a National Historic Landmark. "No man knew the cave; that was an impossible thing. Most of the young men knew a portion of it, and it was not customary to venture beyond the known portion. Tom Sawyer knew as much of the cave as anyone," Twain wrote. An experienced guide will escort you on a one-hour tour with points of interest mentioned in Twain's writings. Walkways are level and smooth, and there are no steps.

While in **Hannibal,** also visit **Cameron Cave.** Cameron is Missouri's newest cave, first discovered in 1925 and opened to the public in 1976. The tour lasts 1¼ hours, and you might be given a lantern to carry while exploring.

❷ Many consider **Rock Bridge State Park,** about 9 mi south of Columbia, to be the most picturesque in the state because of the two caves and many karst features. Call in advance for spelunking tours or a visit to one of the bat caves, where Indiana bats make their home.

❸ While vacationing at the Lake of the Ozarks, thousands of boaters choose to visit **Bridal Cave** in their boats. If you don't have aquatic transportation, you can use the footpath taken by the Osage Indians and see a wedding chapel, Mystery Lake, and massive onyx formations. Don't be surprised if you happen upon a wedding in progress. A

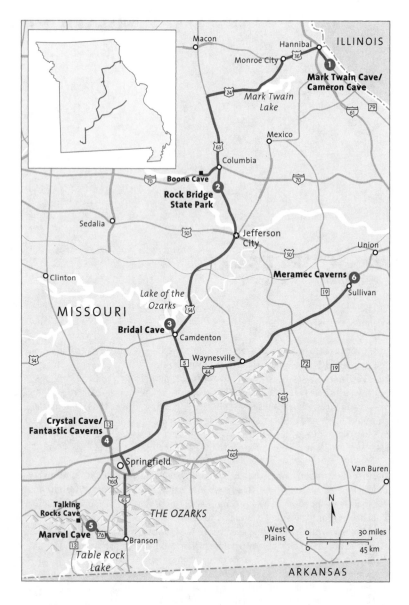

hundred or more are held here each year and uninvited guests are welcomed and expected. Bridal Cave contains more onyx formations per square foot than any other show cave. Spend the night in **Camdenton**, 2 mi south of Bridal Cave.

❹ The Springfield area has two worthy caves. **Crystal Cave** is renowned for Indian symbols and fossils. It's been open to the public for more than 100 years, but the owners have worked hard to keep the cave looking as natural as possible. Although some lighting has been added, the one-hour tour is mostly flashlight and lantern lit.

Fantastic Caverns is a 50-minute jeep tour that follows the route cut by rivers. Lower levels not accessible to visitors are home to such creatures as the Ozark cavefish, bristly cave crayfish, and grotto salamander, all of which are blind after count-less generations of living in darkness. A hydrologist explains these and other facts.

❺ **Marvel Cave** is a part of Branson's Silver Dollar City theme park, and is Missouri's deepest cave at more than 500 feet. The Cathedral Room is 20 stories high, but you don't have to walk back to the top—a tram car will take you. This cave is a National Historic Landmark.

Silver Dollar City also once held claim to **Talking Rocks Cavern,** but after a failed attempt to jazz it up with loudspeakers and echo effects, the cave reverted to private ownership. It's a cave for walkers, however—265 steps up and 265 steps down. There's a beautiful 400-acre nature area aboveground. And if you're afraid of bats, Talking Rocks is one of the few caves devoid of the flying creatures.

❻ To return to Hannibal, retrace your steps north on U.S. 65 to I–44 and travel north-east to Sullivan and a final stop at the **Meramec Caverns,** the first major cave discovery in the state and a hideout for the Jesse James gang. Continue on I–44 into St. Louis, following U.S. 61 back to Hannibal.

Branson

Baldknobbers Hillbilly Jamboree. Comedy, gospel, and country music abound at this popular spectacle, the first of the many shows in Branson. | 2835 W. Rte. 76 | 417/334–4528 | www.baldknobbers.com | $21 | Mar.–mid-Dec., Mon.–Sat.

Branson Scenic Railway. A restored depot is the launching point for a railroad ride through the Ozark Mountains. | 206 E. Main St. | 417/334–6110 or 800/287–2462 | www.bransontrain.com | $19 | Mid-Mar.–Dec., Mon.–Sat. 9, 11:30, and 2; June–July and Oct., also at 5.

Silver Dollar City. The 1880s-style park 5 mi west of Branson on Route 76 offers train and wagon rides, water rides, hands-on crafts, and music shows. | Rte. 76, 388 Indian Point Rd. | 417/338–2611 or 800/475–9370 | www.silverdollarcity.com | $37 | Apr.–May,

MISSOURI RULES OF THE ROAD

License Requirements: To drive in Missouri, you must be at least 16 years old and have a valid driver's license.

Right Turn on Red: You may turn right on red anywhere in the state, *after* a full and complete stop, unless otherwise posted.

Seat Belt and Helmet Laws: Missouri requires all front-seat occupants in cars and persons under 18 years of age operating or riding in a truck to wear safety belts. Children ages 4 to 16 must be secured in a safety belt. All kids under age 4 must be in a child safety seat. Missouri does not require motorcycle and bicycle riders to wear a helmet.

Speed Limits: The speed limit on most Missouri interstates is 70 mph, except where posted in and around large cities. The speed limit on state highways is 65 mph, except where posted. Be sure to check speed limit signs carefully.

For More Information: Contact the **State Department of Motor Vehicles** | 573/526–3669 | www.dor.mo.gov/mvdl/.

Tues.–Sun. 9–7; June–Aug., daily 9–7; Sept.–Oct., Tues.–Sun. 9:30–6; Nov.–Dec., Wed.–Sun. 1–10.

Missouri's deepest cave, **Marvel Cave,** is within Silver Dollar City. Admission to the cave is included in park admission.

Table Rock Dam and Lake. On the main stream of the White River, about 6 mi southwest of Branson, the dam was built as part of an effort to generate electricity, decrease flooding, and provide recreation opportunities. Construction was completed in 1958 at a cost of $66 million. | 5272 Rte. 165 | 417/334–4101 | www.tablerocklake.org | Visitor center: Apr.–Oct., daily 9–5; Mar., Nov.–Dec., weekends 9–5. Tours: Apr.–Oct., daily hourly except noon; Mar., Nov.–Dec., weekends hourly except noon.

Talking Rocks Cavern. Guided tours through this cave, considered one of Missouri's most beautiful, reveal the unusual auditory phenomenon that inspired its name. | Rte. 13, ¹/₂ mi south of Rte. 76 | 417/272–3366 | www.talkingrockscavern.com | $14 | Feb.–Dec., daily 9:30–6.

Dining

Buckingham's Restaurant and Oasis. American. Buckingham's provides the fanciest dining in this part of the state, with steak, seafood, and pasta dominating the menu. The staff prepares some dishes table-side. The restaurant's big-game motif includes a mural of safari animals and a hand-carved cherrywood bar in the lounge. | 2820 W. Rte. 76 | 417/337–7777 | AE, D, DC, MC, V | Closed Sun. | $$$

Contrary Mary's. American. Bright and airy, this restaurant resembles a country garden, right down to the live plants. It serves freshly prepared home-style food, including chicken-fried steak, baked ham, pork chops, pasta, and fresh-baked desserts. | 3292 Shepherd of the Hills Expressway | 417/334–7700 | AE, D, MC, V | $

Gwen's Home Cannery. American. Home-canned goods decorate the walls and shelves of this family-friendly restaurant a few blocks from Branson's theaters. Specialties include beef dishes and a marinated chicken breast served with mushrooms, peppers, onions, and mozzarella cheese. | 1810 W. Rte. 76 | 417/334–5756 | No credit cards | Closed late Dec.–Mar. No dinner Sun. | $–$$

Sadie's Sideboard and Smokehouse. American. Get some great barbecue or sample the ample buffet (available for breakfast, lunch, and dinner) at this spacious and friendly family restaurant. | 2230 W. Rte. 76 | 417/334–3619 | AE, D, MC, V | Closed mid-Dec.–Feb. | $

Lodging

Best Western Mountain Oak Lodge. A free shuttle to the Silver Dollar City amusement park runs from this hotel, which is ¹/₂ mi away from the site. It's also convenient to other area attractions. Rooms have views of the Ozark hills, and are away from the traffic and congestion of the Branson strip. Café, room service, cable TV, tennis court, indoor pool, wading pool, hot tub, video game room, laundry facilities, business services, meeting rooms. | 8514 Rte. 76, Branson West, 65737 | 417/338–2141 or 800/868–6625 | fax 417/338–8320 | www.bestwestern.com | 146 rooms | AE, D, DC, MC, V | Closed Jan.–Feb. | CP | $

Days Inn. In the heart of Branson's Theater District, this chain motel is within 1 mi of 15 theaters and is convenient to area shopping, dining, and attractions. Cable TV, pool, wading pool, hot tub, playground, business services, some pets allowed (fee). | 3524 Keeter St., 65616 | 417/334–5544 or 800/329–7466 | fax 417/334–2935 | www.daysinn.com | 425 rooms | AE, D, DC, MC, V | CP | $$

Lodge of the Ozarks. This lodge aims for an upscale English feel, with wood trim and decorative tile throughout. Restaurant, snack bar, some refrigerators, cable TV, pool, hair salon, hot tub, massage, bar, video game room, business services. | 3431 W. Rte. 76, 65616 | 417/334–7535 or 800/213–2584 | fax 417/334–6861 | www.lodgeoftheozarks.com | 190 rooms | AE, D, MC, V | CP | $–$$

Radisson. The in-house veteran's memorial at this upscale chain is a popular attraction, even for those who are not guests at the hotel. More than 500 feet of wall space is dedicated to those who served in the armed services since World War I. You can easily walk from the hotel to several theaters including the Grand Palace and the Andy Williams Moon River Theatre. Restaurant, in-room data ports, in-room safes, some in-room hot tubs, cable TV with video games, 2 pools, gym, hot tub, sauna, bar, concierge, business services, meeting rooms. | 120 Wildwood Dr. S., 65616 | 417/335–5767 or 888/566–5290 | fax 417/335–7979 | 427 rooms, 27 suites | AE, D, DC, MC, V | $$

Southern Oaks Inn. This motor inn, across from the Shoji Tabuchi Theater and close by the IMAX theater, prides itself on its friendly staff. Rooms are spacious with king- or queen- size beds; you have a choice of interior or exterior corridor entry. Some in-room hot tubs, some refrigerators, cable TV, 2 pools (1 indoors), hot tub, laundry facilities, business services. | 3295 Shepherd of the Hills Expressway, 65616 | 417/335–8108 or 800/324–8752 | fax 417/335–8861 | www.southernoaksinn.com | 147 rooms | AE, D, MC, V | CP | $

Camdenton

Bridal Cave. Weddings are conducted year-round in this cave 2 mi north of town. Another area shows a boat sunken in an underground pool. | Lake Rd. 5-88 | 573/346–2676 | www.bridalcave.com | $12 | Daily 9–6.

Camden County Museum. A small collection focusing on the lives of early county residents is in a building that once served as the Linn Creek School. The town of Linn Creek was relocated when the Bagley Dam was built. Classrooms contain themed exhibits on weaving, vintage and antique household furnishings, tools, and banking. The historical society hosts five dinner theaters here throughout the year. | N. U.S. 54 at Rte. V., Linn Creek | 573/346–7191 | Free | Apr.–Oct., weekdays 10–4.

Ha Ha Tonka State Park. The remains of a castle built in 1905, a natural bridge, springs, and caves invite exploration in this 2,993-acre park on limestone bluffs overlooking the Lake of the Ozarks. There are also a 7-mi hiking trail, two docks, and fishing facilities. Take U.S. 54 to Route D to reach the park. | Rte. D | 573/346–2986 | www.mostateparks.com/hahatonka.htm | Free | Daily 8–dusk.

Pomme de Terre State Park. Camp, swim, hike, or fish for muskie in one of the many coves of Pomme de Terre Lake. Reach the park by taking Route 64 9 mi to Route 64B. | Pittsburg | 417/852–4291 | www.mostateparks.com/pommedeterre.htm | Free | Daily dawn–dusk.

Dining

Baron's Bistro. American. Baron's specializes in American and European cuisine. Prime rib, steaks, and seafood top the menu, and some dishes are prepared table-side. | 8 Bridal Cave Rd. | 573/346–6369 | AE, DC, MC, V | Closed Tues.–Wed. No lunch | $$

Lodging

Castleview Bed and Breakfast. Four-poster beds and marble-top tables accent this Victorian-style clapboard home next to the Ha Ha Tonka State Park. All rooms have private baths. Room TVs; no kids under 12. | Rte. D, 65020 | 573/346–9818 or 877/346–9818 | www.lakelinks.com/castleview | 4 rooms | MC, V | BP | $

Old Kinderhook Resort. The lake's only gated community, this 638-acre resort has an 18-hole Tom Weiskopf golf course as well as lake access. The spacious cottages have decks overlooking the golf course and cozy rattan furniture for a comfortable evening before the fireplace. 2 restaurants, in-room data ports, some in-room hot tubs, cable TV, 18-hole golf course, pro shop, tennis court, pool, exercise equipment, dock, boating, fishing, bar, recreation room, concierge. | 5480 Lake Rd. | 573/346–3952 or 888/346–4949 Ext. 402 | fax 573/346–3958 | www.oldkinderhook.com | 38 cottages | AE, D, MC, V | $$

Columbia

Flat Branch Park. The statewide Katy Trail may be accessed via the 8.9 mi spur trail that starts at this 1-acre downtown city park. | 4th and Cherry Sts. | 573/874–7460 | www.gocolumbiamo.com/parksandrec/parks/ | Daily dawn–dusk.

Nifong Park. The park includes walking trails, the 1855 Maple Wood home, a community theater, and a fine arts gallery operated by the Boone County Historical Society in conjunction with the city parks department. The Heritage Festival each September draws thousands to this park. | Off U.S. 63 at Nifong Blvd. and Ponderosa Dr. | 573/874–7460 or 573/443–8936 | www.gocolumbiamo.com/parksandrec/parks/ | Museum $2 | Park daily dawn–dusk. Museum Apr.–Oct. daily 1–5, Nov.–Mar. Fri.–Sun. and Wed. 1–4.

Rock Bridge Memorial State Park. Spelunking expeditions through the Devil's Icebox and Connor's Cave are a big attraction at this 2,273-acre state park. Fifteen miles of trails cross over and through a number of geological features. | 7 mi south of Columbia on U.S. 63 | 573/449–7402 | www.mostateparks.com/rockbridge.htm | Free | Daily dawn–dusk.

Shelter Gardens. Roses, cacti, and conifers are among the 15,000 annuals and perennials in this 6-acre public garden on the grounds of Shelter Insurance Company. Included is a sensory garden with signage in Braille, and a one-room schoolhouse. It's a popular choice for weddings and is the site of free summer concerts. | 1817 W. Broadway | 573/214–4715 | www.shelterinsurance.com | Free | Daily dawn–dusk.

Dining

Boone Tavern. Continental. This tavern in the heart of town is decorated with historical photos of Columbia. Try the chicken cordon bleu or the steak. There's open-air dining in a gazebo. There's also a Sunday brunch. | 811 E. Walnut St. | 573/442–5123 | AE, D, DC, MC, V | $–$$

Flat Branch Pub and Brewing. American/Casual. Sample many different beers, pizzas, and such specialties as chicken *fuente* (chicken, onions, and peppers rolled in a flour tortilla with a spicy enchilada sauce, cheddar and jack cheese, olives, and scallions). Kid's menu available. | 115 S. 5th St. | 573/499–0400 | AE, D, DC, MC, V | ¢–$

Trattoria Strada Nova. Italian. This downtown eatery is popular with the business crowd, who come for the northern Italian cuisine of seafood and steaks. The wine list is impressive. | 21 N. 9th St. | 573/442–8992 | AE, D, DC, MC, V | Closed Sun. | $$

Hannibal Cameron Cave. The tours of this 9-acre cave are lantern-lit in order to best preserve the natural geological conditions of the 6 mi of interconnecting mazes. | Rte. 79 | 573/221–1656 or 800/527–0304 | www.marktwaincave.com/history | $14 | Early July–Labor Day, daily 8–8; Labor Day–early Nov., daily 9–5; early Nov.–early July, daily 9–4.

Mark Twain Cave. This cave, south of Hannibal, is where Tom and Becky were lost, and where Injun Joe hid his treasure in the fictional stories by Mark Twain. The guided tour lasts one hour. | Rte. 79 | 573/221–1656 or 800/527–0304 | www.marktwaincave.com | $12 | Apr.–May and Labor Day–early Nov., daily 9–6; June–Labor Day, daily 8–8; Nov.–Apr., daily 9–4.

Mark Twain Museum and Boyhood Home. The original two-story home in which Samuel Clemens spent much of his childhood is at the center of this site, which also includes Clemens's father's law office and other sites frequented by the author while growing up here. | 208 Hill St. | 573/221–9010 | www.laurai.com | $6 | June–Aug., daily 8–6; Mar., Mon.–Sat. 9–4, Sun. noon–4; May, daily 8–5; Apr., Sept.–Oct., daily 9–5.

Springfield

Crystal Cave. A great variety of formations, including black stalactites and crystals, await you at this cave, which occasionally holds tours (about 90 minutes) lit by flashlights and lanterns. | 7225 N. Crystal Cave La. | 417/833–9599 | www.wcnet.net/adc/crystal.htm | $9 | Daily 9–1:15.

Fantastic Caverns. This hour-long tour via jeep takes you along the path of an ancient underground river. | 4872 N. Farm Rd. 125 | 417/833–2010 | www.fantasticcaverns.com | $16.50 | May–Oct., daily 8–6.

Laura Ingalls Wilder–Rose Wilder Lane Museum and Home. East of Springfield in nearby Mansfield, this house is where the *Little House* books were written and where Laura, Almonzo, and Rose made their home. | 3068 Rte. A, Mansfield | 417/924–3626 or 877/924–7126 | www.lauraingallswilderhome.com | $8 | Mar.–Oct., Mon.–Sat. 9–5, Sun. 12:30–5:30.

Dining

Aunt Martha's Pancake House. American. Pancakes are always available at this Springfield institution that has been serving stacks since 1964. Burgers, chicken-fried steak, and twice-baked potatoes round out the menu. | 1700 E. Cherokee St. | 417/881–3505 | No credit cards | Closed Mon. No dinner Sun. | ¢–$

Lambert's Cafe. Southern. Lambert's is known as the home of "throwed rolls"—the waiters actually throw the dinner rolls at you like baseballs as they walk through the dining room. Besides possibly getting clobbered in the head with a roll, you can expect hearty servings of roast beef, chicken and dumplings, fried okra, and homemade cobblers. It's also not uncommon for the staff to walk through the dining room with a huge pot of black-eyed peas or fried potatoes and put a spoonful on your plate, whether you asked for it or not. Lambert's is 5 mi south of Springfield on U.S. 65. | 1800 W. Rte. J., Ozark | 417/581–7655 | AE, D, MC, V | $

Sullivan

Meramec Caverns. A hideout of the Jesse James gang, this was the first major cave discovery in the state. At exit 230, follow the signs as you go south on Route W. | I–44 West, Exit 230, Stanton | 573/468–3166 or 800/676–6105 | www.americascave.com | $14 | Nov.–Jan., daily 9–4; Mar. and Oct., daily 9–5; Apr. and Sept., daily 9–6; May–June, daily 9–7; July–Labor Day, daily 8:30–7:30.

Meramec State Park. More than 40 caves and many miles of river await canoers and spelunkers in this 6,896-acre park. The visitor center has a large aquarium filled with fish from the Meramec River. | 2800 S. Rte. 185 (Exit 226 off I–44), Sullivan | 573/468–8155 | www.mostateparks.com/meramec.htm | Daily.

Dining

Country Market Restaurant. American. Order from the menu or sample the buffet at this 24-hour diner off I–44. The fried chicken is particularly popular, but steaks, pasta, and sandwiches are also available. Breakfast is available all day. | 825 N. Loop Dr. | 573/860–8900 | AE, D, MC, V | $

Du Kum In. American. The lacy linen window curtains and wall-mounted plate collection give this restaurant a country feel, as do the fried chicken and homemade pies. | 101 Grande Center | 573/468–6114 | MC, V | Closed Mon.–Tues. | ¢–$

Homer's Bar-B-Que. Barbecue. Pork steaks are the specialty at Homer's, a small restaurant with a rustic interior. Ribs, chicken, and beef brisket are also available. | 693 Fisher Dr. | 573/468–4393 | No credit cards | Closed Sun.–Wed. | $

MONTANA

BEARTOOTH HIGHWAY
A DRIVE ALONG THE ROOF OF THE ROCKIES

Distance: 69 mi   Time: 3 hours
Overnight Break: Cooke City or Red Lodge

With mountain switchbacks and high-altitude views of Montana and Wyoming's snowcapped peaks, giant glaciers, and sprawling valleys with deep-blue alpine lakes, the Beartooth Highway ranks among North America's premier scenic byways. The route is impassable and closed to traffic for much of the year, open only from approximately June to October (depending on weather conditions).

Driving from east to west means you'll have a long, steep uphill climb to the 10,970-ft summit of Beartooth Pass, with narrow switchbacks that can be troublesome for large motor homes and travel trailers, but you'll save your brakes. To avoid glare, you may want to drive east to west in the morning and west to east in the afternoon. The towns of Red Lodge and Cooke City, at the east and west starting points respectively, have full services, including lodging, gasoline, and food. The Beartooth Highway passes 10 national forest campgrounds with picnic tables, fire grates, drinking water, and toilets, but no hookups. Daytime summer temperatures generally average in the 70s, but sudden snowstorms have been reported in every month of the year.

Montana's snowy winters can make for hazardous driving, when sudden storms commonly block highways. You should prepare for the unexpected with winter survival kits of snow tires or chains, a shovel and window scraper, flares or a reflector, a blanket or sleeping bag, a first-aid kit, sand, gravel or traction mats, a flashlight with extra batteries, matches, a lighter and candles, paper, nonperishable foods, and a tow chain or rope.

Even when the highway is formally closed to automobiles, snowmobilers may travel the route and enjoy a spectacular winter wonderland.

❶ **Red Lodge** (U.S. 212 and Route 78) is a historic mining town in Rock Creek Valley at the base of the Beartooth Mountains. In winter it is a magnet for skiers; in summer you can hike, bike, golf, fish, and just look around. The **Beartooth Nature Center** features native North American animals. Directly out of Red Lodge, the Beartooth Highway enters Custer National Forest, one of the three national forests it bisects

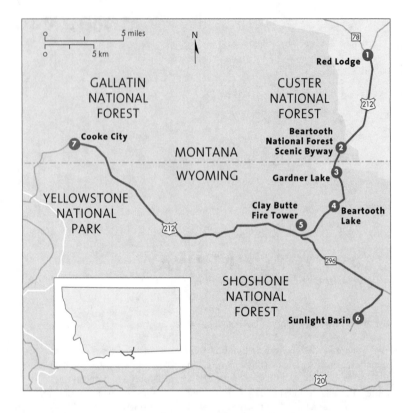

as it skirts the Montana–Wyoming border adjacent to the eastern edge of Yellowstone National Park; the others are the Gallatin and Shoshone national forests.

❷ Along **Beartooth National Forest Scenic Byway** you get incredible vistas to the south and west—snowcapped peaks, glaciers and alpine lakes, colorful wildflowers, and far-reaching plateaus. Tiny patches of snow and ice remain up here much of the year, often tinted pink from algae. Winter weather can last into July.

❸ Continuing southwest on U.S. 212, you'll come to the **Gardner Lake** parking lot, a trailhead for the Beartooth Loop National Recreation Trail, which traverses 10 mi of rolling alpine landscape typically found in the Arctic. Note how plants have adapted to this severe climate. View Sawtooth Mountain to the southwest; across the valley to the north, a black fang rock formation known locally as the Bear's Tooth juts up from the surrounding forest.

❹ Further along on U.S. 212 (approximately 7 mi west of Beartooth Pass), **Beartooth Lake** is at the base of Beartooth Butte. Summer fishermen like its 21-site campground and boat launch. You'll find lots of good hiking and can reach the 100-foot Beartooth Falls on an easy ½-mi trail along a creek.

❺ **Clay Butte Fire Tower** is a beautiful 3-mi detour from U.S. 212. Its visitor information center is open in summer, and from the top of the tower you get a spectacular view of Granite Peak (Montana's highest at 12,799 feet) to the northwest, the North Absaroka Wilderness and Yellowstone National Park to the west, the Clarks

Fork Valley and Absaroka Mountains to the southwest, and the Bighorn Mountains to the east.

6 West of Beartooth Pass you leave the alpine vegetation and descend through a forest of spruce, fir, and lodgepole pine mixed with stands of aspen. To the south and west is the North Absaroka Wilderness; with the Beartooth Wilderness it blankets nearly a million acres. At the junction with Route 296 (also known as Chief Joseph Scenic Highway) you can take a side trip into the remote **Sunlight Basin** to sightsee, camp, hike, and fish. To reach the basin, travel 20 mi southeast on Route 296, then west on the county road for 15 mi.

7 Head back to the intersection of Route 296 and U.S. 212 and proceed west to **Cooke City** on the Montana–Wyoming border. Along the way you'll skirt the Clarks Fork of the Yellowstone River, climb over the summit of Colter Pass, then travel through some of the burn areas from raging 1988 fires. Among the charred snags you can see forest regrowth, birds, and, at times, grizzly and black bears, bighorn sheep, mountain goats, moose, and marmots.

Cooke City, a mining town with a colorful past is now a friendly, small resort community where you can hike, horseback ride, fish, climb, and—in winter—ski. After Cooke City (where you can spend the night if you're inspired to linger), the byway drops through Silver Gate and ends at the Northeast Gate to Yellowstone National Park.

Cooke City

Dining
Grizzly Pad. American/Casual. This small diner is a favorite with locals. It features homemade biscuits and gravy, homemade pies, chili, and the best milk shakes in town. Breakfast is available and you can get picnic lunches to go. | 315 Main St. | 406/838–2161 | MC, V | $

MONTANA RULES OF THE ROAD

License Requirements: Montana recognizes valid driver's licenses from other states and countries. The minimum driving age is 15 with driver training and 16 without.

Right Turn on Red: Right turns on red are allowed, unless otherwise posted.

Seat Belt and Helmet Laws: The driver and all passengers in motor vehicles on Montana roadways must wear seat belts. Law-enforcement officers will not pull you over if you're not wearing a seat belt, but they will ticket you if you commit other infractions while unbelted. Children two and younger must be in a federally approved child-restraint device. Children ages two to four who weigh no more than 40 pounds must also be secured in a child-restraint device. All motorcycle riders under 18 years of age must wear a helmet in Montana. Those over 18 may choose whether or not to wear a helmet.

Speed Limits: The maximum speed on the state's interstate highways is 75 mph; non-interstate roadway limits are 70 mph daytime and 65 mph at night. Trucks over one-ton capacity have interstate speed limits of 65 mph and non-interstate limits of 60 mph daytime and 55 mph at night.

For More Information: Contact the **Montana Highway Patrol** | 406/444–3780.

Miner's Saloon. American/Casual. You'll find nothing fancier than consistently good food here: pizza, sandwiches, salads, and pasta. Try the fish tacos, the steak sandwich, and the buffalo burgers. This is a good place for families. | U.S. 212 | 406/838–2214 | No credit cards | $

Lodging

Alpine Motel. A variety of clean, updated rooms and two apartment-size, two-bedroom suites are available. The suites have full kitchens. Some kitchens, laundry facilities, some pets allowed; no a/c, no room phones, no smoking. | Main St., 59020 | 406/838–2262 or 888/838–1190 | http://ccalpinemotel.com | 25 rooms, 2 suites | AE, D, MC, V | $

High Country Motel. Some of the rooms in this Beartooth mountains motel have kitchens and fireplaces. Some refrigerators, some pets allowed; no a/c, no room phones. | U.S. 212, 59020 | 406/838–2272 | 15 rooms, 4 kitchenettes | AE, D, MC, V | $

Skyline Lodge Bed and Breakfast Guest Ranch. This three-story lodge has spacious, bright rooms, with shiny hardwood floors and balconies from which you can gaze at mountain grandeur. The hunting theme is thankfully understated, save for some mounted antlers in the communal living room. Early check-in (1 PM) gives you plenty of time to go horse-back riding, fishing, or snowmobiling. The lodge is 3 mi east of Cooke City. Hot tub, fishing, recreation room, airport shuttle, no-smoking rooms; no a/c, no room phones, no room TVs. | 737 U.S. 212, 59020 | 877/238–8885 | www.flyfishyellowstone.com/lodge.htm | 5 rooms | AE, D, MC, V | $

Red Lodge

Beartooth Nature Center. Animals that have been injured and cannot be released into the wild again live at this nonprofit center. You might see bears, elk, mountain lions, and deer, and a variety of birds. | 2nd Ave. E, in Coal Miner's Park | 406/446–1133 | www.beartoothnaturecenter.org | Mid-May–mid-Oct., daily 10–5:30; mid-Oct.–mid-May, daily 9–1, weather permitting.

Cooney Reservoir State Park. You'll find great walleye- and rainbow trout–fishing in the reservoir here. The park has a campground with 75 sites, hiking trails, a boat ramp, and a swimming beach. Note that pets are restricted. To reach the park, drive 22 mi southwest of Laurel on U.S. 212, then 8 mi west of Boyd on the county road. | 406/445–2326 | www.fwp.state.mt.us | $5 per vehicle | Daily.

Custer National Forest. The forest sprawls across Montana, South Dakota, and North Dakota, and is home to Montana's highest mountain, Granite Peak, about 10 mi north of Cooke City off the northeast corner of Yellowstone National Park. | South on U.S. 212 | 406/446–2103 | www.fs.fed.us/r1/custer/ | Daily dawn–dusk.

Peaks to Plains Museum. See the family heirlooms of two lady bronco riders, the Greenough sisters, and their brother, Turk, who was married to famous fan dancer Sally Rand. Exhibits on fur trading, a Finnish kitchen, and a coal-mine replica are among the highlights. | 224 S. Broadway | 406/446–3667 | $3 | Weekdays 8–5, weekends 1–5.

Red Lodge Historic District. Built during the coal-mining boom between 1883 and 1910, Red Lodge still has many traces of its ethnic roots. Neighborhoods bear names like Finn Town, Little Italy, and "Hi Bug"—a school-yard tag invented by kids to describe where the English-speaking upper class lived. In August, the four-day Festival of Nations takes over town. | Main St. | 406/446–1718 or 888/281–0625 | Daily.

Red Lodge Mountain Ski Area. Licensed day care and 30 acres of extreme chute skiing are selling points of this facility, one of the northern Rockies' top ski areas. It also has 70 trails and groomed slopes and 60 acres of tree skiing, plus rentals and a ski school. It's on the south edge of town off U.S. 212, in Custer National Forest. | 05 Ski Run Rd. |

800/444–8977 or 406/446–2610 | www.redlodgemountain.com | Late Nov.–Apr., daily 9–4, weather permitting.

Dining

Arthur's Grill at the Pollard. American. Fresh flowers enhance this elegant spot in the beautiful 19th-century Pollard hotel. The menu varies from steaks to buffalo burgers, pasta to seafood. Arthur's has an excellent wine cellar, a good choice of microbrews, and a full bar. | 2 N. Broadway Ave. | 406/446–0001 | AE, D, MC, V | $–$$

Bridge Creek Backcountry Kitchen and Wine Bar. American/Casual. As the "backcountry" in the name implies, the Bridge Creek keeps things casual and relaxed. Dinner might feature all-natural beef or fresh seafood. An excellent lunch menu offers up sandwiches, pasta, soup, and salads. There are several good microbrews on tap and an extensive wine list. A small patio provides some outdoor seating. | 116 S. Broadway Ave. | 406/446–9900 | MC, V | $–$$

Old Piney Dell. American. You'll find heavy dishes such as Wiener schnitzel and prime rib at this Western-style restaurant in the Rock Creek Resort. This place has the best Sunday brunch deal. | Rock Creek Rd. | 406/446–1196 | AE, D, DC, MC, V | No lunch Mon.–Sat. | $–$$

Lodging

The Pollard. Buffalo Bill was here. In fact, the Pollard hosted quite a number of Wild West characters in its heyday. The 1893 hotel has been restored, keeping parts of the original lobby intact. The rooms lean more toward the "modern conveniences" side, rather than the historic, but you'll find some nice touches like sleigh beds scattered throughout. The oak-panel sitting room has a roaring fireplace, the perfect backdrop for sipping a drink and spinning yarns. Restaurant, gym, hot tub, lounge, sauna, business services; no smoking. | 2 N. Broadway Ave., 59068 | 406/446–0001 or 800/765–5273 | www.pollardhotel.com | 39 rooms | AE, D, MC, V | $–$$$

Rock Creek Resort. This resort complex is tucked into the shadow of the Beartooth mountains along beautiful Rock Creek. There are several different types of accommodations: rooms in the Beartooth Lodge are standard motel fare, and rooms in the Twin Elk are more rustic-looking, with exposed beams. There are also condos; a town house, which can accommodate up to six people; and a private cabin with a hot tub and a big stone fireplace. 2 restaurants, some kitchenettes, cable TV, indoor pool, exercise equipment, hot tub, lounge, shop, Internet, meeting rooms; no a/c, no smoking. | 4 mi south of Red Lodge | 800/667–1119 | fax 406/237–9851 | www.rockcreekresort.com | AE, D, DC, MC, V | $$–$$$

Yodeler Motel. Within walking distance of historic downtown, the Yodeler Motel has spiffy rooms, some with saunas or hot tubs. One unit has a full kitchen. In-room data ports, some kitchens, some in-room hot tubs, cable TV, hot tub, some pets allowed, no-smoking rooms. | 601 S. Broadway, 59068 | 406/446–1435 or 866/446–1435 | www.yodelermotel.com | 22 rooms | AE, D, DC, MC, V | $

BOZEMAN TRAIL
FROM LITTLE BIGHORN NATIONAL BATTLEFIELD TO BOZEMAN

Distance: 200 mi   Time: 2 days
Overnight Break: Billings

After a double dose of Bighorn in the southeast, you'll move northwest to Montana's largest city, then west to Bozeman, one of the state's most attractive communities.

Weather permitting, you can drive through the Crow and Northern Cheyenne reservations and entrances to Yellowstone National Park, skirt the bank of the Yellowstone River and the fringes of the Gallatin National Forest, climb Bozeman Pass, and descend into Gallatin Valley.

1 At the junction of I–90 and U.S. 212 near Crow Agency, **Little Bighorn Battlefield National Monument** memorializes one of the last armed efforts of the Northern Plains people to preserve their way of life. You'll learn the significance of June 25–26, 1876, when an overconfident lieutenant colonel named George A. Custer and his 7th Cavalry came face to face with the fiercest warriors of the Sioux, Cheyenne, and Arapaho. Programs, films, tours, and interpretive exhibits help paint the picture.

2 **Bighorn Canyon National Recreation Area** has stunning canyon scenery and trails where you can hike, boat, fish, and camp. On Route 313 south of Hardin, 525-foot-high **Yellowtail Dam** creates picturesque, 71-mi-long **Bighorn Lake,** surrounded by the canyon's spectacular limestone walls. Below the dam, the **Bighorn River** is one of Montana's best year-round trout streams.

3 In **Hardin** you'll find a full range of visitor services, restored buildings, picnic areas, and shops. Off I–90 at Exit 497 is the Big Horn County Historical Museum and Visitor Information Center for regional history and interpretation.

4 **Billings** is eastern Montana's cultural, commercial, and educational center, with many museums, art galleries, theaters, colleges, and stores. The Visitor Center and Cattle Drive Monument on South 27th Street near I–90 commemorate Montana's centennial cattle drive. Spend the night in Billings.

5 **Pompeys Pillar National Historic Landmark** is 28 mi east of Billings off I–94. In 1806, Captain William Clark carved his name on the sandstone butte—the only remaining physical evidence along the trail of the Lewis and Clark Expedition. In season, you can take interpretive tours along the Yellowstone River.

6 West of Billings on I–90 is **Columbus,** which is along the Yellowstone River in the foothills of the scenic Absaroka-Beartooth mountains.

7 **Big Timber** is off I–90 40 mi west of Columbus. There you get an impressive view of the Crazy Mountains, and can visit museums, galleries, antiques shops, historic sites, and the **Yellowstone River Fish Hatchery.**

8 Continue roughly 32 mi west on I–90 to **Livingston.** This is the original gateway to Yellowstone National Park; surrounded by the Gallatin National Forest and granite peaks, Livingston is built on the banks of the scenic Yellowstone River, the longest free-flowing river in the United States and one of America's top trout streams.

9 Nestled in the green cradle of the Gallatin Valley and surrounded by a half-dozen mountain ranges, **Bozeman** is a small town with big-city amenities. At the base of the Bridger Range, it is an ideal place from which to start exploring Yellowstone National Park, Big Sky, and numerous Lewis and Clark historic sites. Historic Main Street is the nucleus of the community and also the original Bozeman Trail. Walk through the campus of Montana State University or the **South Wilson Historic District,** a residential area where houses range from stately mansions to small cottages.

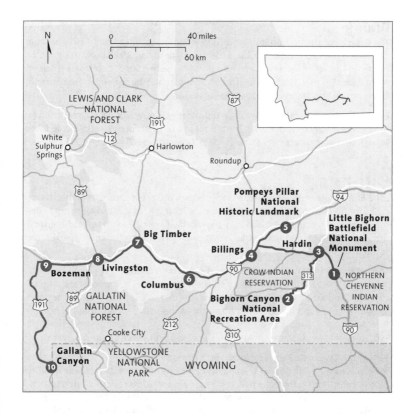

⑩ **Gallatin Canyon** is an 80-mi drive south of Bozeman on U.S. 191, following the Gallatin River as it skirts the snowcapped Spanish Peaks then enters the northwest corner of Yellowstone National Park.

Big Timber

Crazy Mountain Museum. Exhibits represent the history of Big Timber, Sweet Grass County, and the Crazy Mountains. Highlights include the Cremer Rodeo and a room dedicated to pioneers, with artifacts dating to the late 1890s. Other exhibits include a detailed miniature of Big Timber in 1907, the restored Sourdough School House, and a "stabbur"—a reconstruction of an early Norwegian grain storehouse. | Cemetery Rd., I–90 Exit 367 | 406/932–5126 | Free | Memorial Day–Labor Day, Tues.–Sun. 1–4:30 or by appointment.

Greycliff Prairie Dog Town State Park. Loved and hated by Westerners, these perky, burrowing creatures are undeniably fascinating to observe. At this large prairie-dog town, a preserved habitat, you can wander the trails for easy viewing. Watch out for snakes. | Greycliff, I–90 Exit 377 | 406/247–2940 | www.fwp.state.mt.us | May–Sept., daily dawn–dusk.

Halfmoon Park. North of town, follow Big Timber Creek into the fabled Crazy Mountains. The campground is equipped with vault toilets, picnic area, water; a public parking area makes day hikes possible. Big Timber Falls (also known as Halfmoon Falls) is an easy 1/2-mi walk from the campground. Blue Lake (good fishing) is 5 1/2 mi farther up the trail. Go 1 mi north on U.S. 191, then 12 mi west on Big Timber Canyon Road. | Big Timber Canyon Rd. | 406/932–5155 | $5 per vehicle.

Dining

The Grand. Continental. Built in 1890, this restaurant within a hotel has an elegant dark-green color scheme and antique paintings. The dining is casual, with a popular prime rib special on weekends and occasional game specials of antelope, ostrich, or buffalo. Locally raised lamb and beef are also popular, and the seafood is flown in fresh twice weekly. | 139 McLeod St. | 406/932–4459 | D, MC, V | $$–$$$

Prospector Pizza. American/Casual. Casual and inexpensive, this local favorite serves up breakfast, lunch, and dinner. Try the mesquite-smoked ribs, pizza made from scratch, and homemade pies. | 121 McLeod St. | 406/932–4846 | AE, D, MC, V | ¢–$

Billings

Lake Elmo State Park. This urban day-use park attracts visitors to picnic, swim, sailboard, and fish. A display in the Fish, Wildlife & Parks headquarters on-site provides interpretative information about the park. Take U.S. 87 north to Pemberton Lane, then drive ½ mi west. | 2300 Lake Elmo | 406/247–2940 | www.fwp.state.mt.us/parks | Free | Daily dawn–dusk.

Moss Mansion Historic House Museum. The elegant, old-world Moss Mansion offers an unusual blend of architectural styles. The rich tapestries and woodwork, original furniture, and artifacts add warmth and authenticity to this historic 1903 sandstone structure. A one-hour tour captures early turn-of-the-20th-century life as the Preston Boyd Moss family lived it. | 914 Division St. | 406/256–5100 | www.mossmansion.com | $6 | June–mid-Sept., Mon.–Sat. 9–4, Sun. 1–4; mid-Sept.–May, daily 1–3.

Pictograph Cave State Park. People who hunted woolly mammoths in the Yellowstone Valley documented their lives with paintings in caves that you can still explore. The pictographs, ¼ mi in from the park center, are almost 5,000 years old. Bring binoculars for the best view. Special workshops and events are conducted regularly. Take the Lockwood Exit off I-90. | Coburn Rd. | 406/247–2940 | www.pictographcave.org | $5 per vehicle | May–Sept., daily dawn–dusk.

Pompeys Pillar National Historic Landmark. Captain William Clark carved his name on this sandstone butte in 1806. Stop at the visitor center to inquire about interpretive tours. | 28 mi east of Billings, I–94 Exit 23, along Yellowstone River | 406/875–2233 | www.mt.blm.gov/pillarmon/ | $5 per vehicle | May–Sept., daily 8–8.

ZooMontana. The zoological and botanical gardens here specialize in northern-latitude temperate species. There's a separate children's zoo. Take Exit 443 off I–90; follow Zoo Drive to Shiloh Road and make a left. | 2100 S. Shiloh Rd. | 406/652–8100 | www.zoomontana.org | $6 | Daily 10–4.

Dining

Bruno's. Italian. Everything at Bruno's is made from scratch, the pasta included. The fresh, hot bread sticks are excellent accompaniments to every meal. A kid's menu is available. | 2558 Grand Ave. | 406/652–4416 | No credit cards | No lunch Sun. | $–$$

Golden Belle. American. Billings's most elegant restaurant is downtown in the historic Northern Hotel. Try the beef, specially aged in-house, or one of the fresh-catch specials. Reservations are essential for dinner. | 19 N. 28th St. | 406/245–2232 | AE, D, MC, V | $$$

The Granary. American. The Granary is actually in a refurbished historic flour mill. Naturally aged beef, hand-cut daily, is on the menu, along with seafood and poultry. There is an extensive list of microbrews and fine wines. Reservations are essential. | 1500 Poly Dr. | 406/259–3488 | AE, D, MC, V | $$–$$$$

Rex. American. Built in 1910 by Buffalo Bill Cody's chef, this restaurant was saved from the wrecking ball and restored in 1975. Now it's a Black Angus–certified steak house with plenty of seafood specials nightly. You can also try the Rex Patio Bar and Grill. | 2401 Montana Ave. | 406/245–7477 | AE, D, DC, MC, V | $$–$$$

Lodging

C'Mon Inn. The rooms are contemporary, spacious, and comfortable. Consider splurging on a suite with an in-room Jacuzzi. Microwaves, minibars, cable TV, indoor pool, exercise equipment, hot tub, business services. | 2020 Overland Ave., 59102 | 406/655–1100 or 800/655–1170 | fax 406/652–7672 | http://cmoninn.com/billings-mt-hotel.htm | 80 rooms, 8 suites | AE, D, MC, V | CP | $

★**Josephine B & B.** This lovely historic home within walking distance of downtown has five themed rooms—ranging from frilly Victoriana to sunny country to more subdued jewel-tone modernity. Some in-room data ports, cable TV, library. | 514 N. 29th St., 59101 | 406/248–5898 or 800/552–5898 | www.thejosephine.com | 5 rooms, all with private bath | $–$$

Northern Hotel. Traditional elegance and hospitality await you at this historic hotel in downtown Billings. A massive fireplace is the centerpiece of the lobby, a common gathering place for guests and locals. The Golden Belle Restaurant serves American cuisine in an atmosphere that's fancier than usual for Montana. Restaurant, cable TV with movies and video games, in-room VCRs, exercise equipment, hair salon, massage, lounge, casino, shops, meeting rooms, Internet, business services, airport shuttle, free parking, some pets allowed; no smoking. | 19 N. Broadway, 59101 | 406/245–5121 or 800/542–5121 | fax 406/259–9862 | 160 rooms | AE, D, DC, MC, V | $–$$

Bozeman

American Computer Museum. Geared for all ages, this exhibit includes thousands of artifacts that tell the story of information and communication from the beginning of time to the present. It is only the second museum in the world dedicated entirely to the history of the computer. | I–90 Exit 306, turn north to Bridger Park Mall | 2304 N. 7th Ave., Suite B | 406/582–1288 | www.compuseum.org | $3 | June–Aug., daily 9–5; Sept–May, Tues.–Wed. and Fri.–Sat. noon–4; Thurs. 4–8.

Bridger Bowl Ski Area. You will find everything a skier could want here, 16 mi northeast of Bozeman. More than 60 runs cover 2,000 acres of Gallatin National Forest. There are 2,000 vertical feet of lift-served terrain, with 500 additional vertical feet on nearly 400 acres. It's 16 mi north of Bozeman on Route 86. | 15795 Bridger Canyon Rd. | 406/586–1518 or 800/223–9609 | www.bridgerbowl.com | Dec.–Apr., daily 9–4.

Gallatin County Pioneer Museum. The building served as the county jail for 70 years and the site for a hanging in 1924. The gallows and several jail cells remain. You'll find hundreds of artifacts, automobiles, Northern Plains crafts, and a model of nearby Fort Ellis. | 317 W. Main St. | 406/522–8122 | www.pioneermuseum.org | Mid-May–mid-Sept., daily 10–4:30; mid-Sept.–mid-May, Tues.–Fri. 11–4; Sat. 1–4.

Gallatin National Forest. The national forest includes the Absaroka Wilderness and part of the Beartooth Wilderness. Tour scenic Gallatin Canyon, an 80-mi drive south of Bozeman on U.S. 191 along the Gallatin River. The road skirts the Spanish Peaks and enters the northwest corner of Yellowstone Park. You can fish, go white-water rafting, and watch wildlife. | Forest Supervisor's Office: 10 E. Babcock Ave. | Bozeman Ranger Station: 3710 Fallon St. | 406/587–6701 or 406/932–5155 | www.fs.fed.us/r1/gallatin | Daily.

Museum of the Rockies. This museum at the south edge of the Montana State University campus has lifelike displays and rooms full of flora and fauna, as well as the Kirk Hill Nature Trail, a world-class dinosaur display, living-history farm, and a planetarium. | 600 W. Kagy Blvd. | 406/994–2251 | www.montana.edu/wwwmor | $9.50 | Mid-June–Labor Day, daily 8–8; Labor Day–mid-June, Mon.–Sat. 9–5, Sun. 12:30–4.

Dining

Gallatin Gateway Inn. Continental. The dining room of this inn is a white linen and candlelight kind of place complete with mountain views; a less formal dining area and a bar are also on-site. Try the prime rib or salmon. It's 12 mi southwest of Bozeman. | 76405 Gallatin Rd. (U.S. 191) | 406/763–4672 | Reservations essential | AE, D, MC, V | No lunch | $$$–$$$$

John Bozeman's Bistro. Eclectic. The Bistro features an ever-changing menu with lots of fresh specials daily. The kitchen does an excellent job with steaks, pasta, and seafood, and they regularly introduce customers to regional or ethnic flavors. The restaurant is downtown in the oldest brick building on the National Historic Register. Reservations are essential for dinner. | 242 E. Main St. | 406/587–4100 | AE, D, MC, V | Closed Mon. No dinner Sun. | $$–$$$

Leaf and Bean Coffee House. American. Stop here when you need a break from exploring downtown, and have a light meal or a homemade pastry with coffee or tea. Thursday, Friday, and Saturday you can hear live music. | 35 W. Main St. | 406/587–1580 | MC, V | ¢–$

Montana Ale Works. American. This historic railroad freight depot is now one of the most popular restaurants in town with a lounge and four distinct eating areas, including a billiard room with eight game tables. Selections include salads, pastas, burgers, sandwiches, beef, seafood, and poultry. There are 42 beers and microbrews on tap. | 601 E. Main St. | 406/587–7700 | AE, D, MC, V | No lunch | $–$$

Hardin

Bighorn Canyon National Recreation Area. Straddling the Montana–Wyoming border, Bighorn Canyon gives you stunning canyon scenery and a lake that stretches almost 75 mi. You can boat, swim, fish, hike trails, take naturalist-guided trips, and camp. At the Yellowtail visitor center, rangers present programs about the Bighorn Canyon area and its spectacular limestone canyon walls. | 25 mi south on Rte. 313 | 406/666–2412 | www.nps.gov/bica/ | $5 per vehicle | Daily dawn–dusk.

Bighorn County Historical Museum and Visitor Information Center. The complex sits on 22 acres and includes 20 permanent buildings. The museum focuses on Native American and early homestead settlement. It also serves as an official Montana State Visitor Center. | I–90 Exit 497 | 406/665–1671 | Free | May and Sept., daily 8–5; June–Aug., daily 8–8; Oct.–Apr., weekdays 9–5.

Little Bighorn Battlefield National Monument and Custer National Cemetery. General George A. Custer's 7th Cavalry was defeated by leaders Sitting Bull, Crazy Horse, and Gall, and their Sioux and Cheyenne warriors at this site, which was named a national cemetery in 1879 to protect the graves of cavalry buried here. (The site is a memorial to both the cavalry and Native Americans who fought and died here.) Guided tours are available. An annual reenactment of the battle takes place in early June. | I–90 Exit 510 | U.S. 212 | 406/638–3204 | www.nps.gov/libi | $10 per vehicle; $5 pedestrian | Memorial Day–Labor Day, daily 8 AM–9 PM; Sept., daily 8–6; Oct.–May, daily 8–4:30.

Rosebud Battlefield State Park. The undeveloped site of the 1876 battle between the Sioux and General Crook's infantry set the stage for a Native American victory eight days later at the Battle of the Little Bighorn. You can hike here, but watch for rattlesnakes. To reach the site go 25 mi east of Crow Agency on U.S. 212, then 20 mi south on Route 314, and then 3 mi west on county road. | 406/232–0900 | Free | Daily.

Tongue River Reservoir State Park. The 12-mi-long reservoir is situated among scenic red shale, juniper canyons, and the open prairies of southeastern Montana. Water sports are popular here and the park boasts excellent fishing. Rent boats (there's a boat ramp), fish and swim, and buy groceries from May through August. | Off Rte. 314, 6 mi north of Decker | 406/232–0900 | www.fwp.state.mt.us/parks | $5 per vehicle | Daily dawn–dusk.

Dining

The Lariat. American/Casual. This small family restaurant features home-style cooking and is a favorite with the locals. It offers a full menu for breakfast, lunch, and dinner. Breakfast is served any time. | 721 N. Center Ave. | 406/665–1139 | $–$$

Purple Cow. American/Casual. The shakes and steaks are good at this family restaurant, or try the chicken or salads. | Off U.S. 212 at the north end of town | 406/665–3601 | MC, V | $–$$

Livingston

Depot Center. This museum in a restored Northern Pacific Railroad station has railroad and Western history displays and artwork. | 200 W. Park St. (U.S. 89) | 406/222–2300 | $3 | June–Sept., Mon.–Sat. 9–5, Sun. 1–5.

Firehouse 5 Playhouse. The playhouse presents vaudeville and comedy during the summer and musical productions during the fall and winter. Shows are at 8 PM Friday and Saturday, and 3 PM Saturday and Sunday. | 5237 U.S. 89 S | 406/222–1420 | $12.

Yellowstone Gateway Museum. In a turn-of-the-20th-century schoolhouse, this museum has displays on early settlers, Yellowstone National Park, and area railroad history. | 118 W. Chinook St. | 406/222–4184 | $4 | June–Aug., daily 10–5:30; Sept., daily 11–4; Oct.–May by appointment.

Dining

Livingston Bar and Grille. Continental. This homey and rustic restaurant displays art depicting local history. A creative menu, which changes weekly, includes fresh seafood, rabbit, duck, beef, and pasta dishes. A kids' menu is available. | 130 N. Main St. | 406/222–7909 | AE, D, MC, V | No lunch | $$–$$$

Montana's Rib and Chop House. American. As the name implies, Montana's specializes in barbecued ribs and certified Angus beef steaks. You'll also find seafood and chicken, sandwiches, and luscious desserts. | 119 W. Park St. | 406/222–9200 | AE, D, MC, V | No lunch weekends | $–$$

NEBRASKA

THE FUR TRADE AND THE OREGON TRAIL

FROM OGALLALA TO SCOTTSBLUFF AND CHADRON

Distance: 350 mi   Time: 3 days minimum
Overnight Breaks: Scottsbluff/Gering, Chadron

This is a loop tour that lets you explore the Nebraska Panhandle, a region marked by Native American conflict, fur-trading posts, and the route of the Oregon, California, and Mormon trails. The land is rugged, with outcrops that are the beginning of the Pine Ridge country. You'll see sagebrush and prickly pear, along with small natural lakes and pine forests. Begin your trip in Ogallala and drive west on U.S. 26 to Scottsbluff, then head north on Route 71 to Crawford before turning east on U.S. 20 to Chadron. At Chadron, you can either continue the circle, returning south on U.S. 385 through the Panhandle to Alliance or head east into the cowboy country of the Nebraska Sandhills.

❶ Start in **Ogallala.** To cowboys who drove cattle herds here in the late 1800s, this was the promised land of roaring saloons. **Boot Hill Cemetery** is the resting place of some of those cowboys, while the **Front Street/Cowboy Museum** gives a glimpse into what life was like here when Nebraska was part of the Old West. The **Mansion on the Hill** shows how the wealthy lived during the cowboy period.

❷ As you leave Ogallala, take U.S. 26 west for approximately 27 mi to **Ash Hollow State Historical Park.** Bones of ancient rhinos and mammoths found here may date back 6,000 years, and you can see the ruts where Oregon Trail immigrants skidded their wagons down a steep hill. The interpretive center also has information about the 1855 Battle of Blue Water (also called the Harney Massacre), in which Army troops commanded by General William S. Harney attacked the Lakota in retaliation for a fight the previous year near Fort Laramie that left 28 soldiers dead.

❸ When you've finished exploring Ash Hollow, head west on U.S. 26 for approximately 100 mi to **Chimney Rock National Historic Site.** Chimney Rock was one of the most recognized landmarks on the Oregon Trail. You aren't allowed to get right up to the rock any more, but you can visit a little cemetery just east of it.

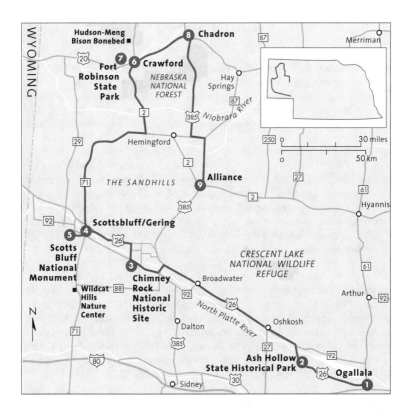

❹ Leaving Chimney Rock, follow U.S. 26 west for about 15 mi to **Scottsbluff/Gering.** Settle in one of these towns—they're separated only by the North Platte River—for a day or so to explore the Oregon Trail sites and take advantage of the towns' recreational opportunities. At the **Wildcat Hills Nature Center,** you can see a herd of buffalo as well as displays related to the flora and fauna of western Nebraska, while the **Wildcat Hills State Recreation Area** provides an area for hiking and camping. The **Farm and Ranch Museum** has some authentic pioneer homes and cabins and lots of old horse-drawn and steam-powered farm equipment, and **Robidoux Pass** has a reconstructed trading post in Carter Canyon.

❺ As the wagon trains headed west, they guided themselves by natural landmarks—and the fortresslike rock now known as **Scotts Bluff National Monument,** 2 mi west of the junction of Routes 71 and 92, was one of their major guideposts. You can hike or drive to the top of the monument for a view of the North Platte River Valley—and see it from afar at places such as Scottsbluff's **Riverside Zoo.**

❻ When you leave Scottsbluff, head north on Route 71 and then take Route 2 for about 74 mi to **Crawford.** Crawford is in the center of an area that was inhabited by Native Americans as far back as 10,000 years ago. About 4 mi north of Crawford on Route 2, turn west onto Toadstool Road, then go 15 mi north to reach the **Hudson-Meng Bison Bonebed,** an archaeological site within the Ogala National Grasslands where excavations have uncovered more than 600 bison skeletons dating to prehistoric times. From mid-May through September, you can see scientists at work at the fossil dig. Before or after that visit, you might want to see some interesting rock formations that look like toadstools at **Toadstool Geological Park,** on Toadstool Road west of Route 2.

7 Heading 3 mi west of Crawford on U.S. 20, you'll come to **Fort Robinson State Park.** Established as a military post during the Plains Indian Wars, Fort Robinson remained in use through World War II, when it was a K-9 training center and the site of a German prisoner-of-war camp. Many of the troops who participated in the major battles (and appalling incidents) of the Plains wars were in companies stationed at Fort Robinson. The state park includes lodging and a restaurant, interpretive programs, and a museum.

8 Going east from Crawford on U.S. 20, **Chadron** is about 20 mi away. Chadron is the home of Chadron State College, where the **Mari Sandoz High Plains Heritage Center** pays tribute to the author of *Cheyenne Autumn* and other books on the history of Nebraska. Chadron's early existence came about in part due to fur-trading posts, and the **Museum of the Fur Trade,** on the site of the 1837 Bordeaux Trading Post, has many artifacts from that era and way of life. Recreational activities abound in **Chadron State Park** and at the **Pine Ridge National Recreation Area,** where motorized vehicles aren't allowed.

9 If you prefer, from Chadron, you can loop south on U.S. 385 to **Alliance** to visit **Carhenge,** a unique reproduction of England's Stonehenge made with 38 cars instead of large blocks of stone. Other sculptures made of automobiles are nearby. If you're interested in Native American and pioneer history, make a stop at the **Knight Museum.** Then continue on south to **Sidney** (140 mi from Chadron) and the **Fort Sidney Museum and Post Commanders Home,** one of the few buildings left of an army garrison built here in the 1880s to protect railroad crews. Once you've reached Sidney, head east on I–80 for about 47 mi to return to Ogallala.

Alliance
Carhenge. This reproduction of England's Stonehenge, in a big field on Route 87 3½ mi north of Alliance, is one of the stranger sights in western Nebraska—instead of

NEBRASKA RULES OF THE ROAD

License Requirements: General driver's licenses are available at age 16, though some special permits for resident youth are allowed.

Right Turn on Red: Unless otherwise posted, right turns on red are permitted *after* a full stop. Left turns on red are allowed where such a turn would not cross an oncoming traffic lane.

Seat Belt and Helmet Laws: Seat belts are required of the driver and all passengers. Children under age six must be secured in a car seat that meets federal guidelines. All motorcycle operators and passengers must wear approved motorcycle helmets.

Speed Limits: The speed limit on the Interstate is 75 mph, except in metropolitan areas around Lincoln and Omaha; on state highways it's generally 60 mph, though some stretches are 55 mph. City and town streets have a speed limit of 25 mph in residential districts, 20 mph in business districts unless otherwise posted. On county roads it's 55 mph or 50 mph on unpaved roads, unless otherwise posted.

For More Information: Nebraska State Patrol | 402/471–4545 | www.nsp.state.ne.us. **Emergency Highway Help Line** | 800/525–5555.

large blocks of stone, it has 38 cars propped up and pointing to the heavens. Nearby, the "car art reserve," as locals call it, has other sculptures made of automobiles. | 308/762–1520 | www.carhenge.com | Free | Daily.

In June, Carhenge observes **Summer Solstice** with a special celebration on the longest day of the year, much as many Britons do at the real Stonehenge and other sites in England. | 308/762–1520 | Free.

Crescent Lake National Wildlife Refuge. Crescent Lake was established as a refuge for nesting and migratory birds, but you may also see antelope and whitetail deer on its 46,000 acres. More than 273 kinds of birds, including eagles, pelicans, and snow and Canada geese, have been spotted here. Fishing is permitted, as well as seasonal hunting in controlled areas, but camping is not. From Alliance, travel east on Route 2 approximately 20 mi to the community of Lakeside and turn south on County Road 250. | 10639 Road 181, Oshkosh | 308/762–4893 | Free | Daily dawn–dusk.

Knight Museum. The emphasis here is on early Nebraska, using artifacts and other exhibits to trace the history of the Native Americans who lived here and the pioneers who came here to live. | 908 Yellowstone Ave. | 308/762–2384 | Free | May–Labor Day, Mon.–Sat. 10–6, Sun. 1–5; Labor Day–Apr., Mon.–Sat. noon–5.

Dining

Elms Restaurant and Lounge. American. Popular with Alliance locals, this restaurant has two main dining areas; one has mirrored walls, red tablecloths, candles, and linen napkins, and the other is more family-oriented, with exposed-brick walls and ceiling fans. Dress is casual in both spaces. Favorite menu items include the 14-ounce rib-eye and chicken-fried steaks. | 1015 E. 3rd St. | 308/762–3425 | www.mallofalliance.com/elms.htm | AE, DC, D, MC, V | $$

Chadron

Chadron State College/Mari Sandoz High Plains Heritage Center. This former campus library honors area native Mari Sandoz, who wrote *Cheyenne Autumn* (later made into a gripping epic film), *Old Jules, Crazy Horse,* and other books about the history and people of western Nebraska. Many original manuscripts and artifacts from the Sandoz home are a part of the exhibits. | 1000 Main St. | 308/432–6066 | www.csc.edu | Free | Weekdays 9–4.

Chadron State Park. It's easy to see why this spot in the beautiful rugged Pine Ridge 8 mi south of Chadron became Nebraska's first state park. Many trails lead through the backcountry, where you may meet wild deer or shy, retreating porcupines. In the evening, you're likely to hear coyotes yipping in the distance. You can tour by jeep, horseback, or just take the hiking and biking trails on your own. There are a crafts center, picnic areas, a lagoon for fishing and paddleboating, camping sites ($8–$12), and 22 cabins for rent ($55–$65). | 15951 U.S. 385 | 308/432–6167 | www.westnebraska.com/ChadronStatePrk.htm | $2.50 | Park year-round; camp sites, May–Nov.; cabins, Apr.–Nov.

Museum of the Fur Trade. On the land where James Bordeaux ran his trading post, the museum and reconstructed outpost display trade goods, weapons, furs and other items relating to the history of fur trading in North America. Furs trapped along the White River are for sale. | 6321 E. U.S. 20 | 308/432–3843 | www.furtrade.org | $2.50 | Late May–Sept., daily 8–5; Oct.–late May, by appointment.

Pine Ridge National Recreation Area. Part of the Nebraska National Forest, this area along the Pine Ridge is one of rugged beauty, with limestone bluffs, buttes, and open ranges. Hiking trails wind through the site, or you can bring your horse and ride. Mountain bikes are permitted, but motorized vehicles are not. It's about 14 mi southwest of Chadron, and one of the best entry points is the Roberts Trailhead off Bethel

Road. The Nebraska National Forest also includes the Ogala National Grasslands and other federally managed reserves in both Nebraska and South Dakota. | Park office: 1240 W. 16th St. | 308/432–4475 | Free | Park daily; office weekdays 7:30–4:30.

Dining
Olde Main Street Inn. American. The best place to eat in Chadron is in the Olde Main Street Inn's dining room. The restaurant specializes in prime rib, buffalo, and lamb, but locals come for the homemade chili. | 115 Main St. | 308/432–3380 | AE, D, MC, V | $–$$

Lodging
Best Western West Hills Inn. The light and airy pale stucco motel sits on a hill near the scenic Pine Ridge, 3 mi from the Fur Trade Museum. The rooms, in soft beiges and browns, include a sitting area with two sofa chairs with a reading lamp. In-room hot tubs, some microwaves, some refrigerators, cable TV, indoor pool, exercise equipment, hot tub, laundry facilities, some pets allowed. | 1100 W. 10th St. | 308/432–3305 | fax 308/432–5990 | 67 rooms | AE, D, DC, MC, V | BP | $–$$

Olde Main Street Inn. This B&B, two blocks north of the town's single stoplight, dates from 1890, and has been run by the women of the O'Hanlon family for four generations. Built like a fort, the three-story brick structure was once headquarters for General Nelson Miles, who commanded U.S. Army troops at Wounded Knee, South Dakota, in 1891. Now a rustic inn of suites and minisuites, it has an 1890 pump well, a running fountain, a fireplace in the dining room, and preserved remnants of the original wallpaper. Restaurant, cable TV, bar, some pets allowed. | 115 Main St., 69337 | 308/432–3380 | www.chadron.com/oldemain | 6 rooms, 3 suites | AE, D, MC, V | BP | $

Our Heritage Bed and Breakfast. A working, family-run ranch since 1887, this B&B is on a clover-dotted prairie, nestled between pine-topped hills, ancient cedar trees, and the fossils-filled Badlands. Accommodations are in a private two-room guest house with a full kitchen. If you wish, you can participate in a "working ranch experience," including fixing fences and feeding livestock. Kitchen, pond, fishing, horseback riding; no a/c. | 1041 Toadstool Rd., 69339 | 308/665–2810 or 308/665–1613 | www.vacation-ranch. com | 2 rooms | No credit cards | BP | $$$

Crawford
Fort Robinson State Park. An active military post for more than 70 years, Fort Robinson has been a state park since 1956 and has long been regarded as Nebraska's premiere state park. Among the well-known incidents of its early days, the fort was the scene of the Cheyenne Outbreak, recounted in Mari Sandoz's book *Cheyenne Autumn* and the film made from her work. Later the fort became a training center for military dogs, and it finally ended its military service as a camp for German prisoners of war during World War II. Today you can ride bicycles, horses, or take a stagecoach ride; fish for trout or swim in an indoor pool; or take a jeep tour to Smiley Canyon to see a buffalo herd. Soldier Creek Wilderness, a 7,794-acre national forest within the park, has 10 mi of trails open year-round. It all starts about 3 mi west of Crawford on U.S. 20. | 308/665–2660 | www.ngpc.state. ne.us/parks/frob.html | $3 | Park daily; organized activities, Memorial Day–Labor Day.

Fort Robinson Museum. The telling is, indeed, in the details at this museum, which traces the history of the fort's military life through the everyday belongings of early cavalry troopers, the Native Americans they fought, and the German POWs detained there during World War II. The museum is on U.S. 20, in the two-story Post Headquarters built in 1905. Be sure to call to confirm open hours as they can vary from season to season. | 3200 U.S. 20 | 308/665–2919 | www.nebraskahistory.org/sites/fortrob/index.htm | $2 | Memorial Day–Labor Day, Tues.–Sun. 10–5; Labor Day–Memorial Day, weekdays 10–5.

Trailside Museum. The former post theater at Fort Robinson is now occupied by the a branch of the University of Nebraska State Museum devoted to the natural history of the region. Its collection of fossils—some of which are 30 million years old—and geological displays are dominated by the 14-foot-high skeleton of a mammoth found north of the fort. | 308/665–2929 | $2 | Memorial Day–Labor Day, daily 9–5.

Hudson–Meng Bison Bonebed. You can watch researchers at work digging for clues to the reason that hundreds of bison died here en masse about 10,000 years ago. Theories range from ancient Native Americans driving them to their deaths to a massive lightning strike and other natural phenomenon, such as prairie fires or hailstorms. The site, within the Ogala National Grasslands, is about 4 mi north of Crawford, then 15 mi west on Toadstool Road, which is gravel. Look for signs. | 1811 Meng Dr. | 308/432–0300 or 308/665–3900 | www.hudsonmeng.org | $4 | Mid-May–Sept., daily 9-5.

Toadstool Geological Park. The terrain looks more like an arid moonscape than part of Nebraska. Trails lead to unusual rock formations throughout the park, on Toadstool Road just west of Route 2. As you hike, you can see tracks left by animals 30 million years ago as they wandered across what was then a wetland. Picnic tables and a campsite ($5) are available. | 308/432–4475 | www.fs.fed.us/r2/nebraska/units/prrd/toadstooltemp.html | Memorial Day–Labor Day, $3 per vehicle; rest of yr, free | Daily, dawn–dusk.

Dining

Frontier Restaurant. American. Booths line the walls and tables occupy the center of this classic American spot with a bar and lounge just beyond big wooden double doors. Beef is a specialty, and the wine list features bottles from Nebraska vineyards. | 342 2nd St. | 308/665–1872 | AE, D, MC, V | $–$$

Lodging

Fort Robinson Lodge. The onetime barracks units of this historic fort have been converted into single guest rooms, and the old officers' quarters are now duplex apartments, all with full kitchens. The rentals list also includes a number of cabins, houses with two to four bedrooms each, and the Peterson Ranch House, with five bedrooms and stalls for your own horses. You can rough it at primitive campsites year-round or park your RV at modernized sites mid-April to mid-November. Rentals require a two-night minimum and a Nebraska Parks Permit and include access to park facilities. Restaurant, snack bar, some kitchens, indoor pool, tennis court, fishing, bicycles, mountain bikes, hiking, horseback riding, horseshoes, shop, some pets allowed; no room TVs. | 3200 U.S. 20, 69339 | 308/665–2900 | fax 308/665–2906 | www.ngpc.state.ne.us/parks/frob.html | 22 rooms, 9 cabins, 25 houses | Closed mid-Nov.–mid-Apr. | MC, V | ¢–$$$

Gering

North Platte Valley Museum and Western History Archives. This regional history museum has the world's largest collection of Oregon Trail artifacts and exhibits that examine the impact of the Oregon, Mormon, and California trails on the development of the valley. A fur trapper's boat, a log cabin, an 1889 homestead dwelling, and a later ranch house, as well as smaller artifacts like tools and weapons illustrate pioneer life in this region. | Overland Trail Rd. and J St. | 308/436–5411 | www.npvm.org | $3 | May–Sept., weekdays 9–4, Sat. 12–4, Sun. 1–4; Oct.–Apr., weekdays 9–4.

Robidoux Pass. As you drive through Carter Canyon, 12 mi from Gering, the ruts you'll see intersecting the gravel road are the visible depressions made by the thousands of wagons that came this way as they headed west. Though the Oregon Trail originally ran south of here, through the Robidoux Pass, which looks much the same today as it did 150 years ago, the route quickly shifted north to the more forgiving landscape by Scotts Bluff National Monument. | Carter Canyon Rd. | Free | Daily.

Scotts Bluff National Monument. Originally called Me-a-pa-te, for "the hill that is hard to go around," this fortress-like rock formation must certainly have seemed just that to pioneers on the Oregon Trail. But they found their way around it, leaving wagon-wheel ruts that can be seen today near the visitor center, on Route 92, 2 mi west of the junction with Route 71. You also can drive to the summit, which overlooks the oldest concrete road in the state, or hike there on the 1⁶/₁₀-mi Saddle Rock Trail. | 308/436–4340 | www.nps.gov/scbl | $5 per vehicle | Memorial Day–Labor Day, daily 8–7; Sept.–May, daily 8–5.

Wildcat Hills State Recreation Area and Nature Center. The nature center, in the rugged Wildcat Hills, is home to a small herd of buffalo. You can hike, bike, or camp along the various trails, but parking at the nature center, 10 mi south of Gering off Route 71, is limited to 20 minutes. | 308/436–3777 | www.ngpc.state.ne.us/parks/wildcat.html | $3 | Grounds and camping, daily; Nature center: Memorial Day–Labor Day, daily 9–5; Sept.–May, weekdays 8–4:30.

Wildlife World at the Wyo-Braska Natural History Museum. More than 350 mounted animals from seven continents are exhibited in this museum in a renovated train station, including Baluchithere, a 30-foot-long dinosaur. | 950 U St. | 308/436–7104 | www.westnebraska.com/wildlifeworld.htm | $3.50 | May–Sept., weekdays 9–5, Sat. 10–4; Oct.–Apr., Tues.–Sat. 10–4.

Dining

Gaslight Restaurant and Lounge. American. Chandeliers throw soft, gold light onto the wooden tabletops and etched-glass panels engraved with scenes and symbols of the area's vibrant past. Locals often come here, especially for the "Family Meal," which includes a serving of chicken, shrimp, or beef, along with a salad, and a side dish. The Gaslight also makes its own coleslaw from scratch. | 3318 10th St. | 308/632–7315 | D, MC, V | $$–$$$

Lodging

Circle S Motel. Along the routes of the Oregon Trail and the Pony Express, this 1950s brick motel on Route 92 offers ground-level rooms in a mostly commercial area about 8 mi from the Wildcat Hills Nature Center and Scotts Bluff National Monument. Cable TV, some pets allowed. | 400 M St. | 308/436–2157 | fax 308/436–3249 | 30 rooms | MC, V | ¢

Ogallala

Ash Hollow State Historical Park. You can follow a walkway along Windlass Hill to look down at the deep ruts made when immigrants on the Oregon Trail locked the wheels on their wagons and skidded down to the spring below. But archaeological records show that humans were using this canyon off Route 26 (about 3½ south of Lewellen), long before that, and bones of ancient rhinos and mammoths found here may date back 6,000 years. You can find out about the history in the visitor center, as well as tour a restored schoolhouse and take a hike along a nature trail. | 308/778–5651 | www.ngpc.state.ne.us/parks/showpark.ihtml | $3 | Grounds daily dawn–dusk; visitor center, Tues.–Sun. 8–4.

Boot Hill Cemetery. Some of those who died with their boots on during the time when Ogallala was the land of saloons and dance halls ended up here, their graves marked by wooden planks. | 10th and Parkhill Dr. | 308/284–4066 or 800/658–4390 | Free | Daily.

Front Street/Cowboy Museum. This re-creation of the town's main street as it was in the 1880s, when Ogallala was called both the "Queen of the Cowtowns" and the "Gomorrah of the Plains," includes some saloonlike structures, but you can take your kids to the Crystal Palace Revue's musicals without worrying about the content. | 519 E. 1st St. | 308/284–6000 | Museum, free; Crystal Palace Dancehall Revue, $4 | Museum, daily 9–9; dance hall, Memorial Day–mid-Aug., shows daily at 7:15.

Haybale Church. Made in 1928 from bales of hay that were then plastered over, this church is the only one of its kind in the United States. A note on the door will tell you where to find the key. Two blocks west and a block south, in the City Park on Route 61, you also can see the world's smallest courthouse, as documented by *Ripley's Believe It or Not*. The key for that is in the modern courthouse next door. | Arthur City Park, Main St., Arthur | 308/284–4066 or 800/658–4390 | Donation suggested | Daily.

★ **Lake McConaughy State Recreation Area.** This is as close as you get to the ocean in Nebraska, and Lake McConaughy, known as "Big Mac," almost feels like an ocean with 36,000 acres of surface water created when part of the North Platte River was dammed in 1941. Just 8 mi north of Ogallala, Big Mac has 100 mi of shoreline with white-sand beaches, a multitude of campsites, and facilities for water sports. Keep your eyes open around the Lone Eagle area because a particular bald eagle dropped in from the power company's nearby eagle sanctuary, seemed to like the name, and continues to hang around here. You'll know you're in Big Mac country when you follow Route 61 across the top of the 3½-mi-long Kingsley Dam. | 308/284–8800 | www.lakemcconaughy.com | $3 | Park year-round; campsites May–mid-Sept.

Lake Ogallala State Recreation Area. Often called the "little lake," this 320-acre body of water was created with fill dirt removed during the building of Kingsley Dam. It's on Route 61, about 8 mi from Ogallala, at the eastern end of the Lake McConaughy complex. You'll find boating and fishing facilities as well as 116 campsites and a controlled shooting area for the fall hunting season. | 308/284–8800 | http://ngpc. state.ne.us/parks | $3; camping, $3–$14 | Park daily; camping May–mid-Sept.

Mansion on the Hill. Harkening back to the money the cattle business could make, this three-story Italianate Victorian home, built in 1887, has been restored to its original condition and is furnished with antiques from the cattle-drive era. | 1004 W. 10th, at Spruce St. | 308/284–4066 | $2 | Memorial Day–Sept. 15, Tues.–Sun. 9–4.

Dining

Hill Top Inn. American. This casual Southwestern-theme restaurant, overlooking Lake McConaughy, is known for its prime ribs and shrimp. | 197 Kingsley Dr. | 308/284–4534 | AE, D, MC, V | Closed Jan.–Mar. | $–$$

Junie Mae's Roadhouse Barbecue. Barbecue. A picture of a winged pig greets you when you arrive at Junie Mae's, a whimsical introduction to some serious barbecue. You can dine indoors in the homey redwood building or outside on a deck, north of Kingsley Dam and overlooking Lake McConaughy. The menu includes prime rib, brisket, and barbecued chicken. There's also a beer garden, plus plenty of espressos and cappuccinos. | 1815 Rte. 61N | 308/726–2626 | No credit cards | Closed Tues.–Wed. and Nov.–Mar. | $

Ole's Big Game Steakhouse And Lounge. American. The buffalo burgers and chicken-fried steak are local favorites, but the decor may end up being the most memorable part of the meal. The late Ole Herstedt, who opened his tavern one minute after Prohibition ended in 1933, hunted on every continent—and mounted more than 200 big-game trophies on these wood-panel walls. | 107 N. Oak St., Paxton | 308/239–4500 | D, MC, V | $

Scottsbluff

Lake Minatare State Recreation Area. A stone lighthouse is a photographer's favorite here, and this park, 6 mi west and 8 mi north of Scottsbluff off U.S. 26, has a full range of water activities around its 2,000-acre lake. Ice fishing is popular in winter. | 291040 The Point Rd. | 308/783–2911 | www.ngpc.state.ne.us/parks | $3 | Grounds, mid-Jan.–mid-Oct., daily; camping, May–mid-Oct.; lighthouse, Apr.–Oct., daily 9–8.

Riverside Zoo. More than 175 specimens of animals, including spider monkeys, mountain lions, and prairie dogs, live here in simulated natural habitats. The Scotts Bluff National Monument is visible across the river. | 1600 S. Beltline Hwy. W | 308/

630–6236 | $2.50 | May–Sept., weekdays 9:30–4:30, weekends 9:30–5:30; Oct.–Apr., daily 10:30–4:30.

West Nebraska Arts Center. This downtown center in the former Carnegie Library has a number of artists-in-residence as well as rotating exhibits in the visual arts gallery, local and visiting performing arts programs, and a children's theater. | 106 E. 18th St. | 308/632–2226 | www.nebraskarts.com | Free | Weekdays 9–4, Sat. 1–5.

Dining

18th Street Bar & Grille. American/Casual. You'll find pool tables and a big-screen TV at this casual restaurant and bar; hamburgers and finger foods are the only items on the menu. | 1722 Broadway | 308/632–6977 | MC, V | Closed Sun. | ¢–$

El Charrito Restaurant and Lounge. Mexican. The metal building may not look like much, but inside, you'll find Tex-Mex classics such as pork chili, guacamole, and sopaipillas, as well as the expected enchiladas, tacos, and burritos. You order at the counter before sitting in the dining room among pictures of western Nebraska's natural landmarks. | 802 21st Ave. | 308/632–3534 | DC, MC, V | Closed Mon. | ¢–$

Lodging

Barn Anew Bed and Breakfast. In this converted barn, built in 1907, you could be sleeping a few yards from—or even on—paths taken by Oregon Trail wagon masters. The dining room has a four-wall mural depicting life around the barn in the first days of the 20th century, and a minimuseum is housed in a barracks, which was originally part of a 1940s prisoners-of-war camp. No room TVs. | 170549 County Rd. L | 308/632–8647 | fax 308/632–5518 | www.prairieweb.com/barnanew | 4 rooms | AE, D, DC, MC, V | BP | $

Candlelight Inn. Rooms here are spare, but have homey touches like fabric-draped night tables and country quilts. Each is decorated differently, B&B style, and a few have canopy beds. Microwaves, refrigerators, cable TV, pool, exercise equipment, bar, airport shuttle. | 1822 E. 20th Pl., 69361 | 308/635–3751 or 800/424–2305 | fax 308/635–1105 | www.candlelightscottsbluff.com | 56 rooms | AE, D, DC, MC, V | CP | $

Fontenelle Inn Bed and Breakfast. This small country inn, built in 1917, has a veranda on the second floor and a leisure room where you can relax after sightseeing. Lunch, dinner, and box lunches are available. No kids under 12, no smoking. | 1424 4th Ave., 69361 | 308/632–6257 | fax 308/632–2726 | 4 rooms | MC, V | BP | $–$$

Sidney

Fort Museum and Post Commander's Home. The residence of the army post commander and the first hospital General Walter Reed was assigned to is among the few remaining buildings of the army garrison built here in the 1880s to protect railroad crews. The museum has period military uniforms and Native American dress. | 1153 6th Ave. | 308/254–2150 | Free | Late May–early Sept., daily 9–1 and 1–3.

NEVADA

THE NEVADA LAKESIDE
STATELINE TO CRYSTAL BAY

Distance: 27 mi   Time: 1 day
Overnight Break: Incline Village

An exhilarating drive up the east shore of Lake Tahoe begins at the high-rise casinos of Stateline, but quickly leaves behind the neon and noise. Unlike the California shore of the lake, which is lined with more than a dozen towns, this side is mostly undeveloped, with forested mountainsides, rocky coves, sandy beaches, alpine lakes, and small marinas. And just about the time you're ready for civilization again, the glittering casinos of Crystal Bay appear.

❶ Begin the drive north on U.S. 50 in **Stateline.** Four major and two minor casinos make up the action, clustered on the flats a short hike from the lake. A small residential area hugs the hills above the high-rises, chalets, and condos, close to the sprawling Heavenly Valley Ski Resort.

❷ Head 3 mi north on U.S. 50 and turn left onto Elk Point Road and drive ½ mi on a dirt road to reach **Nevada Beach.** The nearest public lake access to Stateline on the Nevada side, this large Forest Service facility has a sandy beach, picnic areas, and a 54-site campground.

❸ Four miles north on U.S. 50 is **Zephyr Cove.** Although it's the largest settlement between Stateline and Incline Village, it's a relatively tiny resort, with a beach, marina, campground and RV park, riding stables, and lodge. The 550-passenger stern-wheeler MS *Dixie II* and the 20-passenger trimaran *Woodwind* sail from Zephyr Cove.

❹ **Cave Rock,** 4 mi north on U.S. 50, is 25 yards of solid stone; U.S. 50 passes through it via one of Nevada's few tunnels. This monolith towers over a parking lot, a lakefront picnic area, and a boat launch.

❺ Drive 8 mi northeast on U.S. 50, then 2 mi north on Route 28 to reach **Lake Tahoe–Nevada State Park,** which preserves 3 mi of shoreline and a 10-mi-by-5-mi clump of the Carson Range rising from the lake. Spooner Lake (north of the junction) has a

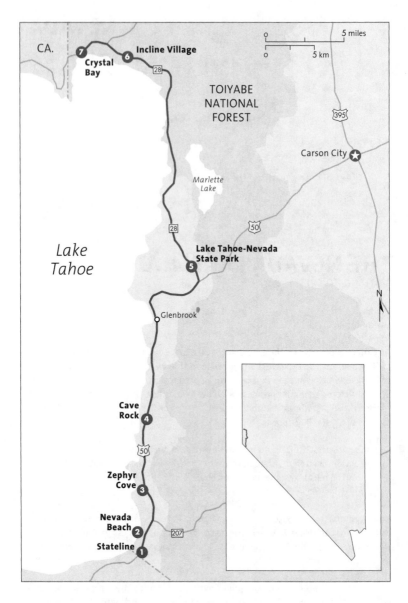

nature trail and the trailhead for a 5-mi hike through North Canyon to Marlette Lake. Sand Harbor (8 mi north on Route 28) is the focal point of the park; it has a beach, rocky cove, and nature trail, and in summer gets very crowded by noon.

❻ Go 13 mi farther north on Route 28 to find **Incline Village,** one of Nevada's few master-planned towns, dating back to the early 1960s; it's still privately owned. There are several places to eat and most are visible from the roadside. Have a quick bite at one of the casual sit-down restaurants, such as Hacienda De La Sierra. Check out Lakeshore Drive to see some of the most expensive real estate in Nevada. If you're tempted to linger, spend the night in Incline Village.

7 Just 3 mi more on Route 28 will take you to the end of the tour, **Crystal Bay,** which has a cluster of low-rise casinos. The historic Cal-Neva, owned for three years by Frank Sinatra, is literally bisected by the state line. In the once-famous and Sinatra-built Indian Room, you'll find the two thick stripes painted down the center—gold for California and silver for Nevada.

Incline Village

Diamond Peak Ski Resort. Diamond Peak has a fun family atmosphere, and is smaller and less crowded than many of the super ski resorts nearby. The 1-mi Crystal chair-lift rewards you with the best views of the lake of any local ski area. There's a half-pipe run for snowboarders and 22 mi of cross-country skiing. Free shuttles run continuously from the ski area around Incline Village and Crystal Bay. | 1210 Ski Way | 775/831–3211 (24-hr snow phone), 775/832–1177 | www.diamondpeak.com.

Lake Tahoe–Nevada State Park. Preserving a full 3 mi of shoreline and 22 square mi of prime Sierra wilderness, the focus of the park is Sand Harbor Beach State Recreation Area, one of the largest and most popular sandy beaches on the lake. You can follow the short nature trail to explore Sandy Point and have a lesson in Tahoe ecology. The park runs along most of Route 28, near Sand Harbor. | 775/831–0494 | http://parks.nv.gov/lt.htm | $5 at Cave Rock and Spooner Lake entrances; $6 May–Sept.; $3 Oct.–Apr. at Sand Harbor entrance | Daily.

Mount Rose Ski Area. With a vertical drop of 1,440 feet, this is one of the highest ski areas around Tahoe. It's geared toward intermediate and advanced (though beginners will find plenty of gentle slopes and an excellent first-timer ski package). It's also the closest skiing to Reno, so it's a popular resort and the parking lots fill up fast. Snowboarders have their own terrain park. Ski shuttles run from downtown Reno. | 22222 Mount Rose Hwy. | 775/849–0704, 800/754–7673 outside NV | www.skirose.com.

Ponderosa Ranch and Western Theme Park. No, the popular 1960s television series *Bonanza* was not based on this ranch at the south end of town off Route 28. It's the

NEVADA RULES OF THE ROAD

License Requirements: To drive in Nevada you must be at least 16 and have a valid driver's license. Nevada also honors out-of-state driver's permits. You must be at least 15 years old and be with an adult who has a legal license.

Right Turn on Red: Right turns on red are permitted everywhere.

Seat Belt and Helmet Laws: All occupants in the vehicle must wear seat belts. Children under 6 years old and 60 pounds must ride in a child-restraint system. Motorcyclists and their passengers are required to wear helmets at all times.

Speed Limits: In some places on I–80 and I–15 you can drive 75 mph. In other places, and on the U.S. highways, the speed limit is 70. It's a quick 65 mph on the interstates in the heart of Las Vegas and Reno.

For More Information: Contact the **Nevada Department of Motor Vehicles** at | 877/368–7828 | www.dmvnv.com.

other way around: the Ponderosa is a theme park based on the television show. It centers on the Cartwright ranch house; you'll also find a petting zoo and a collection of antique vehicles. Have a chuckwagon breakfast, take a wagon ride, and watch a shoot-out. | 100 Ponderosa Ranch Rd. | 775/831–0691 | www.ponderosaranch.com/ | $11.50 | Mid-Apr.–Oct., daily 9:30–6.

Dining

Lone Eagle Grille. American. The Lone Eagle is a cozy place that's great for pre- or après-ski drinking or dining. The restaurant consists of a cabin with two fireplaces; open-air dining is right on the beach. Dungeness crab cakes, spit-roasted duck, and braised lamb shank are among the favorites. The menu also includes such mouthwatering dishes as mesquite-grilled ahi tuna, venison medallions, and New Zealand lamb chops. There's live entertainment weekends. Reservations are recommended. | Country Club Dr. at Lakeshore | 775/832–3250 | AE, D, DC, MC, V | $$$–$$$$

Lodging

Hyatt Regency Lake Tahoe. A self-contained resort half a block from its own beach, this place has virtually everything. The large rooms are both rustic and sophisticated, and you can also relax in the spa or spend some time and money in the 24-hour casino. 3 restaurants, minibars, some microwaves, some refrigerators, cable TV, tennis court, pool, gym, hot tub, massage, beach, bicycles, bars, children's programs (ages 3–12), business services. | 424 rooms; 24 lakeside cottages | 111 Country Club Dr. | 775/832–1234 or 888/899–5019 | fax 775/831–7508 | www.laketahoehyatt.com | AE, D, DC, MC, V | $$–$$$$

Inn at Incline. The Inn at Incline is one of the few motels in a town full of condos, so be sure to book in advance. Cable TV, indoor pool, hot tub, sauna, business services; no a/c. | 38 rooms | 1003 Tahoe Blvd. | 775/831–1052 or 800/824–6391 | fax 775/831–3016 | www.innatincline.com | AE, D, MC, V | $–$$$

Stateline

Cave Rock. A towering slab of solid granite, this rock is sacred to the Washoe Indians. A picnic area and boat launch are among the other attractions. | 11 mi north on U.S. 50 | $5 | Daily 10:30–5.

Nevada Beach. Beach, picnic areas, and a 54-site campground are the big draws of this large Forest Service facility. Make camping reservations as far ahead as possible (up to four months in advance). | Left on Elk Point Rd. | 530/573–2600 or 800/280–2267 | $5 | Daily until 8 PM | May–Oct.

Dining

Chart House. Steak. A lake view and nautical theme match the menu, which has a lot of fresh fish and seafood. Sesame-crusted salmon; seared, peppered ahi tuna; and grilled swordfish are specialties. Steaks are served as well. A kids' menu is available. | 392 Kingsbury Grade (Rte. 28), 2 mi east off U.S. 50 | 775/588–6276 | fax 775/588–4562 | www.chart-house.com | AE, D, DC, MC, V | No lunch | $$–$$$

Llewellyn's. Continental. Llewellyn's is on the 19th floor in Harveys Resort and Casino and offers every diner a spectacular view of Lake Tahoe. You'll find scrumptious entrées such as smoked duck, lobster tails, and wild boar tenderloin. There's a champagne brunch every Sunday. | In Harveys Hotel & Casino | 775/588–2411 or 800/553–1022 | Reservations essential | AE, D, DC, MC, V | $$–$$$$

INTO THE DESERT
LAS VEGAS TO ELY ON I–15 AND U.S. 93

Distance: 175 mi   Time: 2 days
Overnight Break: Caliente

This tour takes you on a little-traveled and scenically varied stretch of country north-east of Las Vegas. After 75 mi of barren desert, you enter a well-watered strip of south-eastern Nevada: green valleys lush with grass and towering cottonwoods, a string of lakes and springs, alfalfa fields backed by rugged and bare mountains, washes carved by time, and a handful of small towns for gassing up the car.

❶ Twenty-two miles northeast of Las Vegas on I–15 (or 60 mi north on U.S. 93) lies **Pahranagat National Wildlife Refuge.** Two unexpected lakes, improbably in the desert, cover 700 acres and preserve a habitat for hundreds of species of migrating and resident birds. Follow the old road at Upper Lake to the lakeside campgrounds.

❷ Take U.S. 93 15 mi north of Upper Pahranagat Lake to **Alamo,** a small and somewhat remote farming and ranching center that went its own quiet way from the 1880s till the 1950s—when the Atomic Energy Commission began aboveground nuclear testing at the Nevada Test Site just on the other side of the Pahranagat Range. The explosions rocked the town, and the residents were required to wear radiation badges. But since the Test Ban Treaty of the early 1990s, peace has returned to Alamo.

❸ **Ash Springs,** 7 mi north of Alamo, is another small settlement with two gas stations; a minimarket; an on-again, off-again eatery; and a primitive public warm spring: take a right across from R Place Texaco (ignore the No Trespassing sign) and park under the big cottonwood.

❹ After leaving Ash Springs, go 5 mi north to Route 375 and continue 36 mi northwest to **Rachel.** This former mining town of no more than 100 residents has achieved inter-national notoriety as the closest town to Groom Lake, also known as Area 51. Only 25 mi south of Rachel, and inaccessible from the town, this top-secret Air Force research facility has reportedly hosted extraterrestrial aircraft and, some believe, extraterrestrials themselves. UFO enthusiasts from all over converge for get-togethers at the Little A'Le'Inn, Rachel's only bar, restaurant, and motel. Route 375 has been desig-nated the Extraterrestrial Highway by the Nevada Department of Transportation.

❺ **Caliente,** 43 mi east of Rachel on U.S. 93 is a small railroad town with a big Spanish Mission–style depot. This city with less than 1,000 people was a favorite writing spot of Zane Grey. A 20-mi side trip to the end of scenic Rainbow Canyon (turn on Route 317 at the south end of Caliente) travels along sheer polychrome canyon walls, past many railroad trestles and bridges, and ranches. This is the best place to overnight, though camping by Cathedral Gorge is also possible.

❻ In 1935, **Cathedral Gorge** (15 mi north of Caliente on U.S. 93, then right 1 mi) became one of Nevada's first four state parks. The cliffs and canyons are the results of continual water erosion in the siltstone and clay shale.

❼ Continue 12 mi north to **Pioche,** which, like most towns in Nevada, started out as a mining camp. Known as one of the toughest, not to mention the most corrupt, towns in the Old West, Pioche still has several original buildings including the court-

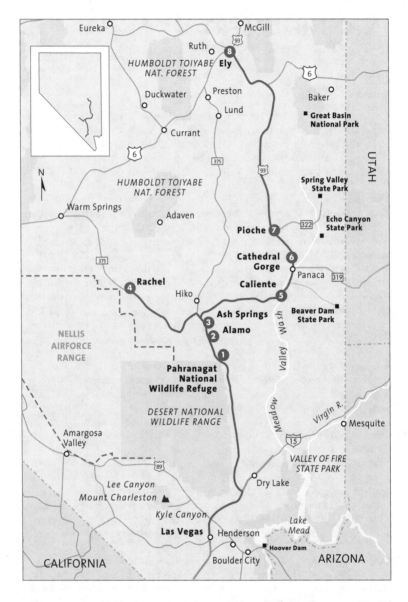

house, an opera house, a firehouse, and a couple of mercantiles; most are within walking distance of each other. There's also the cemetery aptly named Boot Hill.

❽ You can head back to Las Vegas from Pioche or continue on for another 109 mi north to **Ely.** In the 1870s, Ely was just a place to park your stagecoach or pick up your mail, but less than 20 years later, it became the White Pine County seat, with a whopping population of 200—most of whom were miners. With a rich history in copper mining (the last viable mine closed in 1997), Ely's best known attraction is its railroad museums; visitors can even take rides on the famous ghost train. Of course, the real reason to travel up this far is to get a taste of **Great Basin National Park,** which has more than 200 small basins throughout steep mountain ranges, meadows, limestone caves, and the southernmost permanent glacier on the continent.

Caliente

Beaver Dam State Park. Remotest of the 22 Nevada state parks, Beaver Dam is right on the Utah state line, 34 mi east of Caliente. You get hiking trails, cliffs, canyons, a trout-stocked reservoir, and a great campground, not to mention the long dusty 28-mi drive on a graded gravel road. | Off U.S. 93 | 775/726–3564 | http://parks.nv.gov/bd.htm | $3 | May–Oct.

Caliente Railroad Depot & Boxcar Museum. The chamber of commerce, city hall, and the library all use this space, and most of the walls are covered with local artwork. The Boxcar Museum is in an old boxcar, and covers the history of Lincoln County from prehistoric times through the railroad (which founded the town) and nuclear fallout (from the Nevada Test Site next door). | 100 Depot St. | 775/726–3129 | Depot, free; museum, $1 | Weekdays 10–2.

Cathedral Gorge State Park. This unusual desert wash, a million years old and once part of an ancient lake bed, has walls made of soft clay, carved by time and weather into some wondrous shapes. Paths pass through tight canyons and secondary washes; you can also take a 4-mi nature trail from the walls to the campground. | U.S. 93, Panaca | 775/728–4460 | http://parks.nv.gov/cg.htm | $3 | Daily.

Echo Canyon State Park. This park is in the verdant Meadow Valley Wash, around a small earthen dam and reservoir 12 mi east of Pioche. The campground is usually full of anglers fishing for rainbow trout. | Rte. 323 | 775/962–5103 | http://parks.nv.gov/ec.htm | $3 | Daily.

Lodging

Caliente Hot Springs Motel & Spa. The rooms are a little frayed around the edges, but the stay is worth it for the use of the hot baths: private rooms with 3-feet-deep Roman hot tubs filled with sulfur-free 105°F water. Some in-room hot tubs, cable TV. | 18 rooms | U.S. 93 N | 775/726–3777 | fax 775/726–3513 | MC, V | ¢–$

Rainbow Canyon Motel. Built in 1935, the motel is one of the oldest in Caliente. It's also the smallest with only six rooms. The price is right, though. Cable TV. | 6 rooms | 884 A St. | 775/726–3291 | AE, MC, V | ¢

Shady Motel. This motel has been in the same family for the past 40 years, but the old buildings are long gone, replaced with new, more comfortable accommodations. Some microwaves, some refrigerators, cable TV, no-smoking rooms. | 28 rooms | 450 Front St. | 775/726–3106 | AE, MC, V | ¢

Ely

Cave Lake State Recreation Area. High in the pine and juniper forest of the big Schell Creek Mountains that hem in Ely to the east, this is an idyllic spot, where you can spend a day fishing for rainbow trout and a night sleeping under the stars. Arrive early; it gets crowded. | 20 mi east on U.S. 93 | 775/728–4460 | http://parks.nv.gov/cl.htm | $3 | Daily; access may be restricted in winter.

Great Basin National Park. This is one of the newest and smallest national parks in the country, and preserves the second-highest mountain peak in Nevada. It also has the state's only permanent ice field and an extensive network of eroded-granite caves. The visitor center has exhibits on the flora, fauna, and geology of the park, plus books, videos, and souvenirs for sale; a coffee shop is attached. You can also tour Lehman Caves, an extensive network of underground caves with countless stalactites and stalagmites. | Rte. 488, Baker | 775/234–7331 | www.nps.gov/grba | Free; Lehman Cave tours $4–$8 | Year-round; visitor center daily 8–4:30.

Nevada Northern Railway Museum. The Nevada Northern Railroad ran from its yard in east Ely to the copper mines in nearby Ruth to the smelter in nearby McGill and up to the main transcontinental line in the northeast corner of the state. When the mines and mill shut down in the early 1980s, the railroad followed suit, abandoning a $50 million operation. Eight years later, the townspeople turned the whole operation into the most authentic museum in Nevada. | 1100 Ave. A | 775/289–2085 or 866/407–8326 | http://nevadanorthernrailway.net | Train rides $18–$25 | Daily 9:30–4.

Ward Charcoal Ovens Historic State Monument. You can see this row of ovens, the largest in one spot in Nevada, in the desert south of Ely. They were used to turn piñon and juniper into charcoal, which was then used for refining silver and copper from the local ore. It's worth the 12 mi drive to take in this well-preserved piece of Nevada mining history. | U.S. 6/50 | http://parks.nv.gov/ww.htm | $3 | Daily.

Dining

Red Apple Family Restaurant. American/Casual. This casual family-friendly restaurant offers the best eats in Ely. Portions are big, prices are small, and the waitstaff is happy to see you. Here you just may eat the best chicken-fried steak or meat loaf you've ever had. | 2060 Aultman St. | 775/289–8585 | AE, D, DC, MC, V | $

Las Vegas

Bellagio Las Vegas. A 12-acre lake fronts this opulent hotel and the Bellagio Botanical Gardens is full of living flowers, shrubs, and trees. The Fountains of Bellagio is a signature outdoor spectacle. | 3600 Las Vegas Blvd. S | 702/693–7111 or 888/744–7687 | www.bellagio.com | Sun.–Thurs. 10–6, Fri.–Sat. 10–9.

Liberace Museum. Costumes, cars, photographs, even mannequins of the late entertainer make this museum the kitschiest place in town. | 1775 E. Tropicana Ave. | 702/798–5595 | www.liberace.com | Mon.–Sat. 10–5, Sun. 1–5.

Mirage Hotel and Casino. Every 15 minutes from dusk to midnight, the signature volcano in front of the Mirage erupts. Behind the Mirage, eight Atlantic bottlenose dolphins live in a 2.5-million-gallon saltwater Dolphin Habitat, the largest in the world. | 3400 Las Vegas Blvd. S | 702/791–7111 or 800/627–6667 | www.themirage.com | Secret Garden Mon.–Tues. and Thurs.–Fri. 11–5, weekends 10–5; Dolphin Habitat weekdays 11–7, weekends 10–7.

Stratosphere Casino Hotel & Tower. The view from the tower—the tallest observation tower in the United States—and the thrill rides at the top make it worth the extra effort to get to this hotel-casino. | 2000 Las Vegas Blvd. S | 702/380–7777 or 800/380–7732 | www.stratospherehotel.com | Rides Sun.–Thurs. 10 AM–1 AM, Fri.–Sat. 10 AM–2 AM.

Venetian Resort-Hotel-Casino. Various Venetian landmarks are meticulously recreated here. The Grand Canal Shops, a 90-store mall, is complete with a reproduction of Venice's Canalozzo; gondolas ply the waterway. | 3355 Las Vegas Blvd. S | 702/733–5000 | www.venetian.com | Wax museum daily 9:30–11; Hermitage-Guggenheim museum daily 9:30–8:30.

Dining

The Buffet at Bellagio. American. This is one of the most beautifully decorated buffet rooms in town. But the design isn't the main attraction here; even the most discerning foodie should find something to like with selections that include Kobe beef (yes, Kobe beef) and the requisite king-crab legs. | Bellagio Las Vegas, 3600 Las Vegas Blvd. | 702/693–7111 | AE, D, DC, MC, V | $–$$$

Dona Maria. Mexican. You'll forget you're in Las Vegas after a few minutes in this relaxed and unpretentious cantina. All of the combinations and specials are good, but the best play here is to order the enchilada-style tamale (with red or green sauce). | 910 Las Vegas Blvd. S | 702/786–6358 | AE, D, DC, MC, V | ¢–$

Little Buddha. Pan-Asian. It may sound like a mixed metaphor—a Las Vegas branch of an Asian restaurant from Paris—but France's Buddha Bar has achieved world fame for its food and its music. Try such Pacific Rim wonders as Hawaiian smoked pot stickers and curry shrimp in banana leaf. | The Palms, 4321 W. Flamingo Rd. | 702/942–7777 | AE, D, DC, MC, V | $–$$

Pioche

Boot Hill. Pioche's rough-and-tumble reputation sprang from miners' attempts at protecting their claims. Disputes taken to court were often determined by bribery rather than facts, so who owned a claim became a matter of who could shoot first. Mine owners imported hired gunmen—in boom times, more than 20 gunslingers came to Pioche every day—and solved the property issues with a quick bullet rather than a slow trial. You'll find more than a few of those men who died with their boots on buried at Boot Hill, Pioche's Old West cemetery. | Daily | Free.

Brown Hall–Thompson Opera House. One of the last three standing 19th-century theaters in Nevada, the opera house stood as social anomaly in a town known for its lawlessness. It once served as the community's movie theater, but now stands vacant. In 1984 it merited a listing in the National Register of Historic Places. Renovations are underway to bring it to its former glory. | 69 Main St.

Million Dollar Courthouse. In 1871 Pioche was designated the seat of Lincoln County, but it needed a courthouse. Originally contracted to be built for $16,400, numerous problems with materials, declines in revenue, high interest on bond payments, and graft turned the project into a costly endeavor. When the last payment for the courthouse was made in 1936, the final cost to Lincoln County was $1 million. | Lacour St. | 775/962–5182 | Daily 10–4.

Dining

Grubsteak Dinner House. American. Right on Main Street, looking as rustic and rugged as the original buildings in Pioche, the Grubsteak offers typical American fare with a few Tex-Mex dishes thrown in for good measure. Try the chicken tamales or go for the stick-to-your-ribs entrées such as T-bone steak and pork ribs. Kids' menu available. | Main St. | 775/962–5527 | AE, D, MC, V | No lunch | ¢–$

Rachel

Area 51. This infamous spot is a tiny nub in the northeast corner of the vast 3.5-million-acre Nellis Air Force Range. According to sketchy and unconfirmed media reports, Area 51, also dubbed Dreamland, has been a super-secret military installation since the 1950s, where the Air Force has tested top-secret aircraft. Some people also believe that the government stores and does research on UFOs and even collects and studies extraterrestrial beings here. It's illegal to approach the installation; military police have complete authority (not only can they arrest you and take away your cameras, they have orders to use deadly force, if necessary) to prevent intrusions. The closest you can get to the base is to take Groom Lake Road (off Route 375 between mile markers 34 and 35); you'll see signs, surveillance cameras, orange posts marking the base's border, and possibly guards with guns. That's when you stop.

Highway 375. The 98-mi road that runs through southeast Nevada from U.S. 93 to U.S. 6, was named the "Extraterrestrial Highway" by the state's tourism office when public interest was piqued by the hit TV show *The X-Files*. Today, thanks to its proximity to Area 51 and to the mysterious "Black Mailbox," where the installation's mail was supposedly delivered (it's really the mailbox of the only rancher in the area), it is a pilgrimage site for UFO enthusiasts from around the world and the preferred spot to watch the skies at night.

Dining

Little A'Le'Inn. American/Casual. This is the main gathering spot in Rachel and, naturally, it has a UFO theme (try their famous Alien Burger). Along with the restaurant, there's a gift shop and a wall full of UFO photos to peruse. If you feel inclined to spend the night, there are a few standard motel rooms—TVs and VCRs are provided so that you can partake of the video library, which includes many documentaries about Area 51 and UFOs. | Rte. 375 | 775/729–2515 | www.littlealeinn.com | AE, D, MC, V | ¢

NEW MEXICO

CIRCLING NORTHERN NEW MEXICO
SANTA FE, TAOS, AND THE FRONTIERS OF NEW SPAIN

Distance: Approximately 425 mi   Time: 4 days
Overnight Breaks: Raton, Santa Fe, and Taos

During the 16th and 17th centuries, Spanish conquistadors pushed frontier bound-aries hundreds of miles from what is now Mexico into areas they dubbed "New Spain." Through considerable hardship and loss of life, they created new settlements among the piñon forests, in many cases displacing or attempting to enslave the Pueblo Indians of this remote northern section of New Mexico. Attractions on this drive tell the story of these Spanish explorers and settlers, the Native Americans they attempted to conquer, and the later arrivals—early Mexican and American travelers who intro-duced their own cultures into an ethnic mix that is uniquely New Mexico.

    Much of the trip is on two-lane state highways. Snow and ice may temper your speed if you take this tour in winter; spring and fall are ideal times to travel, because of milder temperatures and the greenery and wildflowers that come alive during warm weather.

❶ Arrive in **Santa Fe** early and spend the day sightseeing in what state residents have nicknamed "The City Different," because it's unlike any other U.S. city in architecture, topography, and culture. Spend the night in a Santa Fe hotel or bed-and-breakfast.

❷ Enjoy a leisurely breakfast and leave Santa Fe around 10 AM, which will give you plenty of time to get to **Chimayó.** Take U.S. 84/U.S. 285 north out of Santa Fe. When you reach Pojoaque (about 17 mi from Santa Fe), turn right and take Route 503 about 5 mi to its junction with Route 98. Take the left branch and follow Route 98 to Chimayó. After lunch, save enough time to visit the **Santuario de Chimayó Church** and **Ortega's Weaving Shop,** within walking distance of each other. Eight generations of the Ortega family have been weaving here, and their works of textile art are breathtaking.

❸ Pick up Route 98 again to Route 76, turn right, and proceed northeast through the ageless Hispanic towns of Truchas and Las Trampas. From Las Trampas, another 6

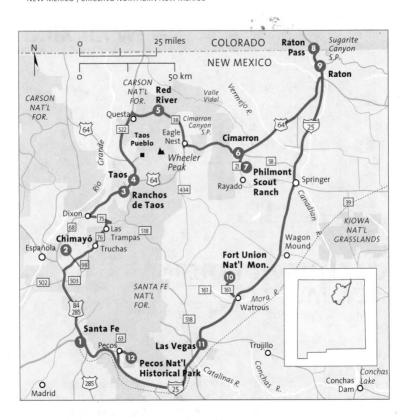

mi farther on Route 76 will bring you to the junction with Route 75. Observe the stunning, tree-lined red mesas and sloping canyons along the way. Turn left (west) and follow Route 75 through Dixon to Route 68 (about 14 mi). Turn right (north) and follow Route 68 21 mi to **Ranchos de Taos,** with the much-photographed **San Francisco de Asís Mission Church** on your right.

❹ Follow Route 68 2 mi north into **Taos.** With the Plaza as your base of operations, tour this sleepy Spanish town's many museums, historic residences, and art galleries. However, keep in mind that during peak tourist seasons the streets can be jammed with vehicles moving at a snail's pace. It's best to abandon your car somewhere and tour the town on foot.

Taos was famous during the early part of the 20th century as an artists' colony, and the village is full of references to those noted painters (Ernest Blumenschein, Bert Phillips, Irving Couse, Joseph H. Sharp, Oscar Berninghaus, among others) and writers (D. H. Lawrence, Frank Waters, and Mabel Dodge Luhan) who made their homes here. Famed mountain man Kit Carson lived in Taos for several years, and today the **Kit Carson Home and Museum** has been preserved much as it was during his lifetime. Spend the night in Taos.

❺ Leave Taos and travel north on U.S. 64 about 4 mi. Where U.S. 64 and Route 522 split, take U.S. 64 west about 8 mi to the bridge crossing the Rio Grande Gorge, the second-highest suspension bridge in the U.S. Parking the car near the bridge and strolling across it is well worth the time, as you will find no better place to appreciate the view of the wild Rio Grande Gorge. Retrace your steps on U.S. 64 until you come back to the Route 522 split, turn north on 522 and continue to the town of Questa, about 20 mi up the road. At Questa, take Route 38 east about 13 mi to **Red River,** a resort town known for its nearby ski slopes.

6 Continuing on Route 38 south about 18 mi brings you to the village of **Eagle Nest,** where you pick up U.S. 64 east and proceed about 24 mi through the grandiose, steep granite canyons of Cimarron Canyon to **Cimarron.** The town was once the administrative seat for the gigantic Maxwell Land Grant, which spread over 2 million acres of northern New Mexico and southern Colorado. Take a look at the historic **St. James Hotel,** which was started in 1880 as a saloon by Henri Lambert, onetime personal chef to both President Abraham Lincoln and General Ulysses S. Grant. Over the next several years, legend has it that as many as 26 men were killed within its walls. See the **Old Aztec Mill Museum** (across the street from the hotel) and other nearby attractions.

7 If you have ever been a Boy Scout, you'll want to make a short side trip to see the historic **Philmont Scout Ranch.** The original land in Philmont Ranch (nearly 36,000 acres) was given to the Boy Scouts in 1938 by Waite Phillips, an Oklahoma oilman. Three years later, more acreage was donated, and today the ranch consists of around 140,000 acres. After visiting Philmont, return to Cimarron and proceed north on U.S. 64 toward Raton about 40 mi.

8 Pick up I–25 at Raton and head north several miles toward the Colorado border and through **Raton Pass,** an ancient Indian trading route noted for its steep precipices and panoramic views of green valleys. Turn around on the other side of the Pass and proceed back along I–25 to Raton.

9 You should allow yourself some time to visit historic downtown **Raton** and its sights. The town offers an impressive walking tour that highlights the **Santa Fe Railroad Depot,** one of the few remaining vestiges of Raton's once thriving rail facilities, as well as a number of commercial buildings, theaters, hotels, and saloons, dating from the mid- to late-19th century and all remarkably well preserved. There are a number of fine lodging facilities in Raton, so plan on spending the night there.

10 Leave Raton early and proceed south on I–25 through Maxwell and Springer until you arrive at Exit 366 (about 89 mi). Follow Route 161 north about 8 mi to **Fort Union National Monument.** Stop by the visitor center for orientation about the fort's importance along the old Santa Fe Trail, then walk among its ruins for a sense of what military life was like on the Southwestern frontier.

11 Leaving Fort Union, follow Route 161 back to I–25 and continue southwest about 20 mi to **Las Vegas.** Visit the many shops clustered around the town Plaza. Return to I–25 and continue toward Santa Fe.

12 Follow I–25 south for about 40 mi to Exit 307, where you'll leave the interstate and head north about 5 mi to **Pecos National Historical Park.** As in the case of Fort Union, you will want to hike the short trail to fully appreciate this deeply moving and spiritual place. The visitor center maintains a theater, a fine museum, a well-stocked bookstore, and squeaky-clean rest rooms.

Leaving Pecos, return north on Route 63, turn left onto Route 50, and continue west to I–25, proceeding another 20 mi back to **Santa Fe.**

Chimayó

Galeria Ortega. The premier gallery in the region features art, gifts, music, Southwestern books, and foods of New Mexico. It's next door to Ortega's Weaving Shop. | Rtes. 98 and 76 | 505/351–2288 | Mon.–Sat. 9–5 (late Mar.–late Oct., also Sun. 11–5).

Ortega's Weaving Shop. The Ortega family of Chimayó has been weaving outstanding products for eight generations; their shop displays samples of their best wares, and there are daily demonstrations of the weaving process. | Rtes. 98 and 76 | 505/351–4215 | Mon.–Sat. 9–5.

★**Santuario de Chimayó.** Legend states that a mysterious light came from the ground on Good Friday in 1810, giving the site of this small frontier adobe church healing properties. The shrine is a National Historic Landmark and is pleasantly free of crass commercialism. Thousands come here each Holy Week. | Rte. 98 | 505/351–4889 | Free | Daily 9–5:30.

Chapel of Santo Niño de Atocha. Just 200 feet away from the main church, this small chapel built in 1857 is said to have miraculous healing powers. It's named after a boy saint brought from New Mexico who, it is said, lost one of his shoes as he wandered the countryside helping people; it is tradition to place shoes at the foot of his statue as an offering. | Free | Daily 9–5:30.

Dining

Leona's de Chimayó. Mexican. Flavored tortillas—from jalapeño to blueberry–chocolate to pesto—are the specialty of this fast-food burrito-and-chili stand at one end of the Santuario de Chimayó parking lot. Anticipate summer crowds. | 4 Medina La. | 505/351–4569 | AE, D, DC, MC, V | Closed Tues.–Wed and Nov.–Apr. No dinner | ¢

★**Rancho De Chimayó.** Mexican. This restaurant, in a century-old adobe hacienda tucked into the hillside, is still owned and operated by the family that first occupied the house. The interior has whitewashed walls and hand-stripped vigas; a fireplace makes winter dining all the more cozy. In summer, a terraced patio shaded by catalpa trees is available for outdoor dining. | Rte. 98, Chimayó | 505/351–4444 | AE, D, DC, MC, V | Closed Mon. and Nov.–May | $–$$

NEW MEXICO RULES OF THE ROAD

License Requirements: The driving age in New Mexico is 16. As a visitor driving an automobile in New Mexico you must have a valid driver's license from your home state.

Right Turn on Red: A driver can turn right on a red light after coming to a full stop.

Seat Belt and Helmet Laws: State law requires automobile drivers and passengers to use seat belts. Motorcyclists and passengers under the age of 18 are required by law to wear helmets. Children riding in automobiles must be restrained in the back seat, and if they are age four or under, they must be restrained in a children's car seat secured in the back seat.

Speed Limits: Individual speed limits are posted in all municipalities. Most interstates maintain a 75-mph speed limit, depending on location.

For More Information: Contact the **New Mexico Highway Hotline** | 800/432–4269.

Cimarron

Cimarron Canyon State Park. Palisades Sills, a 400-foot granite formation, dominates this state park 12 mi west of Cimarron on U.S. 64. There's superb rainbow and trout fishing here. It's a good place to stop for a morning or afternoon hike. | U.S. 64 | 505/377–6271 | www.emnrd.state.nm.us/nmparks | $4 per vehicle | Daily.

Old Aztec Mill Museum. Today the 1864 mill houses four floors of photos, clothing, tools, and memorabilia depicting life in Colfax County from the 1860s forward. | Rte. 21 | 505/376–2913 | $2 | May–Sept., Mon.–Sat. 9–5 and Sun. 1–5; Oct.–Apr., Mon.–Sat. 9–5.

Philmont Scout Ranch. The 140,000-acre Philmont Ranch, 4 mi south of Cimarron on Route 21, is the world's largest private youth camp, which was donated to the Boy Scouts of America by Oklahoma oilman Waite Phillips. If you visit the ranch, you can see the Kit Carson Museum and the Philmont Museum, as well as the Villa Philmonte, Waite Phillips's original summer home. | Rte. 21 | 505/376–2281 | Free | July–Aug., daily 8–6; Sept.–June, Mon.–Sat 8–noon and 1–5.

Kit Carson Museum. Built on a portion of the original fort founded by Kit Carson and Lucien Maxwell, which is 2 mi south of the main Philmont offices, this interpretive museum has both hands-on exhibits and displays that demonstrate turn-of-the-20th-century mountain man life. Hosts, dressed in 1880s period costumes, talk about the history and legends of the area, and you can try your hand at blacksmithing or black powder rifle shooting. | Rte. 21 | 505/376–2281 | Free | June–Aug., daily 8–5.

The Philmont Museum and Seton Memorial Library. Across the street from Philmont's main offices and base camp, this museum exhibits photographs, artifacts, and information about the history of the area and the ranch; it also has the extensive book collection of Ernest Thompson Seton, famed naturalist and founder of the Boy Scouts. | Rte. 21 | 505/376–2281 | Free | July–Aug., daily 8–6; Sept.–June, Mon.–Sat. 8–noon and 1–5.

Villa Philmonte. Built in 1927, this lavish Mediterranean-style villa was the summer home of oil tycoon Waite Phillips until 1941. The collection here includes brilliantly colored Oriental rugs, intricate tile work, antique furnishings, and numerous works of art, as well as photographs of regular guests like Theodore Roosevelt. Reservations for tours must be made at the Philmont Museum and Seton Memorial Library next door. | Rte. 21 | 505/376–2281 | $4 | June–Aug., daily 8–5, tours every ½ hour; Sept.–May, tours by appointment only.

St. James Hotel. Dating back to 1872, this still active hotel has sheltered such characters as Zane Grey, Wyatt Earp, Doc Holliday, Annie Oakley, Clay Allison, and Buffalo Bill. Sightseeing in the lobby is free if you have dinner or drinks at the hotel; ask about the ghost in Room 18. | 17th and Collinson Sts. | 505/376–2664 | Daily.

Dining

Colfax Tavern. American/Casual. Also known as Cold Beer, New Mexico, this tavern 11 mi east of Cimarron has been open since Prohibition. In addition to an ongoing card game and Shiner Bock on tap, there are Saturday-night dances and a winter *Jeopardy!* tournament. The menu includes green-chili burgers, pizza, spaghetti on Monday, and brisket on Wednesday. | U.S. 64 | 505/376–2229 | No credit cards | $

Las Vegas

Fort Union National Monument. During its heyday, Fort Union—at a critical point along the Santa Fe Trail about 30 mi north of Las Vegas—was the largest U.S. military establishment in the entire Southwest. Completed in 1869, it served as a supply center for smaller installations across the region. The arrival of the Santa Fe Railroad in the 1880s put the fort out of business, as trains began to bypass the fort and speed much-needed army equipment directly to its destinations. | Rte. 161 | 505/425–8025 | $3 | Memorial Day–Labor Day, daily 8–6; Labor Day–Memorial Day, daily 8–4.

Las Vegas National Wildlife Refuge. Observe American eagles, waterfowl, and a large variety of other wildlife species from your vantage point in this refuge 6½ mi southeast of Las Vegas. It's one of the premier birding sites in the Southwest. | Rte. 281 | 505/425–3581 | Free | Daily; visitor center weekdays 8–4:30.

Storrie Lake State Park. The lake 6 mi north of Las Vegas has a visitor center and offers windsurfing, fishing, boating, waterskiing, camping, and picnicking facilities. It's a favorite place to catch rainbow and German brown trout. | Rte. 518 | 505/425–7278 | $4 | Park daily; visitor center Apr.–Aug., daily 8–8.

Theodore Roosevelt Rough Riders' Memorial and City Museum. Teddy Roosevelt recruited many members of his Rough Riders regiment from New Mexico and the surrounding territory. After the Spanish–American War, Roosevelt's veterans chose Las Vegas as their reunion site, and over the years the town became the repository for many Rough Riders artifacts. | 727 Grand Ave. | 505/454–1401 Ext. 283 | Free | Nov.–Apr., weekdays 9–noon and 1–4, Sat. 10–3, Sun. noon–4; May–Oct., Sat. 10–3, Sun noon–4.

Dining

Blackjack's Grill. Italian. The steaks here are the best in town, and the Old Mexico pork tenderloins, seafood enchiladas, flan, and New York cheesecake are also worthy. The romantic dining room and the more casual patio by the garden are both equally pleasant. | 1133 Grand Ave. | 505/425–6791 or 888/448–8438 | AE, D, MC, V | $–$$

El Rialto Restaurant & Lounge. Mexican. Perfectly blended margaritas set the mood for the fajitas, enchiladas, and chiles rellenos at this popular restaurant. In an historic 1890s building, El Rialto is packed with antiques. | 141 Bridge St. | 505/454–0037 | AE, D, MC, V | Closed Sun. | ¢–$$

Estella's Restaurant. Mexican. Don't be put off by the modest appearance: Estella's, which has been smothering burritos in green chili since 1950, is one of the best places to stop for a bite. | 148 Bridge St. | 505/454–0048 | No credit cards | Closed Sun. No dinner Mon.–Wed. | ¢–$$

Raton

Capulin Volcano National Monument. Walking along the rim of Capulin Mountain, you'll see parts of five states. The volcano is young—only about 60,000 years old—but it has been dormant long enough for you to descend into its crater for a look around. It's 29 mi east of Raton on U.S. 64/U.S. 87 to Capulin, then 3½ mi north. | Off Rte. 325 | 505/278–2201 | www.nps.gov/cavo | $5 per vehicle | Memorial Day–Labor Day, daily 7:30–6:30; Labor Day–Memorial Day, daily 8–4.

Maxwell National Wildlife Refuge. Home to dozens of species of waterfowl, plus bald eagles and deer, this is the site of some of the best trout fishing in northern New Mexico. It's 23 mi south of Raton, 4 mi northwest of Maxwell. | Off Rte. 505 | 505/375–2331 | www.southwest.fws.gov/refuges/newmex/maxwell.html | Free | Daily.

Raton Museum. Artifacts from Raton's past, a fine photo collection, regional artwork, and old musical instruments are just a few of the varied items in this museum. | 218 S. 1st St. | 505/445–8979 | Free | Memorial Day–Labor Day, Tues.–Sat. 9–5; Labor Day–Memorial Day, Wed.–Sat. 10–4.

Sugarite Canyon State Park. The site of an early coal mining camp that drew miners from all over the world, this gem of a park is 7 mi northeast of downtown Raton. Sugarite has some of the state's best hiking, camping, wildflower viewing, fishing, and bird-watching. Hikes in the park range from the easy ½-mi Grande Vista Nature Trail to the pleasant 4-mi jaunt around Lake Maloya to the challenging Opportunity Trail. "Caprock" is the name given to the park's striking basaltic rock columns, which were formed millions of years ago by lava from a nearby volcano; climbing is permitted on these sheer cliffs. | Rte. 526 | 505/445–5607 | $4 | Park daily 8–6.

Dining

Pappas' Sweet Shop. American. Pappas' is a place of pleasant nostalgia, with collectibles and antiques throughout the spot. It's no longer a sweets shop; instead, simple but good steaks, pasta, and seafood are served. | 1201 S. 2nd St. | 505/445–9811 | AE, D, MC, V | Closed Sun. | $–$$$

Lodging

Best Western Sands. All rooms at this Best Western are spacious and comfortable; Luxury Wing rooms have extras, such as Kona coffee and Neutrogena amenities. Restaurant, in-room data ports, some minibars, cable TV, outdoor pool, hot tub, playground, business services. | 300 Clayton Rd., 87740 | 505/445–2737 or 800/518–2581 | fax 505/445–4053 | www.bestwestern.com | 50 rooms | AE, D, DC, MC, V | CP | $

Budget Host Melody Lane Motel. Affordable and unpretentious are the key words in describing the Budget Host chain, but fear not: the rooms here are clean and comfortable and this quiet motel is adequate for a quick stopover. Minibars, cable TV, some pets allowed (fee). | 136 Canyon Dr., 87740 | 505/445–3655 or 800/421–5210 | fax 505/445–3461 | www.budgethost.com | 27 rooms | AE, D, DC, MC, V | CP | ¢–$

El Portal. El Portal is an eccentric hostelry in a restored 1885 building. The lobby is filled with antiques—a vintage Royal typewriter is among the items—and has a working fireplace. Many rooms have themes: for instance, the Holiday Room has autographed photos of Hollywood stars. The rooms aren't high on amenities, but the price is right. Restaurant, some kitchenettes, cable TV, some pets allowed. | 101 N. 3rd St., 87740 | 505/445–3631 or 888/362–7345 | 15 rooms, 39 apartments | MC, V | ¢

Red River

Pioneer Canyon Trail. Take this 3-mi-long auto trek and go back more than 100 years to the days when gold and copper were mined in the surrounding mountains. The trip is two to three hours long if you stop at all of the sites. The trail starts behind the Arrowhead Lodge. | Pioneer Rd. | 505/754–2366 | Daily.

Red River Ski Area. Fifty-eight trails and a 1,600-foot vertical drop are the high points of this ski area. | Pioneer Rd. | 505/754–2223 or 800/341–7669 | www.redriverskiarea.com | Thanksgiving–late Mar.

Dining

Old Tymers' Café. American/Casual. You can start your day with fresh biscuits, French toast, or an omelet at this restaurant. The lunch menu includes barbecued brisket sandwiches, chili dogs, and hamburgers. | 210 Main St. | 505/754–2951 | D, MC, V | ¢–$

Shotgun Willie's. Barbecue. The meat here is smoked for 30 hours over hickory and mesquite and then served with Willie's special-recipe barbecue sauce. Try the barbecued chicken sandwich, the sliced brisket, or the charbroiled burger. | Main and Pioneer Sts. | 505/754–6505 | No credit cards | ¢–$

Sundance. Mexican. Fajitas or burritos are good bets in this Southwestern-style restaurant. Throw back a margarita or some sangria in front of the fireplace. | 401 High St. | 505/754–2971 | AE, D, DC, MC, V | Closed Apr.–mid-May. No lunch Sept.–Mar. | $

Santa Fe

Cristo Rey Church. The largest adobe structure in the United States, this church is considered by many to be the finest example of pueblo-style architecture anywhere. It was completed in 1940 to commemorate the 400th anniversary of Francisco Vásquez de Coronado's exploration of the Southwest. | Canyon Rd. and Cristo Rey St. | 505/983–8528 | Free | Daily 8–7.

Georgia O'Keeffe Museum. One of many painters who moved to Santa Fe in the early part of the 20th century, Georgia O'Keeffe settled near the city and focused some of her most famous paintings on Southwestern themes. This private museum contains 130 of her works. O'Keeffe's favorite foods are for sale in the café. | 217 Johnson St. | 505/995–0785 | www.okeeffemuseum.org | $8 | Nov.–July, Mon., Tues., Thurs., Sat. 10–5, Fri. 10–8; Aug.–Oct., also open Wed. noon–8.

Institute of American Indian Arts Museum. Native American art from a range of tribes, including those from Alaska and the Southwest, are displayed at this handsomely renovated former post office. You'll find paintings, photography, sculptures, prints, and other crafts. | 108 Cathedral Pl. | 505/983–8900 | www.iaiancad.org | $4 | June–Sept., daily 9–5; Oct.–May, Mon.–Sat. 10–5 and Sun. noon–5.

La Fonda. A *fonda* (inn) has stood on this site facing the southeast corner of the Plaza since 1610, though the current structure dates to 1922. Architect Isaac Hamilton Rapp, whose Rio Grande–Pueblo Revival structures put Santa Fe style on the map, was the original architect; it was remodeled in 1926 by architect John Gaw Meem. Because of its proximity to the Plaza, La Fonda has been a gathering place for actors, politicos, and cowboys. | 100 E. San Francisco St. | 505/982–5511 or 800/523–5002 | www.lafondasantafe.com | Free | Daily.

Museum of Fine Arts. Santa Fe's oldest art museum opened in 1917 and contains one of the finest regional collections in the United States, displaying the work of many early New Mexico artists who settled and worked around Santa Fe and Taos. | 107 W. Palace Ave. | 505/476–5072 | www.nmculture.org | $7 | Tues.–Sun. 10–5.

Museum of Spanish Colonial Art. This 5,000-square-foot adobe museum occupies a building designed in 1930 by acclaimed architect John Gaw Meem. It has one of the most comprehensive collections of Spanish Colonial art in the world. Objects here, dating from the 16th century to the present, include retablos, elaborate santos, tinwork, straw appliqué, furniture, ceramics, and ironwork. | 750 Camino Lejo | 505/982–2226 | www.spanishcolonial.org/museum.shtml | $6, 4-day pass $15 (good at all 5 state museums in Santa Fe) | Daily 10–5.

New Mexico State Capitol. Sometimes called the Roundhouse, New Mexico's capitol building is built in the shape of a Zia sun symbol. Artwork by regional artists adorns the lobby. | Paseo de Peralta and Old Santa Fe Trail | 505/986–4589 | Free | June–Aug., weekdays 8–7; Sept.–May, weekdays 8–5.

★ **Palace of the Governors.** The oldest public building in continuous use in the United States, this humble-looking one-story adobe structure is the headquarters of the Museum of New Mexico. Part of the fun in visiting Santa Fe is to walk under the portals of the palace and view all the wonderful handmade jewelry, the work of native New Mexicans, for sale on blankets lining the street. The museum, bookstore, and printing shop on the premises are all must-sees. | Palace Ave. (north side of the Plaza) | 505/476–5100 | www.nmculture.org | $7 | Tues.–Sun. 10–5.

Pecos National Historical Park. On land donated by actress Greer Garson, 2 mi south of Pecos and 26 mi southeast of Santa Fe, this park presents the fascinating story of one of the largest prehistoric pueblos in the Southwest. Take the walking tour and visit the museum and bookstore. | Rte. 63 (I–25), Pecos | 505/757–6414 | $3 | Memorial Day–Labor Day, daily 8–6; Labor Day–Memorial Day, daily 8–5.

★**San Miguel Mission.** This 1610 church had its roof burned during the Pueblo Revolt of 1680; the church was restored and enlarged in 1710. The mission served as a place of worship for Spanish soldiers and settlers and Native American converts. | 401 Old Santa Fe Trail | 505/983–3974 | Free | Mon–Sat. 9–5, Sun. 10–4.

Sena Plaza. In the heart of downtown, this plant- and tree-filled plaza, complete with songbirds, is filled with modern shops and eateries. | Between E. Palace Ave. and Nusbaum St., and between Washington and Otero Sts.

Dining

★**Cafe Pasqual's.** Southwestern. Regional and Latin American specialties have been served here for decades: huevos Motuleños (black beans and eggs over a blue-corn tortilla with tomatillo sauce and goat cheese) and chili-rubbed, pan-roasted salmon are the stars of the menu. The restaurant's murals are by Oaxacan artist Leo Uigildo-Martinez. Breakfast is also available. | 121 Don Gaspar Ave. | 505/983–9340 | AE, MC, V | $$–$$$

★**Plaza Restaurant.** American/Casual. Vintage photos adorn the walls of this diner, in operation since 1918. The eclectic menu includes spicy pasta, blue-corn enchiladas, and New Mexico meat loaf. | 54 Lincoln Ave. | 505/982–1664 | AE, D, MC, V | $–$$

Zia Diner. American. Try one of the weeknight blue-plate specials at this upscale diner, or just enjoy a thick slice of strawberry-rhubarb pie. Service is fast and friendly, and the food is fresher and more imaginative than typical diner fare. Patio dining is also available. | 326 S. Guadalupe St. | 505/988–7008 | AE, MC, V | $–$$

Lodging

Adobe Abode. Rooms in this B&B near the Georgia O'Keeffe Museum contain objects the owner has gathered from around the world. Each room has its own theme: for instance, the Bloomsbury has a restrained English feel and an antique wicker bed, the Cabin in the Woods has bright red walls and Adirondack furniture, the Bronco has all sorts of cowboy detritus from hats to boots to lassos incorporated into the room. Dining room, cable TV. | 202 Chapelle St., 87501 | 505/983–3133 | fax 505/424–3027 | www.adobeabode.com | 5 rooms, 1 suite | MC, V | CP | $–$$

★**Hotel Santa Fe.** The light and airy rooms and suites at this handsome Pueblo-style three-story hotel near the Plaza are done in traditional Southwestern style, with locally handmade furniture, wooden blinds, and Pueblo paintings; many have balconies overlooking the city lights. Restaurant, minibars, cable TV, pool, hot tub, bar, laundry facilities, laundry service, business services, airport shuttle. | 1501 Paseo de Peralta, 87501 | 505/982–1200 or 800/825–9876 | fax 505/984–2211 | www.hotelsantafe.com | 40 rooms, 89 suites | AE, D, DC, MC, V | $$$

Santa Fe Motel and Inn. Furnishings are basic at this motel, five blocks from the Plaza, but bright linens and funky, multicolor tile work in the bathrooms, make it quite an upgrade from other motor inns. The casitas in the back have more space and privacy, and some have fireplaces. Some kitchenettes, some microwaves, some refrigerators, cable TV, some in-room VCRs, business services. | 510 Cerrillos Rd., 87501 | 505/982–1039 or 800/999–1039 | fax 505/986–1275 | www.santafemotelandinn.com | 13 rooms, 8 casitas | AE, D, DC, MC, V | CP | $–$$$

Spencer House. This cozy 1920s adobe house is furnished with English and American colonial antiques. Bathrooms are spacious; some rooms have fireplaces. The living room has a fireplace as its centerpiece—and the requisite rocking chair to go in front of it. Dining room, some in-room hot tubs, cable TV; no kids under 12. | 222 McKenzie St., 87501

| 505/988–3024 or 800/647–0530 | fax 505/984–9862 | www.spencerhousesantafe.com | 6 rooms | AE, MC, V | BP | $$–$$$

Taos

Carson National Forest. Surrounding Taos and spanning almost 1½ million acres across northern New Mexico, the forest has over 50 recreation sites, including lakes, the Wheeler Peak Wilderness Area, and Pecos Wilderness Area. You can hike, bike, fish, or ski, or just look at the wildflowers. | Headquarters: 208 Cruz Alta Rd. | 505/758–6200 | www.fs.fed.us/r3/carson | Free | Headquarters weekdays 8–4:30.

D. H. Lawrence Ranch and Memorial. The author of *Lady Chatterley's Lover* was one of the first writers to come to the region. The ranch where Lawrence lived for almost two years, 15 mi north of Taos, is now an education and conference center. The house is not open to the public, but you can visit the memorial where Lawrence's ashes were scattered and where his wife Frieda is buried. | Rte. 522, San Cristobal | 505/776–2245 | Free | Daily 8:30–5.

Fechin Institute. Built between 1927 and 1933 by artist Nicolai Fechin (who died in 1955), this adobe house is a showcase of daring colorful portraits and landscapes. | 227 Paseo del Pueblo Norte | 505/758–1710 | $4 | Wed.–Sun. 10–2.

Governor Bent Home and Museum. Newly appointed New Mexico governor Charles Bent was killed in this house during the Taos Revolt of January 1847 by a mob protesting the U.S. annexation of New Mexico. See the hole in the wall through which Bent's wife and children tried to escape. | 117A Bent St. | 505/758–2376 | $2 | Daily 10–5.

Rio Grande Gorge Bridge. A view of this deeply carved canyon with a tiny ribbon of the Rio Grande below greets you as you walk across this bridge. Sometimes you can see river rafters bobbing far below you. Unfortunately, graffiti covers the railings of this famous bridge, but nature more than compensates. | U.S. 64, 11 mi northwest of Taos | No phone | Daily.

San Francisco de Asís Church. Restored in 1979, this Spanish Mission–style church dates to the 18th century. It is most famous for the painting *Shadow of the Cross,* by Henri Ault, on which each evening the shadow of a cross appears over Christ's shoulder. The phenomenon is unexplained. | Rte. 68, 500 yards south of Rte. 518, Rancho de Taos | 505/758–2754 | Free | Mon.–Sat. 9–4; mass Sun. at 7, 9, and 11:30.

Taos Plaza. At the heart of the Taos downtown area, the Plaza is one of the oldest parts of the city. By a special act of Congress, the U.S. flag flies 24 hours a day here in honor of Kit Carson's stand against the Confederacy during the Civil War. | Don Fernando Rd. | No phone | Daily.

★ **Taos Pueblo.** For nearly 1,000 years the mud-and-straw adobe walls of Taos Pueblo have sheltered Tiwa-speaking Native Americans. A United Nations World Heritage Site, this is the largest multistory pueblo structure in the United States. The pueblo today appears much as it did when the first Spanish explorers arrived in New Mexico in 1540. Bread is still baked in *hornos* (outdoor domed ovens) and artisans of the Taos Pueblo produce and sell (tax-free) traditionally handcrafted wares. Respect the RESTRICTED AREA signs that protect the privacy of residents and native religious sites. | 2 mi north of Taos on Paseo del Pueblo Norte (Rte. 68) | 505/758–9593 or 505/758–1028 | www.taosvacationguide.com/history/pueblo.html | $10 | Daily 8–5; closed during certain ceremonies and funerals.

Taos Ski Valley. Included in many top-10 ski resort lists in the United States, this resort is 18 mi northeast of Taos. It has a ski school and 72 runs, though there is no snowboarding permitted. | Taos Ski Valley Rd. (Rte. 150) | 505/776–2291, 800/776–1111 (accommodations) | www.skitaos.org | Slopes late Nov.–early Apr.; summer chairlift May–Oct., Thurs.–Mon. 10–4:30.

Dining

Apple Tree. Contemporary. Dine indoors, surrounded by original art, or sit out in a courtyard, where you can watch the sparrows come to beg crumbs. Try the grilled lamb or chicken fajitas. The wine list is outstanding. The restaurant is one block north of the Plaza. | 123 Bent St. | 505/758–1900 | AE, D, DC, MC, V | $$–$$$

Orlando's. Southwestern. Frequented by locals, this family-run restaurant serves chicken enchiladas, blue-corn enchiladas, and shrimp burritos, to name a few. Eat in the cozy dining room or call ahead for takeout. | 114 Don Juan Valdez La. | 505/751–1450 | No credit cards | ¢–$

★ **Trading Post Café.** Contemporary. The marinated gravlax appetizer here is exceptional, and the paella is a bounty for two. Try the homemade raspberry sorbet or the flan. To park, turn east onto Route 518 (Talpa Road) north of the restaurant, and then walk back along Talpa Road to get to the entrance. | 4178 Paseo del Pueblo Sur, Ranchos de Taos | 505/758–5089 | AE, D, DC, MC, V | Closed Mon. | $–$$$

Lodging

Casa Benavides Bed & Breakfast Inn. One block from the Plaza, this B&B combines the charm of an old Taos adobe with modern luxuries. Rooms are furnished with antiques and original artwork, and there is a lovely courtyard in the main building. Many rooms have fireplaces and skylights. Some kitchenettes, some refrigerators, cable TV, some in-room VCRs, hot tubs; no phones in some rooms, no TV in some rooms. | 137 Kit Carson Rd., 87571 | 505/758–1772 or 800/552–1772 | fax 505/758–5738 | www.taosnet.com/casabena | 33 rooms | AE, D, MC, V | CP | $$–$$$

★ **Hacienda del Sol.** Mabel Dodge Luhan, an heiress who drew literati to the region, owned this pueblo-style house. Most rooms have kiva-style fireplaces (choice of wood-burning or gas-fired), Southwestern handcrafted furnishings, and original artwork. This is one of the most romantic places to stay in Taos. Three rooms have steam baths. Dining room, picnic area, minibars, business services; no a/c, no smoking. | 109 Mabel Dodge La., 87571 | 505/758–0287 | fax 505/751–0319 | www.taoshaciendadelsol.com | 11 rooms (2 with shower only), 2 suites | AE, D, MC, V | BP | $$–$$$

Hotel La Fonda de Taos. On Taos Plaza, this adobe hotel has many antiques and a collection of erotic paintings by D. H. Lawrence (which can be viewed for a small fee). The hotel is steps away from the town's shops, galleries, and restaurants. No TV in some rooms, no smoking. | 108 S. Plaza, 87571 | 505/758–2211 or 800/833–2211 | fax 505/758–8508 | www.hotellafonda.com | 24 rooms | AE, MC, V | $–$$$

Old Taos Guesthouse. Once an adobe hacienda, this B&B is on 7½ acres of land. All rooms have private entrances and private baths. Some rooms have skylights or fireplaces. The outdoor hot tub has a magnificent view. Some kitchenettes, hot tub; no room phones, no smoking. | 1028 Witt Rd., 87571 | 505/758–5448 or 800/758–5448 | fax 505/758–5448 | www.oldtaos.com | 9 rooms | D, MC, V | BP | $–$$

ON THE TRAIL OF BILLY THE KID
FROM LAS CRUCES TO THREE RIVERS

Distance: Approximately 350 mi   Time: 4–5 days
Overnight Breaks: Alamogordo or Cloudcroft, Las Cruces, Ruidoso

Of all the outlaws associated with the history of New Mexico, the most notorious by far was Billy the Kid. He is said to have killed 21 men during the late 1800s, including Lincoln County Sheriff William Brady. Finally, another sheriff, Pat Garrett, tracked down the rebellious young outlaw and shot him dead. This tour of the south-central section of the state passes through sites with links to the Kid, including the towns of Old Mesilla, Lincoln, and White Oaks. Along the way you'll also see the White Sands National Monument, the Space Hall of Fame, and the natural beauty of the state. Weather conditions in this region are mild year-round, except for parts of winter in the highlands and some rare desert snowstorms.

❶ The tour begins in **Las Cruces,** New Mexico's second-largest city. Las Cruces was established in 1848, when the U.S. Army placed a small military post there. Five years later, when the Gadsden Purchase was ratified, the entire region became American territory. Get your bearings for the many sights in this area at **Las Cruces Museum of Natural History.**

❷ On the outskirts of Las Cruces is the historic village of **Old Mesilla.** For a brief period during the Civil War, it was the unofficial capital of the Confederate Territory of Arizona. Billy the Kid was once incarcerated for murder in Mesilla, but escaped. Today the cluster of shops and restaurants lining the **Old Mesilla Plaza** offers crafts and food. Spend the night in Las Cruces.

❸ Leaving Las Cruces, take I-25 to U.S. 70 northeast and drive the 25 mi to the entrance of the **White Sands Missile Range.** You will pass through a security station (be sure your driver's license and car insurance papers are up-to-date, because they will be checked). If you happen to be here on the first Saturday in either April or October, you will be able to tour the Trinity Site, where America's first atomic bomb was detonated. But keep in mind it's a long drive north—about 145 mi from Las Cruces—to the Socorro, New Mexico area, where you enter the far northern end of the missile range, so plan on an extra day if you want to tour the facility.

❹ After you leave the range, turn back northeast on U.S. 70 and drive until you see the entrance (about 30 mi) to **White Sands National Monument** on your left. This natural wonder encompasses nearly 200,000 acres of glistening gypsum dunes.

❺ After viewing the dunes, follow U.S. 70 into **Alamogordo,** a good place to spend the night. A must-see here is the **New Mexico Museum of Space History,** a four-story cube perched on the side of a mountain. It honors the men and women who have made their marks on space research and exploration, and even offers simulated space walks on Mars. **The Alameda Park Zoo** is one of the oldest animal parks in the Southwest and is home to hundreds of domestic and foreign species.

❻ Leaving Alamogordo northward on U.S. 54, proceed until you arrive at the highway's junction with U.S. 82, which you will take to the town of **Cloudcroft.** In the early 1900s surveyors gave the romantic name to the town after spying a single white cloud hovering over a nearby meadow, which in the Old English vernacular is "croft." Today it's a mountain retreat that has great year-round temperatures and one of the nation's highest golf courses. While there, visit the **National Solar Observatory at Sacramento Peak,** the national center for the study of the sun. (You might want to consider staying overnight in Cloudcroft instead of at Alamogordo, if only to experience The Lodge, a truly unique place.) Pick up Route 244 at Cloudcroft and follow it through the Mescalero Apache Indian Reservation to its junction with U.S. 70.

❼ Follow U.S. 70 eastward into the picturesque Sacramento Mountain town of **Ruidoso** and spend the night. Nearby is the **Hubbard Museum of the American West,** which displays a variety of Native American artifacts, horse-drawn vehicles, original art, and

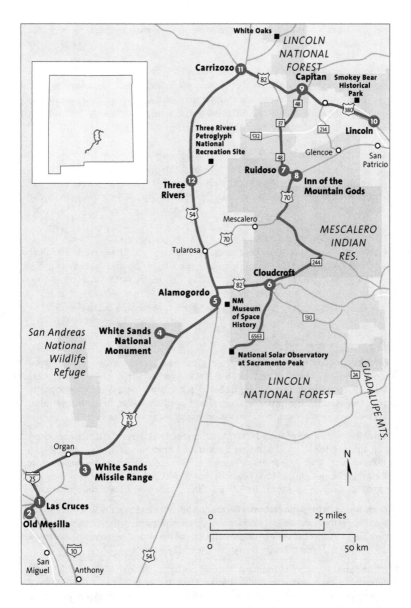

antiques. Brush up on your Billy the Kid lore at the **Billy the Kid National Scenic Byway Visitor Center,** adjacent to the museum.

❽ Just outside Ruidoso, on the Mescalero Apache Indian Reservation, is the **Inn of the Mountain Gods,** which reopens in fall 2004. The Mescalero Apache-owned inn offers luxurious accommodations, fine dining, golf, tennis, boating, fishing, and gambling, including poker and bingo.

❾ Leave Ruidoso on Route 48 and drive north to **Capitan,** the home of the **Smokey Bear Historical Park.** Smokey, the survivor of a 1950 forest fire near town, was the inspiration for the cartoon mascot adopted by the National Council for Forest Fire Prevention. You'll see Smokey's grave site here, as well as the **Smokey Bear Museum,** which contains an exhibit of Smokey memorabilia.

⑩ Proceed east on U.S. 380 to **Lincoln.** Billy the Kid reportedly spent the night at the Ellis Store Country Inn at Mile Marker 98. Prepare to spend at least half a day in Lincoln. Tour the restored frontier town and site of Billy's last escape from the law: he met his end at the hand of Sheriff Pat Garrett near Lincoln in the town of Fort Sumner. The Kid is buried at Fort Sumner Military Cemetery.

⑪ Backtrack on U.S. 380 to Capitan and then continue until you reach **Carrizozo.** Twelve miles northeast of here, via U.S. 54 and Route 349, lies the legendary ghost town of **White Oaks**—an old haunt (no pun intended) of Billy the Kid—which once boasted a population of 4,000, supporting three churches, two hotels, four newspapers, and many saloons.

⑫ Returning to Carrizozo, continue southward along U.S. 54 through the village of Oscuro to the community of **Three Rivers** and the turnoff to **Three Rivers Petroglyph National Recreation Site** on your left. Here, more than 500 ancient drawings and rock carvings grace the cliffs overlooking the Tularosa basin. Spend as much time as you can spare here to enjoy the interpretive trail and other outdoor activities.

Return to U.S. 54 and proceed southward on your way back to **Las Cruces.**

Alamogordo

Eagle Ranch. You'll find the largest grove of pistachio trees in New Mexico here—some 12,000 trees—4 mi north of the White Sands Mall. Tour the farm, linger in the art gallery, and buy some nuts to take home. | 7288 U.S. 54, at U.S. 70 | 505/434–0035 or 800/432–0999 | www.eagleranchpistachios.com | Free | Ranch Mon.–Sat. 8–6, Sun. 9–6. Tours Sept.–May, weekdays at 1:30; June–Aug., weekdays at 10 and 1:30.

New Mexico Museum of Space History. Space and early rocketry exhibits, a planetarium, and outdoor displays and parks are among the attractions at this facility 2 mi east of downtown Alamogordo. IMAX movies with space and nature themes also are shown at the site. | Top of NM Hwy. 2001 | 505/437–2840 or 877–333–6589 | Museum $2.50, IMAX movie $6 (daytime) $6.50 (evening) | Daily 9–5, IMAX movies hourly.

Three Rivers Petroglyph National Recreation Site. Ancient Indians, who lived in the area between AD 1000 and 1350, carved thousands of pictures on the surrounding rocks here about 35 mi north of Alamogordo. It's one of the largest petroglyph sites in the United States. | County Rd. B30 | 505/525–4300 | $2 | Daily.

★**White Sands National Monument.** Encompassing 275 square mi, this is the largest deposit of gypsum in the world. It's 15 mi southwest of Alamogordo. | Off U.S. 70 | 505/679–2599 or 505/479–6124 | $3 | Visitor center Memorial Day–mid-Aug., daily 8–7; mid-Aug.–Memorial Day, daily 8–5.

Dining

Compass Rose. Continental. Patterned after a Bavarian-style pub, this unusual establishment has wooden-bench seating. Try the salads and hot sandwiches, including Reubens, pepper steaks, and the "ultimate ham and cheese." | 2203 E. 1st St. | 505/434–9633 | AE, D, MC, V | ¢–$$

Margo's Mexican Food. Mexican. Chalupas (beans, meat, and cheese served on crisp tortillas) are the specialty at this casual, family-owned spot. In winter try *menudo,* steaming-hot hominy and tripe. | 504 1st St. | 505/434–0689 | AE, D, MC, V | ¢–$

Lodging

Best Western Desert Aire. You'll find larger-than-average rooms in this attractive adobe-and-brick building. This is probably the best place amenities-wise to stay in Alamogordo proper. In-room data ports, some microwaves, cable TV, pool, hot tub, sauna, laundry facilities, some pets allowed (fee). | 1021 S. White Sands Blvd., 88310 | 505/437–2110 | fax 505/437–1898 | www.bestwestern.com | 99 rooms | AE, D, DC, MC, V | CP | $

Comfort Inn & Suites. On Alamogordo's main street, this lovely two-story motel is within walking distance of three restaurants. Some microwaves, refrigerators, cable TV, pool, hot tub, laundry facilities, business services. | 1020 S. White Sands Blvd., 88310 | 505/434–4200 or 800/255–5061 | fax 505/437–8872 | 91 rooms | AE, D, DC, MC, V | CP | $

Holiday Inn Express. Rooms at this comfortable, two-story hotel are accessible from an interior hallway, which reduces ambient noise. It's two blocks from the junction of U.S. 54 and 70. In-room data ports, cable TV, pool, hair salon, laundry facilities, laundry service, business services, some pets allowed. | 1401 S. White Sands Blvd., 88310 | 505/437–7100 or 800/465–4329 | fax 505/437–7100 | www.hiexpress.com | 108 rooms | AE, D, DC, MC, V | CP | $

Carrizozo

Sierra Blanca Brewing Co. New Mexico's largest microbrewery offers samples and free tours. | 503 12th St. | 505/648–6606 | Free | Daily 9–4.

Valley of Fires Recreation Area. After the lava from an erupting volcano flowed here 1,500 years ago, it cooled and formed a jagged black landscape called the Malpais, now home to bald and golden eagles and many varieties of cactus. Hiking is permitted on the nature trail. The area is 4 mi west of Carrizozo. | U.S. 380 | 505/648–2241 | $5 | Visitor center daily 8–4.

Dining

Four Winds Restaurant. American/Casual. Made-from-scratch cinnamon rolls, soups, hefty steaks, and burgers draw truckers, bikers, and travelers to this family-run diner. | U.S. 54/U.S. 380 | 505/648–2964 | MC, V | ¢–$$

Outpost Bar & Grill. American. One of New Mexico's venerable green chili–hamburger joints, the Outpost is a well-weathered bar decorated with elk racks and the mounted heads of many other critters. Enjoy some hand-cut french fries while watching the big-screen TVs or shooting pool. | 415 Central | 505/648–9994 | No credit cards | ¢–$

Roy's Gift Gallery. Café. Named for the owner, Roy Dow, this old-fashioned ice-cream parlor dishes out malts and sundaes at a 1935 working soda fountain. Store fixtures date to the 1880s. | 1200 Ave. E | 505/648–2921 | Closed Sun. | MC, V | ¢

Cloudcroft

Lincoln National Forest, Sacramento Ranger District. Hiking, backpacking, and fishing are among the activities at this large reserve. | 61 Curlew St. (off U.S. 82) | 505/682–2551 | www.fs.fed.us/links/forests.shtml | Free | Daily.

National Solar Observatory. At an altitude of 9,200 feet, the National Solar Observatory hosts research scientists from around the world. During the day you can take a self-guided tour, wander the grounds, and peek through one of the telescopes. | Rte. 6563 | 505/434–7000 | www.sunspot.noao.edu | Free | Visitor center Mar.–Dec., daily 10–6; Jan.–Feb., weekends 10–4. Self-guided tours daily dawn–dusk; May–Sept, guided tours Sat. at 2 PM.

Sacramento Mountains Historical Museum. In a restored log cabin, this small museum displays pioneer and railroad artifacts from the region. | U.S. 82 | 505/682–2932 | $1 | Mon.–Tues. and Fri.–Sat. 10–4, Sun. 1–4.

Dining
Rebecca's. Continental. Dine in a turn-of-the-20th-century atmosphere with a mountain view in The Lodge's restaurant, named for a flirtatious redheaded ghost who is said to haunt the hallways in search of a new lover. Try the shrimp, steak, or chateaubriand for two. | 1 Corona Pl | 505/682–2566 | AE, D, DC, MC, V | $$–$$$$

The Western Bar and Café. American. Alleged to have the best omelets (try the Mexico omelet with green chili, cheese, tomatoes, and ham) and chicken-fried steak in New Mexico, this landmark has served locals and visitors for half a century. Bring the family for a hearty meal, or come for karaoke night on a Thursday and get to know the locals. | 86 Burro St. | 505/682–2445 | No credit cards | ¢–$$

Lodging
★ **The Lodge.** Judy Garland and Clark Gable are among the past guests at this Victorian lodge. The Bavarian-style interior seems right out of a gothic novel. Rooms have period antiques and ceiling fans. Affiliated with the lodge is the off-premises Lodge Pavilion, a rustic 10-room B&B. Restaurant, some in-room data ports, some kitchens, some microwaves, some refrigerators, 9-hole golf course, pool, gym, some hot tubs, outdoor hot tub, sauna, croquet, horseshoes, volleyball, cross-country skiing, snowmobiling, lounge, some pets allowed (fee). | 1 Corona Pl. | Box 497, 88317 | 505/682–2566 or 800/395–6343 | fax 505/682–2715 | www.thelodgeresort.com | 61 rooms | AE, D, DC, MC, V | $$–$$$$

Las Cruces
Historical Museum of Lawmen. In the front lobby of the Sheriff's Office you'll find displays of weapons used by law-enforcement officers and criminals. Nifty vehicles out front include an 1865 horse buggy, an 1880s hay wagon, and a 1949 classic Ford police car. | 750 N. Motel Blvd., Suite 8 | 505/525–1911 | Free | Weekdays 8–5.

New Mexico Farm and Ranch Heritage Museum. Agricultural and ranching exhibits cover the history, heritage, and science of farming and ranching in New Mexico in this museum 1½ mi east of Las Cruces. | 4100 Dripping Springs Rd. | 505/522–4100 | $3 | Mon.–Sat. 9–5, Sun. noon–5.

White Sands Missile Range. The Range Museum displays historical exhibits and outside, missiles and rockets. Twice a year you can tour the Trinity Site, where the first atomic bomb in the United States was detonated. To reach the range turn east off U.S. 70, 25 mi northeast of Las Cruces; take the access road 5 mi to the gate and stop to obtain a visitor's pass. Note that you must have a current driver's license and insurance to enter, as well as photo identification for all passengers. | U.S. 70 | 505/678–1134 | www.wsmr.army.mil | Free | Museum weekdays 8–4, weekends 10–3; Trinity site: 1st Sat. in Apr. and 1st Sat. in Oct., 8–2.

Dining
My Brother's Place. Mexican. Try the tostadas *compuestos*—a concoction of red or green chili, meat, pinto beans, and cheese in a crispy tortilla cup—and wash it down with wine by the pitcher or several varieties of Mexican beer. For dessert, try an empanada (Mexican pastry) or the crème caramel. | 334 S. Main St. | 505/523–7681 | AE, D, DC, MC, V | Closed Sun. | ¢–$

Nellie's. Mexican. It's tough to find seating in this tiny, diner-style restaurant, but that's because the food is incredible—the locals eat here in droves. The chiles rellenos are mouthwatering. | 1226 Hadley Ave. | 505/524–9982 | No credit cards | No dinner | ¢–$

Si Señor. Mexican. A popular business lunch and dinner spot, this restaurant has pleasant and spacious Southwestern-style rooms. Entrées emphasize three distinct chili sauces—Las Cruces green (mild and flavorful), Deming red (spicy), and a variety described as "smoke," also known as Hatch green (very spicy). | 1551 E. Amador Ave. | 505/527–0817 | AE, D, MC, V | $–$$

Lodging

Hilltop Hacienda B&B. This inn, minutes from downtown Las Cruces, has mountain views and lovely gardens. Rooms are furnished with family heirlooms, and an extra, private kitchen is available for guests. Dining room, kitchen, library; no kids under 12, no smoking. | 2600 Westmoreland, 88012 | 505/382–3556 | fax 505/382–3556 | www.zianet. com/hilltop | 3 rooms | AE, D, MC, V | BP | $

★ **Lundeen Inn of the Arts.** Built in 1890, this adobe hotel is furnished with antiques, and there's an art gallery on the property; each room is named for an artist. There are fireplaces in the suites. Picnic area, some kitchenettes, some microwaves, some refrigerators, cable TV, some in-room VCRs, gym, library, business services, some pets allowed. | 618 S. Alameda, 88005 | 505/526–3326 | fax 505/647–1334 | www.innofthearts.com | 21 rooms, 7 suites | AE, D, DC, MC, V | BP | $

T.R.H. Smith Mansion Bed and Breakfast. Each room in this historic B&B has a regional theme: the Americas Room is the largest and has furniture from Latin America, the European room has warm green walls and flower-print upholstery, the Southwest Room has cowboy bric-a-brac and nightstands fashioned out of Native American drums, and the Polynesian Room has rattan furniture and decorative mosquito netting draped around the bed. Dining room, in-room data ports, billiards, some pets allowed; no smoking. | 909 N. Alameda Blvd., 88005 | 505/525–2525 or 800/526–1914 | fax 505/ 524–8227 | www.smithmansion.com | 4 rooms | AE, D, MC, V | BP | $–$$

Lincoln

Lincoln State Monument. Eleven individual sites around town comprise the monument, including the San Juan Mission, the Tunstall Mercantile Store Museum, and the Lincoln County Courthouse Museum. | Lincoln | 505/653–4372 | www.museumofnewmexico.org | $6 pass grants entry to 7 historic structures; $2.50 per site | Daily 8:30–5.

    Historic Lincoln Visitors Center. Native Americans, buffalo soldiers, and the history of the "Five Day Battle"—as the Lincoln County War is known locally—are the subjects of some of the exhibits here. | Main St./U.S. 380 | 505/653–4025 | www. museumofnewmexico.org | Daily 8:30–5.

    Lincoln County Courthouse Museum. Billy the Kid escaped from this building while he was awaiting his execution. Exhibits contain historical documents, including a letter from Billy to Governor Lew Wallace. | Main St. | 505/653–4372 | www.museumofnewmexico.org | Daily 8:30–5.

    Tunstall Store Museum. When the state of New Mexico purchased this store in the 1950s, boxes of old inventory—some dating back to the 19th century—were discovered and are now on display. John Chisum and Alexander McSween had their law offices here as well. | Main St. | 505/653–4049 | www.museumofnewmexico.org | Daily 8:30–5.

Dining

Ellis Store Country Inn. Contemporary. Wild game is the specialty here, but a choice of 10 entrées and several delicious desserts are available nightly. The food is complemented by fine china and crystal and the intimacy of the oldest house in Lincoln County. | U.S. 380, Milepost 98 | 800/653–6460 | Reservations essential | AE, D, MC, V | $$$$

Wortley Pat Garrett Hotel. American. Pot roast and mashed potatoes are the main attraction here, but you might also want to sample the green-chili stew. Desserts include cobblers and a pineapple upside-down cake. | U.S. 380 | 505/653–4300 | No credit cards | Closed Nov. 1–Apr. 27. No dinner | ¢–$

Old Mesilla

Gadsden Museum. Three blocks from the Mesilla Plaza, this museum displays a variety of Native American and early Spanish artifacts. A painting commemorating the Gadsden Purchase is a highlight. | W. Barker Rd. at Rte. 28 | 505/526–6293 | $2 | Mon.–Sat. 9–11 and 1–5.

Stahmann Farms. With over 4,000 acres, this is the largest family-owned pecan orchard in the world. You can drive through the orchard on Route 28 or stop by the farm store to sample and buy products made from pecans. | 22505 Rte. 28 S, La Mesa | 505/526–8974 or 800/654–6887 | Free | Store Mon.–Sat. 9–6, Sun. 11–5.

Dining

Double Eagle. Continental. On the east side of Mesilla Plaza, this restored Territorial-style hacienda still has its century-old wall coverings. The Sunday champagne brunch is worth the trip. Ask to be seated in the covered courtyard, which has a skylight. | 308 Calle Guadalupe | 505/523–6700 | AE, D, DC, MC, V | $–$$$

La Posta de Mesilla. Mexican. This restaurant, in a former stagecoach stop for the Butterfield Overland Mail and Wells Fargo stages, serves up Southwestern favorites. Chiles rellenos and red or green enchiladas are among the offerings; the chefs follow recipes dating back more than 100 years. | 2410 Calle de San Albino | 505/524–3524 | AE, D, DC, MC, V | Closed Mon. | ¢–$

★**Mesón de Mesilla.** Continental. People drive from all over southern New Mexico and even west Texas to dine in this restaurant—in the Mesón de Mesilla B&B—known for seared sturgeon in pesto, chateaubriand for two, and filet mignon. If you stay in the inn, you'll enjoy the restaurant's gourmet breakfasts. A guitarist plays on weekends. | 1803 Avenida de Mesilla | 505/525–2380 | AE, D, DC, MC, V | $$–$$$

★**Old Mesilla Pastry Cafe.** Café. Known for delicious baked goods and delicious pizzas, as well as such specialty foods as buffalo and ostrich meat, this café is a good stop for breakfast or lunch. | 2790 Avenida de Mesilla | 505/525–2636 | AE, MC, V | Closed Mon., Tues. No dinner | ¢–$

Ruidoso

Billy the Kid National Scenic Byway Visitor Center. Adjacent to the Hubbard Museum of the American West, this is the headquarters for information about Lincoln County, Billy the Kid, and the Scenic Byway. | U.S. 70 E, Ruidoso Downs | 505/378–5318 | www. byways.org | Daily 10–5.

Hubbard Museum of the American West. The heritage of the horse is celebrated here: browse more than 10,000 horse-related artifacts, as well as exhibits documenting the history of the American West. Note one of the world's largest equine sculptures, 255 feet long, by local artist Dave McGary. | 841 U.S. 70 W, Ruidoso Downs | 505/378–4142 | $8 | Daily 9–5.

Lincoln National Forest, Smokey Bear Ranger District. The Smokey Bear Ranger District Headquarters in Ruidoso manages approximately 375,000 acres of the more than 1 million acres of pristine Lincoln National Forest. Semi-desert plants, piñon pine, and juniper mingle with high-elevation grasses and flowering plants for a spectacular four-season display of colors. The forest covers four New Mexico counties and is popular for hiking, camping, and fishing. There are many access points around town. | Ruidoso Headquarters: 901 Mecham Dr. | 505/257–4095 | Free | Daily.

Smokey Bear Historical State Park. Dedicated to real forest fire survivor Smokey Bear, this park 22 mi north of Ruidoso in Capitan includes a museum operated by the village of Capitan that documents the life and times of the bear cub. Smokey lived out his life in the National Zoo in Washington, DC, and died in 1976; his grave is in the park. | 118 Smokey Bear Blvd., Capitan | 505/354–2748, 505/354–2298 (museum) | www.emnrd.state.nm.us/forestry/smokey.htm | $1 | Daily 9–5.

Dining

La Lorraine. French. A French Colonial interior with flower arrangements and chandeliers sets the perfect mood for traditional French cuisine, including chateaubriand, beef bourguignonne, and sausage-stuffed quail. | 2523 Sudderth Dr. | 505/257–2954 | AE, MC, V | Closed Sun. | $$–$$$$

Lincoln County Grill. American/Casual. The locals come here for quick service and good, inexpensive food. Step up to the counter to order hearty Texas chili, old-fashioned hamburgers, or chicken-fried steak. At breakfast you can have eggs served with fluffy, homemade biscuits. Tables are covered with old coffee, tea, and tobacco tin images. | 2717 Sudderth Dr. | 505/257–7669 | AE, D, MC, V | ¢–$

Pub 48. American/Casual. Opened by the Sierra Blanca Brewing Company, this pub, with an adobe brick fireplace and wood ceiling, has a cozy, mountain-cabin feel. Try such microbrews as nut-brown ale while sampling pizzas or barbecued brisket. | 441 Mechem Dr. | 505/257–9559 | AE, MC, V | Closed Tues. | ¢–$$

Lodging

Best Western Swiss Chalet Inn. In the mountains 3 mi north of Ruidoso, this charming, simple resort hotel resembles, just as its name implies, an elegant mountain Swiss chalet. It's a 16-minute drive from Ski Apache slopes. The restaurant serves German and American food. Restaurant, room service, cable TV, some in-room VCRs, pool, hot tub, sauna, bar, laundry facilities, business services, some pets allowed. | 1451 Mechem Dr., 88345 | 505/258–3333 or 800/477–9477 | fax 505/258–5325 | www.ruidoso.net/swisschalet | 82 rooms | AE, D, DC, MC, V | CP | ¢–$

High Country Lodge. This mountain resort is tucked beside a quiet mountain lake 5 mi north of Ruidoso. It has large two-bedroom cabins, all with fully equipped kitchens and front porches, some with fireplaces. Picnic area, kitchens, cable TV, tennis courts, pool, hot tub, sauna, playground, business services, some pets allowed (fee); no a/c. | Rte. 48, Alto, 88312 | 505/336–4321 or 800/845–7265 | www.ruidoso.net/hcl | 32 2-bedroom cabins | AE, D, DC, MC, V | $–$$

★**Park Place Bed & Breakfast.** Guests at this cozy lodge are blessed with both hospitality and privacy. You can choose seclusion in your own luxurious space or stroll into an inviting lobby where you might meet up with other guests for conversation or games in front of a toasty fireplace. Turn off U.S. 70 north onto Sudderth Drive, turn left on Thomas Street, then right on Reese Drive to cross the river. In-room VCRs, tennis court, outdoor hot tub, fishing, croquet, horseshoes, volleyball. | 137 Reese Dr., 88345 | 505/257–4638 or 800/687–9050 | fax 505/630–0127 | www.ruidoso.net/parkplace | 3 rooms | AE, MC, V | $–$$

NORTH DAKOTA

NORTH DAKOTA FRONTIER
FROM BISMARCK TO WILLISTON TO MEDORA

Distance: 475 mi   Time: 4 days
Overnight Breaks: Bismarck, Medora, Williston

Native American history, frontier exploration, and early cowboy living are the highlights of this tour. You'll travel from the bluffs overlooking the Missouri River to the open prairie, wind through the majestic Badlands, and finish in the cow town of Medora. At the height of summer, ripening grain fields bow to the ever-present wind, the "big lake"—Lake Sakakawea—glistens, and the rugged terrain of the Badlands wears deep hues of sandy browns and taupes. Spring and fall seasons release sudden splashes of color in this otherwise subtle landscape. Don't forget that the Missouri River forms the dividing line between the Central and Mountain time zones. This tour is not recommended for winter; many of the sights will be closed, and the roads may be covered with snow or ice.

❶ As North Dakota's capital city, **Bismarck** prides itself on its well-maintained residential areas, bustling downtown and shopping districts, and its many sights. Across the Missouri River, sister city **Mandan** was once called the Gateway to the West by novelist John Steinbeck. Mandan is a logical starting place for a busy day of sightseeing. Start with **Fort Abraham Lincoln State Park,** the headquarters for General Custer and the 7th Cavalry. On the fort grounds, the Custer House has been reconstructed and hosts tours. Also at the park is **On-A-Slant Indian Village,** with re-created dwellings—called earth lodges—from the Mandan people, who lived there from 1650 to 1750. After visiting the park and exhibits, head to Mandan and the **Five Nations Arts** for one-of-a-kind gifts—including quillwork, beadwork, star quilts, and sculptures—made by Native American artists. Just across the street and down a block is **Mandan Drug,** where you can get a sandwich, some homemade soup, and old-fashioned hard ice cream. After lunch, head for Bismarck and the **State Capitol,** where you can enjoy a free tour of the 19-story art deco building. Across the street is the **North Dakota Heritage Center,** home to a museum with numerous period exhibits, from a woolly mammoth to a 1940s tractor. For an evening of entertainment, consider dinner and gaming at **Prairie Knights Casino.** Spend the night in Bismarck.

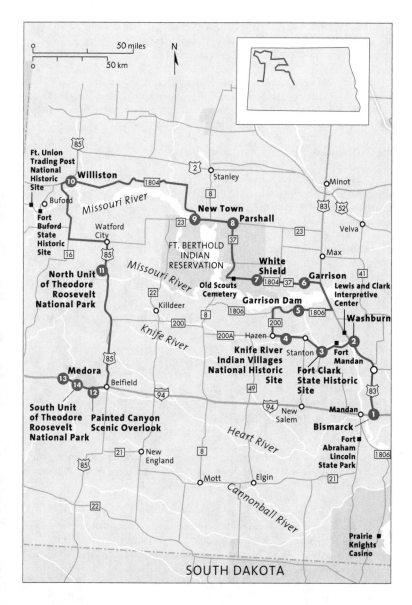

❷ Begin day two with a pleasant drive north to **Washburn,** where you can visit the **Lewis and Clark Interpretive Center.** Exhibits include artifacts from nearly every major tribe encountered by the explorers. From the center, turn west on Route 200A and watch for signs for **Fort Mandan,** only 1½ mi away on Route 17. Fort Mandan is a replica of the 1804–05 winter quarters used by Lewis and Clark and their expedition.

❸ Return to Route 200A and travel west, past rolling ranch lands and farm fields to **Fort Clark State Historic Site,** the spot of a former fur-trading post. Although nothing remains, plaques tell the history of commerce and tragedy: during the summer of 1837, a passenger steamboat brought smallpox to the nearby Mandan Indian village, wiping out 90 percent of its people.

❹ Continue west on Route 200A about 8 mi to Stanton and **Knife River Indian Villages National Historic Site,** which was inhabited for thousands of years. Enjoy the exhibits and a visit to a full-size reconstructed earth lodge.

❺ Get back on Route 200A and travel west 3 mi to Hazen, then north 19 mi on Route 200 to Pick City, and then east on Route 1806. Enjoy the panoramic rolling farmland along the route, and then prepare to drive over the jaw-dropping **Garrison Dam** from Pick City to Riverdale. The mile-long dam, built between 1947 and 1954, created Lake Sakakawea from the Missouri River and generates hydroelectric power. Free tours are available weekdays.

❻ From Garrison Dam, continue on Route 1806 and connect with U.S. 83. Travel north 12 mi on U.S. 83, and turn west on to Route 37, which will take you to **Garrison.** A fun stop here is the **North Dakota Fishing Hall of Fame,** where the state's best anglers are honored.

❼ Traveling west from Garrison, Route 37 becomes Route 1804. Continue on 1804 as you enter the Fort Berthold Indian Reservation, home of the Three Affiliated Tribes—Mandan, Hidatsa, and Arikara. About 1 mi into the reservation is **White Shield,** named for a famous Arikara chief who served as a scout for Gen. George A. Custer. Just 3 mi west of White Shield is the **Old Scouts Cemetery.** This small, serene cemetery is the final resting place for war veterans and some of Custer's Arikara scouts.

❽ Continue on Route 1804 as it veers north and becomes Route 37 once again; continue on to **Parshall,** about 25 mi. Houses and pastures dot the reservation's hills, interspersed with the occasional gorgeous gully dotted with Juneberry bushes. Parshall is home to the **Paul Broste Rock Museum,** a must-see collection of specimens from around the world. After you've visited the museum, turn west on Route 23 and travel along the north edge of the reservation.

❾ Just 17 mi west of Parshall, **New Town** is the seat of tribal government. Here you can find the **Three Affiliated Tribes Museum.** Continue west on Route 1804 to **Williston,** and make this your stopping place for the evening.

❿ Begin day three of your tour with a jaunt to two forts just west of **Williston** on Route 1804. The first stop is **Fort Buford State Historic Site,** just 21 mi from Williston. A military post established in 1866, Fort Buford is noted for its famous prisoners, Sitting Bull and Chief Joseph. Drive 2 mi west, again on Route 1804, and you'll see **Fort Union Trading Post National Historic Site** clearly from the road. Between 1828 and 1867 this post dominated the fur trade along the upper Missouri River.

⓫ From Williston, travel south on U.S. 85 about 60 mi and take in the beauty of the prairie, dotted with ranches and an occasional tree. Then prepare for a startling change of scenery, as the dramatic buttes that make up the Badlands begin to appear. The **North Unit of Theodore Roosevelt National Park** is a primitive area where you might spot the buffalo and deer roaming, eagles and hawks soaring, and prairie dogs scampering. After touring this portion of the park, continue south on U.S. 85 about 50 mi and connect with I–94, traveling west.

⓬ **Painted Canyon Scenic Overlook** is your next breathtaking stop. The visitor center overlooks a panoramic view of the Badlands.

⑬ Just off I–94 is the very walkable frontier town of **Medora,** founded by a French nobleman and named for his American wife. Have a look at their 26-room mansion, the **Chateau de Mores State Historic Site.** Depending on the hour you can begin to explore the park described at the next stop, or you can knock off for the day and have dinner in Medora, where you'll also want to spend the night.

⑭ After breakfast, head over to the **South Unit of Theodore Roosevelt National Park,** the entrance of which is a mile across from the Chateau de Mores. The visitor center has a film and exhibits, and just a short walk away is the **Maltese Cross Ranch Cabin,** from one of Theodore Roosevelt's two North Dakota ranches. The drive through the South Unit shows off more of the Badlands' incredible terrain. After having lunch in Medora, check out the many museums, including the **Medora Doll House, Museum of the Badlands, and Harold Schafer Heritage Center.** If you'd like to purchase something special, travel to Beach just 26 mi west and visit **Prairie Fire Pottery.** The owner supplies the world's zoos with animal-print tiles and handcrafts exquisite pottery with a unique, shimmery glaze.

To return to Bismarck, travel east along I–94 from Beach (about a 2½-hour trip) or Medora (about a 2-hour trip).

Bismarck

North Dakota Heritage Center. The state's largest museum and archive has permanent exhibits covering Native Americans, immigrants, dinosaurs, and tractors. | 612 E. Boulevard Ave. | 701/328–2666 | www.state.nd.us/hist | Free | Oct.–Apr., weekdays 8–5, Sat. 9–5, Sun. 11–5; May–Sept., daily 8–4:30.

Prairie Knights Casino and Lodge. Blackjack, slots, video poker, keno, and poker tables await you at this Vegas-style casino, the fanciest of the five reservation casinos. No tipping is allowed in the casino and restaurants. A 96-room lodge is adjacent to the casino. Nearby, the Marina at Prairie Nights on Lake Oahe has ramps, slips, a picnic area, and RV sites. | 3932 Rte. 24 | 701/854–7777, 800/425–8277 in ND | www.prairieknights.com | Free | Daily.

NORTH DAKOTA RULES OF THE ROAD

License Requirements: The minimum driving age in North Dakota is 16.

Right Turn on Red: You may turn right on a red light after stopping when the intersection is clear of both pedestrians and vehicles, unless otherwise posted.

Safety Belt and Helmet Laws: North Dakota law requires all front-seat occupants over the age of 18 to wear safety belts. Children under age 3 must be properly secured in an approved child-restraint seat, and children ages 3 to 10 must be properly secured in either an approved child-restraint seat or a safety belt. Motorcyclists under the age of 18 must wear a helmet.

Speed Limits: The speed limit is 70 mph on interstate highways, except when otherwise posted around major cities. On all other primary and secondary highways, the speed limit is 65 mph unless otherwise posted.

For More Information: Contact the **North Dakota Department of Transportation** | 701/328–2500 general information, 701/328–7623 road reports, 800/472–2121 emergency assistance | www.state.nd.us/dot.

State Capitol. The 19-story building is the state's tallest and one of only three U.S. state capitols without a traditional dome. The structure, with a moderne-style exterior and art deco interior, was built in the early 1930s after a Christmas fire destroyed the original. Tours are available hourly, excluding lunch time (noon). | 600 E. Boulevard Ave. | 701/328–2480 | Free | Memorial Day–Labor Day, weekdays 8–4, Sat. 9–4, Sun. 1–4; Labor Day–Memorial Day, weekdays 8–4.

Dining

Bistro 1100, An American Café. Eclectic. Ostrich, wood-fired burgers, and Greek pizza are among the diverse choices at this relaxed eatery with an open kitchen. In nice weather, you can eat outside on a deck overlooking downtown and the railroad tracks. | 1103 E. Front Ave. | 701/224–8800 | AE, MC, V | Closed Sun. | $$–$$$

Los Amigos. Mexican. Expect authentic and homemade food here; favorites include traditional tamales and chiles rellenos—with mouthwatering hot sauce and the right dash of cilantro. Kids' menu. | 431 S. 3rd St. | 701/223–7580 | AE, D, DC, MC, V | Closed Sun. | $–$$

North American Steak Buffet. Steak. All-you-can-eat is the key phrase here. The prix fixe includes several kinds of salads, hot-foods bars, and desserts. No alcohol. | 2000 N. 12th St. | 701/223–1107 | AE, D, MC, V | $

★ **Peacock Alley Bar and Grill.** American/Casual. In what was once the historic Patterson Hotel, this restaurant was the scene of countless political deals, captured in period photographs. Choices might include pasta salads, soups, sandwiches, Cajun firecracker shrimp, and pan-blackened prime rib. There's also a Sunday brunch. | 422 E. Main Ave. | 701/255–7917 | AE, D, DC, MC, V | No dinner Sun. | $$

Lodging

Best Western Doublewood Inn. At I–94 and U.S. 83, this two-story motel is ¼ mi from the State Capitol. The indoor pool is adjacent to an outdoor courtyard with a modest but well-cared-for garden. Restaurant, room service, meeting rooms, microwaves, refrigerators, cable TV, some in-room VCRs, indoor pool, hot tub, sauna, bar, playground, laundry service, business services, airport shuttle, some pets allowed (fee). | 1400 E. Interchange Ave., 58501 | 701/258–7000 or 800/554–7077 | fax 701/258–2001 | www.bestwestern.com | 143 rooms | AE, D, DC, MC, V | BP | $

Comfort Suites. A 97-foot water slide into the pool makes this hotel popular with families. Although it is several miles from downtown, it's off I–94 near one of Bismarck's two malls. Aside from shopping, there are a dozen restaurants and a movie theater within walking distance. Some in-room hot tubs, cable TV with movies, indoor pool, exercise equipment, gym, hot tub, laundry service, business services, meeting rooms, video game room, airport shuttle. | 929 Gateway Ave., 58503 | 701/223–4009 or 800/228–5150 | fax 701/223–9119 | www.comfortsuites.com | 60 suites | AE, D, MC, V | CP | $–$$

Expressway Suites. Part of a regional chain, this simple hotel offers spacious suites at low prices. It is within walking distance of Kirkwood Mall, several restaurants, the Bismarck Civic Center, and Lake Oahe, and a short drive from the zoo. The Expressway Inn next door has simpler rooms. Microwaves, refrigerators, cable TV with movies and video games, indoor pool, hot tub, some in-room hot tubs, bar, business services. | 180 Bismarck Expressway, 58504 | 701/222–3311 or 888/774–5566 | fax 701/222-3311 | www.expresswayinnandsuites.com | 64 suites | AE, D, DC, MC, V | CP | $–$$

Garrison

Audubon National Wildlife Refuge. More than 200 bird species live in this 14,300-acre refuge. On a 7½-mi driving tour you might see Canada geese and white-tailed deer. | 3275 11th St. NW, Coleharbor | 701/442–5474 | www.fws.gov | Free | Daily dawn–dusk.

Garrison Dam. The fifth-largest earthen dam in the world, Garrison controls flooding on the Missouri River and generates electricity. Finished in 1954, the dam also created Lake Sakakawea and a related recreation industry. The powerhouse includes a vast network of power stanchions, high-voltage lines, and transformers. Tours of the power plant are conducted by the U.S. Army Corps of Engineers. | Box 517, Riverdale | 701/654–7411 | Free | Memorial Day–Labor Day, noon–4.

Lake Sakakawea. The third-largest man-made lake in the United States starts just south of Williston and extends more than 178 mi to the southeast, where it stops at the Garrison Dam. Access to the lake is fairly easy, with more than 1,300 mi of publicly owned shoreline. Walleye, northern pike, and salmon create exceptional sportfishing. From Garrison, go 25 mi south on Route 200 and follow the signs; the lake is 1 mi north of Pick City. | 701/654–7411 | www.nwo.usace.army.mil.

Lake Sakakawea State Park. Next to the Garrison Dam, this park has a full-service marina with 80 slips, two large boat ramps, and campsites. About 220,000 people visit the park each year. From Garrison, go 25 mi south on Route 200 and follow the signs; the park is 1 mi north of Pick City. | Riverdale | 701/487–3315 | www.state.nd.us/ndparks | $5 | Daily; campgrounds mid-May–early Oct.

Dining

Four Seasons Restaurant and Ice Cream Parlor. American/Casual. In a plain concrete block building you can find an assortment of sandwiches, such as chili cheeseburgers and turkey clubs, and buffalo steak. Try the grilled chicken-and-bacon melt. Sunday brunch. | 182 N. Main St. | 701/463–2044 | No credit cards | ¢–$

Lake Road Restaurant. American/Casual. The restaurant is known for hamburgers and a few German dishes, such as *knoephle* soup. On Route 37, 6 mi west off U.S. 83. | Rte. 37 | 701/463–2569 | MC, V | ¢–$

Stoney End. Steak. Originally built as a WPA project in the 1930s, the restaurant has fieldstone inside and out, two stone fireplaces—one in the dining room and one in the Cabin Fever lounge—and art throughout the building. The menu has certified Black Angus beef and prime rib (only on weekends). Kids' menu. | Rte. 37, 1 mi east of Garrison | 701/337–5590 | DC, MC, V | Closed Sun. No lunch | $–$$

Totten Trail Lounge. American/Casual. Stuffed and mounted hunting trophies—from fish to deer—adorn the walls at this roadside café and lounge. The supreme pizza (sausage, pepperoni, onions, peas, and mushrooms) and the burgers are popular. | 1412A U.S. 83 NW, Coleharbor | 701/337–5513 | AE, MC, V | ¢–$

Mandan

Five Nations Arts. In an old railroad depot, this shop sells traditional and contemporary arts and crafts from 200 regional Native American artists. Several weekends every year, Native American artists come and work in-house. | 401 W. Main St. | 701/663–4663 | www.5nationsarts.com | May–Sept., Mon.–Sat. 9–7, Sun. noon–5; Oct.–Dec., Mon.–Sat. 10–6, Sun. noon–5; Jan.–Apr., Mon.–Sat. 10–5.

Fort Abraham Lincoln State Park. Rich in Native American and military history, this 1870s fort began as a fur-trading post in the 1780s. By 1872 it had been renamed for Lincoln, and it soon became the home of the 7th Cavalry and General George A. Custer. The officers' quarters that Custer shared with his wife, Libby, have been restored to their 1876 appearance, when the doomed general left on his expedition to the Little Big Horn. Also in the 75-acre park are reconstructed barracks, a commissary store, and infantry blockhouses. You'll also find trails and a campground in the park. | 4480 Fort

Lincoln Rd. | 701/663–9571 or 701/663–1464 | www.state.nd.us/ndparks | $5 | Memorial Day–Labor Day, daily dawn–dusk.

On-A-Slant Indian Village was inhabited by Mandan Native Americans between 1650 and 1750. About 1,000 people lived in the village, but by the early 1800s, most had been wiped out by smallpox. Four reconstructed earth lodges give a sense of the Mandan people's world. The village is listed on the National Register of Historic Places.

Dining

★**Mandan Drug.** American. The pharmacy and other original pieces of this former drugstore are still intact, including the stools, a jukebox with 1960s songs, and a player-piano. Try the Sakakawea sandwich with turkey breast, cream cheese, and cranberry sauce. Follow up with an old-fashioned cherry soda or a brown cow—a root beer float with chocolate syrup—and then take home some delicious handmade candy. | 316 W. Main St. | 701/663–5900 | MC, V | Closed Sun. No dinner | ¢

Medora

Burning Hills Amphitheatre. Built into a bluff, the seven-story amphitheater hosts nightly performances of the Medora Musical every summer. If you sit near the top, you can enjoy a panoramic view of the Badlands and, if you're lucky, you'll see bison grazing in the distance. The amphitheater seats almost 3,000 people. | 701/623–4444 or 800/633–6721 | www.medora.com | Memorial Day–Labor Day.

Chateau De Mores State Historic Site. A French nobleman and his wife, Medora, constructed this 26-room mansion in 1883. The couple entertained Theodore Roosevelt during his Dakota ranching days and hosted extravagant hunting parties. The chateau is restored to its glory days and offers interpretive tours during the summer. About 1 mi from the chateau is the De Mores Memorial Park, the spot indicated by a lone-standing brick chimney, all that remains of the beef-packing plant. | 1 Chateau La. | 701/623–4355 | www.state.nd.us/hist/chateau/chateau.htm | Adults $6 | Mid-May–mid-Sept., daily 8:30–6, mid-Sept.–mid-May by appointment only.

Medora Doll House. Antique dolls and toys fill almost every inch of this small house, built by the Marquis de Mores in 1884. Also known as the von Hoffman House, it's listed on the National Register of Historic Places. | 485 Broadway | 701/623–4444 or 800/633–6721 | www.medora.com | $4 | Memorial Day–Labor Day, daily 10–7.

Museum of the Badlands. In this collection is one of the region's most extensive exhibits of Plains Native American artifacts, along with personal items of Apache chief Geronimo. | 195 3rd Ave. | 701/623–4444 or 800/633–6721 | www.medora.com | $4 | Memorial Day–Labor Day, daily 10–7.

Prairie Fire Pottery. Handmade stoneware pottery and terra-cotta tiles with wildlife tracks are displayed in a studio and showroom. The studio supplies 27 different animal-track tiles to zoos and parks worldwide. | 127 Main St. E, Beach | 701/872–3855 | Mon.–Sat. 9–6 or by appointment.

Dining

Chuckwagon Cafeteria. American. Though known for ribs, chicken, and steaks, this restaurant also has a sandwich shop and bakery. Note the photographs of the early days of Medora and an extensive collection of Indian arrowheads. The prix fixe buffet is available for breakfast and lunch. | 250 3rd Ave. | 701/623–4444 or 800/633–6721 | AE, D, MC, V | Closed Labor Day–Memorial Day | $

Rough Rider Hotel Dining Room. American. Barbecued buffalo ribs, prime rib, and huge hamburgers are the big draw here. Photos of Theodore Roosevelt hang on the rustic walls. | 301 3rd Ave., at Main St. | 701/623–4444 or 800/633–6721 | AE, D, MC, V | $$–$$$

Trapper's Kettle. American. You'll see plenty of traps and kettles here, though perhaps the most unusual aspect of the decor is the salad bar, which is in a canoe. The chili topped with cheese is a favorite; also popular are the hearty frontier-style scones. Breakfast served. | 83 U.S. 85 N at I–94, Belfield | 701/575–8585 | AE, D, DC, MC, V | ¢–$

Lodging

AmericInn Motel and Suites. Glowing wood and western themes accentuate this motel. The two-story cement-block building is in a commercial area three blocks from downtown; restaurants and stores are nearby. Some in-room hot tubs, some microwaves, some refrigerators, cable TV, indoor pool, hot tub, sauna, laundry facilities, business services, meeting rooms, some pets allowed. | 75 E. River Rd. S, 58645 | 701/623–4800 or 800/634–3444 | fax 701/623–4890 | www.americinn.com | 56 rooms, 8 suites | AE, D, DC, MC, V | CP | $

★**Rough Riders Hotel.** Built in 1883, this downtown hotel is operated by the Theodore Roosevelt Medora Foundation, a nonprofit organization that restores historic Medora. Rooms on the second floor have country-western antiques, brass beds, patchwork quilts, and red velvet drapes. There's a restaurant on the first floor. Parking is on the street. Guests have pool privileges at Badlands Hotel, four blocks away. Cable TV, meeting rooms; no smoking. | 301 3rd Ave., 58645 | 701/623–4444 or 800/633–6721 | fax 701/623–4494 | www.medora.com | 9 rooms | AE, D, MC, V | EP | $$

New Town

Four Bears Bridge. Named for the Mandan and Hidatsa Chief, Four Bears, this narrow bridge spans a mile of Lake Sakakawea, making this the longest bridge in the state. It's 4 mi west of New Town. Construction on a new, wider bridge was begun in spring 2003, and should be finished by 2005. | Rte. 23 | 701/627–4477 | www.fourbearsbridge.com.

4 Bears Casino and Lodge. An economic force for the reservation, this Las Vegas–style casino offers slots, blackjack, roulette, poker, bingo, and craps. It also has special events, including concerts, rodeos, car shows, and boxing. It's 4 mi west of New Town, off Route 23 just across the Four Bears Bridge. | 202 Frontage Rd. | 701/627–4018 or 800/294–5454 | www.4bearscasino.com | Free | Sun.–Thurs. 8 AM–2 AM, Fri.–Sat. 24 hours.

Old Scouts Cemetery. You'll see headstones for some of Custer's Arikara scouts, though they aren't buried here; it's actually the resting place of military personnel and war veterans from later conflicts. Note that all headstones face east into the rising sun. | 701/627–4477 | Daily.

★**Paul Broste Rock Museum.** Built from uncut granite and cement by a local recluse in the 1960s, this stone building houses a private collection of 5,000 rocks, agates, minerals, and crystals. | N. Main St., Parshall | 701/862–3264 | www.parshallndak.com/rockmuseum.htm | $4 | May–Oct., daily 10–5; or by appointment.

Three Affiliated Tribes Museum. The history of the Mandan, Hidatsa, and Arikara cultures are explored at this diverse museum through artifacts and crafts. Take note of the dresses decorated with elk teeth. It's four miles west of New Town next to Four Bears Casino, off Route 23. | 701/627–4477 | $3 | Apr.–Veterans Day, daily 10–6.

Van Hook Marina. Known locally as "fisherman's paradise" for its walleye, this little resort area has campgrounds, guide and fish-cleaning services, a boat ramp, and a bait shop whose owners are world-class walleye anglers. | 1801 Van Hook | 701/627–3811 | May–Aug., daily 6:30 AM–10 PM; Sept.–early Oct., daily 6:30 AM–8 PM.

Dining

Lucky's Café at 4 Bears Casino. American. Try the walleye or the T-bone steak at this casino restaurant. Note that Thursday through Sunday dinner is buffet only. | 202 Frontage Rd. | 701/627–4018 or 800/294–5454 | AE, D, MC, V | $

Riverside. American. Paintings of western scenes decorate this restaurant, which is popular for the prime rib feasts it offers on most weekends. A kids' menu is available. | 358 Main St. | 701/627–4403 | AE, MC, V | No lunch weekends | ¢–$

Scenic 23. American. Families and summer anglers enjoy tucking into steak, lobster, and the prime rib here. A kids' menu is available. | 1803 Van Hook | 701/627–3949 | AE, D, MC, V | Closed Sun. No lunch | $

Theodore Roosevelt National Park

Maah Daah Hey Trail. Hike and ride horses or mountain bikes on this 120-mi trail. Its name means "grandfather" or "be here long" in the Mandan language. The trail passes through the rugged Badlands and the Little Missouri National Grasslands. Maps are available through the U.S. Forest Service. | U.S. Forest Service, 1511 E. Interstate Ave., Bismarck | 701/225–5151 | Daily.

North Unit. More rugged than the South Unit, the North Unit may permit chance meetings with bison, mule deer, and elk. You can take a 14-mi loop trail to the Oxbow Overlook, or other self-guided trails that wind in and out of ravines. At the visitor center, 15 mi south of Watford on U.S. 85, you can see a slide show about the park before making your visit. | 701/842–2333 | www.nps.gov/thro | $5 per person or $10 per vehicle | Park daily; visitor center Memorial Day–Sept., daily 9–5:30.

Painted Canyon Scenic Overlook. Catch your first glimpse of Badlands majesty here and learn more about the area from the wildlife and geology exhibits in the visitor center. | 201 E. River Rd., Medora | 701/623–4466 | www.nps.gov/thro | Park daily; visitor center mid-June–Labor Day, daily 8–6; Apr.–mid-June, daily 8:30–4:30; Sept.–mid-Nov., daily 8:30–4:30.

South Unit. A 36-mi scenic loop takes you by prairie dog towns, coal veins, and panoramic views of the Badlands. Self-guided trails, most under 1 mi long, introduce you to the area's geology, ecology, and history. At the Medora Visitor Center, a 13-minute film describes the park. | 315 2nd Ave., Medora | 701/623–4466 | www.nps.gov/thro | $5 per person or $10 per vehicle | Daily. Visitor Center: mid-June–Labor Day, daily 8–8; Labor Day–mid-June, daily 8–4:30.

　　Elkhorn Ranch Site. When Theodore Roosevelt came to the Badlands in the 1880s, he became a cattle rancher. The ranch was one of his ventures and is in the National Register of Historic Places. Today there are no buildings or signs here. Make sure to check at the South Unit Medora Visitor Center for road- and river-fording conditions. The ranch is 35 mi north of the visitor center on gravel roads. | 701/623–4466 | www.nps.gov/thro | $10 per vehicle | Daily.

　　Peaceful Valley Shadow Country Outfitters. This outfitter offers a way to see the South Unit as cowboys and frontiersmen might have seen it a century ago. Guides lead you on some of the park's 80 mi of marked horse trails after a round of lessons; separate excursions are available for more experienced riders. A five-hour ride costs $75, a 2½-hour ride $35, a 90-minute ride $20, and a pony ride for the kids is $7. | 7 mi north from South Unit Visitor Center | 701/623–4568 or 701/677–4260 off-season | Memorial Day–Labor Day, daily.

Washburn

Fort Clark State Historic Site. A fur-trading post built in 1830 near the Missouri River, 15 mi west of Washburn off U.S. 83, the fort burned down in 1860. Today, you can reconstruct its history with the help of markers along a walking trail. The site is on the National Register of Historic Places. | 701/328–2666 | Free | Daily.

Fort Mandan. Built in the shape of a triangle on the banks of the Missouri River just west of Washburn, this fort was Lewis and Clark's home through the winter of 1804–05. It's fully restored and on the National Register of Historic Places. | 2 mi west of the Lewis and Clark Interpretive Center on County Rd. 17 | 701/462–8535 | www.fortmandan.com | $5 | Memorial Day–Labor Day, daily 9–7; Labor Day–Memorial Day, daily 9–5.

Freedom Mine. Freedom Mine is one of the 10 largest coal mines in the United States. Its lignite feeds three power stations and a gas plant. You can arrange a tour by calling 24 hours ahead, or drop in for one of the scheduled tours. | 204 County Rd. 15, Beulah | 701/873–2281 | Free | Tours Mon.–Thurs. at 9, 11, and 1.

Knife River Indian Villages National Historic Site. Sacagawea met Lewis and Clark here and became their guide and translator in the early 1800s. But community life at this site goes back 8,000 years, and flourished until the mid-19th century, when disease started taking its toll on the Native American people in the region. | County Rd. 37, Stanton | 701/745–3309 | www.nps.gov/knri | Free | Mid-May–Labor Day, daily 7:30–6; Labor Day–mid-May, daily 8–4:30.

Lewis and Clark Interpretive Center. Lewis and Clark's voyage of discovery to this area in 1804–1806 is the focus of this center, where you can see a hand-carved replica of the 4-ton canoes the explorers used. All the Native American groups Lewis and Clark met are represented by objects and artifacts, and there are 1830s illustrations by Karl Bodmer. | 2576 8th St. SW | 701/462–8535 | www.ndlewisandclark.com | $5 | Memorial Day–Labor Day, daily 9–7; Labor Day–Memorial Day, daily 9–5.

Dining

Dakota Farms Family Restaurant. American. Sit at a booth by the front window and watch the highway traffic while breakfasting on ham and eggs, or retire to the dining area in the back to enjoy a rib steak. | 1317 Border La. | 701/462–8175 | D, DC, MC, V | ¢–$

Lewis and Clark Café. American. Antique wagon wheels and old photos help this small-town café serve up history with its meals. Try the burger or the steak named for Lewis and Clark. Kids' menu available. | 602 Main St. | 701/462–3668 | No credit cards | No dinner Sun. | ¢–$

Williston

Buffalo Trails Museum. Epping, 22 mi northeast, is a small town with a big museum. In seven buildings you will find antiques and fossils, but the most unusual items are the re-created dentist's office, sickroom, and parlor with life-size papier-mâché figures. From Williston, head east on U.S. 2. Turn right onto Route 42 and follow signs to the museum. | Rte. 42, Epping | 701/859–4361 | $3.50 | Memorial Day–Labor Day, Tues.–Sat. 10–4, Sun. 1–5; Labor Day–Memorial Day, by appointment.

Fort Buford State Historic Site. Built in 1866 near the concourse of the Missouri and Yellowstone rivers, this military post was the site of Sitting Bull's surrender in 1881. The officers' quarters are now a museum, and in the soldiers' cemetery you can hunt for unusual, sometimes humorous headstones. There is also a reproduction of an 1870s army barracks. | 15349 39th La. NW | 701/572–9034 | $5 | Mid-May–mid-Sept., daily 9–6; mid-Sept.–mid-May, by appointment.

Fort Union Trading Post National Historic Site. Admire the impressive palisade and three-story bastions of Fort Union from the highway. John Jacob Astor's American Fur Company built the fort, which dominated trade on the upper Missouri River from 1828 to 1867. | 15550 Rte. 1804 | 701/572–9083 | www.nps.gov/fous | Free | Memorial Day–Labor Day, daily 8–8; Labor Day–Memorial Day, daily 9–5:30.

Lake Park Drive-In. See a movie at one of relatively few drive-in theaters still running in the country. Ticket prices are for the nightly double feature. The show goes on at dusk, but come early so the kids can enjoy the playground. | U.S. 2 North | 701/572–9137 | $7 | Apr.–Sept., daily at 9:45 PM.

Dining
Dakota Farms Family Restaurant. American. The Dakota Farms serves breakfast all day, and has a reputation for fair prices and good service. Come in for all-you-can-eat fish on Fridays. | 1906 2nd Ave. W | 701/572–4480 | D, MC, V | ¢–$

Gramma Sharon's Cafe. American. Would you expect to find anything less than home-cooked meals—the omelets and the mashed potatoes from scratch are particularly good—in a place named Gramma's? But unlike your gramma's kitchen, this one is open 24 hours. | U.S. 2 and 85 | 701/572–1412 | D, MC, V | ¢–$$

Lunch Box. American/Casual. New and old lunch boxes are everywhere in this café, which serves up soups, salads, sandwiches, and omelets. Try the almond chicken salad or the roast beef on a fresh pita, and homemade chili and pies. Note that the café closes at 4. | 20 W. Broadway | 701/572–8559 | No credit cards | Closed Sun. No dinner | ¢–$

Lodging
Airport International Inn. This two-story hotel with clean, modern rooms is six blocks from the airport and 4 mi from downtown. The restaurant serves mainly fish and steak dishes and strives for a romantic feel with soft lighting and candles at every table. Restaurant, indoor pool, hot tub, bar. | 3601 2nd Ave. W, 58801 | 701/774–0241 | fax 701/774–0318 | 144 rooms | AE, D, DC, MC, V | EP | ¢–$

El Rancho Motor Hotel. This Southwestern-style motel six blocks from downtown is well known for its restaurant. Rooms are large and modern. Restaurant, in-room data ports, cable TV, bar, laundry service, some pets allowed (fee). | 1623 2nd Ave. W, 58801 | 701/572–6321 or 800/433–8529 | fax 701/572–6325 | 91 rooms | AE, D, DC, MC, V | EP | $

Lund's Landing Marina Resort. Cedar camping cabins have knotty-pine interiors and camp furniture with bunk beds. The cabins have no running water; shower and toilets are in the main building. You can rent kayaks, pontoons, and fishing boats here, and there's a kids' fishing dock. The resort is 22 mi east of Williston in Ray on Route 1804. Picnic area, refrigerators, dock, boating, fishing, some pets allowed; no room phones, no room TVs, no smoking. | 11350 Rte. 1804, Ray 58849 | 701/568–3474 | www.lundslanding.com | 6 cabins (shared shower only) | MC, V | Closed Dec.–Apr. | MAP | $–$$

OUACHITA NATIONAL FOREST ALONG U.S. 59
TRAVELS INTO THE OLD CHOCTAW NATION

Distance: 140 mi   Time: 2–3 days
Overnight Break: Poteau

Drive along U.S. 59 to the pine-covered heart of the old Choctaw Nation and the Ouachita Forest. ("Ouachita" is the French spelling of two Choctaw words *owa* and *chito*, for "big hunt.") The highway weaves in and out of protected wilderness areas—advance planning is a must, since the few available overnight accommodations are booked months in advance. Campers have an easier time of it, since there are hundreds of both improved and unimproved campsites available. The most scenic times to travel are in the spring, when the dogwoods are in bloom, or in the fall: southeastern Oklahoma's fall foliage is definitely the state's showiest.

❶ Begin at the **Overstreet-Kerr Living History Farm,** 10 mi south of **Sallisaw.** Life in Indian Territory is re-created here, and period demonstrations include the making of sorghum, soap, and brooms, as well as territorial farming and gardening.

❷ The attractions for the next five stops on this tour are in the environs of the cozy river valley town of **Poteau,** named for a nearby river. **Spiro Mounds Archaeological State Park** contains 11 earthen mounds used by the Mound Builder civilization from AD 600 to 1450. The mounds have yielded burial treasures, including engraved shells, embossed copper plates, stone tools, textiles, and prehistoric lace.

❸ A purported Viking rune stone thought to have been carved with hieroglyphics around AD 900 can be seen at **Heavener Runestone State Park.** At 1,000 feet above the city of Heavener, the park offers a panoramic view of the valley below, great sunsets, a visitor information center, a nature trail, and picnic tables. Plan to stay the night in Poteau.

❹ The **Peter Conser Historic House Site** is the restored 19th-century residence of a prominent politician, businessman, and captain of the Choctaw Lighthorsemen, an elite tribal law-enforcement corps that patrolled Indian Territory.

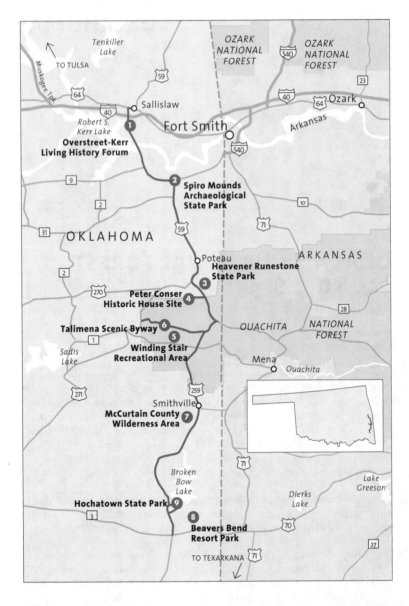

❺ Bordering the Peter Conser Historic House Site is the 1.7-million-acre **Ouachita National Forest,** the South's oldest national forest and the largest shortleaf pine forest in the country. In addition to the pines, white and scrub oak, hickory, dogwood, and other varieties of trees blanket the blue-tinged faces of the Winding Stair Mountains. The 26,445-acre **Winding Stair Recreation Area** is home to numerous scenic lookouts and campgrounds, including **Cedar Lake Campground** and **Cedar Lake Equestrian Camp.** Cedar Lake Campground has an 84-acre lake, hiking trails, and RV and tent campsites, and is a trailhead for the 46-mi long Ouachita Trail. Cedar Lake Equestrian Camp is known as the "Cadillac of horse camps," as it provides individual corrals and hot showers for both horse and rider.

❻ The **Talimena Scenic Byway** (Route 1) intersects U.S. 259 15 mi south of the northern edge of Ouachita National Forest. The state's first scenic byway proceeds westward, scaling the peaks of the Winding Stair and Rich mountains. The road, built purely for its scenic potential, is named for its two end points: Mena, Arkansas, and Talihina, Oklahoma. There are numerous scenic turnouts and picnic stops along the 54-mi-long route. **The Robert S. Kerr Memorial Arboretum and Nature Center** has a visitor information center, and three interpretive trails designed to educate hikers about tree species.

❼ A 1-mi walking trail at the 14,000-acre **McCurtain County Wilderness Area** has markers designating prime wildlife viewing stops.

❽ The pine-studded, 3,500-acre **Beavers Bend Resort Park** is built around the Mountain Fork River and Broken Bow Lake. It's Oklahoma's most-visited park, with miles of hiking trails. Inside the park, the **Forest Heritage Center** traces the history of the area back to prehistoric times with painted murals and artifacts. The center is built around an atrium with a hundred-year-old oak-log cabin moved to the park from the Kiamichi Mountains.

❾ Beavers Bend Resort Park adjoins the McCurtain County Wilderness Area as well as **Hochatown State Park. Cedar Creek Golf Course,** at the Hochatown park, was carved out of the pine woods with chain saws and machetes; it has a winding mountain stream and a revolving cast of wildlife, including wild turkeys and bald eagles.

Broken Bow

Beavers Bend Resort Park. Oklahoma's most popular state park encompasses 3,522 densely forested acres, where you can hike, fly-fish, boat, swim, horseback ride, and golf. There are also a nature center, the Forest Heritage Center; a miniature train; canoe and paddleboat rentals; 47 cabins; a 40-room lakefront lodge; RV sites; and 18 camping areas. | 10 mi north of Broken Bow on Rte. 259A | 580/494–6300 | www.touroklahoma.com | Daily.

OKLAHOMA RULES OF THE ROAD

License Requirements: Home state licenses are honored for non-residents.

Right Turn on Red: Permitted throughout the state *after* a complete stop, unless otherwise posted.

Seat Belt and Helmet Laws: Seat belts are mandatory for drivers, front-seat passengers, and back-seat passengers under the age of 13; child restraints are mandatory for children under four years of age. Safety helmets are required for motorcyclists under age 18; face shields, goggles, or windscreens are mandatory. Motorcyclists are required to use their headlights at all times, even during daylight hours.

Speed Limits: 75 mph on turnpikes; 70 mph on interstate highways; 65 mph on most state highways; and 55 mph on most county roads. Residential and business-district limits are set by local ordinance.

For More Information: Contact the **Oklahoma Public Information Office** | 405/425–7709.

Forest Heritage Center. The center covers the evolution of the forest from prehistoric times. Exhibits include life-size dioramas, wood carvings, natural-history exhibits, antique chain saws, Choctaw artifacts, and a century-old cabin. | 580/494–6497 | Daily 8–8.

Hochatown State Park. Abutting Beavers Bend Resort Park and the McCurtain County Wilderness Area, this park, nestled in the foothills of the Kiamichi Mountains, has the 18-hole Cedar Creek Golf Course as its centerpiece. The park has three entrances a few miles north of the Beaver Bend main entrance. | Rte. 259A | 580/494–6451 | Daily dawn–dusk.

McCurtain County Wilderness Area. More than 14,000 acres comprise the last sizable expanse of old growth oak–shortleaf pine forest in the nation. Flying squirrels, bobcats, red and gray foxes, and 100 species of birds have been spotted in the wilderness area which has a 1-mi walking trail with markers designating prime viewing spots. | 25 mi north of Broken Bow, 8 mi east of U.S. 259 | 800/528–7337.

Poteau

Cedar Lake Campground. An 84-acre lake, hiking trails, and RV and tent campsites can be found on this 200-acre campground. | Holson Valley Rd., 3 mi west of U.S. 59 S | 918/653–2991 | Daily.

Cedar Lake Equestrian Camp. Tent and RV campsites are equipped with individual corrals for horses and hot and cold showers for both horses and humans. | Holson Valley Rd., 3 mi west of U.S. 59 S | 918/653–2991.

Heavener Runestone State Park. A 12-ft-by-10-foot granite slab bearing eight runic letters some claim were left behind by Viking explorers in AD 900 is the centerpiece of this state park. Grounds include a hiking trail, a picnic area, a playground, and a gift shop. Day-use only; camping available at nearby Lake Wister State Park. | U.S. 259, 12 mi south of Poteau | 918/653–2241 | www.touroklahoma.com | Daily dawn–dusk.

Ouachita National Forest. This forest comprises 1.7 million acres of mountains, ridges, lakes, and streams in southeast Oklahoma and west-central Arkansas. More than 200,000 acres of the nation's largest shortleaf pine forest have been set aside for such activities as camping, hiking, mountain biking, horseback riding, hunting, and fishing. Ouachita National Forest is broken into two parts; use U.S. 259, which runs north through both sections to enter and exit the forest. For east–west exploration, use Route 63 or Talimena Scenic Byway (Route 1). | 918/653–2991 weekdays, 918/567–2046 weekends | www.fs.fed.us/oonf/ouachita.htm | Daily.

Robert S. Kerr Memorial Arboretum and Nature Center. Three interpretive trails and an unstaffed visitors center provide information about tree species, soil conditions, and Native American traditions. | On Rte. 1 (Talimena Scenic Byway) 1½ mi east of U.S. 259 | 918/653–2991.

Winding Stair Recreation Area. You can camp, picnic, and hike at this scenic area. | Rte. 1, 2 mi west of U.S. 259.

Peter Conser Historic House Site. The 1894 two-story home of the captain of the Choctaw Lighthorsemen has been restored and is open for tours. | Conser Rd. 3 mi west of U.S. 59 | 918/653–2493 | Wed.–Sat. 10–5, Sun. 2–5.

Spiro Mounds State Archaeological Center. The state's only archaeological park provides glimpses of the 60 tribes that lived in the area from 600 to 1450. Eleven earthen burial and ceremonial mounds excavated here have yielded thousands of religious and ornamental objects. A resident archaeologist gives guided tours. | 18154 1st St., Spiro | 918/962–2062 | Free | Wed.–Sat. 9–5, Sun. noon–5.

Talimena Scenic Byway. The 54-mi road links Talihina, Oklahoma, in the west to Mena, Arkansas, in the east. It's most popular when the fall foliage is at its peak, and in spring when the dogwood trees are in bloom. There are a number of scenic turnouts and picnic areas. | 918/567–3434 | Daily.

Dining

La Huerta. Mexican. This restaurant is known for its homemade salsa, tacos, burritos, enchiladas, and combination dinners. And there's plenty of cold beer to wash everything down. Lunch specials are very reasonably priced. | 3115 N. Broadway | 918/649–0086 | AE, MC, V | $

Warehouse Willie's. American. Sporting wacky decor—a toy train runs around the second-floor dining room—in a converted warehouse, this restaurant serves excellent gumbo and grilled steaks, shrimp, pork chops, and burgers. Popcorn pops while you wait. | 300 Dewey Ave. | 918/649–3400 | Closed Sun.–Mon. | MC, V | $–$$

Lodging

Best Western Traders Inn. This reliable chain motel is within walking distance of restaurants and shops. Rooms have king-size or double beds. The lounge has karaoke every Thursday night. In-room data ports, cable TV, pool, hot tub. | 3111 N. Broadway, 74953 | 918/647–4001 | fax 918/647–9555 | www.bestwestern.com | 75 rooms | AE, D, DC, MC, V | CP | $

Days Inn & Suites. This Days Inn tries to stand a cut above the average motel decor from the five chandeliers in the lobby to the dark wood and deep tones of the guest rooms. Some two-bedroom suites have wet bars and whirlpool tubs. In-room data ports, microwaves, refrigerators, cable TV, exercise equipment, meeting rooms. | 1702 N. Broadway, 74953 | 918/647–3510 | 62 rooms | AE, D, MC, V | CP | $

Kerr Country Mansion Inn. The former home of Oklahoma statesman Robert S. Kerr was constructed from native timber and stone and has spectacular views of the river valley. A tiny museum and a K-shape swimming pool are other quirky features of the inn. It's 6 mi southwest of Poteau. Cable TV, pool, meeting rooms. | 1507 S. McKenna, 74953 | 918/647–8221 | 20 rooms | MC, V | CP | $

Sallisaw

Overstreet-Kerr Living History Farm. Once the residence of Indian Territory settlers, the grounds include a restored 1895 home and historic strains of grains, vegetables, and livestock that would have been used by the Choctaws in the late 19th century. | U.S. 59, Keota, 10 mi south of Sallisaw | 918/966–3396 | $3 | Fri.–Sat. 10–4.

Robert S. Kerr Lake. Boating, fishing, sailing, campsites, and a swimming beach are the highlights of this 42,000-acre lake. Boat rentals are available at the marina. | U.S. 59, 15 mi west of Sallisaw | 918/489–5541, 918/775–4522 marina | Daily dawn–dusk.

Sequoyah's Home. The one-room cabin built by Cherokee linguist Sequoyah after he moved to Indian Territory from Tennessee in 1829 has exhibits about the Cherokee alphabet he invented, as well as information about the Cherokee Nation. | Rte. 101, 10 mi northeast of Sallisaw | 918/775–2413 | Free | Tues.–Fri. 9–5, weekends 2–5.

Sequoyah National Wildlife Refuge. Migratory geese, ducks, and other waterfowl flock to this 28,000-acre reserve at the confluence of the Canadian and Arkansas rivers. Refuge facilities include a photo blind, hiking trails, and observation towers; fishing, hunting, and boating are permitted. Take I-40 to the Vian exit and follow the county road 3 mi south to the reserve. | Rte. 1, 10 mi west of Sallisaw | 918/773–5251 | http://southwest.fws.gov/refuges/oklahoma/sequoy.html | Daily.

OREGON

OREGON COAST
FROM ASTORIA TO BROOKINGS

Distance: Approximately 306 mi (without detours)Time: 3–4 days
Overnight Breaks: Bandon, Cannon Beach, Gold Beach, Newport, Yachats

A drive along the Oregon coast is at once dramatic and dazzling. Passing through small beach towns, fishing villages, and maritime resorts, U.S. 101—conveniently, the only roadway you'll need for this tour—dips, climbs, and curves through stretches of forest and along rocky headlands, windswept cliffs, and pristine white-sand beaches. Numerous state parks, overlooks, and scenic byways provide access to ocean vistas, historic lighthouses, and marine wildlife sanctuaries. Best of all, the amazing splendor of the Oregon coast is accessible to the public.

The weather along the coast is generally mild, especially south of Gold Beach, but it is unpredictable. Winds seem ever-present and temperatures definitely dip when the sun goes down. Pack a raincoat along with your swimsuit.

1 Astoria is where the mighty Columbia River empties into the Pacific, 96 mi west of Portland on U.S. 30. Maritime history buffs should stop in at the **Columbia River Maritime Museum** to see memorabilia salvaged from the almost 2,000 ships that have foundered in the treacherous waters; you can also explore a fully operational U.S. Coast Guard ship. Tour **Flavel House,** to see inside a restored mansion from the 1880s. The observation platform atop the 125-foot **Astoria Column** offers a view over Astoria, the Columbia River, and the Coast Range.

2 Having finally reached the Pacific Ocean, the explorers Lewis and Clark spent the rainy winter of 1806 in a small wooden fort that has been faithfully replicated at **Fort Clatsop National Memorial,** 5 mi south of Astoria on Alt. U.S. 101.

3 Seaside (12 mi south of Astoria on U.S. 101), one of the most tourist-oriented towns on the Oregon coast, has a long, sandy beach with a 2-mi boardwalk surrounded by hotels and restaurants.

4 Cannon Beach (10 mi south of Seaside on U.S. 101), another popular tourist mecca, is named for a cannon that washed ashore from a schooner in 1846. There are plenty

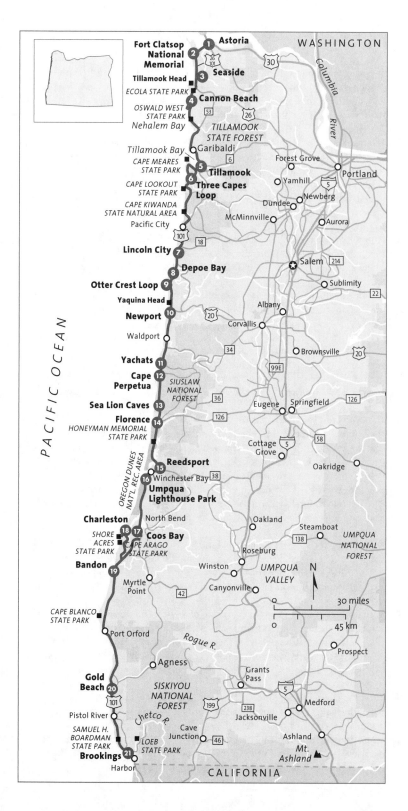

WASHINGTON

1 Astoria

Fort Clatsop
National
Memorial
2

3 **Seaside**

Tillamook Head

ECOLA STATE PARK

4 **Cannon Beach**

OSWALD WEST
STATE PARK
Nehalem Bay

TILLAMOOK
STATE FOREST

Tillamook Bay Garibaldi

CAPE MEARES
STATE PARK

5 **Tillamook**

CAPE LOOKOUT
STATE PARK
6 **Three Capes**
Loop

CAPE KIWANDA
STATE NATURAL AREA

Pacific City

Lincoln City **7**

Depoe Bay
8

Otter Crest Loop **9**

Yaquina Head

Newport **10**

Waldport

Yachats **11**

Cape **12**
Perpetua

SIUSLAW
NATIONAL
FOREST

Sea Lion Caves **13**

Florence **14**

HONEYMAN MEMORIAL
STATE PARK

OREGON DUNES
NAT'L. REC. AREA

Reedsport **15**

16 Winchester Bay

Umpqua
Lighthouse Park

Charleston

North Bend

SHORE
ACRES
STATE PARK
18 **17**

Coos Bay

CAPE ARAGO
STATE PARK

Bandon
19

Myrtle
Point

CAPE BLANCO
STATE PARK

Port Orford

Rogue R.

Agness

Gold
Beach **20**

Pistol River

SIKIYOU
NATIONAL
FOREST

SAMUEL H.
BOARDMAN
STATE PARK
LOEB
STATE PARK

Brookings **21**

Harbor

Chetco R.

Cave
Junction

CALIFORNIA

Columbia River

Forest Grove

Yamhill
Portland

Dundee Newberg

McMinnville

Aurora

Salem

Sublimity

Albany

Corvallis

Brownsville

Eugene Springfield

Cottage
Grove

Oakridge

Oakland

Steamboat

UMPQUA
NATIONAL
FOREST

Roseburg

Winston

UMPQUA
VALLEY

Canyonville

Grants
Pass

Prospect

Jacksonville Medford

Ashland

Mt.
Ashland

N

30 miles

0

45 km

of places to shop in this hamlet—one of the more upscale resort towns on the Oregon coast—but the real glory of the place is its broad beach, great for walking and kite flying, and presided over by a formidable offshore monolith known as **Haystack Rock.** Spend the night in Cannon Beach.

5 Tillamook (40 mi south of Cannon Beach on U.S. 101), surrounded by lush green fields, has long been known for its dairy industry. Stop in at the **Tillamook County Creamery** to sample the cheese and ice cream that have made this town famous. A lesser known entity, yet one worth exploring, is the **Latimer Quilt and Textile Center,** a wonderful, interactive museum and educational center which preserves, promotes, displays, and facilitates the creation of textile arts.

6 From Tillamook, take the **Three Capes Loop** (marked turnoff in town), a 35-mi scenic byway that passes three headlands—**Cape Meares, Cape Lookout,** and **Cape Kiwanda**— as it winds along the coast, rejoining U.S. 101 just south of **Pacific City.**

7 Lincoln City (16 mi south of Pacific City on U.S. 101), the most popular destination on the Oregon coast, is chock-full of tourist amenities along the Coast Highway and has plenty of shops and galleries.

8 From the tiny harbor at **Depoe Bay** (12 mi south of Lincoln City on U.S. 101), excursion boats run by **Tradewinds** head out on whale-watching cruises, conditions permitting. Some of the gigantic gray whales that annually migrate along the Oregon coast break away from the pod to linger year-round in Depoe Bay.

9 The **Otter Crest Loop** (5 mi south of Depoe Bay, off U.S. 101) scenic byway winds along the cliff tops to **Cape Foulweather,** a 500-foot headland, and down to a fascinating sea cave known as the **Devil's Punchbowl** before rejoining U.S. 101 north of Newport. Once you are back on U.S. 101, take the well-marked turnoff to **Yaquina Head,** where the gleaming white **Yaquina Bay Lighthouse,** activated in 1873, acts as the focal point for what has been designated by the Bureau of Land Management as an Outstanding Natural Area. On the rocky offshore islands you can often see harbor seals, sea lions, cormorants, murres, puffins, and guillemots.

10 Newport (12 mi south of Depoe Bay on U.S. 101) has an old **Bayfront** area where you'll find galleries, stores selling fresh crab and fish, and good seafood restaurants. As you leave Newport, signs on the south side of Yaquina Bay Bridge will direct you to the famous **Oregon Coast Aquarium,** a $4\frac{1}{2}$-acre complex.

11 Yachats (pronounced YA-hots, 23 mi south of Newport on U.S. 101) is a small, attractive coastal hamlet with B&Bs, restaurants, and a rocky, surf-pounded beach with tide pools. The highway follows the shoreline's contours through town and leads you to **Yachats State Park,** where on the north side of **Yachats River** outlet you can practically hand-feed seagulls. Yachats is a pleasant place to spend the night.

12 Towering 800 feet above the Pacific, **Cape Perpetua** (9 mi south of Yachats on U.S. 101) is the highest lookout point on the Oregon coast. For more information on this 2,700-acre scenic area, popular with hikers, naturalists, campers, and beachcombers, stop by the **Cape Perpetua Visitors Center.** A well-marked Auto Tour winds through Siuslaw National Forest to the $\frac{1}{4}$-mi **Whispering Spruce Trail,** where the views extend some 150 mi north and south and 37 mi out to sea.

⑬ On U.S. 101, 11 mi south of Cape Perpetua are the **Sea Lion Caves,** one of the Oregon Coast's premier attractions.

⑭ Just 13 mi south of the sea lions is the restored waterfront Old Town in **Florence.** This town is a good source of seafood restaurants and the jumping-off point for the **Oregon Dunes National Recreation Area** (visitor center south side of Umpqua River Bridge), an awesome 41-mi-long stretch of dunes with forests, lakes, and camping facilities.

⑮ In **Reedsport** (20 mi south of Florence on U.S. 101) you may want to stop at the **Umpqua Discovery Center,** where the chief attraction is the *Hero,* the laboratory ship used by Admiral Byrd on his expeditions to the Antarctic.

⑯ Some of the highest sand dunes in the country are found in **Umpqua Lighthouse Park** (turnoff 6 mi south of Reedsport on U.S. 101). The **Umpqua River Lighthouse,** built in 1861, flashes its warning beacon from a bluff overlooking the south side of Winchester Bay.

⑰ **Coos Bay** (27 mi south of Reedsport on U.S. 101), a former lumber town, lies on the largest natural harbor between San Francisco and Seattle's Puget Sound. The town itself is not particularly attractive, but west of it there are three oceanfront parks.

⑱ Head first to **Charleston** (7 mi west of Coos Bay on Newmark Ave.), a small fishing village; the road becomes Cape Arago Highway as it loops into town. **Sunset Bay State Park** (2 mi south of Charleston off Cape Arago Highway) has a protected lagoon where you can actually swim (if you're brave enough for the cold waters) without worrying about currents and undertows. **Shore Acres State Park** (1 mi south of Sunset Bay State Park) is the setting for a garden—part of a former seaside estate—that incorporates formal English and Japanese design elements. **Cape Arago State Park** (1 mi south of Shore Acres State Park) overlooks the **Oregon Islands National Wildlife Refuge,** a breeding ground for seabirds and marine mammals. From Cape Arago State Park you'll have to backtrack to Coos Bay to regain U.S. 101.

⑲ Massive sea stacks, miles of uncrowded white sandy beaches, and dramatic bay sunsets make **Bandon** an inviting coastal haven. A must-see attraction is the **West Coast Game Park,** America's largest wild animal petting park, where more than 450 exotic animals among 75 species are available for touching and viewing. Bandon's a great overnight spot.

⑳ At **Gold Beach** (35 mi south of Cape Blanco on U.S. 101), the fabled **Rogue River,** one of the few U.S. rivers to merit Wild and Scenic status from the federal government, pours into the Pacific. Beaches here are uncrowded and the scenery is some of Oregon's most delightful: soft, sandy beaches complemented by rugged rocks and sea stacks. The town's seasonal tourist industry is based largely on fishing and jet-boat trips up the Rogue. For more information, contact **Rogue River Mail Boat Trips** or **Jerry's Rogue Boats.** Gold Beach is a prime overnight destination.

㉑ Nearly 90% of the nation's potted Easter lilies are cultivated in **Brookings** (27 mi south of Gold Beach on U.S. 101). With its mild year-round climate, this southern part of the Oregon coast is sometimes referred to as Oregon's Banana Belt. The town, at the mouth of the Chetco River, is equally renowned as a commercial and sport-fishing port.

Astoria

Astoria Column. Follow scenic drive signs to Coxcomb Hill to see this 125-foot monument, which is listed in the National Register of Historic Places. It was built in 1926 on the site of the first permanent U.S. settlement west of the Rockies. A spiral staircase leads up to a viewing platform where you get a 360-degree panoramic view of the Astoria Bridge, the Pacific Ocean, and the Columbia River. | Daily.

The Astoria Riverfront Trolly. "Old 300" is a beautifully restored 1913 streetcar that travels for 4 mi along Astoria's historic riverfront. Get a close-up look at the waterfront, from the Port of Astoria to the East Morring Basin; the Columbia River; and points of interest in between. | 1095 Dwayne St. | 503/325–6311 | www.oldoregon.com | $1 per boarding; $2 all-day pass | Memorial Day–Labor Day, weekdays 3–9, weekends noon–9; Labor Day–Memorial Day, weekends noon–dusk.

★ **Columbia River Maritime Museum.** The star of this downtown waterfront museum is the U.S. Coast Guard lightship *Columbia*. There are also exhibits and artifacts relating to lighthouses, shipwrecks, navigation, fishing, and naval history. | 1792 Marine Dr. | 503/325–2323 | www.crmm.org | $8 adults | Daily 9:30–5.

Flavel House. Built by Captain George Flavel, a Columbia River bar pilot, this 1885 Queen Anne Victorian home has six fireplaces with hand-carved mantels and tiles imported from Italy, Holland, Belgium, and Algeria. | 441 8th St. | 503/325–2203 | $5 | May–Sept., daily 10–5; Oct.–Apr., daily 11–4.

★ **Fort Clatsop National Memorial.** Capts. Meriwether Lewis and William Clark camped here during the winter of 1805–06. A replica of their fort is the high point of the 125-acre park, which is 5 mi southeast of Astoria. Demonstrations on making candles and clothing, smoking meat, building canoes, and firing flintlocks add life to the expedition displays. | 92343 Ft. Clatsop Rd. | 503/861–2471 | www.nps.gov/focl | $3 | Labor Day–mid-June daily 9–5; mid-June–Labor Day daily 8–6.

Fort Stevens State Park. Fort Stevens is the only military installation in the continental U.S. to have been fired upon since the War of 1812. The park, 6 mi southwest of Astoria, has a museum of U.S. military history, a blacksmith shop, guided tours, and daily Civil

OREGON RULES OF THE ROAD

License Requirements: To drive in Oregon, you must be at least 16 years old and hold a valid driver's license.

Speed Limits: The maximum speed limit in any city and on urban interstates and highways is 55 mph, while on rural interstate highways it is 65 mph. The maximum speed allowed in residential districts and public parks is 25 mph.

Right Turn on Red: A right turn may be made onto a two-way street *after* stopping at a red light and yielding as necessary, unless otherwise noted.

Seat Belt and Helmet Laws: Safety belt use is mandatory for all drivers and passengers in all available seating positions when the vehicle is in motion. Children under four who weigh 40 pounds or less are required to be in an approved child safety seat. All motorcycle operators and passengers and moped operators are required to wear helmets at all times.

For More Information: Contact **Oregon Driver and Motor Vehicles Services** at | 503/945–5000.

War–era cannon and rifle demonstrations. On Labor Day weekend a Civil War reenactment is staged. | Warrenton Hammond Rd. | 503/861–1671 or 800/551–6949 | www. oregonstateparks.org | $3 per car | May–Oct., daily 10–6; Nov.–Apr., daily 10–4.

Josephson's. One of the Oregon coast's oldest commercial smokehouses, Josephson's uses alder wood for all its processing and specializes in Pacific Northwest Chinook and coho salmon. | 106 Marine Dr. | 503/325–2190 | fax 503/325–4075 | www.josephsons.com | Weekdays 8–5:30, weekends 10–5:30.

Dining

Gunderson's Cannery Cafe. Seafood. Gunderson's in-season seafood is prepared fresh and never fried. The lime prawns, halibut burger, or crab and shrimp cakes are good choices. Homemade soups, focaccia pizza, breads, and desserts are also available. The café is in a turn-of-the-20th-century cannery overlooking the Columbia River. | 1 6th St. | 503/325–8642 | D, DC, MC, V | No dinner Sun.–Mon. | $–$$$

Home Spirit Bakery Café. Contemporary. In an 1891 Queen Anne house with a river view, this unusual restaurant is filled with artifacts from the 1902–1912 Arts and Crafts period. It's known locally for its baked goods. Lunch is served weekdays; Thursday through Saturday there's also a prix-fixe dinner with a choice of four entrées: seafood, chicken, red meat, and vegetarian. The price of the meal depends on the night; Saturday is highest. | 1585 Exchange St. | 503/325–6846 | No credit cards | Closed Sun.–Mon. No dinner Tues.–Wed. | $$–$$$

Ship Inn. Seafood. The Ship Inn is well known among locals and savvy tourists for its famous fish (halibut is used) and chips. But don't overlook the many other seafood dishes prepared with a Pacific Northwest flair. | 1 2nd St. | 503/325–0033 | AE, D, MC, V | $–$$$

Bandon

Bandon Dunes Golf Resort. The resort features two distinct Scottish links–style courses, both set on a lovely stretch of sand dunes slightly above the Pacific Ocean, overlooking more than 20 mi of undisturbed shoreline. There are also a full spectrum of accommodations options, two full-service restaurants, two lounges, golf shops, and a 32-acre practice center. | 57744 Round Lake Dr. | 541/347–4380 or 888/345–6008 | www.bandondunesgolf.com.

Bullards Beach State Park. This park at the confluence of the Coquille River and the Pacific Ocean offers picnicking, fishing, camping, bicycling, and hiking. Within the park is the refurbished, nonoperational Coquille River Lighthouse, built in 1896, and a pioneer cemetery. From June through September the park's amphitheater offers entertainment five nights a week. | Off U.S. 101 north of Bullards Bridge, 2 mi north of the city | 541/347–2209 or 541/347–3501 | www.oregonstateparks.org | Daily.

Coquille River Museum. This 4,000-square-foot museum and exhibit space has more than 1,500 photographs of historical Bandon and artifacts from the Na-So-Mah Native American tribe, which inhabited the area for more than 2,000 years. The collection includes handwoven baskets, stone tools, and clay works. The museum collection also includes maritime memorabilia. | Old City Hall, 270 Filmore | 541/347–2164 | $2 | Mar.–Nov., daily 10–4; Dec.–Feb., Mon.–Sat. 10–4.

Sprague Community Theater. Throughout the year, this 250-seat theater presents live productions of musicals, comedies, and concerts from the Bandon Playhouse, Bandon Youth Theater, and other community groups. Quality musicals such as *Chicago, Man of La Mancha,* and *The Nutcracker* have drawn local patrons as well as visitors. Call for show and ticket information. | Bandon City Park, 1202 11th St. SW | 541/347–7426.

★**West Coast Game Park.** Thanks to visitor attendance, West Coast Game Park Safari has become Oregon's largest, totally self-supporting wildlife attraction. There are more than 450 animals and 75 species; visitors can meet, interact with, take pictures of, and walk among free-roaming tame wildlife. The park is 7 mi south of Bandon. | 46914 U.S. 101 | 541/347–3106 | www.gameparksafari.com | $11 | June 15–Labor Day, daily 9–7; Labor Day–June 15, daily 10–4.

Dining
Bandon Baking Company & Deli. Delicatessens. The only scent stronger than the salty sea air is the aroma of fresh-baked bread emanating from this establishment. You'll have a tough time deciding among the huge selection of loaves, especially the cinnamon swirl, cranberry nut, and jalapeño-and-cheese. There are also muffins, scones, bagels, pastries, and cookies—including snickerdoodles and a molasses-ginger concoction. For something hearty, you can build your own sandwich. Note that the bakery closes at 5 PM. | 160 2nd St. | 541/347–9440 | No credit cards | No dinner | ¢

★**Wheelhouse Restaurant & Crowsnest Lounge.** Seafood. As any restaurant with an ocean view should, the Wheelhouse has great seafood—fresh oysters, clams, prawns, and salmon are just some of the choices. The extensive selection of aged steaks, rich pastas, and chicken dishes such as cilantro-pesto chicken, charbroiled with feta cheese and jalapeño is also impressive. The wine list favors Pacific Northwest vintages. | 125 Chicago St. | 541/347–9331 | MC, V | $–$$$

Lodging
Sunset Oceanfront Lodging. This property has such a variety of lodgings—from standard motel rooms to studios all the way to duplexes and beach houses—that there's something for every budget; all but the cheapest rooms have ocean views. Some rooms have fireplaces, decks, and patios. In-room data ports, some kitchenettes, cable TV, indoor pool, spa, laundry facilities, concierge, meeting room, some pets allowed (fee). | 1865 Beach Loop Dr., 97411 | 541/347–2453 or 800/842–2407 | www.sunsetmotel.com | 70 rooms, 3 beach houses, 2 duplexes, 3 triplexes | AE, D, MC, V | ¢–$$

Brookings
Alfred A. Loeb State Park. In a fragrant myrtle forest on the Chetco River 10 mi from Brookings, this park offers some of the best salmon and steelhead fishing in Oregon. | Off U.S. 101 | 541/469–2021 or 800/551–6949 | www.oregonstateparks.org | Daily.

Azalea Park. Five varieties of the flower bloom at this park on the edge of town, which also includes a playground filled with imaginatively designed wooden equipment. | Off N. Bank Chetco River Rd. | 800/535–9469 | Daily.

Brandy Peak Distillery. Witness the art of brandy-making the old-fashioned way at this family-owned distillery. Fruits are ripened to peak flavor, fermented, and slowly distilled in wood-fired-pot stills for natural flavoring and aromas—no additional coloring or flavoring is added. Samples of grappa, pear, and grape brandies are provided. The distillery is just north of Brookings on U.S. 101; take Carpenterville Road and drive 4 mi to Tetley Road, and turn right. | 18526 Tetley Rd. | 541/469–0194 | www.brandypeak.com | Mar.–Jan., Tues.–Sat. 1–5; Jan.–Mar. by appointment only.

Harris Beach State Park. From here, you can watch gray whales migrate in spring and winter. Bird Island, also called Goat Island, is a National Wildlife Sanctuary and a breeding site for rare birds. There is a campground with RV hookups, tent sites, and four yurts. | U.S. 101 | 541/469–2021 or 800/551–6949 | www.oregonstateparks.org | Daily.

Samuel H. Boardman State Park. Highlights of this park 4 mi north of Brookings include a view of Arch Rock and Natural Bridges, as well as a 27-mi-long section of the Oregon

Coast Trail for hikers. The park is 12 mi long, running along the rugged, steep coast. | U.S. 101 | 541/469–2021 or 800/551–6949 | www.oregonstateparks.org | Daily.

Dining

Chetco Seafood Co. Seafood. Homemade chowder is the house specialty here; fish favorites are the grilled cod or halibut. All dishes comes with hearty sides, such as baked potatoes and coleslaw. | 16182 Lower Harbor Rd. | 541/469–9251 | MC, V | $

Smuggler's Cove. Seafood. Fishing vessels docked in the next boat basin and picture windows looking out to sea lend a salty ambience to this low-key restaurant. The daily seafood specials—usually halibut and salmon—are good bets; try the fish-and-chips or the crab melt for lunch. | 16011 Boat Basin Rd. | 541/469–6006 | MC, V | $–$$

Cannon Beach

Ecola State Park. A winding road along Tillamook Head will lead you to an extraordinary view of the Pacific Ocean. You might see elk and deer as you drive through the forest. The park is 2 mi north of Cannon Beach. | U.S. 101 | 503/436–2844 or 800/551–6949 | www.oregonstateparks.org | $3 per vehicle | Daily.

Neahkahnie Mountain. A road with some hair-raising curves climbs to 700 feet as it winds around the flank of this 1,661-foot mountain, south of Cannon Beach. The views are dramatic. Carvings on nearby beach rocks and Native American legends have given rise to a tale that a fortune in gold doubloons from a sunken Spanish galleon is buried somewhere on the mountainside. | U.S. 101.

Oswald West State Park. Several different trails wind through the park, leading to the beach and the Cape Falcon overlook. | Ecola Park Rd. | 503/436–2623 or 800/551–6949 | www.oregonstateparks.org | Mar.–Nov., daily.

Dining

★ **The Bistro.** Contemporary. Flowers, candlelight, and classical music enhance the three-course prix-fixe dinners at this 12-table restaurant. The menu includes imaginative Continental-influenced renditions of fresh local seafood and such specials as lamb, prawns, oysters, and Pacific seafood stew. | 263 N. Hemlock St. | 503/436–2661 | Reservations essential | MC, V | $$–$$$

Dooger's. Seafood. Like the original Dooger's in Seaside, the Cannon Beach branch serves superb seafood and steaks in a casual, contemporary setting. Don't pass up the clam chowder. | 1371 S. Hemlock St. | 503/436–2225 | AE, MC, V | $–$$

Lazy Susan Café. Café. A favorite for breakfast in Cannon Beach, this laid-back spot welcomes you with omelets, waffles, hot cereal, home fries, and fresh-baked scones. | Coaster Sq., 126 N. Hemlock St., 97110 | 503/436–2816 | No credit cards | Closed Tues. No dinner Sun.–Mon., Wed.–Thurs. | $

Lodging

Cannon Beach Hotel. Walk to the beach and downtown shopping from this restored, turn-of-the-20th-century, European-style inn close to Haystack Rock. There's a cozy fireplace in the lobby, and some rooms have fireplaces, too. Restaurant, some in-room hot tubs, cable TV, hot tub, business services. | 1116 S. Hemlock, 97110 | 503/436–1392 | fax 503/436–2101 | www.cannonbeachhotel.com | 9 rooms | AE, D, DC, MC, V | ¢–$$

Grey Whale Inn. This charming inn, in operation since 1948, is in a quiet residential neighborhood, just a five-minute walk from the beach. All the rooms are individually decorated with original artwork, done either by the owners or local artists. Some kitchenettes, cable TV, in-room VCRs; no smoking. | 164 Kenai St., 97110 | 503/436–2848 | 5 rooms | MC, V | $$

★**Hallmark Resort.** For the greatest spectrum of accommodations in Cannon Beach, choose from 28 different room styles at this resort, which has options for families, couples seeking romance, and guests with pets. Large suites have gas fireplaces and views of Haystack Rock. In summer the hotel hosts Saturday night beach bonfires. Some in-room hot tubs, some kitchenettes, refrigerators, cable TV, 2 indoor pools, exercise equipment, hot tub, laundry facilities, business services, pets allowed in some rooms (fee). | 1400 S. Hemlock, 97110 | 503/436–1566 or 888/448–4449 | fax 503/436–0324 | www.hallmarkinns.com | 142 rooms, 63 suites, 4 cottages | AE, D, DC, MC, V | $$–$$$$

Coos Bay

Cape Arago Lighthouse. The lighthouse is on a rock island just 12 mi south of Coos Bay. The original was built here in 1866 but was destroyed by storms and erosion. A second, built in 1908, suffered the same fate. The current one was built in 1934—so far, so good. The lighthouse is connected to the mainland by a bridge. Neither are open to the public, but there's an excellent spot to view this lonely guardian and much of the coastline: from U.S. 101, take Cape Arago Highway to Gregory Point, where it ends at a turnaround, and follow the short trail.

Cape Arago State Park. This park 14 mi southwest of Coos Bay juts out into the Pacific Ocean, making it a good place to watch for whales. If you take the north cove trail, you might also spot seals and sea lions. | Cape Arago Hwy. off U.S. 101 | 541/888–8867 | www.oregonstateparks.org | Daily.

Charleston Marina Complex. The marina includes a launch ramp, a store where you can buy tackle and marine supplies, a 110-space RV park, a motel, restaurants, and gift shops. Fishing charters also set out from here. | 4535 Kingfisher Dr., Charleston | 541/888–2548 | www.charlestonmarina.com | Daily.

Golden and Silver Falls State Park. Twenty-four miles north of Coos Bay on U.S. 101, this park's old-growth forest, sprinkled with maidenhair ferns, hides two natural wonders. Silver Falls pours over a 200-foot-high semicircular rock ledge. One-quarter mile to the northwest, thundering Golden Falls is even more impressive, especially in the spring. | No phone | www.oregonstateparks.org | Daily dawn–dusk.

Shore Acres State Park and Botanical Gardens. Once the grand estate of a pioneer timber baron, Shore Acres, on rugged sandstone cliffs high above the ocean, has gardens planted with flowers from around the world. | Cape Arago Hwy. | 541/888–3732 or 541/888–8867 | $3 per vehicle | www.oregonstateparks.org | Daily 8–dusk.

Sunset Bay State Park. The park includes cliffs and beaches, and a campground with 29 full hookups, 34 electrical and 72 tent sites, and 4 yurts. The lagoon is protected from the sea, making it one of the few places on the Oregon coast where you can swim without worrying about currents or an undertow. You can also hike to Shore Acres and Cape Arago state parks from here. | Cape Arago Hwy., off U.S. 101 | 541/888–4902 or 800/551–6949 | www.oregonstateparks.org | Daily.

Dining

★**Blue Heron Bistro.** American. Subtle preparations of local seafood, chicken, and pasta are served up at this busy bistro. The innovative soups and desserts are excellent. A skylight brightens the dining room, which has natural-wood accents, blue linen, and a tile floor. | 100 W. Commercial St. | 541/267–3933 | AE, D, MC, V | $–$$

Kum-Yon's. Pan-Asian. This tiny spot on the main drag serves up satisfying and inexpensive Asian food, including sushi, sashimi, and kung pao shrimp. The noodle dishes are always a good bet: portions are large, and you can select your own mix of fish, meat, and vegetable accompaniments. | 835 S. Broadway | 541/269–2662 | fax 541/267–3821 | AE, D, MC, V | Closed Mon. | ¢–$

Portside. Seafood. The view of the harbor through the restaurant's picture window is pretty and peaceful. Try the steamed Dungeness crab, bouillabaisse, or fresh salmon. On Friday night there's an all-you-can-eat seafood buffet. | 8001 Kingfisher Rd., Charleston | 541/888–5544 | AE, DC, MC, V | $

Depoe Bay

Depoe Bay Park. With its narrow channel and deep water, the park's tiny harbor is one of the most protected on the coast. It supports a thriving fleet of commercial- and charter-fishing boats. The Spouting Horn, a natural cleft in the basalt cliffs on the waterfront, blasts seawater skyward during heavy weather. | South on U.S. 101 | 541/765–2889 | www.stateoforegon.com/depoebay/chamber | Daily.

Tradewinds. Every year a few of the gigantic gray whales migrating along the coast decide to linger in Depoe Bay and, for more than six decades, Tradewinds has operated cruises to watch them. The skippers are all marine naturalists who give a running commentary. The ticket office is at the north end of Depoe Bay Bridge. | U.S. 101 | 541/765–2345 or 800/445–8730 | www.tradewindscharters.com | $15.

Florence

Devil's Elbow State Park. Heceta Head Lighthouse is among the sights in this park 13 mi north of Florence. Also seek out the natural caves and tide pools. | U.S. 101 | 800/551–6949 or 541/997–3851 | www.oregonstateparks.org | Daily.

    Heceta Head Lighthouse. The beacon that shines from this lighthouse in Devil's Elbow State Park, visible for more than 21 mi, is the most powerful on the Oregon coast. A trail leads from the lighthouse to Heceta House, a pristine white structure said to be haunted by the wife of a lighthouse keeper whose child fell to her death from the cliffs shortly after the beacon was lit in 1894. The house, which was once the light keeper's residence, is now one of Oregon's most remarkable B&Bs. The lighthouse is accessed via a $\frac{1}{2}$ mi-long trail from the parking lot in Devil's Elbow State Park. | U.S. 101 | 541/997–3851 | www.hecetalighthouse.com | $3 per vehicle | Memorial Day–Labor Day, tours daily by appointment.

Jessie M. Honeyman Memorial. Two miles of sand dunes lie between the park and the ocean. Within the park are two natural freshwater lakes and the second-largest campground in the state. | U.S. 101 | 541/997–3851 | www.oregonstateparks.org | $3 per vehicle | Daily.

Sea Lion Caves. A cliff-top elevator descends to the floor of this cavern, near sea level, where Stellar and California sea lions and their fuzzy pups can be viewed. In spring and summer the sea lions are on the rocky ledges outside the cave; during fall and winter they are usually inside the cave. Gray whales are visible during their northern and southern migrations, from October to December and from March to May. | U.S. 101 | 541/547–3111 | www.sealioncaves.com | $7 | Daily 9–sunset.

Dining

Bridgewater Seafood Restaurant. Seafood. Freshly caught seafood—25 to 30 choices nightly—is the mainstay of this creaky-floored Victorian-era restaurant in Florence's Old Town. Also available are steaks, pastas, chicken, burgers, and sandwiches. | 1297 Bay St. | 541/997–9405 | MC, V | $–$$

Clawson's Windward Inn. Seafood. Clawson's is one of the south coast's most elegant eateries. It prides itself on its fresh seafood—try the Chinook salmon fillets poached in Riesling or the shrimp and scallops sautéed in white wine—but steak, pastas, and salads round out the menu. | 3757 U.S. 101 N | 541/997–8243 | D, MC, V | ¢–$$

Mo's. American. Mo's chain of family-style restaurants has been an institution on the Oregon coast for more than four decades. At this location, built right out over the water, bay-front views and down-home service complement the fresh seafood. Don't miss the creamy clam chowder. | 1436 Bay St. | 541/997–2185 | D, MC, V | $–$$

Gold Beach

Cape Sebastian State Park. The parking lots here are more than 200 feet above sea level. At the south parking vista you can see up to 43 mi north to Humbug Mountain. Looking south you can see nearly 50 mi toward Crescent City, California, and the Point Saint George Lighthouse. A deep forest of Sitka spruce covers most of the park. | U.S. 101 | 800/551–6949 | www.oregonstateparks.org | Daily.

★ **Official Rogue River Mail Boat Hydro-Jet Trips.** Experience the wildlife, scenery, and history of the Rogue River Canyon on the first Rogue River boat line. The original boats still deliver the U.S. mail to the remote village of Agness, just as they have since 1895. Deer, eagles, osprey, elk, fox, grouse, otters, vultures, heron, loon, hawks, bears, and seals are commonly spotted along the route, so bring lots of film. You can get a reasonably priced lunch at one of the lodges in Agness. | 94294 Rogue River Rd. | 541/247–7033 or 800/458–3511 | www.mailboat.com | $34–$75 | May–Oct., daily; call for hours.

Prehistoric Gardens. Late sculptor E. V. Nelson created colorful life-size replicas of dinosaurs. The "Dinopark" is 15 mi from Gold Beach in a rain forest filled with giant ferns. | U.S. 101 | 541/332–4463 | $7 | Daily, 9–dusk; call for hours in winter.

Dining

Grant's Pancake and Omelette House. American. What better way to start your morning than with a heaping stack of buttermilk pancakes topped with melted butter and raspberry syrup? Light lunch items such as sandwiches and salads are also available. | 29790 Ellensburg Ave. | 541/247–7208 | No dinner | D, MC, V | ¢–$

Nor'wester Seafood. Continental. The Nor'wester overlooks the spot where the Rogue River spills into a marina; boats, sea lions, and pelicans provide dinnertime entertainment. Start with the clam chowder and then work your way through simple, tasty dishes, such as grilled salmon or marinated New York steak with sautéed mushrooms. | 29971 Harbor Way | 541/247–2333 | AE, MC, V | Closed Dec.–Jan. No lunch | $–$$

Port Hole Cafe. Café. This casual spot in the Old Cannery building on the waterfront serves a wide selection of appetizers, salads, soups, sandwiches, and entrées. Their specialties include fish and chips and pork chops. Breakfast is also available. | 29975 Harbor Way | 541/247–7411 | MC, V | ¢–$

Lodging

Sand 'N' Sea Motel. This property offers great accommodations overlooking the crashing surf for affordable rates. It's within walking distance of restaurants and shops. Most rooms have balconies or patios. Some microwaves, some minibars, exercise equipment, hot tub. | 29362 Ellensburg Ave. (U.S. 101), 97444 | 541/241–6658 or 800/808–7263 | www.sandnseamotel.com | 48 rooms, 1 beach house | AE, D, DC, MC, V | CP | $–$$

★ **Tu Tu' Tun Lodge.** Immaculate guest rooms complete with fresh flowers, views of the Rogue River, and the highest quality beds are just some of the features of this exquisite family-owned lodge. The main lodge has a massive stone fireplace, intimate bar, small library, and nationally recognized restaurant where four-course prix-fixe dinners are served. You'll receive tons of personal attention, so much so you'll feel like a long-lost member of the family. Pool, laundry facilities. | 96550 N. Bank Rogue, 97444 | 541/247–6664 or 800/ 864–6357 | www.tututunlodge.com | 16 rooms, 2 suites, 2 houses | D, MC, V | $$$–$$$$

Newport

Bayfront. With its tall-masted fishing fleet, well-worn buildings, seafood markets, and art galleries and shops, Newport's old Bayfront is an ideal place for an afternoon stroll. So many male sea lions loiter near crab pots and bark from the piers that local people call the area the Bachelor Club.

Devil's Punch Bowl State Natural Area. A rocky shoreline separates this day-use park from the surf. It's a popular whale-watching site just 9 mi north of Newport and has excellent tide pools. | U.S. 101 | 541/265–9278 | Daily.

★**Oregon Coast Aquarium.** One of the most popular attractions in the state, this 39-acre complex contains re-creations of offshore and near-shore Pacific marine habitats, all teeming with more than 15,000 coastal dwellers and 500 species of life from playful sea otters to a 60-pound octopus. A favorite exhibit is Passages of the Deep, an amazing walk through a 200-foot clear underwater tunnel that provides a 360-degree view of swimming sharks and rays. Plan to spend at least three hours here. | 2820 S.E. Ferry Slip Rd. | 541/867–3474 | www.aquarium.org | $10.75 | July–Labor Day, daily 9–8; Labor Day–Memorial Day, daily 10–5; Memorial Day–June, daily 9–6.

Yaquina Bay State Park. At the north end of Yaquina Bay near its outlet to the Pacific, this park is home to a historic lighthouse that in more recent years was used as a Coast Guard Lifeboat Station. It's been restored and is now open to the public. | U.S. 101 S | 541/867–7451 | Daily.

   Yaquina Head Lighthouse. Ninety-three-foot tall Yaquina Head Lighthouse is the tallest on the Oregon Coast. Guided morning tours are limited to 15 people. | 4 mi north of bridge in Newport | 541/574–3100 | $5 per vehicle | Mid-June–mid-Sept., daily noon–4. In winter, call ahead.

Dining

Canyon Way Restaurant and Bookstore. Seafood. Cod, Dungeness crab cakes, bouill-abaisse, and Yaquina Bay oysters are among the popular dishes at this Newport dining spot, which is up the hill from the center of the Bayfront. There's also a deli counter for take-out. | 1216 S.W. Canyon Way | 541/265–8319 | AE, MC, V | Closed Sun.–Mon. | $

Tables of Content. Contemporary. In this restaurant at the literary-themed Sylvia Beach Hotel, the setting is unadorned, with family-size tables; the main plot is a prix-fixe menu that changes nightly; and the central character might be local seafood, like grilled salmon fillet in a sauce Dijonnaise (but you can choose among four entrées, one of them vegetarian). | 267 N.W. Cliff St. | 541/265–5428 | Reservations essential | AE, MC, V | No lunch | $$

Whale's Tale. Seafood. Casual and family-oriented, this bay-front restaurant serves fresh local seafood, thick clam chowder, fish-and-chips, burgers, and sandwiches. Breakfast is also available. | 452 S.W. Bay Blvd. | 541/265–8660 | AE, D, DC, MC, V | Sept.–May closed Tues.–Thurs. | ¢–$

Lodging

Hallmark Resort Newport. All guest rooms have balconies from which you can enjoy panoramic ocean views. Some rooms have fireplaces. Room configurations vary: choose from one queen-size bed with a small sitting area, two queen-size beds and a full living room and kitchenette, three queen-size beds (with one tucked up in a loft space), or a king-size bed with a hot tub. Restaurant, in-room data ports, some kitchenettes, indoor pool, laundry facilities, some pets allowed (fee). | 744 S.W. Elizabeth St., 97365 | 541/265–2600 or 888/448–4449 | www.hallmarkinns.com | 158 rooms | AE, D, MC, V | $–$$$

★**Sylvia Beach Hotel.** Antiques-filled rooms are named for famous writers at this 1913 vintage beachfront hotel. A pendulum swings over the bed in the Poe room. The Christie, Twain, and Colette rooms are the most luxurious; all have fireplaces, decks, and ocean views. A well-stocked, split-level library has decks, a fireplace, slumbering cats, and comfortable chairs. Restaurant, library; no room phones. | 267 N.W. Cliff St., 97365 | 541/265–5428 | 20 rooms | AE, MC, V | $–$$$

Tyee Lodge. This 1940s house in Agate Beach is on a bluff—a nearby trail leads down to the beach. The guest rooms all have fireplaces, pine furniture, and views of the ocean through towering Sitka spruce trees. Breakfast is served family-style in a bay-windowed room facing the ocean. During the 1950s Composer Ernest Bloch lived next door. Dining room; no kids, no smoking. | 4925 N.W. Woody Way, 97365 | 541/265–8953 or 888/553–8933 | www.tyeelodge.com | 5 rooms | AE, D, MC, V | $$–$$$

Pacific City

Cape Lookout State Park/Cape Kiwanda State Natural Area. The coastal bluffs make this a popular hang-gliding and kite-flying area. The park, 1 mi north of Pacific City, has views of the ocean and easy access to the beach. The Cape Lookout Trail, 10 mi north of Pacific City, follows the headland for more than 2 mi. | Whiskey Creek Rd. | 800/551–6949 | www.oregonstateparks.org.

Three Capes Scenic Route. The coastal drive begins in Tillamook and winds for about 25 mi through Oceanside and south to Pacific City. Highlights are Cape Lookout State Park (above) and the Cape Meares Lighthouse. | West of U.S. 101.

Reedsport

Dean Creek Elk Viewing Area. A large herd of Roosevelt elk can be seen at this 1,000-acre site with pasture, woodlands, and wetlands. | Rte. 38 E | 541/756–0100 | Daily.

Oregon Dunes National Recreation Area. The Oregon Dunes stretch along the coast from Florence to North Bend. You'll find fine beaches, campgrounds, boat launch ramps, and picnic areas. Hiking trails pass through green areas that are home to many species of wildlife. All-terrain vehicles are permitted in some areas. | Visitor Center, U.S. 101 and Rte. 38 | 541/271–3611 | Daily.

Umpqua Discovery Center. Exhibits about early settlers are the focus of this educational and cultural center. Other displays explain the history of Native Americans and early explorers. | 409 Riverfront Way | 541/271–4816 | $5 | Daily 9–5.

Umpqua Lighthouse State Park. This 65-foot lighthouse and museum is at the entrance to Winchester Bay in the Oregon Dunes. A campground, 4 mi from Reedsport, surrounds Lake Marie; recreational activities on the lake include nonmotorized boating and swimming. | Off U.S. 101 | 541/271–4118 or 800/551–6949 | www.oregonstateparks.org | Daily.

William M. Tugman State Park. On Eel Lake near the town of Lakeside, this little-known park is surrounded by a dense forest of spruce, cedar, fir, and alder. Recreational activities include fishing, swimming, canoeing, and sailing. | U.S. 101 S | 541/888–4902 or 800/551–6949 | www.oregonstateparks.org | Daily.

Seaside

Ecola State Park. Ecola State Park, 5 mi south of Seaside, is a playground of sea-sculpted rocks, sandy shoreline, green headlands, and panoramic views. The main beach can be crowded in summer, but Indian Beach has an often deserted cove and explorable tide pools. | U.S. 101 | 800/551–6949 | www.oregonstateparks.org | $3 day use, per vehicle | Daily dawn–dusk.

Saddle Mountain State Park. It's a 2½-mi hike from the parking lot to the summit of Saddle Mountain. The park's campground, which is 14 mi north of Seaside, has 10 primitive sites. | Off U.S. 26 | 800/551–6949 or 503/436–2844 | Mar.–Nov., daily.

Seaside Aquarium. Jellyfish, giant king crab, octopus, moray eels, wolf eels, and other sea life hold court at this aquarium on the 2-mi-long beachfront Promenade. You can also feed the harbor seals. Note that during winter, the aquarium sometimes closes Monday and Tuesday; call ahead to confirm the hours. | 200 N. Promenade | 503/738–6211 | $6.50 | Daily 9–5.

Tillamook Head. Follow signs on U.S. 101 south of Seaside until you reach a parking area; from there, a 2-mi hike will bring you to the 1,100-foot-high viewing point atop Tillamook Head. You'll be able to see the Tillamook Rock Light Station, a mile or so out to sea. The lonely beacon, built in 1881 on a straight-sided rock, towers 41 feet above the ocean. Decommissioned in 1957, it is now a columbarium, used to bury human remains. | U.S. 101 | 800/551–6949 | www.oregonstateparks.org.

Dining

Dooger's Seafood and Grill. Seafood. The original Dooger's (the sister restaurant is in Cannon Beach) serves up superb seafood and steaks in a casual, contemporary setting. Don't pass up the famous clam chowder. | 505 Broadway | 503/738–3773 | MC, V | $–$$

Sam's Seaside Café. American/Casual. Half a block from the boardwalk and beach, this quiet, casual spot serves inexpensive burgers, salads, seafood dishes, and homemade cakes and pies at lunch and dinner. Sam's stays open until midnight. | 104 Broadway | 503/717–1725 | AE, MC, V | ¢–$

Tillamook

Blue Heron French Cheese Company. In business since 1979, Blue Heron specializes in Camembert, Brie, and other French cheeses. There's a petting zoo, a deli with seating, and a gift shop that carries Oregon wines, jams, mustards, and other products. You can eat outside at picnic tables. A popular addition is a tasting room where you can sample the products of Oregon wineries. | 2001 Blue Heron Dr. | 503/842–8281 or 800/275–0639 | fax 503/842–8530 | www.blueheronoregon.com | Memorial Day–Labor Day, daily 8–8; Labor Day–Memorial Day, daily 9–5.

★ **Latimer Quilt and Textile Center.** The center is dedicated to the preservation, promotion, creation, and display of the fiber arts. Spinners, weavers, beaders, and quilters can be found working on projects in the Quilting Room and may engage you in hands-on demonstrations. Rotating exhibits range from costumes, cloth dolls, crocheted items from the 1940s and 1950s, exquisite historical quilts dating from the early to mid-1800s, basketry, and weavings. | 2105 Wilson River Loop Rd. | 503/842–8622 | $2.50 | Tue.–Sat. 10–4, Sun. noon–4.

Pioneer Museum. The displays in Tillamook's 1905 county courthouse include Native American, pioneer, logging, and natural history exhibits, plus antique vehicles and military artifacts. Most popular are the collections of dolls, quilts, and guns. | 2106 2nd St. | 503/842–4553 | fax 503/842–4553 | $3 | Mon.–Sat. 8–5, Sun. 11–5.

Tillamook County Creamery. The largest cheese-making plant on the West Coast, 2 mi north of Tillamook, draws more than 750,000 visitors each year. Here the milk from local Holstein and brown Swiss cows becomes ice cream, butter, and cheddar and

Monterey Jack cheeses. You can see exhibits and get free samples. | 4175 U.S. 101 N | 503/842–4481 | fax 503/842–6039 | www.tillamookcheese.com | June–mid-Sept., daily 8–8; mid-Sept.–May, daily 8–6.

Tillamook Naval Air Station Museum. During World War II, blimps patrolled the coast to watch for enemy submarines and were based at this site in massive hangars. Today, the remaining hangar is home to a museum that displays vintage aircraft. | 6030 Hangar Rd. | 503/842–1130 | www.tillamookair.com | $9.50 | Daily 10–5.

Dining

Artspace. Eclectic. Everything is homemade at this eatery in Bay City, 6 mi north of Tillamook. The menu may include garlic-grilled oysters and vegetarian dishes, all beautifully presented—often with edible flowers. And if you reserve in advance, you'll get a complimentary appetizer for your thoughtfulness. | 9120 5th St., Bay City | 503/377–2782 | No credit cards | Closed Sun.–Wed. | $–$$

Cedar Bay. Steak. People come to this casual downtown restaurant for chowders made from scratch and desserts such as marionberry cobbler and chocolate cheese-cake. Steaks, prime rib, and seafood are also big draws. | 2015 1st St. | 503/842–8288 | MC, V | $–$$

Roseanna's. Seafood. Roseanna's is in a rustic 1915 building on the beach opposite Three Arch Rock; you might be able to watch sea lions and puffins while you eat. The casual beach vibe gets slightly more dressed up in the evening, with candlelight and fresh flowers. Fresh halibut or salmon, poached baked oysters, or Gorgonzola seafood pasta are must-tries. | 1490 Pacific Ave., Oceanside | 503/842–7351 | MC, V | $–$$

Yachats

★**Cape Perpetua Visitors Center.** The Interpretive Center is inside the Siuslaw National Forest and provides information about the cultural and natural history of the central Oregon Coast. The 2,700-acre Cape Perpetua Scenic Area was created to protect the area's Sitka spruce rain forest. | U.S. 101 | 541/547–3289 | May, Wed.–Sun. 10–4; June–Labor Day, daily 9–5; Labor Day–Apr., weekends 10–4.

Neptune State Park. You can look for wildlife, watch the surf, or gaze at Cumming Creek from benches set on the cliff above the beach. It's also a great spot for whale watching. Low tide provides access to a natural cave and tide pools. | U.S. 101 S | 800/551–6949 | www.oregonstateparks.org | Daily.

Sea Rose. Sea Rose, 6 mi south of Yachats, sells seashells from Oregon and around the world, plus gift items and souvenirs. A free museum displays shells and sea life. There's an exhibit of glass fishing floats, including a giant clam. | 95478 U.S. 101 | 541/547–3005 | fax 541/547–5197 | Memorial Day–Labor Day, daily 9:30–6; Labor Day–Memorial Day, daily 10–5.

Strawberry Hill. Strawberry Hill, just south of Yachats, is one of the best spots on the Oregon coast to view harbor seals resting on rocky islets just offshore, and to see the starfish, anemones, and sea urchins exposed at low tide. | U.S. 101.

Tillicum Beach Campground. Three and a half miles north of Yachats, this oceanside campground is so popular that there's a 10-day stay limit. Stairs provide access to the beach. Open year-round, there are 61 sites. | U.S. 101 | 541/563–3211 | Daily.

Yachats Ocean Road State Recreation Area. The Yachats River meets the Pacific Ocean here just 1 mi from Yachats. Whale watching is a popular activity. | U.S. 101 to Yachats Ocean Rd. | 541/997–3851 or 800/551–6949 | www.oregonstateparks.org | Daily.

Dining

The Joes' Town Center Cafe. American/Casual. This cafe is adorned by pencil sketches, marquetry, and stained glass created by local artists. Choose from fluffy omelets; homemade soups, including clam or smoked salmon chowder, vegetarian lentil, and a tortilla soup; salads; hot and cold sandwiches; and burgers. A full bakery stocks fresh scones, muffins, cookies, pies, and bread. | 4th St. and Rte. 101 | 541/547–4244 | AE, MC, D, V | Closed Wed. No dinner | $–$$

Lodging

The Fireside Motel. The Fireside Motel, the sister property to the Overleaf Lodge, offers a more casual atmosphere. The setting is no less spectacular and most rooms have oceanfront views and balconies on which to enjoy them. Some units have gas fireplaces. Minibars, cable TV, some pets allowed (fee). | 1881 U.S. 101 N., 97498 | 541/547–3636 | www.overleaflodge.com/fireside | 42 rooms | AE, D, MC, V | $

Ocean Cove Inn. These comfortable, spacious ocean-view quarters have wicker furnishings, handmade quilts, and hardwood floors. Decks to watch the beautiful sunsets, affordable rates, and excellent service make this a great choice. Prospect Avenue is off U.S. 101, at the south end of downtown. Microwaves, minibars, cable TV. | 180 Prospect Ave., 97498 | 541/547–3900 | www.oceancoveinn.com | 4 rooms | MC, V | $

★ **Overleaf Lodge.** Revel in the rugged beauty of crashing waves against the rocky shoreline from an oceanfront room—or from the shoreline trail that meanders in front of the lodge. Accommodations are spacious and many offer patios, balconies, or picture windows to admire dramatic coastal sunsets. Excellent, warm service includes guided nature walks and marshmallow bonfire sing-a-longs on summer weekends. Some kitchenettes, microwaves, in-room VCR's, exercise equipment, massage, laundry facilities. | 280 Overleaf Lodge La., 97498 | 541/547–4880 or 800/338–0507 | www.overleaflodge.com | 39 rooms | AE, D, MC, V | CP | $–$$

THE COLUMBIA RIVER GORGE, THE HIGH DESERT, AND MT. HOOD

INTO CENTRAL OREGON AND BACK TO PORTLAND

Distance: Approximately 624 mi   Time: 3–4 days
Overnight Breaks: John Day, Hood River, Mt. Hood

This drive highlights the exceptional variety of Oregon's topography and focuses on three areas of scenic grandeur: the Columbia River Gorge, the high desert country in central Oregon, and Mt. Hood. Start from the hub of a beautiful downtown area, Portland—Oregon's largest city—and head east toward Troutdale and the gorge.

The journey enters some semiremote areas; all roads are paved and marked, but a good Oregon road map is essential. Late spring and early autumn are the best times to make this trip. Winter snows on Mt. Hood can last until April; summer daytime temperatures east of the mountains can be sizzling, although the nights cool off considerably.

❶ Oregon's largest city, **Portland,** could mark the beginning, end, or both points of the tour.

❷ The town of **Troutdale** (13 mi east of Portland on I–84) marks the beginning of the **Columbia River Gorge National Scenic Area.**

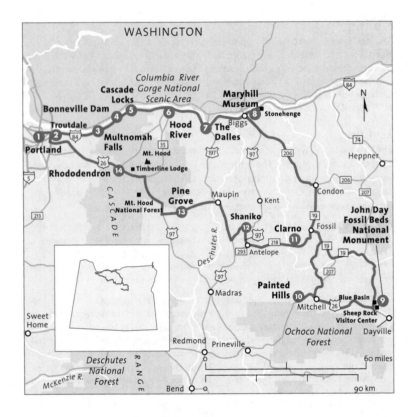

❸ From here **Multnomah Falls** (20 mi east of Troutdale on I–84), the nation's fifth-highest waterfall, pours down some 620 feet in a double-decker torrent. Paved walking paths climb up the hillside to a bridge overlooking the cataract.

❹ Dedicated in 1937 by President Franklin D. Roosevelt, **Bonneville Dam** (5 mi east of Multnomah Falls on I–84) was the first federal dam to span the Columbia. If you want to tour this historic hydroelectric behemoth, there is a visitor center (Exit 40 from I–84) on Bradford Island.

❺ The locks that gave the town of **Cascade Locks** (4 mi east of Bonneville Dam on I–84) its name were built in 1896 to tame the rapids that bedeviled early pioneers heading west toward the Willamette Valley on rafts. Between mid-June and late September you can view the awesome Gorge scenery aboard the stern-wheeler *Columbia Gorge*.

❻ In the past decade, thanks to the strong, ever-present winds blowing down the Columbia Gorge, **Hood River** (17 mi east of Cascade Locks on I–84) has become the self-proclaimed windsurfing capital of the world. Chances are you'll see dozens of windsurfers racing back and forth across the river. **Hood River,** in one of Oregon's prime fruit-growing regions, offers a full array of restaurants and accommodations.

❼ In pioneer days, **The Dalles** (20 mi east of Hood River on I–84) marked the end of the Oregon Trail. From here, would-be settlers had to decide whether to continue west via rafts, braving the treacherous rapids of the Columbia River, or trek overland across Mt. Hood. For a glimpse into the town's 19th-century pioneer and military past, visit the **Ford Dalles Museum.**

❽ Without a doubt, the most unusual cultural attraction in the Columbia Gorge is **Maryhill Museum** (20 mi east of The Dalles on I–84, 2 mi north of Biggs on U.S. 97, 1 mi east of Rte. 14), on the Washington side of the river. An even stranger landmark in this unpopulated desert country is the replica of **Stonehenge** (3 mi east of the museum off Route 14), also part of Maryhill Museum.

❾ Formed by explosive volcanic activity during the Cenozoic era, 5 to 50 million years ago, the geological formations that make up the **John Day Fossil Beds National Monument** cover hundreds of square miles but are divided into three "units." Driving south through the dry, shimmering heat of central Oregon, it may be difficult to imagine this area as a humid, subtropical forest filled with 50-ton brontosauruses and 50-foot-long crocodiles. The eroded hills and sharp, barren-looking ridges contain the richest concentration of prehistoric plant and animal fossils in the world.

Head first to the **Sheep Rock Visitor Center** (Route 19; approximately 155 mi southeast of Biggs; 84 mi south and east to Ruggs on Route 206, 41 mi south on Route 207, 30 mi south on Route 19), where exhibits, a video, and handouts outline the significance of the John Day Fossil Beds. Winding through the impressive **Blue Basin** (2 mi north of the Visitor Center on Route 19), a badlands canyon with sinuous blue-green rock spires, is the **Island in Time Trail,** where trailside exhibits explain the area's 28-million-year-old fossils.

❿ The fossils at **Painted Hills** (37 mi west of Sheep Rock on U.S. 26), the second unit of the John Day Fossil Beds, date back about 33 million years and reveal a climate that had become noticeably drier than that of the Sheep Rock area. Take the $^3/_4$-mi **Carroll Rim Trail** for a commanding view of the hills, or enjoy the view from the parking lot at the trailhead, about 2 mi beyond the picnic area.

⓫ The 48-million-year-old fossil beds at **Clarno** (64 mi north of Painted Hills on Route 19) have yielded the oldest fossils in the national monument. Another trail climbs $^1/_4$-mi from the second parking lot to the base of the **Palisades,** a series of abrupt, irregular cliffs created by ancient volcanic mud flows.

⓬ **Shaniko** (23 mi northwest of Clarno on Route 218) is the closest thing to a ghost town in central Oregon. But there is life here, though the days when the dusty boardwalked hamlet was a gathering spot for ranchers and Basque sheepherders are long gone.

⓭ If the high desert has made your eyes hungry for green and your skin eager for some moisture, relax: Just west of **Pine Grove** (52 mi northwest of Shaniko; 12 mi southwest on U.S. 97, 25 mi north on Route 197, 13 mi west on Route 216) the drive begins to climb north through the 1.1-million-acre **Mt. Hood National Forest.** A panorama of densely forested Cascade peaks and valleys unfolds as you ascend the southern slope of 11,325-foot **Mt. Hood,** the highest mountain in Oregon.

⓮ Near **Rhododendron** (39 mi north of Pine Grove on U.S. 26; 14 mi west on Route 216, 25 mi north on U.S. 26), you are approaching the summit of Mt. Hood. Take the well-marked turnoff from U.S. 26 for the final ascent to **Timberline Lodge** (Timberline Road), the highest spot in Oregon accessible by car. Breathtaking views of forested mountain peaks cupping jewel-like alpine lakes open up along the winding road. From here, follow U.S. 26 southwest back towards Portland.

The Dalles

Celilo Park. Local tribes taught the Corps, who still operate Celilo Lake and park, new methods of catching and preserving salmon. Besides fishing, you can swim, windsurf, kite board, and boat here. There are both day use and camping facilities, and picnic areas. | Exit 99 off I-84 | 541/296-1181 | Free | Daily.

Columbia Gorge Discovery Center-Wasco County Historical Museum. Exhibits highlight the geological history of the Columbia Gorge, back 40 million years when volcanoes, landslides, and floods carved out the area. Also here is the Wasco County Historical Museum, which focuses on 10,000 years of Native American life and exploration of the region by white settlers. | 5000 Discovery Dr. | 541/296-8600 | www.gorgediscovery.org | $6.50 | Daily 10-6.

The Dalles Dam and Reservoir. At this hydroelectric dam just east of the Bonneville Dam you can ride the free Dalles Dam Tour Train to the fish ladder and powerhouse. There's also a sturgeon pond at the visitor center. | Exit 87 (in summer) or exit 88 other times off I-84 | 541/296-1181 | Free | Dam daily; Train tour May-Sept., Wed.-Sun. 8-4 (departs every half hour).

Fort Dalles Museum. This 1856 doctor's office, a museum since 1905, illustrates pioneer and 19th-century life through personal effects such as clothing, guns, and an early hand-washing machine. In addition, there's a collection of early automobiles, including a 1904 Electric Studebaker and a 1908 Knox—and some old hearses, too. | 500 W. 15th St. | 541/296-4547 | $3 | Apr.-Sept., daily 10-5; Oct.-Mar., weekends 10-5.

Maryhill Museum of Art. One of the Columbia Gorge's most unusual cultural attractions is in a castlelike mansion, perched high on a cliff. It contains the largest collection of Rodin sculptures and watercolors west of the Mississippi; prehistoric Native American tools and baskets; and the charming "Théâtre de la Mode," a miniature fashion show devised by French couturiers after World War II. Three miles east of the museum, off Route 14, is an even stranger landmark in this unpopulated high-desert country: a replica of Stonehenge, built by Sam Hill as a memorial to soldiers killed in World War I. | 35 Maryhill Museum Dr., Goldendale, WA | 509/773-3733 | www.maryhillmuseum.org | $7 | Mid-Mar.-mid-Nov., daily 9-5.

Mayer State Park. A shimmery blue lake, desertlike plateaus, and a trail with gorgeous river views await you at this park. You can picnic, boat, fish, windsurf, swim, or laze on the beach. | Exit 77 off I-84 | 800/551-6949 | www.oregonstateparks.org | $3 day use, per vehicle | Daily.

Wasco County Courthouse. The museum in this 1859 courthouse, the oldest between the Cascades and Omaha, illustrates the life of pioneers on the Oregon Trail through pictures and old court records. You can visit the jail cells and, if you like, arrange to get married in the courtroom. | 410 W. 2nd Pl. | 541/296-4798 | Free (donation suggested) | May-Sept., Thurs.-Mon. 11-3; June-Aug., Thurs.-Mon. 10-4.

Dining

Bailey's Place. Contemporary. This 1865 building has 10-foot ceilings and period chandeliers to decorate them. Prime rib is the specialty here, but think about the chicken Ole, in a brandy, cream, and mushroom sauce. Desserts include a huckleberry sundae, chocolate-orange cheesecake, and cappuccino mousse cake. | 515 Liberty St. | 541/296-6708 | AE, D, MC, V | Closed Sun.-Mon. | $-$$$

Cousin's Restaurant and Saloon. American. Home cooking rules at this family restaurant with a frontier motif. If you're a meat-and-potatoes person, try the pot roast or turkey supper with all the trimmings. There are also soups and salads to choose from. A kids' menu is available. | 2114 W. 6th St. | 541/298-2771 | AE, D, DC, MC, V | $

Hood River

Bonneville Lock and Dam. Columbia River water passing through this structure's power generation station produces 1 million kilowatts of hydroelectricity, which is enough to supply more than 200,000 single-family homes. The dam's fish hatchery teems with fingerling salmon, fat rainbow trout, and 6-foot-long sturgeon. Tour the fish ladders and power generation station yourself, or take a 30- to 60-minute interpretive tour. | Exit 40 off I–84 | 541/374–8820 | www.nwp.usace.army.mil/op/b | Free | Visitor center daily 9–5; call to schedule tour.

Columbia Gorge. Cascade Locks, about 15 mi west of Hood River, is the home port of this 600-passenger stern-wheeler. Between mid-June and early October the relic ship churns upriver, then back again, on two-hour excursions through some of the gorge's most awesome scenery. Cruises leave from Marine Park in Cascade Locks. | 541/374–8427 | www.sternwheeler.com | Two-hour cruises (no meal) $12.95; longer cruises with meals $26–$36 | Two-hour cruises June–Sept., daily at 10, 12:30, and 3; dinner cruise Fri. at 7 and Sat. at 6; brunch cruise weekends at 12:30.

Flerchinger Vineyards. This winery, one of Oregon's newest, in the scenic Hood River Valley, has a 6-acre vineyard where Riesling and chardonnay grapes are grown. | 4200 Post Canyon Dr. | 541/386–2882 or 800/516–8710 | www.flerchinger.com | Free | Daily 11–5.

Fruit Loop. Either by car or bicycle, tour Hood River Valley's Fruit Loop, a series of vast orchards lining the Hood River. While on the loop, consider stopping at the quaint town of Parkdale to lunch, shop, and snap a photo of Mount Hood's north face. The route begins on Route 35; well-marked signs direct you around the entire 35-mi loop. | www.hoodriverfruitloop.com.

Hood River Vineyards. Chardonnay, sauvignon blanc, pinot noir, cabernet sauvignon, and merlot are among the varieties produced at this 12-acre, family-owned vineyard, which overlooks the Columbia River Gorge and Hood River Valley. Bottles are sold individually—the best sellers are the pinot noir and chardonnay. | 4693 Westwood Dr. | 541/386–3772 | Free | Mar.–Dec., daily 11–5.

Lost Lake. The waters of one of the most photographed spots in the Pacific Northwest reflect towering Mt. Hood and the thick forests that line the lakeshore. This tiny secluded lake has a campground with 125 sites as well as cabins available for overnight stays on the northwest side of Mt. Hood. Aside from tranquility, you'll find ample opportunities for fishing and hiking. Take Hood River Highway south from Hood River to the town of Dee and follow the signs. | Dee Secondary Hwy. in Mt. Hood National Forest | 541/386–6366 | $5 | Mid-May–mid-Oct., daily.

Mt. Hood Scenic Railroad and Dinner Train. This is an efficient and relaxing way to survey Mt. Hood and the Hood River—the route was established in 1906 as a passenger and freight line. You'll chug alongside the Hood River through vast fruit orchards before climbing up steep forested canyons, glimpsing Mt. Hood along the way. There are four trip options: a four-hour excursion, a dinner tour, a brunch tour, or a murder mystery dinner tour. | 110 Railroad Ave. | 541/386–3556 or 800/872–4661 | www.mthoodrr.com | Apr.–Dec., call for schedule.

Dining

Full Sail Tasting Room and Pub. American/Casual. In the former Diamond cannery building, this glass-walled microbrewery with a windswept deck overlooking the Columbia River won major awards at the Great American Beer Festival. Nachos, beer sausage, and other snack foods complement the fresh ales. During the summer months only, there's a grill menu offering chicken, veggie burgers, and salmon burgers. | 506 Columbia St. | 541/386–2281 or 888/244–2337 | MC, V | ¢–$

6th Street Bistro and Loft. Contemporary. The menu here changes weekly but concentrates on Pacific Northwest flavors, right down to the coffee and salads. Try the grilled fresh fish and chicken or, in season, local fresh steamer clams and wild coral mushrooms. This restaurant uses only local and organic food products. | 509 Cascade Ave. | 541/386–5737 | MC, V | $–$$

Stonehedge Gardens. Contemporary. A five-story Italian stone terrace, used for outdoor summer dining, is the most unusual feature of this restaurant, though the rest of it isn't too shabby, either: this 1898 house is on 6½ acres of gardens; the interior is embellished by detailed woodwork and stained-glass windows. The menu has a mix of Northwest and Continental dishes that include locally raised organic beef filet mignon and seared ahi tuna. | 3405 Cascade St. | 541/386–3940 | AE, MC, V | $–$$$

Lodging

Beryl House. A 1910 Craftsman farmhouse stands amid apple and pear trees 4 mi from Hood River and 3 mi from the Columbia River Gorge. Upstairs, braided rugs, Mission-style furnishings, and the original fir floors, add up to a comfortable stay. There's a wraparound porch, and breakfast may be served on a sundeck overlooking the pear trees. No room phones, no room TVs, no smoking. | 4079 Barrett Dr., 97031 | 541/386–5567 | www.berylhouse.com | 4 rooms | MC, V | BP | $

Columbia Gorge Hotel. This property is fully restored to its turn-of-the-20th-century beauty. No two rooms are alike, but each one is decorated with handcrafted wood antique furnishings, floral wallpaper, and quaint trinkets. A champagne and caviar social is held each afternoon. Restaurant, bar, cable TV, business services, some pets allowed. | 4000 Westcliff Dr. | 541/386–5566 or 800/345–1921 | fax 541/387–5414 | www.columbiagorgehotel.com | 40 rooms | AE, D, DC, MC, V | BP | $$$

Hood River Hotel. Public areas at this 1913 landmark are rich in beveled glass, warm wood, and tasteful jade-and-cream-color fabrics. Rooms have fir floors, Oriental rugs, four-poster beds, and skylights. There's a lively lobby bar and a Mediterranean-inspired restaurant. Restaurant, café, some kitchens, gym, hot tub, sauna, bar. | 102 Oak St., 97031 | 541/386–1900 | fax 541/386–6090 | www.hoodriverhotel.com | 33 rooms, 9 suites | AE, D, DC, MC, V | $–$$

Inn of the White Salmon. This quiet and cozy, European-style two-story brick inn on the Washington side of the Columbia River was built in 1937. The common areas and sleeping rooms are filled with antiques and artifacts; all rooms have private bathrooms. Dining room, cable TV, hot tub, some pets allowed (fee). | 172 W. Jewett Blvd., White Salmon, WA 98672 | 509/493–2335 or 800/972–5226 | www.innofthewhitesalmon.com | 11 rooms, 5 suites | AE, D, DC, MC, V | CP | $$–$$$

★**Lakecliff Bed & Breakfast.** Architect A. E. Doyle, who designed the Multnomah Falls Lodge, the Classical Revival public library and Benson Hotel in Portland, also designed this summer home-turned-B&B. The 1908 house, built on a cliff overlooking the river is beautifully maintained and exceptionally comfortable. For summer months, reservations are required at least three months in advance. Dining room, croquet; no smoking. | 3820 Westcliff Dr. (head east from I–84's Exit 62), 97031 | 541/386–7000 | fax 541/386–1803 | www.lakecliffbnb.com | 4 rooms | MC, V | BP | $$

Old Parkdale Inn. This fanciful B&B keeps the spirit of famous artists alive: the Gauguin Room celebrates Paul Gauguin's love of the tropics; the O'Keeffe Suite has a serene Southwestern theme. This is one B&B that not only welcomes children, but actually *encourages* families to stay here—lots of toys and books are provided to occupy energetic youngsters. | 4932 Baseline Rd., 97041 | 541/352–5551 | www.hoodriverlodging.com | 3 rooms | MC, V | BP | $$

John Day

Grant County Historical Museum. Memorabilia from the Gold Rush, including authentic gold nuggets, are on display at this museum. You'll also see Native American artifacts such as utensils and arrowheads made from stone and wood. Other exhibits showcase antique musical instruments like violins, organs, and an old-fashioned graphonala, a machine similar to what's found on carousels, which plays punched-out discs made from metal. | 101 S. Canyon City Blvd., Canyon City | 541/575–0362 or 541/575–1993 | $4 | May 15–Sept., Mon.–Sat. 9–4:30.

★ **John Day Fossil Beds National Monument.** The geological formations that make up the monument cover hundreds of square miles but are divided into three "units"— Sheep Rock, Painted Hills, and Clarno. Located 40 mi west of John Day, they were formed as a result of volcanic activity during the Cenozoic era 5 million to 50 million years ago.

Clarno Unit. The 48-million-year-old beds in the Clarno Unit have yielded the oldest fossils in the national monument. The drive to the beds traverses forests of ponderosa pines and sparsely populated valleys along the John Day River before turning through a landscape filled with spires and outcroppings that attest to the region's volcanic past. A short trail that runs between the two parking lots contains fossilized evidence of an ancient subtropical forest. Another trail climbs $1/4$ mi from the second parking lot to the base of the Palisades, a series of abrupt, irregular cliffs created by ancient volcanic mud flows. | Rte. 218 | 541/575–0547 | Free | Daily.

Painted Hills. The fossils here date back about 33 million years and prove that the climate had been noticeably drier than during Sheep Rock's era. The eroded buff-color hills reveal striking red and green striations that were created by minerals in the clay. Come at dusk or just after it rains, when the colors are most vivid. | Off U.S. 26 | 541/575–0547 | Free | Daily.

Sheep Rock Unit. You will find exhibits, a video, and handouts at the visitor center here. Two miles north of the visitor center on Route 19 lies the impressive Blue Basin, a badlands canyon with sinuous blue-green spires. Winding through this basin is the $1/2$-mi Island in Time Trail, where trailside exhibits explain the area's 28-million-year-old fossils. The 3-mi Blue Basin Overlook Trail loops around the rim of the canyon, yielding some splendid views. | U.S. 26 to Rte. 19 | 541/987–2333 | Free | Labor Day–Memorial Day, weekdays 9–6; Memorial Day–Labor Day, daily 9–6.

★ **Kam Wah Chung and Co. Museum.** This former trading post on The Dalles Military road (1866–67) was a hub for Chinese laborers during the gold rush. The original building now contains thousands of artifacts and relics which illustrate the site's history as a general store, office of a famous herb doctor, a Chinese temple, and the home of two noted members of the local community, Lung On, merchant, and Ing "Doc" Hay, doctor of pulsology and herbal medicine. | 250 N.W. Canton St. | 541/575–0028 | $4 | Mon.–Sat. 9–noon and 1–5, Sun. 1–5.

Malheur National Forest. You can cut through this 1.4-million-acre forest in the Blue Mountains as you drive from John Day to Burns on U.S. 395. It contains alpine lakes, meadows, creeks, and grasslands, while the area wildlife include mule deer, bighorn sheep, antelope, elk, bobcats, and mountain lions. There are 100 mi of trails and within its boundaries is the Strawberry Mountain Wilderness Area. | U.S. 395 at U.S. 26 | 541/575–3000 | Free | Daily.

Dining

Grubsteak Mining Co. Steak. A tangy yet sweet secret-recipe barbecue sauce drenches the ribs and chicken served here, though if you're really hungry, you may just want to tuck into a hefty steak, which comes with baked beans and baked or mashed potatoes. Vegetarians will find a nice selection of soups, salads, and pastas. The Dirty Shame Tavern, next door and owned by the same people, has pool tables and pizza and assorted pub grub. | 149 E. Main St. | 541/575–1970 | AE, D, MC, V | ¢–$$

Lodging

Best Western John Day Inn. Expect to find a good selection of accommodations here for large and small families alike, including one-, two-, and three-bed units. Some rooms have whirlpool tubs. Microwaves, refrigerators, some in-room hot tubs, indoor pool, hot tub, laundry facilities. | 315 W. Main St., 97845 | 541/575–1700 | 39 rooms | AE, D, DC, MC, V | $

Dreamer's Lodge. This two-story hotel in the center of town has close access to the John Day Fossil Beds. Some rooms have interesting photos of the fossil beds. Fishing and golf are nearby. Minibars, cable TV, cross-country skiing, business services, airport shuttle, some pets allowed. | 144 N. Canyon Blvd. | 541/575–0526 or 800/654–2849 | fax 541/575–2733 | 25 rooms | AE, D, DC, MC, V | $

John Day Sunset Inn. This two-level, family-owned property has modest furnishings, decent amenities, and is close to the center of town. A city park is within walking distance. Some microwaves, minibars, cable TV, pool, hot tub, some pets allowed. | 390 W. Main St., 97845 | 541/575–1462 or 800/452–4899 | fax 541/575–1471 | 44 rooms | AE, D, DC, MC, V | ¢–$

Mt. Hood National Forest

Cooper Spur Ski and Recreation Area. On the eastern slope of Mt. Hood, Cooper Spur caters to families and has two rope tows and a T-bar. The longest run is ²/₃ mi, with a 500-foot vertical drop. Call for hours. | Follow signs from Rte. 35 for 3¹/₂ mi to ski area | 541/352–7803.

Mt. Hood Meadows Ski Resort. Mt. Hood's largest resort has more than 2,000 skiable acres, dozens of runs, seven double chairs, one triple chair, one quad chair, a top elevation of 7,300 feet, a vertical drop of 2,777 feet, and a longest run of 3 mi. | 10 mi east of Government Camp on Rte. 35 | 503/337–2222 or 800/754–4663.

★ **Mt. Hood National Forest.** Mt. Hood is the fourth-highest peak in the Cascades—behind 14,000-foot giants Mt. Rainier and Mt. Shasta and 12,300-foot Mt. Adams—towering at 11,000 feet, and crowned by year-round snow. It is a focal point of the 1.1-million-acre forest, which extends south from the Columbia River Gorge for more than 60 mi and includes 189,200 acres of designated wilderness. These woods are perfect for hikers, horseback riders, mountain climbers, and cyclists. The Pacific Crest Trail, which begins in British Columbia and ends in Mexico, crosses at the 4,157-foot-high Barlow Pass. As with most mountain destinations within Oregon, weather can be temperamental and snow and ice are factors to consider as early as October and as late as May. Bring tire chains and warm clothes as a precaution. | U.S. 26 and Rte. 224 | 503/622–4822 or 888/622–4822 | www.fs.fed.us/r6/mthood | $3 day-use, per vehicle | Daily.

Mt. Hood Information Center. For a glimpse into the area's vivid history, stop at the information center in the Mt. Hood Village RV park, and pick up a copy of the *Barlow Road*. This is a great navigational map of the first emigrant road over the Cascades, where pioneers traveled west via ancient Indian trails to avoid the dangers of the mighty Columbia River. Since this forest is close to the Portland metro area, campgrounds and trails are crowded over the summer months, especially weekends. If you want to camp, stop at the forest service desk at the Information Center. | 65000 E. U.S. 26, Welches | 503/622–7674 or 503/622–3360.

Mt. Hood Ski Bowl. The ski area closest to Portland, Mt. Hood Ski Bowl has 63 trails serviced by four double chairs and five surface tows, a top elevation of 5,050 feet, a vertical drop of 1,500 feet, and a longest run of 3¹/₂ mi. Night skiing is a major activity here. You can take advantage of two day lodges, a mid-mountain warming hut, three restaurants, and two lounges. Sleigh rides are conducted, weather permitting. In summer Ski Bowl has go-carts, mountain- and alpine-bike rentals, and pony rides. Eastside Action Park,

¹/₂ mi to the east, has more than 20 kids-oriented attractions. | 53 mi east of Portland, across U.S. 26 from Government Camp | 503/272–3206 | www.skibowl.com.

Timberline Lodge Ski Area. One of the longest ski seasons in North America unfolds at Timberline. The U.S. ski team conducts summer training at this full-service ski area, which also welcomes snowboarders. Timberline is famous for its Palmer chairlift, which takes skiers to a high glacier for summer skiing. The top elevation is 8,500 feet, with a 3,600-foot vertical drop, and the longest run is 3 mi. Lift tickets are $31 on weekdays, $34 on weekends. | Off U.S. 26, Timberline | 503/272–3311 | Sun.–Tues. 9–5 and Wed.–Sat. 9 AM–10 PM; Palmer chairlift June–Aug, daily 7 AM–1:30 PM.

Dining

Cascade Dining Room. Contemporary. Inside this dining room at Timberline Lodge, you'll find a huge stone fireplace and handcrafted furniture; outside is a spectacular view of the Cascades. For dinner, you might choose Angus beef tenderloin, salmon, or rack of lamb. Finish up with chocolate decadence cake or marionberry cobbler. | Timberline Rd., Timberline | 503/622–0700 or 800/547–1406 | AE, D, MC, V | $$–$$$$

Charlie's Mountainview. American. Old and new skis plaster the walls, lift chairs now function as furniture, and photos of famous skiers and other memorabilia are as abundant as the menu selections. Steaks and hamburgers are worthy here, but house specialties include creamy mushroom soup and chicken Caesar salad with dressing made from scratch. | 88462 E. Government Camp Loop | 503/272–3333 | AE, D, MC, V | ¢–$$

Huckleberry Inn. American. Whether it's 2 PM or 2 AM, Huckleberry Inn welcomes you with soups, milkshakes, burgers, sandwiches, and omelets. There are plenty of huckleberry treats, including pies, pancakes, teas, jellies, and a huckleberry-vinaigrette salad dressing. | E. Government Camp Loop | 503/272–3325 | MC, V | ¢–$

Mt. Hood Brew Pub. American. Pizza, pasta, steak, and seafood are among the popular and hearty choices at this family-style pub. Espresso drinks, Oregon wines, and freshly brewed ales are available. Arrive early if you want outdoor seating in the summertime. | 87304 E. Government Camp Loop | 503/622–0724 | AE, D, MC, V | ¢–$

Lodging

Falcon's Crest Inn. At 4,000 feet, on the south flank of Mt. Hood, this 1983 cedar-and-glass chalet has broad mountain views from the floor-to-ceiling glass walls of the second and third floors. You'll be greeted by a complimentary glass of wine or a soft drink and appetizers upon arrival. Restaurant, some in-room hot tubs; no a/c, no room TVs, no kids under 6, no smoking. | 87287 Government Camp Loop, 97028 | 503/272–3403 or 800/624–7384 | fax 503/272–3454 | www.falconscrest.com | 5 rooms | AE, D, MC, V | BP | $$–$$$

Huckleberry Inn. In the heart of Government Camp, this inn is near ski areas, hiking trails, and mountain lakes. Room sizes vary and can accommodate from 2 to 14 people. Pine-wood furnishings and old photos of historical government camp decorate the rooms; some units have lofts. Restaurant. | E. Government Camp Loop, 97028 | 503/272–3325 | www.huckleberry-inn.com | 17 rooms | MC, V | $

Old Welches Inn. This simple white clapboard house and the 8-foot-high stone fireplace on the covered patio are all that remain of the bustling 1890 Welches Hotel, the first structure and oldest hotel on Mt. Hood. The largest of the guest rooms overlooks Resort at the Mountain's golf course, with views of Hunchback Mountain. The cabin, which dates from 1901, overlooks the first hole of the golf course and has a fireplace and kitchen. Picnic area, some microwaves, some refrigerators; no room phones, no TV in some rooms, no kids under 10, no smoking. | 26401 E. Welches Rd. Welches, 97067 | 503/622–3754 | fax 503/622–5370 | www.lodging-mthood.com | 4 rooms, 1 2-bedroom housekeeping cabin | AE, D, DC, MC, V | BP | $–$$$

Thunderhead Lodge. Awesome mountain views and the night lights of the ski bowl ski resort are among the pretty sights at this fun and friendly condominium lodge. Room sizes and capacities vary according to your needs, and there's a rec room with foosball, a pool table, a wet bar, and a fireplace. The outdoor pool is heated. Pool, laundry facilities. | 87451 E. Government Camp Loop, 97028 | 503/272–3368 or 866/622–1142 | www.thunderheadlodge.com | 10 units | MC, V | $–$$

★**Timberline Lodge.** This National Historic Landmark has withstood howling winter storms on an exposed flank of Mt. Hood for more than 50 years. The structure has a handcrafted, rustic feel, from the wrought-iron chairs with rawhide seats to the massive hand-hewn beams. Dining room, snack bar, some in-room data ports, pool, hot tub, downhill skiing, bar, children's programs (ages 4–12), business services; no TV in some rooms. | Timberline Rd., 97028 | 503/272–3311 or 800/547–1406 | fax 503/272–3710 | www.timberlinelodge.com | 70 rooms | AE, D, MC, V | $$–$$$

Portland

Classical Chinese Garden. Step back 400 years to the Ming era of China at this peaceful setting in Old Town/Chinatown. It's the largest Suzhou-style garden outside China, with a lake, bridged and covered walkways, ponds, rocks, statues, waterfalls, courtyards, and plenty of bamboo. | N.W. 3rd Ave. and Everett St. | 503/228–8131 | www.chinesegarden.org | $6 | Apr.–Oct., daily 9–6; Nov.–Mar., daily 10–5.

International Rose Test Garden. Despite the name, these grounds are not an experimental greenhouse laboratory but three breathtaking terraced gardens, where 10,000 bushes and 400 varieties of roses grow. The flowers are at their peak in June and July and September and October. | 400 S.W. Kingston Ave. | 503/823–3636 | www.portlandparks.com | Free | Dawn–dusk.

Japanese Garden. The most authentic Japanese garden outside Japan is nestled among 5½ acres of Washington Park above the International Rose Test Garden. The Tea House was built in Japan and reconstructed here. | 611 S.W. Kingston Ave. | 503/223–1321 | www.japanesegarden.com | $6 | Oct.–Mar., Mon. noon–4, Tues.–Sat. 10–4; Apr.–Sept., Mon. noon–7, Tues.–Sat. 10–7.

Oregon Museum of Science and Industry (OMSI). An Omnimax theater and planetarium are among the main attractions at the Northwest's largest astronomy educational facility. Moored in the Willamette River as part of the museum is a 240-foot submarine, the USS *Blueback*. | 1945 S.E. Water Ave., south of Morrison Bridge | 503/797–4000 | www.omsi.org | Full package $16, museum $7, planetarium $3.50, Omnimax $7, submarine $3.50 | Memorial Day–Labor Day, Fri.–Wed. 9:30–7, Thurs. 9:30–8; Labor Day–Memorial Day, Tues.–Sun. 9:30–5:30.

Pioneer Courthouse Square. Downtown Portland's public heart and commercial soul are centered in this amphitheatrical brick piazza, whose design echoes the classic central plazas of European cities. Directly across the street is one of downtown Portland's most familiar landmarks, the classically sedate Pioneer Courthouse. Built in 1869, it's the oldest public building in the Pacific Northwest. | 701 S.W. 6th Ave. | 503/223–1613.

Pittock Mansion. Henry Pittock, the founder and publisher of the *Oregonian* newspaper, built this 22-room mansion, which combines French Renaissance and Victorian styles. The 46-acre grounds, north of Washington Park and 1,000 feet above the city, have superb views of the skyline, rivers, and the Cascade Range. | 3229 N.W. Pittock Dr.; from W. Burnside St. heading west, turn right onto N.W. Barnes Rd. and follow signs | 503/823–3624 | www.portlandparks.org | $4.50 | Daily noon–4.

Portland Art Museum. The Pacific Northwest's oldest art museum was founded in 1892. Since then, it has acquired a diverse collection of over 33,000 objects and works of art. Exhibits are an eclectic display of European and American painting and sculpture, Asian, Native American, pre-Columbian, African, and contemporary art. There are also numerous prints, drawings, and photographic displays. | 1219 S.W. Park Ave. | 503/226–2811 | www.pam.org | $7.50 | Tues.–Sun. 10–5.

Portland Saturday Market. On weekends from March to Christmas, the west side of the Burnside Bridge and the Skidmore Fountain environs is home to North America's largest open-air handicraft market. You are guaranteed to find treasures of authentic, quirky, and highly crafted goods in addition to a delicious selection of food. | Under west end of Burnside Bridge, from S.W. Naito Pkwy. to Ankeny Sq. | 503/222–6072 | www.saturdaymarket.org | Mar.–Dec., Sat. 10–5, Sun. 11–4:30.

Dining

★ **The Heathman.** Contemporary. Among The Heathman's Northwest specialties are a delightful Dungeness crab, mango, and avocado salad, and a seafood paella. The dining room, scented with wood smoke and adorned with Andy Warhol prints, is a favorite for special occasions. | Heathman Hotel, 1001 S.W. Broadway | 503/790–7752 | AE, D, DC, MC, V | $$–$$$$

Mayas Taqueria. Mexican. Give your order cafeteria-style and then sit along the window inside or at one of the sidewalk tables. The tacos are one of the best deals in town. | 1000 S.W. Morrison St. | 503/226–1946 | MC, V | ¢–$

Mother's Bistro. American. The menu is loaded with home-style favorites—macaroni-and-cheese, chicken and dumplings, and meat loaf. For vegetarians there's a couscous stew. The tables are a bit close together, so don't pick this place if you want privacy. | 409 S.W. 2nd Ave. | 503/464–1122 | AE, D, DC, MC, V | Closed Mon. | $–$$

Pearl Bakery. Café. A light breakfast or lunch can be had at this popular spot known for its excellent fresh breads, pastries, cakes, and sandwiches. The cakes, cookies, croissants, and Danish are some of the best in the city. | 102 N.W. 9th Ave. | 503/827–0910 | No credit cards | Closed Sun. No dinner | $

Shaniko

Shaniko. Oregon's best-known ghost town has all of 25 residents. During its boomtown days of 1900–1911, this railhead town earned the "Wool Capital of the World" title. Several 1900s-era buildings still stand, but the heart of the town burned down long ago in a series of large fires. Local sites include the Shaniko Jail, Antique Car Barn, and Shaniko Wagon Yard. In addition, you'll find several antiques and collectibles stores, a small museum, and the Gold Nugget Saloon.

Shaniko Hotel. When the Shaniko Hotel opened in 1901, the town's population was in the thousands. The restored hotel has a player piano and part of the original counter in the lobby, and the main staircase is wide enough for hoop skirts. You can stay here if you like—there's even a bridal suite. Rooms range from $56–$96. | 4th and E Sts. | 541/489–3441 or 800/483–3441 | www.shaniko.com.

Dining

Shaniko Cafe. American. In the Shaniko Hotel, this café offers home-style cooking of juicy hamburgers, steaks, and hearty pasta salads. There's also a nice selection of soups, including chicken noodle and clam chowder. Top off your meal with a slice of homemade apple pie. | 4th and E Sts. | 541/489–3415 | MC, V | ¢–$

Shaniko Ice Cream Parlor. Cool off here with of homemade ice cream; there are more than 20 flavors to choose from. | 4th St. | 541/489–3392 | No credit cards | ¢

Troutdale

Crown Point State Park. This park is east of Troutdale on a 730-foot-high bluff with an unparalleled 30-mi view down the Columbia River Gorge. Vista House, the two-tier octagonal structure on the side of the cliff, opened its doors to visitors in 1918; the rotunda has displays about the gorge and the highway. | U.S. 30 | 503/695–2230 | www.vistahouse.com | Free | Mid-Apr.–mid-Oct., daily 9–6.

Dabney State Park. About 4 mi east of the Troutdale bridge, Dabney State Park has boating, hiking, and fishing. It's also a popular summer swimming hole. There's also an 18-hole disc golf course. A boat ramp is open from October through May—when no one is swimming. | U.S. 30 | 800/551–6949 | www.oregonstateparks.org | $3 day-use, per vehicle | Daily dawn–dusk.

Multnomah Falls. A 620-foot-high double-decker torrent—and the fifth-highest waterfall in the nation—Multnomah is by far the most spectacular of the cataracts east of Troutdale. The scenic highway leads down to a parking lot; from there, a paved path winds to a bridge over the lower falls. A much steeper trail climbs to a viewing point overlooking the upper falls. | Exit 31 off I–84 | 503/695–2376 | Free | Daily.

Oneonta Gorge. Following the old highway east from Multnomah Falls, you come to a narrow, mossy cleft with walls hundreds of feet high. Oneonta Gorge is most enjoyable during the summer, when you can walk up the streambed through the cool, green canyon. At other times of year, take the trail along the west side of the canyon. The clearly marked trailhead is 100 yards west of the gorge, on the south side of the road. The trail ends at Oneonta Falls, about ½ mi up the stream. You'll need boots or submersible sneakers—plus strong ankles—because the rocks are slippery. | 2 mi east of Multnomah Falls on Historic Columbia River Hwy. | Daily dawn–dusk.

Rooster Rock State Park. The most famous beach lining the Columbia River is here, below Crown Point (access is from the interstate only). Three miles of sandy beaches and a large swimming area make this park popular. One of Oregon's only designated nude beaches is at the east end (not visible to conventional sunbathers). | I–84, 7 mi east of Troutdale | 503/695–2261 | $3 day use, per vehicle | Daily 7 AM–dusk.

Dining

Black Rabbit. Contemporary. This restaurant at McMenamins Edgefield, a historic 25-acre bed-and-breakfast estate, serves all day and offers Northwest cuisine, such as fresh mussels steamed with green curry, lime juice, and basil, as well as traditional favorites, such as New York steak. Dine indoors or out on the outdoor courtyard. | 2126 S.W. Halsey St. | 503/492–3086 | AE, D, MC, V | $$$

★**Multnomah Falls Lodge.** Contemporary. The lodge, built in 1925 and listed on the National Register of Historic Places, has vaulted ceilings and classic stone fireplaces. Wonderful service accents a wide selection of delicious food, such as a zesty apple-wood-grilled salmon, slow-roasted prime rib, and grilled steak. | 50000 Historic Columbia River Hwy. | 503/695–2376 | AE, D, MC, V | $–$$

Stromboli's. American/Casual. The East Coast is well-represented here, with hearty Italian favorites, sizzling Philly cheesesteaks, and hoagies (sub sandwiches). A favorite is the bombsteak, a combination of green chilies, onions, mushrooms, strip steak, and cheeses. Gourmet pizzas, salads, and soups are also available. | 177 E. Historic Columbia River Hwy. | 503/674–2654 | MC, V | No dinner Mon. | $

SOUTH DAKOTA

BLACK HILLS AND BADLANDS
FROM BADLANDS NATIONAL PARK TO
MOUNT RUSHMORE NATIONAL MEMORIAL

Distance: 250 mi   Time: 3 days
Overnight Breaks: Rapid City, Custer or Custer State Park

Stunning buttes, canyons, badlands, and hills will be your driving companions. You'll pass through the exquisitely restored gold-rush town of Deadwood, then retreat to the vast wildlife preserve of Custer State Park. Along the way, you'll visit South Dakota's best-known memorials. Avoid this tour at the height of winter, when heavy snowfall sometimes make roads impassable.

❶ **Badlands National Park** is a 244,000-acre geologic wonderland. Route 240 wiggles through this moonlike landscape on its 32-mi loop off I–90. The Ben Reifel Visitor Center at Cedar Pass, 9 mi south of the interstate, and the White River Visitor Center, in the southern Stronghold Unit off BIA 27, will help acquaint you with the remote area and its wildlife. The roadless 64,250-acre Sage Creek Wilderness Area inside the park is protected from development and is open only to hikers, backpackers, and other outdoor enthusiasts. The only trails within the wilderness area have been created by the hooves of bison.

❷ The town of **Wall** is home to the **Wall Drug Store;** follow the signs. The internationally known emporium of galleries and unusual attractions became famous during the Depression by offering free ice-water to road-weary travelers, a practice that continues today. It now stocks Black Hills gold jewelry, Native American pottery and moccasins, Western clothing, books, art, postcards, curios, and thousands of pairs of cowboy boots. It also owns the **Western Art Gallery Restaurant,** with more than 250 original oil paintings and seating for 530 diners. Try the 5 ¢ coffee and homemade ice cream.

❸ **Rapid City,** 55 mi west of Wall on I–90, is the gateway to the Black Hills and a pleasant stop in its own right. From here it is possible to visit a combination of five national parks, memorials, and monuments on simple day trips, after which you'll want to spend the night. You can stop at the free **Dinosaur Park,** with its commanding views, **Storybook Island,** a free children's fantasyland park, and the **Stavkirke Chapel in the**

Hills, a replica of the 850-year-old Stavkirke in Borgund, Norway. You'll also discover numerous restaurants and a 13-mi bike and walking path through the center of town. The **Journey Museum** examines Black Hills history and culture. For outstanding shopping head downtown or visit the 110-store Rushmore Mall, the largest shopping center in a 300-mi radius, off I–90 on the city's north side.

❹ Begin the following day with the 46-mi drive west on I–90 to **Spearfish,** one of the state's prettiest towns. Set in a broad valley at the mouth of Spearfish Canyon, the town's main attractions are a convention center; historic sandstone buildings; the **Black Hills Passion Play,** presented on an outdoor stage since 1938; and the **Matthews Opera House,** a restored 1906 theater. You might also want to stop by the **D. C. Booth Historic Fish Hatchery,** or the **High Plains Heritage Center and Museum.**

❺ **Spearfish Canyon National Scenic Byway** greets motorists with sheer limestone palisades that tower to the right and left of U.S. 14A as it winds through the 19-mi gorge. The actual entrance to the canyon is in town, on the southwest side of Spearfish. Spearfish Creek splashes along the canyon floor as towering Black Hills spruce scent the air. Several canyon waterfalls, including Bridal Veil and Roughlock, are popular roadside stops.

❻ The twin cities of **Lead/Deadwood,** a bit farther on U.S. 14A, provide the ideal spot to stretch your legs. Visit Lead's **Black Hills Mining Museum** or the Homestake Visitor Center to learn more about mining's impact on the hills. In Deadwood, the **Adams Museum** displays rare artifacts from the town's colorful past. The **Old Style Saloon**

No. 10 bills itself as "the only museum in the world with a bar" and offers music, black-jack, poker, and slots.

❼ Hill City, approximately 40 mi south on U.S. 385, is another mining town turned tourist mecca. Its Main Street has shops and galleries, as well as the **Mount Rushmore Brewing Company,** with good pub grub and a wide selection of microbrews.

❽ Crazy Horse Memorial, the colossal mountain carving of the legendary Lakota leader, is south of Hill City on U.S. 16/385. The memorial's complex includes the **Indian Museum of North America,** which displays beautiful bead and quillwork repre-senting many of the continent's Native nations.

❾ Custer, 5 mi south of Crazy Horse Memorial on U.S. 385, is a friendly community surrounded by some of the most incredible scenery in the Black Hills, including Custer State Park, the Needles Highway, Harney Peak, Wind Cave National Park, and **Jewel Cave National Monument.** Jewel Cave was named for the nailhead and dogtooth spar crystals that line its more than 129 mi of mapped passageways. It is currently ranked as the second-longest cave in the United States (after Kentucky's Mammoth Cave). You can take an elevator down 234 feet, and various tours are offered at different times of the year.

❿ Custer State Park, 5 mi east of Custer on U.S. 16A, has 73,000 acres of scenic beauty, exceptional drives, close-up views of wildlife, and fingerlike granite spires rising from the forest floor. Relax through a hayride and chuckwagon supper, or take a jeep tour into the buffalo herds. Plan on spending the night in Custer or Custer State Park.

⓫ Wind Cave National Park is south of Custer State Park via Route 87 and U.S. 385. The park has 28,295 acres of wildlife habitat aboveground and the world's sixth-longest cave below, with 108 mi of mapped passageways. Six miles farther south on U.S. 385 you come to **Hot Springs.** Here still are more historic sandstone buildings; the

SOUTH DAKOTA RULES OF THE ROAD

License Requirements: To drive in South Dakota, you must be at least 14 years old and have a valid driver's license.

Right Turn on Red: Everywhere in the state, unless otherwise posted, you may make a right turn on red *after* a full stop. Exceptions include one-way streets in Rapid City.

Seat Belt and Helmet Laws: All drivers, front-seat passengers, and passengers under the age of 18 must wear a seat belt. Children under age five may only ride in a federally approved child safety seat, or if they exceed 40 pounds, the child may be secured with a seat belt. Motorcyclists 18 and older are not required to wear a helmet in South Dakota. Minors riding or driving a motorcycle must wear a helmet. Eye protection is required for all motorcy-clists. It is recommended that all motorcyclists have headlights and taillights on at all times.

Speed Limits: The speed limit on South Dakota's two interstates is 75 mph, except as noted near Rapid City and Sioux Falls. Posted limits on state and secondary highways are usually 65 mph, although most Black Hills scenic roadways are set at 55 mph.

For More Information: Contact the **South Dakota Highway Patrol** | 605/773–3105.

amazing **Mammoth Site,** where some 50 of the giant beasts have been unearthed; and **Evans Plunge,** with the world's largest naturally heated indoor swimming pool.

⓬ Take U.S. 18 east, then Route 79 north, then Route 40 west to **Keystone** to visit nearby **Mount Rushmore National Memorial.** Patiently awaiting you are the awesome carved busts of four U.S. presidents, Washington, Jefferson, Lincoln, and Theodore Roosevelt.

Return to Rapid City via U.S. 16A and 16, then follow I–90 east approximately 50 mi to Badlands National Park, your point of origin.

Badlands National Park

Badlands National Park. The 244,000-acre park has 64,000 acres of wilderness, seven marked hiking trails that stretch over 11 mi, and two visitor centers (Ben Reifel Visitor Center at Cedar Pass and the White River Visitor Center). Towering spires, ragged ridgelines, and deep canyons are some of the memorable sights. | Rte. 240, Interior | 605/433–5361 | fax 605/433–5404 | www.nps.gov/badl | $10 per car for 7-day pass; $5 motorcycles and bikes | Daily.

Artifacts from the parklands and educational maps make the **White River Visitor Center Museum** a worthy stop. | Off Rte. 27 57750 | 605/455–2878 | Free | Call for hrs.

Dining

★**Cedar Pass Lodge and Restaurant.** Southwestern. This open-air, full-service restaurant has an exposed beam ceiling and knotty pine walls. Enjoy steak and trout or Indian tacos and fried bread, accompanied by a cold beer or a glass of wine. | Badlands Loop Rd. | 605/433–5460 | AE, D, DC, MC, V | Closed Nov.–Mar. | $

Custer

★**Black Hills National Forest.** Custer is the headquarters for this forest on the western edge of South Dakota. The forest covers 1.2 million acres and makes up almost half of the entire Black Hills region. Teeming with wildlife and natural beauty, it offers fishing, camping, hiking, mountain biking, and horseback riding. | 605/343–8755 | www.fs.fed.us/r2/blackhills | Free.

Cathedral Spires. Granite towers reach above the top of the trees toward the heavens. This registered National Landmark lies on Needles Highway in Custer State Park. | Custer Needles Hwy. | 605/255–4515 | www.custerstatepark.info.

Centennial Trail. A 111-mi trail, Centennial crosses the prairie grasslands near Bear Butte State Park and climbs into the Black Hills high country, skirting lakes and streams, monuments, memorials, and campgrounds until it reaches Wind Cave National Park. Hikers are welcome on the entire trail, which is accessible from 22 trailheads. Portions are open to horseback riders and mountain bikers. | 605/347–5240.

★**Crazy Horse Memorial.** The colossal mountain carving—still in progress—depicts Lakota leader Crazy Horse atop his steed. At the memorial's base are a restaurant and gift shop, as well as work by Crazy Horse sculptor Korczak Ziolkowski. | Ave. of the Chiefs | 605/673–4681 | $9.

Indian Museum of North America. At the base of the memorial is one of the most impressive collections of Plains Indian artifacts in the country. The collection is presented in an airy setting of ponderosa pine. | Ave. of the Chiefs | 605/673–4681 | Free with memorial admission.

Custer County Courthouse Museum. See three floors of artifacts and the region's premier exhibit on General George A. Custer's 1874 Black Hills expedition. Also here is an 1875 log cabin, the first built in the Black Hills. | 411 Mount Rushmore Rd. | 605/673–2443 | $3 | June–Aug., Mon.–Sat. 9–9, Sun. 1–9; Sept.–May, by appointment only.

★ **Custer State Park.** You'll find 114 square mi of preserve alternating among alpine meadows, rolling foothills, pine forests, and fingerlike granite spires. The park is also the home of one of the nation's largest bison herds. There's camping, summer theater, and four rustic mountain retreats. | U.S. 16A (at Rte. 87) | 605/255–4515 | www.custerstatepark.info | May–Oct., $12 per vehicle or $5 per person; Nov.–Apr., $6 per vehicle or $2.50 per person | Daily.

Jewel Cave National Monument. The cave—the world's third-longest—has nearly 130 mi of known passages. It was formed by water dissolving minerals out of the limestone, and exploration is hampered by occasional flooding. You'll see unusual boxwork, frostwork, and popcorn formations as well as stalactites, stalagmites, and crystals. An elevator takes you 234 feet underground to view this incredible maze. The only way to explore the cave is on one of the ranger-led tours; you can picnic or hike aboveground on your own. | U.S. 16 (13 mi west of Custer) | 605/673–2288 | Discovery Tour $4, lantern tour $8, scenic tour $8, spelunking tour $27 | Memorial Day–Labor Day, daily 8–7:30; Labor Day–Memorial Day, daily 8–4; call for tour hours.

Dining

Bavarian Restaurant. German. Murals of German country scenes decorate the dining room of this family-style restaurant and lounge. The popular dish here is *rouladen* (thinly sliced sirloin wrapped with mustard, bacon, and a dill pickle and seared, then baked for several hours until tender). Buffet dining is available, as is a fine selection of German beers. | U.S. 16/385 N | 605/673–4412 | D, MC, V | Call for winter hours | $

Chief Restaurant. American. The big menu at the Chief includes buffalo steaks and burgers, a Philly steak sandwich, kabobs, and prime rib. Many of the tables are set up around a large indoor fountain. There is a salad bar and the service is family-style. | 140 Mount Rushmore Rd. | 605/673–4402 | AE, D, MC, V | Closed Nov.–mid-Apr. | $$

Laughing Water Restaurant. Native American. This airy pine restaurant, with windows facing the Crazy Horse Memorial, is noted for its fry bread and buffalo burgers. There's a soup and salad bar, but you'd do well to stick to the Native American offerings— try the Indian taco and Buffaloski (a Polish sausage made with Dakota buffalo). | Ave. of the Chiefs | 605/673–4681 | AE, D, MC, V | Closed Nov.–Apr. | ¢–$

Lodging

Bavarian Inn. Some rooms at this resort among the pines have views of the Black Hills, and all upstairs rooms open onto balconies with seating areas. The inn is less than 1 mi from downtown. Restaurant, cable TV, tennis court, 2 pools (1 indoor), hot tub, sauna, bar, playground, some pets allowed (fee). | U.S. 16/385 N, 57730 | 605/673–2802 or 800/657–4312 | fax 605/673–4777 | www.custer-sd.com/bavarian | 64 rooms | AE, D, DC, MC, V | $

Blue Bell Lodge and Resort. The modern handcrafted log cabins at this hideaway in Custer State Park have fireplaces, a lodge, picnic tables, and a chapel with regular services in summer. There is a campground on the premises, and hayrides and cookouts are part of the entertainment. A stable offers trail rides and overnight pack trips on old Indian trails. Restaurant, picnic area, kitchenettes, cable TV, hiking, horseback riding, bar, lounge, playground, laundry facilities, meeting rooms, some pets allowed (fee); no a/c, no room phones. | 605/255–4531 or 800/658–3530 | fax 605/255–4706 | www.custerresorts.com | 29 cabins | AE, D, MC, V | Closed Oct.–mid-May | $$–$$$

French Creek Guest Ranch B&B. You can soak up views of the Needles formation while porch-sitting at this luxurious "bed-and-barn" on a 25-acre working horse ranch. The ranch is 1½ mi from Custer State Park. Restaurant, refrigerators, tennis court, sauna, fishing, basketball, hiking, horseback riding, mountain biking, volleyball; no room phones, no room TVs, no kids under 13. | 605/673–4790 or 877/673–4790 | fax 605/673–4767 | www.frenchcreekranch.com | 3 rooms | D, MC, V | CP | $–$$

Deadwood

Adams House Museum. Original furniture and decor are the hallmarks of this 1892 mansion built in Deadwood's Presidential District. The house tells the story of two prominent Deadwood families and the town's shift from a transient gold camp to a wealthy permanent settlement. | 22 Van Buren St. | 605/578–3724 | $5 | May–Sept., Mon.–Sat. 9–6, Sun. noon–4; Oct.–Apr., Mon.–Sat. 10–3.

Adams Museum. The oldest history museum in the Black Hills is an exceptional repository of historic Deadwood memorabilia. There are frequent special exhibits and events. | 54 Sherman St. | 605/578–1714 | Free | May–Sept., Mon.–Sat. 9–7, Sun. noon–5; Oct.–Apr., Mon.–Sat. 10–4.

Broken Boot Gold Mine. Join guides on a journey into an authentic gold mine and pan for gold. If nothing else, you'll receive a souvenir stock certificate. | Upper Main St., U.S. 14A | 605/578–9997 | $4.75 | June–Aug., daily 8:30–5:30; Sept. and May, daily 9–4:30.

Mickelson Trail. Named for the late Governor George S. Mickelson, this 114-mi trail has 14 trailheads, all with parking, toilets, and picnic tables. South Dakota's first rails-to-trails project, the gravel path extends across the backcountry from Deadwood to Edgemont, through four tunnels and over more than 100 bridges. Bicycles and horses are allowed on the trail. A trail pass (required for ages 12 and up) can be purchased at self-service stations at the trailheads. The trailhead in Deadwood in behind the Sherman Street Parking Lot by the creek. | Sherman St. | 605/584–3896 | $2.

Old Style Saloon #10. Thousands of artifacts, vintage photos, and a two-headed calf are among this hangout's decorations. You'll find live entertainment nightly, gaming, and excellent food upstairs at the Deadwood Social Club. A reenactment of "The Shooting of Wild Bill Hickok" happens four times a day during the summer. | 657 Main St. | 605/578–3346 | Free | Memorial Day–Labor Day, Sun.–Mon. 8 AM–2 AM, Tues.–Sat. 8 AM–3 AM; Labor Day–Memorial Day, daily 8 AM–2 AM.

Tatanka: Story of the Bison. This Kevin Costner–owned attraction showcases 17 larger-than-life bronze sculptures of Lakota warriors pursuing a herd of bison over a cliff. The Sweetgrass Grill at Tatanka serves exceptional bison cuisine. An interactive interpretive center tracks the history of the American bison, and an 1840 Lakota encampment with Native interpreters in costume transports visitors to a long-ago life on the Great Plains. | 100 Tatanka Dr. | 605/584–5678 | $6.50 | May–Oct., daily 9–7.

Dining

Creekside Restaurant. American. Part of the Deadwood Gulch Resort, this restaurant resembles an old saloon, complete with a bar from the 1880s. You'll find yourself greeted with hearty breakfasts and plate-size steaks. Some locals say they make the best burgers in town. Their salads are also good, largely due to the homemade apricot dressing and fresh sunflower bread that comes with them. | Rte. 85 S | 605/578–1294 or 800/695–1876 | AE, D, MC, V | $–$$

★ **Deadwood Social Club.** Italian. Light jazz and blues play in the background at this homey and relaxed restaurant, which serves a blend of northern Italian and American cuisines. Try the Portobello mushrooms and garlic in balsamic vinegar for an appetizer, then move on to coriander-crusted tuna, rosemary-and-tomato chicken, or a Black Angus steak with shrimp. The cellar stocks one of South Dakota's best wine selections. Don't leave without having a piece of homemade cheesecake. | 657 Main St. | 605/578–3346 or 800/952–9398 | AE, MC, V | Closed Mon. | $$–$$$

Jake's. Contemporary. Owned by actor Kevin Costner, this may well be South Dakota's premier restaurant experience, with an atrium setting, cherrywood accents, fireplaces, and soft lighting. Try the buffalo roulade, Cajun seafood tortellini, filet mignon, or fresh fish. | Midnight Star Casino, 677 Main St. | 605/578–1555 | Reservations essential | AE, D, DC, MC, V | Closed Sun. No lunch | $$–$$$$

Hill City

Pactola Reservoir. Ponderosa pine forests surround this reservoir in the Black Hills National Forest, which has a public beach, three picnic areas, two scenic overlooks, two campgrounds, two boat-launch facilities, hiking trails, and the Pactola Pines Marina, a full-service facility with pontoon rentals, gasoline, and a convenience store with supplies. | U.S. 385, 15 mi north of Hill City | 605/343–8755 | www.fs.fed.us/bhnf | Free | Mid-May–Sept., daily 8:30–6.

Sheridan Lake. The lake has 400 surface acres and is surrounded by ponderosa pine forests, picnic areas, and hiking trails. Facilities include two public beaches and a full-service marina with slip rental, boat rental, a convenience store, and gasoline. Group and individual campsites are available. You will need to purchase a National Forest Service day-use permit. | 16451 Sheridan Lake Rd., 9 mi north of Hill City | 605/574–2169 | www.sheridanlakemarina.com.

Sylvan Rocks Climbing Lessons and Adventures. Climbing classes ranging from beginner to advanced use Sylvan Rocks as their classroom. Costs range from $125–$500; the maximum number of climbers per guide is three. | 301 Main St. | 605/574–2425 | fax 605/342–1487.

Dining

Alpine Inn. American. European charm finds its way into the Old West at the Alpine Inn. The lunchtime menu changes daily but always includes an array of healthful selections from sandwiches to salads (with no fried food). Note that the dinner menu only has two items: small filet mignon or large filet mignon. | 225 Main St. | 605/574–2749 | No credit cards | Closed Sun. | $

Mount Rushmore Brewing Company. American. Spacious dining is on tap along with a large selection of microbrews and imports at this Black Hills brewery. Tanks, boilers, and pipes are part of the scenery, reminding you that something is always brewing. Specialties are steaks, prime rib, pizza, and hearty pub fare, including the popular "white chili" made from great northern beans and chicken and spices. | 349 Main St. | 605/574–2400 | D, MC, V | Closed Sept.–May | $–$$

Hot Springs

Evans Plunge. Get ready to splash in the world's largest indoor natural warm-water swimming pool. The Plunge also has additional indoor-outdoor pools, waterslides, a sauna, a steam room, and a fitness center. | 1145 N. River St. | 605/745–5165 | $8 | Daily, call for hrs.

★**Mammoth Site of Hot Springs.** More than 50 giant mammoths have already been unearthed from a prehistoric sinkhole where they came to drink 26,000 years ago. You can watch the excavation in progress and take guided tours of this unique discovery. | Southern city limits on U.S. 18 truck bypass | 605/745–6017 or 800/325–6991 | www.mammothsite.com | $6.50 | Daily, call for hours.

Wind Cave National Park. This is the world's sixth-longest cave, and you can explore several of its 108 mi of known passageways on one of five tours. Above ground, discover a 28,000-acre wildlife preserve that is home to bison, pronghorns, and prairie dogs. | U.S. 385 | 605/745–4600 | Free; cave tours $6–$20 | Daily 8–6.

Dining

Elk Horn Cafe. American. Your choices include burgers and steaks that are hand cut on the premises. Eat breakfast on one of two outdoor decks with a view of town. | 310 S. Chicago St. | 605/745–6556 | AE, MC, V | $–$$

Keystone

Beautiful Rushmore Cave. Stalagmites, stalactites, helectites, flowstone, ribbons, columns, and the "Big Room" are all part of a worthwhile tour into the depths of the Black Hills. In 1876, miners found the opening to the cave while digging a flume into the mountainside to carry water to the gold mines below. | 13622 Rte. 40 | 605/255–4384 or 605/255–4634 | www.beautifulrushmorecave.com | $7.50 | May 1–Memorial Day and Labor Day–Oct., daily 9–5; Memorial Day–Labor Day, daily 8–8.

Big Thunder Gold Mine. Tour an underground gold mine, pick up some free gold ore samples, and do a little gold panning of your own here. | Rte. 40 | 605/666–4847 or 800/314–3917 | Tour $7.50; panning $6.50 | May–mid-Oct., daily 8–8.

Cosmos Mystery Area. No one stands up straight and balls roll uphill at this unusual and entertaining attraction. | U.S. 16, 4 mi north of Keystone | 605/343–9802 | www.cosmosmysteryarea.com | $7 | Apr.–Oct., daily 7–7; Nov.–May, call for hrs.

★**Mount Rushmore National Memorial.** One of the nation's most popular attractions is 3 mi from Keystone. Ample visitor facilities complement the giant likenesses of Washington, Jefferson, Lincoln, and Theodore Roosevelt. | Rte. 244 | 605/574–2523 | www.nps.gov/moru | Free, parking $8.

Dining

Buffalo Dining Room. American. You can feast on the very popular buffalo stew—or more standard fare like burgers and pasta—while enjoying views of Mount Rushmore. A "monumental" bowl of ice cream is the best way to end a meal. | Rte. 244 | 605/574–2515 | AE, D, MC, V | No dinner mid-Oct.–early Mar. | ¢–$

Creekside Dining. American. Although this casual dining room does have a great patio view of Mount Rushmore, its menu is by far the best reason to come here. If you still have room after getting through platters of prime rib, buffalo, lamb, chicken, and fish, try the desserts, which include bread pudding and peach cobbler. | 610 U.S. 16A | 605/666–4904 | MC, V | Closed Nov.–May | $$–$$$

Spokane Creek Deli. American. Simple fare like pizza and subs hit the spot at lunch and dinner here. The homemade biscuits and gravy are a must for a hearty breakfast. | U.S. 16A | 605/666–4430 | DC, MC, V | Closed Labor Day–Memorial Day | $

Lead

Black Hills Mining Museum. Displays explore the history of mining in the Black Hills. There are guided tours through simulated tunnels and stopes (underground steps), a video theater, and gold panning activities. | 323 W. Main St. | 605/584–1605 or 888/410–3337 | $4.50, gold panning $5 | May–Aug., daily 9–5; Sept.–Apr., Tues.–Sat. 9–4:30.

Deer Mountain. Ski lessons, rentals, and cross-country trails are available here, as are three lifts and 32 downhill trails with a 700-foot vertical drop. There are several good beginner slopes, and staff caters to novices. | 1000 Deer Mountain Rd. | 605/584–3230 | www.skideermountain.com | Lift ticket $5–$29; rentals $8–$20; lessons $20–$60 | Nov.–Mar., Wed.–Thurs. and Sun. 9–4, Fri.–Sat. 9–9.

Terry Peak. A 1,100-foot vertical drop, 24 trails, and loads of snow account for the popularity of this 400-acre ski area in the Black Hills. The peak has five chairlifts, a rental shop, lessons, and day lodge facilities. Nearly $^3/_4$ of the runs are rated intermediate. | Rte. 85, 3 mi west of Lead | 605/584-2165 or 800/456-0524 | www.terrypeak.com | Lift ticket $10-$35; rentals $10-$20; lessons $45-$150 | Nov.–Apr., daily 9–4.

Dining

Stampmill Restaurant and Saloon. American. Photos gracing the dark-wood and brick interior of this 1892 restaurant trace the history of Lead and its mines. Basic food is available in the saloon; try the Black Angus steak or the French onion soup. | 305 W. Main St. | 605/584-1984 | D, MC, V | ¢–$$

Rapid City

Bear Country U.S.A. Bears, wolves, elk, bighorns, and other North American wildlife roam free in their natural habitat. Bear cubs and wolf pups are housed in a walk-through area. Allow at least 1½ hrs for your visit. | 13820 U.S. 16 S | 605/343-2290 | www.bearcountryusa.com | $12 per adult or $40 per vehicle | May–Oct., daily 8–6.

Black Hills Caverns. Frost crystal, amethyst, logomites, and calcite crystals fill the cave, first discovered by pioneers in the late 1800s. Half-hour and hour tours are available. | 2600 Cavern Rd. | 605/343-0542 | Tour $8, panning $6 | May–Sept., daily 9–5.

Black Hills National Forest. Hundreds of miles of hiking, mountain biking, and horseback riding trails crisscross this million-acre forest on the western edge of the state. Other entry points are Custer, Deadwood, Hill City, Hot Springs, Lead, Spearfish, and Sturgis. | Black Hills National Forest Visitor Center, 803 Soo San Dr. | 605/343-8755 | www.fs.fed.us/bhnf | Free | Park daily, visitor center mid-May–Sept.

Crystal Cave Park. A trout pond and the bones of a hapless explorer are two of the sights on the 45-minute, non-strenuous tours of this crystal-lined cavern. | 7770 Nameless Cave Rd. | 605/342-8008 | $8 | May–Oct. 15, daily 9–6.

Dinosaur Park. Seven life-size replicas of colossal prehistoric reptiles guard the crest of Skyline Drive. | 940 Skyline Dr. | 605/348-0462.

Stavkirke Chapel in the Hills. Norse dragon heads mix with Christian symbols in this chapel, which is held together with pegs. It is an exact replica of the 850-year-old Stav church in Borgund, Norway. Scandinavian immigrant artifacts are displayed next door. | 3788 Chapel La. | 605/342-3880 | Free | May–Sept., 7 AM–sunset.

Thunderhead Underground Falls. Six hundred feet within a mountain, along a deserted mine shaft, you'll find a spectacular waterfall, first discovered by miners while blasting for gold. | 10940 W. Rte. 44 | 605/343-0081 | $5 | May–Oct., daily 9–7:30.

Dining

Circle B Ranch Chuck Wagon Supper & Music Show. American. Chuckwagon suppers include tender roast beef, biscuits, and all the trimmings; buffalo and chicken options are a bit extra. The ranch also offers western music shows, gold panning, and trail and wagon rides. The prix fixe includes all of the above. | 22735 U.S. 385 | 605/348-7358 or 800/403-7358 | Reservations essential | MC, V | Closed Oct.–Apr. No lunch | $–$$

Firehouse Brewing Co. American. The state's first brewpub occupies a historic 1915 firehouse, and it is ornamented throughout with brass fixtures and firefighting equipment. The five house-brewed beers are the highlight of the menu, which also includes pastas, salads, and gumbo. | 610 Main St. | 605/348-1915 | Reservations not accepted | AE, D, DC, MC, V | No lunch Sun. | $–$$

Fireside Inn. Steak. A warm fireside setting complements some of the best beef in the Dakotas. Try the bean soup, New York steak, or the 20-ounce Cattlemen's Cut. | Rte. 44 W | 605/342–3900 | AE, D, MC, V | No lunch | $–$$$

Landmark Restaurant and Lounge. American. Popular for its lunch buffet, this hotel–restaurant also serves dinner specialties that include prime rib, buffalo, freshwater fish, and wild game. | 523 6th St. | 605/342–1210 | AE, D, DC, MC, V | $$–$$$$

Lodging

★ **Alex Johnson Hotel.** Period furnishings fill this nine-floor hotel in operation since 1928. Right in downtown, it's surrounded by shops and restaurants. Restaurant, some in-room hot tubs, some refrigerators, cable TV with movies, bar, meeting rooms, business services, airport shuttle. | 523 6th St., 57701 | 605/342–1210 or 800/888–2539 | fax 605/342–7436 | www.alexjohnson.com | 141 rooms, 2 suites | AE, D, DC, MC, V | $–$$

Best Western Town 'N Country Inn. The five, two-story buildings of this chain motel sit 1 mi from downtown on the road to Mount Rushmore and near Rapid City Regional Hospital. Restaurant, some refrigerators, cable TV, 2 pools, playground, airport shuttle. | 2505 Mount Rushmore Rd., 57701 | 605/343–5383 or 877/666–5383 | fax 605/343–9670 | www.bestwestern.com | 100 rooms | AE, D, DC, MC, V | $–$$

Sweetgrass Inn Bed & Breakfast. Antique furnishings and gingham and floral-print linens fill this Victorian farmhouse. Some rooms have private baths and entrances. Young children are welcome. Some in-room hot tubs, cable TV, in-room VCRs, outdoor hot tub; no room phones. | 9356 Neck Yoke Rd., 57701 | 605/343–5351 or 800/317–6784 | 8 rooms | MC, V | BP | $$–$$$

Spearfish

D. C. Booth Historic Fish Hatchery. This century-old hatchery contains a museum, a historic home, fish ponds, and underwater viewing windows. | 423 Hatchery Circle | 605/642–7730 | http://dcbooth.fws.gov | Free | Museum and home, Memorial Day–Labor Day, daily 9–6; Grounds open year-round, daily dawn–dusk.

High Plains Western Heritage Center and Museum. Western art and artifacts, including bronze sculptures and paintings, are displayed in this modern facility. Outdoors, you can view a sod dugout, a one-room school, a log cabin, and live buffalo, longhorns, and miniature horses. Cowboy poetry and music are performed on Wednesday evenings from Memorial Day to Labor Day. | 825 Heritage Dr. | 605/642–9378 | $4 | Memorial Day–Labor Day, daily 9–8; Labor Day–Memorial Day, daily 9–5.

Spearfish Canyon. Southwest of Spearfish, this canyon is home to more than 1,000 species of plants. The road that winds through the canyon is designated a National Scenic Byway, and meanders along the banks of Spearfish Creek past waterfalls and towering trees. The upper reaches of the canyon provided the backdrop for the closing scenes of Kevin Costner's epic *Dances With Wolves*. | U.S. 14A | 605/642–2626 or 800/626–8013 | Free | Daily.

Dining

Latchstring Restaurant. American. A wonderful view of Spearfish Canyon will accompany your meal at this casual spot. For breakfast try the sourdough pancakes. Popular dinner entrées include fresh trout and steak. | Spearfish Canyon, U.S. 14A | 605/584–3333 | D, MC, V | $–$$

Roma's Ristorante. Italian. Although located in a turn-of-the-20th-century brick building in Spearfish's downtown, the interior of Roma's has a distinctly modern look. The open dining room and kitchen are decorated in muted gold and green tones, 20-

foot-high wine racks climb the walls, and works by local artists grace the loft area. Specialties include the spicy "angry" shrimp and smoked pheasant ravioli. On Wednesday, all wine is half-price. | 701 5th St. | 605/722–0715 | D, MC, V | $–$$

Shoot the Bull Steakhouse. Steak. Ropes, horns, and antlers are scattered throughout this eatery. Try the filet mignon and prime rib. | 539 W. Jackson Blvd. | 605/642–2848 | AE, D, DC, MC, V | No lunch | $–$$$

Wall

National Grasslands Visitor Center. Managed by the U.S. Forest Service, this visitor center focuses on providing information about the national grasslands—Grand River, Fort Pierre, and Buffalo Gap are the three in western South Dakota—with more than 20 exhibits highlighting prairie plants and animals and recreation opportunities. | 708 Main St. | 605/279–2125 | Jun.–Aug., daily 7 AM–8 PM; Sept.–May, daily 8–4:30.

Wall Drug Store. The store's claim to fame during the Depression—offering free ice-water to road-weary travelers—is still appreciated by drivers today. Wall Drug has grown to accommodate four art gallery–dining rooms that seat 520 visitors; its Western Mall has 14 shops. | 510 Main St. | 605/279–2175 | Memorial Day–Labor Day, daily 6 AM–10 PM; Labor Day–Memorial Day, daily 6:30 AM–6 PM.

Dining

★**Elkton House Restaurant.** American. Wood paneling and a sunroom set the tone for this comfortable restaurant. Try the terrific hot roast beef sandwich, served on white bread with gravy and mashed potatoes. A breakfast bar serves fresh fruit and pastries in summer. | 203 South Blvd. | 605/279–2152 | D, MC, V | $–$$

Western Art Gallery Restaurant. American. This restaurant in the Wall Drug Store displays more than 250 original oil paintings, all with a Western theme. Try a hot roast beef sandwich or a buffalo burger. The fresh doughnuts are some of the best in the state. | 510 Main St. | 605/279–2175 | ¢–$

TEXAS

BANDERA TO NEW BRAUNFELS
A HILL COUNTRY TOUR

Distance: 110 mi   Time: 3 days
Overnight Breaks: Fredericksburg, Austin

Hill Country is a scenic area tucked north of San Antonio and west of I–35. Created by an earthquake more than 30 million years ago, the region spans 23 counties and is chock-full of small towns, picturesque lakes, dramatic caves, and historic attractions. Take this drive in April, and the roadsides are a show of wildflower color. Be wary of this tour during heavy rains, however, as many roads are subject to flash-flooding.

❶ Begin your tour in **Bandera.** This community, known as the "Cowboy Capital of the World," is surrounded by numerous dude ranches that provide a chance to take to the saddle for a few days of cowboy fun. Rodeos, country and western music, and horse racing are regular pastimes.

❷ From Bandera, head north on Route 173 for approximately 25 mi to **Kerrville.** The **Y. O. Ranch,** which raises exotic animals in addition to cattle, is here; call to arrange a tour of part of its 40,000 acres. The nearby **National Center for American Western Art** exhibits cowboy-theme paintings and sculpture.

❸ **Fredericksburg** is approximately 25 mi north on Route 16. This German community's old-time storefronts are filled with gift shops, cafés, and bed-and-breakfasts (plan on spending the night here). Downtown, the **National Museum of the Pacific War** concentrates on that theater of World War II, and honors Fredericksburg native Admiral Chester Nimitz, World War II Commander-in-Chief of the Pacific. **Enchanted Rock State Natural Area** is site of the largest stone formation in the West. Easy walks around the rock, and moderate to advanced climbs, are possible. In summer, start early to avoid midday heat.

❹ To get to **Stonewall,** the birth and burial place of Lyndon B. Johnson, from Fredericksburg head east on U.S. 290 for about 10 mi. Visit the **Lyndon B. Johnson State Historical Park,** where you can catch a guided tour of the LBJ Ranch. During the spring, this portion of the drive is lined with blooming peach trees.

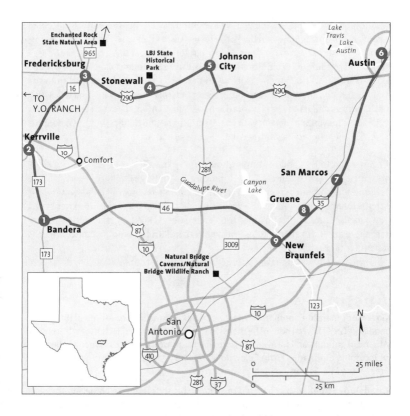

❺ Continue on U.S. 290 14 mi to **Johnson City,** named for Sam Ealy Johnson Sr., LBJ's grand-father. LBJ moved here from Stonewall when he was five years old. Here you'll find the visitor center for the Lyndon B. Johnson National Historic Park. The site includes his boyhood home.

❻ From Johnson City, head east on U.S. 290 for about 40 mi, then north on I-35 into **Austin.** The centerpiece of the city is the **State Capitol.** Guided tours of the building are offered daily.

South of the Capitol is the **Governor's Mansion,** with historic reminders of the many governors of the Lone Star State. On the north side of the Capitol is the **University of Texas at Austin.** On campus, the **Lyndon Baines Johnson Library and Museum** traces the history of Johnson's presidency through exhibits and films. On the eighth floor you can tour a model of the Oval Office as it looked during LBJ's administration. Spend the night in Austin.

❼ Approximately 40 mi south of Austin at Exit 206 off I-35 is **San Marcos,** a favorite with shoppers, who come to browse its massive outlet mall. Find recreation along the banks of the San Marcos River, popular with snorkelers for its clear waters. The waters form the focal point for **Aquarena Center for Continuing Education,** a historic park that dates back to 1928 when A. B. Rogers purchased 125 acres at the headwaters of the San Marcos River to create a grand hotel.

❽ When you've finished shopping, drive to **Gruene** (pronounced Green), a former town that is now actually more of a neighborhood in New Braunfels. From its founding in the 1870s, Gruene was a happening place with a swinging dance hall and busy cotton gin. But when the boll weevil arrived in Texas with the Great Depression, Gruene became a ghost town. Today that former ghost town is alive with small shops and restaurants in old storefronts as well as Texas's oldest dance hall—**Gruene Hall**—which is as lively today as it was in the 1880s. Burlap bags draped from the ceiling dampen the sound, 1930s advertisements plaster the walls, and a U.S. flag with 46 stars still hangs over the dance floor. May to August, rent a couple of inner tubes (one for you, and one for your cooler) in Gruene and float down the Guadalupe River for a few hours—a shuttle will take you back up to town.

❾ By returning to I–35 and continuing south, or by traveling south on Gruene Road, you can reach **New Braunfels.** The self-proclaimed "Antique Capital of Texas" is home to numerous antiques shops, most in the downtown region. The area's water park, **Schlitterbahn** ("slippery road" in German) is huge, right on the Guadalupe River banks. You can also canoe, raft, and inner-tube on the Comal River. Outside of New Braunfels, there are **Natural Bridge Caverns** and **Natural Bridge Wildlife Ranch,** which is a popular family attraction.

From New Braunfels, take Route 46 west for about 50 mi back to Bandera.

Austin

Governor's Mansion. For more than 130 years, Texas governors have lived in this grand, modified-Greek Revival home. The mansion has an impressive collection of 19th-century American antiques and furnishings. Note that tours are sometimes suspended because of incoming dignitaries. | 1010 Colorado St. | 512/463–5516 | www.governor.state.tx.us | Free | Tours Mon.–Thurs. 10–noon, every 20 min.

Guadalupe Street. Also known as "the Drag," this thoroughfare bordering the west side of the University of Texas campus is lined with restaurants, trendy boutiques, and music shops. | Between Martin Luther King Jr. Blvd. and Dean Keeton St.

TEXAS RULES OF THE ROAD

License Requirements: To drive in Texas you must be at least 16 years old and have a valid driver's license.

Right Turn on Red: You may make a right turn on red *after* a full stop anywhere in the state, unless otherwise posted.

Seat Belts and Helmet Laws: All drivers and front-seat passengers must wear seat belts. Children under age four must wear a seat belt, whether seated in the front or back. Children under age two must only ride in a federally approved child safety seat. Motorcyclists under age 21 must wear a helmet; motorcyclists age 21 and over are not required to wear helmets if they have proof of insurance valued over $10,000 or have proof of completion of a motorcycle operations course.

Speed Limits: The speed limit in Texas is 70 mph on limited-access highways, 60 mph on other highways, and 30 mph in urban areas. In heavily traveled corridors limits are often reduced, be sure to check signs carefully.

For More Information: Texas Department of Public Safety | 512/424–2000 | www.txdps.state.tx.us.

★ **Lady Bird Johnson Wildflower Center.** Fields and fields of wildflowers bloom year-round at this 43-acre complex. (Look for the state flower, the bluebonnet, in April.) Wander along the nature trails through color-filled meadows, climb the observation tower for an overview, stroll past stone terraces and cultivated fields, and then stop in the visitor center and the gift shop to learn more about Texas's native plants and to buy a some gorgeous art photographs. Wildflower Café is open for lunch, or you could pack a basket and eat at one of the two picnic areas. | 4801 LaCrosse Ave. | 512/292–4200 | www.wildflower.org | $5 | Grounds Tues.–Sun. 9–5:30; visitor center Tues.–Sat. 9–4, Sun. 1–4; shop Tues.–Sat. 9–5:30, Sun. 1–4.

6th Street. Austin is the live-music capital of Texas; some like to think the scene's even bigger than the one in Nashville, Tennessee. The highest concentration of bars, restaurants, and clubs (more than 50) with nightly music is on 6th Street. Walk past the clubs any evening, and with the variety of music styles played, odds are you can find something to fit your mood. | Between Congress Ave. and I–35.

State Capitol. Pink granite quarried from Granite Mountain, near the town of Marble Falls, was used to construct the state capitol building (the nation's largest, with a cupola 12 feet taller than the U.S. capitol), which houses the governor's office, the Texas legislature, and several other executive state agencies. From 1892 to 1898, hundreds of stonecutters from Scotland along with gangs of Texas convicts cut the stone. Daily tours last from 30 to 45 minutes and take you past 5 mi of wainscoting, impressive stained-glass panels, and numerous paintings of the Texas Revolution. | 11th St. and Congress Ave. | 512/463–0063 | www.tspb.state.tx.us | Free | Weekdays 8:30–4:30, Sat. 9:30–3:30, Sun. noon–3:30.

   Capitol Visitor Center. The visitor center is inside the old General Land Office on the southeast corner of the capitol grounds. Exhibits trace the construction, history, and restoration of the capitol building. One room is dedicated to the writer O. Henry (William Sydney Porter) who worked at the Land Office. | 112 E. 11th St. | 512/305–8400 | Free | Mon.–Sat. 9–5, Sun. noon–5.

University of Texas at Austin. Founded in 1883, this is first and the largest member of the University of Texas system. The active student population is approximately 48,000, but being a UT grad is a way of life—look for Bevo, the longhorn mascot, everywhere from car bumper stickers to tattoos. Take a regular campus tour or the moonlight prowl (8 PM various nights), which is much more anecdotal. | The Tower, Guadalupe between 22nd and 23rd Sts. | www.utexas.edu | 512/471–3434 | Tours free | Visitor tours weekdays 10 AM and 2 PM, Sat. 2 PM.

   Jack S. Blanton Museum of Art. This museum is one of the top 10 university art galleries in the country. The galleries contain 20th-century artwork as well as popular culture items from the late-19th and early-20th centuries. Works from Mexican artists are also on display. | 23rd and San Jacinto Sts. | 512/471–7324 | www.blantonmuseum.org | Mon.–Wed., Fri. 9–5, Thurs. 9–9, weekends 1–5.

Zilker Park. The site of temporary Franciscan missions in 1730 and a former Native American gathering place is now a popular park. The 351 acres along the shores of Lake Austin has trails, a botanical garden, picnic areas, recreational fields, and a natural pool. Barton Springs, which produces from 12 million to 90 million gallons in any 24-hour period, feeds the 300-yard-long swimming pool. | 2201 Barton Springs Rd. | 512/397–1463, 512/476–9044 pool | www.ci.austin.tx.us | Park and botanical garden free, pool $3 | Park and botanical garden daily 7 AM–dusk; pool daily 5 AM–10 PM.

Dining

The County Line. Barbecue. The barbecue here rivals any you've had. Choose your meats (which have been smoking over mesquite and a twig or two of pecan wood for 18–20 hours), then choose your sides—potato salad, coleslaw, beans, and white bread to name a few. This, the original wooden restaurant in a former speakeasy, spawned a chain of rusticated places across the state. | 6500 Bee Caves Rd. | 512/327–1742 | AE, D, DC, MC, V | $–$$

Güeros. Tex-Mex. This spacious and popular restaurant, a former feed store, has high ceilings and tall windows, a rustic bar, and live music. The little tacos *al pastor* (marinated rotisserie-roast pork with pineapple, cilantro, and onions) are stellar, and the fresh-lime margaritas are justly famous. Breakfast is served on weekends. | 1412 S. Congress Ave. | 512/447–7688 | AE, D, DC, MC, V | $

Scholz Garten. Eclectic. Established in 1866, this outdoor beer garden and indoor dining room is a venerable local favorite. In addition to standard casual American fare, the menu includes Tex-Mex, barbecue, and German dishes. | 1607 San Jacinto Blvd. | 512/474–1958 | AE, D, DC, MC, V | Closed Sun. | ¢–$

Threadgill's. Southern. Chicken-fried steak, fried green tomatoes, and massive grilled pork chops are some of the not-too-light Southern dishes to tuck into here. Don't forget the homemade cobbler or the free seconds on vegetable side orders—butter beans, okra and tomatoes, black-eyed peas, and squash casserole are but a few of the options. The building is decorated with vintage Austin memorabilia. | 6416 N. Lamar Blvd. | 512/451–5440 | MC, V | $–$$

Lodging

Austin Motel. Motor Inns were becoming popular in 1938 when the Austin was built. Today it's a colorful, retro-chic place to stay with reasonable rates. Rooms are redecorated all the time, but many have bright-color walls—watermelon, lilac, blue jay—or tropical murals to set them apart from standard motel fare. Room 145 (two double beds) is especially funky, with a lime-green and lemon-yellow polka dot wall. Suites (really just larger rooms) are generally more serene. Some in-room hot tubs, cable TV, pool, free parking, no-smoking rooms. | 1220 S. Congress Ave., 78704 | phone/fax 512/441–1157 | www.austinmotel.com | 41 rooms | AE, D, MC, V | $.

Driskill. The lobby of this landmark downtown hotel has a stained-glass dome and 30-foot-high ceilings. Choose between the traditional rooms with Victorian reproductions in the Driskill Tower, and rooms in the original hotel, which have high ceilings, antiques, and black marble baths. Restaurant, room service, in-room data ports, in-room safes, cable TV with movies, gym, massage, bar, dry cleaning, laundry service, concierge, business services, meeting rooms, free parking, no-smoking rooms. | 604 Brazos St., 78701 | 512/474–5911 | fax 512/474–2214 | www.driskillhotel.com | 176 rooms, 12 suites | AE, D, DC, MC, V | $$$–$$$$

Habitat Suites Hotel. Habitat Suites is a "green" hotel: it does its best to be kind to the environment. For example, the pool is sanitized through an ionization process instead of with chlorine. All suites have contemporary wood-veneer furnishings, large desks, and fireplaces in the living rooms. Duplex two-bedroom, two-bath suites are also available. Kitchens, in-room data ports, cable TV, pool, outdoor hot tub, dry cleaning, laundry facilities; no smoking. | 500 Highland Mall Blvd., 78752 | 512/467–6000 or 800/535–4663 | www.habitatsuites.com | 95 suites | AE, D, DC, MC, V | BP | $–$$

Lakeway Inn. Deluxe rooms and suites have private balconies overlooking Lake Travis, and even standard rooms have water views. All rooms have exposed beams and jewel-tone accents. Walk down to the marina to rent a Jet Ski or pontoon boat for the day; while zipping around the lake, you can stop for breaks at waterside restaurants. The resort is 20 minutes from downtown. Restaurant, room service, in-room data ports, cable TV with movies, golf privileges, 2 pools, lake, health club, spa, outdoor hot tub, boating, jet skiing, marina, 2 bars, Internet, business services, meeting rooms, no-smoking rooms. | Off U.S. 290, 101 Lakeway Dr., 78734 | 512/261–6600 or 800/525–3929 | fax 512/261–7311 | www.lakewayinn.com | 239 rooms, 34 suites | AE, D, DC, MC, V | $$–$$$

Bandera

Bandera County Historic Tours. A walking or driving tour of the county can bring you to the original town jail and county courthouse, historic 11th Street, present-day blacksmiths and saddle makers, and a working ranch. Brochures for self-guided tours are available at the Bandera Convention and Visitor Bureau. | Bandera CVB, 606 Rte. 16 S | 830/796–3045 or 800/364–3833.

Frontier Times Museum. Cowboy paraphernalia, Indian arrowheads, Western show posters, Buffalo Bill memorabilia, and prehistoric artifacts are on display in this museum, established in 1927. | 506 13th St. | 830/796–3864 | $2 | Mon.–Sat. 10–4:30, Sun. 1–4:30.

Dining

Busbee's Barbecue. Barbecue. On the town's main drag, this popular spot serves chicken, brisket, and ribs. As a variation on the usual ultraheavy barbecue meal, the chef will slice your grilled chicken or beef and toss it onto a bed of fresh greens. | 319 Main St. | 830/796–3153 | No credit cards | ¢–$

Cabaret Cafe and Dance Hall. Continental. The circa-1936 dance hall of this all-wood ranch-style restaurant is the second-oldest in Texas and has live music Saturday night. The wait on weekends is worthwhile for a taste of the mesquite-grilled prime rib and fresh fish. | 801 Main St. | 830/796–8166 | AE, MC, V | Closed Mon.–Tues. | $–$$

O.S.T. Restaurant. American. This restaurant has been an institution for more than 75 years; the acronym stands for Old Spanish Trail, which once passed through Bandera. Expect such down-home country-style American food as chicken-fried steak with cream gravy, chopped steak with brown gravy, and fried shrimp. Come early before they run out of the homemade biscuits. | 305 Main St. | 830/796–3836 | D, DC, MC, V | $–$$

Fredericksburg

Enchanted Rock State Natural Area. The 640-acre granite outcropping here is the largest stone formation in the West; it places second nationally to Georgia's Stone Mountain. Follow the path through the scrub to the stand-alone rock and up to the top. The climb is fairly steep. If you must go in summer, start early; it gets hot on top of the granite even in February. Picnic facilities and a 60-site primitive campground are also here. Entry into the park is limited during busy weekends; access is sometimes closed from 11 AM to 5 PM. | Off Rte. 965, 18 mi north of Fredericksburg | 915/247–3903 | www.tpwd.state.tx.us | $5 | Daily 8 AM–10 PM.

National Museum of the Pacific War. World War II Pacific Commander Admiral Chester Nimitz, the town's most famous resident, is honored at the museum in a former hotel built by Nimitz's grandfather to resemble a ship. Three stories of exhibits focus on the Pacific theater. Several hotel rooms, the hotel kitchen, and the bathhouse have been restored. Also on the 9-acre site is the Garden of Peace, a gift from the people of Japan. | 340 E. Main St. | 830/997–4379 | www.nimitz-museum.org | $5 | Daily 10–5.

Dining

Cotton Gin Restaurant. Contemporary. You'll find upscale Hill Country cuisine here: the quail has a rosemary and garlic crust and comes stuffed with jalapeños, for example. Although the food has high aspirations, the dining room is down-to-earth casual. A large stone hearth anchors one side of the room and the exposed beams and rafters show off the building's structure from its former use as a cotton gin. | 2805 S. Rte. 16 | 830/990–5734 | Reservations essential | AE, D, DC, MC, V | Closed Sun. No lunch Sat. | $$–$$$

George's Old German Bakery and Cafe. German. You might find solid German fare, such as bratwurst, on the specials board at this casual storefront café, but then again it might be something more familiar like chopped steak or chicken cordon bleu. The fresh-from-scratch rye bread, rich strudels, and big breakfasts are popular. | 225 W. Main St. | 830/997–9084 | No credit cards | No dinner | ¢–$

Lodging

Fredericksburg Bed and Brew. Note the second "B" of this unusual lodging—included in the room rate is a sampler of the Fredericksburg Brewing Co.'s four beers. Eleven of the rooms are above the restaurant–microbrewery (which quiets down at closing, 9 PM or 10 PM nightly); one is on the ground level next to it. Several of the rooms have a Hill Country theme—wrought iron, pine beds, rustic art, and stonework, and three of them overlook Fredericksburg's Main Street. Restaurant, bar; no room phones, no room TVs, no kids, no smoking. | 245 E. Main St., 78624 | 830/997–1646 | fax 830/997–8026 | www.yourbrewery.com | 12 rooms | MC, V | $

Gästehaus Schmidt. The number of B&Bs in town and in the surrounding countryside can be mind-boggling. Gästehaus Schmidt, a reservation service, helps you sort through and find the right one from the more than 175 they represent. Whether you prefer a town house right among the shops and restaurants or a log cabin 5 mi down the road, they'll be able to find you what you want. | 231 W. Main St., 78624 | 830/997–5612 | fax 830/997–8282 | www.fbglodging.com | AE, D, MC, V | $–$$

Peach Tree Inn. A grassy courtyard with a waterfall and large pecan trees provide a pretty setting for this updated 1940s motor hotel. Ten executive suites overlook Barton Creek and have ample work space, separate living rooms, and fireplaces. Some of the original rooms are actually cottages that accommodate two to six people. Some microwaves, some refrigerators, cable TV, pool, horseshoes, playground, meeting rooms, no-smoking rooms. | 401 S. Washington St., 78624 | 830/997–2117 or 800/843–4666 | fax 830/990–9434 | www.thepeachtreeinn.com | 34 rooms, 10 suites | AE, D, MC, V | CP | ¢–$

Johnson City

Lyndon B. Johnson National Historical Park. The former U.S. president moved to town from Stonewall, approximately 10 mi west of Johnson City, when he was five years old. The downtown visitor center has exhibits, informative panels, and artifacts related to the President's life. Two 30-minute films concentrate on LBJ and Lady Bird's accomplishments. Early farm implements are also displayed. From 1913 to 1934 Lyndon Johnson lived in a simple white frame house while Johnson's father, Sam Ealy Johnson Jr. was a state representative. By guided tour you can explore this Boyhood Home next to the visitors center; it's been restored to the condition and furnished according to how it would have looked in the 1920s. | Lady Bird La. off Ave. F | 830/868–7128 | www.nps.gov/lyjo | Free | Daily 8:45–5.

Lyndon B. Johnson State Historical Park. A guest house-turned-welcome center is the reconstructed birthplace of Lyndon Johnson. Board here for the guided bus tours around the LBJ Ranch. The home itself is still inhabited and is not open to the public. The tour is of the working farm and cattle operations. | 14 mi west on U.S. 290, State Park Rd., Stonewall | 830/644–2252 | $3 | Tours daily 10–4.

Dining

Uncle Kunkel's Bar-B-Q. Barbecue. Around Hill Country, barbecue competition is fierce—this joint has won blue ribbons at four state fairs and runs a successful mail-order business. Stop here if you're in the mood for brisket, pork, ribs, or sausage; if you want chicken, be sure to call ahead. | 110 U.S. 281 (at U.S. 290) | 830/868–0251 or 888/814–5900 | MC, V | Closed Mon.–Tues. No dinner | ¢

Kerrville

Hill Country Museum (Capt. Charles Schreiner Mansion). The town's development and the story of Texas Ranger Charles Schreiner are the focus of this local history museum in an 1850s stone mansion. Schreiner came to Kerrville as a young man in the 1850s, and after the Civil War he opened a dry goods store and began acquiring land. Schreiner's company was the first business in America to recognize the value of mohair, a prelude to Kerrville becoming the mohair capital of the world. | 226 Earl Garrett St. | 830/896–8633 | $5 | Mon.–Sat. 10–4:30.

Kerrville-Schreiner State Park. Hike on 7 mi of trails or swim and fish in this 517-acre park on the Guadalupe River. You can rent inner tubes year round. Screened shelters and campsites are available. | 2485 Bandera Hwy. | 830/257–5392 | www.tpwd.state.tx.us | $3 | Daily 8 AM–10 PM.

National Center for American Western Art. Filled with Western-theme paintings and sculpture, this hilltop museum has work by members of the Cowboy Artists of America. | 1550 Bandera Hwy. (Rte. 173) | 830/896–2553 | www.caamuseum.com | $5 | Late May–Aug., Mon.–Sat. 9–5, Sun. 1–5; Sept.–late May, Tues.–Sat. 9–5, Sun. 1–5.

Y. O. Ranch. The ranch once sprawled over more than 600,000 acres; today it spans a mere 40,000 acres. Touring the exotic game ranch (reservation required) is like going on a safari—there are herds of zebra, giraffe, bongo (African antelope), and water buffalo and flocks of red-neck ostrich and emu. You can also go horseback riding, take a nature tour, participate in a trail drive, and stay overnight in an 1880s log cabin. | Off Rte. 41 W, Exit 490, 1736 YO Ranch Rd. NW, Mountain Home | 830/640–3222 or 800/967–2624 | www.yoranch.com | Tour $28 | Tours daily 10 AM.

Dining

Bill's Barbecue. Barbecue. A local fixture for more than 30 years, this rustic dining spot serves up slow-smoked pit barbecue—brisket, sausage, chicken, and ribs. A large combo comes with your choice of three meats and two sides. | 1909 Junction Hwy. | 830/895–5733 | No credit cards | Closed Sun.–Mon. No dinner | ¢–$

Joe's Jefferson Street Cafe. Southern. This casual eatery in an 1890 Victorian mansion has such traditional Texas dishes as steak, gulf shrimp, catfish, and chicken-fried steak. Try a bottle of local Hill Country wine, like that from Grape Creek Vineyards. | 1001 Jefferson St. | 830/257–2929 | MC, V | Closed Sun. No lunch Sat. | $–$$

Rich's Hill Country Cafe. American. A longtime breakfast and lunch spot, Rich's is popular with locals for big pancakes, huevos rancheros (eggs with picante sauce), and breakfast tacos. For lunch, baked chicken, and chicken-fried steak are among the choices. | 806 Main St. | 830/257–6665 | No credit cards | Closed Sun. No dinner | ¢–$

New Braunfels

Canyon Lake. You can boat, picnic, and camp at the many public parks that line this lake. It is a popular destination with anglers in search of catfish, largemouth bass, and, below the dam, rainbow and brown trout. | Rte. 306, 14 mi northeast of New Braunfels, Canyon Lake | 830/964–3341 or 800/528–2104 | www.canyon-lake.net | Free | Daily 7–dusk.

Gruene Dance Hall. Two-step to live country music nightly from June to August and Friday to Sunday the rest of the year. The front-room bar is open nightly. The rustic hall's wood floor is surrounded by long benches, and taller benchlike tables. Big name performances have concert seating and advance ticket sales. | 1281 Gruene Rd., Gruene | 830/606–1281 | www.gruenehall.com | Free–$20 | Weekdays 10 AM–midnight, Sat. 10 AM–1 AM, Sun. 10 AM–9 PM.

Guadalupe River. Rent an inner tube and enjoy a leisurely afternoon floating down the Guadalupe River. Sports outfitters, beer stores, and roadside operations, all rent tubes (about $14 for two to six hours). Most provide shuttle service back from prede-termined points downstream. Rockin' R River Rides is one of the biggest outfitters. | Rockin' R, Gruene and Hunter Rds., Gruene | 888/883–5628 | www.rockinr.com | $14 | Daily 9 AM–dusk, weather permitting.

Natural Bridge Caverns. Named for the rock arch over the entrance, this cave is the largest in the state. North caverns tours start every 30 minutes and last 75 minutes, passing well-lit underground formations on sometimes slippery paths. The hearty—and fit— might opt to reserve a two- to four-hour guided spelunking adventure ($95), using ropes, crawling, and lighted hard hats to navigate. | 11 mi southeast of New Braunfels, 26495 Natural Bridge Caverns (Rte. 3009) | 830/651–6101 | www.naturalbridgecaverns.com | $14 | Late May–Aug., daily 9–6; Sept.–late May, daily 9–4.

Natural Bridge Wildlife Park. See zebras, gazelles, antelopes, and ostriches—and feed them—at this drive-through wildlife ranch. There's a petting zoo with pygmy goats at the entrance. It's 9 mi southeast of New Braunfels. | 26515 Natural Bridge Caverns Rd. (Rte. 3009) | 830/438–7400 | www.nbwildliferanchtx.com | $12 | Late May–Aug., daily 9–6:30; Sept.–late May, daily 9–4.

Schlitterbahn Water Park. Come enjoy the largest tubing park in the world. The Comal River supplies cool springwater at the rate of 24,000 gallons a minute and repli-cates the look and feel of river rapids. Brave the 60-foot Schlittercoaster and the mile-long Raging River tube chute or go for a dip in the 50,000-gallon hot tub with a swim-up bar. | 305 W. Austin St. | 830/625–2351 | www.schlitterbahn.com | $29 | Late Apr.–mid-May, Sat. 10–7, Sun. 10–6; mid-May–late Aug., daily 10–8; late Aug.–late Sept., weekends 10–6.

Dining

The Gristmill. Steak. With floor-to-ceiling windows thrown open to the breezes and terraced decks in the beer garden spilling down the bank to the Guadalupe River, the lines between inside and outside blur at The Gristmill. On one side, crumbling walls have been left unrestored from when this building was a cotton gin in the 1800s. The food is as straightforward as the wooden tables its served on, but it is fresh and flavorful. | 1287 Gruene Rd., Gruene | 830/625–0684 | AE, D, DC, MC, V | $–$$

Huisache Grill. Southwestern. Owners Lynn and Don Forres hired an architect to turn an old train station into a restaurant. The clean lines of the recycled glass-and-wood interior are stylish and the simplicity of the station's whitewashed wood siding fits in nicely. The food is as inventive as the space: grilled pork chops are served on a bed of sliced apples and rum butter, and salmon is topped with Parmesan and baked in parchment paper. | 303 W. San Antonio St. | 830/620–9001 | AE, D, DC, MC, V | $–$$

New Braunfels Smokehouse. Barbecue. Nearly 300 people can sit down for a meal indoors and out at this "tasting house" for the smoked meat business. All the deli meats for sandwiches are processed on-site. Apple dumplings and bread pudding for dessert are excellent. Breakfast is served until 11 AM. | 146 Rte. 46 E | 830/625–2416 | AE, D, MC, V | $–$$

San Marcos

Aquarena Center for Continuing Education. In 1928, A. B. Rogers purchased 125 acres at the headwaters of the San Marcos River, where an artesian spring comes up, to build a resort. He provided glass-bottom boats to cruise Spring Lake, home to many fish (including some white albino catfish) and various types of plant life. Today you can still enjoy a cruise on a glass-bottom boat and see the site of an underwater archaeological dig. Visible is the spot that yielded the remains of Clovis Man, a hunter-gatherer who lived on the San Marcos River 13,000 years ago. | 921 Aquarena Springs Dr. | 512/245–7575 or 800/999–9767 | Boat ride $6 | Daily 10–6.

Calaboose African-American History Museum. Photos and memorabilia document the history and experiences of African-Americans in southwest Texas. There are permanent exhibits on the Tuskegee Airmen, the Buffalo Soldiers, and the Cotton era in the San Marcos area. The museum is in the small, original Hays County Jail building, built in 1873. | 200 Martin Luther King Dr. | 512/393–8421 or 512/353–0124 | $3 | By appointment.

Southwestern Writers Collection. The full name of this museum is the Southwestern Writers Collection and Wittliff Gallery of Southwestern and Mexican Photography. The archival repository contains the works of writers and photographers with links to the Southwest. Exhibits, which change three times a year, have explored Texan music, Mexican women photographers, and Larry McMurtry's writing. | Albert B. Alkek Library, Southwest Texas State University, 601 University Blvd., 7th floor | 512/245–2313 | www.library.swt.edu/swwc/index.html | Free | Mon. and Wed.–Fri. 8–5, Tues. 8 AM–9 PM, Sat. 9–5, Sun. 2–6.

Wonder World. A guided tour lasting 1½ hours covers the entire park, including the 7½-acre Texas Wildlife Park, Texas's largest petting zoo. A miniature train chugs through the animal enclosure, stopping to allow riders to pet and feed white-tailed deer, wild turkeys, and many exotic species. One stop on the tour is Wonder Cave, created during the earthquake that produced the Balcones Fault, an 1,800-mi line separating the western Hill Country from the flat eastern farmland. | 1000 Prospect St. | 512/392–3760 | www.wonderworldpark.com | $16 | June–Aug., daily 8–8; Sept.–May, weekdays 9–5, weekends 9–6.

Dining

Café on the Square and Brew Pub. Tex-Mex. The Café and Pub is in a historic building with a pressed-tin ceiling and Southwestern artwork. It's known for all-day breakfast *migas* (a mixture of scrambled eggs, fried tortilla strips, jalapeños, onions, and tomatoes), enchiladas, fajitas, buffalo burgers, and beer. | 126 N. LBJ St. | 512/396–9999 | AE, D, MC, V | $

Palmer Restaurant. Contemporary. Eat in a courtyard at iron tables with a trickling, tiered fountain and greenery, or in the wood-panel, librarylike dining room. Entrées show a Mexican influence—pasta with an ancho chili-cream sauce and squash, grilled chicken with tomatillos, and a char-grilled tuna with chipotle aioli. | 216 W. Moore St. | 512/353–3500 | AE, D, DC, MC, V | $–$$

BIG BEND COUNTRY TOUR
EL PASO TO DEL RIO

Distance: approximately 1,050 mi   Time: 5 days
Overnight Breaks: Alpine, Big Bend National Park, Del Rio, El Paso

You almost expect to hear dramatic guitar music descend from the heavens as you enter Big Bend country. This is Texas, pardner—the *real* Texas, the stuff cowboy movies are made of. The area stretches from Del Rio, Texas and Edwards Plateau all the way west to El Paso and the Mexico and New Mexico borders. Try imagining yourself astride a tall, rangy cow horse instead of inside that stuffy SUV as you cover this drive of more than 1,000 mi through some of the most uninhabited regions of the United States. Whether you start in Del Rio or El Paso, you'll notice some commonality in the rugged and sometimes stark terrain dotted with hardy mesquite bushes and sticklike protrusions of yucca plants. These are the Chihuahuan Desert's northern-most reaches, but you won't find many sand dunes or statuesque saguaro cacti here: this scrubby desert is instead noted for unique vegetation such as the red-barked evergreen and red berries of the Texas madrone, found in Big Bend and Guadalupe Mountains national parks.

Little changed from its Wild West days, Big Bend Country includes the only true mountains in Texas: the Guadalupe Range, an eastern portion of the Rockies that includes Guadalupe Peak, Texas's tallest at 8,749 feet. South of the Guadalupe Range lie the Davis Mountains, which are a popular getaway for those headed to rugged Big Bend National Park. The park lies right next to the U.S.–Mexico border, tucked into the region formed by a southward dip in the Rio Grande. Here the Chisos Mountains rise to 7,825 feet.

While you won't spend much time on an interstate, rest assured that most Texas highways are in remarkably good condition. This means you can sometimes ride as free as a cowboy on an unfenced range with speed limits as high as 75 mph. Texans love their highways. You will, too. Just be aware that even the desert has its occasional winter storms, so check ahead for weather reports. Rain, too, can create havoc at times with flooded arroyos spewing across roads in low lying areas.

❶ Start the tour in **El Paso,** where you might want to spend a day touring area attrac- tions including historic adobe churches along the **Mission Trail.** In early morning on the next day, head out on Montana Avenue east until the route turns into U.S. 62/180. Drive 110 mi, past the intersection with Route 54, until you reach **Guadalupe Mountains National Park,** where you can hike among 80 mi of trails accessing rugged canyons and juniper forests. Be sure to pack a picnic lunch for midday, because you won't have many dining options in this remote area.

❷ Backtrack to Route 54, where you'll turn south and travel 55 mi to the old mining and ranching town of **Van Horn,** a popular stop for east–west I–10 travelers, including national sports announcer John Madden (who refuses to fly). Eat a late lunch or early dinner at his favorite spot for enchiladas or steak, **Chuy's.**

❸ Take I–10 east 37 mi to Route 118, then drop south for 77 mi to **Alpine,** where you can spend the night here or in one of its neighbors of **Fort Davis** or **Marfa** (all within 30 mi). Alpine, a town of 8,000, is perched at an elevation of 4,485 feet, lofty by Texas standards. The mountainous climate makes the town a popular vacation spot; you can enjoy mountain climbing, horseback riding, rock hunting, and more. At night you might want to drive toward Marfa and see if you can spot its famous mystery lights, little glowing balls in the distance sometimes called "ghost lights."

❹ The next morning, continue your journey down Route 118 from Alpine for 80 mi and then turn west on Route 170 for a few miles for a short side trip to **Terlingua.** During its boom days, quicksilver mines helped the population reach nearly 2,000. When the price of mercury dropped in the 1940s, Terlingua became a ghost town. Thanks in part to tourism generated by adjacent Big Bend Ranch State Park and Big Bend National Park, the area's economy is improving. If you continue west a few more miles, you can visit **Lajitas,** an old cavalry outpost converted into a resort with Old West boardwalk.

❺ Backtrack to the entrance of **Big Bend National Park,** where you should plan to spend the rest of the day. This remote, little-visited national park is a place to get away from it all and enjoy nature along the banks of the Rio Grande. That massive river, which forms part of the border between Texas and Mexico, marks the location of Big Bend. (Picture

a map of the western side of Texas where the river—and thus the state's boundary—makes a big bend . . .well, you figured it out.) A strategic crossroad for thousands of years, the park has witnessed a parade of Comanche, Apache, Spanish conquistadores, U.S. soldiers, Mexican revolutionaries, and many others. Big Bend National Park spans more than 800,000 acres and offers a backdrop of canyons, desert, the Chisos Mountains, more than a thousand plants, and a wide range of animal and bird life. Plan on spending the night at **Chisos Mountain Lodge,** within park boundaries (it's a good idea to make advance reservations for this popular lodge, the only motel available in the park). If the lodge is booked up, exit the park via U.S. 385 and travel to **Marathon** (70 mi north of the center of the park), where you can spend the night at the historic, restored Gage Hotel.

6 From Marathon, turn east on U.S. 90 and drive 175 mi (much of this scenic drive will be alongside the Rio Grande and Mexico) until you reach **Del Rio.** With opportunities for shopping, swimming, hiking, and hunting, Del Rio's got a lot to offer, and calls itself "the best of the border." Perched at the edge of the Chihuahuan Desert, the town of 37,000 is an oasis with lush vegetation, thanks to the San Felipe Springs (artesian wells that gush more than 90 million gallons of water through the town daily). Almost every Del Rio visitor takes at least a short trip to Ciudad Acuña, Mexico, directly across the border. Northwest of Del Rio about 9 mi past the town of Comstock lies a must-see attraction: **Seminole Canyon State Historical Park.** The park has some quiet sites with spectacular views of the Chihuahuan Desert, dotted with cacti and populated with numerous bird species. Of course, you can't overlook the huge water reservoir and bleached rock cliffs of **Amistad National Recreation Area,** popular with anglers and boaters.

⑦ After spending the night in Del Rio, take U.S. 277 north for 86 mi to **Sonora.** This wool and mohair center is best known by travelers because of its convenient location on I–10. Sonora is also home to the most formation-rich caverns in the state.

⑧ From Sonora, turn back west on I–10 for 130 mi until you reach your last stop of **Fort Stockton.** This West Texas community lies in the heart of the Chihuahuan Desert. It's also a designated Texas Main Street city and has refurbished many storefronts to their original appearance. Buildings such as the 1884 jail and the Grey Mule Saloon recall the days when this town was a frontier army post. Overnight here, or return to El Paso via an easy 225-mi drive west on I–10.

Alpine

McDonald Astronomical Observatory. You'll find this spot 6,791 feet above sea level on the rounded peak of Mount Locke in the Davis Mountains. The visitor information center is at the base of the mountain, and on Tuesday, Friday, and Saturday nights, you can join them for "Star Parties"—constellation tours, viewings through telescopes, and a video. The observatory is 43 mi north of Alpine via Route 118. | Rte. 118N off Spur 78, Ft. Davis | 432/426–3640 or 877/984–7827 | vc.as.utexas.edu | $7 | Daily 9–5, tours at 11 AM and 2 PM.

Museum of the Big Bend. Encompassing the contributions of the many groups that once called Big Bend home—Native Americans, Spanish, Mexicans, and Anglo-Americans—this museum is a good starting point for an overview of the region's cultural and natural history. Children will enjoy the Discovery Center with hands-on exhibits. Be sure to see the Chihuahuan Desert Cactus Garden. | Sul Ross State University, off U.S. 90 | 432/837–8143 | www.sulross.edu/~museum/ | Free | Tues.–Sat. 9–5, Sun. 1–5.

Woodward Agate Ranch. Hunt, gather, and collect famed Texas agates and other semiprecious stones on the grounds of this 3,000-acre rock-hunter's paradise. If you're less inspired, you may purchase sample rocks already weighed and cleaned. | Rte. 118, 18 mi south of Alpine | 432/459–2361 | $5 per vehicle | Apr.–Nov., daily 11–4.

Dining

Cueva de León Cafe. Mexican. This popular restaurant has been making quality Mexican food since 1976. Try the chiles rellenos (long, mild green chiles roasted and peeled in-house, stuffed with jack cheese, lightly battered, and deep-fried) and beef fajitas, or sample a little of everything at the Saturday dinner buffet. | 100 W. 2nd St., Fort Davis | 432/426–3801 | AE, D, MC, V | Closed Sun. | ¢–$

Reata Restaurant. American. This popular restaurant is in an 1896 adobe house; the wisteria-covered patio is shaded with pecan and pine trees. The "West Texas cowboy cuisine" draws from a variety of regional influences, and includes chicken-fried steak, wild game such as buffalo, a fish-of-the-day, and Mexican food. | 203 N. 5th St. | 432/837–9232 | Reservations essential | AE, MC, V | Closed Sun. | $$–$$$

Lodging

Hotel Limpia. Built in 1912 and styled in 1944 art deco, this hotel in the town square is constructed of locally mined pink limestone. It boasts the only bar in the county. Rooms are decorated with Victorian and Mission-style furnishings. Restaurant, some kitchenettes, some microwaves, in-room hot tubs, cable TV, bar, business services; no TV in some rooms, no smoking. | Main St., Fort Davis 79734 | 432/426–3237 or 800/662–5517 | www.hotellimpia.com | 36 rooms, 2 guesthouses, 1 cottage | AE, D, MC, V | $–$$$

Hotel Paisano. Once a gathering place for ranchers, this elegant hacienda-style lodge is included on the National Register of Historic Places. While rooms are now spacious and modern, some original touches have been retained, such as old Spanish tile in bathrooms. Restaurant, some kitchens, indoor pool, bar, meeting rooms. | Rte. 17, Marfa 79843 | 866/729–3669 | www.hotelpaisano.com | 33 rooms | AE, D, MC, V | $–$$$

Big Bend National Park Area

Barton Warnock Environmental Education Center. The center serves as one of two entrances to the Big Bend Ranch State Park. The 2-acre Desert Garden, which exhibits plants native to the Chihuahuan Desert, surrounds the center. | Rte. 170, Lajitas | 432/424–3327 | $3 | Daily 8–4:30.

Big Bend National Park. The remarkable geographical and ecological diversity of Texas is beautifully illustrated here. Big Bend is the largest public park in the state, covering 801,163 acres of arid desert, lush floodplains, and much in between. The park is home to more than 1,000 plant species and 500 kinds of birds and mammals. The park maintains hundreds of campsites, both primitive and modern, in addition to a very popular lodge. The visitor centers have brochures, maps, and exhibits on area wildlife and natural history. Rangers are on hand to provide additional information. There are stations in Chisos Basin, Persimmon Gap, and Rio Grande Village.

Panoramic vistas and a quest for the Colima warbler (a domestic bird found only in Big Bend) await you in Chisos Basin, in the forested higher-park elevations. This central site also has hiking trails, a lodge, campground, grocery store, gift shop, and restaurant with scenic views. Hikers soak themselves in the 105°F waters at the Hot Springs historic site alongside the Rio Grande. | Off Rte. 118 | 432/477–2251 | www.nps.gov/bibe/ | $15 | Daily 8–6.

Lajitas Stables. Guided horseback rides are available across the land where the Chihuahuan Desert meets the southwest Rocky Mountains. Tours can last from one hour to five days. | Rte. 170, Lajitas | 432/424–3238 or 888/508–7667 | www.lajitasstables.com | $35 per hour; $130 full-day tour | Daily 9–5.

Terlingua Trading Company. You'll find jewelry, books, gourmet foods, and an extensive selection of Mexican imports in the former headquarters of the Chisos Mining Company. | 100 Ivy St., Terlingua | 432/371–2234 | Free | Daily 9–9.

Lodging

Chisos Mountains Lodge. Though Big Bend National Park has hundreds of campsites, this is the only hotel; it's therefore often booked months in advance during prime spring and fall viewing seasons. Although it isn't fancy, most rooms have private balconies and spectacular views of the mountains and the desert floor. The lodge is far and away the nicest affordable option in the immediate region. From the Alpine/Study Butte entrance, follow Basin Road 22 mi east to its end. Restaurant, some pets allowed; no a/c in some rooms, no room phones, no room TVs. | Big Bend National Park, 79834 | 432/477–2291 | fax 432/477–2291 | www.chisosmountainslodge.com | 72 rooms | AE, D, DC, MC, V | $

Gage Hotel. Travel about 70 mi north of the center of Big Bend National Park on U.S. 385 to reach the tiny ranching community of Marathon and the genuine country charm of the Gage Hotel. Cowboy, Native American, and Hispanic cultures are reflected in furnishings in this historic lodge, built in the 1920s. The expertly crafted gardens and courtyards are worth viewing, even if you aren't a guest. Some rooms do not have private baths. Massage therapy is a plus for weary travelers. Restaurant, some kitchenettes, some microwaves, some refrigerators, pool, massage, bar, shops, some pets allowed (fee); no phones in some rooms. | Off 101 U.S. 90 W, 79842 | 432/386–4206 | fax 432/386–4510 | www.gagehotel.com | 44 rooms, 2 houses | AE, D, MC, V | $–$$$

Lajitas on the Rio Grande. This resort complex has a variety of accommodations in re-created historic lodgings, including officers' quarters. It's surrounded on the east by Big Bend National Park, and on the west by Big Bend State Park. 3 restaurants, some in-room hot tubs, some kitchenettes, minibars, some microwaves, some refrigerators, cable TV, 18-hole golf course, tennis court, pool, pond, hair salon, massage, spa, boating, bicycles, mountain bikes, horseback riding, bar, laundry service, airstrip, no-smoking rooms. | Rte. 170 | 432/424–3471 or 877/525–4827 | www.lajitas.com | 72 rooms, 16 suites, 2 cottages | AE, D, DC, MC, V | $$$$

Del Rio

Amistad National Recreation Area. The construction of Lake Amistad (derived from the Spanish word for "friendship") was a cooperative project between the United States and Mexico. Completed in 1969, the 67,000-acre lake was built as a way to control flooding, provide irrigation for South Texas farms and ranches, and offer water recreation. | Visitor center: U.S. 90, just west of Del Rio | 830/775–7491 | www.nps.gov/amis | Free.

Ciudad Acuña, Mexico. Located across the border in Mexico, this town is a popular shopping destination with many restaurants. | U.S. 90 to the International Bridge | 830/775–3551 or 800/889–8149 | www.ciudadacuna.com.mx.

Judge Roy Bean Visitor Center. This visitor center has information about attractions throughout the state, as well as displays recounting the wild stories of Judge Roy Bean, one of the most famous characters of the Wild West era. Next door is the Jersey Lilly, Judge Bean's courtroom and saloon, where he dispensed frontier justice in the 1880s. | U.S. 90, Langtry | 830/291–3340 | Free | Daily 8–5.

Laughlin Air Force Base. The largest pilot training installation in the country, this base has more operational aircraft than any other in the Air Force. Tours last 2½ hours and leave from the Del Rio Chamber of Commerce on the second and fourth Wednesday of every month. | 561 Liberty Dr., Suite 6 | 830/298–5201 | www.laughlin.af.mil | Free.

Seminole Canyon State Historical Park. This park was occupied by prehistoric man about 8,500 years ago. Today you can see pictographs as part of a 90-minute guided tour (a somewhat strenuous 1-mi hike; bring water, as there are no drinking facilities in the canyon). Camping is possible in the park. | U.S. 90, 45 mi south of Del Rio | 830/292–4464 | www.tpwd.state.tx.us/park/seminole/ | $2 | Daily 8–5.

Val Verde Winery. Established by Italian immigrant Frank Qualia in 1883, this is the oldest winery in Texas. Tours and tastings are available. | 100 Qualia Dr. | 830/775–9714 | Free | Mon.–Sat. 10–5.

Dining

Avanti. Italian. Avanti's glistening white building with pink entryway is a distinctive structure in Del Rio and one of the town's nicest eateries. The owner is Italian, and you'll find authentic versions of calamari and Venetian chicken on the menu, though you'll also find certified Angus beef and Texas lamb. Murals and white tablecloths create a cozy, languid mood. Reservations are essential on weekends. | 600 E. 12th St. | 830/775–3363 | AE, D, MC, V | $–$$

Crosby's. Mexican. Crosby's is a popular place to stop for dinner before crossing back over the border to Del Rio. This American-run outpost serves up Mexican and Continental fare; try the quail or the *tortillas portuguesas* (sliced, fried tortillas with cheese sauce). | 195 Hidalgo, Ciudad Acuña | 877/772–2020 | MC, V | ¢–$$

Memo's. Tex-Mex. Near the San Felipe Creek, this endearing hangout has Saltillo tile floors and a piano bar. Since 1936, it's been serving up dishes from both sides of the border, though the enchiladas always sell the best. Piano jams take place every Tuesday and Thursday night, with occasional appearances by country stars. | 804 E. Losoya St. | 830/774–8104 | AE, D, MC, V | Closed Sun. | ¢–$

Lodging

Best Western Inn. This two-story chain motel offers extra perks like cherrywood furniture in the rooms, and complimentary cocktails every evening. It's within walking distance of restaurants. In-room data ports, cable TV, pool, hot tub, laundry facilities, business services, some pets allowed. | 810 Ave. F, 78840 | 830/775–7511 | fax 830/774–2194 | 62 rooms | AE, D, DC, MC, V | CP | $

Laguna Diablo Resort. This rustic resort—erected as a dude ranch in 1944—is made of native stone and rough-sawn wood. All apartments have a covered porch and are within 100 feet of the water. Units are available on a daily or monthly basis. Kitchenettes, laundry facilities. | 1 Sanders Point Rd., 78840 | 830/774–2422 or 866/227–7082 | www.lagunadiablo.com | 10 apartments | D, DC, MC, V | $

Villa Del Rio Bed & Breakfast. Iron gates, columns, archways, and a shaded courtyard make this 1887 historic mansion an elegant gateway to Del Rio's Wild West past. Palms, pecan trees, and magnolias line the grounds, created by early residents who were among founders of the huge, nearby Lake Amistad dam and reservoir. Rooms have hardwood floors and some offer views overlooking the courtyard and fountain. A two-bedroom cottage with Mission-style furnishings is next to a vineyard. Some kitchens. | 123 Hudson Dr., 78840 | 830/768–1100 or 800/995–1887 | fax 830/768–3167 | www.villadelrio.com | 3 rooms, 1 cottage | AE, MC, V | BP | $–$$$

El Paso

Chamizal National Memorial. This memorial celebrates the resolution of century-long boundary disputes between Mexico and the United States. Both sides converted their lands into national parks. The El Paso side houses a border-history museum, a theater, and a graphic arts gallery. The Mexican side has been developed into acres of botanical gardens and includes an interesting archaeological museum. | 800 S. San Marcial St. | 915/532–7273 | www.nps.gov/cham | Free | Daily 8–5.

El Paso Mission Trail. Passing through El Paso's oldest Mexican and Native American districts—neighborhoods filled with notable restaurants, craft shops, and antiques stores—this famed trail leads to three active missions and several other historical sites. | Off I–10, 12 mi east of downtown | 915/534–0677 | http://missiontrail.elp.rr.com | Free | Daily dawn–dusk.

    Mission Socorro. Mission Socorro was established in 1682. The present building was constructed in 1843 and is known for its fine *vigas* (carved ceiling beams) and bell tower. | 328 S. Nevaraz Rd. | 915/859–7718 or 800/351–6024.

    Mission Ysleta. The formal name of the oldest Spanish mission in the Southwest is Nuestra Señora del Carmen. The original mission was established here in 1681 for the Tigua Indians, after they were expelled in the Pueblo Rebellion. Flood waters destroyed the original structure and several subsequent structures. The building that stands today was built in 1851; its familiar silver dome was added in the 1880s. | 100 Old Pueblo Rd. | 915/858–2588.

    San Elizario Presidio. This fort was built to protect the missions. Its chapel is still in use. | 1556 San Elizario Rd. | 915/534–0630 or 800/351–6024.

    Tigua Indian Reservation. The reservation is adjacent to Mission Ysleta. Stop by to purchase native pottery and taste homemade bread baked in adobe ovens. | 119 S. Old Pueblo Rd. | 915/859–7913, 915/860–7777 casino.

El Paso Museum of Art. The museum's diverse collections include classic European sculptures, Mexican folk art, local photography, and contemporary installations. A portrait of George Washington is a highlight. | El Paso Dr. between Main Dr. and San Francisco Ave. | 915/532–1707 | www.elpasoartmuseum.org | Free | Tues.–Sat. 9–5, Sun. noon–5.

Fort Bliss. Established as an outpost to guard against Indian attack in 1848, the facility was later used by Confederate soldiers. Today the base is the site of the largest air-defense establishment in the nation and headquarters for the U.S. Army Air Defense. | Pershing and Pleasanton Rds. | 915/568–3137 | Free | Daily 9–4:30.

Guadalupe Mountains National Park. This gorgeous park is home to Guadalupe Peak, the highest patch of land in Texas at 8,749 feet, and El Capitan, a massive limestone formation rising 8,085 feet. In winter people visit the park to see snow, in fall to see the colorful foliage, and in spring and summer to glimpse the smooth red bark of the madrone tree, which grows wild nowhere else in the state. Camping is permitted, but overnight facilities in the park are very scant. Bring water—this is desert country with limited amenities. | U.S. 62/180, Pine Springs,110 mi from El Paso | 915/828–3251 | www.nps.gov/gumo | $3 | Daily dawn–dusk; visitor center 8–4:30.

Hueco Tanks State Historical Park. The natural rock formations in this 860-acre park served as rainwater reservoirs for native settlers some 10,000 years ago. Today it's a haunt for rock climbers, and a good site for a hike or a picnic. Among other attractions are some 2,000 Indian pictographs (guided tours are available), 190 bird species, and 10 varieties of wildflowers. Advance reservations are essential. | 6900 Hueco Tanks Rd., off U.S. 62/180, 32 mi northeast of El Paso | 915/857–1135 | www.tpwd.state.tx.us/park/hueco/hueco.htm | $4 | Daily dawn–dusk.

Transmountain Road. This road, just off I–10 west of town, takes you through Smuggler's Gap, a dramatic cut across the Franklin Mountains. | Free | Daily.

Dining

Jaxon's. Southwestern. More than 500 archival photos and a mural depicting El Paso history crowd the walls of this busy restaurant, which also serves home-brewed beer. Favorite dishes include tortilla soup, Santa Barbara beef, and Jaxon's rib eye (served with sautéed onions and green chili strips). | 4799 N. Mesa St. | 915/544–1188 | www.jaxons.com | AE, D, DC, MC, V | ¢–$$

La Hacienda. Mexican. The oldest continually operating restaurant in El Paso serves Mexican and New Mexican cuisine. Try the steak Tampiquena (steak topped with onions, tomatoes, long green chilies, and cheese) or the Old El Paso Combo, an assortment of tacos and enchiladas. Lighter is available on the covered patio out back. | 1720 W. Paisano Dr. | 915/533–1919 | fax 915/533–3636 | AE, D, MC, V | $–$$

La Nortena y Cafe Deluxe. Mexican. Dine in a former jailhouse at this good spot for border-style Mexican cuisine, with tasty choices such as *salpicon* (spicy minced-meat salad), quesadillas, *chilorio* (venison sausage), chili-roasted corn, and more. | 212 W. Overland Ave. | 915/533–0533 | DC, MC, V | ¢–$$

State Line. Barbecue. Enjoy the outdoor patio as you wait for your table in the nostalgic dining room. Fred Astaire and Ginger Rogers grace the walls and music of a time gone by fills the classic jukebox. Don't miss the beef and pork ribs and the homemade desserts. | 1222 Sunland Park Dr. | 915/581–3371 | AE, D, DC, MC, V | $–$$$

Lodging

Camino Real Hotel. The Camino Real is distinguished by its high-ceiling Dome Bar over which is a 1912 Tiffany stained-glass dome of rich blues. The rest of this historic hotel is more understated, with refurbished, spacious rooms with contemporary furnishings. 2 restaurants, coffee shop, room service, bar, cable TV, pool, gym, sauna, meeting rooms, airport shuttle, parking, business services, some pets allowed. | 101 S. El Paso St. | 915/534–3000 or 800/769–4300 | fax 915/534–3024 | www.caminoreal.com | 359 rooms | AE, D, DC, MC, V | $$–$$$

Courtyard by Marriott El Paso Airport. You can fly into the nearby El Paso International Airport, rent a car, and make this lodge a convenient stopover for beginning or ending your driving tour. Time your arrival or departure to take advantage of inexpensive weekend rates. A courtyard full of greenery and pool area provide a mini-outdoor sanctuary. Contemporary rooms are spacious, with separate seating areas. Restaurant, in-room data ports, some minibars, cable TV, pool, gym, laundry service, meeting rooms, airport shuttle. | 6610 International Dr. | 915/772–5000 or 800/321–2211 | fax 915/772–5009 | www.marriott.com | 90 rooms | AE, D, DC, MC, V | $–$$$

Fort Stockton

Annie Riggs Memorial Museum. Built in 1899 as a hotel, today this museum is filled with local history exhibits and memorabilia from Camp Stockton. | 301 S. Main St. | 432/336–2167 | $2 | Daily 10–5.

Historic Fort Stockton. The original and reconstructed buildings from the 1858 fort include officers' quarters, a guardhouse, and a jail. It's off U.S. 290. | 300 E. 3rd St. | 432/336–2400 | $2 | Mon.–Sat. 10–1 and 2–5.

Paisano Pete. This 22-foot fiberglass bird is allegedly the largest roadrunner statue in the world. | Dickenson Blvd. and Main St. | 800/334–8525 | Free | Daily.

Dining
Comanche Springs Restaurant. American. Local history and cowboy art cover the walls and booths of this restaurant, which serves a Mexican-American buffet daily. Eat the "Sitting Bull," a 5-lb burger, in under an hour and it's free. | 2501 W. I–10 | 432/336–9731 | AE, D, MC, V | ¢–$$

Sonora

Caverns of Sonora. An underground stream system helped dissolve and carve the many passages of this natural wonder, estimated to be up to 1 million years old. Guided tours are available. | Rte. 1989 Caverns of Sonora Rd. | 325/387–3105 | $15–$20 for tours | Mar.–Labor Day, daily 8–6; Labor Day–Apr., daily 9–5.

Historic Walking Tour. Pick up a brochure and map at the chamber of commerce for this self-guided walking tour which will lead you to historic homes, the former jailhouse, and the Old Santa Fe Depot. | 707 N. Crockett St. | 325/387–2248 | Free | Daily.

Dining
La Mexicana Restaurant. Mexican. Flour tortillas are made fresh daily at this colorful restaurant, and the meat is carefully char-grilled. For dessert, the flan and the ice-cream sundaes win kudos, but it's the creamy trés léches cake that will keep you coming back for more. | 308A U.S. 277 N | 325/387–3401 | AE, D, DC, MC, V | ¢–$

Van Horn

Culberson County Historical Museum. The local history exhibits here in the Clark Hotel include Native American artifacts and frontier memorabilia. | 112 W. Broadway | 432/283–8028 | Free | Daily.

Smokehouse Auto Museum. This classic car museum at the Smokehouse Restaurant boasts a large collection of restored autos. Also on view are memorabilia related to the auto. | 905 W. Broadway | Free | Mon.–Sat. 6 AM–10:30 PM.

Dining

Chuy's Restaurant. Mexican. You may have heard about Chuy's from sports announcer John Madden, the unofficial celebrity sponsor of the restaurant. Enchiladas and fajitas are popular choices on the menu, as are Chuy's seafood and steak. | 1200 W. Broadway | 432/283–2066 | AE, D, DC, MC, V | ¢–$

Smokehouse. Barbecue. The Smokehouse has several rooms with different moods and themes from sports and aviation memorabilia to antiques. In addition to their specialty of smoked meats, the restaurant also has steaks, sandwiches, and Mexican food. | 905 W. Broadway | 432/283–2453 | AE, D, DC, MC, V | $$–$$$

KINGSVILLE TO ARANSAS NATIONAL WILDLIFE REFUGE
SOUTH TEXAS TOUR

Distance: 117 mi Time: 6 hrs to 2 days.
Overnight Break: Corpus Christi

Cruise through the Coastal Bend, a region spanning Rockport, Aransas Pass, Port Aransas, Corpus Christi, and inland to Kingsville. Once a magnet for travelers in the days of buccaneers and Spanish conquistadors, the region today draws both sea and nature lovers. Bird-watchers from around the globe come for a chance to view more than 400 species that winter here. The area is dotted with birding and hiking trails, guided tour boats, and other attractions that lend themselves to copious picture-taking.

❶ Begin your tour at the expansive **King Ranch,** which was founded in 1853 by Capt. Richard King. It ranks as one of the largest spreads in the world, spanning 825,000 acres, larger than Rhode Island. Today it's home to more than 60,000 cattle and 300 quarter horses and welcomes visitors from around the world. Take a guided tour, in air-conditioned minibus comfort, departing from the visitor center.

❷ Next stop is **Kingsville,** at the intersection of Route 141 and U.S. 77. The town named for the nearby ranch also offers several ranching attractions. The **King Ranch Museum** centers on the history of the ranch, including a photo essay on life on the ranch in the 1940s. Nearby is the **King Ranch Saddle Shop,** opened after the Civil War to supply the ranch with saddles; today it produces expensive purses, belts, luggage, chairs, and, of course, saddles.

❸ From Kingsville, head north on U.S. 77 for about 25 mi, then east on Route 44 for about 10 mi into **Corpus Christi.** One of America's 10 busiest ports, Corpus Christi has a bustling waterfront with tour boats, shrimp boats, and deep-sea fishing charters. The **Corpus Christi Museum of Science and History** has life-size replicas of the *Niña, Pinta,* and *Santa María.* Across the Harbor Bridge, the **Texas State Aquarium** showcases the aquatic animals and habitats indigenous to the Gulf of Mexico. Next door, the **U.S.S. *Lexington* Museum on the Bay** is set in the most decorated aircraft carrier in U.S. Naval history. Spend the night in Corpus Christi.

❹ Don't miss a stop on **Padre Island** for beachcombing, fishing, and swimming. Once you cross the causeway and bridge to the island, take a left on Route 22. Turn off at the sign for **Bob Hall Pier** to reach the lighted fishing pier, paved parking lot, and campgrounds. Continue on to the entrance of **Padre Island National Seashore,**

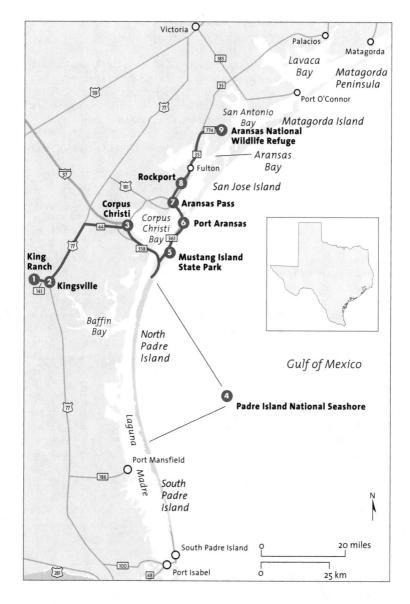

about 7 mi farther. The park has nature trails, a windsurfing beach, miles of undeveloped sand, and a visitor center containing exhibits on the region. You can drive on the beach for the first few miles, after that it's four-wheel drive only for the rest of the 70-mi shoreline. North of the park, surfers take advantage of small wave action created by a surf pier at **J. P. Luby Surf Park** on Route 361, and campers can enjoy covered picnic areas and overnight hookups at **Padre Balli Park** on Route 22.

5 When you've finished exploring the park, retrace your steps and return north, driving past the island bridge where the road becomes Route 361. For wave action, turn off towards **J. P. Luby Surf Park,** popular with surfers and teenagers cruising the beach.

Or continue northeast 2 mi to **Mustang Island State Park.** The park has 1½ mi of beach camping and a stable that rents out horses for beach jaunts.

❻ Perched on the northern tip of Mustang Island via Route 361 is **Port Aransas,** known as "Port A" among Texans. Spend an afternoon out in the Gulf aboard a deep-sea fishing cruise. Large group boats, taking as many as 100 passengers, provide bait and tackle; serious anglers looking for big-game fish, such as marlin and shark, can book charters. For a chance to see dolphins, stop by the Roberts Point Park on Route 361. Dolphins often chase the ferries as they make their way across the ship channel. If you'd like to learn more about marine life, visit the small aquarium at the **University of Texas Marine Science Institute.**

❼ Stay on Route 361 to **Aransas Pass,** which is more a genuine fishing village and less a tourist destination than many other coastal communities. (Many of its 7,000 residents are employed in the fishing industry.) The **Seamen's Memorial Tower,** a monument to the fishermen lost at sea, marks the entrance to the working harbor.

❽ Ten miles north of Aransas Pass on Route 35 is **Rockport.** The town is considered a bird-watching paradise, with more than 500 species on record. Rockport's position on a major bird flyway (the Central Flyway) has made it an international birding destination. It's particularly known for migrating passerines, shorebirds, waterfowl, birds of prey, and hummingbirds. History buffs will also find plenty of activities in Rockport–Fulton. The **Fulton Mansion State Historic Structure,** refurbished by the Texas Parks and Wildlife Department, was somewhat of a futuristic home when first built in 1876. For an even earlier look at coastal life, stop by the **Texas Maritime Museum,** which traces maritime history from the Spanish shipwrecks off the Gulf coast to the offshore oil industry.

❾ **Aransas National Wildlife Refuge** is the winter (late October–early April) home of the endangered whooping crane, a statuesque white bird with a red crest, 4-feet tall with a 7-foot wingspan. A self-guided drive—with trails, observation towers, and spotting scopes—allows you the opportunity to see the whooping cranes, as well as many other species of birds, and alligators. Displays at the visitor center explain more about the delicate ecology of the region. To get closer to the shy whoopers from the water, take a boat tour from Rockport.

To return to Kingsville, take Route 35 north from the Aransas National Wildlife Refuge to Route 239 west, and proceed for about 10 mi to U.S. 77. Proceed south on U.S. 77 for about 90 mi into Kingsville.

Aransas Pass

Conn Brown Harbor. The nexus of Aransas Pass, this harbor is home to fish-packing houses and the site of commercial shrimp boats docking and departing. Rent a boat to visit the coastal islands of Mustang and St. Joseph, picnic, or visit the Seaman's Memorial Tower, dedicated to those who were lost at sea. | 35 N to Stapp Ave., turn right | 361/758–2750 | Daily.

Dining

Nopalitos Restaurant. Mexican. The brightly painted dining area of this local favorite is festooned with sombreros, serapes, and neon signs (one in the shape of Mexico). Try the grilled beef fajitas, or the beef shank-and-vegetable soup. The namesake nopalitos (spineless cactus) are served in scrambled eggs at breakfast. | 306 E. Goodnight St. | 361/758–1080 | AE, D, DC, MC, V | ¢

Corpus Christi

Asian Cultures Museum and Educational Center. Art and artifacts from Japan, China, Korea, and the Philippines are on display in a minimalist setting. Look for ancient stone Buddhas, delicate porcelain dolls, and minutely detailed models of pagodas. | 1809 N. Chaparral St. | 361/882–2641 | www.geocities.com/asiancm | $5 | Tues.–Sat. 9–5.

Bob Hall Pier. The fishing pier on Padre Island off South Padre Island Drive extends beyond the third sandbar into the Gulf of Mexico; rod, reel, and bait may be purchased or rented. | 15820 Rte. 22 | 361/949–7437 | $1 | Daily 24 hrs.

Corpus Christi Museum of Science and History. Exhibits cover everything from small dinosaurs to Spanish shipwrecks. Don't miss the "Seeds of Change," designed by the Smithsonian's National Museum of Natural History; it traces the European discovery of America through dioramas. | 1900 N. Chaparral St. | 361/883–2862 | www.cctexas.com | $10 | Tues.–Sat. 10–5, Sun. noon–5.

Heritage Park. This park has nine historic homes dating from 1851. Each has been restored and some are used by civic groups for their headquarters. The Galvan House hosts art exhibits. Concerts and performances take place on the lawn. | 1581 N. Chaparral St. | 361/883–0639 | Park free, tours $4 | Mon.–Sat. 10–2; tours Wed.–Thurs. 10:30, Fri.–Sat. 10:30, 12:45.

Padre Island National Seashore. First established in 1962, this 70-mi stretch of unblemished seashore is a haven for beachcombers, boaters, and swimmers. Go in spring to enjoy wildflowers, bird watching, and windsurfing; in summer to view nesting sea turtles; and in winter to collect shells. You can drive along parts of the island, but a four-wheel-drive vehicle is required to explore most areas. Hiking trails abound and swimming is permitted on all beaches, though lifeguards are on duty only at Malaquite Beach, from Memorial Day to Labor Day. Camping facilities are available at Malaquite Beach and Bird Island Basin. The Malaquite Beach Visitor Center, open year-round, has educational programs, brochures, a small museum, and a concession stand. | 20301 Park Rd. | 361/949–8173 or 361/949–8068 | www.nps.gov/pais | $5 per vehicle | Park daily 24 hrs; visitor center late May–Aug., daily 8:30–6, Sept.–late May, daily 8:30–4:30.

South Texas Institute for the Arts. Traditional and modern works by artists connected with Texas are on view at this museum by the bay. The building was designed by Phillip Johnson. | 1902 N. Shoreline Blvd. | 361/825–3500 | www.stia.org | $3 | Tues.–Sat. 10–5, Sun. 1–5.

Texas State Aquarium. Aquatic animals and habitats indigenous to the Gulf of Mexico are showcased through exhibits and outdoor tanks. Dolphin Bay takes up more than 30,000 square feet, and contains more than 400,000 gallons of water, to hold nonreleasable dolphins. Handlers are present to teach you more about these marine mammals. | 2710 N. Shoreline Blvd. | 361/881–1200 or 800/477–4853 | www.texasstateaquarium.com | $12 | Late May–early Sept., Mon.–Sat. 9–6, Sun. 10–6; early-Sept.–late May, Mon.–Sat. 9–5, Sun. 10–5.

U.S.S. _Lexington_ Museum on the Bay. Five self-guided tour routes give you a close look at the most decorated aircraft carrier in U.S. Naval history, called "The Blue Ghost." Volunteers are often men and women (this was one of the first female training carriers) who served aboard and are happy to share their history. | 2914 N. Shoreline Blvd. | 361/888–4873 or 800/523–9539 | www.usslexington.com | $10 | Late May–early Sept., daily 9–6; early Sept.–late May, daily 9–5.

Dining

Blackbeard's on the Beach. American. Laid-back Blackbeard's, with its beach-shack allure, is popular for its mounds of fried shrimp and fierce margaritas. It's down the beach from the U.S.S. *Lexington* Museum on the Bay and the Texas State Aquarium. | C.C. Beach, 3117 Surfside Blvd. | 361/884–1030 | AE, D, DC, MC, V | ¢–$

Crawdaddy's. Cajun/Creole. The restaurant's claim to fame is its Cajun boil, a dish of shrimp, crawfish, crab claws, sausage, corn on the cob, and new potatoes, all boiled together in a powerfully spicy broth. For the less adventurous, there are relatively tame dishes such as red beans and rice. Look for the live crawfish walking slowly over the tubs full of ice and beer. | 414 Starr St. | 361/883–5432 | AE, D, MC, V | $–$$

La Bahia. Mexican. A satisfying blend of authentic Mexican and Tex-Mex fare awaits you here. The hip, stylish interior has exposed brick, high ceilings, arched doors and windows, and richly textured wall treatments. The flour and corn tortillas are homemade, the breakfast taquitos are available all day, and the full bar is open late. | 224 N. Mesquite St. | 361/888–6555 | AE, D, DC, MC, V | No dinner Sun. | ¢–$

Water Street Seafood Co. and Oyster Bar. Seafood. Daily fresh catch specials are chalked up on a large board in the cavernous dining room. The regular menu favorite is the embrochette (shrimp and oyster wrapped in bacon, served with a tangy remoulade sauce). The back building is the Oyster Bar and the front is the Seafood Co.; both have the same menus. | 309 N. Water St. | 361/881–9448 or 361/882–8683 | AE, D, DC, MC, V | $$

Lodging

Bayfront Inn. A three-tier terra-cotta fountain and elaborate brickwork set the Spanish tone for the exterior of the Bayfront Inn. Rooms are basic-motel style—clean with fairly nondescript furniture—but the downtown location is excellent. Ask for a bay-view room ($10 extra). In-room data ports, cable TV, pool, laundry facilities, meeting rooms, no-smoking rooms. | 601 N. Shoreline Blvd., 78401 | 361/883–7271 or 800/456–2293 | fax 361/883–2052 | www.bayfrontincc.com | 110 rooms | AE, D, DC, MC, V | CP | $–$$

Holiday Inn Sunspree Resort. The only real hotel on Padre Island, this resort attracts sun and sand lovers. Seascape murals, aquariums, and terrariums decorate the lobby. Oceanfront rooms have balconies facing the Gulf of Mexico. Light floral spreads and curtains complement the blond-wood cabinets and headboards set against guest rooms' salmon-color walls. Restaurant, microwaves, refrigerators, cable TV with video games, 2 pools, outdoor hot tub, gym, sauna, fishing, bar, video game room, shop, children's programs (ages 5–11), laundry facilities, Internet, business services, no-smoking rooms. | North Padre Island, 15202 Windward Dr., 78418 | 361/949–8041 or 888/949–8041 | fax 361/949–9139 | www.holiday-inn.com | 149 rooms, 4 suites | AE, D, DC, MC, V | $$–$$$

Ocean House B&B. You can stay in one of the mansionlike homes that line bay-front Ocean Drive between town and Padre Island. All the suites in the main and garden houses have large sitting areas and king or two queen beds. Bougainvillea and palms surround the tile-edge pool. Dining room, some kitchens, cable TV, some in-room hot tubs, in-room VCRs, pool; no smoking. | 3275 Ocean Dr., 78404 | 361/882–9500 | fax 361/884–5894 | www.oceansuites.com | 5 suites | AE, D, DC, MC, V | BP | $$$–$$$$

Villa del Sol. Perched on the Gulf's edge, this condominium hotel has breathtaking views of the bay. Each one-bedroom unit has a full kitchen, a living room, and a private balcony. The condos are individually decorated, but pastels and white rattan seem to be popular choices. The complex is on C.C. Beach near the U.S.S. *Lexington* Museum; the downtown area is just over the Harbor Bridge. Picnic area, kitchens, cable TV, 2 pools, wading pool, outdoor hot tub, fishing, volleyball, laundry facilities, no-smoking rooms. | 3938 Surfside Blvd. | 800/242–3291 | fax 361/883–7537 | www.villa-delsol.com | 238 apartments | AE, D, DC, MC, V | $–$$$

Kingsville

King Ranch. Sprawling across 825,000 acres, the King Ranch traces its history to 1853 when it was founded by Capt. Richard King, who made his fortune on Rio Grande riverboats. Take a guided tour of the working ranch in air-conditioned buses. Still one of the largest in the world, the ranch developed the Santa Gertrudis and King Ranch Santa Cruz breeds of cattle, as well as the first registered American quarter horse. | Santa Gertrudis Ave. or Rte. 141, 1½ mi west of town | 361/592–8055 or 800/333–5032 | www.king-ranch.com | $7 | Mon.–Sat. 9–4, Sun. noon–5.

King Ranch Museum. The history of the *vaqueros* (cowboys), King Ranch, and the founding ranch families is conveyed through exhibits that include a collection of saddles, and antique carriages and cars. | 405 N. 6th St. | 361/595–1881 | www.king-ranch.com | $2 | Mon.–Sat. 10–4, Sun. 1–5.

King Ranch Saddle Shop. The King Ranch Saddle Shop carries on the tradition of saddle making, with exquisite detail and hand-tooled ornamentation. The large store also produces and sells fine purses and belts, luggage, briefcases and organizers, and leather chairs. You can also buy items with the ranch's brand, a running W, on it— dishes, cups, flatware, coasters, shirts, hats, bedding. | 201 E. Kleberg | 361/595–1881 | www.krsaddleshop.com | Mon.–Sat. 10–6.

Dining

King's Inn. Seafood. Devotees drive the 45 minutes from Corpus Christi to eat perfectly coated, delicately fried seafood. Main dishes are served family-style, by the pound— orange roughy, catfish, shrimp, scallops, frogs' legs, oysters—as are side dishes like avocado salad, garden fresh sliced tomatoes, and french fries. | Rte. 628, Loyola Beach, 5 mi south of Kingsville off U.S. 77 | 361/297–5265 | MC, V | $–$$$

Port Aransas

Fisherman's Wharf. Cast off on regular offshore five- and eight-hour fishing excursions aboard the 100-foot, twin-hull *Wharf Cat* (with an air-conditioned cabin and a concession stand). Rods, reels, bait—and someone to help you net your big catch— are all included, with no licenses necessary. The marina also rents smaller offshore vessels and runs a summer sunset evening cruise. | 900 N. Tarpon St. | 361/749–5448 or 800/605–5448 | www.wharfcat.com | $40–$60 | Daily 8 AM and 2 PM.

Mustang Island State Park. The 3,500-acre park has 5 mi of open beaches and such facilities as freshwater showers, picnic tables, and tent and RV camping. You can drive on the beach here. | Rte. 361, 14 mi south of Port Aransas | 361/749–5246 | www.tpwd.state.tx.us | Free | Daily 24 hrs.

San Jose Island. Pirate Jean Lafitte is said to have camped here. Large iron rings, thought to have been used to tie up his group's small boats, were discovered at the site. Even today, the island is accessible only by boat, and there are no public facilities. It is a quiet getaway for fishing, beachcombing, swimming, or shelling. The Jetty Boat leaves year-round from the Woody's Sport Center marina. | 136 W. Cotter St. | 361/749–5252 | www.woodysonline.com | $10 | Daily 6:30–6.

University of Texas Marine Science Institute. Students of oceanography, ecology, marine chemistry, and botany train at this branch of the University of Texas, located on 82 beachfront acres. Stop by the visitor center for a self-guided tour or to view exhibits and films (3 [pm]) on Texas Gulf life. | 750 Channel View Dr. | 361/749–5246 | www.utmsi.utexas.edu | Weekdays 8–5.

Dining

Crazy Cajun. Cajun. Butcher paper covers the wooden tables; if you order the Hungry Cajun, waiters deposit a heap of pepper-spiced shrimp, crawfish, crab, sausage, corn, and potatoes directly onto the paper. On weekends, live Cajun-style music keeps the joint jumping. | 303 E. Beach St. | 361/749–5069 | AE, D, MC, V | No lunch weekdays | ¢–$$

Pelican's Landing Restaurant. Seafood. This bustling eatery specializes in locally caught fish, shrimp, oysters, and crab cakes, served before a magnificent waterfront view of Lake Texoma. | 337 Alister St. | 361/749–6405 | AE, D, DC, MC, V | $–$$

Lodging

Port Royal Resort. A huge lagoon-shape pool—with palm tree–clad islands and a swim-up bar—takes center stage at this U-shape condominium rental. The beach is just beyond the pool and all the one-, two-, and three-bedroom units have views of both. Tropical prints and fabrics define the beach-oriented decorations. You can rent horses for a ride on the beach nearby. A three-night minimum is imposed during spring break and July through August. Restaurant, kitchens, cable TV, 2 tennis courts, pool, hot tub, volleyball, bar, shop, playground, meeting rooms, no-smoking rooms. | Mustang Island, 3 mi south of town, 6317 Rte. 361, 78373 | 361/749–5011 or 800/242–1034 | fax 361/749–6399 | www.port-royal.com | 210 apartments | AE, D, MC, V | $$–$$$$

Rockport

Aransas National Wildlife Refuge. The National Park Service set aside this 54,829-acre refuge as the prime wintering ground for the endangered whooping crane and 300 other bird species. You can hike or drive the paved, 15-mi loop to see some of the area's other critters, including bats, armadillos, bobcats, feral hogs, and alligators. Be sure to climb the observation tower to peer through scopes at the whooping cranes (late October to early April). The Wildlife Interpretive Center has more information about area species. A boat tour can take you from Rockport out to the birds' protected area. | 25 mi north of Rockport on Rte. 35, then east on Rte. 774 to Rte. 2040 | 361/286–3559 | http://southwest.fws.gov | Free | Park daily dawn–dusk, interpretive center daily 8:30–4.

Connie Hagar Cottage Sanctuary. More than 6 acres of bay-side trails run through this sight, named after the woman who helped put Rockport on the birding map. The bay is ideal for sighting many shore bird species. Just follow signs along Broadway until you see bird-watching platforms across the street from the bay. | Church and 1st Sts. | 361/729–6445 or 800/242–0071 | Daily dawn–dusk.

Copano Bay Causeway State Park. A lighted fishing pier, public boat ramp, picnic area, and bait shop are among the attractions at this 6-acre facility. | Rte. 35, 5 mi north of Rockport | 361/729–8519 | www.tpwd.state.tx.us | $1.75 per fishing rod | Daily 24 hrs.

Goose Island State Park. The "Big Tree," considered one of the largest oak trees in the world, is in this 314-acre park. It's thought to be more than 1,000 years old, and is 35 feet in circumference and 44 feet tall. | Rte. 35 to Rte. 13, 12 mi north of Rockport | 361/729–2858 | www.tpwd.state.tx.us | $2 | Daily 8 AM–10 PM.

Rockport Birding Adventures. From November through March take a three-hour boat tour on the M.V. *Skimmer* to view the whooping cranes that winter in Aransas National Wildlife Refuge. The boat holds less than 30 people, so it can navigate closer to the birds than the larger charters—but reservations also fill up quickly. | Harbor-front, N. Fuller Beach Rd. | 877/892–4737 | www.rockportadventures.com | $30 | Nov.–Mar., Wed.–Mon. 10:30 and 1.

Rockport Center for the Arts. The center's galleries, classrooms, pottery studio, and sculpture garden are used to exhibit local and theme-based artwork. The landscaped grounds are a tranquil place to unwind. | 902 Navigation Circle | 361/729–5519 | www.rockportartcenter.org | Free | Tues.–Sun. 10–4, Sat. 1–4.

Lodging

Hoopes' House Bed & Breakfast. Bird-watchers flock into this big, yellow Victorian home (circa 1892). A mural in the sunroom depicts many of the sea and shorebirds that call Rockport home from November through March. Victorian antique beds and dressers furnish the high-ceiling guest rooms with crown molding; clawfoot tubs, small tiles, and fluffy bathrobes are on hand in the bathrooms. Ask if one of the four rooms in the original home is available. Cable TV, library; no kids under 12. | 417 N. Broadway, 78382 | 361/729–8424 or 800/924–1008 Ext. 300 | www.hoopeshouse.com | 8 rooms | AE, MC, V | BP | $$

UTAH

FROM SALT LAKE
INTO THE MOUNTAINS
SALT LAKE CITY TO WASATCH-CACHE NATIONAL FOREST

Distance: 90 mi   Time: 2 days
Overnight Break: Park City

The first portion of this mountain drive, from Salt Lake City to Park City, is a perfect short getaway for families, couples or solo travelers wanting to commune with nature. After resting in Park City, you'll set out into the rolling country of Heber Valley and into the pristine beauty of the Wasatch-Cache National Forest. Don't try to do the entire drive in winter: Route 150 may be closed due to snow, and although Park City is great fun if you're into winter sports, lodging rates double during ski season.

❶ From **Salt Lake,** I–80 runs through Parley's Canyon toward Park City. This is Utah's original toll road, devised by enterprising Mormon settler Parley P. Pratt; he stationed his home midway and charged settlers a fee to pass through the canyon, the easiest route into the Salt Lake valley.

❷ Proceed 20 mi east on I–80, then south for approximately 5 mi on Route 224 into Park City. Main Street in **Park City** is an easy up-and-down walk of less than a mile. Shopping is its chief interest, but take time to enjoy the art galleries on both sides of the street and settle on a good place for dinner. Spend the night in Park City.

❸ Leaving Park City, head east on Route 248 approximately 7 mi to the **Kamas Ranger District Office** to determine the road conditions and gather information before heading into the **Wasatch-Cache National Forest.**
     The **Uinta Mountains** will be visible to the east for the remainder of this tour. They are one of only a few mountain ranges in North America running on an east–west axis.

❹ The Provo River parallels the road along much of this drive. **Upper Provo River Falls** (22 mi east of Kamas on Route 150) is a lovely place to stretch your legs or stop for a picnic or snack. Walkways near the road follow the river past a series of small cascades, and you can choose a meditative spot along the rocky shores where the water creates the perfect mood music.

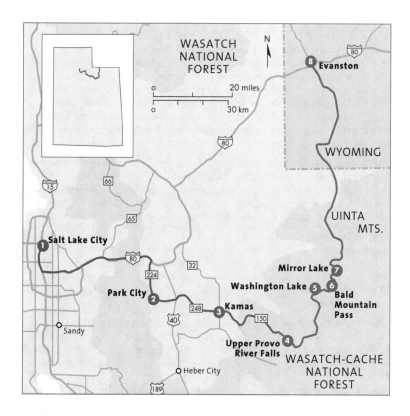

5 As the highway continues to climb in elevation, there are several signed turnoffs leading to small lakes. Some of these roads may be suitable only for high-clearance vehicles, but others are maintained and paved with gravel and have developed picnic and camping areas. Some access short hikes to lakes nestled in thick pine forests. **Washington Lake** (approximately 27 mi northeast of Kamas on the west side of Route 150) is particularly beautiful in summer when wildflowers are in bloom.

6 Continue along Route 150 for another 5 mi or so to **Bald Mountain Pass,** where the road climbs to 10,687 feet, an elevation close to the timberline. You'll see tree stands thin out and open into meadows, at their greenest in summer. The area has been carved by glaciers and the moraines left by glacier action can be recognized as bumpy hills curving across stream valleys with angular rock fragments not rounded by stream action.

7 Another mile on Route 150 will take you to beautiful **Mirror Lake,** on the northeastern descent from Bald Mountain, about 1 mi from the top of the pass. This alpine lake's tranquil waters beautifully reflect the sky and the ring of pine trees surrounding the shore. No motorboats are allowed, so it's a lovely place to spend a quiet afternoon; the only sound you'll hear is the whip of fly-fishing rods as enthusiasts test the water for trout.

8 To finish this drive, you can either continue north to **Evanston,** Wyoming (32 mi north on Route 150), then take I–80 back into the Heber Valley (approximately 40 mi southwest), or go back the way you came (33 mi southwest to Kamas).

Park City

Alpine Slide, Gorgoza Skate Park, and Little Miners' Park. In summer, the resort center at Park City Mountain Resort transforms ski operations into facilities for other sports. The Alpine Slide begins with a chairlift ride about halfway up the mountain, then special "sleighs" carry sliders down 3,000 feet of winding concrete and fiberglass track at a breathtaking pace. In winter, the Gorgoza Skate Park has a snow-tubing course. The Little Miners' Park has children's rides: a mini-Ferris wheel, a slow-moving train, and an airplane ride. There's also a miniature golf course. | Park City Mountain Resort | 435/647–5333 | www.parkcitymountain.com | June–Sept., weekdays 2–9, weekends 11–9.

The Canyons. The fifth-largest ski resort in the country, this establishment is also open year-round for hiking, biking, and horseback riding. In winter, snowboarders remain loyal to the place, one of the first in Utah open to them. With 3,625 acres, though, the mountain has plenty of room for everyone to coexist peacefully. | 4000 The Canyons Dr., north on Rte. 224 | 435/649–5400 or 888/226–9667 | fax 435/649–7374 | www.thecanyons.com.

Deer Valley Resort. Deer Valley is considered Utah's most upscale resort—and is proud of it. Open year-round, the resort has lift-assisted mountain biking in summer, as well as hiking and riding. The vertical drop is 3,000 feet, serviced by 18 lifts, including a gondola and six high-speed quads. The 84 runs and six powder bowls yield a total of 50% intermediate terrain. | 2250 Deer Valley Dr. S | 435/649–1000, 435/649–2000 snow report | www.deervalley.com.

Utah Winter Sports Park. Take a two-hour ski-jumping lesson at the official training site for the U.S. Nordic and freestyle ski teams. Choose the 18- or 38-meter hill, and use your own equipment or rent it from the park. There are public recreational rides on the bobsled–luge track. After the snow melts, you can watch the free-style skiers train on an artificial slope, landing in a huge splash pool. | 3000 Bear Hollow Dr., off Rte. 224 | 435/658–4200 | fax 435/647–9650 | www.saltlake2002.com | Daily.

Dining

Claimjumper. American. In the center of historic Old Town, this lively restaurant is pure Americana, from its hardwood floors, green drapes, and grand stone fireplace

UTAH RULES OF THE ROAD

License Requirements: The minimum driving age in Utah is 16. All drivers must have a valid driver's license.

Speed Limits: On major highways the speed limit is 55 mph, particularly in urban areas. Speed limits range from 65 to 75 mph on interstate highways in rural areas, but watch out: "rural areas" are determined by census boundaries, so their delineation may seem arbitrary to the casual driver.

Right Turn on Red: Generally, right turns are allowed on a red light *after* the vehicle has come to a complete stop, unless otherwise posted.

Seat Belt and Helmet Laws: Utah law requires seat belt use for drivers, front-seat passengers, and all children under 10. Children under the age of two are required to be in federally approved safety seats. Helmet use is mandatory for motorcyclists and passengers under the age of 18.

For More Information: Utah Department of Motor Vehicles | 801/965–4518. **Utah Highway Patrol** | 801/297–7780.

to its emphasis on steaks, prime rib, and burgers. All the beef is aged, and cooked to your request. | 573 Main St. | 435/649–8051 | AE, D, DC, MC, V | $$–$$$

Eating Establishment. American. Near the top of Main Street, this affordable local favorite is known for its hearty keep-you-skiing-all-morning breakfasts and its barbecue dinner specials. | 317 Main St. | 435/649–8284 | AE, D, MC, V | $–$$

★**Glitretind.** Continental. Glitretind humbly describes itself as a "European mountain bistro," but it's really more of a grand lodge. The menu highlights such wild game dishes as grilled buffalo and venison, but also offers lunch sandwiches on thick, crusty bread and dinners of Asian duck, baked salmon, and tender steaks. In warm weather, you can eat on the deck, with a view of the Heber and Deer valleys. | Stein Eriksen Lodge, 7700 Stein Way | 435/649–3700 | AE, D, DC, MC, V | $$$–$$$$

Morning Ray Café & Bakery. American. The Continental crowd favors this bakery café that serves specialty breads, bagels, pastries, and substantial omelets, pancakes, and quiches. Wooden chairs and tables and yellow-toned walls with local art make the space inviting. | 268 Main St. | 435/649–5686 | AE, MC, V | No dinner | ¢–$

Royal Street Cafe Contemporary. Beautiful, creative, colorful food is what you'll find at this Deer Valley resort restaurant. Many people make a meal out of appetizers, but don't skip one of the sumptuous entrées, such as the spinach, goat cheese, and smoked-tomato enchiladas. | Silver Lake Lodge, 7600 Royal St. | 435/645–6724 | AE, D, DC, MC, V | $–$$

Lodging

Best Western Landmark Inn. Park City hotels can get pricey, so this chain inn off I–80 is a good alternative. Rooms are standard but pleasantly furnished, and a relaxing poolside area and a separate recreation area make this a good bet for families. Restaurant, in-room data ports, minibars, cable TV, indoor pool, gym, hot tub, laundry facilities, some pets allowed (fee). | 6560 N. Landmark Dr., 84098 | 435/649–7300 or 800/548–8824 | fax 435/649–1760 | 92 rooms, 14 suites | AE, D, DC, MC, V | $$$

Chateaux at Silver Lake. You have a choice of single hotel rooms or one-, two-, three-, or four-bedroom suites at this complex. The rooms and units are spacious and posh with fireplaces, kitchens, dining rooms, and jetted tubs. In-room data ports, refrigerators, microwaves, some kitchens, cable TV, pool, hot tub, exercise equipment, business services, laundry facilities. | 7815 Royal St. E, 84098 | 435/658–9500 or 800/453–3833 | fax 435/658–9513 | www.chateaux-deervalley.com | AE, D, DC, MC, V | $$$–$$$$

1904 Imperial Hotel. Built in 1904 as a boarding house for miners and travelers, the hotel has been restored to a more upscale turn-of-the-20th century Western Victorian style. Cable TV, hot tub; no a/c. | 221 Main St., 84060 | 435/649–1904 or 800/669–8824 | fax 435/645–7421 | www.1904imperial.com | 10 rooms, 2 suites | AE, D, MC, V | $$–$$$$

Shadow Ridge. The basic hotel rooms here have the same amenities as the lavish suites, making them a good value for a modest price. The hotel is at the base of the Park City Mountain Village. Restaurant, some microwaves, cable TV, pool, exercise equipment, hot tub, laundry facilities, business services. | 50 Shadow Ridge Dr., 84060 | 435/649–4300 or 800/451–3031 | fax 435/649–5951 | 150 rooms, 50 suites | AE, D, DC, MC, V | $$–$$$

Salt Lake City

★**Alta Ski Area.** Alta is the perennial favorite of serious local skiers. There's no glitz, no fancy cuisine, and no fashion show on the slopes, just an excellent ski school, incredible powder snow, and a mountain that some consider a sort of monument to the sanctity of skiing. Alta limits the uphill capacity of its lifts per hour, thus limiting the number of skiers on the mountain so as to "protect the skiing experience." | Big Cottonwood

Canyon, east on Rte. 152 | 801/359–1078 or 801/742–3333 | www.altaskiarea.com | Mid-Nov.–mid-Apr.

★**Snowbird Ski and Summer Resort.** When it opened in the 1970s, Snowbird was on the cutting edge of ski trends, and it has managed to stay there ever since. Snowbird has black diamond runs all over the mountain. A gondola that holds 125 people takes you to deep powder bowls. At the base, several angular buildings provide upscale lodging, fine dining, and such amenities as swimming pools, tennis courts, and a full-service spa, all of which are open throughout the year. | Little Cottonwood Canyon, east on Rte. 210 | 801/742–2222 or 800/385–2002 | fax 801/947–8227 | www.snowbird.com | Mid-Nov.–late Apr.

State Capitol. On a hill at the north end of State Street, the capitol building, completed in 1915, is built in Renaissance Revival style. Depression-era murals in the rotunda depict events from Utah's past. Knowledgeable volunteer guides lead free hourly tours. | 300 N. State St. | 801/538–1563 or 801/538–3000 | Weekdays, hours vary.

★**Temple Square.** The 10-acre plot is the very center of Mormonism. The square blooms with bright gardens in spring, summer, and fall; thousands of colored lights illuminate the buildings and trees during the holiday season. Two visitor centers house exhibits and art with religious themes. Bordered by Main Street and North, South, and West Temple streets. | North Visitors' Center, 50 W. North Temple | 801/240–2534 | www.saltlake.org/slc | Daily.

    Tabernacle. The Mormon Tabernacle Choir performs on Thursday and Sunday in the squat, oval-shape, domed Tabernacle. You can also attend the extra rehearsals scheduled weekly. | Temple Square | 801/240–4872 | Thurs. evening, Sun. morning.

Utah Museum of Natural History. The museum's largest hall holds the skeletons of dinosaurs and other prehistoric creatures. An exhibit on rocks and minerals includes information on mining in Utah. Also on display is a collection of more than 1,000 pieces of Indian art, including jewelry and elaborate masks. | 1390 E. President's Cir., off East 200 S | 801/581–4303 | www.umnh.utah.edu | $6 | Daily.

Dining
★**The Aerie.** Continental. Elegant dining and breathtaking views unite here on the 10th floor of the Cliff Lodge at Snowbird, at the base of the mountain. The dining room is decorated with Chinese art from the owner's collection. Specialties include rabbit ravioli and duck breast with fresh seasonal fruit sauce. There's a sushi bar in winter. Breakfast is served in winter only. | Rte. 210 | 801/742–2222 Ext. 550 | Reservations essential | AE, D, DC, MC, V | No lunch | $$–$$$

Cuchina. Continental. Cuchina is equal parts bakery, Italian deli, coffee shop, and candy store. Its breakfast scones are justifiably famous; lunch and dinner yield such entrées as meat loaf with garlic potatoes, chicken orzo salad with feta cheese and raisins, and salmon fillets stuffed with cheeses and herbs. Outdoor dining is on a porch with a view of the garden. | 1026 E. 2nd Ave. | 801/322–3055 | MC, V | ¢–$

Lamb's Restaurant. American. Said to be Utah's oldest restaurant (in operation since 1919), Lamb's is in a historic building in the heart of downtown. The interior and furniture from 1939 remain. Specials include beef tenderloin Stroganoff, baby beef liver, fresh trout and halibut, and a variety of lamb dishes. | 169 S. Main St. | 801/364–7166 | AE, D, DC, MC, V | Closed Sun. | $$–$$$

Porcupine Pub and Grille. Eclectic. The decor is modern Southwestern chic, but the menu really gets around: cherry-barbecue salmon, Thai chicken, a Portobello mushroom sandwich, and tequila-lime pasta are a few examples. It's south of downtown, at the mouth of Big Cottonwood Canyon. | 3698 E. Fort Union Blvd. | 801/942–5555 | AE, D, MC, V | $$–$$$

UTAH COLOR COUNTRY
ZION, BRYCE, AND GRAND STAIRCASE–ESCALANTE NATIONAL MONUMENTS

Distance: Approximately 140–170 mi   Time: 3 days
Overnight Breaks: Springdale, Bryce Canyon National Park, Escalante, or Boulder.

The singular beauty of red-rock terrain awaits you on this drive through southern Utah. The tour treats you to some stunning, diverse landscapes and incorporates pieces of three designated scenic byways and two national parks. Winter driving in the Bryce Canyon and Boulder areas can be snowy and icy, so plan accordingly.

❶ It's easy to spend a full day in the western portion of **Zion National Park,** your first stop. To avoid high-season traffic, leave your car at one of the shuttle stops in Springdale. You can also park at the visitor center and pick up a shuttle into Zion Canyon, where private vehicles are not allowed May through October. Do stop at the visitor center for a fantastic overview of the park's geology and natural history. You can also find out about ranger-guided hikes or lectures for the day. There are a multitude of hiking trails for all fitness levels; for a nice level walk into one of the park's most popular areas, take the shuttle to the end of the road and enjoy the paved Riverside Walk. On this trail you'll not only walk beside the waters of the Virgin River, but alongside towering cliffs dripping with hanging gardens. For a good workout, try Emerald Pools Trail or Angels Landing. Don't miss the walk up to Weeping Rock.

❷ If you're not camping in the park, spend the night in one of the many excellent **Springdale** (south of the park on Route 9) motels, lodges, or bed-and-breakfasts. Springdale has plenty of restaurants as well.

After a good night's sleep, head east on gradual switchbacks to pass through the **Zion–Mt. Carmel Tunnels,** a highlight of the drive. A testimony to American ingenuity, the tunnels were cut through the massive canyon walls in the late 1920s. East of the tunnels, the landscape changes dramatically as you emerge into the light between ancient sand dunes embossed by the work of wind and water. Route 9 takes you to **Zion's East Entrance.**

❸ From Route 9, turn north (left) onto U.S. 89 at Mt. Carmel Junction and drive through verdant **Long Valley,** which is naturally irrigated by the Virgin River and bordered by yellow-, red-, and white-banded cliffs. After 44 mi, turn east on Route 12 toward Bryce Canyon.

❹ Drive 15 mi on Route 12 to reach the junction with Route 63, which leads to the park boundary of **Bryce Canyon National Park.** During summer months your best bet is to use the park's optional shuttle bus to enjoy the **Scenic Drive,** the park service road running south from the park entrance for 37 mi. You can, however, take your own vehicle into the park if you wish. Stop at as many overlooks as time allows. With reservations, you can stay the night inside the park at its quiet, rustic lodge. Otherwise, select one of the motels just outside the park boundaries.

In the morning, watch how the rising sun makes the hoodoo (a natural column or pinnacle of rock) formations of Bryce seem to shift shape and color. Spend a couple of hours further exploring the park. Stroll the easy Rim Trail or, for a memorable walk into the amphitheater, choose the Navajo/Queen's Loop Trail. When you're ready to rest your legs and get back into the car, return to Route 12 and head east.

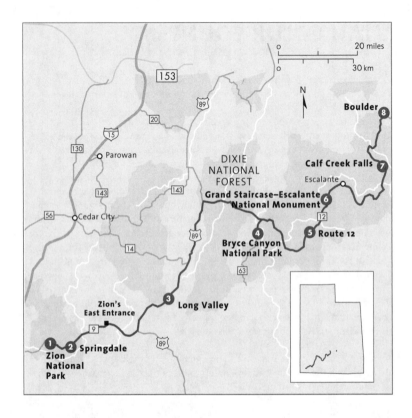

❺ Utah Scenic Byway Route 12 is one of only 20 American roads recognized by the U.S. National Scenic Byways Program and it is an adventure not to be missed. The 29-mi stretch between Escalante and Boulder takes you over the top of a narrow hogback (a ridge with a sharp summit and steeply sloping sides). You'll want to gaze across the horizon toward the thousands of acres of the Grand Staircase–Escalante National Monument, but best to keep your eyes on the road! It is not for the faint of heart nor for those afraid of narrow, winding mountain roads, but it's worth all the palpitations. Once you pass Boulder you'll enter a cool alpine swath with awesome views into the valley.

❻ Enter **Grand Staircase–Escalante National Monument.** Many of the monument's most incredible landscapes and features—slot canyons, rock-art panels, ancient ruins, twisted river courses—are deep inside formidable mesas. Continue to the town of **Escalante** (30 mi northeast on Route 12) to eat, fill up the tank, and pick up bottled water.

❼ From Escalante, travel north to the signed parking area for **Calf Creek Falls** (20 mi north on Route 12). If you're so inclined, take the 2$\frac{1}{2}$-mi hike to the falls. (Don't forget to carry plenty of water.) A brochure at the trailhead locates more than 20 points of interest along this level path, including Anasazi ruins, interesting petroglyphs, some abandoned late-19th-century farming equipment, and wildlife. At the canyon's end, an impressive waterfall plunges from the top of a sandstone cliff. After hiking back to the trailhead, take a moment to rest and replenish your water supply before returning to Escalante to spend the night.

❽ Alternatively, continue driving another 29 mi to **Boulder,** and spend the night where the temperatures are a bit cooler. While there, stop off at the **Anasazi State Park** to learn about the ancient cultures indigenous to this area.

Boulder

Anasazi State Park. Anasazi is a Navajo word interpreted to mean "ancient enemies." What the Anasazi called themselves we will never know, but today their descendants, the Hopi people, prefer the term ancestral Puebloan. This state park is dedicated to the study of that mysterious culture, with a largely unexcavated dwelling site, a museum with interactive exhibits, and a reproduction of a six-room pueblo. | 460 N. Rte. 12, Boulder | 435/335–7308 | http://parks.state.ut.us | $5 per vehicle | Memorial Day–Labor Day daily 8–6, Labor Day–Memorial Day daily 9–5.

Dining

★**Hell's Backbone Grill.** Contemporary. One of the best restaurants in southern Utah, this remote spot on Route 12 is worth the drive from any distance. The menu is inspired by Native American, Western range, Southwestern, and Mormon pioneer recipes. The owners, who are also the chefs, use only fresh, organic foods that have a historical connection to the area. Outdoor dining overlooking a tiny pond on the grounds of Boulder Mountain Lodge is a treat. | 20 N. Rte. 12 | 435/335–7464 | AE, D, MC, V | Closed Nov.–Mar. | $$–$$$

Lodging

★**Boulder Mountain Lodge.** The best place to stay on Route 12 is this wonderful lodge with a 5-acre pond. Pastoral grounds provide a sanctuary for ducks, coots, and other waterfowl, and horses graze in an adjacent meadow. Large, modern rooms with balconies or patios offer gorgeous views of the wetlands. The main lodge contains a great room with fireplace, and there's a fine art gallery and remarkably good restaurant on the premises. Restaurant, outdoor hot tub, some pets allowed (fee); no smoking. | 20 N. Rte. 12, 84716 | 435/335–7460 or 800/556–3446 | fax 435/335–7461 | www.boulder-utah.com | 20 rooms | D, MC, V | $

Bryce Canyon National Park

Bristlecone Loop. At the southernmost edge of the park, right off Rainbow Point, this short 1½-mi trail enters briefly into Bryce Canyon's conifer forest, and, in places, offers spectacular 270-degree views of the surrounding canyon country. | Daily.

Navajo Loop Trail. The Navajo Loop is actually a "down, and then back up the way you came." It is short, only 1½ mi round-trip, but from the trail's beginning at Sunset Point to the turnaround deep in the canyon, it's a drop of 520 feet. You get the best view of many of Bryce's most famous formations—Thor's Hammer, The Pope, and Temple of Osiris among them—from this trail. Rangers lead guided trips on the Navajo Loop at least twice a day. | Daily, except when icy or snowpacked.

Queen's Garden Trail. Considered the "easiest" trail into Bryce Canyon, the Queen's Garden hike begins at Sunrise Point. Round-trip, this jaunt is 1½ mi, and its 320-foot descent is more gradual than that of most of the park's other trails. The route is marked with signs offering geological information on the pillars, hoodoos, balanced rocks, and spires on every side. Stories of the origin of formation names, like Gulliver's Castle and Queen Victoria, also make for interesting reading. | Daily, except when icy or snowpacked.

Rim Trail. Skirting the edge of Bryce Canyon for 5½ mi, this trail is probably the most complete way to see and enjoy the bizarre and beautiful geology of Bryce. Though the distance may sound a bit daunting (particularly if you don't arrange for a shuttle or someone with a car to meet you at the trail's end), the path is fairly level and rated easy to moderate. The ½-mi stretch between Sunrise and Sunset points sees the most traffic as there are amazing vistas along the way. You'll also find plenty of benches nicely positioned for resting and enjoying the views. | Daily, most of year.

Sunrise and Sunset Points. The ½-mi stretch between these two overlooks is paved and level, well-adapted for wheelchairs or strollers. These viewpoints are two of the park's most impressive, with sweeping panoramas of the colors, erosional forms, and mysterious landscapes for which Bryce Canyon is known. | Daily.

Dining

Bryce Canyon Lodge. American. The restaurant in the middle of this historic 1924 lodge is the only place to dine within the park. Many menu items change each year, but you should be able to sample Utah mountain red trout or wagon-wheel pasta with marinara sauce anytime you go. | 1 Bryce Canyon | 435/834–5361 | Reservations essential | AE, D, DC, MC, V | Closed Nov.–Mar. | $–$$

Bryce Canyon Pines Restaurant. American. Known for homemade soups like tomato broccoli and corn chowder, and for fresh berry and cream pies, this homey, antiques-filled restaurant 6 mi northwest of the park entrance dishes up quality comfort food. | Rte. 12 | 435/834–5441 | AE, D, DC, MC, V | ¢–$$

Lodging

Best Western Ruby's Inn. This large two-story inn is the closest accommodation outside the park, with spacious rooms and a comfortable lobby. It's a good place to stay if you want easy access to such organized activities as chuckwagon cookouts, trail rides, and helicopter and ATV tours. Restaurant, picnic area, cable TV, in-room VCRs, 2 indoor pools, cross-country skiing, laundry facilities, business services, some pets allowed (fee). | Rte. 63, 1 mi off Rte. 12 | 435/834–5341 or 800/468–8660 | fax 435/834–5265 | www.rubysinn.com | 368 rooms | AE, D, DC, MC, V | $–$$

★**Bryce Canyon Lodge.** Built in 1925, this lodge has been named a National Historic Landmark. It's a great place to come for peace and quiet—no TVs here. You can stay in spacious motel rooms or in cabins; both are within walking distance of the canyon's rim. Restaurant, laundry facilities, business services. | 1 Bryce Canyon, 84717 | 435/834–5361, 303/297–2757 (reservations) | fax 435/834–5464 | www.brycecanyonlodge.com | 40 cabins, 70 motel units, 3 suites, 1 studio | AE, D, DC, MC, V | Closed Nov.–mid-Apr. | $–$$

Bryce Canyon Pines. Some of the pine-panel rooms in this motel have fireplaces and kitchens. There's a campground here, too. The property is 6 mi from Bryce Canyon. Restaurant, cable TV, pool, horseback riding, business services. | Rte. 12, Milepost 10 Bryce, 84764 | 435/834–5441 or 800/892–7923 | fax 435/834–5330 | www.brycecanyonpinesl.com | 50 rooms | D, DC, MC, V | $

Bryce Canyon Resort. This rustic lodge is across from the local airport and 3 mi from the park entrance. Cabins and cottages are also available for those seeking a tad more privacy. Restaurant, in-room data ports, cable TV, indoor pool, laundry facilities. | 13500 E. Rte. 12, 84717 | 435/834–5351 or 800/834–0043 | fax 435/834–5256 | 57 rooms, 2 suites | MC, V | $

Escalante

Escalante State Park. The park was created to protect a huge repository of fossilized wood and dinosaur bones. It takes very little time on either of the two brief interpretive trails before you start to feel like an expert on things that are petrified. You'll see twisted and partially buried pieces of wood, and entire fallen forests. Another feature of the park is Wide Hollow Reservoir, with its associated wetlands. You can fish for trout in the reservoir, and go birding at the wetlands, one of the few bird-watching sites in southern Utah. | 710 N. Reservoir Rd. | 435/826–4466 | www.utah.com/stateparks/escalante.htm | $4 | Daily dawn–dusk.

Grand Staircase–Escalante National Monument. At a little over 1 million acres, the national monument dominates any map of southern Utah. Only a few roads go into the depths of the monument, none of which you should try to negotiate in a standard passenger car. Nevertheless, you can still experience and enjoy these fabulous landscapes; guided tours, including bicycle, four-wheel-drive, and backcountry hiking trips, are readily available; the Bureau of Land Management (BLM) maintains a list of guides and outfitters permitted to operate inside the monument. Advance reservations are suggested. Route 12 provides access to the monument. | Escalante Interagency Visitor Center: 755 W. Main St., Escalante | 435/865–5100 general info, 435/826–5499 Escalante Visitor Center | www.ut.blm.gov/monument | $5 | Park daily 8 AM–10 PM; visitor center weekdays 8–4:30.

Kodachrome Basin State Park. As soon as you see it, you'll understand why the park earned this name from the National Geographic Society. The sand pipes seen here are found no other place in the world. You can hike any of the trails to spot some of the 67 pipes in or around the park. The short Angels Palace Trail takes you quickly into the park's interior, up, over, and around some of the badlands. | Cottonwood Canyon Rd., 9 mi southeast of Cannonville | 435/679–8562 | http://parks.state.ut.us | $5 | Daily 6 AM–10 PM.

Lower Escalante River. Some of the best backcountry hiking in the area lies 15 mi east of Escalante on Route 12, where the river carves through striking sandstone canyons and gulches. You can camp at numerous sites along the river for extended trips, or you can spend a little time in the small park where the highway crosses the river. | 435/865–5100 | Daily.

Lodging

Escalante Outfitters. Stay here if you're on a budget—and not fussy about amenities. There are seven double-occupancy log bunkhouses (three with double beds, four with bunk beds); all share a common bathhouse. Coffee shop, picnic area, fans; no a/c. | 310 W. Main St., 84726 | 435/826–4266 | fax 435/826–4388 | www.arof.net/~slickroc/escout | 7 bunkhouses | MC, V | ¢

Escalante's Grand Staircase Bed & Breakfast Inn. Rooms in this inn have skylights, tile floors, log furniture, and murals reproducing area petroglyphs. You can relax on the outdoor porches or in the library or make use of the bike-rental shop and explore the adjacent national monument. Dining room, cable TV, hot tub, bicycles, library. | 280 W. Main St., 84726 | 435/826–4890 | fax 435/826–4889 | www.escalantebnb.com | 5 rooms | MC, V | CP | $–$$

Prospector Inn. This three-story brick building on Main Street is the largest hotel in town. Restaurant, cable TV, business services. | 380 W. Main St., 84726 | 435/826–4653 | fax 435/826–4285 | 50 rooms | AE, MC, V | $

Springdale

O. C. Tanner Amphitheater. This performance venue is set amid huge sandstone boulders at the base of the enormous red cliffs spilling south from Zion National Park. *The Grand Circle* is a multimedia presentation on the Southwest that shows nightly at dusk from Memorial Day to Labor Day. In summer, live concerts are held at the amphitheater each weekend. | Lion Blvd. | 435/652–7994 | www.dixie.edu/community | May–Oct., daily.

Springdale Fruit Company. Surrounded by apple orchards, this small market is an interesting and healthy stop. The store carries freshly squeezed juices, organic fruit and vegetables, a huge variety of trail mix concoctions, and bakery items. A picnic area is behind the market. | 2491 Zion Park Blvd. | 435/772–3222 | Daily 8–dusk.

Zion Canyon Theatre. A 37-minute film, *Zion, Treasure of the Gods,* is shown once an hour in a 500-seat auditorium on a screen 80 feet wide and 6 stories high. | 145 Zion Park Blvd. | 435/772–2400 or 888/256–3456 | www.ziontheatre.com | Apr.–Oct., daily 9–9; Nov.–Mar., daily 11–7.

Dining

★**Bit and Spur Restaurant and Saloon.** Mexican. This restaurant has been a legend in Utah for more than 20 years. A seasonal menu offers a variety of familiar Mexican entrées, including burritos, tacos, and tostadas, but the kitchen also gets creative. Get here early so you can eat outside and enjoy the lovely grounds and great views. | 1212 Zion Park Blvd. | 435/772–3498 | Reservations essential | D, MC, V | No lunch | $–$$

Bumbleberry Inn. American. This local favorite is famous for its bumbleberry (a combination of "burple" and "binkel" berries) concoctions, such as a homemade pie, bumbleberry pancakes, and stuffed French toast. The salmon fish-and-chips, burgers, marinated chicken breast, fresh trout, and steak specials are also popular. | 897 Zion Park Blvd. | 435/772–3611 | D, MC, V | $

Zion Pizza and Noodle Company. Italian. This eatery in the former Springdale Mormon church serves salads, calzones, and crispy pizzas baked in slate ovens. Eat on the patio or on the front apron overlooking Zion Park Boulevard. Beer and ale are on tap. | 868 Zion Park Blvd. | 435/772–3815 | AE, D, MC, V | Closed Dec. | ¢–$

Lodging

Canyon Ranch Motel. These small cottage facilities tucked away from the highway are peaceful and well appointed. Rooms are basic and bright, and the pleasant lawn area has large shade trees and picnic tables. Picnic area, pool, hot tub. | 668 Zion Park Blvd., 84767 | 435/772–3357 | fax 435/772–3057 | 22 rooms in cottages | AE, D, MC, V | $

★**Cliffrose Lodge and Gardens.** Flowers decorate the 5-acre grounds of this family-friendly, charming lodge. Comfy rooms will keep you happy after a long hike, and from your balcony you can continue to enjoy views of the towering, colorful cliffs. The Virgin River is just outside your door; you can have a picnic or barbecue by its banks. The Cliffrose is within walking distance of the Zion Canyon visitor center and the shuttle stop. Cable TV, pool, outdoor hot tub, beach. | 281 Zion Park Blvd., 84767 | 435/772–3234 or 800/243–8824 | fax 435/772–3900 | www.cliffroselodge.com | 36 rooms | AE, D, MC, V | $$

★**Desert Pearl Inn.** Every room at this posh inn is a suite, with vaulted ceilings and thick carpets, plus cushy throw pillows, Roman shades, oversize windows, bidets, sleeper sofas, and tile showers with deep tubs. The pool area is exceptionally beautiful, with a double-size hot tub, and showers and rest rooms at poolside. In-room data ports, in-room safes, kitchenettes, refrigerators, cable TV, in-room VCRs, pool, outdoor hot tub, shops. | 707 Zion Park Blvd., 84767 | 435/772–8888 or 888/828–0898 | fax 435/772–8889 | www.desertpearl.com | 60 suites | AE, D, MC, V | $$

The Harvest House. This attractive pioneer-house inn with large wraparound porch caters to hikers and peace-and-quiet seekers. You can relax on the deck overlooking the koi pond or in the hot tub, which has a view of Watchman Peak, or spend time in the quiet, tasteful rooms, none of which has a telephone or television. It's a half-mile from the park entrance. Hot tub; no room phones, no room TVs. | 29 Canyon View Dr. | 435/772–3880 | fax 435/772–3327 | 4 rooms | MC, V | CP | $–$$

Zion National Park

Bicycling. The paved, 3½-mi Pa'rus Trail winds along the Virgin River in Zion Canyon. You can take guided tours both in the park and on land south of the park. Electric bikes, tandem bikes, mountain bikes, children's bikes, and helmets for all ages can be rented by the hour, the half-day, or all day in Springdale, south of Zion Canyon. Bicycles are not recommended on the park road and are not allowed on park trails except for the Pa'rus. | Bike Zion, 1458 Zion Park Blvd. (Rte. 9) | 435/772–3929 | Scenic Cycles, 205 Zion Park Blvd. (Rte. 9) | 435/772–2453.

Emerald Pools Trail. The trailhead for an easy-to-moderate hike to this series of pools and waterfalls lies across the street from the Zion Park Lodge, about 6 mi north of the park's main south entrance. You can walk to the Lower Emerald Pools in about an hour to see waterfalls cascading off the red cliffs into a series of pools. Getting to the Upper Pools is a bit more difficult and takes about an hour longer. | Zion Canyon Rd. | 435/772–3256 | Daily.

Riverside Walk. Beginning at the Temple of Sinawava shuttle stop at the end of Zion Canyon Scenic Drive, this trail is a delightful 1-mi round-trip stroll along the Virgin River. The river gurgles by on one side of the trail; on the other side, wildflowers bloom out of the canyon wall in fascinating hanging gardens. This is the park's most popular trail; it is paved and suitable for baby strollers and for wheelchairs with assistance. A round-trip walk takes about an hour and a half. | Zion Canyon Scenic Dr., about 5 mi north of Canyon Junction.

Zion Canyon Visitor Center. Unlike most national park visitor centers, which are filled with indoor displays, the center at Zion presents almost all of its visitor information in an appealing outdoor exhibit area. Beneath shade trees beside a gurgling brook, displays help you plan your stay in the park and introduce you to the geology, flora, and fauna of the area. | At the South Entrance to the park | 435/772–3256 | www. nps.gov/zion | Apr.–Oct., daily 8–7; Nov.–Mar., daily 8–5.

Zion Human History Museum. For a complete overview of the park with special attention to human history, stop at the museum. Exhibits explain how humans interacted with the geology, wildlife, plants, and unpredictable weather in the canyon. Displays focus on the human history of Zion Canyon from prehistory to the present. | Zion Canyon Scenic Dr., about 1 mi north of the South Entrance | 435/772–3256 | www.nps.gov/zion | May–Sept.

Dining

Zion Lodge Restaurant. American. Photographs of the early days of this national park make interesting study while waiting for a table in the dining room. The casual lunch fare includes sandwiches, burgers, and sack lunches for hikers. Dinner choices include pastas, chicken-fried steak, and some seafood. You can eat on the porch for a grand view. Reservations are essential from June through August. | Zion Canyon Scenic Dr., 3.2 mi north of Canyon Junction | 435/772–3213 | MC, V | $$–$$$

Lodging

Zion Lodge. Knotty pine woodwork and log and wicker furnishings accent the lobby. Lodge rooms are modern but not fancy. The historic Western-style cabins (which date from the 1930s) have gas-log fireplaces. This is a place of quiet retreat, so there are no televisions. The lodge is within walking distance of trailheads, horseback riding, and, of course, the shuttle stop. This popular destination requires reservations at least six months in advance. Restaurant; no room TVs. | Zion Canyon Scenic Dr., 3.2 mi north of Canyon Junction | 435/772–3213 or 303/297–2757 | fax 435/772–2001 | www.zionlodge. com | 121 rooms | AE, D, DC, MC, V | $–$$

WASHINGTON

THE SEATTLE LOOP
A VOLCANO AND WINE TOUR

Distance: approximately 530 mi   Time: 4–7 days
Overnight breaks: Mt. Rainier National Park, Vancouver, Yakima

This is a fun tour that will take you to the two tallest volcanic peaks in Washington, Mt. Rainier and Mt. Adams, and to the most violent, Mt. St. Helens, which blew its top in 1980 and still rumbles occasionally. Along the way you can opt to tour the Yakima Valley with its numerous wineries.

   Before setting out on a winery tour, obtain the most recent free edition of the Washington Wine Commission's guide booklet, *Touring the Washington Wine Country,* by contacting the Commission at 206/667–9463 or wawinectr@aol.com. Alternately, you can contact Appellation Yakima Valley at 866/846–9881 for a copy of the guide or pick one up at Sagelands, the first winery you'll encounter on the route.

❶ Begin your tour in **Seattle.**

❷ From Seattle, head south on I-5 to Route 7. Continue south on Route 7 to Elbe and turn onto Route 706 to reach **Longmire,** the main southern gateway to Mt. Rainier National Park. Be sure to fill up your car before you enter the mountains; the few gas stations in the backcountry charge a premium for gasoline. You can check the weather forecast on AM 710 or AM 1000. You might also want to tune in AM 1610, the radio frequency on which the state broadcasts warnings (if you hear only static that's good news: nothing bad is happening).

❸ **Mt. Rainier National Park** has celebrated its 100th anniversary, despite fears that it is being trampled to death because too many visitors walk its trails and crush its wildflower meadows. If you're worried about summer crowds, you might want to approach the mountain from the northeast, via Route 410 from Enumclaw. This winding road takes you past the Sunrise entrance of the park, and over Cayuse and Chinook passes down the Naches Valley—an ancient route over the Cascades used by Indians and American immigrants—to Yakima. It also has a picnic area with wildflowers and some great views of the mountain if you don't have time to stop and hike. The advantage of having taken the southern route, however, is that you

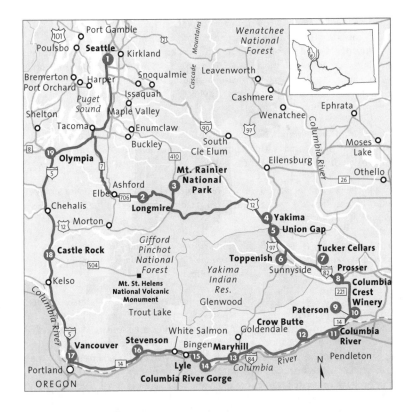

can stay at either Longmire or Paradise, in the shadow of the mountain. Reservations are essential in this area, especially in summer.

4 After you've had your fill of the park head east, cross the Cascade Crest on U.S. 12 through White Pass, and descend the Tieton River Valley to the Naches River and head south on I–82 into **Yakima,** a pleasant but sprawling agricultural metropolis. Yakima is the gateway to Washington wine country, and therefore another perfect place for an overnight stay.

Note that the drive from Mt. Rainier to Yakima is about 100 mi and, because of winding roads, may take as much as three hours. Give yourself plenty of time to stop and look around, since both of the pass roads wind through spectacular scenery. The tall mountain looming to the south is Mt. Adams, at 12,276 feet, Washington's second-tallest mountain.

5 When you're finished exploring Yakima, head southeast on I–82 for about 5 mi to **Union Gap** and take Exit 40 to Wine Country Road. Nearly all of the Yakima Valley wineries are situated within 1 or 2 mi of this road, which winds through the valley to Hogue Cellars (Exit 82 in Prosser). The **Sagelands** is the first winery you'll come to; here you can pick up the most recent Washington Wine Commission booklet to help you choose which wineries you'll visit. Among the wineries you don't want to miss are **Kiona, Hogue, Chinook, Hinzerling** (Washington's oldest family-owned winery—still housed in a converted garage), **Portteus,** and **Covey Run.** The latter sits high up on a slope north of **Zillah,** with great views of the valley (which should, in spring, be white with apple, cherry, or apricot blossoms or pink with blooming peach trees), the green Horse Heaven Hills, and the snowcapped peak of Mt. Adams.

Note that if you don't plan on visiting any wineries, you can shorten your trip by heading south to the Columbia Gorge by taking U.S. 97 for approximately 25 mi from Union Gap to Toppenish, and then traveling another 60 mi across the Horse Heaven Hills via Satus Pass to Goldendale and Maryhill. Pick up the itinerary at Maryhill and continue west through the gorge.

❻ After you finish exploring Wine Country Road, make a stop at the excellent tribal museum at the Yakama Nation Cultural Center in **Toppenish** (you can't miss it; follow signs directing you to the casino).

❼ In addition, you might want to stop at **Tucker Cellars,** off U.S. 12 just east of **Sunny-side,** and buy fresh Yakima Valley asparagus (some of the best in the West) at this winery's farm stand.

❽ The Yakima Valley is level and only some 80 mi long, giving you plenty of time to slow down and explore (there are 40 wineries just in this valley). From Toppenish, head south on Route 22 for about 35 mi to **Prosser.**

❾ From Prosser, take Route 221 south across the **Horse Heaven Hills** to **Paterson** on the Columbia River (about 26 mi or 40 minutes). Don't look for a "town" at Paterson. All you'll find are a couple of houses and a highway junction. Be sure to fill up your car here; there will be no gas station for more than 100 mi. This road winds steeply up the hillside from Prosser. Stop at turnouts for great views of the Yakima Valley. Once you've reached the top, you'll find yourself on a rolling plain of wheat. A century ago, these hills were covered with bunch grass and wild horses ran free.

❿ Before you descend to the river, you might want to stop at **Columbia Crest winery.** This facility looks like a French country château and is known for its red wines.

⓫ From Paterson, turn right/east (downriver) on Route 14 and you'll run into the **Columbia River.** At this point the river runs through a steep-walled rock-sided canyon that's green for only a short time in spring (except for irrigated fields, vineyards, and orchards).

⓬ The next stop is **Crow Butte,** 14 mi west of Paterson in the Umatilla National Wildlife Refuge. Take a trail to the top (370 feet above the river) and see some great views of the river—which is contained here by John Day Dam and also known as Lake Wallula—and of local wildlife. At the foot of the butte are dunes and a sandy beach. Best of all, in summer the water is warm enough for swimming.

⓭ From Crow Butte, Route 14 runs west to **Maryhill** (Paterson to Maryhill is 65 mi; two hours of driving time if you don't stop at Crow Butte). Take the short detour on U.S. 97 up the hill to the Flemish château at the **Maryhill Museum of Art.** It has a spectac-ular view of river and mountains and an equally spectacular collection of Rodin sculp-tures. Nearby is **Maryhill Winery,** the state's newest destination winery.

⓮ Return to Route 14 and enter the **Columbia Gorge.** The gorge is some 80 mi long and has some truly beautiful scenery. As you drive down the Washington side of the river, you'll get a good view of the tall waterfalls dropping from the cliffs of the Oregon side. The Washington side has fewer falls, because here the rock tilted and caused massive landslides, which has led, instead, to white-water rivers raging down from the mountains.

🚖 One such river, the **Klickitat,** still has Indian fishing scaffolds near **Lyle** (30 mi, 40 minutes west of Maryhill on Route 14). In season (usually fall) you can watch Native Americans dip-netting salmon here.

🚖 From Lyle continue downriver on Route 14, through Bingen (which has a winery), to **Stevenson,** which has an excellent interpretive center about the gorge. That 28-mi drive should take about 40 minutes. West of Skamania, 834-foot-tall Beacon Rock has a trail to the top with great views of the gorge.

🚖 From Beacon Rock, continue downriver to **Vancouver** (Stevenson to Vancouver is 50 mi or 1½ hours of driving time without stops). Vancouver was founded in 1825 by the Hudson's Bay Company as Fort Vancouver, a fur-trading depot. Today the modern city, 8 mi north of Portland, is flourishing following an extensive downtown renovation. Vancouver also has comfortable lodgings and is a good stopover before continuing to Mt. St. Helens.

🚖 After you've rested, take I–5 north to **Castle Rock** (48 mi north of Vancouver or about 50 minutes of driving time), then drive east on Route 504 to the Coldwater Ridge Visitor Center on the eastern edge of **Mt. St. Helens National Volcanic Monument.** At Castle Rock's **Cinedome Theater** (Exit 49 off I–5), a 30-minute film *The Eruption of Mount St. Helens* plays every 45 minutes from 9 AM to 6 PM.

🚖 Return to I–5 and drive north to Seattle via I–5 (116 mi or about two hours of driving time). You might want to take some extra time to visit the state capital of **Olympia.** Even if you decide to have dinner in Olympia, you can easily drive back to Seattle that evening (it's about an hour's drive from Olympia to Seattle, depending on traffic).

The Seattle Loop map

WASHINGTON RULES OF THE ROAD

License Requirements: Washington drivers must be at least 16 years old, possess a valid driver's license, and carry proof of insurance.

Right Turn on Red: Permitted throughout the state unless posted signs state otherwise.

Seat Belt and Helmet Laws: Seat belts are mandatory for the driver and for all passengers. Children four–six years old and 40–60 pounds must be strapped into approved safety seats. Motorcyclists must wear helmets.

Speed Limits: Speed limits on highways and interstates vary from 60 to 70 mph. Follow posted signs.

For More Information: Call the **Traffic Safety Commission** | 360/753–6197.

Castle Rock/Kelso

Castle Rock. The site takes its name from a tree-covered knob that once stood on the banks of the Cowlitz River and served as a navigational landmark for Hudson's Bay Company trappers and traders. The landscape changed dramatically when the 1980 Mt. St. Helens eruption filled the Toutle and Cowlitz Rivers with hot volcanic mush. Castle Rock's location on I–5 at the Spirit Lake Highway makes it a major point of entry for the Mt. St. Helens National Volcanic Monument. | Visitor center: Rte. 504 | 360/274–2100.

Kelso Visitor and Volcanic Information Center. Stop here for directions to Mt. St. Helens and information on its sights and amenities. | 105 Minor Rd. | 360/577–8058 | fax 360/578–2660 | Free | May–Oct., daily 8–6; Nov.–Apr., Wed.–Sun. 9–5.

Mt. St. Helens National Volcanic Monument. This 8,365-foot-high mountain is one of a string of volcanic Cascade Range peaks. The mountain is most easily reached via the Spirit Lake Memorial Highway (Route 504), which has unparalleled views of the mountain and the surrounding Toutle River Valley. Stop at the Mt. St. Helens Visitor Center at mile-marker 5 to pick up maps. You can also hire guides here to take you into the volcano's blast zone for overnight camping. Weyerhauser/Hoffstadt Bluff Visitors Center (Route 504, 27 mi east of I–5) is run by Cowlitz County and has the only full-service restaurant along the highway. The Coldwater Ridge Visitor Center, at mile-marker 43, documents the 1980 eruption and the devastation it wrought on the Toutle River Valley. Johnson Ridge Observatory, 53 mi east of I–5, has the most spectacular views of the crater and lava dome. Also, be sure to check out Ape Cave, the longest lava tube in the Americas at 12,810 feet. Passes to the park are available at visitor centers and Cascade Peaks Restaurant and Gift Shop on Forest Road 99. The Northwest Forest Pass, $5 per vehicle per day, is required to park at trailheads, visitor centers and other forest facilities. | Rte. 504 | 360/247–3900 general info, 360/274–2100 for Mt. St. Helens Visitor Center, 360/274–2131 for Coldwater Ridge Visitor Center | $3 per day per facility or $6 per day for a multicenter pass.

Maryhill

Maryhill Museum of Art. An oddity in the wilds of the Columbia River canyon, this is a first-rate Flemish château–style museum high on a bluff overlooking the river. It was built in the 1920s by railroad magnate Sam Hill; today it holds, among other things, an excellent collection of Rodin sculptures. | 35 Maryhill Museum Dr. | 509/773–3733 | fax 509/773–6138 | www.maryhillmuseum.org | $7 | Mid-Mar.–mid-Nov., daily 9–5.

Maryhill Winery. Washington's newest destination winery has panoramic views of the Columbia River and Mt. Hood. This is a great place to stop as you wind your way to Vancouver. | 9774 Rte. 14 | 509/773–1976 | www.maryhillwinery.com | Daily 10–6.

Mt. Adams Recreation Area. This 12,276-foot-tall mountain, northwest of Goldendale, is enclosed by a wilderness area and by the Yakama Indian Reservation. Camping and hiking is permitted in the latter only by permission of the tribe; call the Mt. Adams Ranger Station or the tribe's Forestry Development Program for information. | Between Yakima Valley and Columbia Gorge | 509/395–2501 Mt. Adams Ranger Station, 509/865–5121 Ext. 657 Forestry Development Program | fax 509/395–3424 | $5 | July–Sept. dawn–dusk.

Mt. Rainier National Park

★ **Grove of the Patriarchs.** A small island of 1,000-year-old trees in the Ohanapecosh River, protected from the fires that have afflicted surrounding areas, is one of the park's most stunning features. A 2-mi loop trail that begins west of the Stevens Canyon entrance heads over a small bridge through an old-growth forest.

Longmire Museum. Glass cases here display samples of preserved plants and stuffed animals from Mt. Rainier National Park, including the friendliest-looking cougar you're ever bound to see. | Rte. 706, 6 mi east of Nisqually entrance, Longmire | 360/569-2211 Ext. 3314 | Free with park admission | July–Labor Day, daily 9–5; Labor Day–June, daily 9–4:15.

Rainier Mountaineering. This highly regarded mountaineering school teaches the fundamentals of mountaineering at one-day classes held during the climbing season, which lasts from late May through early September. | Ashford | 360/569-2227 or 888/892-5462 | www.rmiguides.com.

Sunrise Visitor Center. Heading north from the Grove of the Patriarchs, you'll reach the White River and the Sunrise Visitor Center, from which you can watch the alpenglow fade from Mt. Rainier's summit. The center has exhibits on this region's alpine and subalpine ecology. | 70002 Rte. 410 E, Enumclaw | 360/569-2211 Ext. 2357 | July 4–Oct. 1, daily 9–6.

Trail of Shadows. The $\frac{1}{2}$-mi trail, which begins just across the road from the National Park Inn, passes colorful soda springs, James Longmire's old homestead cabin, and the foundation of the old Longmire Springs Hotel, which was destroyed around the turn of the 20th century.

Dining
Paradise Inn. American. The full-service dining room at the Paradise Inn serves simple, healthy dishes, such as salmon and salads for lunch, and heavier fare, including bourbon buffalo meat loaf, Mediterranean chicken, and poached salmon with blackberry sauce for dinner. The lodge also has a small snack bar and a cozy lounge. | Rte. 706, Ashford | 360/569-2275 | AE, D, DC, MC, V | Closed Nov.–mid-May | $–$$

Lodging
Cowlitz River Lodge. The location can't be beat here at this comfortable two-story family motel off the highway in Packwood, the southeastern gateway to Mt. Rainier National Park. Cable TV, hot tub, conference room, laundry facilities. | 13069 U.S. 12, 98361 | 360/494-4444 or 888/305-2185 | fax 360/494-2075 | www.escapetothemountains.com | 32 rooms | AE, DC, MC, V | CP | $

National Park Inn. A large stone fireplace is the centerpiece of the common room at this otherwise generic country inn, one of only two in the park, and the only year-round lodging. The small rooms mix functionality with such backwoods touches as wrought-iron lamps and antique bentwood headboards. A large restaurant serves decent American fare. The inn is 6 mi east of the Nisqually entrance. Restaurant, shop; no a/c, no room phones. | Rte. 706, 98304 | 360/569-2275 | 25 rooms, 18 with bath | MC, V | BP (in winter) | $–$$

Paradise Inn. With its hand-carved Alaskan cedar logs, decorative woodwork designed by German architect Hans Fraehnke, polished parquet floors, stone fireplaces, and glorious mountain views, this 1917 inn is loaded with charm. Restaurant, snack bar, lounge, shop. | Rte. 706, Ashford 98304 | 360/569-2275 | fax 360/569-2770 | www.guestservices.com/rainier | 127 rooms, 96 with bath | AE, D, DC, MC, V | Closed Nov.–mid-May | $–$$

Olympia
★**Capitol Campus.** Olympia's main attraction is the cluster of buildings on a bluff above Capitol Lake. The grounds surrounding the Legislative Building contain memorials, monuments, rose gardens (at their best in summer), and Japanese cherry trees (usually in glorious bloom by March). The 1920s Conservatory is open year-round on weekdays

from 8 to 3 and also on weekends in summer. | Legislative Bldg., Capitol Way between 10th and 14th Aves. | 360/586–8687 | Free | Tours daily on the hr 10–3.

Downtown. Compared to the elegance of the capitol campus, the area north (downhill) of the state capitol and the government office buildings, used to appear grungy, until about 10 years ago, when young people moved in and revitalized the urban core. There's now a healthy sprinkling of cafés, used-book stores, record shops, and boutiques. The lively Olympia Farmer's Market, on Capitol Way near the Port of Olympia, is open April–December, Thursday–Sunday. At night, there's a lively (and safe) bar scene. Part of downtown is on a peninsula, which reaches into Budd Inlet to the north, with its working waterfront.

Olympic National Forest. This forest surrounds Olympic National Park on the east, south, and northwest sides. There's lots to do here, from the excellent trout fishing to hiking. It can be reached from many roads which branch off U.S. 101. From Olympia, it's best to take I–5 to U.S. 101 northeast to Exit 104. | 360/956–2400 | fax 360/956–2430 | www.fs.fed.uf/r6/olympic | Free | Headquarters: May–Sept., weekdays 8–4:30.

Yashiro Japanese Garden. A symbol of the sister-city relationship between Olympia and Yashiro, Japan, this garden has a waterfall, a bamboo grove, a koi pond, and stone lanterns. | Union and Plum Sts. | no phone | Free | Daily dawn–dusk.

Dining

Ben Moore's Cafe. American/Casual. This old-fashioned café serves such homey fare as oyster and geoduck (a huge, tasty northwestern clam) tempura, plus the ubiquitous hamburgers and microbrews. | 112 4th Ave. | 360/357–7527 | MC, V | $–$$

Falls Terrace. American. This elegant, multilevel restaurant has large windows offering an unobstructed view of the cascading Tumwater Falls. Steaks, burgers, and seafood are as fancy as the food gets. There is dining on the deck, but you have to be over 21. | 106 S. Deschutes Way | 360/943–7830 | AE, D, DC, MC, V | $$–$$$$

The Fishbowl Brew Pub. American/Casual. Great beer and great nibbles, such as whole-wheat-crust pizzas, are to be had at this pub across the street from—and affiliated with—Fish Brewing Company. | 515 Jefferson Ave. | 360/943–3650 | MC, V | $–$$

Wagner's. Café. Wagner's, both a bakery and a deli, is a local landmark, serving sumptuous pastries and delectable sandwiches. | 1013 Capitol Way | 360/357–7268 | MC, V | ¢–$

Prosser

Chinook Wines. East of Prosser is a small family winery run by Kay Simon and Clay Mackey, vintners regionally renowned for splendid merlot, chardonnay, and sauvignon blanc wines created specifically to complement Northwest cuisine. | Wine Country Rd. east of I–82 | 509/786–2725 | May–Oct., weekends noon–5.

Chukar Cherry Company. You haven't lived until you've devoured a box of chocolate-covered Chukar cherries. The family-owned farm store carries dried and chocolate-covered cherries and berries, preserves, and pie filling. | 320 Wine Country Rd. | 509/786–2055 or 800/624–9544 | www.chukar.com | Mon.–Sat. 8–6, Sun. 10–5.

Hinzerling Vineyards. The oldest family-owned winery in the Yakima Valley specializes in estate-grown cabernet and late-harvest gewürztraminer and Riesling wines. A small two-room inn and restaurant (serving boarding house–style dinners Friday and Saturday) are located on the property. | 1520 Sheridan Ave., off Wine Country Rd. | 509/786–2163 | www.hinzerling.com | Daily 11–5.

Hogue Cellars. Numerous awards have been bestowed upon Hogue Cellars, which is a few blocks east of Chinook. There's a tasting room here, along with picnic areas and a gift shop that carries Hogue wines—cabernet sauvignon, merlot, and fumé blanc among them—and the family's famous pickled beans and asparagus. | Wine Country Rd. at I–82, Exit 82 | 509/786–4557 | Daily 10–5.

Pontin del Roza. This winery is named for its owners, the Pontin family, and the grape-friendly southern slopes of the Yakima Valley, known as the Roza. The winery produces Rieslings, chenin blancs, chardonnays, sauvignon blancs, and cabernet sauvignons. | 35502 N. Hinzerling Rd. | 509/786–4449 | Daily 10–5.

Yakima River Winery. Owners John and Louise Rauner began making wine under the Yakima River label in 1977. Today the winery specializes in barrel-aged red wines and dessert wines. | 143302 N. River Rd., off Wine Country Rd. | 509/786–2805 | www.yakimariverwinery.com | Daily 9–5.

Dining
Wine Country Inn. This restaurant alongside the Yakima River serves lunch, dinner, and Sunday brunch in a pretty spot overlooking the grass- and tree-lined banks of the Yakima River. In warm weather you can dine on an old-fashioned porch. Choose from classic American soups and salads, and meat and vegetable dishes. | 1106 Wine Country Rd. | 509/786–2855 | AE, MC, V | No dinner Mon.–Tues. | $–$$

Seattle
Capitol Hill. With its mix of theaters and churches, coffeehouses and nightclubs, stately homes and student apartments, Capitol Hill demonstrates Seattle's diversity better than any other neighborhood—Seattle's youth culture, old money, and gay scene all converge on the lively stretch of Broadway East between East Denny Way and East Roy Street.

Experience Music Project. Seattle's most controversial landscape addition is a 140,000-square-foot interactive museum celebrating American popular music. Exhibits include a Jimi Hendrix gallery containing the world's largest collection of Hendrix memorabilia. | 5th Ave. between Broad and Thomas Sts. | 206/770–2700 | www.emplive.com | $19.95 | May 23–Sept.1, Sun.–Thurs. 9–6, Fri. and Sat. 9–9; rest of yr, daily 9–5.

★ **Pike Place Market.** Besides a number of restaurants, you'll find booths selling fresh seafood, produce, cheese, Northwest wines, bulk spices, tea, coffee, and arts and crafts. Although wandering at will is fun, you can get a free market map (available at several locations around the market) to help you get around. | Pike Pl. at Pike St., west of 1st Ave. | 206/682–7453 | www.pikeplacemarket.org | Mon.–Sat. 9–6, Sun. 11–5.

Seattle Art Museum. Postmodern architect Robert Venturi designed this five-story museum to be a work of art in itself. The museum's extensive collection surveys Asian, Native American, African, Oceanic, and pre-Columbian art. | 100 University St. | 206/654–3255 | www.seattleartmuseum.org | $7; free 1st Thurs. of month | Tues.–Sun. 10–5 (Thurs. until 9).

Space Needle. The distinctive exterior of the remodeled 520-foot-high Space Needle can be seen from almost any Downtown spot. The view (especially at sunset) from the inside out is even better. The observation deck, a 42-second elevator ride from street level, yields 360-degree vistas of the entire region. | 5th Ave. and Broad St. | 206/443–2111 or 800/937–9582 | www.spaceneedle.com | $11 | Sun.–Thurs. 9 AM–11 PM, Fri.–Sat. 9 AM–midnight.

Washington Park Arboretum. The 230-acre arboretum has more than 40,000 native and exotic trees, shrubs, and vines, belonging to some 4,800 different species and cultivars. | 2300 Arboretum Dr. E | 206/543–8800 | depts.washington.edu/wpa | Free | Park daily 7 AM–sunset; visitor center daily 10–4.

Dining

★**Dahlia Lounge.** Contemporary. Romantic Dahlia worked its magic on Tom Hanks and Meg Ryan in *Sleepless in Seattle.* Crab cakes, served as an entrée or an appetizer, lead an ever-changing regionally oriented menu. Other standouts are seared ahi tuna and near-perfect gnocchi. | 2001 4th Ave. | 206/682–4142 | Reservations essential | AE, D, DC, MC, V | No lunch weekends | \$\$–\$\$\$\$

El Puerco Lloron. Mexican. This funky, cafeteria-style diner has some open-air terrace seating on the Pike Place Market Hillclimb, offering views of Elliott Bay on sunny days. It's also got some of Seattle's best and most authentic Mexican cooking—simple, tasty, and inexpensive. | 501 Western Ave. | 206/624–0541 | AE, MC, V | \$

Gravity Bar. Vegetarian. Sprout-filled sandwiches and other healthful foods are dished up at this congenial juice bar with a sci-fi–industrial ambience. | 415 Broadway E | 206/325–7186 | No credit cards | ¢–\$

Siam. Thai. Thai cooking is so ubiquitous in Seattle that it almost can be considered mainstream cuisine. With this amount of competition it's a testament to Siam that it's so popular. Start your meal with the city's best *tom kah gai*, a soup of coconut, lemongrass, chicken, and mushrooms, or the satay. | 616 Broadway | 206/324–0892 | AE, MC, V | No lunch weekends | \$

Stevenson

Columbia Gorge Interpretive Center. Dwarfed by the dramatic basalt cliffs that rise behind it, this museum stands on the north bank of the Columbia River Gorge, 1 mi east of Bridge of the Gods on Route 14. Exhibits illustrate the geology and history of the region. | 990 S.W. Rock Creek Dr. | 509/427–8211 or 800/991–2338 | \$6 | Daily 10–5.

Dining

Dining Room at Skamania Lodge. American/Casual. The wood ceilings, booths, and floors of this cavernous dining room give it a warm glow. Two miles east of the Bridge of the Gods on Highway 14, the restaurant overlooks the Columbia River Gorge. Salmon, crab cakes, scrumptious rack of lamb, and prime rib are some of the dishes cooked in the wood-burning oven. | Skamania Lodge Way | 509/427–7700 | Reservations essential | AE, D, DC, MC, V | \$\$–\$\$\$

Sunnyside

Tucker Cellars. Tucker makes 20,000 gallons of wine—cabernet sauvignon, chardonnay, Riesling, gewürztraminer, and muscat canelli—each year. The Tucker family market, a roadside farm stand east of Sunnyside on U.S. 12, sells splendid homegrown fruits and vegetables. | 70 Ray Rd., off Yakima Valley Hwy. | 509/837–8701 | Apr.–Oct., daily 9–5; Nov.–Mar., daily 9–4:30.

Washington Hills. Brian Carter, one of Washington's most respected wine makers, crafts Washington Hills, Apex, and W. B. Bridgman wines—several whites, a red, and a blush—here. You can picnic in the winery's English gardens. | 111 E. Lincoln Ave., off Yakima Valley Hwy. | 509/839–9463 | Daily 11–5:30.

Dining

Dykstra House. American. In a wine valley with, as yet, few restaurants, the Dykstra house in Grandview has held its own for more than a decade. The food served in this

1914 mansion is simple and flavorful. Friday night dinners are Italian; the grand Saturday night dinners revolve around chicken, beef, or fish. The wines come from nearby Yakima Valley vineyards. | 114 Birch Ave. | 509/882–2082 | Reservations essential | AE, D, DC, MC, V | Closed Sun.–Mon. No dinner Tues.–Thurs. | $$–$$$

El Conquistador. Mexican. The broad menu at this Mexican restaurant includes everything from burritos and fajitas to shrimp sautéed with green peppers and onions and served with a tangy salsa. | 612 E. Edison Ave. | 509/839–2880 | MC, V | No lunch | ¢–$

Taco Wagons. Tex-Mex. These large vans usually position themselves at street corners at lunch and dinner times, or head for the fields and processing plants. The fare they dish up is simple, tasty, and inexpensive: soft tacos, made from handmade tortillas. It's difficult to find food this good and fresh at most area restaurants. | ¢

Tillicum Restaurant. American. A favorite spot among locals, this eatery has a traditional range of dishes including steaks, seafood, barbecued ribs, and pastas. But what Sunnyside residents prefer over everything else is the succulent prime rib. | 410 Yakima Valley Hwy. | 509/837–7222 | AE, D, MC, V | $–$$

Toppenish

American Hop Museum. The United States' only hop museum, this center focuses on the history of the hop industry. Among the many items on display are antique tools and implements, photographs, and memorabilia. | 22 S. B St. | 509/865–4677 | www.americanhopmuseum.com | Donation | May–Sept., daily 11–4.

Fort Simcoe Historical State Park. These residential quarters of an old army fort, erected in 1856, look more like a Victorian summer retreat than a military establishment. This 200-acre day-use heritage park on the Yakama Indian Reservation has an interpretive center and two officers' buildings open to the public. | 5150 Fort Simcoe Rd. | 509/874–2372 | www.parks.wa.gov | Free | Apr.–Sept., daily 6:30 AM–dusk; Oct.–Mar., weekends 8 AM–dusk.

Murals. The Toppenish Mural Association began commissioning murals in 1989 to draw commerce to the small town. The resulting 60-plus colorful paintings throughout the town, in a variety of styles by artists from around the region, commemorate the town's history and Western spirit. You'll find mural visitor guides and tour maps at Toppenish businesses, the Mural Society Visitors Center (across Toppenish Avenue from Old Timers Plaza) and Chamber of Commerce offices.

Yakama Nation Cultural Heritage Center. This museum tells the story of the Yakama nation; a huge longhouse serves as ceremonial center for dance performances and social functions. | South on U.S. 97 | 509/865–2800 | fax 509/865–5749 | $4 | Daily 8–5.

Union Gap

Sagelands Vineyard. This winery, east of Union Gap, is owned by California's Chalone Group and produces cabernet sauvignon, merlot, pinot noir, and chardonnay. The main building has a huge stone fireplace and a commanding view of the upper valley. Outside is a pleasant picnic area, flanked by roses. | 71 Gangl Rd., off Thorpe–Parker Rd. | 509/877–2112 | Mar.–Oct., daily 11–5:30; Nov.–Feb., daily noon–5.

Dining

Miner's Drive-in. American/Casual. This local landmark is always busy. Fast service and a large menu keep customers satisfied; the restaurant cooks everything to order. There's both indoor and outdoor seating. The drive-in is open late for those logging long hours on the road. | 2415 S. 1st St. | 509/457–8194 | AE, DC, MC, V | ¢–$

Vancouver

Clark County Historical Museum. Indian artifacts, the first piano north of the Columbia (built in 1836), an 1890 country store, a 1900 doctor's office, and more are on display here. | 1511 Main St. | 360/695–4681 | Free | Tues.–Sat. 11–4.

Columbia River Waterfront Trail. Bike, skate, jog, or stroll the 4 mi promenade that follows the Columbia River. Visit the Old Apple Tree along the way and stop to enjoy the scenic vistas. | Wintler Park | 360/696–8171.

Fort Vancouver National Historic Site. This splendidly reconstructed fort, with squared-log buildings, an encircling palisade, and corner bastions, was first established here by the Hudson's Bay Company in 1825. In summer, park rangers dress in period costume and demonstrate various pioneer skills. | 1501 E. Evergreen Blvd. | 360/696–7655 | www.nps.gov | Free | Daily.

Gifford Pinchot National Forest. A vast forest of evergreens stretches from Mt. St. Helens east to Mt. Adams, and north to Mt. Rainier. This is one of the oldest forests in Washington and is named for the first Chief of the Forest Service. It is accessible via Routes 14, 25, or 503. | Forest Headquarters 10600 N.E. 51st Cir. | Free | Daily.

Pearson Air Museum. This museum display vintage aircraft—often in working order. | 1115 E. 5th St. | 360/694–7026 | fax 360/694–0824 | www.pearsonairmuseum.org | $5 | Tues.–Sun. 10–5.

Dining

Beaches Restaurant. American/Casual. This restaurant, directly on the water, has gorgeous views up and down the river. The menu includes pastas, wood-fired-oven pizzas, fresh fish, steak, and salads. In the summer, the restaurant gets really lively with antique-car cruise-ins and beach volleyball games. | 1919 S.E. Columbia River Dr. | 360/699–1592 or 503/222–9947 | AE, D, DC, MC, V | $–$$$

Hudson's Bar & Grill. American. Don't let the "Bar & Grill" in Hudson's name lead you astray. This happens to be Vancouver's most notable restaurant offering fine dining at Heathman Lodge. Executive chef Mark Hosak creates noteworthy Northwest cuisine, such as Dungeness crab–stuffed halibut and oven-roasted venison. | 7801 N.W. Greenwood Dr. | 360/254–3100 or 888/475–3100 | AE, D, DC, MC, V | $$–$$$$

Puffin Cafe. Caribbean. Just 16 mi east of Vancouver in Washougal is a funky little floating restaurant hidden among the docks of the Port of Camas-Washougal Marina. Locals flock here for festive open-air dining or a quick bite after they haul in their boats. Ample portions of coconut shrimp, zesty fish tacos, and other Caribbean-style offerings make for a fine day at the beach indeed. | 14 S. A St. | 360/335–1522 | MC, V | $–$$

Lodging

Heathman Lodge. From the Tempur-pedic ultracomfy mattresses to the restaurant, which is worth a visit in itself, Heathman Lodge aims to spoil its guests. Though it's only five minutes away from Westfield Shoppingtown Vancouver, the alpine-style lodge with massive hand-hewn logs manages to feel secluded from its urban surroundings. Restaurant, in-room data ports, microwaves, minibars, in-room hot tubs, cable TV, in-room VCRs, indoor pool, gym, hot tub, sauna, video game room. | 7801 N.W. Greenwood Dr., 98662 | 360/254–3100 or 888/475–3100 | fax 360/254–6100 | www.heathmanlodge.com | 121 rooms, 22 suites | AE, D, DC, MC, V | $–$$

Shilo Inn–Downtown Vancouver. In the heart of downtown, this hotel is close to the Vancouver National Historic Site and is directly off I–5. There are several restaurants within walking distance. Some microwaves, some minibars, cable TV, pool, gym, hot tub, sauna, steam room, laundry service, business services, some pets allowed (fee).

| 401 E. 13th St., 98660 | 360/696–0411 or 800/222–2244 | fax 360/750–0933 | www.shiloinns.com | 118 rooms | AE, D, DC, MC, V | CP | $

Vintage Inn. This 1903 Craftsman-style mansion sits in the heart of downtown, close to the Vancouver National Historic Reserve and many restaurants. Antiques fill all the rooms to the extent that some refer to it as a small museum. A working fireplace occupies one room, while in another French doors lead to a sleeping porch. No room phones, TV in common area, no smoking. | 310 W. 11th St., 98660 | 360/693–6635 or 888/693–6635 | www.vintage-inn.com | 4 rooms | MC, V | BP | $

Yakima

Historic North Front Street. Yakima's old Northern Pacific Depot (1910) looks a bit like a California mission that got lost on a trip north. Today it houses America's oldest brew pub. Other old business buildings line Front Street, across from the depot. Nearby downtown buildings of historic interest include the 1915 Miller Building (E. Yakima Ave. and N. 2nd St.), the U.S. Post Office (S. 3rd and Chestnut Sts.), the 1915 Masonic Temple (321 E. Yakima Ave.), St. Michael's Episcopal Church of 1889 (E. Yakima and S. Naches Aves.), and the Capital Theater (Yakima Ave. and N. Front St.). | 509/248–2021 | fax 509/248–0601 | Free | Daily.

Painted Rocks. Here, 7 mi northwest of Yakima, you'll see remnants of Native American pictographs, some of which were destroyed by a 19th-century irrigation project. | U.S. 12 | 509/248–2021.

White Pass Village. This full-service ski area southeast of Mt. Rainier has condominiums, a snack bar, a grocery store, and a gas station. It has a base elevation of 4,500 feet, a summit elevation of 6,000 feet, and a vertical drop of 1,500 feet. The open woods of the eastern slopes are popular with cross-country skiers. An all-day lift ticket is $37. | U.S. 12 | 509/672–3101 | fax 509/7672–3123 | www.skiwhitepass.com | Nov.–Apr.

Yakima Area Arboretum. The 46-acre arboretum, south of the river, has a small Japanese garden. It is part of a series of parks connected by a paved path along the river. The river's riparian woodland has a dense overstory, which makes for shady walking or biking in the heat of summer. | 1401 Arboretum Dr. | 509/248–7337 | fax 509/248–8197 | www.ahtrees.org | Free | Daily dawn–dusk.

Yakima Valley Museum. In addition to Yakama Indian clothing and beadwork, the museum, in Franklin Park, houses a comprehensive collection of horse-drawn vehicles, and a replica of Chief Justice William O. Douglas's office. | 2105 Tieton Dr. | 509/248–0747 | fax 509/453–4890 | www.yakimavalleymuseum.org | $3 | Tues.–Sun. 11–5.

Dining

★ **Birchfield Manor.** Contemporary. This 1910 Yakima Valley farmhouse has the most elegant dining room in Washington wine country. Little has changed since it served as the mansion's sitting and dining room, and the owners have a knack for making you feel like you're visiting a private home for dinner. The owner/chef also knows Yakima Valley wines like few others. | 2018 Birchfield Rd. | 509/452–1960 | Reservations essential | Closed Sun.–Wed. | AE, DC, MC, V | $$$–$$$$

Deli De Pasta. Italian. The food is tasty and the atmosphere is very simpatico at this Italian café. | 7 N. Front St. | 509/453–0571 | AE, MC, V | Closed Sun. | $$–$$$$

Gasperetti's. Contemporary. Yakima's favorite socialite hangout offers comfortable, chic dining in its elegant space, dishing up such traditional fare as steak, as well as Italian and Northwest dishes featuring locally grown produce. | 1013 N. 1st St. | 509/248–0628 | AE, MC, V | Closed Sun.–Mon. No lunch Sat. | $–$$$

Grant's Brewery Pub. American/Casual. America's oldest brewpub is a Yakima institution. The usual pub grub—burgers, salads, sandwiches—accompanies the suds daily and there's live jazz on weekends. | 32 N. Front St. | 509/575–2922 | MC, V | $

Lodging

Apple Country Bed and Breakfast. From the windows of this 1911 Victorian, which sits in the middle of a working ranch, you can spy quail, pheasants, gophers, and even coyotes. The rooms, with a mixture of antiques and contemporary furnishings, have spectacular views of the valley. Cable TV, some in-room VCRs, laundry facilities, some pets allowed; no smoking. | 4561 Old Naches Hwy., 98937 | 509/972–3409 or 877/788–9963 | fax 509/965–1591 | www.applecountryinnbb.com | 3 rooms | D, MC, V | BP | $

★ **Birchfield Manor.** The only true luxury accommodation in the valley sits on a perfectly flat plateau in Moxee City, 2 mi outside Yakima, surrounded by fields and grazing cattle. The Old Manor House contains a great restaurant and four upstairs rooms. A newer cottage house maintains the country ambience while providing every modern convenience. Restaurant, pool; no kids under 8. | 2018 Birchfield Rd., 98901 | 509/452–1960 or 800/375–3420 | fax 509/452–2334 | www.birchfieldmanor.com | 11 rooms | AE, DC, MC, V | $$–$$$

Orchard Inn Bed and Breakfast. The name isn't just for show: this inn is in the middle of a true cherry orchard, in which you are invited to take strolls. You'll find the cherry theme throughout the contemporary house. It's 7 mi northwest of downtown Yakima. In-room hot tubs, laundry facilities; no smoking. | 1207 Pecks Canyon Rd., 98908 | 509/966–1283 or 888/858–8284 | www.orchardinnbb.com | 3 rooms | AE, D, MC, V | BP | $

Touch of Europe Bed and Breakfast Inn. The many charms of this gracious and well-preserved 1889 Queen Anne Victorian on the National Historic Register include the box-beam ceiling, extensive mill-work, and stained-glass windows. Guests are treated to fresh flowers, Italian chocolates, and baskets filled with fresh Yakima Valley fruit. Dining room; no kids under 17, no smoking. | 220 N. 16th Ave., 98902 | 509/454–9775 or 888/438–7073 | www.winesnw.com/toucheuropeb&b.htm | 3 rooms | AE, MC, V | BP | $–$$

FROM THE POWDER RIVER TO THE PARKS
SUNDANCE TO JACKSON HOLE

Distance: 488 mi   Time: Minimum 5 days
Overnight Breaks: Buffalo, Sheridan, Cody, Yellowstone National Park, Jackson

On this drive you'll see Wyoming's premier attractions, including Devils Tower, the first national monument; Yellowstone, the first national park; and other outstanding sites, from Grand Teton National Park to the world-class Buffalo Bill Historical Center; the Medicine Wheel, an ancient Native American ruin; and spectacular mountains, basins, and plains. For the best driving conditions, travel either in September and early October or late May and early June, when you'll encounter fewer cars and people; note that you won't be able to do this entire tour in winter as some of the roads close, particularly those in Yellowstone.

❶ Begin at **Sundance,** (I–90, Exit 187 or 189, 19 mi east of South Dakota) which introduces you to the region's Native American culture; the town is named not for the robber-bandit of movie fame, but for the Native American ritual held each summer. However, the Sundance Kid did spend time in jail in the town, which is where he earned his nickname.

❷ From Sundance take U.S. 14 north to Route 24 and follow Route 24 north to **Devils Tower,** which rises from the Belle Fourche River valley and is a sacred site for Native Americans. Popular with climbers, the tower has 7 mi of hiking trails, camping, picnicking, and a visitor center.

❸ Follow Route 24 back to U.S. 14 and proceed southwest to Moorcroft, where you pick up I–90 and proceed west to **Gillette** (Exit 132). This is a coal-mining town with great public facilities. Gillette is a great place to stop for lunch after a morning at Devils Tower. Continue your drive west on I–90 across the rolling grasslands of the Powder River Basin.

❹ Nearly 70 mi west of Gillette, at the intersection of I–90 and I–25, is **Buffalo,** which became nationally known in 1892 when cattlemen raised an "army" and invaded Johnson County in an attempt to eliminate rustlers. The cattlemen killed two

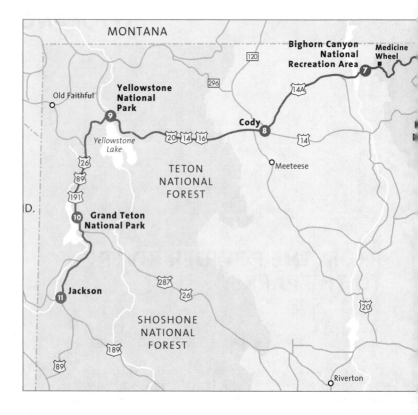

cowboys before Buffalo townspeople surrounded the invaders, who were subsequently rescued by the U.S. Army. Spend the night in Buffalo.

❺ When you're finished exploring Buffalo, continue on I–90 for about 12 mi to **Fort Phil Kearny** (Exit 44), a military post on the Bozeman Trail from 1864 to 1866. Nearby are the sites of the 1866 Fetterman Massacre and the 1867 Wagon Box battle. The fort has an interpretive center, and guides can direct you to the battle sites on Route 193 and U.S. 87. Take the latter to Big Horn and the Bradford Britton Memorial, which displays works by Charles Russell and Frederic Remington.

❻ From the battle sites, continue on U.S. 87 along the east face of the Bighorn Mountains for about 23 mi to **Sheridan** (I–90, Exit 20). Visit the King Museum and enjoy walking around the historic town center. Stay overnight in Sheridan.

❼ From Sheridan, head west on I–90 to Exit 9, where you get onto U.S. 14 and cross the Bighorn Mountains through the **Bighorn National Forest.** At Burgess Junction continue west on U.S. 14A to **Medicine Wheel,** where a short hike takes you to a Native American site. Then follow U.S. 14A down into the Bighorn Basin. The road is steep and curvy, so take it slow and enjoy the incredible view. **Bighorn Canyon National Recreation Area** is at the bottom of the mountain.

❽ Continue west on U.S. 14A for approximately 40 mi to **Cody** (U.S. 14A and U.S. 14/16/ 20). Cody is named for Wild West scout and showman Buffalo Bill Cody. One of the five major museums at the **Buffalo Bill Historical Center** focuses on his life. The five

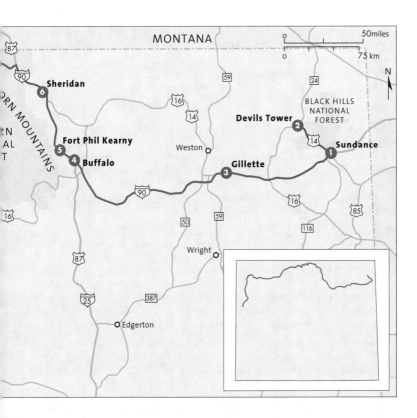

museums—the Plains Indian Museum, the Buffalo Bill Museum, the Cody Firearms Museum, the Draper Natural History Museum, and the Whitney Gallery of Western Art—are in the same complex and have outstanding collections and diverse activities. Consider an overnight in Cody.

The rest of this tour is about 177 mi and will take you through Yellowstone National Park and Grand Teton National Park and into the town of Jackson.

9 **Yellowstone National Park** (52 mi west of Cody on U.S. 14/16/20 or Rtes. 120 and 296) is America's first national park and has a deserved reputation as one of the best, with its boiling mud pots, steaming and spouting geysers, spectacular waterfalls, and diverse wildlife. The Yellowstone roads range from very good, with new pavement, to poor, with potholes, though thanks to improved funding there are more of the former and fewer of the latter. Plan to travel slowly on the basic figure-eight road system. If you travel early in the morning or late in the evening, you may see black or grizzly bears or wolves. Remember that all the animals in Yellowstone are wild; keep your distance. Find lodging in the park and spend the night.

10 **Grand Teton National Park** (south of Yellowstone National Park, north of Jackson on U.S. 26/89/191) encompasses the spectacular Grand Teton Mountain range and much of broad Jackson Hole. From either of the roads crossing the valley you can see the majestic Tetons, and you will often catch glimpses of the Snake River. You can hike, bike, fish, boat, ride horses, camp, and picnic. You may want to climb these mountains, but such excursions are only for skilled climbers. Companies in Jackson Hole can teach you the ropes—literally.

⑪ Continue south on Route 26/89/191 to **Jackson** (U.S. 189 and Rte. 22). It's compact, so you can park and walk to most hotels, motels, restaurants, and downtown attractions. The town has a Western flair and manages to maintain a folksy feeling most of the time. Stay overnight in Jackson.

The quickest way back to Sundance is to retrace your route.

Buffalo

Bighorn National Forest. The Bighorn Mountains—roughly between Buffalo and Tensleep in the south and Sheridan and Lovell in the north—make up one of the many huge areas of public land in north-central Wyoming. You can camp, hike, ride, fish, and in winter, snowmobile. The Cloud Peak Wilderness Area, with 189,000 acres, has enough room for backpacking and horse packing. Elevations range from 8,500 to 13,165 feet. | Buffalo Ranger District, 1425 Fort St., Buffalo | 307/684–1100 | www.fs.fed.us/r2/bighorn | Free | Daily.

Clear Creek Trail. Signs bearing a buffalo symbol mark the Clear Creek Trail, which includes about 11 mi of trails following Clear Creek through Buffalo and past historic areas. The trail has both paved and unpaved sections. Along the way you'll see the Occidental Hotel (made famous by novelist Owen Wister in *The Virginian*), a brewery and mill, and the site of Fort McKinney, now the Veterans' Home of Wyoming. You can walk, cycle, or skateboard on the trail. Pick up a map at the Chamber of Commerce. | 55 N. Main St. | 307/684–5544 or 800/227–5122.

Fort Phil Kearny Site. In 1866 the army established several forts along the Bozeman trail from central Wyoming to Montana's gold fields. Fort Phil Kearny was one of the posts established along the trail to protect travelers from skirmishes between the U.S. military and the Northern Plains Indians. The Native Americans opposed it fiercely, raided routinely, and won several decisive battles before forcing the military to withdraw from the region in 1868. Although the Native Americans promptly burned the fort, the site is now marked and the original foundations are still visible. | 528 Wagon Box Rd. | 307/684–7629 | $1 WY residents; $2 nonresidents | Mid-May–Sept., daily 8–6.

WYOMING RULES OF THE ROAD

License Requirements: To drive in Wyoming you must be at least age 16 and have a valid driver's license (15-year-olds with valid learner's permits may drive as long as there's a licensed driver over 18 in the front passenger seat).

Speed Limits: Wyoming speed limits are 65 mph on state and U.S. highways and 75 mph on interstate highways for all vehicles.

Right Turn on Red: Right turns on red are allowed throughout the state unless posted otherwise.

Seat Belt and Helmet Laws: Drivers must wear seat belts; child restraints are required for infants and children 8 years of age or younger and weighing 80 pounds or less.

Road and Travel Reports: Reports from Wyoming Department of Transportation (available October–April), provide the most up-to-date road conditions. Call 800/996–7623.

For More Information: Contact the **Wyoming Department of Transportation** | 307/777–4484 | http://dot.state.wy.us.

Jim Gatchell Museum of the West. You'll see detailed dioramas of the Powder River Basin Indian conflicts and the Johnson County Invasion of 1892 at this museum, which started as the private collection of a local resident. | 100 Fort St. | 307/684–9331 | www.jimgatchell.com | $4 | Mid-Apr.–Dec., daily 9–7; Dec.–mid-Apr., call for hrs.

Dining

Art Works Too & Cowgirl Coffee Cafe. American. This funky coffeehouse in an 1890s stone-front building is a popular local hangout. A backyard sitting area has its own sculpture garden. Try the organic coffee or tea with chips, fudge, biscotti, or brownies. | 94 S. Main St. | 307/684–1299 | D, MC, V | ¢

Colonel Bozeman's. Southwestern. Good food amid Western memorabilia is what you'll find at Colonel Bozeman's, which is on the Bozeman Trail. Favorites include the buffalo steak and the prime rib. Outdoor dining is available on the deck. | 675 E. Hart St. | 307/684–5555 | AE, D, MC, V | $-$$

Wagon Box Inn. American. This bright and spacious cabin in the Bighorn Mountains is surrounded by ponderosa pines. It serves steak, seafood, burgers, and sandwiches. The huge wine selection is unmatched in the area. It's 15 mi northwest of Buffalo on I–90. | 108 N. Piney Rd., Story | 307/683–2444 | AE, D, DC, MC, V | $$-$$$$

Lodging

Best Western Crossroads Inn. Near the Bighorn Mountains and I–25, this large, modern hotel has spacious rooms and convenient access to the interstate. Restaurant, pub, room service, in-room data ports, cable TV, outdoor pool, hot tub, recreation room, playground. | 75 N. Bypass, 82834 | 307/684–2256 | fax 307/684–2256 | www.bestwestern.com | 60 rooms | AE, D, MC, V | CP | $$

Blue Gables Motel. A cluster of small log cabins, each equipped with either two double beds or one queen-size bed, makes up the majority of this motel. There are also a grassy area for folks to set up their tents ($20 per night) and a two-bedroom house ($134 per night) you can rent by the night or by the week. Coffee shop, picnic area, some microwaves, some refrigerators, outdoor pool, laundry facilities, some pets allowed, no-smoking rooms; no room phones. | 662 N. Main St., 82834 | 307/684–2574 or 800/684–2574 | www.bluegables.com | 17 cabins, 1 house | D, MC, V | $

Z-Bar Motel. The quiet cabins of this motel at the base of the Bighorn Mountains are in a huge shaded yard, complete with tables and a barbecue grill. Some kitchenettes are available—ideal if you are traveling with pets or children. Picnic area, some kitchenettes, cable TV, playground, some pets allowed (fee). | 626 Fort St., 82834 | 307/684–5535 or 888/313–1227 | fax 307/684–5538 | 4 rooms, 22 cabins | AE, D, DC, MC, V | ¢-$

Cody

Buffalo Bill Historical Center. One of the West's finest museums, this is actually several museums rolled into one, showcasing art, firearms, natural history, and the Wild West of Buffalo Bill Cody. The center also has educational courses and presentations. | 720 Sheridan Ave. | 307/587–4771 | www.bbhc.org | $15 for two-day ticket | Apr., daily 10–5; May, daily 8–8; June–mid-Sept., daily 7 AM–8 PM; mid-Sept.–Oct., daily 8–5; Nov.–Mar., Tues.–Sun. 10–3.

Buffalo Bill Museum. This museum is dedicated to the incredible life of William F. "Buffalo Bill" Cody. Shortly after Cody's death, some of his friends took mementos of the famous scout, fighter, and Wild West showman and opened the museum in a small log building. It is now in the historical center and includes huge posters from the original Buffalo Bill Wild West and Congress of Rough Riders shows.

Cody Firearms Museum. Started as the Winchester Museum, the Cody Firearms Museum was rededicated in 1991; it is comprehensive, tracing the history of firearms through thousands of models on display, from European blunderbusses to Gatling guns and modern weapons. Included are examples of Winchester and Browning arms, as well as a replica of an arms manufacturing plant.

Plains Indian Museum. The history of the Plains Indians is highlighted here with information about the Sioux, Blackfeet, Cheyenne, Crow, Shoshone, and Nez Perce.

Whitney Gallery of Western Art. The West's greatest artists are a part of this wing, which has art by Frederic Remington, Charles M. Russell, Albert Bierstadt, George Catlin, and Thomas Moran, and contemporary artists, including Harry Jackson, James Bama, and Peter Fillerup.

Buffalo Bill State Park. The Buffalo Bill Reservoir is the focus of the park, and you can indulge in all sorts of water sports here, as well as hike, camp, and picnic nearby. | 47 Lakeside Rd. | 307/587–9227 | http://wyoparks.state.wy.us/buffalo1.htm | $4 | Park year-round; campground May–Sept.

Buffalo Bill Dam and Visitor Center. Bricks with the names of local residents form the sidewalk in front of the visitor center. You can walk across the actual dam, peering over to see the lake to the west or the outflow to the east. | East end of reservoir | 307/527–6076 | Free | May–Sept., daily 8–8.

Cody Nite Rodeo. Some towns have intermittent rodeos; Cody has had one every night since 1938. It's a training ground for tomorrow's world-champion cowboys and a competition arena for some of today's best rodeo hands. | Stampede Park, 1143 Sheridan Ave. | 307/587–5155 | www.comp-unltd.com/~rodeo/rodeo.html | $10–$12 | Memorial Day–Labor Day.

Shoshone National Forest. The first national forest, Shoshone is a catch-all for various outdoor activities, including hunting, fishing, hiking, and mountain biking. You can ride horses in hospitable weather and snowmobile and cross-country ski once the snow falls. | U.S. 14/16/20 | 307/527–6241 | www.fs.fed.us/r2/shoshone | Free | Daily.

Tecumseh's Wyoming Territory Old West Miniature Village and Museum. Dioramas depict early Wyoming Territorial, Native American history, and Western events. | 142 W. Yellowstone Hwy. | 307/587–5362 | $3 | June–Aug., daily 8 AM–9 PM; May and Sept., daily 10–6.

Trail Town. Started by a local archaeologist, Trail Town is a collection of historic cabins, homes, and buildings, including one that served as a hideout for Butch Cassidy and the Sundance Kid. There is a cemetery with seven relocated graves, including that of Jeremiah "liver-eatin'" Johnson. | 1831 Demaris Dr. | 307/587–5302 | www.oldtrailtown.com | $6 | Mid-May–Sept., daily 8–8.

Dining

Cassie's Supper Club. American. Early in the evening Cassie's is low-key, but at about 9 PM the band warms up and the dancing begins. Only a mile from the rodeo, Cassie's gets downright rowdy; it's certainly the best place in Cody to do some boot-scooting. Steaks, prime rib, and hamburgers are the mainstays along with seafood and chicken. | 214 Yellowstone Ave. | 307/527–5500 | AE, MC, V | $$–$$$

Cody Coffee Company and Eatery. American. This is a great place to grab lunch and take in the views of Spirit and Rattlesnake mountains. Excellent Italian grilled sandwiches are served, as are homemade muffins and cinnamon rolls, freshly squeezed juices, smoothies, and coffee drinks. | 1702 Sheridan Ave. | 307/527–7879 | No credit cards | No dinner | ¢–$

Maxwell's. Eclectic. A turn-of-the-20th-century Victorian house with huge windows and a porch is the setting of this slightly more upscale family restaurant. The baby-back ribs are always a good bet, and the Mediterranean pizza with Greek olives, feta cheese, and fresh tomatoes is also a great selection. | 937 Sheridan Ave. | 307/527–7749 | AE, D, MC, V | $–$$

Proud Cut Saloon. Steak. "Kick-ass cowboy cuisine"—steaks, prime rib, shrimp, fish, and chicken—is the order of the day here. The cowboy theme is dominant throughout this popular watering hole, which is decorated with vintage photographs of Cody country and large game mounts. | 1227 Sheridan Ave. | 307/527–6905 | D, MC, V | $–$$

Stephan's. Contemporary. This intimate restaurant is a Cody favorite, and an alternative to cowboy kitsch: instead of game mounts, you'll find palm plants, real tablecloths, and subdued earth-tone Western art. Specialties include filet mignon stuffed with Gorgonzola, sun-dried tomatoes, and Portobello mushrooms; and Southwest shrimp kebab grilled and scored with jalapeños and pepper jack cheese. | 1367 Sheridan Ave. | 307/587–8511 | AE, MC, V | $–$$$

Lodging

Holiday Inn. The hotel is part of a big complex that contains the Bottoms Up Lounge and QT's Restaurant. Amenities include an outdoor courtyard with a pool, and a convention center. Restaurant, room service. In-room data ports, cable TV, pool, bar, business services, airport shuttle, no-smoking rooms. | 1701 Sheridan Ave., 82414 | 307/587–5555 | fax 307/527–7757 | 184 rooms | AE, D, DC, MC, V | $–$$

Irma Hotel. An ornate cherrywood bar sent by the Queen of England in 1904 is one of the highlights of this hostelry, which is named for Buffalo Bill's daughter. The hotel was built in 1902, and some rooms have an early-20th-century Western style, with brass beds and period furniture. During the summer, locals stage gunfights on the porch. Restaurant, bar. | 1192 Sheridan Ave., 82414 | 307/587–4221 | fax 307/587–4221 | www.irmahotel.com | 40 rooms | AE, D, DC, MC, V | $

Ponderosa Campground. Located within walking distance (three blocks) of the Buffalo Bill Historical Center, this is a large facility with separate areas for tents and RV's. You can even stay in a tepee, or pitch your own tepee or tent in the primitive camping area (no nearby facilities)—known as the OK Corral—in the canyon above the Shoshone River. Flush toilets, dump station, drinking water, laundry facilities, showers, grills, picnic tables. | 1815 8th St., 82414 | 307/587–9203 | 137 RV sites, 50 tent sites | No credit cards | Closed Nov.–Apr. | ¢

Rimrock Dude Ranch. One of the oldest guest ranches on the North Fork of the Shoshone River, Rimrock offers both summer and winter accommodations and activities, from winter snowmobile trips to Yellowstone National Park to summer horsepacking trips into the park and surrounding mountain country. Dining room, refrigerators, pool, airport shuttle; no smoking. | 2728 N. Fork Hwy., 82414 | 307/587–3970 or 800/208–7468 | fax 307/527–5014 | www.rimrockranch.com | 9 cabins | MC, V | FAP | $$$$

Gillette

Cam-Plex. It's worth investigating what's on at this multi-use facility; it could be anything from a rodeo to a concert to a craft show. | 1635 Reata Dr. | 307/682–0552, 307/682–8802 (tickets) | www.cam-plex.com.

Keyhole State Park. You can fish, boat, and swim at this state park. Camping and picnic areas are available, and the marina has a shower house and restaurant. | 353 McKean Rd. | 307/756–3596, 307/756–9529 marina info | http://wyoparks.state.wy.us/keyhole1.htm | $2 WY residents; $4 nonresidents | Daily.

Rockpile Museum. Local historical artifacts, from bits and brands to rifles and sheep wagons, make up the collection here. | 900 W. 2nd St. | 307/682–5723 | Free | June–Aug., Mon.–Sat. 9–8 and Sun. 12:30–6:30; Sept.–May, Mon.–Sat. 9–5.

Dining

Bailey's Bar and Grill. Eclectic. This bar and grill has something of an identity crisis: the interior is that of an English pub, but the food ranges from American-style sandwiches at lunch to Mexican dishes at dinner. | 301 S. Gillette Ave. | 307/686–7678 | AE, MC, V | ¢–$

Packard's Grill. American. Families are the main patrons of this large, airy establishment. Favorites include prime rib and Southern-style dishes. A kids' menu is available. | 408 S. Douglas Hwy. | 307/686–5149 | AE, D, DC, MC, V | No dinner Sun. | ¢–$

Grand Teton National Park

Hiking Trails. Hiking is one of the best ways to see the park. You can get trail maps and information about hiking conditions from rangers at the park visitor centers at Moose or Colter Bay. Popular trails are those in the Jenny Lake area, the Leigh and String lakes area, and the Taggart Lake Trail, with views of Avalanche Canyon.

Jackson Lake. The biggest of the Grand Teton Park's glacier-scooped lakes, Jackson Lake, in the northern reaches of the park, was enlarged by construction of the Jackson Lake Dam in 1909. You can fish, sail, and windsurf and stay at the campgrounds and lodges that dot the shoreline. | U.S. 89/191/287 and Teton Park Rd.

Jenny Lake. Named for the Native American wife of mountain man Beaver Dick Leigh, this pristine mountain lake south of Jackson Lake draws boaters and hikers. You can use the trails surrounding the lake. | Teton Park Rd.

Menor's Ferry. The ferry on display is not the original, but it is an accurate re-creation of the craft built by Bill Menor in the 1890s, and it demonstrates how people crossed the Snake River before bridges were built. | Signal Mountain Summit Rd.

Moose Visitors Center. At the park's south entrance, this is a good place to start any visit to Grand Teton National Park. You'll find information about all activities, a decent resource room where you can purchase maps and books, and knowledgeable people who can tell you what to expect on trails and lakes.

★**Signal Mountain.** North of Moose and midway between Moose and Moran, Signal Mountain got its name when a search party looking for a missing valley resident agreed that whoever found him would light a signal fire atop the mountain, which would be visible throughout Jackson Hole. Though the missing man was dead by the time he was found, searchers burned the signal fire anyway. The narrow road (not suitable for RVs) leads to an overlook with spectacular views of Jackson Hole. | Teton Park Rd.

Dining

Dornan's. Barbecue. Hearty portions of beef, beans, potatoes, stew, and hot coffee and cold lemonade are the standbys at Dornan's, which is easily identified by its tepees. Locals know it for the beef and barbecue cooked over wood fires. You can eat inside the tepees if it happens to be raining or windy; otherwise, enjoy your meal at outdoor picnic tables with views of the Snake River and the Tetons. | 10 Moose Rd. | 307/733–2415 | MC, V | $$

Jackson Lake Lodge Pioneer Grill. American. Seat yourself at the winding counter at this homey luncheonette. You'll find nothing more complicated than great comfort food like bacon and eggs, vegetable lasagna, and rotisserie chicken. Huckleberry pancakes—and anything from the old-fashioned soda fountain—are real treats. | U.S. 89 N | 307/543–2811 Ext. 1911 | AE, DC, MC, V | Closed early Oct.–late May | ¢–$

Jenny Lake Lodge Dining Room. Continental. Elegant—jackets are required—yet rustic, this is Grand Teton National Park's finest dining establishment. The breakfast and dinner menus are offered prix fixe; lunch is à la carte. Reservations are essential for dinner. | Jenny Lake Rd. | 307/733–4647 | AE, DC, MC, V | Closed Oct.–May | $$$$

Lodging

Colter Bay Village. Colter Bay Village, near Jackson Lake, has splendid views and an excellent marina and beach for the windsurfing crowd. Regular cabins have a variety of set-ups, and most have their own baths. The tent cabins aren't fancy—concrete floors, hanging bunks, and canvas exteriors—but they do keep the wind and rain off; rest room facilities are shared. There is also an RV park with showers, a service station, and marina. 2 restaurants, boating, hiking, bar, shops, laundry facilities. | Off U.S. 89, Moran 83013 | 307/733–3100 or 800/628–9988 | fax 307/543–3143 | 166 cabins, 66 tent cabins, 112 RV spaces | AE, DC, MC, V | Closed late Sept.–late May | ¢–$$

Jackson Lake Lodge. Two large fireplaces adorn the lounge, Native American designs decorate the walls, and huge picture windows look out at Willow Flats, below Jackson Lake Dam. There are 30 smaller rooms in the main lodge; the rest, in one-story motor-lodge–style buildings, are preferable. Some rooms have Teton views—and a higher price tag as a result. You can arrange for horseback riding, float trips, and boating excursions. 2 restaurants, pool, boating, hiking, horseback riding, bar, recreation room, business services, meeting rooms, airport shuttle. | U.S. 89 north of Jackson Lake Junction, Moran 83013 | 307/733–3100 or 800/628–9988 | fax 307/543–3143 | www.gtlc.com | 385 rooms | AE, DC, MC, V | Closed late Oct.–mid-May | $$$–$$$$

Signal Mountain Lodge. This lodge, built of volcanic stone and pine shingles, sits on the eastern shore of Jackson Lake. The lobby has a fireplace, a piano, and Adirondack furniture; guest rooms are clustered in cabinlike units, some with kitchenettes, many with lake views. You can rent boats, take scenic float trips, or fish. 2 restaurants, kitchenettes, boating, fishing, bar, shops. | Teton Park Rd., Moran 83013 | 307/543–2831 | 79 rooms | Closed mid-Oct.–early May | AE, DC, MC, V | $–$$$

Spur Ranch Log Cabins. Located at the popular and busy Dornan's in Moose, these log cabins have views of the Grand Teton range. They range from small one-bedroom cabins to large two-bedroom units. Turn left at Moose Junction to reach the property. 2 restaurants, grocery, kitchens, boating, fishing, mountain bikes, hiking, cross-country skiing, bar, wine shop, shops; no a/c, no room phones, no room TVs. | U.S. 26/89/191, 83012 | 307/733–2522 | fax 307/739–9098 | www.dornans.com | 8 1-bedroom cabins, 4 2-bedroom cabins | D, MC, V | $$–$$$$

Jackson

Bridger-Teton National Forest. In the hundreds of thousands of acres of forest, some wilderness, you'll find both developed and backcountry campsites, and can hike, fish, hunt, and study nature. | 340 N. Cache St. | 307/739–5500 | www.fs.fed.us/btnf | Free; campground fees $10–$15 | Daily.

Grand Targhee Ski and Summer Resort. Just one hour from Jackson, Grand Targhee gets more than 500 inches of snow annually. The mountain village has five restaurants, shopping, lodging, and skiing. You can get there on the Targhee Express, daily round-trip coaches, from Jackson and Teton Village mid-December through late March. Follow Route 22 over Teton Pass and turn right onto Route 33; in Driggs, ID, turn right and follow Little Avenue six blocks to a fork, then bear left onto Ski Hill Road and follow to Grand Targhee. | 307/353–2300, 800/827–4433 snow reports | www.grandtarghee.com | $38–$59 daily passes | Dec.–early Apr., daily 9:30–4.

Jackson Hole Museum. Learn how Deadwood Bar got its name, or the story of Jackson's all-female town government. Historic photos, artifacts, and displays are part of the museum exhibits. You can also take walking tours of downtown and historic sites. | 105 N. Glenwood St. | 307/733–2414 (summer only), 307/733–9605 | $3 | Early Sept–late May, weekdays 8–5; late May–early Sept., Sat. 9:30–6 and Sun. 10–5.

National Elk Refuge. More than 7,000 elk spend the winter in the National Elk Refuge, which was established in 1912 to save starving herds. The animals migrate to the refuge grounds in late fall and remain until early spring. Trumpeter swans live here, too, as do bald eagles, coyotes, and wolves. In winter, you can take one of the regular wagon and sleigh rides through the herd; the sleigh rides leave from the National Wildlife Art Museum. | Visitor center, 532 N. Cash St. | 307/733–9212 | http://nationalelkrefuge.fws.gov | $13 sleigh ride only; $15 combination ticket including National Wildlife Art Museum | Visitor center, daily 8–5.

National Wildlife Art Museum. A collection of wildlife art—most of it devoted to North American species—is displayed in the 12 galleries that have both permanent and traveling exhibits. You can also look outward, using one of the spotting scopes, to watch wildlife at the National Elk Refuge. | 2820 Rungius Rd. | 307/733–5771 | www.wildlifeart.org | $6, $15 combination ticket including the National Elk Refuge | Nov.–Sept., daily 8–5; Oct., Mon.–Sat. 9–5 and Sun. 1–5.

Snow King Resort. At the western edge of Jackson, Snow King Resort has 400 acres of ski runs in the daytime and 110 acres for night skiing, plus an extensive snow-making system. | 400 E. Snow King Ave. | 307/733–5200 or 800/522–5464 | $15–$35 | Dec.–Apr., daily; snow-tubing park weekdays 4–8 and weekends noon–8.

Dining

★ **The Bunnery.** Café. The Bunnery, which is tucked into a tiny spot in the Hole-in-the-Wall Mall, is where locals go for breakfast. It's usually busy, so there may be a short wait, but the food's worth it. Sandwiches are available at lunchtime. | 130 N. Cache St. | 307/733–5474 | MC, V | No dinner | ¢–$

Jedediah's House of Sourdough. American. Be prepared to knock elbows with local families at this friendly, noisy restaurant, a block east of the town square. Jedediah's is in a 1910 home and is filled with photos of old Jackson. Try the sourdough pancakes or Teton taters and eggs. | 135 E. Broadway | 307/733–5671 | AE, D, MC, V | $–$$

The Snake River Grill. American. You may spot a celebrity or two at this restaurant overlooking the town square, or you may just be in the company of discerning locals. Choose from fresh fish, free-range meats, and organic produce; you'll find buffalo short ribs, vegetarian pasta with mushrooms and artichokes, as well as grilled elk chops. The Grill has an extensive and celebrated wine list. | 84 E. Broadway | 307/733–0557 | AE, D, MC, V | No lunch | $$–$$$$

Lodging

Antler Motel. No motel in Jackson is more convenient to the Town Square than the Antler, one block south. Some rooms have fireplaces, but these are otherwise standard motel accommodations. There is a complimentary ski shuttle during winter. Restaurant, cable TV, exercise equipment, indoor hot tub, sauna, laundry facilities, meeting room, no-smoking rooms. | 43 W. Pearl St., 83001 | 307/733–2535 or 800/483–8667 | fax 307/733–2002 | www.townsquareinns.com | 110 rooms | AE, D, MC, V | $$$–$$$$

Cowboy Village Resort. Stay in your own small log cabin with covered decks and barbecue grills. There is a ski wax room, and both the START Bus and Targhee Express buses that service the ski areas stop on the property. Some kitchenettes, hot tub, laundry facilities, no-smoking rooms. | 120 S. Flat Creek, 83001 | 307/733–3121 or 800/962–4988 | fax 307/739–1955 | 82 cabins | AE, D, MC, V | $

★**Parkway Inn.** Each room has a distinctive look, with oak or wicker furniture, and all are filled with antiques, from 19th-century pieces onward. This inn is homey and comfortable enough that you might want to settle in for longer than one night. Indoor pool, gym, hot tub, no-smoking rooms. | 125 N. Jackson St., 83001 | 307/733–3143 or 800/247–8390 | fax 307/733–0955 | www.parkwayinn.com | 37 rooms, 12 suites | AE, D, DC, MC, V | CP | $$$

★**Wort Hotel.** Locals have been gathering at this Jackson landmark since the early 1940s, and you can view the history of the town through the photos and clippings posted in the lobby. Completely renovated after a fire in the 1980s, the spacious rooms now have lodgepole furniture and comfortable armchairs. Junior suites have large sitting areas. Restaurant, room service, cable TV, exercise equipment, hot tub, bar, business services, no-smoking rooms. | 50 N. Glenwood, 83001 | 307/733–2190 or 800/322–2727 | fax 307/733–2067 | www.worthotel.com | 60 rooms | AE, D, DC, MC, V | $$$$

Sheridan

Bighorn National Forest. No region in Wyoming has a more diverse landscape—lush grasslands, alpine meadows, rugged mountaintops, canyons, and deserts. | 307/684–1100 | www.fs.fed.us/r2/bighorn | Free | Daily.

Bradford Brinton Memorial. Once the Quarter Circle A Ranch, owned by Bradford Brinton, this is now a memorial to a family known for fine art collections and an elegant home. The displays include art by Charles M. Russell, Frederic Remington, and John James Audubon, among others. You'll also see antique furnishings, quilts, rare books, and other memorabilia. | 239 Brinton Rd., Big Horn | 307/672–3173 | www.bradfordbritonmemorial.com | $3 | May 15–Labor Day, daily 9:30–5.

King's Saddlery and Museum. Don King started making saddles decades ago, and he's been collecting them for just as long. His craft is on full display in this small downtown museum, along with other cowboy gear. The Saddlery itself is still in business, run by King's sons, and it has a tradition for making some of the finest saddles in the world, even crafting them for royalty. The Kings also make King Ropes, used by professional rodeo cowboys and ranchers. Hundreds of ropes (some of them in neon colors) fill racks at the back of the store, and you'll likely find one or more cowboys there trying them out. | 184 N. Main St. | 307/672–2702 or 800/443–8919 | Free | Mon.–Sat. 8–5.

Main Street Historic District. Historic buildings, most still used by businesses, line Main Street. You can get a map from the chamber of commerce. | 307/672–8881.

Trail End Historic Center. When John B. Kendrick brought the first cattle into this area, he established himself as one of the "elite" citizens. Kendrick became Wyoming's governor and a senator, and he lived in this elegant Flemish Revival home completed in 1913. The furnishings at the state historic site are authentic Kendrick items. | 400 Clarendon Ave. | 307/674–4589 | www.trailend.org | $1 WY residents; $2 nonresidents | June–Aug., daily 9–6; Sept.–May, call for hrs.

Dining

Sanford's Grub, Pub, Brewery. American/Casual. The name pretty much says it all. This is a noisy place that caters to a college crowd, but the burgers and sandwiches are worth the ruckus and the brews are equally good. Particularly popular is the Big Horn Wheat brew. | 1 E. Alger Ave. | 307/674–1722 | ¢–$$

Silver Spur. American. You might have to look twice at this place: you'll look hard just to find it and harder before you decide to give it a chance. Give the Silver Spur the benefit of the doubt—though it's small and undistinguished, the helpings here are cowboy-size, and the omelets are worth the leap of faith. | 832 N. Main St. | 307/672–2749 | No credit cards | ¢–$$

Sugarland Restaurant at the Holiday Inn. American. Surprisingly good for a chain hotel restaurant, the Sugarland is a quiet and pleasant choice for when you tire of fast food. The menu is diverse, but showcases reliable beef, seafood, and pasta dishes. | 1809 Sugarland Dr. | 307/672–8931 | AE, D, DC, MC, V | $–$$

Lodging

Big Horn Mountain KOA Campground. The pleasant, shady, and relatively peaceful campground 3½ mi from Sheridan makes roughing it easy with numerous amenities and extras such as miniature golf, basketball courts, fishing, and an on-site snack bar. A convenient stopover point for those going on to Yellowstone, it also has five cabins ($29–$79) that sleep four or five and a bunkhouse that sleeps up to eight. Miniature golf, pool, hot tub, sauna, fishing, playground, laundry facilities, Internet. | 63 Decker Rd., 82801 | 307/674–8766 or 800/562–7621 | www.koa.com | 40 tent sites, 100 trailer slots, 5 cabins, 1 bunkhouse | D, MC, V | Closed early Oct.–Mar. | ¢

Mill Inn Motel. An old mill is incorporated into this motel, which is on the National Register of Historic Places. You'll find large guest rooms with pastel spreads, drapes, and rugs. The lobby and breakfast room are decorated with Western art prints, boots, and saddles. Exercise equipment, some pets allowed. | 2161 Coffeen Ave., 82801 | 307/672–6401 | www.sheridanmillinn.com | 45 rooms | AE, D, MC, V | CP | $–$$

Sundance

Devils Tower National Monument. Native American legend has it that Devils Tower was formed when a tree stump turned into granite and grew taller to protect some stranded children from a bear. Geologists say that the rock tower is the core of a defunct volcano. Northwest of Sundance (take U.S. 14 and then Route 24 north), it was a tourist magnet long before a spaceship landed on it in the movie *Close Encounters of the Third Kind.* You'll find 7 mi of hiking trails, a campground, a picnic area, and a visitor center. Hulett, a few miles northeast of the monument, is the closest town with services. | Rte. 24 | 307/467–5430 (Hulett Chamber of Commerce) | www.nps.gov/deto | $8 | Park year-round; visitor center Apr.–Sept., daily 8–7:30; Oct.–Mar., daily 8:30–4:30; Campground Apr.–Oct.

Vore Buffalo Jump. Thousands of buffalo bones are piled atop each other at the Vore Buffalo Jump on Frontage Road, where Native Americans forced buffalo to fall to their deaths in the era when hunting was done with spears. | 307/283–1000.

Dining

Aro Restaurant and Lounge. American. Standards at this large downtown diner include burgers, prime rib, burritos, Reuben sandwiches, and a huge "Devils Tower" brownie sundae. | 205 Cleveland St. | 307/283–2000 | D, MC, V | $

Country Cottage. American. Flowers, gifts, and simple meals, including sandwiches, are sold at this one-stop shop. | 423 Cleveland St. | 307/283–2450 | MC, V | ¢–$

Log Cabin Cafe. American. Locals crowd this small log-cabin restaurant for its burgers, steaks, and seafood. It's 3 mi from town. | U.S. 14 | 307/283–3393 | MC, V | $

Yellowstone National Park

Yellowstone Highlights. You can't run out of "firsts," "mosts," or "lasts" when it comes to describing Yellowstone National Park—it was the world's first national park; it is the largest national park in the lower 48; and it is, with surrounding wildlands, the center of the last truly intact temperate ecosystem. Follow Route 20 from Cody into the East Entrance of the park. | 307/344–7381, 307/344–2386 TDD | www.nps.gov/yell.

Back Basin. The huge, though unpredictable, Steamboat Geyser is one of the attractions here. Though Steamboat only performs about once a year, when it does, it shoots 300 feet into the air.

Grand Canyon of the Yellowstone. A cascading waterfall and rushing river carved this canyon, which is 24 mi long and 1,200 feet deep. The red and ochre canyon walls are topped with emerald-green forest.

Lower Geyser Basin. The Great Fountain Geyser is the most spectacular of the attractions at Lower Geyser Basin. But you'll find bubbling mud pots, blue pools, fumaroles, pink mud pots, and the minigeysers at Fountain Paint Pots here as well.

Mammoth Hot Springs. Elk who graze nearby are frequent visitors to these multi-color terraces, which were formed by slowly flowing hot mineral water.

Midway Geyser Basin. The Grand Prismatic Spring and Excelsior Geyser Crater are at Midway Geyser, which has some beautiful, richly colored, bottomless pools.

★ **Norris Geyser Basin.** The hottest and oldest such basin in Yellowstone is constantly changing. Some geysers or hot springs might suddenly stop flowing, but others blow and hiss into life. Among the features at Norris are Whirligig Geyser, Whale's Mouth, Emerald Spring, and Arch Steam Vent.

Old Faithful–Upper Geyser Basin. The long-standing centerpiece of Yellowstone is Old Faithful. The mysterious plumbing of Yellowstone has lengthened Old Faithful's eruption cycle somewhat in recent years, but the geyser still spouts the same amount of water–sometimes reaching to 140 feet—and pleases spectators every 80 minutes or so. Elk and buffalo commonly share the area.

Porcelain Basin. The Porcelain Basin is a small geyser area that has a 1-mi boardwalk often crammed with people, but it's a good place to watch the ground bulge and push from underground pressure.

Tower-Roosevelt. You can use the riding trails and have cookouts in this area, check out the Petrified Tree, and hike on trails through the Lamar Valley or to Specimen Ridge with its unusual fossils.

West Thumb. A small geyser basin and views of Lake Yellowstone are worth stopping for at West Thumb, which also has a visitor center and a warming hut.

Yellowstone Lake. North America's largest mountain lake was formed by glaciers. You can boat and fish or simply sit along the shore and watch the waves. In the winter you might see otters and coyotes.

Dining

★**Lake Yellowstone Hotel Dining Room.** American/Casual. This double-colonnaded dining room off the hotel lobby will have you gazing through the big square windows at the lake. As this is one of the park's most elegant restaurants, it tends to attract an older. Try the prime rib prepared in a dry marinade of thyme, rosemary, and garlic or the chicken with wild mushroom sauce. Reservations are required for dinner. | Lake Village | 307/344–7901 | AE, D, DC, MC, V | Closed Oct.–mid-May | $$–$$$

Mammoth Hot Springs Hotel. American. After exploring Yellowstone, you'll welcome the quiet of the Mammoth Hot Springs Hotel dining room. The service is low-key, and the menu varied, with beef, chicken, and pasta dishes. Dinner reservations are essential. | Mammoth Hot Springs | 307/344–7311 | AE, D, DC, MC, V | $$–$$$$

Old Faithful Snow Lodge. American. Whimsical touches abound here, from wood etched with figures of park wildlife to intricate lighting that resembles snowcapped trees. This is the only place in the park, aside from Mammoth, where you can enjoy a relaxing, sit-down lunch or dinner in winter. The menu offers the standard beef, chicken, and pasta options. | Old Faithful Area, off Rte. 20 | 307/344–7311 | AE, D, DC, MC, V | Closed Apr. and Nov. | $$–$$$$

Roosevelt Lodge. American. At this rustic log cabin in a pine forest, the menu ranges from barbecued ribs to hamburgers and steak. Chuckwagon cookouts—reservations essential—involve one- or two-hour trail rides. | Tower-Roosevelt Area | 307/344–7311 | AE, D, DC, MC, V | Closed Sept.–early June | $$–$$$$

Lodging

Cascade Lodge. This motel-style facility, which doesn't get much fancier than pine wainscoting and brown carpets, is amid the trees above the Grand Canyon of the Yellowstone. The property is at the farthest edge of the Canyon Village, which means it's quiet since it's away from the major traffic, but it's also a hike to the nearest dining alternatives. 2 restaurants, cafeteria, picnic area, hiking, horseback riding, bar, shops; no a/c, no room TVs, no smoking. | North Rim Dr. at Grand Loop Rd. | 307/344–7901 | fax 307/344–7456 | www.travelyellowstone.com | 40 rooms | AE, D, DC, MC, V | Closed early Sept.–early June | $$

Lake Lodge. The main lodge, a part of which dates to the 1920s, has views of Yellowstone Lake and is nestled among pine groves. Although the basic cabin-style accommodations are similar to other facilities in the park, the cozy lodge and semi-secluded site at the far end of Lake Village Road make this a better choice. Cafeteria, bar. | Canyon Village, 82190 | 307/344–7901 | fax 307/344–7456 | www.travelyellowstone.com/ | 186 cabins | Closed mid-Sept.–mid-June | AE, D, MC, V | $–$$

Old Faithful Inn. An architectural wonder built in 1903, the log building of this inn has a six-story lobby with huge rock fireplaces. Some rooms have views of Old Faithful. Restaurant, some refrigerators, bar; no a/c, no phones in some rooms. | Old Faithful, 82190 | 307/344–7901 | fax 307/344–7456 | www.travelyellowstone.com | 327 rooms (246 with private bath), 6 suites | AE, D, DC, MC, V | Closed mid-Oct.–Apr. | $–$$$

HISTORIC TRAILS TREK
TORRINGTON TO EVANSTON

Distance: 455 mi   Time: Minimum of 4 days
Overnight Breaks: Casper, Green River, Lander, Rock Springs

On this drive you can cross the same ground pioneers did when they traveled to Oregon, Utah, and California some 150 years ago. In many ways the landscape has changed little in the intervening years. You can make this trip at any time, but spring, summer, and fall are best because all the visitor centers are open and you'll be less likely to run into a snowstorm on South Pass. Bear in mind, though, that the pass is 7,550 feet high, so you could hit snow even in July or August.

❶ Begin at **Fort Laramie National Historic Site** (U.S. 26, 20 mi west of Torrington), which became the most important site on the Oregon-California-Mormon trail route because it was a provisioning point and, after 1849, a U.S. Army post. Actual ruts of the historic emigrant trails cross the fort grounds.

❷ Continuing west on U.S. 26, you'll come to Register Cliff and the Guernsey Ruts, both near **Guernsey,** where 1840s pioneers would congregate to bathe. A mile northeast of town is Guernsey State Park, where you can swim and boat.

❸ From Guernsey continue west on U.S. 20/26 for 15 mi to I–25, then head north on I–25 to **Ayres Natural Bridge,** off the interstate between Douglas and Glenrock.

Overland emigrants sometimes visited this rock outcrop that spans LaPrele Creek, and now it's a popular small picnic area and campsite.

❹ After taking in the beauty of the bridge and its surroundings, head north on I–25 for approximately 40 mi to **Casper** (I–25, U.S. 20/26, and Route 220). Several major trails converged here as emigrants crossed the North Platte River and continued west along the Oregon-California-Mormon routes to the Sweetwater River valley or headed north to Montana's gold fields over the Bozeman or Bridger trails. No community existed here during the migration period, but **Fort Caspar,** which originally went by the name Platte Bridge Station, was a military installation during the later years of overland travel. Spend the night in Casper.

❺ **Independence Rock State Historic Site** (60 mi west of Casper on Route 220) is one of the best-known of all trail sites along the entire 2,000-mi corridor from Missouri to Oregon or California, and pioneers almost always mentioned it in their journals. You can stretch your legs at a rest area, perhaps by climbing to the top of the rock, where you'll see some of the emigrant names carved in the granite. Then continue west on Route 220 to the **Mormon Trail–Martin's Cove Visitors Center** at the Sun Ranch.

❻ Leaving Independence Rock, continue west on Route 220/U.S. 287 to **Lander** (U.S. 287). Lander is off the main emigrant trail route, but it is a good place to hang your hat for the night.

❼ Backtrack south out of Lander on U.S. 287 to Route 28. **South Pass City State Historic Site** (off Route 28 between Lander and Farson) is only a few miles from the most important site of the entire route—South Pass—the long, low pass over the Rocky Mountains used by early travelers to cross the Continental Divide. South Pass City was a gold town established in 1869 and is the birthplace of women's suffrage in Wyoming.

❽ From South Pass City, head west on Route 28 to Farson then travel south on U.S. 191 40 mi to **Rock Springs** (on I–80, exit 104). You can spend the night at Rock Springs, a historic coal-mining town or **Green River** (I–80, exits 89 and 91) 12 mi west, which also owes its prosperity to mining. At the **Flaming Gorge National Historic Area** (south on U.S. 191 or Route 530) you can boat, fish, camp, bike, and hike.

❾ After you've explored Rock Springs, head west on I–80 for approximately 60 mi to the **Fort Bridger State Historic Site** (I–80, exit 48), the emigrants' major trading and provisioning point—the first they had seen since leaving Fort Laramie.

❿ Continue west out of Fort Bridger on I–80 to **Evanston** (Exit 3), a town that got its start as a Union Pacific hell-on-wheels town.

To return to Fort Laramie, head east on I–80 to Rawlins, north on U.S. 287/Route 789 to Route 220, then east into Casper. From Casper, follow I–25 south back to U.S. 26, which leads east into Fort Laramie.

Casper

Casper Mountain and Beartrap Meadow Parks. Rising to the east of the city, Casper Mountain is a recreational paradise where you can hike and fish in summer and cross-country and downhill ski in winter. The Crimson Dawn Museum is the original log-cabin home of Neal and Jim Forsling, who settled in the area with their daughters in 1915. She and her daughters and their friends built the first trails in the woods around

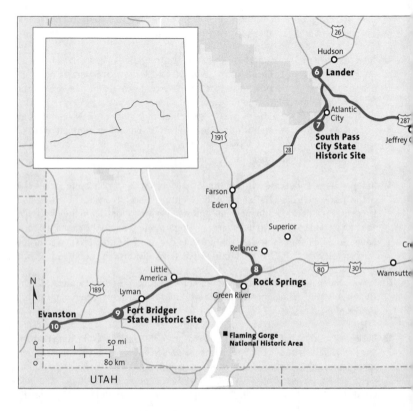

Crimson Dawn Park. Today those same trails are marked with shrines and plaques commemorating the mythical "Enchanted Witches and Elves of Casper Mountain." | Casper Mountain Rd. | 307/235–9325 | Free | Park daily; museum, mid-June–mid-Oct., Sat.–Thurs. 11–7.

In Skunk Hollow along Elkhorn Creek, 8 mi south of Route 251, the **Lee McCune Braille Trail** is a ¹/₃-mi route with rope handrails and 37 stops with print and Braille markers describing the scenery. | Casper Mountain Rd. | 307/235–9325 | Free | June–Sept., depending on snowfall.

Casper Mountain is rated a premier **bird-watching** area, and the local Murie Audubon Society offers both a hotline and guides. | 307/265–2473.

Casper Planetarium. Watch multimedia programs on astronomy and space here. | 904 N. Poplar St. | 307/577–0310 | $2.50 | Sept.–May, 1st and 2nd Thurs. and every Sat. at 7 PM; June–Aug., daily at 4, 7, 8 PM.

Fort Caspar Museum. A small museum re-creates the post at Platte Bridge, which became Fort Caspar after the July 1865 battle that claimed the lives of several soldiers, including Lt. Caspar Collins. A post depicts life at a frontier station in the 1860s. | 4001 Fort Caspar Rd. | 307/235–8462 | www.fortcasparwyoming.com | $2 | June–Aug., Mon.–Sat. 8:30–6:30 and Sun. 12:30–6:30; May and Sept., Mon.–Sat. 8–5 and Sun. noon–5; Oct.–Apr., weekdays 8–5 and Sun. 1–4.

Independence Rock. The turtle-shape granite outcrop became an important site on the Oregon-California-Mormon trails. Pioneers carved their names in the rock, and many are still legible 150 years later. | Rte. 220 | 307/577–5150 | http://wyoparks.state.wy.us/irock1.htm | Free | Daily.

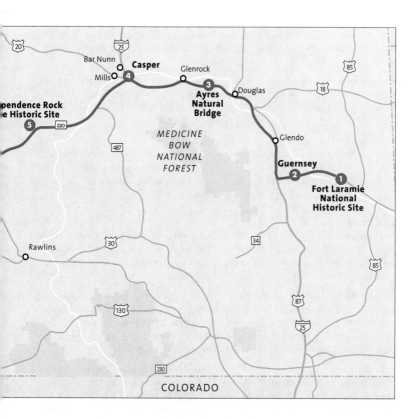

Mormon Trail Handcart Visitor Center. Opened for the 1997 sesquicentennial of the Mormon Trail, this visitor center at the Sun Ranch interprets general trail travel, and particularly the plight of the handcart pioneers in the Willie and Martin Companies, who became stranded in this area in 1856. You can walk the Mormon Trail, and handcarts are available. There's a picnic area, but no food is sold. | 50 mi southwest of Casper on Rte. 220 | 307/324–5218 | Free | Daily.

Nicolaysen Art Museum and Discovery Center. Known locally as The Nic, this art museum has a permanent collection with works by Conrad Schweiring, as well as traveling exhibits. The Discovery Center is an interactive arts-and-crafts area for children. | 400 E. Collins Dr. | 307/235–5247 | www.thenic.org | Free | Tues.–Fri. 10–7.

Platte River Parkway. The natural beauty and historic significance of the North Platte River are preserved along this 4-mi paved trail with access points at Amoco Park at 1st and Poplar streets, at the Historic Trails Overlook east of the Casper Events Center, and between Morad Park and Fort Caspar. | Rte. 220 | 307/577–1206 | Daily.

Dining

Armor's Silver Fox. Contemporary. Locals will tell you this is their favorite place to eat, particularly if someone else is picking up the tab. Quiet, with cozy booths, this restaurant has a diverse menu and extensive wine list. Start with crab cakes, fried green tomatoes, or escargot, then have blackened prime rib or the fresh fish special. | 3422 S. Energy La. | 307/235–3000 | AE, D, DC, MC, V | $$–$$$

El Jarro. Mexican. El Jarro has good food and margaritas—the latter probably lending to the noise level, which can get quite high. The local favorite is the green chili. | 500 W. F St. | 307/577–0538 | D, MC, V | ¢–$$

Paisley Shawl. American. Don't let the nondescript exterior of the Hotel Higgins, where this dining room is located, fool you. Inside you'll find some of the best dining in Wyoming. Specialties include steak and prime rib. | 416 W. Birch, Glenrock | 307/436–9212 | AE, D, MC, V | Closed Sun.–Mon. | $$–$$$

Poor Boy's Steakhouse. Steak. Reminiscent of a frontier mining camp, this steak house has blue-and-white-checked tablecloths and chair backs, quick service, and large portions of steak, seafood, or chicken. A local favorite is the Moonshine Mama (grilled chicken breast with mushrooms and Monterey Jack and cheddar cheeses). | 739 N. Center | 307/237–8325 | AE, D, MC, V | No lunch Sun. | $–$$

Lodging

Hotel Higgins. The 1916 building looks a little questionable on the outside, but the interior is a delight. Rooms are furnished in Victorian style. Restaurant, bar; no a/c in some rooms. | 416 W. Birch, Glenrock, 82637 (I–25 Exit 165) | 307/436–9212, 800/458–0144 (outside WY) | fax 307/436–9213 | www.hotelhiggins.com | 10 rooms | D, MC, V | CP | $

Parkway Plaza. Guest rooms are large and quiet, with double vanities, one inside the bathroom and one outside. The public areas have Western furnishings. Restaurant, in-room data ports, cable TV, indoor pool, hot tub, gym, bar, business services. meeting rooms, no-smoking rooms. | 123 W. E St., 82601 | 307/235–1777 | fax 307/235–8068 | www.parkwayplaza.net | 243 rooms, 22 suites | AE, D, MC, V | $

Radisson. The rooms are large and done in muted blue, green, and mauve. There are Jacuzzi suites and alcove suites in addition to standard rooms. Restaurant, coffee shop, room service, in-room data ports, some in-room hot tubs, cable TV, indoor pool, hair salon, hot tub, bar, airport shuttle, some pets allowed. | 800 N. Poplar St., 82601 | 307/266–6000 | fax 307/473–1010 | www.radisson.com | 229 rooms | AE, D, DC, MC, V | $–$$

Evanston

Bear River State Park. Wildlife, from ducks and Canada geese to herds of bison and elk, is abundant in the park, and you can hike and ski on the trails, which have picnic shelters. The park connects to Evanston's Bear Pathway, a paved trail that for much of its length is fully accessible to people with disabilities. | 601 Bear River Dr. | 307/789–6547 | www.state.wy.us/bear1.htm | Free | Daily dawn–dusk.

Fort Bridger State Historic Site. Started in 1842 as a trading post by mountain man Jim Bridger, Fort Bridger was owned by Bridger and his partner Louis Vasquez until 1853, when Mormons took control of it. The Mormons deserted the area and burned the original Bridger post as the U.S. Army approached during the so-called Mormon War of 1857. The site then became a frontier military post until it was abandoned in 1890. Many of the original military-era buildings remain and have been restored. The largest mountain-man rendezvous in the intermountain West occurs annually at Fort Bridger over Labor Day weekend, attracting hundreds of buckskinners and Native Americans and thousands of visitors. | 37000 Business Loop I–80 | 307/782–3842 | www.state.wy.us/bridger1.htm | $2 WY residents; $4 nonresidents | Mar.–Apr., weekends 9–4:30; May–Sept., daily 9–5:30; Oct.–Nov., daily 9–4:30; Bridger/Vasquez Trading Co. May–Sept., daily 9–5:30.

Dining

Don Pedro's Family Mexican Restaurant. Mexican. You can't get more authentic than this small, family-owned and -operated restaurant that serves up sizzling Mexican fare. Try the fajitas or the special *molcajete* (a stew of beef and chicken). | 909 Front St. | 307/789–9244 | MC, V | $

Legal Tender. American. This quiet restaurant, in the Best Western Dunmar Inn, serves seafood and steaks. The lounge has live entertainment on weekends and karaoke on Wednesday. | 1601 Harrison Dr. | 307/789–3770 | AE, D, DC, MC, V | $–$$

Main Street Artisans Cafe & Gallery. Café. Recharge with an espresso at this cozy eatery and art gallery. The homemade muffins are favorites, as are the mesquite chicken sandwich and fresh tomato-basil soup. | 927 Main St. | 307/789–4991 | MC, V | ¢

Green River

Flaming Gorge Days. A golf tournament, bull-riding competition, parade, arts festival in the park, and concerts are all part of Flaming Gorge Days, held each June. | Green River Chamber of Commerce, 541 E. Flaming Gorge Way, Suite E | 307/875–5711 | Bull-riding competition $6–$8; concerts $25–$30.

Green River. Stroll along the Green River as you explore the same river that John Wesley Powell did when he began his expeditions in 1869. | Green River Chamber of Commerce: 541 East Flaming Gorge Way | 307/875–5711 or 800/354–6743.

    Expedition Island. This island, which served as the starting point for two of John Wesley Powell's expeditions down the Green and Colorado Rivers, can be accessed off 2nd Street, southwest of the railroad yard in Green River. You can stroll along a paved walkway which has plaques providing facts about Powell and other Green River adventurers who followed in his footsteps.

    Green Belt Nature Area. Downstream from Expedition Island on the south bank of the river is the Green Belt Nature Area, with interpretive signs and nature paths where you will see waterfowl and a variety of birds.

    Scott's Bottom Nature Area. Farther south along the river is Scott's Bottom Nature Area, where you'll find more interpretive signs related to local wildlife.

Lodging

Little America. This one-stop facility sits alone in the Little Colorado Desert, and it can be a real haven if the weather becomes inclement. The rooms are large and comfortable. There are also a full-service fuel station and convenience store. Restaurant, pool, gym, bar, shop, playground, laundry facilities, business services. | I–80 20 mi west of Green River, 82929 | 307/875–2400 or 800/634–2401 | fax 307/872–2666 | www.littleamerica.com | 140 rooms, 18 with shower only | AE, D, DC, MC, V | $–$$

Oak Tree Inn. This two-story inn in four buildings on the west side of town is 20 mi from Flaming Gorge and has views of unique rock outcroppings above the city. Restaurant, some refrigerators, exercise equipment, hot tub, laundry facilities, some pets allowed (fee); no smoking. | 1170 W. Flaming Gorge Way, 82935 | 307/875–3500 | fax 307/875–4889 | 192 rooms | AE, D, DC, MC, V | $

Lander

Arapaho Cultural Center Museum and Heritage Center. Art and artifacts related to the Arapaho tribe are included in the collection of this museum, which is off Route 137. The center is also the site of the historic St. Michael's Episcopal Mission. | St. Stephens Rd. | 307/332–3040 | Free | Weekdays 9–5, Sat. 1–4.

Shoshone National Forest, Washakie District (Wind River Mountains). Known simply as the Winds, this is Wyoming's most rugged mountain range. It's a great place for mountain biking, hiking, climbing, dogsledding, cross-country skiing, and snowmobiling. The Continental Divide National Scenic Trail crosses the backbone of these mountains, and is a popular snowmobile trail in the winter. Lander is one of the gateway communities to this vast area that includes national forest and wilderness lands. Contact the Wind River Visitors Council or Shoshone National Forest for information on outfitters in the area. | Wind River Visitors Council, 337 E. Main St., Riverton | 307/856–7566 or 800/645–6233 | www.wind-river.org | Shoshone National Forest, Lander District Office | 307/332–5460 | Daily.

Shoshone Tribal Cultural Center. Shoshone art and artifacts are part of the collections at this center that also has information about the two most famous Shoshones: Chief Washakie and Sacajawea, guide to Lewis and Clark. A small gift shop sells authentic Shoshone crafts and beadwork. There are one- to four-hour tours of historic sites on the Wind River Reservation. | 31 Black Cove Rd., Fort Washakie | 307/332–9106 or 307/332–3177 | $30–$150 tours | Weekdays 8–4:45.

South Pass City State Historic Site. Established during the South Pass Gold Rush of 1868, South Pass City was a model mining town and the birthplace of women's suffrage in Wyoming. Many of the original buildings survive and have been restored. The small museum gives an overview of the South Pass gold district, and at certain times during the summer season you can try your hand at panning for gold in the cold stream that runs through town, which is off Route 137. | South Pass City Rd. | 307/332–3684 | www.state.wy.us/sphs/south1.htm | $2 WY residents; $4 nonresidents | Mid-May–early Sept., daily 9–5:30.

Dining
Atlantic City Mercantile. Steak. You'll feel as if you've stepped directly into an old western when you enter this downtown building, with its long mirrored back bar and collection of mismatched tables and chairs. At times a honky-tonk piano player is on hand. In summer, steaks are cooked on an open-flame grill in the back of the building. The menu also includes chicken, seafood, and sandwiches. | 100 E. Main St., Atlantic City | 307/332–5143 | D, MC, V | $$–$$$

Gannett Grill. American/Casual. This crowded, noisy place serves large sandwiches and hand-tossed New York–style pizza. | 148 Main St. | 307/332–8228 | D, MC, V | ¢–$$

Svilars. Steak. Inside this small, family-owned restaurant you'll find what many natives say is the best food in all of Wyoming. A meal might begin with *sarma* (cabbage rolls) or other appetizers, and ought to be followed by a tremendous and tasty steak. | 175 S. Main St., Hudson | 307/332–4516 | No credit cards | Closed Sun. and every other Mon. No lunch | $$$–$$$$

Lodging
Blue Spruce Inn. Named after the five enormous spruce trees on the property, this 1920s brick home has a huge front porch with a swing, and beautiful gardens. Rooms have themes—Civil War, Native American, brass, and floral—and are cozy and individually decorated with items acquired during the hosts' travels. Library; no TVs in some rooms, no smoking. | 677 S. 3rd St., 82520 | 307/332–8253 or 888/503–3311 | fax 307/332–1386 | www.bluespruceinn.com | 4 rooms | AE, D, MC, V | CP | $

Hart Ranch Hideout. There's a re-created Old West Town at this RV park and campground 9 mi southeast of Lander on U.S. 287 (1 mi south of the junction with Route 28). The campground is beside the Little Popo Agie (pronounced pa-po-sha) river. You can take a hay ride or swim in the river. There are showers, picnic tables, grills, and drinking water available to all sites. Restaurant, fishing, hiking, horseshoes, shops, playground, laundry facilities, some pets allowed. | 9 mi southeast of Lander on U.S. 287 | 307/332–3836 or 800/914–9226 | 65 RV sites, 20 tent sites | D, MC, V | ¢

Pronghorn Lodge. The sculpture garden that spreads through Lander starts at this downtown motel. Some rooms have kitchens. Restaurant, some refrigerators, cable

TV, hot tub, laundry facilities, some pets allowed (fee). | 150 E. Main St., 82520 | 307/332–3940 | fax 307/332–2651 | www.wyoming.com/~thepronghorn | 56 rooms | AE, D, DC, MC, V | CP | $

Rock Springs

Western Wyoming Community College Natural History Museum. Dinosaurs are among the prehistoric animal and plant specimens on display here. Species range in age from 180 million to 67 million years old. Look for the fossilized fish and the baby alligator. The dinosaurs are placed throughout the building, and the museum has rotating exhibits. | 2500 College Dr. | 307/382–1600 | Free | Daily 8–7.

Dining

Bitter Creek Brewery. American/Casual. Choose from 18 different burgers and wash your meal down with Bob, a local brew that has won awards at brew fests in Denver and Laramie—or try a Coal Porter (a dark beer that symbolizes the coal mining heritage of this community). | 604 Broadway | 307/362–4782 | AE, D, MC, V | ¢–$$

Boschetto's European Market. Continental. Rock Springs's population has been a melting pot of nationalities since its earliest settlement as a coal mining town. Boschetto's, a European-style market and deli, with its varieties of cheese, sausage, spaghetti, and other foods, caters to the variety of folks living in the city. | 6717 Broadway | 307/382–2350 | AE, D, DC, MC, V | ¢–$

Lodging

Holiday Inn. Guest rooms at this pleasant chain are bright and spacious; ground-floor rooms have exterior entrances. You can curl up in front of the lobby's fireplace in winter or enjoy a dip in the indoor pool any time. Restaurant, some refrigerators, indoor pool, gym, hot tub, bar, meeting rooms, airport shuttle, some pets allowed (fee). | 1675 Sunset Dr. | 307/382–9200 | fax 307/632–1064 | www.holidayinnrockies.com/hotels/rkswy.html | 113 rooms, 1 suite | AE, D, DC, MC, V | $

Ramada Limited. This reliable chain has cherrywood furniture in the rooms; breakfast is served by the fireplace in the dining room. Located on the west side of town—take Exit 102 off I–80—the Ramada will put you one block from the city's White Mountain Mall. In-room data ports, outdoor pool, gym, laundry service. | 2717 Dewar Dr., 82902 | 307/362–1770 or 888/307–7890 | fax 307/362–2830 | www.ramada.com | 129 rooms, 2 suites | AE, D, DC, MC, V | CP | $

Index